In-Work Poverty in Europe

Bulletin of Comparative Labour Relations

VOLUME 111

Founding Editor

The series started in 1970 under the dynamic editorship of Professor Roger Blanpain (Belgium), former President of the International Industrial Relations Association. Professor Blanpain, Professor Emeritus of Labour Law, Universities of Leuven and Tilburg, was also General Editor of the International Encyclopedia of Laws (with more than 1,600 collaborators worldwide) and President of the Association of Educative and Scientific Authors Authors. He passed away in October 2016.

General Editor

In 2015 Frank Hendrickx, Professor of labour law at the Faculty of Law of the University of Leuven (Belgium) joined as a co-Editor. Frank Hendrickx has published numerous articles and books and regularly advises governments, international institutions and private organisations in the area of labour law as well as in sports law. He is the Editor-in-Chief of the European Labour Law Journal and General Editor of the International Encyclopaedia of Laws.

Introduction

The Bulletins constitute a unique source of information and thought-provoking discussion, laying the groundwork for studies of employment relations in the 21st century, involving among much else the effects of globalization, new technologies, migration, and the greying of the population.

Contents/Subjects

Amongst other subjects the Bulletins frequently include the proceedings of international or regional conferences; reports from comparative projects devoted to salient issues in industrial relations, human resources management, and/or labour law; and specific issues underlying the multicultural aspects of our industrial societies.

Objective

The Bulletins offer a platform of expression and discussion on labour relations to scholars and practitioners worldwide, often featuring special guest editors.

The titles published in this series are listed at the end of this volume.

In-Work Poverty in Europe

Vulnerable and Under-Represented Persons in a Comparative Perspective

Founding Editor
Roger Blanpain

General Editor
Frank Hendrickx

Edited by
Luca Ratti

Contributors

Ann-Christine 'Ankie' Hartzén
Sonja Bekker
Eleni De Becker
Nicola De Luigi
Alexander Dockx
Marion Evers
Antonio Garcia-Muñoz
Christina Hiessl
Mijke Houwerzijl
Giulia Marchi
Aleksandra Peplińska
Paul Schoukens
Monika Tomaszewska
Vincent Vergnat
Ester Villa
Nuna Zekić

Wolters Kluwer

Published by:
Kluwer Law International B.V.
PO Box 316
2400 AH Alphen aan den Rijn
The Netherlands
E-mail: lrs-sales@wolterskluwer.com
Website: www.wolterskluwer.com/en/solutions/kluwerlawinternational

Sold and distributed by:
Wolters Kluwer Legal & Regulatory U.S.
7201 McKinney Circle
Frederick, MD 21704
United States of America
E-mail: customer.service@wolterskluwer.com

Disclaimer: This book is one of the outputs of the research project *WorkYP – Working, Yet Poor*. The *WorkYP* Project received funding from the European Union's Horizon 2020 research and innovation programme under Grant agreement No 870619.

The content of this book reflects only the authors' view and the Research Executive Agency is not responsible for any use that may be made of the information it contains.

ISBN 978-94-035-4996-5

e-Book: ISBN 978-94-035-4997-2
web-PDF: ISBN 978-94-035-4998-9

Notes on Contributors

Ann-Christine 'Ankie' Hartzén is a postdoctoral researcher in labour law at the Department of Business Law, Lund University, Sweden. Her current research is dedicated to the issue of in-work poverty within the framework of the Horizon 2020 project 'Working, Yet Poor'. Apart from in-work poverty, Ankie's research interests focus on labour law, collective bargaining systems and its impact on labour markets, especially for vulnerable persons. In line with this, she also holds a deep interest in the European Social Model and international aspects of collective bargaining systems, not least through her previous work on the European Social Dialogue.

Sonja Bekker is an associate professor at Utrecht University, the Netherlands and Tilburg University, the Netherlands. Her research deals with European Social Policy, in particular focusing on vulnerable groups in the labour market and EU governance modes. At Utrecht University, the Netherlands, Bekker is Programme Director of the research cluster Empirical Legal Research into Institutions for Conflict Resolution (ERI) and Member of the Future of Work hub. Bekker has published extensively on the European Semester of socio-economic coordination, youth unemployment, and workers with flexible jobs. Moreover, she is researching the digital welfare state.

Eleni De Becker is a postdoctoral researcher at the KU Leuven (Institute for Social Law), Belgium where she works on the project 'Work Yet Poor'. Eleni works also as a teaching assistant at the Institute for Social Law and is an affiliated researcher at the Free University of Brussels, Belgium. Eleni obtained her PhD at the KU Leuven, Belgium in 2018 where she analysed the right to social security in the EU. She also worked as a lawyer for a Brussels law firm from 2018 to 2021.

Nicola De Luigi is Full Professor of Sociology at the University of Bologna, Italy and is currently a member of the Scientific Committee of the Ph.D. in Political and Social Sciences. His research deals with interactions among social policies, labour market and social practices.

Alexander Dockx is currently a researcher at the KU Leuven, Belgium connected to the Institute for Social Law, where he works on the project 'Work Yet Poor'. Before that, he specialized in Belgian public law and wrote about aspects of Belgian procedural law.

Marion Evers is an expert in the field of HRM and employment law. She strives to bring together the interests of employers and employees, in order to improve working conditions and performance as much as possible. She has worked as a researcher in in-work poverty at Utrecht University, the Netherlands.

Antonio Garcia-Muñoz is a postdoctoral researcher at the University of Luxembourg, Luxembourg where he works for the Horizon 2020 Project 'WorkYP: Working, Yet Poor', on in-work poverty and European social citizenship. Previously he has worked at Goethe University, Frankfurt, Germany, for the European Centre of Expertise (ECE) in the field of labour law, employment and labour market policies and at Castilla-La Mancha University, Spain.

Christina Hiessl is a senior researcher of Goethe University, Frankfurt, Germany (since 2019), visiting professor of Yonsei University, Seoul, South Korea (since 2014) and recently appointed BOFZAP Professor of Labour Law at KU Leuven, Belgium (as of October 2022). She is a member of the European Centre of Expertise in the field of labour law (ECE) and the Korean Society for Social Security Law, and coordinating coach of the German team in the Hugo Sinzheimer Moot Court Competition.

Mijke Houwerzijl is Full Professor of Labour Law at Tilburg University, the Netherlands (since 2011). She is co-editor of a leading Dutch labour law journal (*Tijdschrift Recht en Arbeid*; since 2006), external board member of the Institute for Labour Law and Industrial Relations in the EU *(IAAEU* in Trier; since 2018) and she chairs the Dutch Department of the International Society for Labour and Social Security Law (ISLSSL; since 2010). Until recently, she also was an endowed Professor of European and Comparative Labour Law at the University of Groningen, the Netherlands (2010–2020).

Giulia Marchi is a postdoctoral researcher at the University of Bologna, Italy and is currently working on Horizon 2020 Project 'Working, Yet Poor'. Her research explores social clauses and protections for employees in outsourcing processes in the field of Italian and EU labour law and the right to fair and adequate wage.

Aleksandra Peplińska, PhD in Psychology, Institute of Psychology, University of Gdańsk, Poland. She is author of numerous publications, including articles, book chapters and books focused mostly on work psychology, organization and management, and quality of life. Particular emphasis in these publications lies on the relationship between the professional situation and its well-being, quality of life and work, including those excluded from the labour market – not only homeless, long-term unemployed, but also stigmatized, discriminated in the labour market – for example, people with disabilities or women. She is Member of European Association of Work and Organizational Psychology and Polish Psychological Association.

Luca Ratti is an Associate Professor of European and Comparative Labour Law and Director of the Master in European Law (I year) at the University of Luxembourg. Since February 2020, he is the coordinator of the Horizon 2020 project 'WorkYP: Working, Yet Poor', focused on in-work poverty and European social citizenship (2020-2023). He currently holds a Jean Monnet Chair in European labour law on the Sustainability of the European Social Model for the years 2022 to 2025).

Paul Schoukens is Full Professor of European, International and Belgian Social Security Law at the KU Leuven (Institute for Social Law), Belgium and Tilburg University, the Netherlands. He is specialized in European, international, comparative and Belgian social security law. He is also responsible for the student exchange programme at the Faculty of Law and Criminology at the KU Leuven, Belgium.

Monika Tomaszewska is Associate Professor at the Department of Labour Law at the Faculty of Law and Administration of the University of Gdańsk, Poland. She is author of several dozen publications, including book chapters, articles, glosses, and entries in lexicons on legal topics published in Polish as well as foreign periodicals focusing mostly on fundamental and social rights. She is an expert in numerous European programmes related to the migration of people, freedom to provide services, posting of workers. She is research manager of the prestigious three-year programme implemented under Horizon 2020-SC6-GOVERNANCE-2019 enhancing social rights and EU citizenship – Working Yet Poor – focusing on the reasons for poverty and social exclusion, the causes of which do not lie in unemployment.

Vincent Vergnat obtained a PhD in Economics at the University of Strasbourg, France in December 2017 and was Research Associate at the Luxembourg Institute of Socio-Economic Research (LISER), Luxembourg and the University of Luxembourg, Luxembourg from 2018 to 2022. He works now as a statistician expert in the French public health insurance since 2022. Very interested in multidisciplinarity, his research focuses on poverty, inequality and labour supply.

Ester Villa is an Associate Professor of Labour Law at the University of Bologna, Italy. Her research explores the forms of protection of employees in the outsourcing processes, the competition between collective agreements as a problem to guarantee the right of an adequate wage and the collective rights of self-employed.

Nuna Zekić is Associate Professor at the Department of Private, Business and Labour Law at Tilburg University, the Netherlands. Her expertise lies in the area of labour law and more precisely, dismissal law, flexible employment, equal treatment, and collective bargaining. She has published extensively on these issues, including articles on platform work and foundations of labour law. At Tilburg Law School, she teaches Dutch and International Labour Law at bachelor and master levels. She acts as a deputy judge at the 's-Hertogenbosch appeal court.

Summary of Contents

Table of Contents

CHAPTER 1

The Challenge of Defining, Measuring, and Overcoming In-Work Poverty in Europe: An Introduction

Luca Ratti, Antonio García-Muñoz & Vincent Vergnat

The present introductory chapter presents the concept of in-work poverty, describes its incidence and recent evolution in the European Union, and provides an overview of the causes behind this phenomenon against the background of policy debates at EU and national level. To better understand what is at stake when we refer to in-work poverty, it is key to have an accurate idea of how it is measured and what are the limitations of existing indicators, reason why this introduction includes an explanation on these two issues. Another section is devoted to explain why the focus of this book is on particular groups of workers for the study of in-work poverty. Finally, an overview of the book's structure and a brief description of each chapter are provided.

§1.01 IN-WORK POVERTY IN THE EUROPEAN UNION

In-work poverty is a reality for too many persons in the European Union (EU). As recorded in a 2021 Resolution of the European Parliament (EP) on inequalities,[1] about 20.5 million people experienced in-work poverty in 2017. Moreover, in the last decade

1. European Parliament, *Resolution of 10 February 2021 on reducing inequalities with a special focus on in-work poverty* (2019/2188 (INI)).

this phenomenon is on the rise,[2] even if in the last years statistical information describes certain stability or even a slight decrease of the percentage of in-work poor.[3]

Despite this scenario, in-work poverty only recently gained visibility. Policy debates with an exclusive focus on the topic are still rare, particularly at national level. Indeed, in-work poverty is to a great extent still perceived as part of the overall goal to reduce poverty with the result that quite often there is no specific focus on the problematic of those who, despite being working, are poor.[4]

The present book aims to contribute to a better knowledge and understanding of in-work poverty, thus equipping policy makers at EU and national level with more targeted tools to tackle this social problem.

The most original element of the present book is its focus on certain groups of workers in the labour market. We refer to these groups as 'Vulnerable and Under-Represented Persons' (VUPs), to convey the idea that individuals belonging to these groups are often in a vulnerable situation in the labour market and/or not adequately represented and protected by labour law institutions, including trade unions (via collective bargaining coverage or otherwise). The idea and composition of the VUPs has its origins in the Research Project 'Working, Yet Poor',[5] in which all the authors in this volume are involved.

This introduction presents, first, the concept of in-work poverty, offering a brief description of the many causes behind this phenomenon. It continues with a description of the incidence and recent evolution of the phenomenon in the EU. Section 1.02 deals with the indicators used at EU level to measure in-work poverty. Section 1.03 explains the methodological reasons behind the focus of the analysis in some particular groups of workers, referred to as VUPs or VUP groups. Section 1.04 presents detailed statistical information on the incidence of in-work poverty in such VUP groups. Finally, §1.05 describes the structure and main contents of the present book.

[A] The Concept of In-Work Poverty

The concept of in-work poverty in the EU is a relative one and entails two dimensions: 'work' and 'poverty'.[6] A person must fulfil, therefore, two cumulative requisites to be considered as 'working poor': first, the person must have worked during a period of time and, second, the income of the household where the person lives, in comparison with the median income levels of the country's households, must fall below a certain threshold.

---

2. Ramón Peña-Casas; Dalila Ghaliani; Slavina Spasova & Bart Vanhercke, *In-work poverty in Europe. A study of national policies*, p. 7 (European Social Policy Network, 2019).
3. This percentage was 9.4% in years 2017 and 2018, to slightly decrease down to 9.2% in 2019, although the data for this last year are still an estimation. Eurostat. In-work at-risk-of-poverty rate by age and sex – EU-SILC survey [ilc_iw01].
4. Ramón Peña-Casas et al., *In-work poverty in Europe*, *supra* n. 2, pp. 12-13.
5. *Working, Yet Poor* is a research project funded under the European Union's Horizon 2020 programme. More information is available in the Project's website: https://workingyetpoor.eu/.
6. *See* Eurofound, *In-work poverty in the EU*, p. 5 (Publications Office of the European Union, 2017).

In the EU, that threshold is met when the yearly equivalized disposable income is below 60% of the national household median income level (*see* more in detail §1.02). The 60% threshold goal is an arbitrary convention aiming at identifying a minimum level of income that is necessary to cover those necessities that are basic relative to the society where the individuals live.

In-work poverty and material deprivation are not equivalents. Material deprivation measures absolute poverty and is built taking into consideration the capacity of individuals to access a number of items included in a basket of basic goods and services (*see* §1.02). In-work poverty, being a relative concept, refers to the position of the individual in a given society, and its functional capacity to participate in the social and political life of the community where he/she lives.[7] Therefore, it is possible to experience in-work poverty even when a person lives in a household with no material deprivation (and vice versa). In the EU, levels of material deprivation tend to be lower than in-work poverty levels.

Another particularity is that in-work poverty combines an individual measure of work with a household dimension of relative income. This means that the composition of the household, as well as the work intensity thereof, are of great importance: even when an individual's employment conditions (wages, number of people employed, etc.) remain constant, it is possible that the poverty status changes over time due to variations in the household composition or changes in the household's work intensity.[8]

There are a number of challenges when it comes to the measurement of in-work poverty and how the indicators are elaborated. These challenges, as well as the strengths and shortcomings of indicators, are discussed more in detail (*see* §1.02).

[B] Drivers of In-Work Poverty

Research shows that in-work poverty is a complex and multidimensional phenomenon with manifold and intertwined causes. These causes or factors are typically grouped into distinct categories for their study, according to their nature. Individual and household factors are the two main categories,[9] although some studies add institutional factors as a third and heterogeneous group of causes.[10] The following paragraphs provide a description of these three groups.

(a) *Individual factors* refer both to the employment situation of individuals and to their socio-demographic characteristics. Each of these subgroups is in turn composed of multiple factors.

---

7. A relative concept of poverty means that poverty is understood in terms of the standard of living of the society in question. *See* Ive Marx & Karl Van den Bosch, How poverty differs from inequality. On poverty measurement on an enlarged EU context: conventional and alternative approaches, pp. 7-9 (Centre for Social Policy, University of Antwerp, 2008), https://ec.europa.eu/eurostat/documents/1001617/4577263/1-1-I-MARX.pdf.
8. Eurofound, *In work-poverty*, *supra* n. 6, p. 5.
9. Ramón Peña-Casas et al., *In-work poverty in Europe*, *supra* n. 2.
10. Eurofound, *In work-poverty supra* n. 6, pp. 7-14.

Among the employment-related causes, one is probably the first to come to mind: having a *low wage*. However, research shows that there is no strong correlation between low salaries and in-work poverty. It is important to keep in mind that poor workers differ from low-wage workers. As explained by Salverda, a low-wage worker in the EU is a person whose hourly earnings (excluding employer paid social contributions and payroll taxes) is less than two-thirds of median hourly earnings.[11] It is, therefore, a *relative* concept (because it depends on the distribution of wages in the population) and an *individual* concept (the situation of the household as a whole is not considered). In addition, low pay is measured on gross hourly earnings while poverty is based on equivalent household disposable income measured over a full year. The data used by Salverda show a higher incidence of low pay than in-work poverty in all the EU countries except Sweden.[12] Although the risk of poverty is higher for a low-paid worker, the weak correlation between these two indicators shows that low wage is only a weak determinant of in-work poverty.[13] Many low-paid workers are secondary earners in a household, and the first earner ensures that the household is not below the poverty line.[14] Indeed, due to the household dimension, the impact of low pay on an individual's risk of in-work poverty depends largely on the composition of the household where she/he lives. Finally, there are wide differences among EU Member States: in most Southern European Member States and also in Lithuania, Hungary, Luxembourg, Sweden, Latvia, Austria, and France, more than one-fifth of low-wage employees are poor, while less than one-tenth of low-wage employees are poor in Slovenia, Ireland, and Czech Republic.[15]

The second most relevant factor related to the employment situation is the *type of contract*: temporary and part-time workers are in the EU at a higher risk to experience in-work poverty than workers with indefinite and full-time contracts. Work-intensity seems to be especially problematic, since part-time workers can face additional difficulties because their access to social benefits may be hampered when eligibility is based on the number of hours effectively worked.[16] The self-employed also face a higher risk of in-work poverty than employees in most EU Member States, although the data on the income of

11. Wiemer Salverda, Low earnings and their drivers in relation to in-work poverty, in *Handbook on In-Work Poverty* 26-49 (Henning Lohmann & Ive Marx eds., Edward Elgar Publishing 2018).
12. *Ibid.*
13. *See* Bertrand Maître, Brian Nolan, & Christopher T. Whelan, *Low-pay, in-work poverty and economic vulnerability: a comparative analysis using EU-SILC*. Manchester School, 80(1), 99-116 (2012); Salverda, Low earnings and their drivers *supra* n. 11.
14. *See*, for example, on Germany, Marco Gießelmann & Lohmann Henning, The different roles of low-wage work in Germany: regional, demographical and temporary variances in the poverty risk of low-paid workers, in *The Working Poor in Europe*, 96-123 (Hand-Jürgen Andreß & Henning Lohmann eds., Edward Elgar Publishing, 2008).
15. European Commission, *Employment and Social Developments in Europe 2016*, pp. 84-93 (Publications Office of the European Union, 2016).
16. Jeroen Horemans & Ive Marx, In-work poverty in times of crisis: do part-timers fare worse? (ImPRovE Working Papers 13/14, Herman Deleeck Centre for Social Policy, University of Antwerp, 2013).

self-employed persons in surveys should be considered with caution, given the risk of underestimation of self-assessed income by the self-employed population.[17]

When it comes to *socio-demographic characteristics* of the working poor, the level of education, gender, age, and country of birth seem to be the most relevant factors on the risk of in-work poverty. Even if these individual characteristics may be in themselves factors triggering in-work poverty, they can also cumulate in the same person in a sort of intersectionality, seriously increasing the overall risk to be working poor.[18] Educational level is the most relevant of the socio-demographic characteristics that may play a role in the risk to experience in-work poverty. The higher the level of education, the lower the in-work poverty rate. Second comes the country of birth. Being born abroad implies a higher risk of in-work poverty when compared with native populations. Research shows that part-time and temporary work are more widespread among foreign-born workers and that a bigger proportion of immigrants have elementary occupations.[19] Surprisingly, age and gender seem to be less relevant in relation to in-work poverty levels[20] and no uniform patterns exist across Member States with respect to these two characteristics.[21] The fact that the gender difference is not significant is paradoxical, given the disadvantage of women in the labour market in terms of wages, working time, occupation, and career progression. This gender paradox is largely explained by the fact that in-work poverty is measured at household level, which poses questions about how resources are shared within the household. Research shows that if household income was to be assessed individually and not at the household level, the risk of in-work poverty would be higher for women than for men.[22]

(b) *Household factors* refer both to the size and the composition of the household, as well as to the work intensity of its members. Indeed, the composition of the household seems to be one of the most important factors in connection to in-work poverty, and existing research suggests that it may be even more important than the individual dimension for the understanding of the phenomenon.[23] Data show that the risk of in-work poverty is much higher for people living in a household with children. In particular, single parents or coupled parents with three or more children experience a higher risk.[24] The household's overall work intensity – defined as the ratio of the total number of months that all working-age household members have worked during the

17. Ramón Peña-Casas et al., *In-work poverty in Europe, supra* n. 2, p. 33.
18. *Ibid.*, p. 25.
19. Eurofound, *In work-poverty, supra* n. 6, p. 8.
20. Ramón Peña-Casas et al., *In-work poverty in Europe, supra* n. 2, p. 26.
21. Eurofound, *In work-poverty, supra* n. 6, p. 8.
22. Sophie Ponthieux, Gender and in-work poverty, in *Handbook on In-Work Poverty* 70-88 (Henning Lohmann & Ive Marx eds., Edward Elgar Publishing 2018).
23. Ramón Peña-Casas et al., *In-work poverty in Europe, supra* n. 2, p. 38.
24. *Ibid.*, p. 39.

income reference year and the total number of months the same household members theoretically could have worked in the same period – is also strongly connected to in-work poverty levels. Logically, the relation between the household work intensity and the individual risk of in-work poverty is inversely proportional: the lower work intensity in the household, the higher the poverty risk of the worker. Workers in low-intensity households with children are the most at risk.[25] Work intensity is often related to institutional and cultural factors and has a gender dimension. Women are more often second earners in the household and tend more often to limit their working time to take care of children. Institutional factors, such as the availability and affordability of childcare or access to flexible work arrangements, can have an important impact on work intensity for women.[26]

(c) As mentioned earlier, some authors add a third set of causes to in-work poverty, grouped under the label '*institutional*'. In its 2017 report, Eurofound lists as institutional factors the following: social transfers, the possibility of the workers to opt-out of the labour market when wages or working conditions are not satisfactory, employment protection and labour market institutions (wage-setting, minimum wage legislation, and collective bargaining). Other institutional factors are access to childcare, tax law, etc. The EP mentions in addition the lack of affordable housing and technological change.[27]

[C] Incidence of In-Work Poverty in the EU: Recent Evolution

What was the incidence of in-work poverty in the EU in 2021? And what has been its recent evolution?

On this point, a caveat is needed: the most recent statistical data on in-work poverty at EU level refer to year 2019 (and even these are still considered as estimation in the European Union Statistics on Income and Living Conditions (EU-SILC) statistics). This means that, at this point of time, it is only possible to assess the situation right before the COVID-19 crisis. In its 2021 Resolution, the EP fears that the economic and social consequences of the COVID-19 pandemic will negatively affect in-work poverty levels. This will start to be visible when statistics of year 2020 become available.

In 2019, the percentage of in-work poor in the EU-27 for employed persons aged 18 and older was 9% (estimated). In the previous years, the percentage remained rather stable at 9.4% (2017 and 2018 for the EU-28), after reaching its peak in 2016 (9.6%). However, going back in time and comparing the data of the last three years

25. *Ibid.*, p. 40.
26. Eurofound, *In work-poverty, supra* n. 6, p. 10.
27. It is also noted by the Parliament that rents are constantly rising in most Member States, leading to overburden rates of housing costs (i.e., when individuals need to spend 40% or more of their equivalized disposable income on housing). European Parliament, *Resolution of 10 February 2021, supra* n. 1.

with the situation before the 2008 crisis, it can be seen that there has been an increase in the levels of in-work poverty in the EU in the last 15 years. The percentage of in-work poverty in 2007 in the EU-27 (without Croatia, but with UK) was 8.3%, whereas in the next years, particularly between 2010 and 2014, the percentage increased every year until 2016 before stabilizing.[28]

Research shows that differences in the levels of in-work poverty among EU Member States are important, and the same can be said about the evolution of in-work poverty within the different countries. In 2019, in-work poverty in the EU ranged from a minimum of 2.9% in Finland to a maximum of 15.7% in Romania. The fact that the levels of in-work poverty have significantly decreased in countries like Greece (where these levels are lower in the years following the 2008 financial crisis than in the pre-crisis period), reflect a significant drop in median incomes rather than an improvement in the situation of the working poor. In this sense, when the poverty threshold is anchored at levels previous to the financial crisis, data are clear in showing that, contrary to the evolution of in-work poverty rates, poverty went up in the countries hit hardest by the crisis.[29]

One of the factors explaining the rise of in-work poverty during the years following the 2008 financial crisis may be the increase in the use of atypical employment. On the one hand, 'a correlation has been found between the rise in non-standard forms of employment and the increased proportion of Europeans at risk of in-work poverty'.[30] On the other hand, due to the contraction of employment during the 2008 financial crisis, there was an important increase in the number of people on atypical employment, including fixed-term (short term) of part-time employment (also involuntary part-time).[31] Therefore, the increased incidence of atypical employment and self-employment, which tend to be clustered in certain households, is relevant.

Even when there are sharp differences between Member States in the levels of part-time work as well as in the levels of temporary employment, data clearly show that, for both types of contracts, the risk of in-work poverty increased on average at EU level, at least between 2007 and 2014.[32]

Differences in the levels of in-work poverty do exist not only between Member States, but also within countries. As it has been described when discussing the causes of in-work poverty, some groups of workers are more likely to be affected by this phenomenon than others. Indeed, in-work poverty is not distributed evenly across the labour market. On the contrary, it tends to concentrate within particular groups, which are therefore more vulnerable.[33]

28. EU-SILC survey -In-work at-risk-of-poverty rate by age and sex.
29. Eurofound, *In work-poverty, supra* n. 6, pp. 16-17.
30. European Parliament, *Resolution of 10 February 2021, supra* n. 1.
31. ETUI, *Benchmarking Working Europe 2019*, 'Labour market and social developments' chapter, 2019.
32. Eurofound, *In work-poverty, supra* n. 6, pp. 22-24.
33. Ramón Peña-Casas et al., *In-work poverty in Europe, supra* n. 2, pp. 49-51.

[D] The Policy Debate on In-Work Poverty in the EU

The policy debate on in-work poverty at EU level has evolved in the recent years. Certainly, concern about in-work poverty has been steadily growing at the same pace as in-work poverty gained visibility and became distinguishable from the broader problem of 'poverty'. The first step on this process took place in 2003, when the EU agreed on a specific indicator to measure in-work poverty by introducing 'in-work at-risk-of- poverty' as part of the EU's set of social inclusion indicators.[34] Since then, in-work poverty became more visible, which was in turn the first step towards a targeted approach to this phenomenon.

The fight against in-work poverty was seen until very recently as part of the overall goal to reduce poverty in the EU, with the consequence that a more specific focus on in-work poverty was missing. The EU 2020 strategy, which had as one of its headline targets to reduce the number of poor by at least 20 million by year 2020, identified the unemployed as a particularly vulnerable group. Therefore, one of the main priorities in the last decade, and especially in the aftermath of the 2008 economic crisis, has been to strive for higher levels of employment. Social policy was informed accordingly at EU level. This approach, however, proved not to be the most adequate to tackle in-work poverty, since getting people into work is not always enough.[35]

The 2008 financial crisis, which became an economic crisis in the EU in the following years, provoked an increase on unemployment levels as well as in the use of non-standard forms of employment and self-employment, but, 'despite the seemingly obvious relationship between (in-work) poverty and hard economic times, the story of in-work poverty during the crisis years is far from simple'.[36]

In 2014, the Social Protection Committee urged EU countries to address the problems of the working poor.[37] However, the qualitative change would come later, with the European Pillar of Social Rights (EPSR), where for the first time in-work poverty was recognized as one of the problems that the EU social agenda had to address.

In particular, Articles 6 and 12 of the EPSR are directly relevant for in-work poverty. Article 6 states that 'workers have the right to fair wages that provide for a decent standard of living' and that 'adequate minimum wages shall be ensured, in a way that provide for the satisfaction of the needs of the workers and his/her family in the light of national economic and social conditions (...). In-work poverty shall be prevented'. Article 12 states that 'regardless of the type and duration of their employment relationships, workers, and, under comparable conditions, the self-employed, have the right to adequate protection'. Furthermore, although in a less direct way, nearly all the other principles in the EPSR, such as equal opportunities and access to the

---

34. Ive Marx & Brian Nolan, *In-work poverty*, p. 11 (GINI discussion paper 51, 2012).
35. Eurofound, *In work-poverty*, *supra* n. 6, p. 4.
36. *Ibid.*, p. 15.
37. Social Protection Committee, Social Europe: many ways, one objective: Annual report of the Social Protection Committee on the social situation in the European Union (2013), (Publications Office of the European Union, 2014).

labour market (principles 3 and 4), fair working conditions, social protection and inclusion are relevant to in-work poverty.[38] The EPSR is, therefore, a point of reference in the fight against in-work poverty in the EU.

In the framework of the implementation of the EPSR, the Commission has released an Action Plan[39] establishing the objective of reducing the number of people at risk of poverty or social exclusion by at least 15 million by 2030. A number of legislative initiatives contribute to substantiate the EPSR Action Plan. In October 2020, a proposal for a Directive on adequate minimum wages was presented by the Commission.[40] In November 2021, the EP's Committee on Employment and Social affairs presented a revised text which was adopted by the Plenary.[41] Similarly, in December 2021, the Commission has presented a proposal for a Directive on improving working conditions of platform workers.[42]

Among the policy actors, the EP has been particularly active in the EU debate on in-work poverty, stressing the importance of having a decent income, including a decent wage, on several occasions.[43] In its last resolution of 10 February 2021, the EP urged the Commission and the Member States to take action against in-work poverty by, among other measures, developing instruments such as minimum incomes, minimum wages, and minimum pensions, promoting collective bargaining, reinforcing available and affordable public services, guaranteeing equal access to education, training, and digitalization, reinforcing the European anti-poverty strategy, fighting tax avoidance, developing housing policies, and ensuring decent working and employment conditions in the digital economy.[44]

Despite the described evolution of the policy debates and discourse at EU level, at national level the 'policy debates and proposals for reforms (...) have only very rarely been framed as explicitly targeting [in-work poverty]' and the debate on in-work poverty remains to a large extent 'underdeveloped in policy discourse and action'.[45]

§1.02 HOW DO WE MEASURE IN-WORK POVERTY?

Measuring poverty and thus in-work poverty is not an easy task. There are different ways to define poverty. Poverty is, indeed, a multidimensional phenomenon, and focusing only on monetary aspects can be considered too restrictive. However, data on living conditions may be more difficult to collect than income. In addition, determining a threshold below which a person is considered poor is difficult and may be arbitrary.

38. Ramón Peña-Casas et al., *In-work poverty in Europe, supra* n. 2, p. 8.
39. European Commission, *The European Pillar of Social Rights Action Plan* (SWD (2021) 46 final).
40. European Commission, COM (2020) 682 final.
41. European Parliament, *Draft legislative resolution on the proposal for a directive on adequate minimum wages in the European Union.*
42. European Commission, COM (2021) 762 final.
43. European Parliament, Resolution of 14 April 2016 on meeting the anti-poverty target in the light of increasing household costs (2015/2223 (INI)) and European Parliament Resolution of 19 January on the European Pillar of Social Rights (2016/2095 (INI)).
44. European Parliament, *Resolution of 10 February 2021, supra* n. 1.
45. Ramón Peña-Casas et al., *In-work poverty in Europe, supra* n. 2, pp. 12 and 84.

Finally, the question of how to define a worker is critical. Surveys question people about their current employment status or about a retrospective calendar of activity over a reference period during which transitions in or out of work may be important. The definition of a worker is, therefore, crucial.

[A] The European Measure of Poverty

Before defining in-work poverty, it is important to understand how poverty is measured in Europe. In 1975, the European Council defined the poor as 'individuals or families whose resources are so small as to exclude them from the minimum acceptable way of life of the Member State in which they live'.[46] This definition assumes a relative approach to poverty: an individual is poor if he/she has a lower standard of living than the others living in the same country. Following these considerations, the European *at-risk-of-poverty (AROP)* indicator measures the proportion of the population with a standard of living below 60% of the median standard of living in a specific country (60% of the median is known as 'the poverty line'). To define the standard of living, the definition uses the disposable income, which corresponds to gross income (from work, capital, etc.) plus social benefits received (public pensions, means-tested or non-means-tested benefits) minus direct taxes (social insurance contributions, income tax, property taxes, etc.). More concretely, it is the income that a household has at the end of the month, or year, to consume or save. Disposable income is measured at the household level, implying that all the incomes of the members of the household are added together. Eurostat defines a household as 'a social unit having common arrangements, sharing household expenses or daily needs and living in a shared common residence'.[47]

Disposable income, per se, cannot be used directly to measure the standard of living because household size also matters. For example, if two households have the same disposable income of 2,000 EUR, and if one household is composed of 2 adults and the other one of 2 adults and 2 children, the standard of living is not the same. The second household, composed of 4 persons, requires more money to meet the needs of all household members or to get the same level of well-being. In addition, not every individual requires the same amount of money to meet their needs, in particular when comparing children and adults. Children generally have fewer needs than adults do. Living together also creates some economies of scale because some expenditures are pooled (e.g., the housing costs, internet access, etc.). A couple does not need twice the income of a single to reach the same level of well-being. The measure of the standard of living therefore corresponds to the disposable income adjusted for household size and economies of scale: the 'equivalized disposable income'. The adjustment is

46. Council Decision of 22 July 1975 concerning a programme of pilot schemes and studies to combat poverty (75/458/EEC).https://eur-lex.europa.eu/legal-content/EN/TXT/PDF/?uri=CELEX:31975D0458&from=EN (accessed 15 Dec. 2021).
47. Eurostat, Glossary: Household social statistics, Statistics Explained (2021). https://ec.europa.eu/eurostat/statistics-explained/index.php?title=Glossary:Household_-_social_statistics (last accessed 15 Dec. 2021).

conducted by using an equivalence scale. The equivalence scale used by Eurostat is known as the *OECD-modified scale*. This scale takes the value 1 for the first adult in the household, 0.5 for additional adults aged 14 and over, and 0.3 for children under 14. The standard of living therefore corresponds to the disposable income divided by the OECD-modified scale. Consequently, the poverty line corresponds to 60% of the median of the distribution of equivalized disposable income per individual observed in the population.

Disposable income and equivalence scale are measured at the household level, then each member of the household has the same equivalized disposable income but the unit of measurement for the *at-risk-of-poverty* rate is the individual. This indicator is known among poverty experts as the headcount measure of poverty. In other words, the *at-risk-of-poverty* rate measures the share of the individuals in a country who are under the poverty line.

The *at-risk-of-poverty* indicator is country-specific: two households in two countries with the same equivalized disposable income can be categorized as poor in one country and not in the other, because the poverty lines are defined according to the median equivalized disposable income observed in each country. In addition, as the median equivalized disposable income can change from one year to the next, the *at-risk-of-poverty* rate can rise even if the standard of living of poor households has risen (but more slowly than the median). Therefore, this indicator has some limitations for comparisons across countries or over time. In addition, it focuses only on some monetary aspects; the wealth, savings, and debts are not considered. Other non-monetary aspects are also not measured in the *at-risk-of-poverty* rate such as in-kind transfers (from public services) or the material situation of households (for example, it does not provide information on whether the household is living in a decent dwelling). On the other hand, this indicator is very useful for comparing the situation of different groups of the population in a specific country. Finally, the *at-risk-of-poverty* rate is also an inequality indicator by measuring the share of the population away from the median standard of living observed in the country.

[B] Measuring In-Work Poverty

As defined by Lohmann, an in-work poor person is a working person who lives in a poor household.[48] The previous section defined what a poor is. The current one describes how to define a worker for statistical purposes.

The International Labour Organization (ILO) defines the currently active population, or the labour force, as 'persons above a specified minimum age who during a specified brief period, either one week or one day [...] fulfil the requirements for inclusion among the employed or the unemployed'.[49] This definition includes therefore

48. Henning Lohmann, The concept and measurement of in-work poverty, in *Handbook on In-Work Poverty* 7-25 (Henning Lohmann & Ive Marx eds., Edward Elgar Publishing 2018).
49. International Labour Organization (ILO), *Resolutions Concerning Economically Active Population, Employment, Unemployment and Underemployment*, paras. 8-9, Adopted by the 13th International Conference of Labour Statisticians (October 1982).

paid employment, self-employment, and unemployment. In the first two categories, a person can be defined, according to ILO, as *'at work'* or *'with a job/enterprise but not at work'*.[50] The former actually worked for a wage/profit or family gain over the reference period while the latter, although formally related to the firm/institution and having already worked for it, did not perform any work over the reference period (because of holidays, illness, etc.).

As stated in the definition of labour force, individuals must fulfil a number of requirements to be regarded as employed or unemployed. Thus, ILO defines the minimum working time to be considered as employed as one hour of work over the reference period (one week or one day). This very large condition allows to define unemployment accordingly as the total lack of work. This condition, like that of the age limit or the reference period, is arbitrary and could be modified according to the research topic or the data available. For example, the reference population used by Eurostat to calculate the *in-work at-risk-of-poverty rate* is composed of the individuals who declared to be employed 'for more than half the total number of months for which information on any status is available during the income reference period'.[51] The reference period is one year.

Academic studies have shown that using different definitions of a worker lead to different results in terms of in-work poverty.[52] The more demanding a criterion on employment is, the more workers in less-stable employment arrangements are excluded from the statistics. Definitions may also change the gender structure of the working poor population, especially in countries where the working time of men and women differ greatly. In addition, the definition of a worker can have an important effect on the evolution of the in-work poverty rate. For example, if the unemployed are not taken into account in the definition of a worker and if the number of unemployed increases after a crisis (especially if the newly unemployed are the former low-paid workers who are more likely to be working poor), a fall in the in-work poverty rate can be observed, but this does not mean that the economic situation of the population is improving. The definition of a worker is a key question when focusing on vulnerable and under-represented groups of workers as in this book because part of them may be excluded if the definition of workers is strict in terms of duration of employment periods.

To sum up, the *in-work at-risk-of-poverty rate* used by Eurostat measures the share of workers (in employment at least 7 months during the year of reference) who are in a household living below the poverty line. In-work poverty is therefore a concept that has both an individual (work) and collective (household needs and resources) dimension. Also, as mentioned in previous sections, being in-work poor does not

---

50. *Ibid.*, para. 9.
51. Laura Bardone & Anne-Catherine Guio. *In-work poverty – New commonly agreed indicators at the EU level*, Eurostat, Statistics in Focus, 5/2005, p. 2 (2005).
52. *See*, for example, Sophie Ponthieux, *Assessing and analysing in-work poverty risk*, in *Income and living conditions in Europe*, 307-328 (Anthony Atkinson & Eric Marlier eds., Office for Official Publications of the European Communities, 2010); Eric Crettaz, *Poverty and material deprivation among European workers in times of crisis*, International Journal of Social Welfare, 24, 312-323 (2015); Henning Lohmann, *The concept and measurement*, *supra* n. 48.

necessarily mean having a low wage or a precarious job, but may be related to high needs of the household and/or low work intensity of other household members. Conversely, a person with a low wage may not be poor because the income of other households and/or the level of national social protection of workers is high and allows the household to exceed the poverty line. As a result, the factors explaining in-work poverty are more complex than only labour market characteristics and low-paid employment. Therefore, the fight against in-work poverty does not only involve measures on employment but also more general policies such as access to childcare to allow parents to work, family policies to compensate for the presence of children, etc.

[C] Alternative Measures of Poverty

Measuring poverty by income can be criticized. Many scholars have highlighted that the well-being of an individual, and hence inequality and poverty of a population, is dependent on many dimensions of human life, such as housing, education, life expectancy, and income is just one of these dimensions.[53] Alternative indicators have therefore been developed to address this reality.[54] This section describes those used by Eurostat.

To include others dimension than income to measure economic vulnerability, the EU has adopted the *material deprivation index*. Material deprivation is defined as '*the inability to afford some items considered by most people to be desirable or even necessary to lead an adequate life*'.[55] The difficulty with this kind of indicator is to determine the list of material elements considered necessary for a decent life. The Social Protection Committee of the European Commission has defined the *material deprivation rate* as the share of the population living in households not able to afford at least three out of the following nine items:[56,57] 1) to pay rent or utility bills; 2) to keep home adequately warm; 3) to face unexpected expenses; 4) to eat meat, fish or a protein equivalent every second day; 5) to have a week's holiday away from home, or could not afford (if wanted to); 6) having a car; 7) having a washing machine; 8) having a colour TV; 9) having a telephone.

A variant of this indicator measures the *severe material deprivation (SMD)* if at least four (instead of three) items are lacking.

53. *See* Peter Townsend, *Poverty in the United Kingdom* (Penguin, 1979); Amartya, Sen, *Inequality Re-examined* (Harvard University Press, 1992).
54. For a review of some of them, *see* Agnieszka Swigost, *Approaches towards social deprivation: Reviewing measurement methods.* Bulletin of Geography. Socio-economic series (38), 131-141 (2017).
55. Eurostat, Glossary: Material deprivation, Statistics Explained, 2021. https://ec.europa.eu/eurostat/statistics-explained/index.php/Glossary:Material_deprivation (last accessed 15 Dec. 2021).
56. Note that the indicator looks at the household's ability to afford some goods and services. For example, if a household does not have a colour TV by choice but is able to afford one, it is not going to be considered deprived for colour TV.
57. Social Protection Committee – Indicators Sub-Group, Portfolio of EU social indicators for the monitoring of progress towards the EU objectives for social protection and social inclusion: 2015 update (Publications Office of the European Union, 2015).

The *material deprivation index* is an absolute index of poverty and common to all EU countries. As opposed to the '*at-risk-of-poverty*' rate discussed earlier, the material deprivation index does not depend on the entire distribution of the variables of interest. The list of items considered in the material deprivation index is somewhat arbitrary, and alternatives may be preferred. For example, Guio, Gordon, and Marlier proposed a statistically more accurate and adequate index to measure deprivation in Europe.[58] This alternative measure is called *social and material deprivation index* at the EU level. This indicator includes some deprivation in some more social aspects of life. Social deprivation can be seen as a situation in which an individual cannot fully participate in the life of the community, while material deprivation is the situation in which an individual cannot live with dignity.[59] To this end, the *social and material deprivation index* is composed of 13 items including variables related to community life. Some items are measured at the household level and others at the individual level.[60] At the household level the items are: 1) face unexpected expenses; 2) one week annual holiday from home; 3) avoid arrears (in mortgage, rent, utility bills, and/or hire purchase instalments); 4) afford a meal with meat, chicken, or fish or vegetarian equivalent every second day; 5) keep their home adequately warm; 6) a car/van for personal use; 7) replace worn-out furniture. The list of individual items includes: 8) replace worn-out clothes with some new ones; 9) have two pairs of properly fitting shoes; 10) spend a small amount of money each week on him/herself ('pocket money'); 11) have regular leisure activities; 12) get together with friends/family for a drink/meal at least once a month; 13) have an internet connection. An individual suffered from *material and social deprivation* if he/she could not afford (whether he/she wants it or not) at least 5 items out of the 13.

To integrate employment into the analysis of socio-economic disadvantage of household, the EU uses the indicator of work intensity. If the total number of months (in full time equivalent and over the last 12 months) worked by working age individuals (18-59 years old, excluding students aged 18-24) in a household is less than 20% of the theoretical number of months that can be worked by these members, then the household is considered to be at *very low work intensity* also known as *(quasi-) joblessness* household. The indicator of *people living in households with very low work intensity* used by Eurostat therefore measures the proportion of persons under 60 living

58. Anne-Catherine Guio, David Gordon, & Eric Marlier, *Measuring material deprivation in the EU: Indicators for the whole population and child-specific indicators*. Eurostat Methodologies and working papers (Office for Official Publications of the European Communities, 2012); *See* also Anne-Catherine Guio et al., *Improving the measurement of material deprivation at the European Union level*. Journal of European Social Policy, 26, 219-333 (2016); Anne-Catherine Guio & Eric Marlier, Amending the EU material deprivation indicator: impact on size and composition of deprived population, In *Monitoring social inclusion in Europe* 193-208 (Anthony Atkinson, Anne-Catherine Guio & Eric Marlier eds., Publications office of the European Union, 2017).
59. For a deeper discussion on deprivation, *see* Peter Townsend, *Deprivation*, Journal of Social Policy, 16(2), 125-146 (1987).
60. Eurostat, Glossary: Material and Social deprivation, Statistics Explained (2021). https://ec.europa.eu/eurostat/statistics-explained/index.php?title=Glossary:Severe_material_and_social_deprivation_rate_(SMSD) (last accessed 15 Dec. 2021).

in a *quasi-joblessness* household.[61] This indicator may reflect difficulties in entering or staying in the labour market. Since labour income is the primary source of income for the majority of households, a low level of work intensity increases the vulnerability to poverty. At the same time, employment is also a means of social integration and the lack of work can lead to social deprivation as well. This indicator is measured at the household level because the (quasi-) absence of work for one household's member can affect the well-being of other household's members.

To conclude, it has been shown that measuring poverty is difficult because of its multidimensional and dynamic nature. Choices must be made in order to follow this phenomenon over time. At the European level, the leading indicator is the *at-risk-of-poverty* rate, which is a monetary and relative measure of poverty. However, another indicator, the *at-risk-of-poverty or social exclusion*, is used in Europe to extend the measurement of poverty to dimensions other than income. This indicator integrates not only the *at-risk-of-poverty* indicator but also the *severe material deprivation* and *very low work intensity* into a single indicator. All of these indicators can be declined at the level of workers and thus complete the indicator of *in-work at-risk-of-poverty rate.*

[D] In-Work Poverty: Limits and Measurement Issues

The previous sections explained that defining poverty and defining work is not easy, but yet another important difficulty exists: the collection of data needed to calculate these indicators and their inherent limitations.

Poverty and social exclusion indicators are measured at the EU level using the EU-SILC survey. The EU-SILC survey interviews every year a sample of households and individuals about their income, their living conditions, and their labour market situation. In addition to being rich in information, this survey has the advantage of having a harmonized structure at the European level, which facilitates international comparisons. However, surveys have often the disadvantage of not covering the population as a whole like homeless or people living in institutions (prisons, hospitals, etc.). In addition, survey data can also suffer from measurement error (e.g., error in the level of income received by the household in the reference year).[62] In addition, the temporality of the data is another important issue. The time it takes for data to be collected and processed means that they are available only for two or three years after the survey. The evolution of poverty is therefore observed with a certain delay.

61. The upper age limit of 60 is questionable but has been retained for the calculation of the official indicator. For a discussion, *see* Terry Ward & Erhan Özdemir, *Measuring low work intensity – An analysis of the indicator*, (ImPRovE Discussion Paper n° 13/09, 2013); Sophie Ponthieux, Risk of poverty or social exclusion over time: a focus on (quasi-) joblessness, in *Monitoring social inclusion in Europe*, 299-315 (Anthony Atkinson, Anne-Catherine Guio, & Eric Marlier eds., Publications office of the European Union, 2017).

62. In some countries, survey data are linked to administrative data for more reliability. Readers interested in the details of the method used in this survey may refer to Emilio Di Meglio et al., Investing in statistics: EUSILC, in *Monitoring Social Inclusion in Europe* 51-61 (Anthony B. Atkinson, Anne-Catherine Guio & Eric Marlier eds, Luxembourg: Publications Office of the European Union, 2017).

Recently, *nowcasting* methods have been developed to determine the current value of indicators based on past values and assumptions of changes in demographics, labour market, and macroeconomics conditions, but these complex methods are beyond the scope of this chapter.[63] Finally, in EU-SILC, the reference year for income and employment history is the calendar year before the survey, while the data on living conditions and the demographic structure of the household refer to the survey year. It is then assumed that employment and incomes do not change rapidly over time, and that the use of employment and income data from the previous year is a good approximation of the current situation. This hypothesis, defensible in 'normal times', is less credible in times of crisis when transitions are more numerous.[64] All these limitations should be kept in mind when discussing the indicators.

§1.03 VULNERABLE AND UNDER-REPRESENTED PERSONS (VUPs): A METHODOLOGICAL TOOL TO STUDY IN-WORK POVERTY

It is now time to turn to the most original contribution of the present book to current research: its focus on specific clusters of workers that are particularly vulnerable in the labour market, labelled as VUPs.

VUPs or VUP Groups stands for 'Vulnerable and Under-Represented Persons'. The research Project 'Working, Yet Poor' has identified four groups of workers that are especially vulnerable to experience a higher risk of in-work poverty. These are low- or unskilled employees with standard employment contracts employed in poor sectors (VUP Group 1), solo and dependent self-employed persons and bogus self-employed (VUP Group 2), flexibly-employed workers (VUP Group 3), and casual and platform workers (VUP Group 4). The focus on VUPs is a conscious methodological option. As research and empirical data show, in-work poverty is not evenly distributed across the labour market.[65] Some particular groups are disproportionally affected by in-work poverty, whereas for others the risk of in-work poverty is much lower.

The institutional and regulatory framework plays a role in the uneven distribution of in-work poverty across the labour market, in defining and perpetuating differences among different groups of workers. Key aspects include the type of contract, collective bargaining coverage, structure of the companies operating in a given sector, etc. The study of these aspects and their impact on in-work poverty levels may shed light on the role of regulation in the prevalence and persistence of the phenomenon.

At policy level, the idea that in-work poverty affects with more intensity particular groups of workers is also becoming more relevant. In this sense, in the 2021

63. *See*, for example, Jekaterina Navicke, Olga Rastrigina, & Holly Sutherland, *Nowcasting Indicators of Poverty Risk in the European Union: A Microsimulation Approach*, Social Indicators Research, 119(1), 101-119 (2014).
64. Terry Ward & Erhan Özdemir, *Measuring low work intensity, supra* n. 61.
65. One of the key findings of the European Social Policy Network report on in-work poverty is precisely that 'in certain categories of the population the risk of in-work poverty is significantly higher'. *See* Ramón Peña-Casas et al., *In-work poverty in Europe, supra* n. 2, p. 10.

EP Resolution shows an awareness of this reality in statements such as '*some categories of workers (…) are at particularly high risk of in-work poverty and social exclusion*'; '*workers affected by in-work poverty often work in jobs with unacceptable working conditions, such as working without collective agreement (…)*' or '*overall, part-timers, and in particular involuntary part-timers, have a higher poverty risk when combining different risk factors, including a low wage, unstable jobs (…)*',[66]

In the same EP resolution, particular attention is devoted to atypical employment:

> 'whereas a correlation has been found between the rise in non-standard forms of employment and the increased proportions of Europeans at risk of in-work poverty; whereas 16, 2% of those working part-time or on temporary contracts are more exposed to the risk of in-work poverty, compared to 6,1% of those on permanent contract'; 'whereas the contraction of employment during the financial crisis in 2008 created a dramatic increase in the number of people in atypical employment, short-term work and part-time employment, including involuntary part-time; whereas part-time workers are most likely to work in basic or lower-level service occupations and sectors and have among the highest in-work poverty risk levels (…).[67]

It seems therefore useful to draw the attention on those particular groups that are more at-risk of in-work poverty. This will allow a more targeted approach that may offer valuable information on the institutional factors influencing in-work poverty.

This approach may also be more effective, since only those particular clusters in the labour market that concentrate on a higher percentage of in-work poor are under scrutiny. Arguably, such targeted approach will also be more successful in detecting the very concrete and particular problems that may affect the identified groups. Furthermore, the potential solutions and policy proposals to tackle in-work poverty arising from a targeted approach are more likely to be responsive to the particular circumstances and problems of the VUP groups.

With the focus on the VUP groups, the present book proposes a comparative exercise, where the central goal is to get an accurate and updated picture of how labour laws and social security regulations may influence the levels of in-work poverty for those workers included in the VUP groups.

It is important to keep in mind that the proposed VUP groups do neither correspond to legal categories *stricto sensu*, nor is their composition exactly the same in the different countries although they have in common that they group together workers that are in a more precarious position in the labour market.

The idea of vulnerability, which is at the core of the proposed groups, is rarely a legal category or autonomous legal concept.[68] It can be linked to the idea of precariousness that is explicitly used in the European Pillar of Social Rights connected to abuse

66. European Parliament, Resolution of 10 February 2021, *supra* n. 1.
67. *Ibid.*, Paras AZ and BF.
68. In some EU Member States, recent laws in the framework of the COVID-19 pandemic have introduced concepts such as 'economic vulnerability' (in Spain, Article 5 of Royal Decree Law 11/2020), albeit there is no such general legal concept of vulnerable worker in the EU.

of atypical contracts,[69] although the link between precarity and atypical contracts is not automatic.[70] Even if precariousness is also not an autonomous legal concept, its use is gaining momentum at EU level.[71] In any case, it has an analytical meaning: 'precarious work' is used to refer to those employment arrangements that deviate from the normative reference point, represented by the standard employment relationship. More recently, this concept also incorporates the idea of a work arrangement that does not comply with EU, international and national standards and laws and/or does not provide sufficient resources for a decent life or adequate social protection.[72] The latter is the approach taken by the EP in 2017.[73]

The VUP groups identified in this book aim at capturing those clusters of workers for whom the levels of in-work poverty are, statistically, more intense than the average. In this sense, these groups are labelled as 'vulnerable'. They correspond to those sections of the workforce that are normally associated with precarious work and vulnerability in the labour market, either because their employment status deviates from the standard employment relationship (VUP groups 2 and 3), because they are in jobs that may not provide sufficient resources for a decent life (VUP Group 1) or because their employment arrangements do not correspond altogether to existing legal categories, with the risks normally associated to informal or under-regulated forms of work (VUP Group 4). The definition of the VUP Groups in the present volume builds on the definitions used in the Project 'Working, Yet Poor', and more specifically on the operational definitions prepared by a team of researchers of the University of Bologna.

[A] VUP Group 1: Low- or Unskilled Employees with Standard Employment Contracts Employed in Poor Sectors

VUP Group 1 refers to low- or unskilled standard employment in poor sectors. In defining the boundaries of this group, three concepts are relevant: the concept of employee, the concept of low-or unskilled worker, and the concept of 'poor sector'.

For the purposes of VUP Group 1 employees are those persons who, under a contract of employment or as a part in an employment relationship, are obliged to perform work or services for another party in return for remuneration and subordinated to this other party. This other party is the employer. Subordination refers to a

69. European Pillar of Social Rights, principle 5, '... *Employment relationships that lead to precarious working conditions shall be prevented, including by prohibiting abuse of atypical contracts*'.
70. Carole Lang, Isabelle Schömann, Stefan Clauwaert, Atypical Forms of Employment Contracts in Times of Crisis (ETUI, 2013), p. 5.
71. For a study of the legal meaning of 'precarious work' at EU and national level *see* Kenner, J., Florczak, I and Otto, M., *Precarious Work: The challenges for Labour Law in Europe* (Edgar Elgar, 2019).
72. *See* for a discussion of the concept of 'precarious work' in the EU and its evolution Florczak, I and Otto, M., Precarious work and labour regulation in the EU: current reality and perspectives., in Kenner, J., Florczak, I and Otto, M., *Precarious Work: The challenges, supra* n. 71.
73. European Parliament resolution of 4 July 2017 on working conditions and precarious employment (2016/2221(INI)).

situation where the following criteria, either jointly or independently, apply: work directions, work control, and integration.[74]

In this group the employment relation corresponds to the 'normative' full-time, open-ended employment contract, also referred to as 'standard' contract. The goal is to capture here low paid work, excluding those working on atypical contracts, with the objective to get a better understanding of the extent to which low salaries are problematic in relation to in-work poverty.

The notion of low- or unskilled employees refers to employees performing generally basic and repetitive tasks, which require limited autonomy of judgment and of initiative in the execution of the tasks and very little, if any, education or training[75] (*see* §1.04).

VUP Group 1 is key to define which sectors are poor. Low-wage earners, in statistical terms, are 'those employees earning two-thirds or less of the national median gross hourly earnings.'[76] Building on this definition, the Project 'Working, Yet Poor' considers that a sector is poor when 20% or more of employees within the sector are low-wage earners.

Under these parameters, five sectors have been identified as 'poor sectors' at EU level, namely: accommodation and food service activities; administrative and support service activities; arts, entertainment, and recreation; wholesale and retail trade; repair of motor vehicles and motorcycles and other service activities[77] (*see* §1.04 for more details). Obviously, there are differences among Member States, as reflected in the national chapters in this book.

The element of vulnerability in VUP Group 1 is, therefore, neither to be found in the contractual arrangements, nor in the flexibility within the contract (part-time work, etc.), but rather in the occupation and sector where these workers carry out their activity.

[B] VUP Group 2: Self-Employed Persons (Particularly Bogus Self-Employed and Solo/Economically Dependent Self-Employed Persons)

VUP Group 2 refers to solo- and bogus self-employment, which are two subtypes of self-employed persons. It is, therefore, necessary to define first the concept of self-employed that is implied. For the purposes of VUP Group 2, self-employed persons are

74. Bernd Waas & Guss H. VanVoss, *Restatement of Labour Law in Europe. The concept of Employee* (Hart publishing, 2017, xxiii). In their definition however, the term 'work instructions' is used instead of 'work directions'.
75. This definition builds on the definitions of the International Standard Classification of Occupation (ISCO-08) from the International Labour Office and the proposal elaborated by the research team of Bologna University for the Working, Yet Poor Project (inspired in the definition offered by the Italian Institute of Statistics, ISTAT).
76. Eurostat, *Earnings statistics*, Statistics explained (2021), https://ec.europa.eu/eurostat/statistics-explained/index.php/Earnings_statistics#Low-wage_earners.
77. NACE rev. 2 classification. *See* EUROSTAT, Statistical classification of economical activities in the European Community, part. IV, Structure and Explanatory Notes, in https://ec.europa.eu/eurostat/documents/3859598/5902521/KS-RA-07-015-EN.PDF.

those persons who perform an activity under a contract that is not formally a contract of employment. This definition builds on the binary divide between employees and self-employed in EU law.[78]

Dependent solo self-employed are defined in VUP Group 2 as own-account workers who are completely or mainly engaged by a firm or principal and whose remuneration mainly or totally depends on the income generated from the business relationship with the said firm or principal.

Independent own-account workers, i.e., those working for various clients or firms under a contract of service or of purchase, at their own account and at their own risk, are excluded from VUP Group 2.[79] The dividing line between dependent and independent own-account workers is, however, not easy to be drawn, as there are borderline cases.

The notion of dependency may refer to personal and economic dependency or only to economic dependency. Personal and economic dependency exists when own-account workers perform their work within the principal's organization or in such a manner that allows the employer to have a certain degree of control and/or a certain power to give instructions.[80] Economic dependency, where the self-employed person, although economically dependent on one or a main principal, is autonomously present on the market, and/or uses its own assets and/or is entitled to freely organize their work.[81]

On their part, bogus self-employed persons are those workers that, despite being formally defined as self-employed, perform the same tasks in the same way as those employees employed by the same firm or principal.[82] Here there are two problems, a first one is the difficulty to differentiate between bogus self-employed and solo dependent self-employed.[83] The second is that bogus self-employed are, by definition, not visible in statistics.

Research shows that in the majority of EU countries, solo self-employed often experience a very high risk of in-work poverty, particularly in those countries where many of the self-employed work in the agricultural sector.[84] For this reason, it is interesting to study to what extent labour law and social security regulations affect solo self-employed, and how, in connection to in-work poverty.

---

78. *See* CJEU C-268/99, *Jany and others*, of 20 November 2001 [ECLI:EU:C:2001:616].
79. In *Confederación Española de empresarios de estaciones de servicio*, the CJEU established that service providers are independent traders as long as they determine their own conduct on the market independently from the principal and bear the financial or commercial risks without operating as auxiliaries within the principal's undertaking. *See* CJEU C-217/05, *Confederación Española de empresarios de estaciones de servicio*, of 14 December 2006 [ECLI:EU:C:2006:784].
80. These workers are, therefore, at the border with bogus self-employment. Nicola Countouris, *The Changing Law of the Employment Relationship*, p. 72 (Ashgate, 2007).
81. This definition builds on Eurofound, Self-employed workers: industrial relations and working conditions (European Union Publications Office, 2010). In this case, the problems of delimitation are mostly with independent own-account workers.
82. As defined in paragraphs 36 and 42 of *FNV Kunsten*. CJEU C-413/13, *FNV Kunsten*, of 4 December 2014 [ECLI:EU:C:2014:2411].
83. See this problem, discussing EU law in Nicola Countouris, The Concept of 'Worker' in European Labour Law: Fragmentation, Autonomy and Scope, ILJ, Vol. 47, 2018, pp. 211-215.
84. Ramón Peña-Casas et al., *In-work poverty in Europe, supra* n. 2, p. 33.

The element of vulnerability in this group arises from the fact that labour law protections, including access to social security, either do not or only partially apply to the solo self-employed, whereas the material situation of many of them, both in the type of work they perform and in the income they receive, is similar to that of employees.

[C] VUP Group 3: Flexibly-Employed Workers (e.g., Fixed-Term, Agency Workers, Involuntary Part-Timers)

VUP Group 3 brings together three categories of atypical employment: temporary work, agency work, and (involuntary) part-time work.

Fixed-term workers included in VUP Group 3 are those persons having an employment contract where the end of the employment contract is determined by objective conditions such as reaching a specific date, completing a specific task, or the occurrence of a specific event.[85]

Agency workers included on VUP Group 3 are those persons having an employment contract with a temporary-work agency with a view to being assigned to a user undertaking to work temporarily under its supervision and direction.[86]

The group of involuntary part-time workers includes those employees whose normal hours of work are formally less than the normal hours of work of a comparable full-time worker,[87] being in this situation against their will or due to family care needs.[88]

Research shows that temporary workers, and particularly part-time workers have a much higher risk to experience in-work poverty than indefinite, full-time workers.[89] VUP Group 3 is particularly interesting because atypical employment has increased in the recent years in Europe and because such an increase seem correlated with higher levels of in-work poverty.[90] Besides, the EU level plays a central role in the regulation of these forms of atypical work and, therefore, this group is a logical target for intervention at EU level. Furthermore, the main characteristics of the forms of atypical work included in this VUP Group, such as temporariness (fixed-term work), low work

85. This builds on the definition in Directive 1999/70/EC of 28 June 1999 concerning the framework agreement on fixed-term work. The definition also includes very short-term contract. *See* CJUE C-486/08, *Zentralbetriebsrat der Landeskrankenhäuser Tirols*, of 22 April 2010 [ECLI: EU:C:2010:215].
86. This definition builds on Article 3 of Directive 2008/104/EC on temporary agency work.
87. This is the definition of part-time enshrined in Clause 3 of Directive 97/81/EC of 15 December 1997 concerning the Framework Agreement on part-time work.
88. For the purposes of VUP Group 3, a person is an involuntary part-timer in the following situations: usually works full-time but is working part-time because of economic slack; usually works part-time but is working fewer hours because of economic slack; is working part-time because full-time work could not be found; signed a part-time contract concerning a certain number of hours but works actually longer without being paid for the excess hours (or is paid less than it should be according to the hours actually worked) or is employed on a part-time basis for reasons connected to family care.
89. Eurofound, *In work-poverty, supra* n. 6, pp. 18-25.
90. European Parliament, Resolution of 10 February 2021, *supra* n. 1, para AZ and BF.

intensity (part-time work), or contingency[91] (temporary agency work), are very often associated to precariousness and vulnerability.[92]

[D] VUP Group 4: Casual and Platform Workers

VUP Group 4 finally refers to both casual and platform workers, in an attempt to shed light on the incidence of in-work poverty on this rather heterogeneous group of workers, often described as 'precarious'. This is not, however, an easy endeavour, given the limitations in the available information. The element of vulnerability in this group has its origins in the lack of (adequate) regulation, resulting in deprivation or very limited access to labour law protections, including access to social security.

For the purposes of VUP Group 4, a casual worker is a person whose work is irregular or intermittent. This includes formally self-employed as well as employees.

The concept of intermittent work refers to short-term contracts concluded to conduct a specific task, often related to an individual project or seasonally occurring jobs. The intermittent worker is required to fulfil a task or complete a specific number of working days.

The category of casual work includes on-call work that involves a contractual relationship in which the principal does not continuously provide work for the worker. Rather, he/she has the option of calling the worker in as and when needed. Some contracts indicate the minimum and maximum number of working hours. So-called zero-hour contracts do not specify minimum working hours, and the principal is not obliged to ever call in the worker.[93]

Finally, platform workers included in VUP Group 4 are those individuals using an app or a website to match themselves with customers, in order to perform specific tasks or to provide specific services in exchange for payment. This notion includes two subcategories: crowdworkers and workers-on-demand via app.[94] Crowdworkers are those persons that complete a series of tasks through on-line platforms (which put in contact an indefinite number of organizations, business, and individuals through the Internet). The nature of the tasks performed on crowdwork platforms varies considerably: they involve microtasks, extremely parcelled activities, usually menial and monotonous, as well as more complex jobs. Workers-on-demand via app are those performing not only traditional activities such as transport, cleaning, and running errands, but also clerical work with the particularity that the match with potential customers or clients is done through an app.

---

91. For the concept of 'contingent work' in labour law and its usage *see* Antonio Lo Faro, Contingent work: a conceptual framework, in *Core and contingent work in the European Union: a comparative analysis* (Edoardo Ales, Olaf Deinert and Jeff Kenner eds., Hart Publishing, 2017).
92. Carole Lang, Isabelle Schömann, Stefan Clauwaert, Atypical Forms of Employment Contracts, *supra* n. 70.
93. This definition builds on the work done by the research team of the University of Bologna for the 'Working, Yet Poor' Project and on the definitions used in Eurofound, New forms of Employment report (Publications Office of the European Union, 2015).
94. Valerio De Stefano, The rise of the 'just-in-time workforce': on-demand work, crowdwork, and labor protection in the 'gig-economy', in CLLPJ, 2016.

§1.04 HOW DOES IN-WORK POVERTY AFFECT THE DIFFERENT VUPS IN THE EU? A STATISTICAL DESCRIPTION

Given the focus of the present book on the four mentioned groups of VUP groups, we must now examine how they are identifiable in the existing statistical data. Labour market data are generally derived from European Labour Force Surveys (LFS). However, these surveys do not provide an in-depth view of the income and living conditions of the households surveyed. As in-work poverty includes not only labour market status but also poverty and the link between the two, the analysis of VUP groups will focus on EU-SILC data.[95]

To be in line with the European *in-work at-risk-of-poverty* indicator, the population of the VUPs included in our definition is restricted to individuals considered as 'in-work'. In-work covers the population, aged from 18, living in private households who are declared to be at work 'for more than half the total number of months for which information on any status is available during the income reference period'.[96] The income reference period in EU-SILC is one year (in most countries, the calendar year before the survey). This definition of a *worker* is more restrictive than in LFS, as it is based on a period of one year and not on a specific moment in time (in the LFS, persons in employment are 'persons who during the reference week worked at least one hour for a pay or profit gain' or who were temporarily absent of the job/business).[97] Therefore, the results on the composition of VUPs may differ from one source to another as it focuses on two slightly different populations.

The advantage of the EU-SILC data and its definitions is that they allow for an analysis of the living conditions of households where one member is employed and has been so for most of the year. This avoids including individuals whose income is not representative of their situation in the reference year. For example, if a person has spent 11 months unemployed and 1 month in employment during the reference year, the income over the reference period is more likely to be representative of his/her situation as unemployed rather than as employed. However, this definition may seem arbitrary, and the academic literature has explored alternative methods of defining a person in employment for the purpose of measuring in-work poverty.[98] In the context of this book, the analysis is aligned with the definition used by Eurostat.

In the rest of this section, the words *employment* or *workforce* will refer to those who are considered as 'in-work' according to the Eurostat definition. Moreover, the statistics presented are calculated for the 27 EU members (i.e., excluding the United

95. This report is based on data from Eurostat (EU-SILC, 2007-2019). The responsibility for all conclusions drawn from the data lies entirely with the authors.
96. Laura Bardone & Anne-Catherine Guio. In-work poverty – New commonly, *supra* n. 51, p. 2.
97. Eurostat, EU labour force survey – methodology, Statistics explained (2021), https://ec.europa.eu/eurostat/statistics-explained/index.php?title=EU_labour_force_survey_-_methodology#EU-LFS_concept_of_labour_force_status (last accessed 15 Dec. 2021).
98. *See*, for example, Sophie Ponthieux, *Assessing and analysing*, supra n. 52; Eric Crettaz, *Poverty and material deprivation, supra* n. 52; Henning Lohmann, *The concept and measurement, supra* n. 48.

Kingdom) from 2007 to 2019 (except for 2007, 2008, and 2009 where data for Croatia are not available).

[A] VUP Group 1: Low- or Unskilled Standard Employment

VUP Group 1 includes *low- or unskilled employees with standard employment contracts employed in poor sectors*. To define low- or unskilled employment with EU-SILC, we built on the International Standard Classification of Occupation (ISCO-08) from the International Labour Office.[99] Following this classification, skill is defined as 'the ability to carry out the tasks and duties of a given job. For the purpose of ISCO-08, two dimensions of skill are used to arrange occupations into groups. These are *skill level* and *skill specialization*'.[100] The classification thus makes it possible to define 4 levels of skill for the occupations:

- Level 1: occupations that 'typically involve the performance and routine physical or manual tasks'.[101] It includes 'office cleaners, freight handlers, garden labourers and kitchen assistants.[102]
- Level 2: occupations that 'typically involve the performance of task such as operating machinery and electronic equipment; driving vehicles; maintenance and repair electrical and mechanical equipment; and manipulation, ordering and storage information'.[103] It includes 'butchers, bus drivers, secretaries, accounts clerks, sewing machinists, dressmakers, shop sales assistants, police officers, hairdressers, building electricians and motor vehicle mechanics'.[104]
- Level 3: occupations that 'typically involve the performance of complex technical and practical tasks that require an extensive body of factual, technical and procedural knowledge in a specialized field'.[105]It includes 'shop managers, medical laboratory technicians, legal secretaries, commercial sales representatives, diagnostic medical radiographers, computer support technicians, and broadcasting and recording technicians'.[106]
- Level 4: occupations that 'typically involve the performance of tasks that require complex problem-solving, decision-making and creativity based on an extensive body of theoretical and factual knowledge in a specialized field'.[107] It includes 'marketing managers, civil engineers, secondary school teachers, medical practitioners, musicians, operating theatre nurses and computer systems analysts'.[108]

99. International Labour Office, International Standard Classification of Occupations 2008 (ISCO-08): Structure, group definitions and correspondence tables, Volume I (2012).
100. *Ibid.*, at 11.
101. *Ibid.*, at 12.
102. *Ibid.*, at 12.
103. *Ibid.*, at 12.
104. *Ibid.*, at 12.
105. *Ibid.*, at 13.
106. *Ibid.*, at 13.
107. *Ibid.*, at 13.
108. *Ibid.*, at 13.

For the purpose of the present analysis, the group of low- or unskilled workers is restricted to workers in occupations at level 1 or 2.

Regarding the economic sector of activity, the poor sectors were defined as the least remunerative sectors. Thus, a poor sector is a sector in which more than 20% of employees are low-wage earners. Low-wage earners (following Eurostat definitions) are persons whose hourly earnings (excluding the social contributions and payroll taxes paid by the employer) is less than two-thirds of the national median gross hourly earnings.[109] At the EU level, five economic sectors meet this definition (following the Structure of Earnings Survey from Eurostat):

(1) Accommodation and food service activities (41.88%, EU 28, 2018).
(2) Administrative and support service activities (32.60%, EU 28, 2018).
(3) Arts, entertainment and recreation (24.49%, EU 28, 2018).
(4) Wholesale and retail trade; repair of motor vehicles and motorcycles (22.70%, EU 28, 2018).
(5) Other service activities (21.39%, EU 28, 2018).

According to the concepts presented earlier, the members of VUP Group 1 are defined as 'in-work' persons having a low- or unskilled occupation and working in one of the five sectors defined as poor.[110]

In 2019, 10.3% of the workforce in EU belonged to VUP Group 1. The share of workers in this group increased slightly from 8.4% in 2008 to 10.3% in 2019. As shown in Table 1.1, compared to all employed, VUP Group 1 members are more likely to be young, women, to have a foreign nationality, and less likely to have a university degree. The level of education of workers has increased in Europe, with the share of employed with a tertiary degree rising from 26.0% in 2007 to 34.9% in 2019. This increase has also affected VUP Group 1, with the share of tertiary graduates rising from 9.5% to 16.5% over the same period.

---

109. Eurostat, *Earnings statistics*, Statistics explained (2021), https://ec.europa.eu/eurostat/statistics-explained/index.php/Earnings_statistics#Low-wage_earners (last accessed 15 Dec. 2021).

110. Due to data constraints (sector of activity grouped in EU-SILC), for the data analysis part, low-skilled workers in the sectors *Real estate activities* and *Professional, scientific and technical activities* were also included in VUP Group 1. However, the bias (to include them) should be relatively small as these sectors represent either a low share of total employment (real estate activities) or the share of low-skilled workers is low (Professional, scientific, and technical activities).

Table 1.1 Composition of VUP Group 1 in the European Union (27), in 2019

	All Employed	*Employees Only*	*VUP 1: Employees in Low-Skilled Occupation and in Poor Sectors*
Age group (%)			
18-34	26.1	27.5	29.4
35-49	40.3	40.3	41.3
> =50	33.6	32.2	29.3
Gender (%)			
Women	46.3	48.0	49.6
Men	53.7	52.0	50.4
Nationality (%)			
Country of residence	91.9	91.5	90.0
Other	8.1	8.5	10.0
Education (%)			
Lower secondary/Primary of less	16.7	15.9	21.8
Upper secondary or post-secondary non-tertiary	48.5	48.9	61.6
Tertiary	34.9	35.2	16.5

Source: EU-SILC/Eurostat

Reading guide: Among the employed, in Europe, in 2019, 26.1% are in the 18-34 age group, while there are 29.4% in this age group among the VUP Group 1.

In-work poverty affects 9.0% of workers in 2019 in Europe as shown in Table 1.2. Focusing only on employees, 7.2% of them are in poverty. VUP Group 1 workers are more often affected by poverty compared to the population of employees (7.9% versus 7.2% for the employees). Workers in this group are also more often affected by severe material deprivation (4.3% versus 3.1% for employees) and by material and social deprivation (10.3% versus 7.8% for employees). Over the entire 2007-2019 period, poverty in the VUP Group 1 has fluctuated between 7.0% and 8.4%, while severe material deprivation and material and social deprivation has decreased significantly in recent years. However, this decline in non-monetary indicators is observed for all groups.

Table 1.2 In-Work Poverty and Deprivation Among VUP Group 1 in the European Union (27), in 2019

	All Employed	*Employees Only*	*VUP 1: Employees in Low-Skilled Occupation and in Poor Sectors*
In-work at-risk-of-poverty	9.0	7.2	7.9
Severe material deprivation	3.3	3.1	4.3
Material and social deprivation	8.1	7.8	10.3

Source: EU-SILC/Eurostat.

Reading guide: Among the employed, in Europe, in 2019, 9.0% are at-risk-of- poverty.

Although in-work poverty is higher for VUP Group 1, all workers in this group are not equally affected by the risk of in-work poverty. Thus, the risk of in-work poverty in VUP Group 1 is higher for women (risk of poverty of 8.1% versus 7.6% for men), for people of foreign nationality (16.9% versus 6.9% for those with the nationality corresponding to the country of residence), and for people with a low level of education (14.3% versus 5.0% for tertiary graduates). Workers who have not worked the whole year are also more affected by the risk of poverty in VUP Group 1 (11.8% against 7.8% for those who have worked the whole year). Other factors affect the risk of poverty, such as household composition. Thus, workers in VUP Group 1 living in a household with more than two children under 18 years of age have a poverty risk of 11.7% compared to 6.6% for those living in a household with no children. Finally, being the only worker in the household generates a risk of poverty of 15.2% compared to 3.6% for workers with more than one worker in the household.

[B] VUP Group 2: Solo and Bogus Self-Employment

VUP Group 2 includes solo and bogus self-employed persons. In EU-SILC, the only distinction available is between self-employed with employees and those without employees. For this reason, the sample of VUP Group 2 is restricted to self-employed without employees. This is imprecise but allows us to get as close as possible to this group given the data constraints.

In 2019, 13.3% of workers in Europe were self-employed. A large part of them were self-employed without employees (8.6% of workers in 2019). The share of workers being self-employed has decreased over the period 2007-2019 from 15.4% to 13.3% for all self-employed and from 10.2% to 8.6% for self-employed without employees. As shown in Table 1.3, compared to the total employed population, self-employed are older, more often men, have more often a low level of education and less often of foreign nationality. In addition, self-employed without employees are more often employed in low-skilled jobs than the employed or the self-employed (with or without employees).

Table 1.3 VUP Group 2 Workforce Composition in the European Union (27), in 2019

	All Employed	*All Self-Employed (Including Family Workers)*	*VUP 2: Self-Employed Without Employees*
Age group			
18-34	26.1	17.0	17.1
35-49	40.3	40.4	40.2
> = 50	33.6	42.6	42.7
Gender			
Women	46.3	35.3	35.3
Men	53.7	64.7	64.7
Nationality			
Country of residence	91.9	94.6	94.3
Other	8.1	5.4	5.7
Education			
Lower secondary/Primary of less	16.7	21.3	21.9
Upper secondary or post-secondary non-tertiary	48.5	46.1	46.0
Tertiary	34.9	32.6	32.1
Occupation			
High skill (ISCO-08 level 3 and 4)	42.2	41.3	38.4
Low skill (ISCO-08 level 1 and 2)	57.8	58.7	61.6

Source: EU-SILC/Eurostat.

Reading guide: Among the employed, in Europe, in 2019, 26.1% are in the 18-34 age group, while there are 17.1% in this age group among the VUP Group 2.

As observed in Table 1.4, the self-employed have a much higher risk of in-work poverty than the employed population (23.7% for the self-employed without employees against 9.0% for the employed). Over the entire 2007-2019 period, the self-employed without employees always had a higher poverty rate than self-employed with employees. Regarding dynamics, the self-employed without employees experienced a risk of in-work poverty greater than or equal to 25% between 2014 and 2017 before declining to 23.7% in 2019. The 2019 value is, however, higher than those observed between 2007 and 2009 for this population. At EU level, the self-employed also have a higher risk of material (and social) deprivation than all employed. The rate of severe material deprivation is 4.8% for the self-employed without employees (against 3.3% for the employed) and the rate of material and social deprivation is 11.7% (against 8.1% for the employed). However, these two rates have been decreasing significantly since 2013.

Table 1.4 In-Work Poverty and Deprivation among VUP Group 2 in the European Union (27), in 2019

	All Employed	*All Self-Employed (Including Family Workers)*	*VUP 2: Self-Employed Without Employees*
In-work at-risk-of-poverty	9.0	20.8	23.7
Severe material deprivation	3.3	4.1	4.8
Material and social deprivation	8.1	9.6	11.7

Source: EU-SILC/Eurostat.

Reading guide: Among the employed, in Europe, in 2019, 9.0% are at-risk-of- poverty.

As with Group 1, all self-employed without employees are not affected by the risk of in-work poverty in the same way. In 2019, men are more at risk of in-work poverty than women in VUP Group 2 (25.5% for men in 2019 versus 21.1% for women). This is also the case for foreigners (33.0% compared to 23.1% for workers having the nationality of the country), people with low education level (38.9% compared to 14.0% for university graduates). This increased risk is also observed for those working part-time and/or in low-skilled jobs. Household composition is also an important factor for this group. Self-employed without employees living alone or being the only one worker in the household have a risk of in-work poverty higher than 30%. The risk of poverty also increases with the number of children (22.1% for self-employed without employees living with no children under 18 versus 27.6% for those living with 2 or more children).

[C] VUP Group 3: Fixed-Term, Agency Workers, Involuntary Part-Timers

VUP Group 3 is composed of fixed-term workers, agency workers, and involuntary part-timers. For the statistical analysis, the VUP Group 3 can be decomposed into 2 groups:

(1) *Temporary workers* defined in EU-SILC as workers with work contract of limited duration including seasonal job and 'persons engaged by an employment agency or business and hired out to a third party for the carrying out of a 'work mission' (unless there is a work contract of unlimited duration with the employment agency or business)'.[111]
(2) *Involuntary part-timers* is approximated in the data persons 'in-work' who spent at least half of the period of work (during the reference period) in part-time work and answered to the question 'Reason for working less than 30 hours' with the following reasons:
   (a) Wants to work more hours but cannot find a job(s) or work(s) of more hours.
   (b) Housework, looking after children or other persons.
   (c) Other reasons.

Part-timers in education, disable, who have multiple part-time jobs (total equivalent to a full-time), or who do not want to work more are not considered as involuntary part-timers. The category of involuntary part-timers is not perfectly captured. Some part-timers have worked 30 hours or more (if the legal working time is higher than 30 hours a week), and were therefore not questioned about the reason for part-time, but may be involuntarily part-timer and other part-timers that simply did not answer the question on the 'reason why'. There is, therefore, a risk of underestimating the total number of involuntary part-timers. It is also important to note that some workers are included in both subgroups: temporary workers who are also involuntary part-timers (in 2019, around one involuntary part-timer out of five is on temporary contract).

In 2019, according to Table 1.5, temporary workers in the EU represent 11.3% of workers and involuntary part-timers 4.9% (with the risk of underestimation explained above). In total, VUP Group 3 thus represents 15.2% of workers. While the share of temporary workers has not varied significantly in recent years (between 11.3% and 11.6% since 2012), the share of involuntary part-time workers has fallen from 5.8% in 2014 to 4.9% in 2019. Compared to the employed population, temporary workers are younger, while involuntary part-timers are more concentrated in the 35-49 age group. Involuntary part-timers (including parents caring for children) are overwhelmingly female (86.7% in 2019). VUP Group 3 workers are more likely to be foreigners compared to the total employed population. They are also more likely to have a low

111. Eurostat, *Methodological guidelines and description of EU-SILC target variables- 2019 operation*, p. 302 (2020). https://circabc.europa.eu/sd/a/b862932f-2209-450f-a76d-9cfe842936b4/DOCSILC065%20operation%202019_V9.pdf (last accessed 15 Dec. 2021).

level of education (24.2% have a primary or lower secondary education compared to 16.7% of the employed population) or a low-skilled job (67.5% in VUP Group 3 against 57.8% among employed).

Table 1.5 VUP Group 3 Workforce Composition in the European Union (27), in 2019

	All Employed	*Temporary Workers*	*Involuntary Part-Timers*	*VUP 3*
Age group				
18-34	26.1	51.4	23.4	43.2
35-49	40.3	30.3	46.7	35.3
> =50	33.6	18.2	29.8	21.5
Gender				
Women	46.3	50.1	86.3	60.1
Men	53.7	49.9	13.7	39.9
Nationality				
Country of residence	91.9	85.5	86.7	86.0
Other	8.1	14.5	13.3	14.0
Education				
Lower secondary/Primary of less	16.7	25.3	22.8	24.2
Upper secondary or post-secondary non-tertiary	48.5	44.2	50.6	46.4
Tertiary	34.9	30.4	26.6	29.4
Occupation				
High skill (ISCO-08 level 3 and 4)	42.2	32.8	30.6	32.5
Low skill (ISCO-08 level 1 and 2)	57.8	67.2	69.4	67.5

Source: EU-SILC/Eurostat.

Reading guide: Among the employed, in Europe, in 2019, 26.1% are in the 18-34 age group, while there are 43.2% in this age group among the VUP Group 3.

Table 1.6 shows that workers in VUP Group 3 are at greater risk of in-work poverty than the employed population. In 2019, the risk of in-work poverty reaches 15.7% in VUP Group 3 compared to 9.0% in the employed population. The same findings emerge when considering non-monetary indicators. The index of severe material deprivation in 2019 is 5.6% for VUP Group 3 against 3.3% for the employed and the index of material and social deprivation is 12.4% for the VUP Group 3 against 8.1% for the employed. As with other groups, material (and social) deprivation has been declining for several years.

Table 1.6 In-Work Poverty and Deprivation Among VUP Group 3 in the European Union (27), in 2019

	All Employed	*Temporary Workers*	*Involuntary Part-Timers*	*VUP 3*
In-work at-risk-of-poverty	9.0	16.1	17.3	15.7
Severe material deprivation	3.3	6.2	5.3	5.6
Material and social deprivation	8.1	12.7	13.8	12.4

Source: EU-SILC/Eurostat.

Note: Individuals who are in both temporary workers and involuntary part-timers are at higher risk of poverty but are counted only once in VUP 3, which is why the poverty rate is lower in VUP 3 than in the two groups taken separately.

Reading guide: Among the employed, in Europe, in 2019, 9.0% are at-risk-of- poverty.

VUP Group 3 is heterogeneous and not all workers in this group are affected by in-work poverty to the same extent. Thus, in 2019, in EU, men are more strongly affected by in-work poverty in this group than women (17.6% for men versus 14.4% for women). Similarly, foreigners have a risk of in-work poverty more than twice as high as nationals (28.1% versus 13.7% in VUP Group 3). Even if education is a protective factor against the risk of in-work poverty, workers with tertiary education in VUP Group 3 are more affected by poverty than tertiary graduates among the employed (9.1% for university graduate in VUP Group 3 against 4.3% in the employed population). As with the other groups, single-person households are more affected by poverty (26.8% versus 13.2% for those living in a 2-person household in 2019, in the VUP Group 3). Similarly, workers in VUP Group 3 living in a single-worker household are three times more at risk of poverty than those living in a multi-worker household (30.2% versus 8.5%).

[D] VUP Group 4: Casual and Platform Workers

It is difficult to measure the number of platform workers and no estimate exist for all European countries. However, a research program seeking to estimate the share of platform workers in 14 European countries, calculates that in average for 14 EU countries, platform work affects around 2% of the adult population.[112] This estimate assumes that a platform worker is a worker who obtains the majority of his/her income from this activity. The rate would reach 4% in the UK, between 2.5% and 3% in Germany and the Netherlands and between 1% and 2% in France, Hungary, Italy, Portugal, Lithuania, Spain, and Sweden. The share of platform workers would be less or equal to 1% in Croatia, Finland, Romania, and Slovakia. Alternatives were tested in this study by defining platform workers less strictly. For example, by defining a platform worker as a worker who performs an activity at least 10 hours per week via platforms, the estimate would be 5.6% of the adult population in Europe (between 6.7% in the UK and 2.7% in Slovakia).

The profile of platform workers is also examined in this study. Platform workers are on average younger than offline workers, but they are also more often men and more often with a high level of education. Moreover, a significant part of platform workers has children to support.

Other studies have also focused on estimating this population in Europe. The results are highly dependent on how platform work is defined.[113] However, all of these studies and the underlying data do not allow to analyse the in-work poverty of these workers, since for that information on the composition of the household and on the income (from work, capital, transfers, etc.) received by all members of the household are needed.

> This section has presented statistical information on the VUP groups using data from the EU-SILC survey. Approximations to the definitions of these groups have been necessary because the data do not allow for certain levels of detail. The results presented refer to all countries of the EU with 27 countries. However, European countries are very heterogeneous, whether in terms of economic performance, demographics, social protection systems, or labour market legislation. Therefore, the conclusions and trends presented for the EU as a whole do not necessarily reflect those observed at the level of each EU Member States.

§1.05 VULNERABLE AND UNDER-REPRESENTED PERSONS IN A COMPARATIVE PERSPECTIVE

The present book offers a comparative perspective on the labour law and social security regulations that shape the working conditions of VUP groups. Seven EU Member States are compared, namely Belgium, Germany, Italy, Luxembourg, the Netherlands, Poland, and Sweden.

These countries represent different models in Europe. They are different in terms of size, economy, geography, culture, industrial relations, and welfare State model. Except for the anglo-saxon/liberal model, all the welfare state typologies described in literature are represented: nordic/social democratic (Sweden);

112. Annarosa Pesole et al., *Platform Workers in Europe* (Publications Office of the European Union, Luxembourg, 2018), https://ec.europa.eu/jrc/en/colleem (accessed 15 Dec. 2021).
113. Eurofound, *Employment and working conditions of selected types of platform work*, p. 33 (Publications Office of the European Union, 2018).

continental/conservative (Belgium, Luxembourg, Netherlands, and Germany); southern/familialist (Italy), and eastern european/post-socialist (Poland).[114] The fact that there are four countries of the continental/conservative family helps to illustrate national differences even between countries of a similar geographical area and welfare-state tradition. Indeed, in-work poverty levels are surprisingly varied even between the BENELUX countries, where Belgium (5.1% in 2018) and Luxembourg (11.5% in 2018)[115] have respectively one of the lowest and one of the highest percentages of in-work poverty in the EU.

The comparative perspective proposed in the book is essential to assess the contribution of the different factors (individual, household and, especially, institutional) in different national contexts. Highlighting and comparing similarities and differences in the labour laws and social security regulations allows for a better understanding of the relative importance and impact that different elements have in producing and reproducing in-work poverty. This exercise is developed in a final chapter consisting of a comparative overview of the main findings in the seven national chapters.

In terms of structure, the book is organized into nine chapters. After the introduction (Chapter 1), there are seven chapters presenting the relevant national regulation in the different Member States. These chapters follow a similar structure of analysis, adapted to the national characteristics, to make possible a meaningful comparison. The final chapter (Chapter 9) offers a comparative overview.

As has been explained earlier, the comparison is focused on particular groups of workers: the VUP groups (*see* §1.03). The national chapters have all a similar basic structure. In every chapter, there is an introduction that offers an overview of the national legal framework in connection to in-work poverty, including an explanation on the role of minimum wages, collective bargaining (coverage, role in wage-setting, etc.), and the most relevant social security benefits. Then, the chapters engage with the analysis of the regulation affecting VUP groups. For each of the VUP groups, the national chapters explain their composition at national level, describe the relevant legal framework with a particular impact in a given group, and assess the impact of regulation on the incidence of in-work poverty in each particular group. For VUP Group 3 (atypical work), each of the categories included in the group (fixed-term, agency work, and involuntary part-time) is analysed separately. Finally, the national chapters include a last section with conclusions.

The national chapters show that there are important differences in the incidence of in-work poverty in the different Member States. Consequently, different policy pointers are highlighted in each report.

Belgium is an example of a Member State with a low incidence of in-work poverty, although as in many other places, the proportion of in-work poor has increased in recent years. The chapter shows that working is a good protection against

114. This typology follows closely the clustering of EU Member States by Wim Van Lacker, *The European World of Temporary Employment, gendered and poor? See also* Eurofound, *In work-poverty, supra* n. 6, pp. 12-14.
115. In-work at risk of poverty rate – EU-SILC (ILC_IW01), year 2018, population 18 years and over.

poverty in Belgium, in a labour market where work intensity is relatively low. Although the indefinite full-time contract is still the best protection against the risk of in-work poverty, the Belgian legislation also has several protection mechanisms in place for the different VUP Group. Still, the chapter shows that certain groups of workers, including those in the different VUP Groups under study, face a high risk of poverty. The authors call for a re-thinking of the Belgian labour and social security laws in order to successfully fight existing problems.

The chapter on Germany describes a country not only with an inclusive labour market and high average wage levels, but also with important inequalities among the working population. Rapidly falling collective bargaining coverage and a jobseekers' regime putting substantial pressure on the unemployed to accept every available job have resulted in a remarkably large low-wage sector. The chapter describes ongoing and recently planned reforms that potentially will help to improve workers' protection against poverty.

The chapter on Italy provides the reader with a rich and detailed overview of in-work poverty in that country. Workers in the different VUP Groups are differently affected by the risk of in-work poverty. Those with indefinite and full-time contracts are better protected, but some problems concerning social security protections for low-wage workers are highlighted. The Italian self-employed are also excluded of some protections and benefits, resulting on a higher risk of becoming working poor than the average employee population. Workers of VUP Groups 3 and 4 are in the worse position, although the report shows recent reforms with the potential to improve the situation.

Luxembourg, despite being a vibrant and well-functioning economy, presents one of the highest levels of in-work poverty in the EU. The chapter explores the causes of this situation against the background of a protective and stable legal framework that, nevertheless, fails to shield atypical workers, particularly temporary and part-time workers, from in-work poverty.

The chapter on Netherlands describes a system where flexible work arrangements are widespread and encouraged while legislation fails to some extent to protect 'flexible' workers. The same goes for solo self-employed, a group that suffers the highest risk of in-work-poverty. On the other hand, workers with indefinite contracts working full time seem to be well protected, even in low-wage sectors. As in other Member States, the chapter shows how in-work poverty has become relevant in policy debates and how recent and planned reforms to tackle the issue are on the policy agenda, mostly through limitations to the most flexible forms of employment and protection to vulnerable solo self-employed.

The chapter on Poland describes a labour law regulation that is limited in its scope of application, therefore leaving many individuals outside its protective umbrella. Indeed, the restrictive interpretation of what constitutes an employment relation limits the potential of labour law to improve workers' income and working conditions. At the same time, there have been some improvements offered by collective labour law even to those formally outside of labour law's scope, such as the self-employed. Within the boundaries of labour law, an excess of flexibility and the focus of active labour market policies are also problematic.

The chapter on Sweden shows a country where in-work poverty is not perceived as a problem. Relying on an extensive and well-functioning collective bargaining system, low wages and low incomes do not seem to be an issue in Sweden. The problems are to be found, against a legal background that provides ample room for flexibility, in connection to work intensity. The chapter also reports recent reforms that will potentially have an effect on in-work poverty, although very much will depend on the level of involvement of the social partners in their implementation.

The last chapter of the book is a comparative overview of the national perspectives. In this comparative overview, differences and similarities are highlighted, in an attempt to find patterns and identify common problems and best practices, connecting all the findings of the national chapters.

Chapter 2

In-Work Poverty in Belgium

Eleni De Becker, Alexander Dockx & Paul Schoukens

This contribution[1] offers an overview of the Belgian labour and social security legislation[2] that may have a direct or indirect impact on (the risk of) in-work poverty for the four Vulnerable Under-Represented Persons (VUP) Groups in Belgium.

While Belgium remained one of the European Union (EU) countries with the lowest in-work poverty rates, the percentage of working persons at risk of poverty has increased over the years. The risk of in-work poverty in Belgium particularly affects self-employed persons, temporary workers and low or unskilled workers. Moreover, significant differences exist between the different regions concerning the risk of monetary poverty (for 2020, this was 14.1% overall, 27.8% in the Brussels region, 18.2% in the Walloon region, and 9.3% in the Flemish region), activation rate (for 2020, this was 68.6% overall, 64.6% in the Brussels region, 63.9% in the Walloon region, and 71.9% in the Flemish region) and severe material deprivation (for 2021, this was 11% overall, 20.5% in the Brussels region, 15.8% in the Walloon region, and 6.6% in the Flemish region).

This chapter first discusses, in the introduction, the socio-economic and legal framework surrounding in-work poverty in Belgium. In the following sections, this chapter addresses for each VUP Group the composition of this

1. This chapter is based on the national report for Belgium drafted in the framework of the Working Yet Poor project by A. Barrio, E. De Becker and M. Wouters.
2. We have finalised this chapter on 1 February 2022; amounts of the different social security benefits have been updated on 12 May 2022 and some (planned) changes to the Belgian legislation that occurred between February and May 2022 have been included as well.

group, the relevant legal framework and looks for four hypothetical household groups at their risk of in-work poverty and the obstacles that might arise from the relevant Belgian legal framework.

§2.01 INTRODUCTION

[A] In-Work Poverty in Belgium

Research into the risk of poverty in Belgium highlights important differences between the total population and the working population. For this first group, the poverty risk lies around 15% for the total population (2020)[3] compared to 4.8% for the working population (2019). The risk of severe material deprivation is 1.8% for the working population (2019),[4] while it is 3.9% for the total population (2020).[5]

As such, working offers a good protection in Belgium, having resulted in a lower percentage of working poor in comparison to other EU Member States. For unemployed persons or people that are inactive for other reasons, the poverty risk is significantly higher (49.4% and 35.9%, respectively).[6]

For most people, work is the main pathway to an adequate living standard. This largely stems from the prevalent insider-outsider characteristics of the Belgian labour market. Labour intensity is lower than the EU average and several neighbouring countries (EU average: 72%; the Netherlands and Germany: 80%),[7] but those who work have both a relatively stable job and relatively good conditions of employment. Organisation for Economic Co-operation and Development (OECD) numbers show that around 4% of employees earn a wage lower than 67% of the median income,[8] which is notably lower than, for example, the Netherlands (15%) and Germany (18%).[9]

In particular, persons with a low level of education face difficulties in finding their way to the labour market. The labour intensity of this group of workers remains quasi stable at a low level, resulting in a higher poverty rate.[10] The poverty risk for this

3. Jill Coene, Tuur Ghys, Bernard Hubeau, Sarah Marchal, Peter Raeymaeckers, Roy Remmen & Wouter Vandenholen, *Armoede en Sociale Uitsluiting Jaarboek 2021* 418 (2021).
4. This chapter is based on data from Eurostat, EU-SILC, 2007, 2013, and 2019. The responsibility for all conclusions drawn from the data lies entirely with the authors. The exploitation of the EU-SILC data has been done by the Luxemburgish partner of the 'Working, Yet Poor' project. Unless mentioned otherwise, the data mentioned in this chapter stems from the Eurostat, EU-SILC data.
5. Jill Coene, Tuur Ghys, Bernard Hubeau, Sarah Marchal, Peter Raeymaeckers, Roy Remmen & Wouter Vandenholen, *Armoede en Sociale Uitsluiting Jaarboek 2021* 418 (2021).
6. Jeroen Horemans, Sarah Kuypers, Sarah Marchal & Ive Marx, *De kwetsbare werkende: een profielschets van armoede en financiële bestaanszekerheid bij werkende Belgen - Covivat Policy Note 4 of June 2020* 7-8 (2020); the authors based their findings on EU-SILC data (2018).
7. *Werkzaamheidsgraad*, Statistiek Vlaanderen (8 April 2021), https://www.statistiekvlaanderen.be/nl/werkzaamheidsgraad#:~:text=In%20de%20Europese%20Unie%20(EU27,Duitsland%20(80%2C0%25.
8. As cited in Ive Marx, *Krachtlijnen voor meer werk én minder armoede: sociale bescherming in tijden van arbeidsdiversiteit* 10 (Itinera 2019).
9. *Ibid.*
10. FPS Social Security, *The evolution of the social situation and social protection in Belgium 2020: persistent challenges* 4 (2021).

group of workers has also increased sharply (from 18.7% in 2005 to 32.7% in 2018).[11] While the employment rate of people with a high level of education is only slightly below the EU average (83.8% vs. 84.8%), for those with a low education it does fall far below the EU average (46.3% vs. 55,7%). This is even more the case for women (37%) than it is for men (54.1%).[12]

Belgium is also characterized by a higher amount of (quasi-)jobless households, being among one of the frontrunners at EU level.[13] Quasi-jobless households increasingly consist of the low-skilled, migrants, singles, and families with children, individuals without a personal income or who live on sickness or disability benefits only.[14]

[B] The Belgian Labour Market

Belgian labour market data shows a strong concentration in full-time employment: around 75% of Belgian employees works full-time (period from 2017 to 2021).[15] The number of self-employed persons has been increasing for years, including the number of women working as self-employed persons in their main occupation.[16]

The number of temporary employment contracts fluctuates around 10% of the total working population for the period from 2017 to Q3 2021. Half of these temporary employment contracts are fixed-term contracts or contracts for specific tasks (+/- 5% of the overall group of employees). Temporary agency work constitutes around 22% of the group (+/- 2% of the overall group of employees). Around 25% of the overall group of employees works part-time: 75% of which are women.[17]

[C] High Dependency on Social Security Benefits

The low employment rate in Belgium has resulted in a high dependency on social security benefits even before the COVID-19 pandemic. Noticeably, however, the

11. *Ibid.*, 72 (2021).
12. *Ibid.*, 14-15 (2021).
13. For 2019, the rate of quasi-jobless households in Belgium was 12.4% with only Greece and Ireland performing worse. There are significant differences between regions in Belgium as well: In Flanders, the rate of quasi-jobless households was 7.4%, which is rather high compared to the low risk of poverty in Flanders. *See* Jill Coene, Tuur Ghys, Bernard Hubeau, Sarah Marchal, Peter Raeymaeckers, Roy Remmen & Wouter Vandenholen, *Armoede en Sociale Uitsluiting Jaarboek 2021* 419 (2021).
14. FPS Social Security, *The evolution of the social situation and social protection in Belgium 2020: persistent challenges* 6 (2021).
15. STATBEL (Labour Force Survey), Labour market indicators (retrieved on 28 February 2022) https://statbel.fgov.be/nl/themas/werk-opleiding/arbeidsmarkt/werkgelegenheid-en-werkloosheid#panel-12.
16. Figures for self-employed persons, (retrieved on 13 May 2022), https://economie.fgov.be/nl/themas/ondernemingen/kmos-en-zelfstandigen-cijfers/zelfstandigen-belgie#:~:text=Op%2031%20december%202020%20waren,gedurende%20de%20laatste%20tien%20jaar.
17. STATBEL (Labour Force Survey), Labour market indicators (retrieved on 28 February 2022) https://statbel.fgov.be/nl/themas/werk-opleiding/arbeidsmarkt/werkgelegenheid-en-werkloosheid#panel-12.

number of people reliant on unemployment benefits has decreased since 2014. On the other hand, the number of persons with an invalidity benefit, social assistance benefit, or disability benefit has increased, with the most striking evolution being the continued increase of the number of persons with an invalidity benefit. In 2019, this number exceeded the number of persons with an unemployment benefit for the first time. The number of persons with a social assistance benefit has also increased sharply as from 2015.[18]

The substantial amount of people dependent on a social security benefit has put a lot of pressure on social spending. In 2018, total social protection expenditures amounted to 28.7% of the Belgian GDP.[19] This is about 1% above the EU average (27.9%), at the same level as the Netherlands (28.9%) and below the level of Germany (29.6%) and France (33.7%).[20]

Despite the high amount of beneficiaries, several social security benefits are too low and lie below the at-risk-of-poverty threshold. This certainly applies to social assistance benefits.

In the past years, the Belgian federal legislator has taken initiatives to increase the lowest social security benefits, while through previous measures the legislator also introduced maximum caps for social security benefits. This has put pressure on the principle of equivalence, as higher incomes face a (large) income fall due to those maxima.

The employment rate remained relatively stable (70%) during the COVID-19 crisis while unemployment did increase during the summer of 2020 to 6.9%. Unemployment did, however, decrease again during the autumn of 2020. Although the share of employed persons remained relatively stable, the amount of work available did drop steeply during the lockdown periods in the COVID-19 pandemic. Appeals to temporary unemployment benefits, schemes for a reduced working time and income support measures for self-employed persons by the federal and the regional governments were immediate and massive. For instance, appeals to the temporary unemployment scheme rose to almost 40% of the workforce and appeals to the bridging right for self-employed persons rose to 50% of all self-employed persons.

[D] Basic Characteristics of Belgian Labour and Social Security Law

Belgian labour and social security law are fundamentally linked to both the socio-political decisions they stem from as well as the social relations between employers and employees or the government, institutions, and socially vulnerable parties. Despite the entangled history and overlapping scope of application, the underlying structures, principles, context, and institutional dynamics have contributed to both branches of social law being regarded as independent fields of study.[21]

18. FPS Social Security, *The evolution of the social situation and social protection in Belgium 2020: persistent challenges* 22-23 (2021).
19. *Ibid.*, 7 (2021).
20. *Ibid.*
21. Frank Hendrickx, *Inleiding tot het Belgische Arbeidsrecht* 9 (Die Keure 2019).

Belgian labour law has an unmistakable civil character, with the contractual relationship establishing the labour relations at its centre. It serves as a counterweight to the superior position of the employer. Labour law provides solutions for the factual and legal power imbalances intrinsic to that of contractual relationships as well as for inequalities on the labour market in general. However, employer interests as well as the interests of society at large are also central to labour policy.[22] To this end, Belgian labour law is characterized by a formalized hierarchy between its sources with binding legislation prevailing over the universally binding decisions made by collective bargaining.[23]

Belgian social security law provides solidarity mechanisms to persons who find themselves in (threat of) a situation where they will not receive an income or where they are faced with exceptional costs. The primary solidarity mechanism to counter social risks is monetary support, but various other forms of social provisions are also present in Belgium. Traditionally, solidarity mechanisms in Belgium took the form of either social insurance-based schemes or social assistance schemes. Social insurance granted a subjective right to protection in case a social risk occurred. Social assistance, on the other hand, was dependent on the government granting support after a means test. This traditional demarcation can no longer be upheld as social assistance is nowadays granted as a subjective right, if the legal conditions are fulfilled. Since the Sixth State Reform (2011), the Belgian legislator also transferred certain aspects of social security (such as child care) to the regions and communities. The different state reforms have led to a complicated web of divided competences in the field of social security and social assistance.

[1] Scope of Application of Belgian Labour and Social Security Law

Belgian labour law is applicable only to employees; the (solo) self-employed do not enjoy the protections provided by labour law. The Belgian legislation defines an employee as '*a person, who on the basis of an employment contract, performs work for pay under the authority of an employer*'.[24] Belgian law does mandate a minimum amount of worktime to employment contracts: such a contract has to entail labour at least equivalent to one-third of full-time employment, although some exceptions to this general principle apply.[25] The Belgian social security system is – to a large extent – still a social security system based on one's professional status, with the exception of health care,[26] child care benefits, and social assistance. Different from Belgian labour law, Belgian social security law does provide protection for self-employed persons but

22. *Ibid.*, 1-2.
23. Art. 51 Act of 5 December 1968 on the collective labour agreements and the sectoral committees, 15.1.1969.
24. Art. 2-5 Labour Act of 16 March 1971, 30.3.1971.
25. Royal Decree of 21 December 1992 determining derogations from the minimum weekly working time of part-time workers laid down in Art. 11*bis* of the Act of 3 July 1978 on employment contracts, 30.12.1992.
26. For health care, the Belgian legislation still departs from one's professional status, but the scope of application was extended and now almost the entire population is covered.

differences exist between the protection provided to employed and self-employed persons.

Belgian social security law utilizes similar concepts of an 'employee' and an 'employment contract' as under Belgian labour law. All employment is taken into account for social security purposes, even when limited in time or scope.[27] The scope of the Belgian social security system does not coincide one-to-one with Belgian labour law. Assimilated situations include, for instance, apprenticeships,[28] artists (whose activity is not considered occasional),[29] persons in the cleaning sector (unless proven otherwise),[30] etc. On the other hand, some categories of employees are (partially) excluded from the social security protection provided for employees.[31]

Self-employment is defined in Belgian (social security) legislation as any natural person who exercises a professional activity in Belgium for which he/she is not bound by an employment contract or a statute as a civil servant[32] and who performs activities outside the authority of an employer.[33] A professional activity as a self-employed person presupposes a genuine, profit-making, and sufficiently frequent activity that goes beyond mere asset management.[34] Self-employed persons, their assisting spouses, and other helpers are compulsorily insured in the social insurance system for self-employed persons.[35] The Belgian legislation does not make a distinction between solo self-employed persons and self-employed persons in general.

[2] Protection Provided under the Belgian Social Security Scheme

The Belgian social security scheme is rooted in the Bismarckian system: professional activity and the payment of social contributions on the generated income from that activity form the basis from which to build up social security rights.[36] This idea still constitutes the basic principle of the Belgian social security protection, which can be

27. Koen Nevens & Guido Van Limberghen, *Actuele problemen van het arbeidsrecht* 7 361-406 (2005).
28. Art. 1, §1 1° a) Act of 27 June 1969 revising the Decree Act of 28 December 1944 on social security for employees, 24.1.2011.
29. *Ibid.*, Art. 1*bis*.
30. *Ibid.*, Art. 2/2.
31. For example: Art. 2, §1 Act of 27 June 1969 revising the Decree Act of 28 December 1944 on social security for employees, 24.1.2011.
32. Art. 3, §1 Royal Decree of 27 July 1967 n° 38 organizing the social statute of self-employed persons, 29.7.1967.
33. One of the key element determining the existing of an employment contract in Belgium is whether an activity is performed under the authority of an employer, see Art. 328, 5° a) and Art. 333, §1 Title XIII of the Programme Act of 27 December 2006, 28.12.2006.
34. Court of Cassation, *TSR* 1984, 443, note H. Declercq (13 May 1985).
35. Art. 6 and 7*bis* Royal Decree of 27 July 1967 n° 38 organizing the social statute of self-employed persons, 29.7.1967.
36. Jef Van Langendonck, Yves Jorens, Freek Louckx & Yves Stevens, *Handboek socialezekerheidsrecht – tiende editie* 41 and further (2020).

broken down into three systems: (i) a system for employees, (ii) a system for self-employed persons, and (iii) a system for civil servants. Social assistance is granted in case of need, irrespective of the professional status.

The Belgian social security system for employees includes compulsory medical care insurance,[37] a sickness/ invalidity benefit, a maternity, paternity and parental leave, an industrial accident benefit, an occupational disease benefit, an unemployment benefit, and a (old age and survivors) pension benefit.[38]

The Belgian social security system for self-employed persons includes compulsory medical care insurance, a sickness/ invalidity benefit, a maternity and paternity leave, and a (old age and survivors) pension benefit. Self-employed are not covered by insurances against unemployment, labour accidents and professional diseases.[39]. Self-employed persons are, however, covered by the bridging scheme under which they may be entitled to a benefit if they completely had to stop their self-employed activity due to bankruptcy, serious economic difficulties, or reasons beyond their control.[40] During the COVID-19 pandemic, the bridging scheme was extended, as discussed below.

In Belgium, family benefits were regionalized as part of the Sixth State reform[41] and are now regulated by the Communities.[42] All current regional regulations on family benefits are universal in scope and based on a right of the child.

[3] The Role of Collective Bargaining in Belgium

Belgium generally considers itself to have an extensive industrial relations system and tradition. Article 23 of the Constitution mentions the right to information, consultation, and collective bargaining. However, the Constitution does not explicitly establish the foundation for the collective bargaining system as such. The right to collective bargaining traditionally plays an important role in the shaping of wages and determining labour standards, both in the execution of national law and outside the scope of it.

---

37. Note that the healthcare insurance encompassing medical care in kind has evolved from a work-based scheme to (in practice) a universal scheme due to the extension of the personal scope of application. *See also* Art. 32 Act of 14 July 1994 concerning the obligatory medical insurance coordinated on 14 July 1994, 27.8.1994.
38. Art. 21, §1 Act of 29 June 1981 concerning the general principles of social security for employees, 2.7.1981.
39. Although they can receive a sickness benefit, provided they fulfil the statutory conditions.
40. Art. 4 Act of 22 December 2016 installing a bridging right for self-employed persons, 6.1.2017.
41. While the transfer of competences as a result of the Sixth State Reform was performed between 2011 and 2014, most Laws at Community level concerning family benefits were only enacted in 2018. *See* 3 Céline Romainville & Marie Solbreux, *La sécurité sociale dans l'État federal*, 53-86 (2017).
42. With the exception of the French Community, for which the competence for family benefits is regulated by the Walloon Region. *See* Mathieu Dekleermaker & Laurie Losseau, *Les transferts de compétences intra-francophones en matière sociale consécutifs à la Sixième Réforme de l'État*, 2 Revue Belge de Securité Sociale 445, 445-463 (2015). Nevertheless, for simplification's purposes, all the four entities as a whole are referred to here as 'Communities'.

The Social Pact of 1944 laid the foundation for an overreaching social security system and stable labour relations in Belgium. Collective bargaining is primarily regulated by the Act of 5 December 1968.[43]

Collective bargaining in Belgium takes place on several different levels, being the national level (National Labour Council and the Group of 10), the sectoral level, and the company level. The way social dialogue is organized on the company level depends on the size of the company.

Although most collective agreements are concluded at the (sub-)sectoral levels or at the level of the company,[44] the National Labour Council plays a crucial role, issuing many national collective agreements, as well as opinions on legislative changes. The Group of 10 – consisting of the most representative employer organizations and trade unions – has an important part to play as well, especially in the shaping of wages.

It is important to highlight that collective bargaining in Belgium is only accessible to the 'most representative employee and employer organizations'. This entails that only a few trade unions meet the conditions to conclude legally-sanctioned collective agreements and only three unions are represented at the national level.[45]

In the recent decades, it has become increasingly complex at national level to reach an agreement on (large) labour market reforms and wage negotiations in the Group of 10. At sectoral level, it seems easier to reach an agreement.[46]

It has to be noted that Belgium has one of the highest rates of trade union membership in the EU. In 2019, Belgium had a collective bargaining coverage rate of

43. Act of 5 December 1968 on the collective labour agreements and the sectoral committees, 15.1.1969. Other regulations apply as well, *see* Royal Decree of 6 November 1969 on the determination of the general rules for the functioning of the sectoral committees and sectoral sub-committees, 18.11.1969; Royal Decree of 7 November 1969 on the determination of the deposition modalities of the collective agreements, 22.11.1969; there are also other legal acts relevant for collective bargaining in Belgium, which are not discussed further in this chapter.
44. See for a discussion: *Report on the results of the sectoral consultation in 2017 and 2018*, General Direction for Collective Labour Affairs of the Federal public service – Employment, labour and social dialogue (retrieved on 14 February 2022) https://emploi.belgique.be/sites/default/files/content/publications/FR/Rapport%20concernant%20les%20resultats%20de%20la%20concertation%20sectorielle%20en%202017.pdf and also in a more recent report: *Report on the results of the sectoral consultation in 2019 and 2020*, General Direction for Collective Labour Affairs of the Federal public service – Employment, labour and social dialogue (retrieved on 13 May 2022) https://emploi.belgique.be/fr/publications/rapport-sur-la-concertation-sociale-sectorielle-2019-2020.
45. Belgium's system in which only the most representative trade unions and employers' associations are eligible to conclude collective agreements has been criticized in front of the supervisory bodies of the ILO (Committee on Freedom of Association). In response to these remarks, the legislature tried to clarify what factors determine 'representativity' in Chapter 6 of the Act of 30 December 2009 on various provisions, 31.12.2009.
46. *Report on the results of the sectoral consultation in 2017*, General Direction for Collective Labour Affairs of the Federal public service – Employment, labour and social dialogue, 4-5 (retrieved on 14 February 2022) https://emploi.belgique.be/sites/default/files/content/publications/FR/Rapport%20concernant%20les%20resultats%20de%20la%20concertation%20sectorielle%20en%202017.pdf and also in a more recent report: *Report on the results of the sectoral consultation in 2019 and 2020*, General Direction for Collective Labour Affairs of the Federal public service – Employment, labour and social dialogue (retrieved on 13 May 2022) https://emploi.belgique.be/fr/publications/rapport-sur-la-concertation-sociale-sectorielle-2019-2020.

96%, which means 96% of all Belgian workers are covered by collective agreements.[47] Trade union membership was 49.1% in 2019, while in 2000 this was still 56,6%.[48] While the rate of collective agreement's coverage remained almost identical during the last 20 years, trade union membership has declined over that period.

Self-employed persons, however, are not covered by collective bargaining (*see also* below). Nevertheless, the personal scope of the Belgian law on collective labour agreements can also be read to include economically dependent solo self-employed persons. The scope of application of this act refers not only to employees, but also to persons who perform work under the authority of a person while not working under a labour agreement.[49] This position is, however, not generally accepted in Belgium.

[4] Minimum Wages in Belgium

Minimum wages in Belgium are typically set by the social partners through national and (primarily) sectoral and sub-sectoral collective agreements.

Every two years, an attempt is made by the Group of 10 to conclude an interprofessional agreement.[50] The aim of such an interprofessional agreement is to put forward some of the broader policy directions for the coming two years; their primary goal, however, is to negotiate and agree on the extent to which wages are allowed to increase in the coming years. These wage increases need to consider the boundaries set in the Act of 26 July 1996, which aims to preserve the competitivity of companies in Belgium compared with companies in the neighbouring countries. This is done by pre-emptively estimating how wage costs will rise in neighbouring countries and, on that basis, negotiate a limit on the minimum wage increases at sector and enterprise level in Belgium. This practice has been criticized, since the legislator directly influences the wage agreements between the social partners by means of a biennial study on neighbouring countries' wage costs. As such, the trade unions seek to amend the Act of 26 July 1996, as it considers the margins within which wage increases are possible as too narrow. To this end, collective action has been undertaken in the form of political pressure, petitions, and manifestations.[51] For 2021-2022, the Group of 10 did not reach an agreement on the growth limit; the De Croo government set the growth limit at 0.4%.[52]

---

47. *Collective Bargaining Coverage*, OECD (retrieved on 14 February 2022), https://stats.oecd.org/Index.aspx?DataSetCode=CBC.
48. *Ibid.*
49. Art. 2, §1 Act of 5 December 1968 on the collective labour agreements and the sectoral committees, 15.1.1969; Valeria Pulignano and Frank Hendrickx, *Het sociaal overleg in België: voorbij institutionele en juridische knelpunten*, 1 Over.werk 2019, 156 (2019).
50. *See Interprofessional Agreement*, Federal Public Service – Employment, labour and social dialogue (retrieved on 14 February 2022), https://emploi.belgique.be/fr/themes/concertation-sociale/niveau-interprofessionnel/accord-interprofessionnel-aip.
51. *Sign the petition against the wage act now!*, ACV-CSC (retrieved on 14 February 2022), https://www.hetacv.be/actualiteit/campagnes/loonnormwet.
52. Royal Decree of 30 July 2021 for the execution of the articles 7, §1 of the Act of 26 July 1996 for the stimulation of employment and preventive safeguarding of the competitiveness, 9.8.2021.

The National Labour Council sets the so-called legal minimum wage,[53] which is the guaranteed average minimum monthly income that any full-time employee in the private sector must receive. This amounts[54] to €1,842.28. Previously, different legal minimum wages applied depending on if the person was at least 18 years old, at least 19 years old with at least 6 months of seniority, or at least 20 years old with at least 12 months of seniority.[55] However, when the legal minimum wage was raised by the National Labour Council in Collective Agreement nr. 43/16 on 9 March 2022, this differentiation was repealed.[56] Part-time employees are entitled to remuneration that is proportional to the one of a full-time employee, and hence their applicable legal minimum wage would be correlated with their working time.[57]

Nevertheless, minimum wages are primarily established through the sectoral committees, of which there are 164 in Belgium.[58] The sectoral minimum wages set through these sectoral committees vary greatly depending on the sector or sub-sector.[59] Furthermore, within each sector or sub-sectors, there are different minimum wages depending on the type of activity, the level of education of the employee, and his or her seniority. For example, in the cleaning sector there are differences on the minimum wage depending on the difficulty of the task – e.g., regular cleaning has an hourly minimum wage of €14.10, while cleaning involving disinfection has an hourly minimum wage of €15.59, and higher hourly rates apply to the collection of waste (€16.02) or to truck drivers transporting waste (€16.86).[60]

53. This is the average minimum monthly income (which also takes into account for example the 13th month).
54. These are the gross amounts; all amounts mentioned in this contribution are the amounts applicable at 12 May 2022.
55. See *Remuneration*, Federal Public Service – Employment, labour and social dialogue (retrieved on 14 February 2022), https://employment.belgium.be/en/themes/international/posting/working-conditions-be-respected-case-posting-belgium/remuneration. The legal minimum is set in Art. 3 Collective Agreement n° 43 of 2 May 1988 on the amendment and coordination of collective agreements n° 21 and 23, 2.5.1988. Nevertheless, the amount appearing in that article was updated for the last time in 2008 and, since then, it has been indexed, i.e., raised annually automatically based on the increase in the cost of living.
56. Art. 3 Collective Agreement n° 43/16 of 9 March 2022 on the amendment of collective agreement n° 43 of 2 May 1988 on the guarantee of an average minimum monthly income, 9 March 1988.
57. Art. 9 Collective Agreement n° 35 of 27 February 1981 on certain provisions of labour law on the matter of part-time labour, 27.2.1981.
58. *Institution et composition des commissions paritaires* (retrieved on 14 February 2022), Federal Public Service – Employment, labour and social dialogue, https://emploi.belgique.be/fr/themes/commissions-paritaires-et-conventions-collectives-de-travail-cct/commissions-paritaires-1#:~:text=Tous%20les%20quatre%20ans%2C%20un,commissions%20et%20sous%2Dcommissions%20paritaires.
59. *See*, for the different minimum wages established by each joint committee, *Database of Sectoral Minimum Wages*, Federal Public Service – Employment, labour and social dialogue (retrieved on 14 February 2022), https://salairesminimums.be/index.html.
60. *Sectoral Committee 121: Cleaning*, Federal Public Service – Employment, labour and social dialogue (retrieved on 14 February 2022), https://salairesminimums.be/index.html.

§2.02 VUP GROUP 1: LOW OR UNSKILLED WORK IN STANDARD EMPLOYMENT IN POOR SECTORS

[A] Composition of VUP Group 1

[1] A Small Proportion of the Belgian Workforce

The workers in VUP Group 1 (low or unskilled work in standard employment in poor sectors) make up a fairly small proportion of the entire in-work population in Belgium (7.7% in 2007 compared to 7.9% in 2019). The severe material deprivation rate has stabilized and even decreased in recent years (1.5% in 2019), taking into account the increase in 2013 (4.4%).

[2] With Mostly Male and Young Workers

The majority of the workers in VUP Group 1 are male, whereby this percentage has been increasing over the last decade (57.5% in 2007 compared to 62.9% in 2019). In comparison to workers in standard employment in all low-skilled occupations, there is a higher share of female workers in poor sectors (37.1% compared to 33% in 2019). In general, younger workers are also overrepresented in this group, with higher shares of workers aged between 18 and 34 years old compared to the overall working population. Overall, their risk of in-work poverty has decreased over the last decade, although with an increase in 2013 (2.9% in 2007 compared to 1.8% in 2019). For persons who are aged between 35 and 49 years old, the risk of in-work poverty is higher and has been increasing in recent years, even doubling since 2007 (4% in 2007 compared to 8.2% in 2019). This could indicate that workers who remain in these occupations are faced with difficulties (e.g., raising of children, etc.).

It can be noted that the percentage of people with another nationality in the Belgian labour market has been increasing in recent years. Although the overall number of people with other nationalities working in the Belgian labour market remains rather limited, it is clear that the number of people with another nationality in VUP Group 1 is larger than for the group of employed persons in general. Moreover, this group of persons also has a higher risk of poverty, both in the overall group of employed persons and specifically for VUP Group 1.

[3] Mainly Workers with a Medium Education Level

Most of the employees working in VUP Group 1 have had a medium level of education (i.e., secondary or post-secondary education): 50.5% for VUP Group 1 compared to 36.3% of the working population in Belgium. The figures for the risk of in-work poverty are also lower for people with medium and high education levels, both concerning the overall group of the working population as well as VUP Group 1. Only employees working in VUP Group 1 with a low education level have a significantly higher risk of in-work poverty.

VUP Group 1 employees work mainly in the following sectors (i) trade, transport, accommodation and food services, and information and communication on the one hand and (ii) other services.[61] Whereas in 2007 the number of workers was more or less equally distributed over the various groups, a trend can be observed whereby the number of employees in the group of trade, transport, accommodation and food services, information and communication has increased strongly (2019: 60.9% compared to 39.1% in the group of other services). However, the risk of poverty is higher in the group of employees in the sector of other services and has doubled since 2007 (3% in 2007 compared to 7% in 2019).

[B] Relevant Legal Framework

[1] Unionization and Collective Agreements Coverage

No specific information is available concerning the unionization and coverage of collective agreements in the selected poor sectors. Taking into account the high trade union membership rates and the high coverage of collective agreements, we refer to our remarks made earlier concerning the role of collective bargaining in Belgium. The same findings apply here as well.

[2] Statutory Provisions That Worsen Working Conditions

The workers in VUP Group 1 (which can be considered as the standard employment relationship) enjoy a wide protection under the Belgian labour and social security legislation. Nevertheless, this group of workers also faces a series of obstacles.

The first one is the distinction between intellectual work (i.e., white-collar employees) and manual work (i.e., blue-collar employees and domestic workers). While the distinction between white-collar and blue-collar workers has on certain points been deemed unconstitutional by the Constitutional Court (and hence progressively eliminated), the regulation concerning domestic workers still deviates from the one applied to standard types of employment. For example, domestic workers experience significantly worse conditions regarding the length and amount of their sick pay benefit when compared to white-collar employees.[62] Furthermore, domestic workers' employment contract may not be suspended due to economic causes (unlike in the case of – some – white-collar and blue-collar employees).[63] There are also still some differences in the protection between blue-collar and white-collar employees, e.g., the

61. The other services group includes the following activities: (i) financial and insurance activities, (ii) real estate activities, (iii) professional, scientific and technical activities, (iv) administrative and support service activities, (v) education, (vii) human health and social work activities, (ix) arts, entertainment and recreation, (x) other service activities.
62. Arts. 112 Act of 3 July 1978 on employment contracts, 22.8.1978.
63. See Arts. 112-114 Act of 3 July 1978 on employment contracts, 22.8.1978.

payment of continued pay in the first period of sickness by the employer (which is less advantageous for blue-collar workers).[64]

Second, many aspects of employees' working conditions are established through collective agreements at sectoral or company level. This is, for example, the case for wage indexation and the possibility of suspending an employment agreement due to economic causes.[65] Moreover, while there is a minimum wage established by a collective agreement at intersectoral level, most sectors have established a higher minimum wage through a sectoral collective agreement. This is particularly relevant in sectors where the average wage is close to the minimum wage, as is the case in the accommodation and textile care sectors.[66] This means that the wage protection can differ strongly between sectors, resulting in difficulties to reach an adequate minimum wage in certain sectors.

Third, income-replacement benefits in the Belgian scheme for employees are expressed as a percentage of the previously earned wage. For persons with a low wage, this could mean that they receive an even lower income-replacement benefit: minimum benefits in income-replacement schemes (such as sickness and unemployment), however, also play an important role in providing protection for persons with low wages. Whereas minimum sickness benefits were previously granted only as of the seventh month of sickness, as of 2024, minimum benefits will be provided immediately after the period of guaranteed wage by the employer.

Fourth, Belgian social security benefits should reach (in principle) the at-risk-of-poverty threshold (i.e., 60% of the median equivalized income): a long-heard critique, however, is that this is not always the case. Examples are maternity benefits in case of minimum-wage single-earner households,[67] unemployment benefits concerning minimum wage employees in one-person households,[68] and minimum retirement pensions regarding family households.[69]

[3] Active Policies, Training, and Unemployment Benefits

Employers and employees in Belgium may resort to various programmes in order for employees to obtain training during the employment relationship, such as training vouchers, educational leave programmes, and vocational training courses (with an obligation for employers with ten or more employees of providing training during at

64. Provisions for blue-collar workers: Art. 52 §1 Act of 3 July 1978 on employment contracts, 22.8.1978 and Arts. 3-4 Collective Agreement n°12*bis* of 26 February 1979 concluded in the National Labour Council.
65. *Indexation Leap*, Federal Public Service – Employment, labour and social dialogue (retrieved on 14 February 2022), https://emploi.belgique.be/fr/themes/remuneration/saut-dindex.
66. Maarten Goos, Guy Van Gyes & Sem Vandekerckhove, *Minimum wages and low-wage work in Belgium: an exploration of employment effects and distributional effects - IPSWICH Working Paper 6* (2018).
67. Guido Van Limberghen et al., *L'accès des travailleurs salariés et indépendants à la sécurité sociale en Belgique*, Federal public service – social security 2020, 547 (2021).
68. *Ibid.*, 551.
69. *Ibid.*, 554.

least two days per year).[70] In February 2022, the federal government reached an agreement to raise the number of training days gradually from two to four by 2024. This agreement still needs to be implemented in legislation in the coming months and will also first be discussed further with the social partners. According to the current available information, this obligation would only apply for employers with more than 20 employees.

Despite the obligation to provide two training days per year, Belgium presents a lower rate of low-skilled employees receiving training than the international average, as well as a significant difference between the rate of low-skilled receiving training and the one of high-skilled doing so (20% vs. 65%).[71] Low-skilled workers have been found to be one of the groups experiencing difficulties finding their way to training. In general, the amount of training provided to workers has not significantly increased over the years.[72]

Furthermore, the active labour market policies existing in Belgium, and which seek to promote the re-integration into the labour market of unemployed persons, might drive some un- or low-skilled employees towards less remunerated jobs in a greater way than in the case of more-skilled employees. In this regard, only during the first three[73] to five months of unemployment may a position be considered unsuitable if it does not correspond to the occupation for which the person has been trained, his or her usual occupation, or to a related profession.[74] After that period, the person's skills, training, and talents, and not his former occupation, are taken into account to assess the suitability of the position.[75]

[C] Impact Analysis

In the final part of our discussion of VUP Group 1, this contribution looks at the risk of in-work poverty for four hypothetical households and the obstacles they might face in light of the relevant legal framework. The hypothetical households are the following (i) a single person, (ii) a single person with two children, (iii) a breadwinner with a dependent partner and two children, and (iv) a family where two persons work and two children. All the children are under the age of 18 years old.

VUP Group 1 is the standard employment relationship from the perspective of Belgian labour and social security law. This group is therefore only confronted to a limited extent with obstacles in labour and social security law. In the following section,

70. Art. 15 Act of 5 March 2017 on feasible and manoeuvrable work, 15.3.2017.
71. Federal Public Service – Employment, labour and social dialogue, *Memorandum van de Federale Overheidsdienst Werkgelegenheid, Arbeid en Sociaal Overleg aan de federale regering voor het werkgelegenheidsbeleid in de periode 2019-2024* 16 (retrieved on 13 May 2022) https://werk.belgie.be/sites/default/files/content/news/Memorandum.pdf.
72. *Lifelong learning*, Statbel (retrieved on 14 February 2022), https://statbel.fgov.be/en/themes/work-training/training-and-education/lifelong-learning.
73. In the case of persons of less than 30 years of age or with less than five years of professional experience, *see* Art. 23 Ministerial Decree of 26 November 1991 on the modalities of the application of unemployment regulations, 25.1.1992.
74. *Ibid.*, Art. 23.
75. *Ibid.*

this chapter focuses specifically on the hypothetical households: our comments on the applicability of labour law and social security law for VUP Group 1 are found in previous subsections.

Take, for example, households that are reliant on income-related social security benefits that only constitute a percentage of the previously earned wage. This calculation method will severely affect certain families that already face difficulties in making ends meet. Nevertheless, such benefits only require limited social security contributions, which should help mitigate the income loss. Furthermore, by granting minimum benefits, the Belgian legislator also tries to provide a minimum threshold of social protection.

Relevant for our hypothetical households, are the differences in income-replacement benefits taking into account the household composition. For example, in the case of unemployment, sickness, or old-age, higher benefits are awarded to families with only one breadwinner; on the other hand, lower benefits are awarded in case that person lives in family where the other partner still works (in the case of unemployment and sickness). This way, the Belgian legislator wants to offer additional protection for families for whom the loss of income can be a significant shock as it is their only income.

Other aspects of labour and social security law apply regardless of the family composition.

When looking at the household characteristics of VUP Group 1, we can make following observations concerning the at-risk-of-poverty rate for the different hypothetical households.

Most employees in VUP Group 1 are living in a household with more than two persons (58 %), which might be surprising as most workers in this group do not have children (yet). This could be explained by the large group of younger workers in VUP Group 1, who may still live with their parents or with a larger group of persons. The risk of in-work poverty of this group has also increased since 2007. For smaller households (people living alone or with one other person), the risk of-in work poverty has remained relatively stable over the past few years. The same percentages can be found for the group of employed persons in general as to the household size and the risk of in-work poverty.

Most workers are part of a household where more than one person works (61.5 %). In that case the risk of poverty is only 0.9 %. This also means that the percentage of in-work poverty for employees of VUP Group 1 is completely concentrated in households where only one person works. This group represents 38.5 % of the number of employees in VUP Group 1, of which 12.5 % face a risk of in-work poverty. Taking into account the rather low percentage of a risk of poverty for persons who live alone, mainly workers who live together with a partner with no income out of work and/or of children face a significantly higher risk of in-work poverty.

Half of the workers in VUP Group 1 do not have a child yet. In that case, the risk of in-work poverty is also rather small (1.5 % in 2019), and this percentage is also lower than what we can find for the overall group of employed persons. This can be explained by the higher number of younger workers, who do not have children (yet). It is noticeable that the percentage of the risk of poverty rate increases strongly for families with more than one child. This seems to imply that the household income (income out of not only work but also family benefits) does not seem to suffice for families with more than one child. The group of families with more than two children represent 28.2% of VUP Group 1, of which 11.7% are at risk of poverty (compared to 7.3% of the overall working population), despite the fact that the percentage of employees is relatively similar (2019: 28.2% compared to 26.4%).

If we apply the findings above to our hypothetical households, we see that in particular families where only one person works (single person, single parent, or a breadwinner with a partner) the risk of in-work poverty is higher. This is in particular the case for families with more than two children.

§2.03 VUP GROUP 2: SOLO AND BOGUS SELF-EMPLOYMENT

[A] Composition of VUP Group 2

[1] Difficulty in Measuring In-Work Poverty for Self-Employed Persons

Delving into the workforce composition of VUP Group 2 quickly reveals the limits of the European Union Statistics on Income and Living Conditions (EU-SILC) data. The available data only differentiates between self-employed persons and the self-employed persons without personnel. However, not every self-employed worker without personnel is a solo self-employed worker, as definitions used by the EU-SILC data may differ from those in this study.

The EU-SILC data show that the in-work at-risk-of-poverty rate is three times higher for self-employed persons (including self-employed persons without employees) than it is for the group of the working population (15% for self-employed persons without employees compared to 4.8% of employed persons in general in 2019). In particular for self-employed persons without employees, this rate has increased between 2007 and 2019 (while remaining relatively stable in the case of employees).

The EU-SILC data, as well as other research, show that employees have a lower risk of in-work poverty, whereas the rate of severe material deprivation between employees and self-employed persons does not differ significantly.[76] While self-employed persons face an increased in-work poverty risk, they are thus not necessarily more likely to be materially deprived. As already pointed out by certain scholars (for instance, Horemans and Marx) the at-risk-of-poverty indicator seems not entirely fit to measure poverty among self-employed persons.

76. *See also* the criticism that 'in-work at risk of poverty' rate is not a good criteria to measure living standards among the self-employed; Bruce Bradbury, *The living standards of the low-income self-employed*, 30, n° 4 Australian Economic Review 1997, 374-389 (1997); Jeroen Horemans & Ive Marx, *Poverty and Material Deprivation among the self-employed in Europe: An exploration of a relatively uncharted landscape – IPSWICH Working Paper 2*, 22 (2017); Ingemar Johansson Sevä & Daniel Larsson, *Are the self-employed really that poor? Income poverty and living standard among self-employed in Sweden*, 6 Society, Health & Vulnerability 2015, 1-16.

[2] A Group of Mostly Male and Older Workers

Self-employed persons without employees tend to be older than the overall in-work population. Approximately 44.4% of the self-employed without employees are 50 years or older, compared to 30,2% of the working population. They are also more often to a higher degree male than the working population (69.6% compared to 52,8%). Similar to the overall working population, the at-risk-of-poverty rates for males and females in the group of self-employed persons without employees are rather similar (13.1% compared to 15.9%). Self-employed persons without employees predominantly have the Belgian nationality, although the number of persons with a different nationality who work as self-employed persons without employees is higher as for the working population (11.3% compared to 14.4%).

[3] A Group of Workers Who Mostly Have a High Level of Education and Who Work in a High Skilled Occupation

In terms of education and occupation, the available figures for self-employed persons in general and self-employed persons without employees match those of the entire working population. A slightly higher percentage of self-employed persons have a higher education and work in an occupation with a high skill-level (53.1% and 53.7%, respectively) compared to a low and medium level of education (46.9%) and a low skill-level (45.9%). We do see higher risk of poverty rates for self-employed persons without employees with a low or medium level of education and low skills. The EU-SILC data does not differentiate between low and medium level of education in 2019, though, making the data difficult to interpret.

[B] Legal Framework

[1] Notion

As mentioned earlier, the Belgian social security legislation defines a self-employed person as a person who regularly exercises a professional activity in Belgium for which he/she is not bound by an employment contract or a statute as a civil servant[77] outside the authority of an employer.[78]

The Belgian legislation does not include a separate category of economically dependent self-employed persons.[79]

77. Art. 3, §1 Royal Decree of 27 July 1967 n° 38 organizing the social statute of self-employed persons, 29.7.1967.
78. A key element determining the existing of an employment contract in Belgium is whether an activity is performed under the authority of an employer, *see also* Art. 328, 5°, a) Programme Act of 27 December 2006, 28.12.2006.
79. 3 Viviane Vannes, *Subordination et parasubordination: La place de la subordination juridique et de la dépendance économique dans la rélation du travail* 67 (2017).

Belgian law does not contain a separate definition or legal provision for solo self-employed persons. It also does not differentiate between self-employed persons working through a personal company or as a natural person. We do see that there are self-employed persons who are active through a personal company, as a means to pay less social security contributions and lower taxes. Aside from putting pressure on the financial sustainability of the Belgian social security system,[80] this also makes it difficult to measure poverty among self-employed persons as their exact income is unclear.

Bogus self-employed persons (being factually employees but formally self-employed persons) do not enjoy a separate social statute under Belgian law. In principle, the Labour Relations Act provides parties the freedom to decide their own statute: they can work either as an employee or as a self-employed person. However, the factual execution of the work takes precedence if this contradicts what the parties agreed upon.[81] This means that even though the parties' own qualification serves as an indicator of what the applicable statute is, other indicators need to be regarded as well and may lead to a requalification. These indicators have been the subject of an extensive amount of case-law, with four criteria having been enshrined in law since 2006. These are – in addition to the qualification given by the parties –whether or not the work schedule can be organized freely, whether or not the work itself can be organized freely, and whether or not hierarchal control is present.[82]

The Belgian legislator has developed additional criteria for certain groups, such as persons working in the construction sector, cleaning services, etc.[83] In February 2022, the Belgian federal government also reached an agreement (part of 'the Labour Deal') to develop an additional list of criteria for platform workers to define their employment relationship, as discussed below.[84]

Employees or self-employed persons may also seek advice on which statute is applicable to the Administrative Commission for the regulation of the Labour Relations, which falls under the umbrella of the Federal Administration for Social Security.

80. *Verlaging van de lastendruk op arbeid en mogelijkheden voor de financiering ervan* 156, Hoge Raad van Financien – Afdeling Fiscaliteit en Parafiscaliteit (May 2020, retrieved on 28 February 2022), https://www.hogeraadvanfinancien.be/sites/default/files/public/publications/hrf_fisc_2020_05.pdf.
81. Art. 331 Programme Act of 27 December 2006, 28.12.2006; see for a discussion also: Dieter Dejonghe & Sofie Vitse, *Schijnzelfstandigheid: een analyse van de rechtspraak na 15 jaar Arbeidsrelatiewet* 1 (2021).
82. Art. 333, §1 Programme Act of 27 December 2006, 28.12.2006; see for a discussion also: Dieter Dejonghe & Sofie Vitse, *Schijnzelfstandigheid: een analyse van de rechtspraak na 15 jaar Arbeidsrelatiewet* 16-31 (2021).
83. For the criteria in the construction sector, *see* Royal Decree of 7 June 2013 for the execution of Art 337/2, §3 of the Programme Act (I) of 27 December 2006 concerning the nature of the labour relations that exist for the execution of some construction works, 25.6.2013. For criteria in the cleaning sector, *see* Art. 337/1, §1, 4° Programme Act (I) of 27 December 2006 concerning the nature of the labour relations that exist for the execution of some construction works, 28.12.2006.
84. Stefan Grommen, Lonne van Erp & Johny Vansevenant, *Government reaches labour deal: work week of 4 days and more clarity for food delivery*, vrtNWS (15 February 2022), https://www.vrt.be/vrtnws/nl/2022/02/14/arbeidsdeal/.

[2] ***Obstacles to the Application of Labour Law and Social Security Standards***

[a] *No Application of Labour Law*

Labour law is not applicable to self-employed persons. This is especially important in light of the right to a minimum wage and the right of collective bargaining. For instance, the rules on the minimum wage are not applicable to self-employed persons. The same applies for the right to collective bargaining; the Act of 5 December 1968 states that only employees and persons in a similar position (who work under the authority of another person) fall under the scope of application of this act. Although economically dependent solo self-employed persons could be considered to be in a similar position as employees, this is not a commonly accepted position in Belgium.[85] In general, we can conclude that both solo and bogus self-employed persons do not fall under the scope of application of Belgian labour law.

[b] *Differences in Social Protection Coverage Between Employees and Self-Employed Persons*

Differences between self-employed persons and employees are present in the protection provided by social security legislation, with the protection for self-employed persons being less extensive than those available to employees (*see* higher).

Self-employed persons receive maternity benefits for a shorter duration than employees (12 weeks,[86] as opposed to 15 weeks). Similarly, they receive a flat-rate amount with the amount varying depending on whether the maternity leave is taken up on a full-time or a part-time basis[87] (a gross amount of €782.77 per week for full-time workers during the first four weeks, diminishing to €715.95 afterwards; €391.39 per week for half-time workers during the first four weeks, diminishing to €357.98 afterwards).[88] Meanwhile, social security benefits for employees amount to a percentage of their previously earned wage (approximately 80% of the previous salary and the

85. Valeria Pulignano and Frank Hendrickx, *Het sociaal overleg in België: voorbij institutionele en juridische knelpunten*, 1 Over.werk 2019, 156 (2019).
86. Art. 94 Royal Decree of 20 July 1971 on the institution of an indemnity insurance and a maternity insurance for the benefit of the self-employed and the aiding spouses, 7.8.1971. The benefit has a duration of 13 weeks in the case of a multiple birth, see *Ibid*.
87. Note that the 'part-time' refers to the self-employed persons taking up part-time maternity leave in addition to working part-time, not whether or not the self-employed person usually works part-time instead of full-time.
88. Art. 94 Royal Decree of 20 July 1971 on the institution of an indemnity insurance and a maternity insurance for the benefit of the self-employed and the aiding spouses, 7.8.1971; National institute for sickness and invalidity insurance, *Amount of the flat rate indemnity during your maternity leave as a self-employed* (retrieved on 24 February 2022), https://www.inami.fgov.be/fr/themes/grossesse-naissance/montants/independants/Pages/indemnite-repos-maternite-independant.aspx.

maximum wage that can be take into account is capped).[89] Self-employed persons are also entitled to a childbirth benefit (a single payment for every born child of €1,214.51 for those residing in the Brussels[90] or Walloon region[91] or €1,167.33 for those residing in the Flemish region)[92] as well as 105 vouchers for cleaning and other services related to household chores.[93]

Paternity benefits for self-employed persons have the same duration as for employees (i.e., 15 days, and as of 2023 20 days), but consist of a fixed amount instead of a percentage of the previously earned salary (i.e., for self-employed persons a gross amount of €89.24 or €44.62 for each day depending on whether the paternity leave is on a full-time or half-day basis).[94] Benefits for fathers who are employees amount to 82% of the previously earned, taking into account that there is a cap on the maximum wage.

Different from employees, self-employed persons need to fulfil a waiting period in case that the incapacity for work does not last longer than seven days. In that case, a self-employed person does not receive any sickness benefits.[95]

Self-employed persons receive flat-rate sickness benefits, different from employees (who receive a sickness or invalidity[96] benefit linked to the previously earned income). Both during the first period of incapacity for work (sickness) and during the period of invalidity (after one year of sickness), the amount depends on the family situation.[97] Higher sickness benefits are also granted when a self-employed person had to stop his or her undertaking due to sickness.[98] These flat-rates benefits are equal to the minimum amount received by employees as of the fourth month of sickness.[99]

Self-employed persons – unlike employees – are not covered by labour accidents insurance and professional diseases insurance, although they may receive benefits for a temporary or long-term incapacity resulting from a professional

89. During the first 30 days, an employee receives 82% of their gross wages, afterwards it becomes 75% of that gross wageup until a certain ceiling, of €154,60 per day.
90. *How much family allocations can I receive?*, Famiris (2021, retrieved on 25 February 2022), https://famiris.brussels/fr/faq/combien-d-allocations-familiales-puis-je-recevoir/.
91. *Votre prime de naissance en quelques clics*, Famiwal (retrieved on 25 February 2022), https://primedenaissance.wallonie.be/.
92. *Overview of the amount of child care benefits and other family benefits granted by the Federal government*, Flemish Government (retrieved on 25 February 2022), https://www.groeipakket.be/bedragen; *see also Starting amount (growth package)*, Flemish Government (retrieved on 25 February 2022), https://www.vlaanderen.be/startbedrag-groeipakket.
93. Royal Decree of 12 December 2001 on the voucher cheques, 22.12.2001.
94. *Allocations for paternity and birth*, Social Security Self-Employed Entrepreneurs (retrieved on 14 February 2022), https://www.rsvz.be/nl/faq/vaderschaps-en-geboorte-uitkering.
95. Art. 7 Royal Decree of 20 July 1971 on the institution of an indemnity insurance and a maternity insurance for the benefit of the self-employed and the aiding spouses, 7.8.1971.
96. Invalidity benefits are granted if one is sick longer than one year.
97. Art. 9 Royal Decree of 20 July 1971 on the institution of an indemnity insurance and a maternity insurance for the benefit of the self-employed and the aiding spouses, 7.8.1971.
98. This is only the case when a person has been sick for more than a year and lives together with other persons who have an income.
99. As discussed earlier, minimum benefits for sickness are granted in 2024 as of month 1.

accident/professional disease if they fulfil the legal requirements for temporary or long-term incapacity.[100]

Furthermore, self-employed persons are also excluded from the unemployment benefits scheme available to employees; except when they were previously insured as an employee and fulfil the legal conditions applicable for employee.[101] Nevertheless, they may be entitled to a benefit from the bridging scheme if they have completely stopped their self-employed activity due to bankruptcy, serious economic difficulties, or reasons beyond their control.[102] They also need to fulfil a qualifying period (i.e., having paid social security contributions in the 4 quarters during a reference period of 16 quarters before the take up of the bridging right).[103] If one fulfils the legal conditions, a self-employed person can receive benefits for a period of 12 months.[104] While one can request benefits from the bridging scheme multiple times in a row, the total period of receiving them may not exceed 12 months throughout the entire career of a self-employed person. When a self-employed person receives a bridging right, (s)he also remains insured for health insurance. During the COVID-19 crisis, the measures to receive a bridging right were extended, and self-employed persons could also take this up when they (due to Covid-19 crisis) faced a profit loss or had to quarantine or when they need to take up care for a child. The extension of the bridging right has been prolonged until the first and second quarter of 2022.[105] It remains to be seen in the coming months whether the legislator will reshape the original bridging right (as granted before the COVID-19 crisis) for the period after the COVID-19 crisis. No measures have been taken yet; the Belgian government did however extended the bridging right scheme in April 2022 (running from April to June 2022) for self-employed who face a significant profit loss due to the Russian-Ukrainian conflict.[106]

Furthermore, not all social security benefits awarded to self-employed persons reach the at-risk-of-poverty threshold (i.e., 60% of the median equivalized income).

---

100. See for the personal scope on the regulation on work accidents: Art. 1 Act of 10 April 1971 on work accidents, 24.4.1971.
101. The reference period can be extended (at least with 6 months and max. 15 years) with periods during which the person concerned was not covered by the unemployment insurance for employees, but had another statute (e.g., as a self-employed person), *see* Art. 30 Royal Decree of 25 November 1991 concerning the unemployment regulation, 31.12.1991.
102. Art. 4 Act of 22 December 2016 installing a bridging right for self-employed persons, 6.1.2017.
103. There are also some additional conditions which are not discussed further, *see also* Arts. 5-6 Act of 22 December 2016 installing a bridging right for self-employed persons, 6.1.2017.
104. Some exceptions do apply to this general rule: *see* Art. 7 Act of 22 December 2016 installing a bridging right for self-employed persons, 6.1.2017.
105. The temporary extended bridging right can also be taken up by a self-employed person who has already received a benefit under the classic bridging right for the total maximum duration. The temporary extended bridging right is also not taken into account in calculating the maximum duration of the classic bridging right, *see also* Art. 2 Royal Decree of 21 January 2022 to amend the Act of 23 March 2020 to amend the Act of 22 December 2016 on the institution of a bridging right for the self-employed and for the institution of temporary measures due to COVID-19 for the self-employed, 4.02.2022; no legal measures have been adopted yet to extend the measure until Q2 of 2022: see https://socialsecurity.belgium.be/nl/nieuws/nieuwe-tijdelijke-crisismaatregel-overbruggingsrecht-voor-zelfstandigen-08-04-2022.
106. The applicable legislation has not been adopted yet: *see* https://socialsecurity.belgium.be/nl/nieuws/nieuwe-tijdelijke-crisismaatregel-overbruggingsrecht-voor-zelfstandigen-08-04-2022 (retrieved at 13 May 2022).

For instance, this is the case for incapacity benefits concerning (long-)term incapacitated self-employed person in one-person households[107] and statutory retirement old-age pensions.[108]

Due to the low old-age pensions granted for self-employed persons and the tax advantages granted for second pillar pension schemes, a large group of self-employed persons has such a second pillar pension scheme to build up additional pension rights. According to the available figures, in 2019 almost 64% of the self-employed persons have paid contributions to such a pension scheme.[109]

Despite the obstacles discussed earlier, self-employed persons who are in a state of need can also apply for an exemption from social security contributions for certain quarters. This option is not open for employees. In 2019, 11,716 requests were filed, which is an increase of 16%, compared to the year before.[110]

[3] Unionization and Application of Collective Agreements

Certain employers' associations, such as Union of Self-Employed Entrepreneurs (UNIZO) and Neutral Trade Union for Self-employed Persons (SNI) have been invested in representing the interest of solo self-employed persons and small-sized enterprises. Trade unions traditionally only represented employees, which stems from the scope of application of the Act of 5 December 1968 regulating collective agreements and collective bargaining. More recently, however, trade unions like the Christian trade union have started to provide protection for economically dependent self-employed (or freelancers with precarious conditions).[111] As only three trade unions meet the legal criteria to conclude collective agreements, Belgium does not have a tradition that 'new' trade unions can easily be established. This can lead to a difficult balancing act when both employee and employers' organizations want to represent the dependent and solo self-employed workers. At this time, there is no clarity on this matter, which begs the question if this group is actually represented.

The Act of 5 December 1968 regulating collective bargaining applies not only to employees but also to persons who perform work under the authority of another person. This can mean that also economically dependent solo self-employed persons fall under the scope of application of the Act of 5 December 1968. Whether it is possible to conclude agreements that resemble collective agreements but between self-employed persons and a principal, with them not falling under the scope of the Act of

107. Guido Van Limberghen et al., *L'accès des travailleurs salariés et indépendants à la sécurité sociale en Belgique*, Federal public service – social security 2020, 544 (2021).
108. *Ibid.*, 556.
109. Please note that it concerns self-employed persons who work as a self-employed person as their main activity: *Biennial report concerning the second pillar pension scheme for self-employed persons* 6, FSMA (May 2021), https://www.fsma.be/sites/default/files/media/files/2021-05/wapz_wapbl_wapznp_05-2021_nl.pdf.
110. *Social contributions and exemptions of self-employed*, Federal Public Service – Economy (18 October 2021), https://economie.fgov.be/nl/themas/ondernemingen/kmos-en-zelfstandigen-cijfers/zelfstandigen-belgie/sociale-bijdragen-en.
111. *See United Freelancers*, ACV-CSC United Freelancers (retrieved on 25 February 2022), https://www.unitedfreelancers.be/home-fr.

1968, remains unclear, as discussed earlier. Some authors remark that – notwithstanding possible issues with EU competition law[112] – it should be possible.[113] This 'collective agreement' would then be governed under general civil law, instead of collective labour law. To this day, there has not been any significant case law whether or not this is possible. As such, collective agreements that cover certain self-employed persons are still rather exceptional in Belgium.[114]

[C] Impact Analysis

In the final part of our discussion of VUP Group 2, this contribution looks at the risk of in-work poverty for four hypothetical households, as explained earlier. Our analysis in the following section focuses specifically on the hypothetical households: our comments on the applicability of social security law for VUP Group 2 are found in previous subsections.

Self-employed persons nowadays receive more social protection than a couple of decades ago; nevertheless, several social risks are still not open for self-employed persons, such as unemployment as well as schemes providing protection for labour accidents and occupational diseases.

Looking at the social security benefits granted for self-employment, only flat-rate benefits are provided. This can be explained in light of the difficulties the legislator faces in finding information on the exact income of self-employed persons. Nevertheless, this will constitute a significant loss of income for certain families. The flat-rate benefits provided in the social security scheme for self-employed persons do, however, consider the household composition, similar as for VUP Group 1.

As for the family benefits, we refer to our comments for VUP Group 1.

Other aspects of social security law discussed earlier apply regardless of the family composition. Labour law does not apply for self-employed person, so this element is not discussed further in this part.

When looking at the household composition of VUP Group 2, we can make the following observations concerning the at-risk-of-poverty rate for the different hypothetical households.

A majority of the self-employed persons without employees live in households with more than two persons (approximately 60% in 2019). For this group, the at-risk-of-poverty rate is significantly higher in comparison to the whole group of employed persons (10.8% in 2007 and 18.6% in 2019 compared to 4.9% in 2007 and 5.3% in 2019 for employed persons). The risk of poverty for all self-employed persons and for self-employed persons without employees living in a one-person household is

112. *See also, Approval of the content of a draft for a Communication from the Commission, Guidelines on the Application of EU competition law to collective agreements regarding the working conditions of solo self-employed persons C (2021) 8838 final*, European Commission, 9 December 2021.
113. Conclusion Pierre-Paul Van Gehuchten, *Quel droit social pour les travailleurs de plateformes?* (2019).
114. *See, for example.* 'Sanoma', which is discussed in depth in Daniel Dumont, Auriane Lamine & Jean-Benoît Maisin, *Le droit de négociation collective des travailleurs indépendants* (2020).

also significantly higher than for the overall group of employed persons. Both groups have been confronted with a strong increase in the at-risk-of-poverty rate (respectively 34% and 37.7% in 2013 compared to 17.7% and 9.7% in 2007). In the last couple of years the general at-risk-of-poverty rate has somewhat decreased for single persons, but the percentage of self-employed persons without employees has nonetheless doubled since 2007 (19.1% in 2019).

Only for those living in two-person households, has the at-risk-of-poverty rate decreased strongly and evolved towards the rate that we found for the working population in general.

Furthermore, a higher risk of poverty is mainly found in households where only one person works. A majority of self-employed persons without employees, however, live in households where more than one person works (65.4%).

Regarding the number of children in a household: similarly to VUP Group 1, around half of the self-employed persons without employees does not have any children under the age of 18 years old. This percentage has been increasing over the last decade (51.8% in 2007 compared to 58.1% in 2019), and can perhaps be explained by the fact that more self-employed persons without employees are 50 years or older and might have children above 18 years old. The at-risk-of-poverty rate for this group has remained rather constant, but nevertheless remains higher to that of the whole group of employed persons (10.6% compared to 3.2% in 2019). For households with one or two children under the age of 18 years old, however, the risk-at-poverty rate has risen (sharply). This is the case for both self-employed persons in general and self-employed persons without employees. Similar to VUP Group 1, this seems to imply that the household income (income out of work but also family benefits) does not seem to suffice for families with more than one child.

If we apply the findings above to our hypothetical households, we see that in particular families where only one person works (single person, single parent, or a breadwinner with a partner) the risk of in-work poverty is higher. This is even more so for families with children.

§2.04 VUP GROUP 3: FIXED-TERM, AGENCY WORKERS, INVOLUNTARY PART-TIMERS

[A] Composition of VUP Group 3

[1] General Remarks

The EU-SILC data gathers both temporary workers[115] and involuntary part-time workers in the same category. This makes a specific analysis for either subgroup somewhat difficult. Nevertheless, it remains possible to identify certain trends.[116]

115. Temporary work includes a temporary job or work contract of limited duration. A contract has a limited duration when the termination of the job is determined by objective conditions such as reaching a certain data, completion of a certain assignment, etc. A temporary job includes (i) persons with a seasonal job or (ii) Persons engaged by an employment agency or business and

The percentage of temporary workers and involuntary part-timers constitute around 13% of all employed persons (2019).

The vast majority of fixed-term workers and part-time workers are predominantly working in the category 'other services' (63.5% in 2019).[117] Regardless of the sector temporary workers and involuntary part-time workers work in, their risk of in-work poverty is always higher than for the working population.

[2] A Higher Risk of In-Work Poverty for the Workers In VUP Group 3

The at-risk-of-poverty rate for temporary and involuntary part-time workers is about twice as high as to that of the working population (11.3% compared to 4.8% in 2019). As to the severe material deprivation rate, a clear increase can also be observed over the last decade. The severe material deprivation rate for this group of workers is also significantly higher compared to that of the working population (6.1% compared to 1.8% in 2019).

[3] A Group That Is Predominantly Female and Young

When considering aspects such as age, gender, and nationality for temporary and involuntary part-time workers, it becomes clear that in this group, young and female workers are overrepresented compared to the in-work population as a whole. In 2007 around 50% of temporary and part-time workers were between 18 and 34 years old. Over the last decade, however, this percentage has declined by 10% and the percentage of people over the age of 50 years old has increased sharply, particularly in the period between 2007 and 2013 (13.9% in 2007, compared to 20.7% in 2013 and 21.7% in 2019). Mostly workers aged between 35-49 years old face a higher risk of poverty (17.1%), with lower poverty risks for younger workers (8.6%) and 5.8% for those older than 50 years (2019). This can be explained by the fact that students may also take up temporary work in combination with their studies, and still live together with their parents.

Approximately 71.1% of the fixed-term and involuntary part-timers are women; this number is much higher than what we found for the working population, where the number of female workers fluctuates around 47.2%. However, the risk of in-work poverty is rather similar for both men and women working in temporary jobs or part-time employment, with a slight increase for both groups over the last decade

---

hired out to a third party for the carrying out of a 'work mission' (unless there is a work contract of unlimited duration with the employment agency or business): *see also Glossary – Temporary Employment*, Eurostat (retrieved at 26 February 2022), https://ec.europa.eu/eurostat/statistics-explained/index.php?title=Glossary:Temporary_employment.

116. Information found at national level for the different subgroups of VUP Group 3 is discussed below in our discussion of each of the different subgroups.

117. This sector includes the following groups: financial and insurance activities, real estate activities, professional, scientific and technical activities, administrative and support activities, education, human health and social work activities, arts, entertainment and recreation and other service activities.

(11.4% for women and 11% for men, compared to 9.1% for women and 9.6% for men in 2007). The fact that – despite the higher number of women in VUP Group 3, their risk of in-work poverty is similar to that of men can be explained by the fact that women are often the second earner in the family. This second wage can have an important effect on the overall household income, lifting families out of poverty.

Although temporary and involuntary part-time workers predominantly have the Belgian nationality, the percentage of persons with another nationality within this VUP Group has doubled over the last decade (9.6% in 2007 compared to 17.9% in 2019). An increase which is higher than the increase in persons with another nationality among all employed persons; workers with another nationality also face a higher risk of in-work poverty.

[4] A Group of Low- and Medium-Skilled Workers in a Low-Skilled Occupation

EU-SILC data shows that temporary and involuntary part-time workers are more likely to have a low or medium level of education. Approximately 18.4% of the temporary and involuntary part-time workers had a low level education (compared to 12.6% for the overall working population) and 41.9% had a medium level education (compared to 36.3% for the overall working population). Particularly persons with a low level education in temporary or involuntary part-time work face a high risk of poverty (24.9% compared to 12% for the working population).

For the other groups (medium and high level education), the risk of in-work poverty has remained rather constant over the last decade. Nevertheless, also their risk of in-work poverty remains about twice as high compared to the working population (for temporary workers and involuntary part-time workers this is 11.3% (medium skilled) and 4.9% (high skilled) compared to 5.5% (medium skilled) and 2.5% (high skilled).

As for the skill-level of their occupation, two-thirds of temporary workers and involuntary part-time workers work in a low skill-level occupation (62.5% compared to 51.3% for the group of employed persons in 2019). The risk of in-work poverty for low-skilled workers has remained rather constant over the last decade (12.2% in 2019 compared to 11.2% in 2007). For temporary and involuntary part-time workers with a high skill-level, on the other hand, the risk of in-work poverty has sharply increased over the last decade (6% in 2007 compared to 9.7% in 2019). For temporary and involuntary part-time workers with high skills, the at-risk-of-poverty rate is now almost four times higher than for the working population in general.

As for the type of contract, it is not unexpected that around 60% (58.5% in 2019) work with a temporary contract. However, it is also interesting to note that a large majority of temporary workers and involuntary part-time workers work 12 months (86.1% compared to 94.6% of all employed persons). One would expect to see more irregular work patterns for this group of workers (and thus shorter working periods).

[B] Fixed-Term Employees

[1] Notion

A fixed-term employment contract contains an indication of a fixed date (or event to occur at a fix date), after which the parties are released from their reciprocal obligations, unless parties have decided otherwise.[118] According to the available data from the Belgian administration for statistics (STATBEL) the number of fixed-term workers compared to the overall number of employees is around 10 à 11% (2019, 2020, and 2021)[119].

There are several limits in place in Belgian legislation as to ensure that employers do not make use of fixed-term contracts in order to circumvent the stricter rules that apply for the termination of a contract of indefinite duration.

Successive fixed-term contracts are generally considered to constitute an employment contract of indefinite duration, except in a set of situations, or if the employer is able to prove that these contracts were justified by the nature of the work or by other legitimate reasons.[120]

A fixed-term employment contract may generally be succeeded only by another fixed-term contract (without being considered as a contract of indefinite duration) four times, each contract having at least a duration of three months, and with the total duration of these successive contracts not exceeding two years.[121] Also, successive fixed-term contracts with each lasting at least six months and a maximum combined duration of three years may be performed with the preliminary authorization of the relevant civil servant without being considered as a contract of indefinite duration.[122]

Temporary work can also be performed as a replacement contract or as a contract for the performance of temporary work.[123] Replacement employment contracts under the Act on employment contracts refer to replacements of an employee whose contract is suspended for reasons other than lack of work due to economic causes, bad weather, strike, or lockout.[124] The maximum combined duration is two years.[125] Afterwards, the rules on the end of the contract for indefinite duration apply.

While both successive fixed-term contracts and successive replacement contracts for a period of more than two years are regarded as a contract of indefinite duration, the same did not apply if it was a fixed-term contract being succeeded by a replacement contract and *vice versa*. This difference in treatment was deemed unconstitutional by

118. Art. 7 Act of 3 July 1978 on employment contracts, 22.8.1978; Willy Van Eeckhoutte & Vincent Neuprez, *Compendium Social – Droit du travail contenant des annotations fiscales* 836 (2020).
119. The data for 2021 did not include the month December yet: STATBEL (Labour Force Survey), Labour market indicators (retrieved on 28 February 2022) https://statbel.fgov.be/nl/themas/werk-opleiding/arbeidsmarkt/werkgelegenheid-en-werkloosheid#panel-12.
120. Art. 10 Act of 3 July 1978 on employment contracts, 22.8.1978.
121. *Ibid.*, Art 10*bis*.
122. *Ibid.*
123. Art. 1, §1bis and §2 Act of 24 July 1987 on temporary work, interim work, and the provision of workers to users, 20.8.1987.
124. Art. 11*ter* Act of 3 July 1978 on employment contracts, 22.8.1978.
125. *Ibid.*

the Constitutional Court, citing that the intent of this system was to benefit from a legally prescribed steadiness in one's occupation.[126]

The employment contract for the performance of temporary work is, in turn, a variant of an employment contract that shares similarities with a fixed-term contract. In order to be considered as such, an employment contract must have as its purpose the replacement of a permanent worker, to meet the demands set by a temporary increase in workload or to ensure the performance of exceptional work.[127] If they do decide to operate under the Act on temporary work,[128] several specificities apply to this kind of contracts. Among them, we highlight the possibility of performing several successive contracts without being considered as an open-ended contract, and (when performed for replacing an employee) not having to be limited to a maximum combined duration of two years.[129]

[2] Equal Treatment, Working Conditions, and Social Security Benefits

Fixed-term employees may not be treated less favourably regarding their employment conditions than employees with a contract of an indefinite duration in a comparable situation solely on the grounds that they work with a contract of definite duration.[130] In this regard, 'employees with a contract of indefinite duration in a comparable situation' are persons in a contract of employment of indefinite duration at the same establishment (or, alternatively, working for the same company or in the same branch of activity) performing the same or similar work or function.[131]

There are, however, some instances in which employees under a fixed-term contract of employment are arguably less protected. After the end of the employment contract, an employee does not receive any compensation. Employees with a fixed-term contract are, however, entitled to unemployment benefits (if they fulfil the legal conditions). Furthermore, employees under a fixed-term employment contract who want to end their contract early, have to pay a compensation equal to the amount of remuneration that was remaining until the end of the contract (except if the termination happens during the first half of the – first – fixed-term contract within the parties). This obligation also applies for employers. The amount cannot, however, exceed twice the remuneration corresponding to the length of the period of notice which would have been due if the contract had been concluded without a predetermined term.[132]

126. 93/2021, Constitutional Court (17 June 2021).
127. Art. 1, §2 Act of 24 July 1987 on temporary work, interim work, and the provision of workers to users, 20.8.1987.
128. Act of 24 July 1987 on temporary work, interim work, and the provision of workers to users, 20.8.1987.
129. *Ibid.*, Arts. 1-2 and 3.
130. Art. 4 Act of 5 June 2002 on the non-discrimination principle to the benefit of employees with a fixed-term employment contract, 5.6.2002. The Act also notes that the employer must inform fixed-term employees of vacancies in the company or establishment to ensure that they have the same opportunity as other workers to obtain a vacant post, *see Ibid.*
131. *Ibid.*
132. Art. 40 Act of 3 July 1978 on employment contracts, 22.8.1978.

Fixed-term employees are generally covered by the same social security schemes as employees who work with a contract of indefinite duration. However, different rules apply on the calculation of the qualifying period to provide additional protection. We briefly highlight some elements, as in this chapter they cannot be discussed in detail.

For example, the Belgian legislation equates some days of inactivity with work days for the fulfilment of the reference period to receive unemployment benefits, such as the days during which a person was unemployed. This can be of importance for fixed-term employees or temporary agency employees: days during which they did not work but received an unemployment benefit can thus be taken into account in case they become unemployed in a later stage.[133] The Belgian legislation also allows that employees who become unemployed again within three years after being unemployed, can be exempted from fulfilling a waiting period.[134] This period can also be prolonged taking into account the statutory conditions. Similar rules also apply for example in the case of sickness. In case of sickness the qualifying period will be calculated per hour for seasonal, intermittent, or part-time employees. One falls under this category if an employee is not covered by the social insurance schemes for employees for the hours outside his/her normal working hours and if the employee does not fulfil the conditions for entitlement to unemployment benefits for those hours.[135] This makes it easier for those employees to perform the necessary working days; however, where the number of working days for full-time employees is converted from five to six per week: this is not the case when the working days are calculated per hour (and which thus puts those workers at a disadvantage).[136]

[3] Unionization and Collective Agreement's Application

No information has been found on the specific unionization coverage rate of fixed-term employees. Nor was data found on whether trade unions are able to effectively represent them and grant application of the conditions established by collective agreements.

In principle, fixed-term bilateral work is only regulated by legislation, i.e., Art. 7-11*bis* of Act of 3 July 1978 on employment contracts and the Act of 5 June 2002 on the non-discrimination principle to the benefit of employees with a fixed-term employment contract, not a national collective agreement. It does happen, however, that sectoral bargaining imposes additional rights for fixed-term workers, e.g., such as a

133. *See* the different grounds summed up in Art. 38 Royal Decree of 25 November 1991 concerning the unemployment regulation, 31.12.1991.
134. *Ibid.*, Art. 42, §2.
135. Art. 202 Royal Decree of 3 July 1996 executing the Act of the obligatory medical insurance coordinated on 14 July 1994, 31.7.1996.
136. *Ibid.*, Art. 203, §6-7.

priority rule in case a position (with a contract of indefinite duration) with their employer opens up.[137]

According to a study of 2017, social partners have also developed some actions towards the prevention of abuses and fraud on seasonal work, fixed-term work, and the fight against undeclared sectors in some specific sectors such as the food service industry and agriculture.[138]

[C] Temporary Agency Workers

[1] Notion

Belgian legislation defines temporary agency as a company whose activity consists in hiring temporary agency workers to make them available to users for the performance of temporary work having as its purpose:[139]

- to provide for the replacement of a permanent worker;
- to meet a temporary increase in workload;[140]
- to ensure the execution of exceptional work;[141]
- to make a temporary worker available to a user for the purpose of filling a vacancy, with a view to the permanent engagement of the temporary worker by the user for the same job at the end of the period of provision (this is only allowed three times per vacancy, for a maximum total duration of nine months and not exceeding each month per temporary agency contract).[142]

137. This, however, depends on the specific sectoral or sub-sectoral collective agreements, following database contains an overview of the different sectoral collective agreements: https://emploi.belgique.be/fr/themes/commissions-paritaires-et-conventions-collectives-de-travail-cct/conventions-collectives-0.
138. *Fraudulent contracting of work: Abusing fixed-term contracts, Belgium, Estonia and Spain*, Eurofound (27 July 2017, retrieved on 28 February 2022), https://www.eurofound.europa.eu/publications/information-sheet/2017/fraudulent-contracting-of-work-abusing-fixed-term-contracts-belgium-estonia-and-spain, 11.
139. Arts. 1 & 7, 1° Act of 24 July 1987 on temporary work, interim work, and the provision of workers to users, 20.8.1987.
140. In this case, prior agreement of the trade union delegation is necessary. Furthermore, special limitations exist if the user belongs to the construction sector (namely the impossibility of performing consecutive daily contracts, and the prohibition of using a temporary agency work for longer than six consecutive months). *See* Arts. 10 and 11 Collective Agreement n° 108 of 16 July 2013 concluded in the National Labour Council on temporary work and interim work.
141. Exceptional work are tasks not normally performed by the user for a maximum duration of approximately three months, including preparation of events, unloading of lorries (with the prior agreement of the union delegation of the user company), secretarial work for businessmen temporarily staying in Belgium, performance of specialized tasks requiring a particular professional qualification, overtime work as a result of an accident, inventory and balance sheet work (for a maximum duration of 7 days per calendar year). *See* Art. 6, §1 Collective Agreement n° 108 of 16 July 2013 concluded in the National Labour Council on temporary work and interim work.
142. *Ibid.*, Art. 26.

A temporary employment contract is a contract in which a temporary agency worker undertakes, vis-à-vis a temporary employment agency and in return for remuneration, to perform temporary work for a user for one of the abovementioned aims.[143] A temporary agency worker is a worker who enters into a temporary employment contract to be placed at the disposal of one or more users.[144] Hence, temporary work agencies may only place temporary workers at the disposal of users, and users may only employ temporary workers for the purpose of performing temporary work.[145]

Temporary work agencies must be recognized by the public authorities, with conditions and procedures for recognition varying per region.[146] A temporary work agency may then conclude a fixed-term or open-ended contract with a worker for the performance of temporary agency work. It is allowed that temporary agencies hire a temporary worker through successive daily temporary employment contracts with the same user, but only if the need for flexibility in using such successive daily contracts can be demonstrated by the user and the trade union delegation is previously informed.[147]

The use of temporary agency workers outside these specifically allowed circumstances (i.e., replacement of a permanent worker, temporary increase in workload, execution of exceptional work, and filling a permanent vacancy with the temporary agency worker after the end of a certain period) is prohibited.[148] It is also forbidden for one company to exceed a certain number of temporary workers. Moreover, it is not allowed to use temporary agency workers during a strike.[149]

In certain cases, the temporary work contract will be terminated and the temporary worker and the user shall be bound by a contract of employment for an indefinite period. For instance when the user employs or continues to employ a temporary worker in the aforementioned prohibited circumstances, even though the temporary work agency has notified the user of its decision to withdraw the worker. It

143. Art. 7, 2° Act of 24 July 1987 on temporary work, interim work, and the provision of workers to users, 20.8.1987.
144. *Ibid.*, Art. 7, 3°.
145. *Ibid.*, Art. 21.
146. *See* Decree of Walloon Parliament of 3 April 2009 on the registration or licensing of employment agencies, 5.5.2009; Decree of the Parliament of the German-speaking Community on the licensing of temporary employment agencies and the supervision of private employment agencies, 13.7.2009; Flemish Decree of 10 December 2010 on the private labour mediation, 29.12.2010; Ordonnance of the Parliament of the Brussels-Capital Region of 14 July 2011 on the joint management of the labour market in the Brussels-Capital Region, 10.8.2011.
147. Art. 8*bis* Act of 24 July 1987 on temporary work, interim work, and the provision of workers to users, 20.8.1987; Arts. 33-40 Collective Agreement n° 108 of 16 July 2013 concluded in the National Labour Council on temporary work and interim work.
148. Art. 21 Act of 24 July 1987 on temporary work, interim work, and the provision of workers to users, 20.8.1987.
149. *Ibid.*, Art. 1, §5 Act of 24 July 1987 on temporary work, interim work, and the provision of workers to users, 20.8.1987 and Art. 19 Collective Agreement n° 108 of 16 July 2013 concluded in the National Labour Council on temporary work and interim work.

will also be the case if the user exceeds the number of attempts to fulfil a vacancy through a temporary agency contract.[150]

If the user cannot prove the need for flexibility justifying the performance of successive daily temporary agency contracts (as mentioned above), the temporary employment agency is obliged to pay remuneration to the temporary employee who has been employed on the basis of successive daily temporary employment contracts. In addition to the remuneration, an indemnity is also owed. The amount has to correspond to the remuneration that would have been paid if a two-week temporary employment contract had been concluded.[151]

Administrative or penal sanctions may be imposed under certain circumstances as well. In this regard, a temporary agency would be subjected to an administrative fine of between €80 and €800.[152] Moreover, the performance of temporary agency work in one of the prohibited circumstances abovementioned, or any other lack of compliance with the rules concerning temporary agency work, may result in an administrative sanction (between €200 and €2,000) or a criminal sanction (between €400 – €4,000).[153] These sanctions are multiplied by the number of temporary agency workers involved.[154]

[2] Equal Treatment, Working Conditions, and Social Security Benefits

Workers of temporary agencies are generally entitled to the same remuneration,[155] access to company infrastructure,[156] and measures on well-being at work[157] as if they would be employed as permanent workers by the user. The notion of 'remuneration' includes non-recurring performance-related benefits and bonuses (such as loyalty, production, or end-of-year bonuses) that permanent workers typically receive.[158] It also includes meal vouchers, but only in an equal basis with the user's fixed-term employees (and thus, if these are entitled to less or no meal vouchers than permanent workers under the relevant collective agreement due to objective reasons,[159] then

150. Art. 41 Collective Agreement n° 108 of 16 July 2013 concluded in the National Labour Council on temporary work and interim work.
151. Art. 8*bis* Act of 24 July 1987 on temporary work, interim work, and the provision of workers to users, 20.8.1987.
152. Art. 176 Social Penal Code, 1.7.2010.
153. *Ibid.*
154. *Ibid*; The Social Penal Code put a limit to the number of workers: sanctions can only be multiplied by max. 100 workers: Art. 103.
155. Art. 10 Act of 24 July 1987 on temporary work, interim work, and the provision of workers to users, 20.8.1987.
156. Such as catering services, childcare facilities, and transport services, and unless a difference in treatment is justified by objective reasons, *see Ibid.*, Art. 10*bis*.
157. *Ibid.*, Art. 19; Art. X.2-1 Code wellbeing at work, 2.6.2017.
158. Willy Van Eeckhoutte & Vincent Neuprez, *Compendium Social – Droit du travail contenant des annotations fiscales* 607-608 (2020).
159. Art. 4 Act of 5 June 2002 on the non-discrimination principle to the benefit of employees with a fixed-term employment contract, 5.6.2002.

temporary agency workers would be so too).[160] Nevertheless, collective benefits provided by the user, such as group life insurance[161] or loyalty premiums,[162] are not included. Note that - while the name may imply otherwise - temporary agency workers may just as well have an open-ended contract instead of a fixed-term contract.

The build-up of seniority rights has been adapted to accommodate temporary agency work. Certain periods of non-activity will be taken into account when they do not exceed more than one week. Also periods where the execution of the agreement is temporarily ceased will be taken into account, for as long as the temporary agency worker does not work for another employer during that period in time.[163] If the user stops the temporary agency worker's contract and hires him/her in the exact same function within a period of seven days, then the seniority of the temporary agency worker will be taken into account (but not for more than one year).[164]

The first three working days of an employment contract for temporary agency work are regarded as a trial period, unless parties agreed otherwise. Until the expiry of that period, each of the parties may terminate the employment contract without notice or compensation. Simultaneous probationary periods are not allowed if the temporary agency worker is employed through successive contracts for temporary agency work (for the same function and with the same user).[165]

Some measures have also been taken so as to avoid that temporary agency workers experience negative consequences concerning social security, *see* our discussion on fixed-term work.

[3] Unionization and Collective Agreement's Application

No information has been found on the specific unionization coverage rate of agency workers. Nor was data found on whether trade unions are able to effectively represent them and grant application of the conditions established by collective agreements.

Although equal treatment has been primarily imposed by law, it has still been a struggle to guarantee it for temporary agency workers. Increasing equality is a matter of interplay between legislation and collective agreements providing additional protection. With that goal in mind, the social partners have concluded a substantial amount of successive collective agreements to increase the degree of equality between temporary agency workers and standard employees.[166]

---

160. Willy Van Eeckhoutte & Vincent Neuprez, *Compendium Social – Droit du travail contenant des annotations fiscales* 608 (2020).
161. *See also* RG 3617-03, Labour Court Liège Section Neufchâteau 11th chamber (5 May 2004).
162. *See also* RG 2017/AG/73, Labour Court Ghent 2nd chamber (8 October 2018).
163. Art. 13 Act of 24 July 1987 on temporary work, interim work, and the provision of workers to users, 20.8.1987.
164. Art. 37/4 Act of 3 July 1978 on labour contracts, 22.8.1978.
165. Art. 5 Act of 24 July 1987 on temporary work, interim work, and the provision of workers to users, 20.8.1987.
166. *Ibid. See also* for an overview of the different collective agreements closed at the national level by the National Labour Council: http://www.cnt-nar.be/Cct-theme.htm#travail%20interimaire.

In Belgium there is a separate sector committee for temporary agency work: several collective agreements provide additional protection for temporary agency workers (e.g., in case of sickness and an additional benefit in case of temporary unemployment). Some of those collective agreements only apply in case that there is no similar sectoral agreement in place in the sector of the user where the temporary agency worker works. The collective agreement by the sectoral committee for temporary agency work will thus apply by default. On the other hand, some collective agreements explicitly state that the agreement for the sector of the user applies only when this agreement is more beneficial.

Worth mentioning is also the federation where all the private labour mediation offices and Human Resource service providers (FEDERGON) have a seat. Within this federation, there is an ombudsperson where temporary agency workers can file a complaint in case they face problems with the applicable legislation or their social rights.[167]

[4] Outsourcing and Matching Between Labour Demand and Supply

The use of temporary agency work as a means of externalizing labour is arguably limited by the fact that the use of such type of work may be performed only within the quite limited situations prescribed by the law, as analysed earlier.

[D] Involuntary Part-Time Work

[1] Notion

Belgian legislation defines a 'part-time employee' as an employee whose normal working hours, calculated on a weekly basis or on average over a period of employment of up to one year, are less than those of a full-time worker in a comparable situation.[168] Moreover, Collective Agreement n° 38 concerning part-time work distinguishes this form of work from others (such as casual work, seasonal work, and temporary work) in that it must concern work performed on a regular and voluntary basis for a shorter period than the normal duration.[169]

In 2018, almost 26.8% of all employees worked part-time.[170] Mostly women work part-time (43.5% of women worked part-time compared to the overall number of employees; this was 11% for men). There are also large differences between men and women dependent on the age groups. The number of persons working part-time is

167. *Ombudsperson*, Federgon (retrieved on 27 February 2022), https://federgon.be/ombudsdienst/.
168. Art. 2, 2° Act of 5 March 2002 on the non-discrimination principle to the benefit of part-time workers, 13.3.2002.
169. Art. 1 Collective Agreement n° 35 of 27 February 1981 on certain provisions of labour law on the matter of part-time labour, 27.2.1981.
170. *Kerncijfers – Statistisch overzicht van 2019*, Statbel (2019, retrieved on 28 February 2022), 101, https://statbel.fgov.be/sites/default/files/images/in%20de%20kijker/kerncijfers_2019_r.pdf.

smaller for persons between 25 and 49 years old (39% of women worked part-time compared to the overall number of employees; this was 7.5% for men). Higher numbers of part-time work can be found with workers between 15 and 24 years old (48.4% for women and 24.6% for men compared to the overall number of employees) as they will often combine part-time work with their studies) and older workers (+50 years old, 52.5% for women and 15.1% for men compared to the overall number of employees).[171]

A part-time employment contract typically may not amount to less than one-third of the weekly working time of a full-time employment contract for a person who works in the same category within a company.[172] This rule, however, may not apply[173] to persons excluded from the scope of the law on collective agreements and persons excluded from social security schemes due to the brevity or accessory nature of their employment relationship,[174] as well as to persons performing work through a temporary agency and persons in a sector to which this limit may not be applied (as provided in a collective labour agreement).

Involuntary part-time work does not have its own specific definition provided by law. In Belgium, the share of involuntary part-time work is relatively small, compared to other EU Member States: only 4.5% (2020) of all persons working part-time do so on an involuntary basis (22.1% for the EU in 2020).[175] The number of involuntary part-time workers in Belgium has also decreased since the financial and economic crisis.[176] More men than women seem to work involuntary part-time.[177] It is, however, unclear whether this phenomenon of involuntary part-time work is not underestimated in the available data. For example, in certain sectors the available positions offered are almost all on a part-time basis. In the absence of any full-time jobs, part-time work is the only available option.[178]

171. *Ibid.*
172. Art. 11*bis* Act of 3 July 1978 on employment contracts, 22.8.1978.
173. Royal Decree of 21 December 1992 determining derogations from the minimum weekly working time of part-time workers laid down in Art. 11*bis* of the Act of 3 July 1978 on employment contracts, 30.12.1992.
174. *See* further Arts. 16-18 Royal Decree of 28 November 1969 for the execution of the Act of 27 June 1969 revising the law decree of 28 December 1944 on the social security for workers, 5.12.1969.
175. *Incidence of involuntary part time workers*, OECD (retrieved on 25 February 2022), https://stats.oecd.org/Index.aspx?QueryId=9584.
176. Jeroen Horemans, Ive Marx & Brian Nolan, *Hanging in, but only just: part-time employment and in-work poverty throughout the crisis*, Vol. 5 n°5 IZA Journal of European Labor Studies 1, 3-5 (2016).
177. *How common – and how voluntary – is part-time employment?*, Eurostat (8 June 2018, retrieved on 28 February 2022), https://ec.europa.eu/eurostat/web/products-eurostat-news/-/DDN-20180608-1; *Incidence of involuntary part time workers*, OECD (retrieved on 28 February 2022), https://stats.oecd.org/Index.aspx?QueryId=9584.
178. Timo Lehaen, *Sociale bescherming van onvrijwillig deeltijdse werknemers in armoede* 5 (Masters thesis KU Leuven 2020-2021).

[2] Equal Treatment, Working Conditions, and Social Security Benefits

According to the Act of 5 March 2002, part-time employees may not be treated less favourably than full-time employees in a comparable situation solely on the grounds that they work part-time.[179] 'Full-time employees in a comparable situation' are employees at the same establishment (or, alternatively, working for the same company or in the same branch of activity) having the same type of employment contract and performing the same or a similar type of work or occupation.[180]

Collective Agreement n° 35 also establishes the principle of non-discrimination,[181] as well as the principle of equal treatment with regard to pay.[182] This also entails that the remuneration of a part-time employee must also evolve on the basis of the same scale of seniority as that applied to a full-time employee.[183] Another measure, intended to equalize the treatment of part-time employees, is that employers are obligated to give priority to part-time employees when a full-time position becomes vacant in the company they are working at.[184] This priority right only applies in case that an employee has made a request to his/her employer to receive priority and for job openings for which the part-time worker has the necessary qualifications and if this would mean an increase in the hours worked for more than one month.[185]

Part-time employees are generally covered by the same social security schemes as employees who work on a full-time basis. However, different rules apply on the calculation of the qualifying period to provide additional protection for part-time workers. We briefly highlight some elements, as in this contribution the different elements cannot be discussed in detail. For example, in the case of unemployment, voluntary part-time workers must complete a waiting period which consists of the same number of working days required for full-time employment.[186] For part-time workers, the number of working days is, however, half days. The reference period to fulfil the qualifying period is also extended with six months.[187] Similar rules to fulfil the

179. Art. 4 Act of 5 March 2002 on the non-discrimination principle to the benefit of part-time workers, 13.3.2002. Differences in treatment can exist, however, if they are justified by objective reasons. See *Ibid.*; Michel Davagle, Pierre Delchevalerie & Leen Van Assche, *Le contrat de travail à temps partiel* 27 (Wolters Kluwer 2018).
180. Art. 4 Act of 5 March 2002 on the non-discrimination principle to the benefit of part-time workers, 13.3.2002.
181. Art. 1*bis* Collective Agreement n° 35 of 27 February 1981 on certain provisions of labour law on the matter of part-time labour, 27.2.1981.
182. *Ibid.*, Arts. 9-10.
183. *See also* RG 33896-06, Labour Court Liège Section Liège 5th chamber (18 December 2006).
184. Arts. 152-156/1 Programme Act of 22 December 1989, 14.11.2011; Royal Decree of 2 May 2019 towards the execution of the provisions of the Programme Act of 22 December 1989 on the prioritization of part-time employees in receiving a vacant position at their place of employment, 15.5.2019; *see also* Art. 2 of the Royal Decree that excludes certain workers.
185. Art. 3 Royal Decree of 2 May 2019 towards the execution of the provisions of the Programme Act of 22 December 1989 on the prioritization of part-time employees in receiving a vacant position at their place of employment, 15.5.2019.
186. Art. 33 Royal Decree of 25 November 1991 concerning the unemployment regulation, 31.12.1991.
187. 2 Sophie Remouchamps, *Questions transversale en matière du sécurité sociale* 140 (Larcier 2017).

qualifying period also apply in case of sickness.[188] All part-time workers, however, receive half the amount of unemployment benefits that full-time employees would receive, regardless of in the exact hours worked, which is a disadvantage for those that work more than half-time but less than full-time. Minimum unemployment benefits are also prorated,[189] which is different in case of sickness. Minimum sickness benefits provided to employees are granted, irrespective of the previously worked hours and are granted as of month 7.[190] The Belgian legislation now also provides minimum benefits as of month 4 (2022)[191] but during month 4 to 6 minimum benefits cannot exceed the previously earned wages.[192]

In order to encourage unemployed persons who worked full-time or part-time to take up employment, the Belgian legislation provides the possibility to take up part-time work (for less hours in case one worked previously already part-time) and still receive part of their unemployment benefit.

[3] Unionization and Collective Agreement's Application

Part-time workers are covered by collective agreements in the same manner as full-time workers. In addition to them enjoying the same basic protections as full-time employees, however, part-time workers have also been the subject of agreements made by the social partners on a national level. Through collective bargaining, their position was regulated by Collective Agreement n° 35 on of 27 February 1981 on certain provisions of labour law on the matter of part-time labour.[193]

[E] Impact Analysis

In the final part of our discussion of VUP Group 3, this contribution looks at the risk of in-work poverty for four hypothetical households, as explained above. As the EU-SILC data looked at both the temporary workers and involuntary part-time workers, this impact analysis also looks at the three subgroups of VUP Group 3 together. Our analysis in the following section focuses specifically on the hypothetical households: our

188. Art. 202-203 Royal Decree of 3 July 1996 executing the Act of the obligatory medical insurance coordinated on 14 July 1994, 31.7.1996.
189. 2 Sophie Remouchamps, *Questions transversale en matière du sécurité sociale* 143-144 (Larcier 2017).
190. Book I, Part II, Eveline Anckaert, *Praktijkboek sociale zekerheid voor de onderneming en de sociale adviseur* 294 (Kluwer 2020).
191. The aim is to guarantee a minimum benefit as early as the first month of sickness in 2024, after the period of a guaranteed wage by the employer. This change in the legislation will be introduced gradually.
192. Royal Decree of 17 January 2021 amending, as regards the granting of a minimum daily amount during the first six months of primary incapacity, the Royal Decree of 3 July 1996 executing the Law of the obligatory medical insurance coordinated on 14 July 1994, 26.1.2021.
193. Act of 5 March 2002 on the non-discrimination principle to the benefit of part-time workers, 13.3.2002. *See also Collective Agreements per subject*, National Labour Council (23 April 2020, retrieved on 25 February 2022), http://www.cnt-nar.be/Cct-theme.htm#travail%20a%20temps%20partiel; Collective Agreement n° 35 of 27 February 1981 on certain provisions of labour law on the matter of part-time labour, 27.2.1981.

comments on the applicability of labour law and social security law are found in previous subsections.

Concerning social security law for fixed-term workers and the impact on the hypothetical four households, the analysis for VUP Group 1 applies here as well.

When looking at the household composition of VUP Group 3, we can make the following observations concerning the at-risk-of-poverty rate for the different hypothetical households.

Temporary and involuntary part-time workers are more likely to live in a household of more than two persons. Households with two or more than two persons are subject to lower rates of in-work poverty than single persons (single person: 23.1%, household with 2 persons: 27.8% and households with more than 2 persons: 9.8% in 2019). Temporary or involuntary part-time work does seem to create difficulties for persons to make ends meet. For families with two or more than two persons, this is less the case, and the high share of part-time work taken up by women as second-earners could explain this. Nevertheless, also for families with two or more than two persons, the risk-at-poverty rates are still significantly higher than for the working population, regardless of the household size (2.2% for families with 2 persons and 5.3% for families with more than 2 persons in 2019).

The number of people per household at work also has an important impact on reducing the risk at in-work poverty: 2.5% (2019) (in case more than one person works) compared to 26.2% (2019) (in case that only one person works). In the large majority of households, more than one person works (63.1%, 2019).

More than 54.3% of temporary workers and involuntary part-time workers live in a household with no children (under the age of 18 years): this high number can be explained by the fact that the group of temporary and involuntary part-time workers has a large group of younger workers (39.7% in 2019), who may still live with their parents or with a larger group of persons. Approximately 21.7% of temporary workers and involuntary part-time workers are above 50 years old: they might also have children who already are 18+ years old.

In-work poverty rates are higher for families with children, with an at-risk-of-poverty rate at the same level for households with one child or more. A possible explanation could be that family benefits do not seem to suffice to support workers with the higher costs they face in bringing up children. The temporary and involuntary part-time workers without children face a lower risk of in-work poverty (9.3% in 2019), but this rate nevertheless remains three times higher compared to the working population in general (3.2% in 2019).

If we apply the findings above to our hypothetical households, we see that in particular families where only one person works (single person, single parent, or a breadwinner with a partner) the risk of in-work poverty is higher. This is even more so for families with children.

§2.05 VUP GROUP 4: CASUAL AND PLATFORM WORKERS

[A] Composition of VUP Group 4

VUP Group 4 consists of both platform workers and casual workers. The latter can be divided into two subgroups: intermittent workers and on-call workers. Unfortunately, there is a lack of aggregated data on both casual work and, especially, platform work in Belgium.[194]

The few studies available show that, like in many other EU countries, the use of platform work has spread across Belgium.[195] No data, however, has been found on the risk of poverty of platform workers in Belgium or the features of those platform workers who experience a risk of poverty. Similarly, this lack of systemic information has resulted in a lack of insight on issues between the platform worker and the platform, like conflict resolution mechanisms or notifications on changes to the terms and conditions.[196]

Fiscal authorities have, however, provided data on how widespread platform work is in Belgium. More specifically, data on how many platform workers made use of state-approved digital platforms and the tax advantages related to them. In 2019, this was around 18,458 persons for a monthly average of €102, with foreign-born workers being an important group in specifically transportation and delivery services.[197] A large group of platform workers are paid by transaction and not per hours worked. This leads to unpredictable and unstable income formulas, which constitutes one of the main challenges for platform workers.[198] Note however that there are also non-approved digital platforms operating in Belgium, providing platform work without special tax advantages. They fall outside of the scope of the data provided.[199]

Intermittent work – a subset of casual work – falls under the Belgian regulations on fixed-term contracts. As such, the applicable VUP Group is Group 3, which was discussed earlier.

---

194. Harald Haubens, Karolien Lenaerts & Willem Waeyaert, *The platform economy and precarious work* 18 (European Parliament 2020).
195. Pwc, *Share Economy 2017: The New Business Model* 30-32 (PriceWaterhousCooper 2017).
196. European Centre of Expertise in the field of labour law, employment, and labour market policies, *Thematic Review 2021 on Platform work – Synthesis report* 19 (European Commission 2021); *see also* the research project conducted by prof. dr. Valeria Pulignano at KU Leuven: https://soc.kuleuven.be/ceso/wo/erlm/respectme and Claudia Mara & Valeria Pulignano, *Working for Nothing in the Platform Economy. Forms and Institutional Contexts of Unpaid Labour*, Solidar (2021, retrieved on 25 February 2022), https://www.solidar.org/en/publications/working-for-nothing-in-the-platform-economy-thematic-publication.
197. European Centre of Expertise in the field of labour law, employment, and labour market policies, *Thematic Review 2021 on Platform work – Synthesis report* 9 (European Commission 2021).
198. European Centre of Expertise in the field of labour law, employment, and labour market policies, *Thematic Review 2021 on Platform work – Synthesis report* 19 (European Commission 2021).
199. European Centre of Expertise in the field of labour law, employment, and labour market policies, *Thematic Review 2021 on Platform work – Synthesis report* 9, 17 (European Commission 2021).

The other form of casual work is on-call work, which manifests itself in Belgium through a system of flexi-jobs, discussed below in more detail. In Q4 of 2019, 10.614 employers were making use of flexi-job workers spread over 73,057 places of work.[200] Flexi-jobs are especially prevalent in the hotel and catering sector. In Q1 of 2019, 46% of all flexi-job workers were working in that sector. Of those workers, 49% were between the age of 25 and 39.[201]

Due to a lack of data, this contribution does not include an impact analysis for the four hypothetical households.[202]

[B] Casual Workers

As mentioned, casual work manifests in two forms. The first is intermittent work, which comes with its own subcategories. The second one is on-call work. Both fall under different regulations and appear in different ways in Belgian legislation

Two forms of work existing under Belgian law may be qualified as intermittent work, namely short-term contracts concluded to conduct a specific task[203] and contracts concerning seasonally occurring jobs. For both types of contract, similar rules apply as for fixed-term employment contracts.

For the purposes of this report, on-call work involves a contractual relationship in which the principal does not continuously provide work for the worker but rather has the option of calling the worker in as and when needed. Within the Belgian legal system, the structure that best fits that definition is arguably the flexi-job employment. Already reviewed by the Belgian Constitutional Court and found constitutional,[204] flexi-job contracts are fixed-term[205] employment contracts performed within a flexi-job framework agreement[206] that may be used by employers if:

- it concerns the hospitality, catering, retail, hairdressing/beauty care, or bakery/pastry sectors;[207]

---

200. Guidea, *Monitor Flexi-jobs 2019 Q4* 2 (2019).
201. Guidea, *Monitor Flexi-jobs 2019 Q1* 3 & 11-14 (2019).
202. However, this impact analysis was made for VUP Groups 1, 2, and 3.
203. Arts. 9-11 Act of 3 July 1978 on employment contracts, 22.8.1978; Federal Public Service – Employment, labour, and social dialogue, *Contrat de travail conclu pour une durée déterminée (CDD) et contrat de travail conclu pour un travail nettement défini* (retrieved on 14 February 2022) https://emploi.belgique.be/fr/themes/contrats-de-travail/contrats-de-travail-particuliers/contrat-de-travail-conclu-pour-une.
204. 107/2017, Constitutional Court (28 September 2017).
205. Art. 8 Act of 16 November 2015 on various provisions on social affairs, 26.11.2015. A contract concluded under the same conditions than a flexi-job contract between a temporary employment agency and a temporary worker is considered a flexi-job contract, *see Ibid.*, Art. 3.
206. *Ibid.*, Arts. 6-7.
207. *Ibid.*, Art. 2.

- the person already works as an employee for at least four-fifth of the working time of a full-time employee with one or more other employers in the third quarter preceding the flexi-job;[208]
- and the person to be employed is not employed by the same employer for more than four-fifth of the working time of a full-time employee under a status other than flexi-job.[209]

This means that flexi-jobs are only available to those workers that already benefit from social protection.

Flexi-job employment contracts are not limited to a certain number of hours or days, although the hours worked may not exceed the maximum weekly number of hours established by a sector (which are typically 38 hours, but that may amount up to 50 hours – including overtime – in sectors such as hospitality and catering).[210]

Employers are not obliged to inform flexi-job employees with a variable schedule in advance what their daily working hours are.[211] Because of this, flexi-job contracts have been likened to zero-hours contracts.[212]

Moreover, remuneration from flexi-jobs may be set at €11.12 per hour[213] (hence lower than the minimum wage),[214] and it is not subjected to normal social security contributions and to taxes.[215] The employer must pay a special social security contribution amounting to 25% of the remuneration paid concerning flexi-jobs contracts.[216] Employment resulting from a flexi-job contract is taken into account for the determination of potential social security entitlements.[217] In the same line of thought, work performed in the framework of a flexi-job contract is considered as work for the purposes of unemployment insurance.[218]

---

208. *Ibid.*, Art. 4, §1*ter*; If the person hired is receiving an old-age pension, the requirement of having performed at least four-fifth of the working time of a full-time employee with one or more other employers in the third quarter preceding the flexi-job does not have to be fulfilled, *Ibid.*, Art. 4, §3.
209. *Ibid.*
210. *Working time and rest periods*, Federal Public Service – Employment, labour and social dialogue (retrieved on 25 February 2022), https://emploi.belgique.be/fr/themes/international/detachement/conditions-de-travail-respecter-en-cas-de-detachement-en-1#toc_heading_1.
211. Art. 11 Act of 16 November 2015 on various provisions on social affairs, 26.11.2015.
212. Emile Vandervelde Institute, *Les flexi-jobs, une ineptie sociale et économique: Etat de la question* 6 (2016).
213. *Flexi-jobs*, Socialsecurity.be (retrieved on 25 February 2022), https://www.socialsecurity.be/site_fr/employer/infos/flexi-jobs.htm.
214. Emile Vandervelde Institute, *Les flexi-jobs, une ineptie sociale et économique: Etat de la question* 10 (2016).
215. Art. 38, §1, subpara. 1, 29° Royal Decree of 27 August 1993 for the execution of the Income Tax Code 1992, 19.11.2015 and Art.14-16 Act of 16 November 2015 on various provisions on social affairs, 26.11.2015.
216. Art. 16 Act of 16 November 2015 on various provisions on social affairs, 26.11.2015; Art. 38, §3*sexdecies* Act of 29 June 1981 concerning the general principles of social security for employees, 2.7.1981.
217. See for a discussion also: Selma Lisein, *Les Flexi-jobs Allez hop! Encore un peu plus d'insécurité et de surcharge pour les travailleurs!* 11 (L'atelier des droits sociaux 2019).
218. Art. 18 Act of 16 November 2015 on various provisions on social affairs, 26.11.2015. Marie-Lise Pottier, *Un répertoire des contrats de courte durée* 50 (Wolters Kluwer 2020).

[C] Platform Workers

[1] Notion

A platform worker is defined in this book as an individual who uses an app or a website to match himself/herself with customers, in order to perform specific tasks or to provide specific services on-demand in exchange for payment.[219] Platform workers may belong to two different subtypes, namely crowdworkers (who complete a series of tasks through online platforms for an indefinite number of organizations, business, and individuals through the Internet) and workers-on-demand via app (who perform traditional activities such as transport, cleaning, and running errands, but also clerical work channelled through an app).[220]

The definition of this book generally fits into the concept of platform work used within Belgium. In this regard, the discussion on platform workers in Belgium has primarily focused on the issue of platform workers' employment status, as this status is important for determining their social security and labour law rights. Legislation has been enacted in Belgium to regulate the platform economy, providing a broad definition of what constitutes a platform activity. In addition though, it also provides certain advantages to platforms, such as exempting marginal activity on registered platforms from taxes and social security contributions.[221]

[2] Legal Framework

[a] Platform Workers: Employees or Self-Employed Persons?

Overall, persons performing platform work in Belgium generally do so outside an employment relationship. Some legal cases, however, are challenging that classification and looking to obtain employee status for certain platform workers. In this regard, in October 2020, the Administrative Commission for the Regulation of the Labour Relations agreed with an Uber driver when they claimed to be an employee rather than self-employed person.[222] In its decision, the Administrative Commission noted that there were sufficient indicators establishing the presumption of the existence of an employment relationship.[223] Furthermore, the Administrative Commission stated that

219. Eurofound, *New forms of Employment* (2015).
220. For the distinction between crowdwork and work-on-demand via app *see* Valerio De Stefano, *The rise of the 'just- in-time workforce': on-demand work, crowdwork, and labor protection in the 'gig-economy'*, 71 Conditions of Work and Employment Series, 1-51 (2016).
221. Programme Act of 1 July 2016, 4.7.2016.
222. *Demande de qualification de la relation de travail - Dossier n° 187 – FR – 20200707*, Administrative Commission for the regulation of the labour relations of the Federal public service – Social security (26 October 2020), https://www.commissiearbeidsrelaties.belgium.be/docs/dossier-187-nacebel-fr.pdf.
223. *Ibid.*, 5-7; European Centre of Expertise in the field of labour law, employment, and labour market policies, *Thematic Review 2021 on Platform work – Synthesis report* 32 (European Commission 2021); For more on such criteria, *see* Art. 337/2, §1*ter* Programme Act of 27 December 2006, 28.12.2006.

out of four criteria necessary to reverse such a presumption, three were not fulfilled.[224] Uber, nevertheless, has appealed the decision in front of the Brussels Labour Court.[225] The court has overruled the decision of the Administrative Commission on 8 December 2021; this decision is currently subject of an appeal procedure before the Brussels Labour Court of Appeal.[226]

On 15 February 2022, the Belgian federal government reached an agreement on a general labour reform. As a part of the so-called labour deal, eight criteria were agreed upon to determine whether platform workers are self-employed persons or employees. Criteria that indicate that the platform worker is an employee are the following: if the platform puts an income ceiling in place and if the platform prescribes certain behaviour towards the customer. In addition, several indicators for whether or not the platform workers are self-employed will also be instituted, like having the freedom to accept or refuse tasks at their own discretion. They also need to be able to determine how much they charge for the service provided, as well as being able to refuse service due to certain rates being offered to them. Self-employed platform workers would also need to be able to choose for themselves when they will not be working, be able to build up their own customer relations outside of the platform, and work for third parties. If five out of eight criteria indicate that the platform worker is in fact an employee, there will be a refutable presumption of them being so. In addition, it was agreed in the labour deal that all platform workers will receive protection in case of a labour accident, irrespective of their employment status.[227] For self-employed platform workers, this would mean that they receive additional protection as currently self-employed persons are not insured against labour accidents. Note that the labour deal has yet to be accepted by the social partners and parliament.

[b] Employment and Social Security Rights

In many occasions, platform workers' labour and social security rights depend on their employment status. If a person performs work as an employee for an online platform, then they would be entitled to the same labour and social security rights as members of VUP Groups 1 or 3. Consequently, platform workers experience several measures of protection (e.g., provisions ensuring equality between fixed-term workers, temporary

224. *Demande de qualification de la relation de travail - Dossier n° 187 – FR – 20200707*, Administrative Commission for the regulation of the labour relations of the Federal public service – Social security (26 October 2020), https://www.commissiearbeidsrelaties.belgium.be/docs/dossier-187-nacebel-fr.pdf 7-10.
225. Le Soir, *Uber devant le tribunal du travail de Bruxelles concernant le statut d'un travailleur* (17 February 2021, retrieved on 14 February 2022), https://www.lesoir.be/355764/article/2021-02-17/uber-devant-le-tribunal-du-travail-de-bruxelles-concernant-le-statut-dun.
226. 2021/014148, Labour Court Brussels French-speaking 25th chamber (8 December 2021).
227. Bruzz, *Labour deal: eight criteria to determine if meal courier is bogus self-employed*, 15 February 2022, https://www.bruzz.be/economie/arbeidsdeal-acht-criteria-om-te-bepalen-maaltijdkoerier-schijnzelfstandige-2022-02-15; Stefan Grommen, Lonne van Erp & Johny Vansevenant, *Government reaches labour deal: work week of 4 days and more clarity for food delivery*, vrtNWS (15 February 2022), https://www.vrt.be/vrtnws/nl/2022/02/14/arbeidsdeal/.

agency workers or part-time workers, and standard workers, as well as those limiting the use of temporary (agency) work), but also certain risk factors (e.g., the fact that many labour rights, such as minimum wage or temporary unemployment, depend in part on the economic sector in which work is performed).[228] If, in turn, a person performs platform work as a natural person outside of an employment relationship, their social security rights and obligations depend in a significant part on the level of earnings produced by their activity as a platform worker.

The Act of 1 July 2016 provided a special treatment of income resulting from certain services provided via approved electronic platforms as it concerns the calculation of social security contributions.[229] As a result, natural persons are exempted from social security contributions if they performed services for purposes other than their usual economic activity and did so within the framework of agreements concluded via an approved electronic platform. In addition, the income received through an approved electronic platform may not exceed a certain annual amount (€6.390 in 2022);[230] in that case the income earned is not taken into account for social security purposes and are also subjected to a certain extent to taxes.

As of May 2022, there are 117 electronic platforms registered in the Finance Ministry's list of approved platforms.[231] The list includes platforms such as Deliveroo, Listminut (rebranded as Ring Twice), and Helpper. All platform registered deal with providing services on-demand via an app, and none of them relate to crowdwork.

The regulation installed by the Act of 2016 was expanded on by the Act of 18 July 2018,[232] which the Constitutional Court, in its decision of 23 April 2020, deemed the Act of 18 July 2018 unconstitutional. Thus, its application concerning services rendered after 31 December 2020 was annulled.[233] As a result, from 2021 on, activities performed through approved electronic platforms were once again (fully) regulated by the Act of 1 July 2016.

Other observable challenges between platform work and social security include: placing the social and insurance risks on the shoulders of the platform worker (who might not be able to assume them); platform workers being potentially employed by several platforms simultaneously (with the additional complexity that might involve); potential increase in the use of flexi-jobs or employment contracts consisting of a very

228. *See* earlier the discussion of VUP Group 1 (low- or unskilled standard workers) and VUP Group 3 (fixed-term workers, agency workers, involuntary part-time workers).
229. Programme Act of 1 July 2016, 4.7.2016.
230. *Ibid.*, Art. 22.
231. *Économie collaborative – liste des plateformes agréées*, Federal Public Service – Finances (retrieved on 14 February 2021), https://finances.belgium.be/sites/default/files/downloads/127-economie-collaborative-liste-plateformes-agreees-20210316.pdf.
232. Sarah Ghislain & Myriam Verwilghen, *Le statut social des travailleurs de l'économie de plateforme: état des lieux dans un contexte mouvant (Première partie)*, vol. 28 n° 1382 Journal des tribunaux du travail (2020).
233. 53/2020, Constitutional Court (23 April 2020). For more information on the Act of 18 July 2018 and the arguments presented in front of the court, see Part II, 3, II Yves Jorens, *Social Law 4.0: New Approaches for Ensuring and Financing Social Security in the Digital Age* 13-38 (Nomos 2020).

small number of hours; and risk of lesser training opportunities available to platform workers.[234]

[c] Industrial Relations and Collective Bargaining

In Belgium collective bargaining and the conclusion of collective agreements in the private sector are governed primarily by the Act of 5 December 1968,[235] in which the personal scope is restricted to employees and to persons who, otherwise than under a contract of employment, provide work under the authority of another person.[236] This essentially means that platform workers outside of an employment relationship or an assimilated situation are generally not entitled to exercise the right of collectively organizing through trade unions. The social partners, however, mentioned in the interprofessional agreement for the period 2017-2018 their intention to address the challenges presented by platform work and digitalization.[237] Those challenges were also analyzed by the social partners in both the National Labour Council and the Central Economic Council.[238]

Several employers' organizations (such as UNIZO, and SNI) have traditionally represented solo self-employed persons, a group in which platform workers outside of an employment relationship may fit. Moreover, some platform workers have created associations to represent them (such as the *Collectif des coursier-e-s*) and the christian trade union CSC/ACV has established a sub-division (United Freelancers) specifically focusing on solo self-employed persons.[239] Trade unions have also provided support to platform workers in the case before the Administrative Commission for the Regulation of the Labour Relations and the Brussels Labour Court concerning Uber, and they 'actively aim to identify, inform, organise and represent platform workers, on an individual and group basis'.[240]

Furthermore, during the period in which Deliveroo contracted some of its riders as employees of the cooperative SMart, the socialist trade union (FGTB/ABVV) and

234. Part III, Chapter 3 Yves Stevens, *The Platform Economy* 268 (Intersentia 2019).
235. Act of 5 December 1968 on the collective labour agreements and the sectoral committees, 15.1.1969.
236. *Ibid.*, Art. 2.
237. Interprofessional Agreement for 2017-2018 of 11 January 2017, 11.1.2017, https://www.vbo-feb.be/globalassets/actiedomeinen/sociaal-overleg/interprofessioneel-overleg/ademruimte-om-te-ondernemen-en-te-consumeren/ipa-2017-2018.pdf 6-7.
238. Sem Vandekerckhove & Karolien Lenaerts, *Working conditions and social protection of platform workers in Belgium: Policy measures and stakeholder initiatives* 4 (European Commission 2020).
239. Moreover, the trade union ABVV-FGTB has provided support to platform workers at the early stages of their organization, particularly through the collective GandGent, *see* Anne Dufresne & Cédric Leterme, *Travailleurs de platforme: La lutte pour les droits dans l'économie numérique* 47 (Gresea 2021); European Centre of Expertise in the field of labour law, employment, and labour market policies, *Thematic Review 2021 on Platform work – Synthesis report* 20 (European Commission 2021).
240. Sem Vandekerckhove & Karolien Lenaerts, *Working conditions and social protection of platform workers in Belgium: Policy measures and stakeholder initiatives* 5 (European Commission 2020).

CSC/ACV were reportedly close to the conclusion of a collective agreement with SMart specifically targeting the riders' needs when Deliveroo ceased its partnership with the cooperation.[241]

Even when platform workers were entitled to the right of collectively organizing (for example, because they perform platform work through an employment relationship), they would still be subjected to the same challenges as the members of VUP Groups 1 and/or 3 when doing so. Among these challenges may be highlighted the strict requirements asked from social partners to be considered representative enough for negotiating collective agreements, which has resulted in only three trade unions fulfilling such requirements (i.e., FGTB/ABVV, CSC/ACV, and the liberal trade union (CGSLB/ACLVB)). Hence, while platform workers may create their own representative organizations outside of those three trade unions, the competences of such organizations are very limited (and do not include the negotiation of collective labour agreements).[242]

Another challenge experienced by platform workers is that, while the Belgian collective bargaining system assumes a certain homogeneity within one specific sector or sub-sector, platform work's divergent features compared to other forms of work may result on platform workers' needs not being necessarily the same as other workers within the same sector or sub-sector (and, hence, they are not necessarily addressed within the collective negotiation mechanisms).

Concerning the right to strike, it is questionable whether a traditional interpretation of the right to strike under Belgian law would cover in its scope self-employed platform workers, particularly taking into account the scope of the Act of 5 December 1968.[243] Platform workers in Belgium have, however, performed in occasion protests, strikes, and other actions.[244]

§2.06 CONCLUSIONS

Although Belgium remained one of the EU countries with the lowest in-work poverty rates, the percentage of persons at risk of in-work poverty has increased over the years. Significant differences also exist between the different regions in Belgium. Working offers a good protection against poverty in Belgium: for unemployed persons or people that are inactive for other reasons, the poverty risk is significantly higher. This largely stems from the prevalent insider-outsider characteristics of the Belgian labour market

241. *Annexe Deliveroo*, Smart (2018), https://smartbe.be/wp-content/uploads/2014/01/251017-Deliveroo.pdf, referenced in Jan Drahokoupil & Agnieszka Piasna, *Work in the platform economy: Deliveroo riders in Belgium and the SMart arrangement*, 1 ETUI 1, 10 (2019).
242. Partie IV, 1 Filip Dorssemont & Auriane Lamine, *Quel droit social pour les travailleurs de plateformes?* 333 (Anthemis 2020).
243. *Ibid.*, 311.
244. Sem Vandekerckhove & Karolien Lenaerts, *Working conditions and social protection of platform workers in Belgium: Policy measures and stakeholder initiatives* 5 (European Commission 2020). It should be noted that, by doing so, they might risk being subjected to contractual sanctions, *see* Partie IV, 1 Filip Dorssemont & Auriane Lamine, *Quel droit social pour les travailleurs de plateformes?* 334 (Anthemis 2020).

with a rather low working intensity. In Belgium persons who work have both a relatively stable job and relatively good conditions of employment. On the other hand, there is a large group of persons with a low level of education facing difficulties in finding their way to the labour market.

Looking at the protection provided for the different VUP groups, we see that the standard employment relationship (i.e., full-time employment on the basis of an agreement for indefinite duration) still receives the largest protection in both labour law and social security law. VUP Group 1 can serve as an example of this standard employment relationship. Nevertheless, Belgian labour law has several restrictions in place, limiting the use of temporary work (VUP Group 3) as well as intermittent and on-call work (VUP Group 4). The federal government also plans to take additional protective measures for platform workers. These measures have been criticized in the past for making the Belgian labour market too rigid. Several additional protection mechanisms are also provided in social security law. An example is the measures taken in calculating the reference period; but also the minimum benefits provided in income-replacement schemes. Providing such measures raises the question on the relationship with the received benefits and the contributions paid and the financial sustainability of the Belgian social security scheme. Similarly, one may wonder to what extent the Belgian social security system is still coherent nowadays, taking into account its traditional design as a Bismarckian social security system with a strong focus on social security contributions. The same can be said for the different statuses in place for which no or only limited social contributions and taxes are due (flexi-jobs and platform work on recognized platforms). It is unclear to what extent these measures actually help to activate persons and to provide them an adequate social protection.

Overall, one can conclude that the Belgian legislation has several protection mechanisms in place for the different VUP Group 1, 3, and 4 (to a certain extent). Solo self-employed persons also receive protection under the scheme of self-employed persons; labour law, however, does not apply and the protection provided under social security law is not as elaborate as for employees.

Nevertheless, we do see that certain groups do not find access to the labour market, resulting in a high poverty risk. Certain group of workers do have access to the labour market, but they also face a high risk of poverty. This is in particular the case for the 3 VUP Groups (VUP Group 1, 2, and 3) for which we had data. Rethinking the Belgian labour law and social security law has been high on the agenda for years now, but still remains rather difficult to do in practice. This, nevertheless, seems necessary if one wants to not only activate people who have difficulties finding their way to the labour market but also provide adequate social protection in such a way as not to overburden the public finances.

CHAPTER 3

In-Work Poverty in Germany

Christina Hiessl

Germany provides the example of a country with an inclusive labour market and high average wage levels, but also important inequalities among the working population. Rapidly falling collective bargaining coverage and a jobseekers' regime putting substantial pressure on the unemployed to accept every available job have resulted in a remarkably large low-wage sector. At present, though, Germany stands out by many ongoing and planned reforms with the potential of improving workers' protection against poverty.

§3.01 INTRODUCTION

Throughout the twenty-first century, Germany has stood out for its strong and stable economic growth and favourable labour market developments. It is now among the top performers in Europe in relation to employment and unemployment rates (most notably for the young), and this has not changed in the context of the pandemic crisis. The rise in labour market participation has also benefitted groups with traditionally large gaps in employment rates – older and disabled workers, women (despite the remaining large gender gap), and migrants, particularly regarding the challenging labour market integration of large numbers of refugees.[1]

At the same time, this development has gone hand in hand with rising inequality and most notably an expansion of the low-wage sector.[2] Although German average

1. Bundesregierung, Bundesregierung, Sechster Armuts- und Reichtumsbericht – Lebenslagen in Deutschland. Unterrichtung durch die Bundesregierung, Drucksache 19/29815 (2021) 176 et seqq.
2. Cf. Christina Hiessl, Armut trotz Arbeit im Fokus der EU-Politik: Das "Working, Yet Poor"-Projekt im Kontext, in Sozialer Fortschritt, Armut trotz Arbeit (Bernd Waas & Christina Hiessl ed. 2022, forthcoming).

wages are the fifth highest in the European Union (EU), the share of the low-wage sector in total employment is the sixth largest.[3] This is part of an overall constant rise in inequality ever since the German reunification, which in recent years has been more affected by the rising share of the poorest than that of the richest.[4] In terms of poverty, the rising standard of living has sent material deprivation rates on a long-term downwards trend, while rising inequality has led to almost constant increases of relative poverty levels. In 2019, the poverty rate stood at almost 16% of the general population, its highest value since measurements began in 2005,[5] and everything points towards a spike as a result of the pandemic crisis.[6] In European comparison, notably the poverty rate for the unemployed towers above that of all other Member States,[7] and more recently old-age poverty has been on the rise and is projected to increase more rapidly in future.[8]

In this context, work stands out as the one key way to escape poverty. The in-work poverty rate is just half the general poverty rate, and unlike for the latter there has been a trend reversal after the introduction of a statutory minimum wage in 2015, since when in-work poverty no longer increased but even declined slightly. This does not apply to the self-employed, whose already very high rates continued to increase throughout all measurements.

[A] Main Features of Labour Law, Social Security, and the Role of Collective Bargaining

German labour and social security law is largely restricted to employees. The self-employed are not generally covered by any of the branches of social insurance and thus only entitled to tax-financed benefits that are either universal (such as child allowance) or means-tested (social assistance). There is, however, a complex system of partial inclusions of various groups, defined by criteria that generally relate to their occupation and/or their similarity with employees, in different parts of social security and/or collective and in some cases even individual labour law. *See infra* at §3.03[B].

Germany has a pronounced dual-channel system of worker representation, in which collective bargaining between trade unions and employers' associations (or, more rarely but increasingly, individual employers) is complemented by bargaining processes at company level in which the workers' side is represented by a works

3. *See* Eurostat data at https://ec.europa.eu/eurostat/databrowser/view/ILC_DI05__custom_2192981/default/bar?lang=en and https://ec.europa.eu/eurostat/databrowser/view/earn_ses_pub1n/default/bar?lang=en.
4. Olaf Groh-Samberg et al., Dokumentation zur Generierung Multidimensionaler Lagen auf Basis des Sozio-Oekonomischen Panel (2021) 99.
5. Jonas Pieper et al., Gegen Armut hilft Geld. Der Paritätische Armutsbericht 2020, Deutscher Paritätischer Wohlfahrtsverband Gesamtverband e. V. (2020) 8, 15.
6. Cf. Claudia Czernohorsky-Grüneberg, Herausforderungen bei der Integration in den Arbeitsmarkt – Beitrag des Jobcenters Frankfurt am Main, in Sozialer Fortschritt, Armut trotz Arbeit (Bernd Waas & Christina Hiessl ed. 2022, forthcoming).
7. Surpassing 70% in several years including 2019: *see* data at https://ec.europa.eu/eurostat/databrowser/view/ILC_LI04__custom_2193011/default/bar?lang=en.
8. Pieper et al., *supra* n. 5 at 27.

council. Due to strong co-determination rights, works council agreements emerge as a third relevant source of regulation next to statutory law and collective bargaining agreements in the narrow sense. Since the mid-1990, Germany has experienced a continuous and substantial decline in collective bargaining coverage, which has extended to less than half of dependent workers since the early 2010s.[9] This has happened in the context of a substantial rise in labour market participation and a historic expansion of the low-wage sector. Also coverage by works council agreements is receding, though at a slower pace.[10] Nonetheless, the crucial importance of industrial relations has been highlighted again during the pandemic crisis, when the smooth introduction of frameworks for health and safety and short-time work by the social partners at all levels was an invaluable asset.

[B] Policies and Measures That Directly Impact on In-Work Poverty

The introduction of a general statutory minimum wage in 2015 has halted the rapid expansion of both the low-wage sector and in-work poverty levels, and both have even slightly declined since. This is despite its low level, which was set at EUR 8.50 and made subject to further determination by a bipartite committee, which is to develop it in line with collective bargaining trends. So far, it has remained clearly lower than 50% of the median wage. While its introduction immediately affected just the 11% of the workforce with the lowest wages, the fact that it apparently influenced the size of the low-wage sector as such indicates that also wages closer to the low-wage threshold of two-thirds of the median benefitted, notably via collective bargaining.[11] In practice, violations (in particular by longer actual than contractual working hours) are still estimated to be sizable.[12] Heeding one of its key electoral promises, the recently elected governing coalition has announced to legislate for an extraordinary increase of the statutory minimum wage to EUR 12 per hour in late 2022[13] – which would come close to 60% of the median wage and thus make Germany one of the few countries which (almost) fulfil this core criterion of the 'Kaitz index'.[14]

---

9. Currently, the coverage rate amounts to 43%: Statistisches Bundesamt, Tarifbindung nach Betrieben und Wirtschaftszweigen (2021), https://www.destatis.de/DE/Themen/Arbeit/Verdienste/Tarifverdienste-Tarifbindung/Tabellen/tarifverbindung-betriebe.html.
10. Peter Ellguth, Ost- und Westdeutschland nähern sich bei der Reichweite der betrieblichen Mitbestimmung an, in IAB-Forum, 13/05/2020 (2020).
11. Bundesregierung, *supra* n. 1 at 183.
12. Mindestlohnkommission, Dritter Bericht zu den Auswirkungen des gesetzlichen Mindestlohns. Bericht an die Bundesregierung nach 9 Abs. 4 Mindestlohngesetz (2020); Alexandra Fedorets et al., Lohnungleichheit in Deutschland sinkt, 92 DIW Wochenbericht No. 7/2020 (2020) 97.
13. Bundesregierung, Mehr Fortschritt wagen. Koalitionsvertrag zwischen SPD, Bündnis 90/Die Grünen und FDP (2021), https://www.bundesregierung.de/breg-de/service/gesetzesvorhaben/koalitionsvertrag-2021-1990800, 66; Silvia Helbig, Wirksame Armutsbekämpfung vor allem durch höheren Mindestlohn, in Sozialer Fortschritt, Armut trotz Arbeit (Bernd Waas & Christina Hiessl ed. 2022, forthcoming).
14. *See* European Commission (2020), Impact assessment accompanying the Proposal for a Directive of the European Parliament and of the Council on adequate minimum wages in the European Union, Commission Staff Working Document, SWD/2020/245 final. Available at https://eur-lex.europa.eu/legal-content/EN/TXT/?uri=CELEX%3A52020SC0245, 4 et seqq.

In addition to the general minimum, wage standards based on collective agreements have been made mandatory for a small number of sectors, but the conditions to make collective agreements generally binding are restrictive, and various proposals for a general easing have so far not been successful.

A large-scale overhaul of the social security system for jobseekers in the early 2000s (*see infra* at §3.02[B] for the so-called Hartz reforms) brought a shift to means-tested benefits. Today, only about a third of the unemployed (about 811,000) are entitled to insurance-based, wage-related benefits. Even where insurance periods and other requirements are fulfilled, entitlements are short and can exceed one year only in case of beneficiaries more than 50 years of age with a contributing period of at least the last 30 months. By contrast, 5.307 million individuals are currently receiving the subsidiary means-tested benefit (so-called ALG II benefit) due to households with at least one member capable of working.[15] This benefit provides for the constitutionally guaranteed subsistence level (which avoids material deprivation but is far below the relative poverty line).[16] The strict means test requires the realisation of assets and the deduction of virtually any income, including almost all labour market income above EUR 100. Beneficiaries are required to accept virtually any job they are capable of performing, subject to sanctions. In 2019, the Constitutional Court declared parts of the sanctioning regime invalid and ordered a suspension of all sanction beyond 30% of the benefit, but the law (which envisages benefit withdrawal rates of 60% and even 100%), has not been reformed yet. Importantly, the coalition agreement[17] announces a major overhaul of the regime within the present legislative period.

The fast descent into (relative) poverty in this framework is considered not only the main reason for the aforementioned very high poverty rate of the unemployed, but also an important factor fuelling the expansion of the low-wage sector, as it keeps reservation wages low and forces beneficiaries to accept also work that does not match their qualification level. Non-take-up of means-tested benefits, which is estimated to be around 48.4-63% and particularly high for the in-work poor, is considered related, *i.a.*, to the system's stigmatising effects and the need to apply separately for various components.[18]

The German vocational training system is well known for achieving both a skilled workforce and one of the lowest youth unemployment rates in the EU.[19]

---

15. Among the 3.611 million beneficiaries capable of working, over 1.5 million are unemployed, close to 900,000 are in-work poor. Bundesagentur für Arbeit, Grundsicherung für Arbeitsuchende (SGB II) – Die aktuellen Entwicklungen in Kürze – Januar 2022 (2022), https://statistik.arbeitsagentur.de/DE/Navigation/Statistiken/Fachstatistiken/Grundsicherung-fuer-Arbeitsuchende-SGBII/Aktuelle-Eckwerte-Nav.html.
16. Ulrich Walwei, Aufstocker: Die Kerngruppe der Erwerbsarmut, in Sozialer Fortschritt, Armut trotz Arbeit (Bernd Waas & Christina Hiessl ed. 2022, forthcoming).
17. Bundesregierung, *supra* n. 13 at 75 et seq.
18. Stefan Sell, Die 'Aufstocker' im Hartz IV-System: 10 Milliarden Euro im Jahr 2018 für die „Subventionierung von Lohndumping"? Eine Spurensuche in den offiziellen Daten, in Aktuelle Sozialpolitik (2019), https://aktuelle-sozialpolitik.de/2019/11/14/erwerbstatige-aufstocker-im-hartz4-system; Hermann Buslei et al. Starke Nichtinanspruchnahme von Grundsicherung deutet auf hohe verdeckte Altersarmut, DIW Wochenbericht 49/2019 (2019) 909.
19. *See* Eurostat data at https://ec.europa.eu/eurostat/databrowser/view/tespm080/default/bar?lang=en.

Apprenticeship-based training offered by enterprises ensures that applicants are steered into professions for which there is an actual demand in the market. While this system has been under serious strain due to the COVID-19-related restrictions, training processes could be largely upheld in the great majority of cases, often by innovations based on collective bargaining. The more structural challenges concern the declining number of applicants, fuelled both by demographic changes and by preferences for higher school-based education. In the most recent past, this tendency has no longer been counter-balanced by the influx of refugees and asylum seekers into the vocational training system.[20] Further training beyond the highly institutionalised vocational training system is more fragmented and subject to companies' individual needs, and frequently leaves out those groups most in need of training for their individual employability. This has given rise to calls for more standardisation, enhanced options of subsidising vulnerable groups, and a better involvement of works councils.[21]

The short-time work system, which had been important to the comparatively mild impacts of the financial crisis on the German labour market and the economy in a wider sense, has proved its merits once more during the COVID-19 crisis. Its use was swiftly expanded and operationalised by the social partners, leading to a historic peak of more than seven million short-time workers (about a fifth of the workforce) in May 2020.[22] As in earlier crises, conditions for the receipt of short-time work allowance were eased and benefit levels increased, preventing both dismissals and significant income losses. Debates about possible amendments include most notably calls for higher replacement rates for low-wage earners instead of the current flat-rate system.[23]

[C] Policies and Measures Indirectly Influencing In-Work Poverty

Among the policies of indirect influence on in-work poverty, the probably most debated issues at present concern child benefits and the pension system.

As for the former, a universal age-dependent child allowance is granted irrespective of income, but eventually more beneficial for high-income families due to effects of tax progression. In addition, (near-)poor households whose income would meet the subsistence level for the parents are granted a 'child supplement' to avoid having to

20. Tobias Maier, Vorausschätzung der Ausbildungsplatznachfrage und des Ausbildungsplatzangebots für 2020, in Datenreport zum Berufsbildungsbericht 2020. Informationen und Analysen zur Entwicklung der beruflichen Bildung (Bundesinstitut für Berufsbildung ed. 2020) 62.
21. Frauke Bilger & Alexandra Strauß, Weiterbildungsverhalten in Deutschland 2018. Ergebnisse des Adult Education Survey – AES-Trendbericht: Bundesministerium für Bildung und Forschung (BMBF 2019); BMAS, Weißbuch Arbeiten 4.0 (2017), https://www.bmas.de/SharedDocs/Downloads/DE/Publikationen/a883-weissbuch.pdf?__blob=publicationFile&v=1, 108 et seqq.
22. Thomas Kruppe & Christopher Osiander, Kurzarbeit in der Corona-Krise: Wer ist wie stark betroffen? In IAB-Forum, 30 June 2020, https://www.iab-forum.de/kurzarbeit-in-der-corona-krise-wer-ist-wie-stark-betroffen.
23. Enzo Weber, Jobs retten oder Stillstand finanzieren? Nur mit Qualifizierung dürfte sich Kurzarbeit für den Fiskus auf Dauer auszahlen. IAB (2020), https://www.iab-forum.de/jobs-retten-oder-stillstand-finanzieren-nur-mit-qualifizierung-duerfte-sich-kurzarbeit-fuer-den-fiskus-auf-dauer-auszahlen, 5 et seqq.

apply for means-tested benefits due to child-related expenses. Its amount is gradually reduced to zero for higher-income families. Single parents can receive a maintenance advance if the child's other parent fails to pay maintenance at the legal minimum level. On the one hand, this system has the potential to lift (near-)poor families above the poverty line. On the other, it disadvantages the poorest – as the maintenance grant for single parents (who have the highest poverty rates of all groups) is reduced by the full amount of the child allowance, and both benefits are deducted in full in case of reliance on means-tested benefits such as ALG II. Also, non-take up for these benefits is considered to be even higher than for ALG II.[24] Responding to various calls for a reform that streamlines benefits and targets the poor, the recently elected government has announced to introduce a new regime of basic child security.[25]

Dwindling pension levels in turn are the most important factor of deferred or hidden in-work poverty, as many low-income households would basically need to set aside a sizable share of their net income for supplementary old-age savings to avoid poverty over the life cycle. German first-pillar pension replacement rates have fallen significantly over recent decades, to a level that is well below the Organisation for Economic and Co-operation Development (OECD) average. Without additional savings, a full-time worker earning the minimum wage and retiring in 2030 after 45 years of work will be just above the threshold for receiving means-tested benefits, i.e., clearly below the poverty line. The (voluntary) funded second- and third-pillar pension schemes have proven to be much less affordable than expected, mainly due to capital market developments.[26] This problem has recently been partly addressed by the introduction of a basic pension, which supplements low pension entitlements based on an insurance period of 33 years or more,[27] and more far-going reforms are envisaged by the new administration's coalition agreement.[28]

§3.02 VULNERABLE AND UNDER-REPRESENTED PERSON (VUP) GROUP 1: LOW- OR UNSKILLED STANDARD EMPLOYMENT

[A] Composition of VUP Group 1

While empirical results on low-skilled work on the German labour market diverge depending on the definitions and databases used, all studies indicate that its importance has declined in the recent past, particularly for the lowest-skilled activities. One

24. Bündnis 90/Die Grünen, Antrag: Faire Chancen für jedes Kind – Kindergrundsicherung einführen, Deutscher Bundestag Drucksache 19/14326, 19. Wahlperiode (2019).
25. Bundesregierung, *supra* n. 13 at 100.
26. Ute Klammer, Rentenpolitik zwischen Rollenbildern und Respekt: Verletzen Grundrente & Co. die Grundprinzipien der Gesetzlichen Rentenversicherung – oder helfen sie vielmehr, ihr Sicherungsversprechen einzulösen?, in Neustart in der Rentenpolitik. Analysen und Perspektiven (Blank/Hofmann/Buntenbach ed. 2020) 49.
27. Cf. the Basic Pension Law and Bundesregierung, Lebensleistung verdient Anerkennung. Fragen und Antworten zur Grundrente (2020), https://www.bundesregierung.de/breg-de/aktuelles/kabinett-grundrente-1722964.
28. Bundesregierung, *supra* n. 13 at 73 et seq.

of the most noteworthy unanimous findings of different studies relates to the substantial role of overqualification, which is found to concern around 70% of those performing low-skilled work.[29] Although somewhat less pronounced than in other EU countries, statistics evidence a strong polarisation in the sense that workers who are already in higher-skilled occupations are much more likely to benefit from training than those in low-skilled work.[30]

[B] Relevant Legal Framework

In Germany, the position of groups with a weak position in the labour market was decisively affected by the 'Hartz Reforms' of the early 2000s. Whereas a major part of those reforms focused on the activation of the unemployed as described further in this subsection, they also enhanced employer's flexibility in relying on temporary agency work (*see infra* at §3.04[B][1] for the changes introduced by 'Hartz I'), marginal work and solo self-employment (*see infra* at §3.03[B] for the consequences of 'Hartz II'). Naturally, the competitive pressure from such 'flexible' types of work has particularly affected low-skilled workers, who are generally more easily replaced than skilled employees.

Regarding wages, dwindling affiliation levels in both trade unions and employers' associations have left an ever-declining share of the workforce covered by collective agreements.[31] In a controversial move to halt the fall in membership levels, employers' organisations have installed a model which allows affiliates to opt out of coverage by the collective agreements they negotiate – which further fuelled the oft-cited 'erosion of collective bargaining coverage'.[32] The downward trend in coverage by collective agreements has been ongoing for decades and affects all sectors of the private economy, albeit with sizeable differences among the individual sectors. By 2018, the share of workers covered by a collective bargaining agreement had decreased to 43% (even just 39% if company-level agreements are excluded). That share ranged from 100% in the public service to just 16% in agriculture, forestry, and fishing.[33]

The general expansion of the low-wage sector (comprising, according to OECD standards, those earning less than two-thirds of the median wage) over recent decades to 21.7% of all dependent employees in 2018 naturally affected particularly low- or unskilled workers.[34] The fact that collective agreements were increasingly either not

29. Anja Hall & Ugur Sevindik, Einfacharbeit in Deutschland – wer arbeitet was und unter welchen Bedingungen? Ergebnisse aus der BIBB/BAuA-Erwerbstätigenbefragung 2018 (2020) 19 et seq.
30. *See* Eurostat data at https://circabc.europa.eu/ui/group/d14c857a-601d-438a-b878-4b4cebd0e10f/library/c5a8b987-1e37-44d7-a20e-2c50d6101d27/details.
31. Irene Dingeldey, Wechselwirkungen zwischen Mindestlohn und Tariflohn, in Arbeit 28/1 (2019).
32. Cf. e.g., Reinhard Bispinck & Thorsten Schulten, Das Tarifsystem stabilisieren – wie soll das gehen?, in Mitbestimmung 7-8 (2011) 28.
33. Statistisches Bundesamt, Tarifbindung nach Betrieben und Wirtschaftszweigen (2021), https://www.destatis.de/DE/Themen/Arbeit/Verdienste/Tarifverdienste-Tarifbindung/Tabellen/tarifverbindung-betriebe.html.
34. Thorsten Kalina & Claudia Weinkopf, Niedriglohnbeschäftigung 2018. Erstmals Rückgang, aber nicht für gering Qualifizierte und Minijobber*innen. IAQ-Report, 5 (2020).

covering those workers or setting wage rates far below the low-wage threshold was expressly referred to by the Federal Government in the context of the introduction of the statutory minimum wage.[35] As from the mid-2010s, legislative amendments have sought to counteract or cushion the consequences of this erosion on wages, working conditions, and workers' voice. Key reforms include the introduction of a general minimum wage (cf. the 2015 Minimum Wage Law, MiLoG), sectoral wages (*see* the Posting of Workers Act, AEntG), and a minimum apprenticeship allowance (cf. the Vocational Training Act, BBiG), the easing of conditions for declaring collective agreements universally binding, and the 2021 Works Council Modernisation Act.

Active labour market policies (ALMPs) have been at all the very heart of the aforementioned Hartz reforms. Under the slogan of 'promoting and demanding' (*Fördern und Fordern*), measures of support for the un- and underemployed were combined with strong elements to prevent the social safety net from becoming a 'hammock' for beneficiaries not willing to work. In a paradigm shift, recipients were no longer assumed to be capable and intrinsically motivated to manage their job search and use offers of job matching, counselling, and training services if needed. Instead, such services were henceforth connected to the beneficiaries' duty to participate in them. Former 'limits of reasonableness' were abolished, and beneficiaries of ALG II benefits have since been expected to accept offers of employment even where those do not match their skills level and/or significantly undercut their previous wage level. This is ensured by a combination of low means-tested benefits, strict conditionality, and sanctions in case of non-compliance, as stipulated by the Second Book of the Social Code, SGB II.[36]

Instruments of support by the labour market authorities as devised by the Hartz reforms were scaled back substantially several years after their introduction,[37] but notably measures of skills enhancement have recently been expanded again. The 2018 Participation Opportunities Law (TCG) introduced the possibility to subsidise employers for hiring beneficiaries whose unemployment has lasted for at least two years despite support from the employment authorities. The subsidy amounts to 75% of the wage costs in the first year of the employment relationship and is lowered to 50% in the second year. In case of a dismissal during the subsidising period, the funding amount approved for the last six months must be repaid. The employer must also enable the authority to provide on-the-job support to the beneficiary over the period at issue, without reduction of pay for associated interruptions in the work process (Section 16e SGB II). In addition, Section 16i SGB II now allows for wage subsidies of up to 100%

---

35. Bundesregierung, Entwurf eines Gesetzes zur Stärkung der Tarifautonomie. Drucksache 18/1558 (2014).
36. *See* Dorothee Spannagel & Katharina Molitor, Einkommen immer ungleicher verteilt. WSI-Verteilungsbericht 2019, 440 et seqq.; Ulrich Walwei et al., Hartz IV — Reform einer umstrittenen politischen Maßnahme. Wirtschaftsdienst 99 (2019), https://doi.org/10.1007/s10273-019-2439-3, 235 et seqq.
37. *See* Bundesagentur für Arbeit, Berichte: Analyse Arbeitsmarkt Zeitreihen (Jahreszahlen) Deutschland (2020), https://statistik.arbeitsagentur.de/Statistikdaten/Detail/201812/analyse/analyse-arbeitsmarkt-zeitreihen/analyse-arbeitsmarkt-zeitreihen-d-0-202012-pdf.pdf?__blob=publicationFile.

over five years for companies hiring beneficiaries who have been out of work for six out of the seven preceding years.

Subsequently, the 2018 Qualification Opportunities Act (QCG) and the 2019 Employment of Tomorrow Act (AvmG – in force since October 2020) improved the framework for funding training for workers in low-skilled occupations without the latter having to quit their current jobs. To enable the beneficiaries to obtain a relevant qualification recognised in the dual system, authorities may not only fund training costs and related expenses (travel, accommodation, childcare), but also provide a wage subsidy to the employer. The degree of support depends, *i.a.*, on the size of the company and the characteristics of the worker. Wage subsidies may amount to up to 100% for low-skilled employees in programmes aiming at the completion of a recognised vocational qualification. While funding was and continues to be a discretionary performance, the AvmG has introduced a legal entitlement for workers undertaking the completion of a recognised vocational qualification to have their training costs funded by the competent authority (Section 3 (3) SGB III).

Studies[38] show that employee representatives and notably works councils can play a positive role in improving in-company training opportunities. Works councils' right to co-determine training provision has been strengthened by reforms of the Works Constitution Act (BetrVG) in 2001 and 2021 (cf. the aforementioned Works Council Modernisation Act).

[C] Impact Analysis

Studies examining the impact of the Hartz reforms largely agree that they have contributed to the labour market boom of the twenty-first century,[39] although outcomes vary regarding the scale of their impact notably in relation to the generally favourable environment of strong economic growth over that period.[40] A particularly controversial debate concerns the sustainability of labour market integration achieved by the system.[41] In recent years, about half of former beneficiaries in the ALG II scheme who found a job have re-applied for benefits within several months.[42] This situation

38. E.g., Uwe Cantner et al., Works councils, training activities and innovation: A study of German firms. Jena Economic Research Papers No. 2014-006 (2014); Tobias Wiß, Employee representatives' influence on continuing vocational training: The impact of institutional context. European Journal of Industrial Relations, 23/2 (2017) 169 et seqq.
39. Cf. Benjamin Baykal, Gesellschaftliche Erfolge wahrnehmen – Chancen anerkennen – Brücken nutzen, in Sozialer Fortschritt, Armut trotz Arbeit (Bernd Waas & Christina Hiessl ed. 2022, forthcoming).
40. Walwei et al., *supra* n. 36 at 236; Brigitte Hochmuth et al., Hartz IV and the Decline of German Unemployment: A Macroeconomic Evaluation, Friedrich-Alexander-Universität Erlangen-Nürnberg, Institute for Employment Research (2018).
41. *See*, e.g., Gerhard Bäcker, Arbeitslosenversicherung stärken. Sozialgesetzbuch III und II harmonisieren, Wirtschaftsdienst 99/2019, https://doi.org/10.1007/s10273-019-2439-3, 252 et seqq.; Jürgen Schupp, Hartz- weder Rolltreppe aus der Armut noch Fahrstuhl in die Armut. Wirtschaftsdienst 99 (2019), https://doi.org/10.1007/s10273-019-2439-3, 247 et seqq.
42. *See* Bündnis 90/Die Grünen, Antrag: Ein Zukunftsprogramm gegen Armut – Armut bekämpfen, Teilhabe garantieren, Chancen und Zusammenhalt stärken, Drucksache 19/30394, 19.Wahlperiode (2021).

gives rise to concerns about the consequences for employees' bargaining power in wage negotiations, as employers can 'afford' to offer poorly paid jobs to those whose only alternative is life at barely the subsistence level. Needless to say, workers with an actually low skills level may be particularly disadvantaged when also basically skilled workers are pressurised into competing for low-skilled jobs for lack of immediately available alternatives. In combination with the described erosion of collective bargaining coverage, this fuelled the emergence of exorbitantly low wages in jobs to which no minimum wage standard was applicable.

The introduction of a general statutory minimum wage as described was eventually seen as unavoidable to tackle this development. Unsurprisingly, it has been of particular significance for low-skilled workers in low-wage sectors. Overall, around 11% of all workers earned less than EUR 8.50 gross per hour in 2014, i.e., before the introduction of the minimum wage at that level.[43] Employees in small and medium-sized enterprises (SMEs), East German companies, and businesses not bound by collective agreements were significantly more affected.[44] Ohlert[45] finds that almost 70% of workers in hospitality, but also around or above 50% in the sectors of Other services, Retail trade, Agriculture/forestry/fishing, and Transportation and storage benefitted from having their wage increased to the new statutory minimum.

Regarding support instruments including wage subsidies, the Federal Government[46] recently expressed its conviction that they are reaching the right target group. As of December 2019, around 43,000 employees were supported by an average funding amount per capita of more than EUR 1,200 per month. Proper evaluation of the instruments' effectiveness and possible needs for adaptations would only be possible once the first cohorts have completed the full funding period (i.e., at the end of 2024).

By contrast, the enhanced options for training support have already been subject to first evaluations, with promising results. Klaus et al.[47] find that the number of participants in sponsored in-work up- and re-skilling has doubled between 2016 and 2019, the focus has shifted towards the completion of recognised vocational qualifications, and recently the share of low-skilled workers and non-German nationals has increased. The number of workers whose employer receives a training-related wage subsidy is higher than ever before.[48] Kruppe[49] finds that, all in all, the possibilities of

43. Mario Bossler et al., Auswirkungen des gesetzlichen Mindestlohns auf Betriebe und Unternehmen. Studie im Auftrag der Mindestlohnkommission, Institut für Arbeitsmarkt- und Berufsforschung (2018) 52.
44. Matthias Dütsch & Ralf Himmelreicher, Characteristics contributing to low- and minimum-wage labour in Germany; in Journal of Economics and Statistics, 240/2-3 (2020) 161 et seqq.
45. Clemens Ohlert, Ausmaß der betrieblichen Betroffenheit vom gesetzlichen Mindestlohn anhand der Verdienststrukturerhebung. Bundesanstalt für Arbeitsschutz und Arbeitsmedizin (2021) 5.
46. Bundesregierung, Antwort auf die Kleine Anfrage – Drucksache 19/27973 – Zwei Jahre neue Regelinstrumente zum sozialen Arbeitsmarkt und zu Lohnkostenzuschüssen im Zweiten Buch Sozialgesetzbuch, Bundestagsdrucksache 19/29176, 19. Wahlperiode (2021).
47. Anton Klaus et al., Geförderte Weiterbildung Beschäftigter: Trotz erweiterter Möglichkeiten noch ausbaufähig. IAB-Kurzbericht, 24/2020 (2020) 4 et seqq.
48. *See* Bundesagentur für Arbeit, *supra* n. 37.
49. Thomas Kruppe, Finanzierung der Weiterbildung. Stellungnahme des IAB zur Anhörung in der Sitzung der Projektgruppe 7 der Enquete-Kommission Berufliche Bildung des Deutschen Bundestages am 23.11.2020, 14|2020 (2020) 6, 11.

labour market institutions to support lifelong learning and forward-looking up-skilling have never been wider. At the same time, support in this framework is discretionary, dependent on the cooperation of all actors, and has to be financed from institutions' limited budgets. As long as employers and/or workers are bearing a significant share of the costs, the subsidies often do not reach those most in need of them. This has led to calls for strengthening public investment, e.g., by providing paid training leave in the framework of unemployment insurance.[50] As for the participation of workers' representatives, research indicates that works councils are far from using the rights introduced by the aforementioned reforms of the BetrVG to their full extent.[51]

All in all, despite improvements through ALMPs,[52] concern remain about the Hartz approach having potentially been 'too successful' in bringing the unemployed back to work at any cost. For years, the German unemployment rate has been among the lowest in Europe;[53] companies are suffering significant and increasing difficulties to find skilled workers,[54] and yet a large share of low- and unskilled jobs are occupied by overqualified workers (*see supra* at §3.02[A]). An easing of conditionality requirements to the effect of enabling skilled workers to find a suitable rather than the first available job might eventually also help to 'free' low-skilled occupations for those who face difficulties in improving their skills level.[55] It remains to be seen to what degree such concerns will be addressed by the overhaul of the regime as announced in the coalition agreement (*see supra* at §3.01[B]).

§3.03 VUP GROUP 2: SOLO AND BOGUS SELF-EMPLOYMENT

[A] Composition of VUP Group 2

Germany has always displayed one of the lowest shares of the self-employed among its workforce ever since comparative EU-level measurements began in 2005; the share has declined further in every annual measurement since 2009 and stood at the EU-wide second lowest level (after Luxembourg) in 2020.[56] Just more than half of the German

---

50. *Ibid.*, 11.
51. Simone Janssen & Ute Leber, Zur Rolle von Weiterbildung in Zeiten von Digitalisierung und technologischem Wandel. IAB-Stellungnahme Nr. 5/2020 (2020), 12 et seqq.; Antje Utecht, Transformationsatlas: Personalentwicklung und Qualifizierung. IG Metall Vorstand (2019) 9.
52. Cf. Katharina Erbeldinger, Sicherung auskömmlicher Erwerbsarbeit als Aufgabe für Arbeitsmarkt- und Sozialpolitik – Blick in den Sechsten Armuts- und Reichtumsberichts der Bundesregierung, in Sozialer Fortschritt, Armut trotz Arbeit (Bernd Waas & Christina Hiessl ed. 2022, forthcoming).
53. Cf. Eurostat data at https://ec.europa.eu/eurostat/databrowser/view/tipsun20/default/bar?lang=en.
54. Gudrun Schönfeld et al., Ausbildung in Deutschland – eine Investition gegen den Fachkräftemangel. Ergebnisse der BIBB-Kosten-Nutzen-Erhebung 2017/18. Report 1/2020 (2020) 14 et seq.
55. *See* Katharina Dengler et al., Arbeitsaufnahmen von Arbeitslosengeld-II-Empfängern und die Stabilität der Beschäftigung, Statistik-Tage 2019 (2019); Bäcker, *supra* n. 41, 252 et seqq.
56. *See* Eurostat data at https://ec.europa.eu/eurostat/databrowser/view/LFST_HHSETY__custom_1957254/default/bar?lang=en.

self-employed have no employees of their own, while the same is true for three out of four self-employed persons in EU countries on average.[57]

[B] Legal Framework: Notion; Obstacles to the Application of Labour Law and Social Security Standards; Unionisation and Application of Collective Agreements

Self-employed persons are generally not subject to labour law or mandatory insurance in any of the five branches of social security (health, long-term care, industrial injury, pension, and unemployment insurance). Although healthcare insurance has been mandatory for all German residents since 2009 (Section 193 (3) of the Insurance Contract Act –VVG), self-employed persons without a right to opt into social health insurance (*see infra* in this subsection) only have the option of concluding a commercial insurance contract – with individual risk- (rather than income-)related contributions.

There are several exceptions for specific subgroups, all of whom constitute minorities among the self-employed. The largest one, employee-like persons, are relevant only under labour law. They are defined[58] as self-employed who either dedicate the majority of their working time to or receive the majority of their income from a single client undertaking (or group). For freelancers providing artistic or journalistic services, the threshold in terms of income is reduced from 50% to one-third. Employee-like persons are covered notably by the right to occupational health and safety and data protection, equal treatment, annual leave, and care leave. Moreover, in case of conflicts between the worker and an employer, they can resort to the labour courts.[59] The much smaller group of home workers are defined by the Home Work Law (HAG) as persons who obtain the majority of their income by completing 'assignments' for an organisation on which they depend economically, at home or at a self-chosen workplace (alone or with family members: Section 2 (1) HAG). These workers are covered by a range of labour law protections, being assimilated to employees in the fields of occupational health and safety, youth and maternity protection, annual leave, continuation of payments in case of sickness, notice periods and special dismissal protection. Neither of these two groups is covered by minimum wage legislation, but both can be subject to collective bargaining agreements under the same conditions as employees.

Both categories have been defined many decades ago, in labour market contexts that significantly differed from today's. Thereby, they do not necessarily cover modern

57. *See* Eurostat data at https://ec.europa.eu/eurostat/statistics-explained/index.php?title=Self-employment_statistics.
58. In Section 12a TVG (*infra* n. 59).
59. The provisions are scattered over a number of legal acts – notably Section 2 (2) of the Federal Annual Leave Act (BUrlG), Section 5 (1) of the Labour Court Act (ArbGG), Section 7 (1) of the Home Care Leave Act (PflegeZG), Section 2 (2) of the Occupational Health and Safety Act (ArbSchG), Section 6 (1) of the General Equal Treatment Act (AGG), Section 26 (8) of the Federal Data Protection Act (BDSG), and Section 12a (1) of the Collective Bargaining Agreements Act (TVG).

forms of self-employment displaying significant elements of dependence. Although the century-old concept of the home worker was prevented from receding into complete insignificance by a reform that removed the requirement of a physical work product – and was thus opened to activities such as text editing, translating, participation in surveys, web design, or programming – notably the requirement of work based on specifically allocated assignments prevents the category from being operationalised for groups such as platform workers.[60]

For purposes of social security, only home workers are comprehensively covered like employees, and the contracting party ordering assignments from them is treated like an employer in terms of contribution splitting and payment. Special autonomous schemes covering all branches except unemployment insurance exist for farmers,[61] artists, and writers,[62] and certain regulated professions with a tradition of collective organisation have mandatory accident and/or pension insurance mechanisms in place. Self-employed midwives, maritime pilots, seafarers, and craftsmen (Section 2 (1-2) SGB VI) are I lege covered by statutory pension insurance, and seafarers as well as health or welfare service professionals are covered by accident insurance (Section 2 (1) SGB VII). A non-occupation-specific inclusion of the self-employed exists only for pension insurance, and it is limited to those who work 'essentially only for one client' (Section 9 SGB VI). In practice, this is interpreted as requiring that at least five-sixths of the solo self-employed's total operating income be received solely from one client.[63] Importantly, apart from the special arrangements for home workers, artists, and writers, the self-employed have to finance their social insurance via own contributions without support from the principal (cf. Section 169 (1) SGB VI). This also means that they bear the risk of being charged with retroactive payment obligations in case of errors about their classification – which in practice affects notably those surpassing the five-sixths criterion as described in the previous paragraph.

Voluntary application for social insurance is generally allowed only for statutory pension insurance, which allows for a choice of contribution amounts between certain thresholds (Sections 7, 161 SGB VI). Voluntary healthcare or unemployment insurance is only possible as a prolongation of pre-existing affiliation, for which an application needs to be brought within short timeframes when becoming self-employed. For social health insurance (*see* Section 9 SGB V), this serves to avoid strategies of cherry-picking based on the different calculation rules, as risk-based contributions for private insurance turn out low for the young and much higher for older individuals. Another measure aiming to prevent abuse requires the self-employed enrolled in social health insurance to pay contributions based on a minimum monthly basis[64] even in months

60. Waas, Crowdwork in Germany, in Crowdwork – A Comparative Law Perspective. HSI-Schriftenreihe Band 22 (Waas et al. ed. 2017) 163 et seqq.
61. *See* provisions scattered across the respective parts of the Social Code and some additional acts (e.g., Sections 146 et seqq. SGB V; Law on Farmers' Old-Age Security, ALG).
62. *See* the Artists' Social Insurance Act (KSVG).
63. Helmut Reinhardt & Wolfgang Silber, Sozialgesetzbuch VI: gesetzliche Rentenversicherung: Lehr- und Praxiskommentar (2021) 17.
64. In the context of the COVID-19 crisis, this fictional income was almost halved from EUR 2,284 in 2020 to EUR 1,097.67 in 2021.

when their actual income is low or negative. As for unemployment insurance, affiliation requires a self-employed applicant to have been compulsorily insured for the minimum period be entitled to unemployment benefits immediately before commencing their self-employed activity. They must work in a self-employed capacity for at least 15 hours a week and apply for insurance coverage within three months of founding their business. The fixed contribution amount is calculated based on insured employees' average wages. During the first two years, the contribution is reduced to half its value (cf. Section 28a SGB III).

Plans for mandatory provision for old-age and invalidity risks for the entire economically active population had been tabled by previous governments (cf. a proposal under then Labour Minister von der Leyen in 2012) and were anchored in the previous government's coalition agreement.[65] A key issues paper by the Federal Labour Ministry, postponed several times, *i.a.*, due to the COVID-19 crisis, was finally drafted in December 2020. It envisages an obligation, starting in 2024, of all self-employed under 35 years of age to either apply for coverage in the public pension system or otherwise secure insurance for an equivalent range of risks, i.e., old age, death, and a reduction of earning capacity. The obligation would also apply to self-employed income from a side job, except marginal work (cf. *infra* at §3.04[C][1]). Although the Ministry has repeatedly announced the publication of a draft law by the end of this year, parliamentary documents[66] indicate that the government does not expect the law to pass in the current legislative period.[67] Various studies[68] indicate that a comprehensive pension system for the economically active population (*Erwerbstätigenversicherung*) would also entail macroeconomic benefits, *i.a.* by reducing the number of recipients of (tax-financed) social assistance benefits under the Twelfth Book of the Social Code (SGB XII).[69]

The COVID-19 crisis has shone a light on the fact that the (solo) self-employed are as a rule not covered by short-time work arrangements, which were arguably the major approach to preventing in-work poverty among employees when businesses had to restrict their activity. Structurally, the scheme is part of the unemployment insurance system, so that only home workers (*see supra* last subsection), but no other groups of self-employed are covered by it (cf. Section 103 SGB III).

When the crisis hit, the self-employed obtained an immediate right to apply for a partial compensation of business-related expenditures which could not be avoided even at times of interrupted or significantly reduced business activity. The right to apply for a one-off payment of up to EUR 15,000 between March and May 2020 was

---

65. Bundesregierung, Koalitionsvertrag zwischen CDU, CSU und SPD (2018).
66. Bundestag, Anlage 2 zum Plenarprotokoll 19/220 des Deutschen Bundestags– 19. Wahlperiode – 220. Sitzung. Berlin, Mittwoch, den 14. April 2021.
67. *See* Der Spiegel, Heil will Selbstständige in Rentenkasse einzahlen lassen, Der Spiegel of 9/6/2021, https://www.spiegel.de/wirtschaft/soziales/debatte-ueber-rente-mit-68-hubertus-heil-will-selbststaendige-in-rentenkasse-holen-a-5b5c749d-f738-407b-8667-b617e35d772d.
68. For an overview *see* Rudolf Zwiener et al., Demografischer Wandel und Renten: Beschäftigungspotenziale erfolgreich nutzen, Wirtschaftsdienst 100 (2020) 7 et seqq.
69. Cf. also Johannes Geyer, In die Zukunft ohne Gesamtkonzept: Vorausberechnungen und ihre Probleme, in Neustart in der Rentenpolitik. Analysen und Perspektiven (Florian Blank et al. eds, Nomos 2020) 199 et seqq.

followed up by similar 'bridging aids' that compensated for varying percentages of fixed business expenditure during the further waves of the pandemic.[70] First evaluations confirm that these benefits have been vital to ensure the survival of a non-negligible number of self-employed businesses.[71] While it was thus acknowledged that many businesses would still need to pay their bills even in times of lockdown and restriction of customer contact, the same was not necessarily true for the private bills of the individuals behind those businesses. Once again, the self-employed were tacitly assumed to be capable of dealing with situations of income loss. In the pertinent literature, individuals who were fully liable for their business with their private assets and could only fall back on social assistance were also very much and expressly included in criticisms that relief measures were preventing too many 'necessary insolvencies' – and should thus be denied to those with an over-average turnover decrease relating to comparable undertakings.[72]

Only when the country entered into a second lockdown in November and December 2020 did the government decide to grant those losing 80% or more of their turnover due to the imposed closure of their business (or that of their proven main clients) during these two months a reimbursement of up to 75% of their loss. Due to the complex conditionality of these benefits, effective disbursement was delayed past March 2021 in numerous cases.[73] It was not until mid-February 2021 that the government decided to create a benefit to compensate for income losses among the self-employed in a more general way. As an optional alternative to seeking compensation for fixed expenditure in the first half of 2021, the self-employed could receive a one-off payment (*Neustarthilfe*) at the amount of 50% of their turnover in the first half of 2019, up to EUR 7,500. If their income turned out to be more than 60% lower than in 2019 in the first half of 2021, then beneficiaries were allowed to keep the entire payment; otherwise, they needed to reimburse all or parts of it proportionally.[74] Subsequently, this benefit was renewed for the second half of 2021, with a higher maximum of EUR 9,000.[75]

Finally, the pandemic has cast a spotlight on the degree to which the use of solo and presumed bogus self-employed may be prone to abuse in industrial production

70. Four programmes so far, each covering periods of several months (Überbrückungshilfen I-IV). For an overview of the programmes, which became more generous over time, *see* Jannis Bischof, Die Bedeutung der Kostenstruktur für Effektivität von Staatshilfen, 49 Wirtschaftsdienst 7 (2021) 536 et seqq., https://link.springer.com/article/10.1007/s10273-021-2962-x.
71. Caroline Stiel, Soforthilfe für Selbstständige wirkt vor allem positiv, wenn sie rasch gewährt wird, DIW aktuell 60 (2021) 1. To quantify the impact, the authors find it about half as effective as the start-up grant (*see infra* at §3.03[C]) in its original form.
72. Bischof et al., *supra* n. 69, at 540 et seqq.
73. Johannes Seebauer et al., Warum vor allem weibliche Selbstständige Verliererinnen der COVID-19-Krise sind, DIW Wochenbericht 15 (2021) 268; Stiel et al., *supra* n. 71, at 5; Alexander Kritikos, Nach fünf Monaten Lock-down: Selbständige brauchen endlich eine Perspektive, DIW Wochenbericht 13 (2021) 248.
74. Stiel et al., *supra* n. 71 at 5.
75. For details on the ongoing modifications of the programmes, *see* the ministry's guidelines at https://www.ueberbrueckungshilfe-unternehmen.de/UBH/Navigation/DE/Dokumente/FAQ/Neustarthilfe-Plus/neustarthilfe-plus.html.

chains. After an initial focus on the precarious working and living conditions of seasonal workers in agriculture, attention soon shifted to slaughterhouses.[76]

The meat industry had been criticised for years because of the widespread use of self-employed subcontractors, oftentimes based abroad. Low wages, poor working conditions, and accommodation had repeatedly been subject to parliamentary debate. As demand increased, large butchering and meat processing corporations ended up employing more than 85% of the workers in the industry. Over time, the use of own employees declined in favour of subcontractors who would either be solo self-employed or post their own workers to German slaughter houses.[77] According to a survey by the food workers' union NGG, two-thirds of meat industry workers were self-employed in 2013, frequently working at the end of complex subcontracting chains.[78] A key issues paper by the Labour Ministry of May 2020[79] identified grievances such as 'overcrowding, rampant rents, violations of hygiene, distance and occupational safety regulations (notably lack of protective equipment, insufficient safety distance, no occupational medical care) as well as violations of the minimum wage and working hours law'. After several meat plants had turned into epicentres of COVID-19 outbreaks with dire consequences, intense legislative debates throughout 2020 resulted in an amendment to the Law on Ensuring Workers' Rights in the Meat Industry. As of January 2021, companies of 50+ workers are no longer allowed to engage self-employed contractors in their core business (slaughtering, cutting, and meat processing).

[C] Impact Analysis

The described piecemeal approach to social protection leaves the majority of the solo self-employed without minimum standards for remuneration and without affiliation to any branch of social security. Collective agreements for the self-employed effectively exist exclusively for 'free collaborators' of print, audio, and television companies (to whom the lowered one-third threshold for classification as employee-like applies).[80] For home workers, specific committees (*Heimarbeitsausschüsse*) have been set up at the regional labour ministries, composed of representatives of home workers and their

76. Thorsten Schulten, Arbeitsbedingungen: Neuordnung der Fleischwirtschaft. 100 Wirtschaftsdienst 6 (2020) 393.
77. Gerhard Bosch et al., Kontrolle von Mindestlöhnen (Wiesbaden 2019) 191 et seqq.
78. Bernd Maiweg, Beispiel aus der Praxis – Schlachtindustrie: Zwei Drittel arbeiten mit Werkvertrag, in Werkverträge – Missbrauch stoppen. Gute Arbeit durchsetzen (2015) 12; Thorsten Diepenbrock, Selbständigkeit und Arbeitnehmereigenschaft im Sozialrecht, NZS 2016, 127 et seqq.
79. BMAS, Eckpunkte – Arbeitsschutzprogramm für die Fleischwirtschaft (2020), https://www.bmas.de/SharedDocs/Down-loads/DE/PDF-Pressemitteilungen/2020/eckpunkte-arbeitsschutzprogramm-fleischwirtschaft.pdf?__blob=publi-cationFile&v=3.
80. Wank, § 12a Arbeitnehmerähnliche Personen, in Wiedemann et al. (ed.), Kommentar zum Tarifvertragsgesetz, 8th ed. (2019), 1703 et seqq.; Sabine Blaschke & Veronika Mirschel, Die Genese gewerkschaftlicher Interessenvertretung für Solo-Selbstständige unter besonderer Berücksichtigung des Mediensektors, in Die Unorganisierten gewinnen (Susanne Pernicka & Andreas Aust ed. 2007) 5.

clients, which set compulsory minimum standards for fees and/or other aspects of home work in accordance with Section 18 HAG.

Empirical research[81] has raised doubts about the effectiveness of voluntary insurance options. Although surveys indicate that a majority of the self-employed are either involved in some form of old-age insurance or dispose of private savings, the monetary value of old-age provision indicated in the same surveys shows that most are far from ensuring a living above the poverty line after retirement.[82] Based on estimates about the scale to which this risk is expected to rise as a result of the pandemic,[83] the incumbent Federal Labour Minister concluded that around three out of four million self-employed on the German labour market are not adequately protected, with the solo self-employed particularly affected. The difference between the self-employed and employees was found to be larger than in any other EU Member State.[84]

As for health insurance, a significant share of the self-employed is found to underestimate the substantial increase in risk-dependent contribution rates for private insurance over their lifetime. This reportedly results in some self-employed workers going to extraordinary lengths to obtain a renewed entitlement to insurance under state social security – including moving to a different EU member state temporarily for at least one year, which gives them the right to opt into social security upon their return to Germany.[85] Finally, the number of self-employed workers voluntarily affiliated to unemployment insurance has fallen sharply since the early 2000s. This was related to the gradual discontinuation of a short-lived generous start-up grants scheme (*Gründungszuschüsse*: Section 93 SGB III), initiated in 2006 and originally linked to very favourable conditions for opting into unemployment insurance.[86] After the start-up grant was turned into a discretionary benefit and insurance conditions tightened repeatedly,[87] the number of applications for insurance dropped from 105,000 in 2010 to just more than 23,000 in 2013, 19,000 of whom were admitted to unemployment

81. Antonio Brettschneider & Ute Klammer, Lebenswege in die Altersarmut. Biografische Analysen und sozialpolitische Perspektiven (2016) 408 et seqq.; Karl Brenke & Martin Beznoska, Solo-Selbständige in Deutschland – Strukturen und Erwerbsverläufe. BMAS-Forschungsbericht 465 (2016) 53 et seqq.
82. Karl Brenke, Die allermeisten Selbständigen betreiben Altersvorsorge oder haben Vermögen, DIW Wochenbericht 45 (2016), https://www.diw.de/documents/publikationen/73/diw_01.c.546807.de/16-45-3.pdf; ver.di Selbstständige, Pflichtversicherung? Vorsorgepflicht? Alles anders? Bei der Altersvorsorge geht's um Grundsätze (2021), https://selbststaendige.verdi.de/was-tun_1/rentendebatte.
83. Judith A. Czepek, Flexibler Arbeitsmarkt, unflexible Renten? Diskontinuierliche Lebensverlaufe und ihre Absicherung im Alter, in Neustart in der Rentenpolitik. Analysen und Perspektiven (Florian Blank et al. ed. 2020) 91; Anita Tiefensee, Altersarmut – (k)ein Problem? Aktuelle und zukünftige Entwicklungen in Deutschland, in Neustart in der Rentenpolitik (Florian Blank et al. ed. 2020) 162.
84. Karin Schulze Buschoff, Selbstständigkeit und hybride Erwerbsformen. Sozialpolitische Gestaltungsoptionen. WSI Policy Brief 21, (2018) 5.
85. Wechsel von der privaten zur gesetzlichen Krankenversicherung für Selbständige (2021), https://www.firma.de/unternehmensfuehrung/wechsel-von-der-privaten-zur-gesetzlichen-krankenversicherung-fuer-selbstaendige/.
86. Frank Sowa, Arbeitslosenversicherung für Solo-Selbständige: Eine qualitative Studie zur Antragspflichtversicherung nach § 28a SGB III. IAB-Forschungsbericht 3 (2020) 21 et seqq.
87. Elke Jahn & Angelina Springer, Arbeitslosenversicherung: Auch Selbstständige nehmen Unterstützung in Anspruch, IAB-Kurzbericht 26 (2013) 200 et seqq.

insurance. In 2018, there were just around 3,000 new entries. It is noteworthy that the tightening of insurance conditions – apart from steeply increasing contributions, notably the abolishment of both the opt-in possibility for already established entrepreneurs and the option to receive benefits repeatedly – was decisively linked to Federal Court of Auditors' concerns about possible abuse by self-employed beneficiaries with irregular incomes.[88]

This general lack of unemployment insurance puts self-employed workers at risk to accept very low levels of remuneration, as their only 'exit option' is to file for social assistance.[89] The lack of pension insurance or savings in turn may be seen as hidden in-work poverty, as set out *supra* at §3.01[C].

As for support measures during the COVID-19 crisis, the late introduction and long processing periods for applications for benefits that took income losses into account meant that those self-employed individuals who were essentially 'selling their labour' and thus had no or few fixed operating costs to declare effectively received no payments until more than a year after the onset of the crisis.[90] In the meantime, they were left to use up their financial reserves until the point where the absence of income and personal assets entitled them to social assistance benefits.[91] No retroactive compensation for losses in 2020 was granted. Ironically, even the asset test conducted in case of an application for social assistance has proven to be particularly harsh for many self-employed individuals. Notably, while accrued social pension insurance entitlements cannot be touched in this process, and certain forms of private retirement saving schemes are expressly exempt, this did not necessarily apply to the old-age savings which self-employed individuals had accumulated in the absence of mandatory pension insurance regulation applying to them. Even under the temporarily alleviated conditions at the height of the crisis, assets surmounting EUR 60,000 excluded an entitlement to social assistance benefits, which was the leading cause e.g., for artists' applications to be rejected.[92] This shows how the lack of social insurance coverage in different areas interacts to the disadvantage of self-employed individuals experiencing a temporary loss of income.

The SOEP-CoV survey found that, several months into the crisis, more than two-thirds of self-employed respondents' businesses had been affected between April and July 2020, as a result of regulatory constraints, decline in demand and/or delivery problems. More than half had to reduce their working hours, on average by almost 16.5 hours less per week than before the crisis. Three out of five of all self-employed respondents experienced a decline in earnings, with those affected earning little more than a third of the pre-crisis amount and almost half having liquidity reserves for no more than three months to maintain their activity. Due to self-employed women's high

88. *Ibid.*; Sowa, *supra* n. 86 at 8 et seqq.
89. cf. Schoukens/Weber 2020: 21 et seq
90. Kritikos, *supra* n. 73 at 248.
91. *See* Alexander Kritikos et al., Corona-Pandemie wird zur Krise für Selbständige, DIW aktuell No. 47/2020 (2020) 1.
92. Gerhart Baum, Aufruf zur Nothilfe für freiberufliche Künstler*innen, Kulturrat NRW Press release of 9/06 (2020), https://www.kulturrat-nrw.de/aufruf-zur-nothilfe-fuer-freiberufliche-kuenstlerinnen-09-06-2020/.

likelihood to work in strongly affected sectors, 63% of them suffered income losses. Between 76% and 91% of respondents in the hospitality, tourism, sports, wellness, hairdressing, and cosmetics sectors were not able to work at all at the time of the survey, and 9 out of 10 in those industries had a shortfall in earnings of more than 75%. Between 32% and 49% of the self-employed feared that they would have to stop their activity in the near future despite using all available state support.[93] While concrete statistics seem to be missing to date, there are numerous accounts of cases in which the self-employed gave up their business long before concrete government aid became available for them.[94] These findings are in striking contrast to those for employees, among whom 'only' 15% of respondents reported any decrease in income in the same survey. Such decreases were mostly due to short-time working, which still ensured the maintenance of 60%-87% of wages for lost working hours (and actually more than that, due to the tax effect and often top-ups by employers). Structurally, the scheme is part of unemployment insurance and consequentially excludes the self-employed.

Consequently, it seems noteworthy that the incumbent administration's coalition agreement[95] announces the continuation of the turnover-based ad-hoc benefit to compensate for fallouts from the pandemic for 'as long as needed'. In the long term, it commits to ease access to voluntary unemployment insurance and abolish minimum contribution rates in voluntary social health insurance. Old-age and invalidity provision ensuring an income above the social assistance level after retirement is to become obligatory. While this would finally bring Germany more in line with the prevailing European norm of mandating pension insurance for the entire working population, the envisaged scheme would ensure the recognition of private products with non-income-based contributions.

Finally, the inapplicability of the statutory minimum wage and the only exceptional coverage by collective agreements enables a much larger degree of income polarisation than for employees (i.e., with both very low and very high incomes being much more common), and notably the share of low-wage earners is high among the solo self-employed (27% in 2019[96]).

§3.04 VUP GROUP 3: FIXED-TERM, AGENCY WORKERS, INVOLUNTARY PART-TIMERS

Fixed-term work is currently somewhat less frequent in Germany than on average in the EU, albeit with a growing tendency and clear indications of a strong effect of

93. Irene Bertschek & Daniel Erdsiek, Soloselbstständigkeit in der Corona-Krise, Digitalisierung hilft bei der Bewältigung der Krise, ZEW-Kurzexpertise 20-08 (2020), 3.
94. Kevin Hanschke & Simon Strauß, Sie sterben still, in FAZ of 27/2 (2021); Stiel et al., *supra* n. 71 at 1; Seebauer et al., *supra* n. 71 at 268.
95. Bundesregierung, *supra* n. 13 at 69, 75.
96. Andreas Jansen, Wachsende Graubereiche in der Beschäftigung. Ein interdisziplinärer Forschungsüberblick über die Entstehung und Entwicklung neuer Arbeits-und Beschäftigungsformen in Deutschland. Working Paper Forschungsförderung No 167 (2020) 48 et seqq.; Fedorets et al., *supra* n. 12 at 92 et seqq.

regulatory measures on its incidence among the workforce.[97] The use of temporary agency work is slightly more widespread than for the EU as a whole.[98] The by far most important factor contributing to Germany's high share of atypical work is the prominence of part-time work. The German part-time employment rate is the fourth highest in the EU after the Netherlands, Austria, and Belgium, and the country has the third highest share of workers in all of the low-work-hour categories of 1-9 hours, 10-19 hours, and 25-29 hours of work per week.[99]

[A] Fixed-term Employees

[1] Legal Framework: Notion; Equal Treatment; Working Conditions and Social Security Benefits; Unionisation and Collective Agreement's Application

Section 14 of the Part-time and Fixed-term Employment Act (TzBfG) stipulates that a fixed-term contract can be based either on objective reasons or on a combination of a maximum period and number of renewals. If the conditions are not complied with or the employment relationship is tacitly continued after expiry of the fixed term, then the employment contract is deemed to have been concluded for an indefinite period. An objective reason exists 'in particular' in eight enumerated situations, including the temporary nature of the work, the replacement of another employee, or fixed terms based on a court settlement.

Among these eight reasons, two have given rise to particular controversy. Reason no. 5, i.e., fixed-term contracts for the purpose of testing employees, is now the most commonly used in the private economy according to a survey (IAB-Betriebspanel) conducted in 2018, after a significant shift from the reasons cited in the wake of the financial crisis in 2009.[100] While uncertain economic prospects were still the dominant reason for most companies back then, 42% of respondent companies mainly used the fixed term for testing in 2018. The Federal Labour Court has repeatedly clarified that reliance on this reason must not circumvent the six-month limitation of probationary

---

97. Notably the expansion of its use when fixed-term contracts without objective reason (*see* next subsection) became legal in the early 2000s. *See* Eurostat data at https://ec.europa.eu/eurostat/databrowser/view/LFSQ_ETPGA__custom_1818481/default/table?lang=en and Eric Seils & Helge Baumann, Trends und Verbreitung atypischer Beschäftigung. Eine Auswertung regionaler Daten, WSI Policy Brief Nr. 34/06 (2019) 6.
98. *See* Eurostat data at https://ec.europa.eu/eurostat/databrowser/view/LFSA_QOE_4A6R2__custom_1828104/default/table?lang=en. Note that an unlikely spike to 5.4% in 2020 indicated in that dataset is based on provisional data and contradicts national statistics – *see* PWC, Zeitarbeitsbranche aktuell 2020. Zum Einfluss von COVID-19, 2020, https://www.pwc.de/de/industrielle-produktion/zeitarbeitsbranche-aktuell-2020.pdf).
99. *See* Eurostat data at https://ec.europa.eu/eurostat/databrowser/view/tesem100/default/table?lang=en; https://ec.europa.eu/eurostat/databrowser/view/LFSA_QOE_3A4__custom_1116812/default/table?lang=en.
100. Christian Hohendanner, Befristete Beschäftigung in Deutschland 2018. IAB-Betriebspanel 1996-2018, hochgerechnete Werte (2019).

periods to six months (Section 622 of the Civil Code[101]). Trade unions nonetheless report a high incidence of up to 'years-long' fixed terms concluded for testing.[102] Even more controversially, reason no. 7 allows for a justification by limited budgets in the public sector, where fixed-term contracts are particularly common.[103] The qualification of this as a genuinely objective reason has been questioned, and the Federal Labour Court[104] had asked for a preliminary ruling by the Court of Justice of the European Union (CJEU) on its compatibility with Article 5 of the Fixed-term Directive 99/70/EC. The dispute in that case was later settled, though. Nonetheless, significant doubts remain as to the compliance with EU law.[105] The special provisions for older employees, which were introduced by the First Hartz reform and have become known in the context of the CJEU's *Mangold* and *Lufthansa* rulings, currently permit fixed terms of up to five years for employees over age 52. However, they apply only to employees who, immediately before the start of the fixed-term contract, have been unemployed for at least four months.

Sections 14 (2-3) TzBfG permit fixed terms without an objective reason for a period of two years, to be renewed no more than three times, unless a permanent employment relationship has previously existed with the same employer. Collective agreements are allowed to deviate in terms of both the permitted number of extensions and the maximum duration, and such collective agreements can be made applicable to employment contracts of non-bound employers by means of individual reference.

A pending reform bill published by the Labour Ministry in April 2021[106] plans to reduce the maximum duration of fixed-term contracts without an objective reason from 2 years to 18 months. In addition, companies with more than 75 employees (which are particularly likely to hire for fixed terms) would be allowed to conclude fixed-term contracts without an objective reason with no more than 2.5% of their staff. Fixed terms based on an objective reason other than the nature of the work or a court settlement would also be limited to a maximum of 5 years with the same employer.

Section 4 (2) TzBfG stipulates the principle of equal treatment in relation to a comparable employee with a permanent contract, unless objective reasons justify different treatment. Section 5 provides protection against victimisation.

---

101. *See*, e.g., Federal Labour Court of 25 October 2017 – 7 AZR 712/15; and of 02 June 2010 – 7 AZR 85/09; Müller-Glöge 2021: note 49a.
102. DGB, 'Wir wollen den Missbrauch bei den Befristungen abschaffen', Abteilung Arbeitsmarktpolitik Nr. 1/2020 (2020) 9.
103. Federal Labour Court of 27 October 2010 – 7 AZR 485/09.
104. Decision of 27 October 2010 – 7 AZR 485/09.
105. Notably with a view to the lacking concretisation of the conditions for permissible reliance on this justification in national case law: *see* Müller-Glöge, *supra* n. 101 at note 71a.
106. BMAS, Referentenentwurf des Bundesministeriums für Arbeit und Soziales, Entwurf eines Gesetzes zur Änderung des allgemeinen Befristungsrechts (2021), https://www.arbrb.de/media/BMAS_RefE_Befristungsrest-1.pdf.

[2] *Impact Analysis*

Fixed-term workers' inherent unstable employment situation is combined with an increased likelihood to earn low hourly wages.[107] In its most recent analysis of the low-wage sector (measured by OECD standards), the Federal Statistics Office found it to include 21% of all employees, but 33% of fixed-term workers.[108]

In practice, even if the legal provisions described in the last subsection are complied with, fixed-term employment regularly implies a number of disadvantages. Some of these have to do with legally stipulated employment periods over which certain rights accrue. Several social security entitlements are dependent on prior insurance periods, which may be compromised by unstable and interrupted careers. This applies, e.g., to the requirements for receiving unemployment insurance benefits according to Section 142 SGB III as well as the determination of the period for which the benefit will be granted (Section 147 SGB III). But also several labour law entitlements (e.g., the right to sick pay by the employer) depend on the duration of the employment relationship. Most notably, annual leave entitlements basically come into being after six months of employment (Section 4 of the Federal Annual Leave Act – BUrlG). This has given rise to specific collective agreement-based solutions in sectors with a particularly high share of fixed-term work, notably construction (cf. the Sozialkassen der Bauwirtschaft or SOKA-BAU). Beyond this, collective agreements and individual employment contracts frequently stipulate entitlement regarding wages, leave rights, and dismissal compensation based on seniority. The same is true for entitlements provided for in social plans in case of collective redundancy.[109]

Another disadvantage results from the lack of dismissal protection. Other than a dismissal (cf. Section 1 (2) of the Dismissal Protection Act – KSchG), a non-renewal of a fixed-term contract need not be justified by the employer, which implies a risk of discriminatory or retaliatory non-renewals. The conclusion of fixed-term contracts notably avoids the applicability of special dismissal protection in case of severe disability (Section 168 SGB IX), maternity (Section 17 MuSchG), parental leave (Section 18 BEEG) or care leave (Section 5 Care Leave Act), and various employees with representative functions such as works council members (Sections 15 KSchG and 103 BetVG). Also the works council's right to co-determination under Section 106 of the Works Constitution Act does not apply in case of the expiry of a fixed-term contract. Finally, a number of disadvantages result more indirectly from the high degree of uncertainty about future employment – both for the employee and for third persons. A list of such disadvantages compiled by the German Trade Union Confederation[110] mentions, *i.a.*, reduced chances of getting a rental apartment or a loan from a bank, starting a family,[111] standing for election as works council members,[112] or being

107. Cf. Seils/Baumann, *supra* n. 97.
108. Sandra Klemt & Sabine Lenz, Verdienste, in Datenreport (Statistisches Bundesamt 2018) 173.
109. Nikolai Laßmann et al., Handbuch Interessenausgleich und Sozialplan. Handlungsmöglichkeiten bei Umstrukturierungen (2020) 346.
110. DGB, *supra* n. 102 at 3 et seqq.
111. Compared to permanent workers, fixed-term employees aged 20-34 marry less often and have fewer children (cf. Eric Seils, Jugend und befristete Beschäftigung, WSI Policy Brief 12/2016).

involved in company-provided training.[113] Employees hoping to be promoted to a permanent position by their employer are particularly vulnerable to exploitation, resulting, e.g., in unpaid overtime work.[114] All in all, it is noteworthy that, according to surveys, stable, permanent employment is the most important factor which workers are looking for in a job, taking precedence over flexible working hours or even high income.[115] A survey by the Federal Statistics Office[116] puts the share of employees who consciously chose a fixed-term occupation at only 5.9%.

[B] Temporary Agency Workers

[1] Legal Framework: Notion; Equal Treatment; Working Conditions and Social Security Benefits; Unionisation and Collective Agreement's Application

Temporary agency workers may be hired out only by licenced agencies (Sections 1 (1) and 12 of the Temporary Employment Act, AÜG). For the construction industry, temporary agency work is prohibited in principle (Section 1b), but with certain exemptions – including for companies in the construction industry with their seat in another Member State of the European Economic Area (EEA). The maximum duration of a worker's assignment to one user is limited to 18 months, but collective agreements with trade unions can stipulate a different duration or permit a works council agreement to deviate from it. The stipulations of such a collective agreement can be made applicable also in user companies not bound by it by means of individual agreement, but in that case deviations by works council agreements may regularly not extend the maximum period beyond 24 months, unless a different duration is stipulated by the collective agreement (Section 1 (1b) AÜG). A hiring-out agreement contravening the AÜG is null and void and leads to a retroactive reclassification as an employment relationship between the worker and the user. This consequence can only be prevented by a written demand of the worker to uphold the employment relationship with the agency, to be presented in person to the employment office within one month and subsequently submitted to the employer within three days (Sections 9 et seq. AÜG).

Certain forms of hiring out workers are expressly exempt from the law (cf. Section 1 (1a and 3) AÜG). This includes assignments between users in the same

112. Due to their increased vulnerability to 'retaliatory non-renewal': *see* Berndt Keller, Unsichere Arbeit – unsichere Mitbestimmung. Die Interessenvertretung atypisch Beschäftigter (2018) 19.
113. Only 36% of fixed-term workers are offered such training, compared to 51% of permanent employees (*see* Frauke Bilger et al., Weiterbildungsverhalten in Deutschland 2016. Ergebnisse des Adult Education Survey (AES) (2017) 46).
114. Mario Bossler & Philipp Grunau, Chasing the carrot - actual working hours of fixed-term employees, in Applied Economics Letters, Vol. 26 No. 14 (2019) 1148 et seqq.
115. Anja Crößmann & Lisa Günther, Arbeitsmarkt und Verdienste, in Datenreport (Statistisches Bundesamt 2018) 186 et seqq.
116. Statistisches Bundesamt, Mikrozensus 2018 (2019), https://www.destatis.de/DE/Methoden/Qualitaet/Qualitaetsberichte/Bevoelkerung/mikrozensus-2018.html.

economic sector bound by the same collective agreement, either in the context of a syndicate of several employers cooperating for a project or – if expressly permitted by the collective agreement – for the purpose of avoiding short-time work or layoffs. In the latter case, certain provisions of the law are nonetheless applicable. The same partial exemption applies to assignments within a group of undertakings or only occasional assignments, provided the worker is not hired for the purpose of being hired out. Very recently, the Federal Labour Court[117] has submitted a request for a preliminary ruling to the CJEU concerning the compatibility of one public-sector specific exemption from the AÜG with the Temporary Agency Work Directive 2008/104/EC. That exemption permits a collective agreement in the public sector to provide for a permanent assignment of an employee to a company to which that employee's tasks have been outsourced.

For decades, construction remained the only sector subject to a sectoral ban. This changed only very recently when, as described *supra* at §3.03[B], the COVID-19 crisis exposed the prevalence of precarious working conditions in the meat industry. Although less ubiquitous than the use of self-employed contractors, the use of temporary agency workers (who constituted 8.7% of workers in the industry in 2017[118]) was found to be subjected to essentially the same risks of abuse and precarious working conditions. In force since April 2021, the amended Section 6a of the Law on Ensuring Workers' Rights in the Meat Industry now prohibits the use of temporary agency workers in the core business of the meat industry (slaughtering, cutting, and meat processing). Companies in the butcher's trade with up to 49 employees are exempt. In the course of parliamentary deliberations, the possibility of strictly limited exceptions for three years was introduced, but made dependent on the conclusion of a collective agreement, which has not been the case so far.[119]

The principle of equal treatment of temporary agency workers with the user's own employees is set out in Section 8 AÜG. That provision allows for derogations by collective agreements, which can generally be made applicable in undertakings of non-bound employers in the sector at issue. If the derogation concerns remuneration, it may suspend equal pay up to the first nine months of a worker's assignment to a user, or even longer in case of a step-by-step increase after the first six weeks which ensures that the payment due to a worker after 15 months equals the collectively bargained wage for the sector at issue (Section 8 (4) AÜG). Amendments of the framework for short-time work at the onset of the COVID-19 crisis enabled, for the first time, the coverage of temporary agency workers by publicly subsidised short-time work schemes (cf. Section 11a AÜG and the KuGV).

117. Federal Labour Court of 16 June 2021 – 6 AZR 390/20 (A).
118. Bosch et al., *supra* n. 77 at 220.
119. *See* Frank Specht, Zeitarbeitsbranche legt Verfassungsbeschwerde gegen Heils Kontrollgesetz ein, in Handelsblatt of 12/5/2021, https://www.handelsblatt.com/politik/deutschland/fleischindustrie-zeitarbeitsbranche-legt-verfassungsbeschwerde-gegen-heils-kontrollgesetz-ein/27183538.html.

[2] Impact Analysis

Also temporary agency workers are subject to the combined effect of the inherent instability of their employment situation and the prevalence of low hourly wages.[120] Compared to fixed-term workers, temporary agency workers have an even higher likelihood to work for low wages – 39% according to the Federal Statistics Office.[121]

The option of derogations from equal treatment in Section 8 (2-4) AÜG has been widely used. The two most broadly applicable collective agreements set out wages and working conditions of temporary agency workers for all relevant sectors of the industry. As a result, temporary agency workers are regularly excluded from wage entitlements in line with comparable workers in the user undertaking, usually by reference to the collective agreement in their individual contract, as union membership is very low.[122] While collective agreements frequently provide better rights than the legal minimum for temporary agency workers assigned over long periods (particularly an obligation of the user to take them over as regular workers), they regularly deny any rights to equal treatment in case of (the practically dominant) short-term assignments.[123] The debate about the validity of such clauses in collective agreements and their applicability via reference in individual employment contracts[124] has been reinvigorated when another case involving derogations from the principle of equal treatment by a branch-level collective agreement was brought before the Federal Labour Court. In December 2020, the court asked the CJEU for a preliminary ruling regarding the requirement of 'respecting the overall protection of temporary agency workers' when relying on the deviation option of Article 5 (3) of the Temporary Agency Work Directive.

The AÜG's amendment in 2017, which introduced both the aforementioned maximum duration of 18 months and limitations to the derogation from equal treatment were found to have had visible effects in terms of reducing the number of temporary agency workers, many of whom were taken over into the user undertakings' regular staff.[125] Collective agreements were also no longer allowed to keep wages for temporary agency workers below the statutory minimum wage after the expiry of the transition period for exemption from the Minimum Wage Act in 2017, and overall increasing wage levels have been observed since then.[126]

120. Cf. Seils, *supra* n. 111; Crößmann/Günther, *supra* n. 115.
121. Klemt/Lenz, *supra* n. 108 at 173.
122. Cf. Holger Brecht-Heitzmann et al., TVG – Tarifvertragsgesetz. Kommentar für die Praxis, Frankfurt a. M. (2014) note 163.
123. Berndt Keller, Berufs- und Spartengewerkschaften. Neue Akteure und Perspektiven der Tarifpolitik (2017).
124. Cf. Jutta Gruber, Grundfragen und aktuelle Probleme der arbeitsvertraglichen Bezugnahme auf Tarifverträge (2017) 165.
125. Bundesagentur für Arbeit, Berichte: Blickpunkt Arbeitsmarkt – Entwicklungen der Zeitarbeit (2021).
126. Matthias Kaufmann, Eine Krise im Zeitraffertempo. Leiharbeit unter Druck, Der Spiegel of 23/8/2020 (2020), https://www.spiegel.de/wirtschaft/leiharbeit-in-der-corona-krise-das-schlaegt-voll-auf-die-arbeitnehmer-durch-a-5860683b-790d-4590-a9fd-df9c8c8bc7e1.

The COVID-19 pandemic caused an immediate and significant reduction in the number of temporary agency workers, with about a quarter losing their jobs over the first half of 2020 – which by far exceeded the reduction of 17.8% during the global financial crisis.[127] Income losses reported in surveys amounted to more than 30% on average. This shows the vulnerability of the sector to temporary demand shocks since the former 'prohibition of synchronisation' was abolished by the Hartz reforms. In today's practice, the majority are employed for a fixed term which covers only the assignment to a particular client, or assignments are short enough to allow for a termination during the probationary period. Temporary work agencies benefit by not needing to keep employees on their payroll during stand-by times, though regularly retaining contact details of former employees for further assignments.[128] Other than for employees in general, specific studies about the number of jobs potentially saved by the now possible (*see* subsection § 3.04[B][1]) use of short-time work for temporary agency workers seem to be missing to date. The fact that, in November 2020, the number of temporary workers was still 6.4% below the previous year's figure indicates that they faced a significantly higher risk of being dismissed than regular staff of the user undertakings.[129]

The prohibition of temporary agency work in the meat industry is subject to a constitutional complaint brought by four affected companies in May 2021 and supported by the branch organisations of the temporary agency industry. As has been the case with litigation about the sectoral ban in the construction industry, the complaint primarily relies on a claimed violation of the fundamental right of choosing an occupation under Article 12 (1).[130]

[C] Involuntary Part-timers

[1] Legal Framework: Notion; Equal Treatment; Working Conditions and Social Security Benefits; Unionisation and Collective Agreement's Application

According to Section 2 (1) TzBfG, part-time workers are those whose regular weekly working hours are shorter than those of a comparable full-time worker. Section 4 (1) entitles them to equal treatment *pro rata temporis*. Section 9 TzBfG obliges employers to give priority to their involuntary part-timers when filling a vacancy if the employee has notified their wish for an extension of working hours in writing. In this case, the part-time employee's application for the vacant job can be refused only if another candidate is more suitable for the work in question, the employer has given preference to another part-time employee, or urgent operational reasons do not allow for it. Vice

127. Cf. PWC, *supra* n. 98.
128. Kaufmann, *supra* n. 126.
129. *See* Bundesagentur für Arbeit, *supra* n. 125 at 4.
130. *See* IGZ, Verfassungsbeschwerde gegen sektorales Zeitarbeitsverbot eingelegt, Press release of 12/5/2021 (2021), https://www.ig-zeitarbeit.de/presse/artikel/verfassungsbeschwerde-gegen-sektorales-zeitarbeitsverbot-eingelegt.

versa, Section 9a TzBfG entitles involuntary full-time employees with a seniority of at least 6 months in a company of 45 + workers to a working hours reduction for a period of 1 to 5 years. In this case, a refusal by the employer must be justified by operational reasons or the simultaneous use of this option by other employees, whereby the exact circumstances depend on the size of the company. A new application based on this provision is possible after one year after a justified rejection, or, where the first application has been granted, one year after return to the original working hours.

The legal regime applicable to marginal work ('mini jobs') dates back to 1971, and it has been significantly affected by the Hartz reforms, which were expressly aimed at creating a flexible, attractive type of employment that would bring more individuals into the labour market.[131] Section 8 (1) SGB IV defines marginal employment as work remunerated by a wage which regularly does not exceed the limit of EUR 450 per month (on a second subtype *see infra* at §3.05[B]). If one individual has several low-wage jobs, these are to be added up. It is possible, though, to combine regular (non-marginal) work with a marginal side job without foregoing the applicability of the special regime for the side job. This regime essentially consists in an exemption from income tax and social security contributions, which effectively means that wages are paid 'gross for net'. While the law envisages coverage by pension insurance, it permits the employee to opt out – a possibility which was used by around 80% of marginal part-time workers in the commercial sector and almost 87% in private households in September 2020.[132] Employers, by contrast, need to pay a flat-rate tax and contribution for their marginal workers, amounting to a total of around 31% of the wage (Sections 40a (2) of the Income Tax Act, EStG, 249b SGB V, 32 SGB I: the percentage depends, *i.a.*, on whether the employee has made use of the opt-out from pension insurance). In case of an income between EUR 450 and 1,300 ('midi job'), the employee is subject to full social security coverage, but a reduced rate of contributions is applied compared to earnings above this level (Section 163 (10) SGB VI).

[2] Impact Analysis

Part-time workers' hourly wages are, on average, 20% lower than those of full-time workers, and almost half (47%) of those working less than 20 hours per week belong to the low-wage sector.[133] Marginal part-timers were by far the most likely to see their wages increase as a result of the introduction of a statutory minimum in 2015.[134]

131. Dorothea Voss & Claudia Weinkopf, Niedriglohnfalle Minijobs. WSI Mitteilungen (2012) 5.
132. Rat der Arbeitswelt, Erster Arbeitswelt-Bericht: Vielfältige Ressourcen stäken – Zukunft gestalten. Impulse für eine nachhaltige Arbeitswelt zwischen Pandemie und Wandel (2021), https://www.arbeitswelt-portal.de/fileadmin/user_upload/awb_2021/210518_Arbeitsweltbericht.pdf, 67.
133. Klemt/Lenz, *supra* n. 108 at 170 et seqq.; cf. also Crößmann/Günther, *supra* n. 115.
134. Hans Verbeek et al., Analysepotential von Daten der Amtlichen Wirtschaftsstatistik für die Mindestlohnforschung, Studie im Auftrag der Mindestlohnkommission. Institut für Sozialforschung und Gesellschaftspolitik, Berlin 2020) 61.

The continuous growth in marginal part-time employment (to now more than one-fifth of the German labour force[135]) suggests that tax privileges are a major reason for keeping the volume of work low enough to not cross the threshold of EUR 450. Almost 37% of marginal part-time workers in the commercial sector report earnings just below that threshold. In surveys, every fifth marginal part-time employee expressly refers to the tax law framework as a reason for their current low level of working hours.[136]

Thereby, companies' frequent and growing offer of marginal work is basically a paradox. In theory, marginal employment should be less attractive than other part-time work for the employer, as the aforementioned contribution level of around 31% is significantly higher than the overall rate when regular social security contributions are paid.[137] Various studies assessing the reasons for the 'flexibility gains' regularly invoked by companies as their reason for using marginal work have failed to find any objectifiable advantage, as there is notably no significant difference in terms of administrative effort.[138] A cost advantage only arises from the fact that the combined tax and social security burden of employer and employee for work subject to social security coverage is higher than the employer's burden in case of marginal work. This obviously suggests that the companies participate in the tax privilege by paying marginal workers lower (gross) wages. Time and again, even works councils of larger undertakings have been found to agree to (informal) arrangements stipulating that marginal employees be paid the same *net* wage as other workers for equal work. Apparently, neither workers nor their representatives are likely to invoke this as a violation of Section 4 (1) TzBfG, particularly in view of the lack of social security coverage for work which is artificially kept below the EUR 450 threshold.[139] Individual commenters even doubt the existence of discrimination under labour law in such cases.[140]

Research indicates that the attractiveness of marginal work for companies can lead to part-timers being trapped in low-hours and low-paid employment. In surveys, around a third of mini-jobbers stated having the goal of finding employment subject to social security contributions, and a significant share indicated their employer's opposition as the main barrier.[141] Studies[142] also show that the majority of marginally

135. Markus Grabka & Konstantin Göbler, Der Niedriglohnsektor in Deutschland – Falle oder Sprungbrett für Beschäftigte? (2020), https://www.bertelsmann-stiftung.de/fileadmin/files/BSt/Publikationen/GrauePublikationen/200624_Studie_Niedriglohnsektor_DIW_final.pdf, 26.
136. Gabriele Fischer et al., Stefan, Situation atypisch Beschäftigter und Arbeitszeitwünsche von Teilzeitbeschäftigten, 2015, https://www.iab.de/389/section.aspx/Publikation/k180209301, 50.
137. Voss/Weinkopf, *supra* n. 131 at 6.
138. Fischer et al., *supra* n. 136 at 54.
139. Voss/Weinkopf, *supra* n. 131 at 8 et seqq.
140. Gregor Thüsing, Ungleichbehandlung geringfügig Beschäftigter in Tarifverträgen, in Zeitschrift für Tarifrecht 19/3, 2005) 124.
141. Fischer et al., *supra* n. 136 at 50 et seqq.
142. Kerstin Bruckmeier & Katrin Hohmeyer, Arbeitsaufnahmen von Arbeitslosengeld-II-Empfängern: Nachhaltige Integration bleibt schwierig, IAB-Kurzbericht, No. 2/2018, Institut für Arbeitsmarkt- und Berufsforschung (2018).

employed women attempting to use it as a stepping stone into regular employment do not succeed. Some[143] even find that jobseekers without a mini-job are more likely than those with such a job to realise their wish to enter into regular employment in the medium term. The reasons invoked for these counter-intuitive findings frequently relate to the dominance of low-skilled, auxiliary activities performed by marginal workers, which barely increase the individual's employability. In fact, the privileged treatment of wages below EUR 450 has been found to prompt a sizeable number of skilled workers to work in marginal auxiliary, low-paid activities rather than employment that fits their level of qualification[144] – raising concerns in the light of the aforementioned shortages of skilled labour (*see supra* at §3.02[C]). Based on such findings, the 'Council on the World of Work', commissioned by the Federal Labour Ministry to issue recommendations for reforms, has recently found that the current regime for marginal work has failed to reach its core goals of acting as a stepping stone into employment. The significant side effects, which raise concerns in terms of not only equity and poverty traps, but also macroeconomic inefficiencies and distortion of competition, are thus not considered justified, leading the council to recommend a gradual phasing out of the current regime.[145]

Apart from the special regime for marginal work, other 'institutional factors' contributing to phenomena of involuntary work in the wider sense are the – regionally very different – availability and affordability of childcare and long-term care to alleviate problems of work-life balance. Moreover, despite the significant improvements in terms of rights to use institutional child- and long-term care in the framework of the introduction of a right to childcare (Section 24 SGB VIII), family care remains the more affordable option especially for workers who would expect low wages also in full-time employment.[146] Another issue is a tax law particularity known as spousal splitting. The latter is based on a provision in the Income Tax Act (Section 32 (5) EStG), which essentially provides that spouses be taxed as if both partners had earned precisely 50% of the cumulative income of both spouses in the tax year at issue. This favours couples with one main breadwinner, as the higher income is not subject to the (high) tax rate which would follow from general tax progression rules.[147] The flipside is that it strongly disincentivises an increase of working hours for the 'side earner' (frequently the female partner), as the additional income may be almost completely taxed away if it triggers the applicability of a higher tax rate to the spousal income. The system has been subject to criticism ever since its introduction back in 1958 but has remained essentially unchanged since then.[148]

---

143. Timm Bönke et al., Aufstieg durch Einstieg, Wirkungsanalyse der Arbeitsmarktflexibilisierung seit 2005 (2020), https://diw-econ.de/wp-content/uploads/Aufstieg-durch-Einstieg-in-den-Arbeitsmarkt.pdf.
144. BAuA, Sicherheit und Gesundheit bei der Arbeit 2012, Unfallverhütungsbericht Arbeit (2014), https://www.baua.de/DE/Angebote/Publikationen/Berichte/Suga-2012.pdf?__blob=publicationFile&v=7, 66
145. Rat der Arbeitswelt, *supra* n. 132 at 70 et seqq.
146. *Ibid.*, at 78 et seqq.
147. Jenny Huschke, Und das Thema bewegt sich doch! Gedanken zur Reform der Minijobs, WSI Mitteilungen (2012) 69.
148. Rat der Arbeitswelt, *supra* n. 132 at 73 et seqq.

Finally, involuntary part-time may result from the benefit deduction rules of the ALG II regime (*see supra* at §3.02[B]). As beneficiaries of means-tested benefits are only allowed to keep 20% or less of any income from employment above EUR 100 per month, a long-hour part-time or even full-time job that would not lift the household out of poverty will not increase the household income significantly more than a very low-hours marginal job. Conversely, the strict conditionality requirements demand that beneficiaries accept every job offer, which reportedly forces many to work in low-hour and low-skilled part-time jobs while receiving the benefit – with the mentioned doubts about the effectiveness of such occupations for future employability.[149]

A number of empirical surveys indicate that violations of labour rights are particularly common for part-time workers with low weekly working hours, and most notably mini-jobbers. Between a third and over half of marginally respondents state in surveys that they do not know about their entitlement to continued wage payment during sickness and on public holidays, or do not claim it.[150] Moreover, marginally employed workers are regularly involved only to a very small extent in further training, especially in company qualification measures.[151] Problems of factual undercutting of the minimum wage by longer actual than contractual working hours are particularly relevant for part-time workers. Across all groups, the proportion of employees regularly working unpaid overtime hours has been put to around 10% for full-time, but 38.5% for part-timers, and even more than 50% for marginal part-timers.[152] Various studies raise concerns about employers underpaying recipients of ALG II benefits, benefitting from the fact that those are not entitled to quit their job without facing a sanction, while the wage level barely matters to them (as most of it is deducted from their ALG II benefit anyway).[153]

Due to their exemption from social insurance coverage, marginal workers are entitled neither to unemployment benefit nor to short-time work allowance. This puts them particularly at risk at times of crises. Almost half of mini-jobbers in employment in 2019 were no longer employed in spring 2020.[154] In fact, among all jobs lost between early 2020 and early 2021, mini-jobbers constituted an absolute majority.[155]

149. Irene Dingeldey et al., Geringfügige Beschäftigung im ALG-II-Bezug. WSI Mitteilungen (2012) 33.
150. Fabian Beckmann, Minijobs in Deutschland – Die subjektive Wahrnehmung von Erwerbsarbeit in geringfügigen Beschäftigungsverhältnissen (2019), https://www.springer.com/de/book/9783658236243, 224.
151. Settimio Monteverde, Komplexität, Komplizität und moralischer Stress in der Pflege, in Ethik in der Medizin 4 (2019) 345 et seqq.
152. Alexandra Fedorets et al., Mindestlohn: Nach wie vor erhalten ihn viele anspruchsberechtigte Beschäftigte nicht. DIW Wochenbericht 28/2019, https://www.diw.de/de/diw_01.c.635358.de/publikationen/wochenberichte/2019_28_1/mindestlohn__nach_wie_vor_erhalten_ihn_viele_anspruchsberechtigte_beschaeftigte_nicht.html.
153. Dingeldey et al., *supra* n. 149 at 39.
154. Markus Grabka et al., Beschäftigte in Minijobs sind VerliererInnen der coronabedingten Rezession. DIW Wochenbericht 45 (2020), https://www.diw.de/de/diw_01.c.802083.de/publikationen/wochenberichte/2020_45_1/beschaeftigte_in_minijobs_sind_verliererinnen_der_coronabedingten_rezession.html.
155. Rat der Arbeitswelt, *supra* n. 132 at 64.

§3.05 VUP GROUP 4: CASUAL AND PLATFORM WORKERS

[A] Composition of VUP Group 4

Based on SOEP data, Jaehrling/Kalina[156] find that around 5% of the workforce have been formally employed for on-call work in the period 2011-2017, but almost three times as many have been involved in arrangements requiring their availability on call (*see* next subsection for the contractual setups used). Other studies[157] have pointed out the prevalence of low-skilled assignments and the very frequent combination with marginal work. Reliable data on the incidence of platform work are virtually absent. Various surveys estimate their numbers in Germany to be between 620,000 and 3.5 million, of whom 100,000 to 300,000 accept tasks via a digital platform at least once a month.[158] Regarding the resulting differences between estimates of the share of platform workers among the population (ranging from 0.85 % by Bonin/Rinne 2017 to 10.4 % by Pesole et al. 2018), Schäfer[159] cautions that many studies fail to sufficiently control for factors such as selection bias (e.g., surveys conducted online) and misinterpretation by respondents of the concept of platform work.

[B] Casual Workers: Notion and Relevant Legal Framework

Intermittent work is generally allowed as long as the rules on successive fixed-term contracts are respected. Section 8 (1) SGB III makes work of up to 70 days per year subject to the same exemptions as the EUR 450 mini jobs described *supra* at §3.04[C][1]. On-call work is conditionally permissible in accordance with Section 12 TzBfG. Where the conditions prescribed in that provision are met, the employee can be required to be available on call without on-call time being paid for separately.[160] Notably, under Section 12 (1-3), the agreement must stipulate the length of weekly and daily working hours – otherwise a working time of 20 hours per week and at least three consecutive hours per day is deemed to be agreed. Instead of a specific duration, minimum or maximum working hours can be stipulated.[161] In this case, the weekly working time for which the employee is called to work may only be up to 25% longer than the minimum or 20% shorter than the maximum working time that has been agreed. In addition, the employer must inform the employee of the working hours of a particular day at least four days in advance. These rules are the result of amendments

156. Karen Jaehrling & Thorsten Kalina, Formelle und informelle Formen von Abrufarbeit in Deutschland. Eine Bestandsaufnahme zu Verbreitung und Prekaritätsrisiken. IAQ-Forschung 3 (2019) 10 et seqq.
157. Eva Hank & Jens Stegmaier, Wenn die Arbeit ruft. IAB-Kurzbericht 14 (2018).
158. Jansen, *supra* n. 96 at 104.
159. Holger Schäfer, Crowdwork und Plattformarbeit in Deutschland, IW Kurzbericht No. 79 (2019).
160. Ulrich Preis & Florian Wieg, Weisungsrecht nach Inhalt, Ort und Zeit der Arbeitsleistung in einer mobilen Arbeitswelt – kritische Überlegungen zur Rechtsentwicklung. AuR (2016) 313.
161. *See* Federal Labour Court of 7. 12. 2005 – 5 AZR 535/04.

in 2019, which addressed former abusive practices of companies using on-call workers like full-timers while not guaranteeing more than two working hours per week.[162]

Importantly, collective agreements can deviate both from the necessity to stipulate any standard working time in advance and to inform the worker four days prior to deployment. Once agreed by the social partners for a given sector, such a derogation can be used by contractual reference also by employers not bound by the collective agreement. A number of branch-level agreements use these possibilities, particularly as regards the framework for the predictability of working hours.[163]

[C] Platform Workers: Notion and Relevant Legal Framework

Platform workers' rights depend essentially on whether they are classified as self-employed or employees. In practice, most of them are classified as self-employed, with numerous disputes about the accuracy of this classification,[164] but hardly any case law to this date. On 1 December 2020, the Federal Labour Court[165] ruled for the first time that crowdworkers can basically be classified as employees. The case concerned the performance of on-location micro-tasks such as mystery shopping. The court found that, despite the lack of a formal obligation to work, the platform structure was geared to incentivise users to complete a high number of tasks, and viewed the degree of stability of task completion achieved by the platform equivalent to that of an employer relying on its workers' contractual obligation to work. This view amounts to an important evolution of the well-established understanding of a contractual obligation to work as a *sine qua non* for an employment relationship.[166] Needless to say, this single decision has not resolved legal uncertainties about the classification of the inhomogeneous category of platform workers.[167]

Within days after the judgment, the Federal Labour Ministry announced legislative action to enact clearer rules for the platform economy, and published 10 key points of reform to, *i.a.*, increase platforms' responsibility for their workers, improve social protection, and facilitate transparency, control, and effective implementation.[168]

---

162. Nadine Absenger et al. Arbeitszeiten in Deutschland. Entwicklungstendenzen und Herausforderungen für eine moderne Arbeitszeitpolitik. WSI-Report 19 (2014) 38.
163. cf. Jansen, *supra* n. 96 at 106 et seq.
164. *See*, e.g., Thomas Klebe, Arbeitsrecht 4.0: Faire Bedingungen für Plattformarbeit, in WISO direkt No. 22 (2017).
165. Federal Labour Court of 1 December 2020, 9 AZR 102/20.
166. In line with the text of the law (cf. the lower instance judgments in the same case: Munich Labour Appeals Court, of 4 December 2019 – 8 Sa 146/19; Munich Labour Court of 20 February 2019 – 19 Ca 6915/18).
167. Cf. Werner Eichhorst & Carolin Linckh, Solo-Selbständigkeit in der Plattformökonomie. WISO direkt 28 (2017) 1 et seqq.
168. BMAS, Eckpunkte – Faire Arbeit in der Plattformökonomie (2020), https://www.bmas.de/SharedDocs/Downloads/DE/Pressemitteilungen/2020/eckpunkte-faire-plattformarbeit-kurzfassung.pdf?__blob = publicationFile&v = 1.

[D] Impact Analysis

The described rules on on-call work have been criticised for the lack of any limits for the duration of the stand-by period during which the employee must expect to be called – which may lead to a massive barrier to pursuing other gainful activity especially in case of low working hours and wages below a living income.[169] More generally, observers have noted that in reality forms of on-demand work avoiding the applicability of Section 12 TzBfG have long existed. Zero-hours framework contracts, which formally oblige neither party to offer or accept work, are combined with very short fixed-term employment contracts, at times concluded orally.[170] So far, courts have not reclassified such framework agreements as employment contracts as long as there was no legal obligation to take over any particular shift.[171] It remains to be seen whether the Federal Labour Court's crowdwork judgment will constitute a turning point in this regard. Another possibility of achieving a degree of flexibility akin to on-demand work is the use of working time accounts which stipulate average working hours over a reference period. Jaehrling/Kalina[172] quote court cases illustrating how the use of part-time contracts in connection with working time accounts and regular overtime can enable employers to rely on the factual on-demand availability of their workforce. With a view to digital tools, including apps developed to enable employers to identify and contact workers available for 'voluntary' overtime opportunities as they arise, various commenters[173] have pointed to factual pressure for workers to accept such assignments.

In the literature, there are numerous references to low-wage levels, as well as practices of non-payment of paid sick leave or national holidays by employers' artificial modification of the times when an employee is called to work.[174] One study found these workers' likelihood to belong to the low-wage sector to be 2-3 times higher than the general value of 21% in 2017: 46.2% of all on-call workers, and even two-thirds of those without a contractually agreed aggregate weekly working time.[175]

The heterogeneity and often intermittent nature of platform work make it difficult to capture income developments in a meaningful way.[176] Baethge et al. find that more than half of platform workers use online platforms to earn up to EUR 400 per month,

169. Frank Bayreuther, Die neue Brückenteilzeit und andere Änderungen im TzBfG, in NZA (2018) 1582.
170. *See* Marcus Bieder, Der Nullstundenvertrag – zulässiges Flexibilisierungsinstrument oder Wegbereiter für ein modernes Tagelöhnertum?, in Recht der Arbeit (RdA), No. 6 (2015) 388 et seqq.
171. Cf. the judgments cited by Jaehrling/Kalina, *supra* n. 156 at 7 et seq.
172. *Ibid.*, 8 et seq.
173. E.g., Jan Böwe & Johannes Schulten, Dienstplanung per Smartphone. Magazin Mitbestimmung 12 (2014).
174. Cf. Jansen, *supra* n. 96 at 104 et seqq.
175. *Ibid.*, at 107 et seqq.; Jaehrling/Kalina, *supra* n. 156.
176. *Ibid.*, at 88; Eichhorst/Linckh, *supra* n. 167 at 3.

a third even just up to EUR 200, and only 7% more than EUR 1,500 by performing platform work. The respondents' average working time was six hours per week.[177]

§3.06 CONCLUSIONS

European Union Statistics on Income and Living conditions (EU-SILC) data provide some insight into the in-work poverty risks faced by VUPs in Germany. For the national workforce at large, the German at-risk-of-poverty rates have generally been very close to the EU average.[178]

At a first glance, EU-SILC data as extracted for this project seem to indicate that low-skilled work increases the risk of in-work poverty much less than other factors, and that its importance is even decreasing. These somewhat counter-intuitive results are likely explained by the fact that the very broad definition of low-skilled occupations used for the extracted EU-SILC data (based on ISCO-08 occupational categories 4-9) does not reflect the particularities of the German vocational training system (*see supra* at §3.01[B]). The national labour market generally values (notably apprenticeship-based) skillsets below the tertiary level. By contrast, high poverty risks are evident for those whose education level does not exceed the lower secondary level (twice as high as for those with upper secondary, and thrice higher than for those with tertiary education in virtually all years of measurement[179]). VUP 1 workers performing low-skilled work in a narrower sense therefore constitute a group facing high risks of poverty due to their 'replaceability' for employers. At the same time, as full-time, permanent employees, these workers may be expected to benefit most from ongoing and planned reform initiatives such as the extraordinary increase of the statutory minimum wage (*see supra* at §3.01[B]), the alleviation of pressures on the unemployed to accept any available job (reform of jobseekers' benefits, *see supra* at §3.01[B]), as well as ALMPs focusing on training (*see supra* at §3.02[B]).

In-work poverty rates of the self-employed in Germany are slightly lower than the European average, but still close to thrice as high as for German employees[180] (even more than thrice when focusing solely on the solo self-employed). The probably most crucial factor to consider when comparing in-work poverty rates for VUP Group 2 across countries is that the degree to which the German self-employed are excluded from mandatory social insurance coverage is virtually unparalleled in Europe.[181] This obviously results, ceteris paribus, in higher net incomes for the German self-employed, which reduces in-work poverty risks. The flipside of this is, however, an exceptionally high risk of poverty *out of work*, as the self-employed essentially have nothing but

177. Catherine Bettina Baethge et al., Plattformarbeit in Deutschland: Freie und flexible Arbeit ohne soziale Sicherung, Bertesmann-Stiftung (2019) 22 et seq.
178. *See* Eurostat data at https://ec.europa.eu/eurostat/databrowser/view/ILC_LI04__custom_2207542/default/table?lang=en.
179. *See* Eurostat data at https://ec.europa.eu/eurostat/databrowser/view/ILC_LI07__custom_2208269/default/table?lang=en.
180. *See* Eurostat data at https://ec.europa.eu/eurostat/databrowser/view/ILC_LI04__custom_2207542/default/table?lang=en.
181. *See supra* at §3.03[C].

means-tested benefits (far below the relative poverty line) to rely on when social risks such as sickness, unemployment, disability, or old age materialise. This illustrates that, especially for the self-employed (who are subject to highly diverging levels of social protection across countries[182]), in-work poverty can effectively not be viewed in isolation when the policy goal is one of reducing poverty overall. This is why reform plans such as the expansion of social security coverage for the self-employed (*see supra* at §3.03[C]) can be expected to have a considerable poverty-alleviating potential, even though in-work poverty may even rise as a result. An important side effect of mandatory coverage would be to reduce risks of a downward spiral caused by self-exploitative offers of some self-employed, which do not allow for putting aside even the bare minimum in savings to avoid poverty over the life cycle.

As for VUP Group 3, no separate data exist for temporary agency workers, but fixed-term employees have a three times higher poverty risk than permanent employees, which is also somewhat higher than on average for fixed-term workers in the EU.[183] By contrast, part-time workers' at-risk-of-poverty rates are 'only' twice as high as those of full-timers, and thereby somewhat lower than the respective EU average.[184] For all three subgroups of the VUP 3 category, it seems essential to point out that in-work poverty rates are only reflective of the worker's current situation in the year of measurement, without considering the potentially significant long-term consequences of low-hour work or interrupted careers for avoiding poverty over the life cycle. No specific data are available for VUP 4 workers, for whom these concerns are arguably even more pronounced.

The general development of poverty as measured by EU-SILC[185] indicates that the German in-work poverty rates have fallen more substantially than on average in the EU over the years of strong economic growth prior to 2020, but were subject to an unusually pronounced increase in the context of the COVID-19 crisis. To a certain degree, this may be seen as emblematic for a country where social insurance is characterised by various exemptions (e.g., for mini-jobbers and the self-employed) and particularly unambitious in respect of jobseekers' benefits (which are dominated by the means-tested, tax-funded ALG II scheme as described *supra* at §3.02[B]). Arguably, this generally leads to higher net wages (and thus lower poverty risks) in good times, while a considerable share of the working population is barely protected from falling below the poverty line as soon as crisis hits.

---

182. Cf. Christina Hiessl, Germany: The self-sufficient entrepreneur trope and the pandemic gnawing away at it, in International Journal of Comparative Labour Law and Industrial Relations (2022, forthcoming).
183. *See* Eurostat data at https://ec.europa.eu/eurostat/databrowser/view/ilc_iw05/default/table?lang=en.
184. *See* Eurostat data at https://ec.europa.eu/eurostat/databrowser/view/tessi250/default/table?lang=en. These differences may be related to the fact that part-time work is very widespread in Germany (*see supra* at §3.04[C][2]), so that this group does not constitute a marginalised minority among the workforce. The German fixed-term work rate in turn is lower than the EU average.
185. *See* Eurostat data as referenced in Chapter 1.

CHAPTER 4

In-Work Poverty in Italy*

Ester Villa, Giulia Marchi & Nicola De Luigi

This chapter focuses on in-work poverty in Italy. After introducing the most important elements in the Italian production and regulatory system having an influence on in-work poverty, the focus turns to a targeted analysis of the four Vulnerable and Under-Represented Person (VUP) groups. First, the composition and the direct measures that affect in-work poverty are considered for each VUP group. The measures that indirectly influence in-work poverty of the four VUPs by type of household are then analysed. Finally, some concluding remarks are provided on the strengths and weaknesses of national legislation and on how it affects the different VUP groups.

§4.01 INTRODUCTION

Comparative political economy literature has often described Italy as the 'sick man' of Europe.[1] In terms of economic and employment performance, it lags behind the Nordic and Continental countries.[2] Furthermore, in recent decades, the gap with other Mediterranean countries, like Spain, has widened when considering specific indicators, such as economic growth or the female employment rate.[3] Italian capitalism has experienced difficulties in adapting to the structural changes triggered by the transition

* The chapter is the outcome of a joint discussion between the authors. However, the author of §4.01 and §4.06 is Nicola De Luigi; the author of §4.02, §4.03, and §4.07 is Ester Villa; the author of §4.04 and §4.05 is Giulia Marchi.
1. Andrea Mammone & Giuseppe A. Veltri, *Italy today: the sick man of Europe* (Routledge 2010).
2. OECD, *Strengthening Active Labour Market Policies in Italy, Connecting People with Jobs* (OECD Publishing 2019).
3. Margarita León & Emmanuele Pavolini, *'Social investment' or back to 'familism': the impact of the economic crisis on family and care policies in Italy and Spain*, South European Society and Politics, 19:3, 353-369 (2019).

from a labour-intensive to a knowledge-intensive economy.[4] Accordingly, compared to other advanced economies, the historical distortions that characterise its Welfare State are far from being fixed, and new social risks – including in-work poverty – continue to be poorly covered.[5] The 2008 economic and financial crisis had a profound effect on the country, highlighting and exacerbating its structural weaknesses.

Some factors have a particular influence on in-work poverty, contributing to the development of economic uncertainties among workers and their household members.

First, the structure of the production system is often described as molecular.[6] Indeed, in 2018, micro enterprises (3-9 employees) and small enterprises (10-49 employees) accounted for, respectively, 79.5% and 18.2% of the total production units, while medium enterprises (50-249 employees) and large enterprises (more than 250 employees) covered just 2.3% of the total.[7] Accordingly, more than 55% of the labour force was employed in micro and small enterprises. This specific structure of the production system has delayed the transition to a knowledge-based economy and the development of a high-tech sector.[8] This has had major consequences on the employment rate and the quality of jobs: since the 1990s, the Italian labour market has produced an abundance of precarious, low-skilled, and poorly paid jobs.[9]

Second, the Welfare State has historically been characterised by a functional distortion involving different levels of social risk coverage, with the bulk of resources being focused on the old-age risk.[10] This has created a hypertrophic pension sector with a lack of (or fragmented) protection of other social risks, particularly new ones. More specifically, although poverty has always been a widespread risk, it has never been tackled with a coherent strategy and with ad hoc instruments.[11] However, in 2018, a minimum income guarantee was introduced for the first time in Italy – the Inclusion Income (*Reddito di Inclusione* – REI) – later replaced, in turn, by a new measure, which is more generous in terms of cash benefits, known as Citizenship Income (*Reddito di Cittadinanza* – RdC). Accordingly, the redistribution capacity of the Italian Welfare State has increased in recent years.[12]

Third, in relation to households and family policies, Italy has traditionally followed a male-breadwinner family model, with men going out to work and women

---

4. Silja Häusermann, *The multidimensional politics of social investment in conservative welfare regimes: family policy reform between social transfers and social investment*, Journal of European Public Policy, 25:6, 862-877 (2018).
5. Valeria Fargion & Elisabetta Gualmini, Tra l'incudine e il Martello. Regioni e nuovi rischi sociali in tempo di crisi (Il Mulino 2013).
6. Yuri Kazepov & Costanzo Ranci, *Is every country fit for social investment? Italy as an adverse case*, Journal of European Social Policy, 27, 90–104 (2017).
7. Istat, *Censimento permanente delle imprese 2019: i primi risultati*, https://www.istat.it/it/files//2020/02/Report-primi-risultati-censimento-imprese.pdfIstat (2019).
8. Silja Häusermann, *The multidimensional politics*, *supra* n. 4.
9. Yuri Kazepov & Costanzo Ranci, *Is every country fit*, *supra* n. 6.
10. Maurizio Ferrera, *Il Modello Sud-Europeo di Welfare State*, Rivista Italiana di Scienza Politica 1, 67-101 (1996).
11. Maurizio Ferrera, *Welfare state reform in Southern Europe fighting poverty and social exclusion in Italy, Spain, Portugal and Greece* (Routledge 2005).
12. Giovanni B. Sgritta, *Politiche e misure della povertà: il reddito di cittadinanza*, Politiche Sociali, 1, 39 (2020).

staying at home to look after the children and other dependent relatives.[13] Accordingly, family policies have followed a familistic approach, striving to avoid removing from families (particularly, women) their care responsibilities. Therefore, Italy is characterised by an unsupported family-based structure.[14] For this reason, the dual-earner model, with both parents working full-time, is uncommon, even in the aftermath of the economic crisis.

Regarding the labour market, comparative literature has highlighted that Italy suffers from two interlinked shortcomings: a historically low employment rate - by comparative standards - in conjunction with a high unemployment rate, and the presence of a strong occupational divide, the insider/outsider gap.[15]

Turning our focus to the data on employment, the economic and financial crisis struck Italy profoundly, more so than other European countries. Between 2008 and 2013, the employment rate (20-64 years old) progressively decreased (dropping from 62.9% to 59.7%) and only started to recover from 2014.[16] However, this upturn in the employment rate was not followed by an increase in occupational intensity, namely the total volume of working hours. Indeed, this value still remains lower than the pre-crisis period. When considering the unemployment rate (6.1% in 2007, increasing to 9.2% by 2019), the picture is far from optimistic, with the rate still remaining well above the EU-27 average (7.1%).

These employment data should be analysed in view of the strong segmentation of the Italian labour market, with insiders, on one side, and outsiders, on the other. The former are employed on a full-time and permanent basis, while the latter include unemployed persons and atypical workers.[17] The risk of becoming an outsider in the aftermath of the economic crisis has not diminished, while the pandemic crisis has exacerbated the situation for some outsider groups.

The data discussed should also be considered in view of the recent evolution of both employment legislation and labour market policies.

In relation to its employment legislation, since the 1990s, like most advanced economies, Italy has undertaken a process of deregulating its labour market with a view to increasing its flexibility. However, up until the mid-2010s, this flexibility was only marginally present.[18] Therefore, it did not cover the insiders, but only the newcomers.

The situation changed in the aftermath of the economic and financial crisis. In 2012, the so-called Fornero Reform modified Article 18 of the Workers Statute (Italian Law no. 300/1970), making it less strict. For the first time, the rights of insiders, in

---

13. Chiara Saraceno, *The ambivalent familism of the Italian welfare state*, Social Politics: International Studies in Gender, State & Society, 1, 60-82 (1994).
14. Wolfgang Keck & Chiara Saraceno, *The impact of different social-policy frameworks on social inequalities among women in the European Union. The labour-market participation of mothers*, Social Politics - International Studies in Gender, State & Society, 20:3, 297-328 (2013).
15. Patrik Vesan, *La politica del lavoro*, in *Le politiche Sociali* (Maurizio Ferrera ed., Il Mulino 2019).
16. Eurostat data.
17. David Rueda, *Social democracy inside out: partisanship and labour market policy in industrialized democracies* (Oxford University Press, 2007).
18. Patrik Vesan, *La politica del lavoro, supra* n. 15.

terms of job protection, were included. The Fornero Reform also attempted to restrict the use of atypical employment contracts in order to reduce the amount of precarious jobs. Nevertheless, the real change occurred in the mid-2010s when the Jobs Act was approved in 2014. This Act reduces the rigidity of insiders' employment contracts by introducing new regulations on unlawful dismissals for employees hired after 7 March 2015 (known as '*contratto a tutele crescenti*').[19] The repercussions of this change were extensive, as the flexibility – which was previously marginal – now directly covered labour market insiders. Simultaneously, flexibility at the margins continued to be promoted, with fixed-term contracts being further liberalised. One countertrend was the recognition of employee protections also for hetero-organised collaborations, for which they had previously been excluded.

A partial turnaround occurred in 2018. The coalition government approved the 'Dignity Decree' (*Decreto Dignità*), which involved re-regulating the labour market, making it more difficult for employers to use fixed-term contracts, and increasing the compensation for unlawful dismissals for those hired from 7 March 2015 onwards. During those years, the Constitutional Court ruled on the latter regulation, strengthening the protection applied to circumstances of unfair dismissal.[20]

Although in-work poverty and low-wage work are different concepts, low wages can increase the risk of being poor while in work. Italian legislation does not include any statutory provision establishing a minimum wage, and collective agreements only apply to employers and employees who are members of the signatory trade unions. However, according to established case law, the concept of fair remuneration is determined with reference to the minimum wage rates established by national collective agreements signed by the most representative trade unions in the sector. Although these sector-based minimum wages are relatively high in comparison to the average wage,[21] many issues arise as to their effective functioning, enforcement, and compliance with contractual minimum wages. In addition, this sector-based minimum wage only covers employees and hetero-organised workers.

The COVID-19 pandemic had an immediate and disruptive effect on living and working conditions in Italy and across Europe, exacerbating inequality and poverty, particularly among those social groups which were already experiencing severe hardship. The Italian government introduced many extraordinary – albeit temporary – measures to tackle the economic and social consequences of the pandemic and to support workers and employers. The most important were those aimed at protecting employment levels.[22] From March 2020, individual dismissals and collective redundancies for economic reasons were temporarily suspended. This suspension was

19. More in detail, it covers employees working in companies whose workforce exceeds 15 employees in the same business unit or municipality or 60 people in total; employees on fixed-term contracts converted into open-ended employment contracts after 7 March 2015; and employees on apprenticeship contracts converted into open-ended contracts after 7 March 2015.
20. *See* further §4.02, [B][1].
21. Andrea Garnero, *The dog that barks doesn't bite: coverage and compliance of sectoral minimum wages in Italy*, IZA Discussion Papers, No. 10511 (2017).
22. Dismissal in violation of these rules was considered null. These measures, however, are problematic with regard to the principle of freedom of private economic initiative (Art. 41

gradually extended to 30 June 2021, due to the ongoing pandemic crisis.[23] The block on dismissals was accompanied by the payment of income support to employees whose employment had been suspended. In particular, a wage guarantee fund was set up to respond to the COVID-19 crisis, with simplified rules.[24] Although this protection was strong, the remuneration paid during the suspension period was still lower than it had been before, as the wage guarantee fund only paid a portion of the salary. In addition, employees could also take time off from work to look after their children while educational and teaching services were suspended, and to care for disabled people requiring assistance due to the temporary closure of their facilities.

Self-employed workers were probably the most affected by the COVID-19 pandemic crisis and the least protected against its socio-economic consequences.[25] For these workers, who were not receiving a wage or pension, income-support allowances were introduced.[26]

Regarding labour market policies, until the 2010s, the labour market deregulation was not associated with an increase in social security, in terms of both passive benefits and active measures. In other words, Italian 'flexicurity' was more biased towards flexibility.[27]

Historically, Italian unemployment benefits have not been very generous and their eligibility requirements, in terms of contributions and seniority, are strict.[28] This means that for many workers - mostly outsiders - unemployment risks were not covered. However, in the 2010s, during and in the immediate aftermath of the economic crisis, the picture began to change: the cited Fornero Reform introduced a new unemployment benefit, the ASPI (*Assicurazione sociale per l'impiego*), which was more generous but maintained the contribution and seniority requirements, making it difficult to access for a large number of employees, particularly atypical workers. ASPI was then replaced by a new form of unemployment insurance known as NASPI (*Nuova assicurazione sociale per l'impiego*), which substantially relaxed the eligibility criteria. NASPI has become a quasi-universal benefit covering almost all employees, including atypical ones. A new unemployment benefit was also introduced for non-subordinate

Const.). *See* Franco Scarpelli, *Blocco dei licenziamenti e solidarietà sociale*, Rivista italiana di diritto del lavoro, I, 313 (2020); Carlo Zoli, *La tutela dell'occupazione nell'emergenza epidemiologica fra garantismo e condizionalità*, Labor, 439 (2020).

23. The prohibition on dismissal was introduced for a period of 60 days with Art. 46, law decree No. 18, 17 March 2020, converted in law No. 27/2020. The prohibition was extended to five months by way of Art. 80, law decree No. 34, 19 May 2020. It was subsequently extended by way of Art. 14, law decree No. 104 of 14 August 2020, followed by Art. 12, law decree No. 137/2020, and, lastly, law No. 178 of 30 December 2020.
24. Claudia Carchio, *Gli ammortizzatori sociali alla prova dell'emergenza Covid-19: un'ennesima conferma*, Il lavoro nella giurisprudenza, 5, 454 (2020).
25. The self-employed are usually excluded from wage supplementation schemes and experience a lack of coverage in terms of social security.
26. It applied to self-employed workers, namely professionals not enrolled in official registers, para-subordinate workers enrolled in the INPS (national institute of social security) separate pension scheme, artisans and workers in the entertainment industry.
27. Fabio Berton, Matteo Richiardi & Stefano Sacchi, *Flexinsecurity. Perchè in Italia la flessibilità diventa precarietà* (Il Mulino 2009).
28. Stefano Sacchi & Patrick Vesan, *Le politiche del lavoro* (Il Mulino 2011).

workers (known as Dis-coll). In addition, since 2019, resources have been invested to strengthen public job centres and, following the approval of the National Recovery and Resilience Plan, measures to protect the unemployed have been bolstered.[29]

The data considered in the previous pages can assist us in understanding why the in-work poverty rate in Italy is well above the EU-27 average (9.4%) and is one of the highest among the European Union (EU) Member States. Somewhat unexpectedly, male workers are more likely to be at risk of poverty than female workers (respectively 13.4% vs. 10.6% in 2017). However, these data are not surprising when considering the structure of both the labour market and Italian households. Indeed, the female employment rate is very low by comparative standards, and the dual-earner family model is quite scarce. When employed, women tend to be the second-earners, topping up men's income. In Southern Italy, in particular, the male, single-earner and breadwinner family model is still predominant.

This household structure affects the in-work poverty risk for individuals from various perspectives. First, workers aged 18-24 are slightly better off than those aged 25-54 (respectively, 12.3% and 12.8% in 2017), as a relatively high percentage of younger workers continue to live with their parents. Second, work intensity plays a significant role: in-work poverty risks are much higher in households with medium or low work intensity than those with very high or high work intensity. Finally, there appears to be a strong association between in-work poverty, on one hand, and the number of earners/presence of children, on the other. In-work poverty is higher among single parent and 'traditional breadwinner' families. Once again, these data are very indicative: one condition for lowering the in-work poverty risk in households with children appears to be the presence of two primary earners, thus involving a shift from the traditional male-breadwinner family model to the dual-earner or modern multi-earner model. However, this shift seems a long way off.

§4.02 VUP GROUP 1: LOW OR UNSKILLED STANDARD EMPLOYMENT

[A] Poor Sectors, Composition, and In-Work Poverty Risk

To analyse VUP Group 1, the poor sectors had to be identified: according to Eurostat, in Italy, these are 'administrative and support service activities', 'other service activities', 'accommodation and food service activities' and, finally, 'real estate activities'.[30]

Based upon the general data, according to European Union Statistics on Income and Living Conditions (EU-SILC), in 2018 10.4% of workers belonged to this specific VUP group. This proportion increased over time, confirming that the labour market is experiencing something of a downward trend, with the bulk of new jobs being positioned in the low-skilled/poor sectors.

29. 'Piano Nazionale di Ripresa e Resilienza. Italia Domani'. For further information, https://italiadomani.gov.it/en/home.html.
30. Eurostat, earn_ses_pub1n, extraction: 01.03.2021.

Shifting the focus to the individual variables, the probability of members of this group being at risk of poverty, compared to employees with permanent contracts in standard sectors, is much higher (14.3% vs. 7.5% in 2018). It should also be noted that the in-work poverty phenomenon for VUP Group 1 deteriorated over time: not only did it increase compared to 2007 (12.2%) but when a positive trend occurred in 2013 – when the value slightly decreased (11.4%) – this was then reversed.

The in-work poverty risk has a particular impact on the 18-34 and 34-49 age groups (respectively, 14.2% and 15.2% in 2018). For these age groups, the likelihood of being at risk of poverty decreased between 2007 and 2013, but it increased again in the late 2010s. Conversely, for those aged over 50, the risk remained rather constant, albeit slighting declining over time (from 13.7% in 2007 to 13% in 2018).

When considering the gender variable, *women* are more likely than men to be at risk of in-work poverty (15.2% vs. 13.3%). This risk has constantly increased since 2007. In other words, women belonging to VUP Group 1 were strongly affected by the economic and financial crisis, and their situation did not improve once the economy recovered in the mid-2010s. Once again, the data are not surprising when considering that women are generally paid less than men and that their access to social insurance benefits is more restricted.

Nationality appears to be associated with a much higher possibility of being poor while in work. Almost 32.2% of non-Italian low-skilled employees in poor sectors are at risk of in-work poverty (vs. 9.3% of those with Italian citizenship). Interestingly, between 2013 and 2018, the risk worsened for both natives and migrants, but to a very different extent: for Italians, the risk increased by just 1 percentage point (pp), while for non-Italians, it grew by 10.1 pp.

In terms of *education* levels, it is clear that being highly qualified does not automatically protect workers from the risk of in-work poverty. In VUP Group 1, in 2018, the risk of in-work poverty was higher among those with a low education level (18.7%) than those with medium and higher levels (respectively, 11.5% and 12.1%); however, the latter two values remain quite high. Furthermore, the risks increased sharply for the highly-educated from 2007 to 2018 (from 2.3% to 12.1%). These data confirm the scarce amount of economic returns gained from education in Italy, leading to an increasing share of over-qualified, highly skilled employees working in poor sectors.

In shifting the focus to *household variables*, it is interesting to note that, in 2018, the risk of in-work poverty was higher for single-member households (13.8%) than for those with two or more members (respectively, 5.2% and 7.6%). Furthermore, while, for the latter, the risk decreased between 2013 and 2018, for single-member households, it increased.

The risk of in-work poverty consistently appears to be much higher in single-earner families (23.3%) than in dual-earner households (5.1%). The data once again confirms that the old-fashioned male-breadwinner family model exacerbates in-work poverty risks, particularly for employees in low-skilled occupations and poor sectors. However, it should be noted that for both single and dual-earner households, the risk increased over time, thus revealing a general deterioration of the economic conditions of VUP Group 1 households.

Finally, the data demonstrates that the risk of in-work poverty is associated with the number of children in the household. Before the crisis, the risk was extremely high (27%) for households with more than one child. In 2013, the situation substantially improved, with the risk decreasing by almost 15 pp. However, the data revealed a further decline in 2018. At the end of the 2010s, both households with one child and those with more than one child experienced much higher risks than those with no children (respectively, 18.3%, 20.2% vs. 11.8%). These values suggest that family policy measures undertaken by Italian governments do not seem to be effective in lowering the levels of in-work poverty.

[B] Relevant Legal Framework

In recent years, many legislative reforms affecting those in VUP Group 1 have compounded their precariousness and deteriorated their working conditions, such as regulations on dismissals, active policies, and unemployment benefits. In addition, the wage-setting mechanism is a problematic issue, particularly for employees of VUP Group 1.

[1] Dismissals

Italian Legislative Decree no. 23 of 4 March 2015 introduced a *new system of penalties for unlawful dismissal for those hired from 7 March 2015,*[31] making permanent employment contracts more flexible in terms of the costs of dismissal, thus weakening the protection against unfair dismissals. This decree *reduced the scope for reinstatement in circumstances of unfair dismissal* and *increased the cases in which the employee is only entitled to monetary compensation.*

Reinstatement[32] applies only to discriminatory and invalid dismissals, or dismissals that are considered ineffective in the absence of written notification. In these cases, the employee also receives compensation in an amount equal to the sum of wages lost from the day of dismissal to the day of reinstatement.[33] Reinstatement also applies to disciplinary dismissals that are found to be illegal due to the lack of any justified subjective reason or just cause *if the circumstances do not exist*. In this case, however, the amount of compensation is equal to the wages lost from the day of dismissal to that of actual reinstatement, but they may not be higher than the 12-month standard wage.

31. Employees hired before 7 March 2015, are protected by Art. 18, law No. 300/1970 (so-called Workers' Statute), as amended in 2012, and Art. 8, law No. 604/1966. The latter discipline applies only to employees in firms with less than 15 employees in the productive unit or less than 60 employees at national level.
32. As an alternative to reinstatement, the employee can opt for substitution benefit equivalent to 15 months' worth of standard wage.
33. The compensation must not be lower than 5 months' worth of standard wage.

In other cases of disciplinary and economic dismissals without justified reason,[34] *under the original formulation, only monetary compensation was provided, increasing in accordance with seniority*: the amount of compensation was equal to 2 months' wages per year of service, ranging from a minimum of 4 to a maximum of 24 months (Article 3). This regulation was amended by the '*Decreto Dignità*' (Italian Law no. 96/2018), representing a countertrend compared to other recent reforms. Indeed, it enhanced the compensation for unlawful dismissal, providing that the monetary compensation should not be less than 6 months' wages or more than 36 months' wages.

The Constitutional Court ruled on this regulation in its judgements no. 194/2018 and no. 150/2020. It addressed the issue of the constitutionality of this system, in which the compensation is determined solely based on the dismissed employee's length of service. The court deemed unconstitutional 'the phrase that automatically tied the amount of compensation to the length of service of the dismissed employee'. The court ruled that in treating different situations identically, this inflexible criterion was unreasonable and violated the principle of equality: the detriment caused in the different circumstances by unfair dismissal depends upon a variety of factors. Thus, while length of service is certainly relevant, it is just one of many elements. In conclusion, the contested Article 3(1) was considered unconstitutional with regard only to the phrase 'in an amount equal to two months' wages [...] for each year of service'.[35] As a result, the compensation for unjustified dismissals (Article 3) varies from a minimum of 6 to a maximum of 36 months of remuneration.[36] When determining the amount of compensation, *the courts will primarily take account of the length of service, along with other criteria*, which may be inferred on a systematic basis from the development of legislation imposing limits on dismissals, such as *number of employees, scale of business activity, conduct and circumstances of the parties.*[37]

[2] ***Remuneration***

Regarding wage-setting mechanisms, there are many significant issues, such as wage indexation mechanisms, decentralised collective bargaining, and pirate collective

34. The same rule applies in case of violation of criteria for selecting employees to be dismissed in the case of collective dismissals, and violation of procedural rules in collective dismissals. For formal or procedural violations in the case of individual dismissals, compensation was equal to 1 monthly wage per year of service, ranging, however, between 2 and 12 months (Art. 4).
35. For the same reasons, the court contested Art. 4 with regard to the phrase 'in an amount equal to one monthly salary [...] for each year of service'.
36. Compensation for violation of formal and procedural rules (Art. 4) varies from a minimum of 2 to a maximum of 12 months' worth of remuneration.
37. For a comment on these judgments, *see* Carlo Cester, *Il Jobs Act sotto la scure della Corte costituzionale: tutto da rifare?*, Il lavoro nella giurisprudenza, 163 (2019); Arturo Maresca, *Licenziamento ingiustificato e indennizzo del lavoratore dopo la sentenza della Corte costituzionale n. 194/2018 (alla ricerca della norma che non c'è)*, Diritto delle relazioni industriali, 228-243 (2019); Maria Teresa Carinci, *La Corte costituzionale n. 194/2018 ridisegna le tutele economiche per il licenziamento individuale ingiustificato nel 'Jobs Act', e oltre*, WP C.S.D.L.E. 'Massimo D'Antona'. IT, No. 378 (2018).

agreements.[38] However, for VUP Group 1, the latter is currently the most problematic issue.

As previously described, Italian legislation does not include any statutory provision establishing a minimum wage. When an employee claims before a court that his/her wage does not satisfy the principle of fairness and adequacy envisaged by Article 36 of the Constitution,[39] the court determines the wage level according to Article 2099 of the Italian Civil Code (c.c.). Courts usually refer to the 'basic wages' (*minimi tabellari*)[40] established in national industrial collective agreements. Thus, it is be an industry and contractual – as well as judicial – national minimum wage.

The number of collective agreements has dramatically increased in recent years.[41] This phenomenon and the proliferation of a variety of competing industry collective agreements – which can be applied by the employer regardless of the activity performed – may lead to sharp reductions in wages and deteriorations of working conditions.

First, the multiplicity of collective agreements applicable to a single category – or with partially overlapping scope of application – encourages employers to apply the agreement that envisages the lowest cost of labour.

Second, with the view to deviating from the provisions and protections included in collective agreements stipulated by the most representative social partners in the industry, many firms seek collective agreements negotiated outside the boundaries of their main economic activity, simply to save on labour costs. This practice drives something of a downward trend in collective negotiated minimum wages as, on average, employee salaries covered by pirate collective agreements are estimated to be 15% lower than those covered by other collective agreements.[42]

---

38. There are no set criteria used to define a collective agreement as 'pirate'. Indeed, it is not possible to regard an agreement as such simply because it provides for lower minimum rates than those contained in the collective agreement entered into by the comparatively most representative trade unions. Between the pirate contract and the leader contract, there is a wide 'middle ground' (*see* Marzo Peruzzi, *Viaggio nella 'terra di mezzo', tra contratti leader e pirata*, Lavoro e diritto, 211 (2020). According to some interpretations, pirate contracts are entered into by subjects working in 'collusion' with the employer organisation. *See* Giulio Centamore G., *Contratti collettivi o diritto del lavoro «pirata»?*, Variazioni su temi di diritto del lavoro, 479 (2018); Andrea Lassandari, *Pluralità di contratti collettivi nazionali per la medesima categoria*, Lavoro e diritto, 261-299 (1997).
39. Article 36 of Constitution establishes that workers have the right to fair wages, in accordance with the quality and quantity of their work. Adequate wages shall in any case be guaranteed, such as to ensure them and their families a free and dignified existence.
40. Seniority, special allowances and incentives are excluded. The basic wage rates may be adjusted downwards for apprentices.
41. On this issue, *see* Giulio Centamore, *I minimi retributivi del CCNL confederale Vigilanza privata, sezione Servizi fiduciari, violano l'Art. 36 Cost.: un caso singolare di dumping contrattuale e una sentenza controversa del Tribunale di Torino*, Diritto delle relazioni industriali, 850 (2020); Silvia Ciucciovino, *Fisiologia e patologia del pluralismo contrattuale tra categoria sindacale e perimetri settoriali*, Lavoro e diritto, 185-210 (2020).
42. Daria Vigani & Carlo Lucifora, *Losing control? The effects of pirate collective agreements on wages*, in http://conference.iza.org/conference_files/LaborMarketInstitutions_2019/vigani_d23851.pdf (2019). On this issue, *see* Supreme Court, 20 February 2019, n. 4951. For a comment on this ruling, *see* Lucio Imberti, *Trattamento economico minimo (del socio lavoratore) e c.c.n.l. parametro: chi individua la categoria e il parametro della stessa?*, Labor, 4 (2019).

However, it should be noted that *collective agreements signed by historical unions also sometimes establish an unfair wage level.* As employers can technically apply an industry collective agreement regardless of the activity performed, they sometimes 'choose' the most convenient one, thus leading to downward competition between such agreements.[43] For this reason, employee wages are often inadequate.

There have been many rulings on this issue. In such cases, although employees were entitled to wages established in collective agreements stipulated by the comparatively most representative trade-unions' and employers' associations – in compliance with Article 7, paragraph 4 of Italian Decree Law no. 248 of 2007 on cooperatives' working members – judges considered the remuneration to be in conflict with Article 36 of the Constitution. Indeed, employee wages fell drastically over the years, in some cases by more than 30%, following the takeover of the employer organisation. This wage was considered insufficient to live a dignified existence or to make ends meet.[44] In one case, the court asserted that the remuneration was in conflict with Article 36 of the Constitution as it was lower than the absolute poverty threshold calculated by Istat (the Italian institute of statistics). Indeed, if a wage in line with the absolute poverty threshold was considered adequate, fair remuneration would be 'flattened' to the minimum level.[45]

When the remuneration envisaged by the national collective agreement stipulated by the comparatively most representative trade unions is considered to be in conflict with Article 36 of the Constitution – as in these rulings – the judge then faces the problem of re-determining the remuneration in accordance with the principles of the Constitution. In this respect, many authors highlight the risk of falling into a sort of 'judicial subjectivism'.[46]

This issue is particularly widespread in certain sectors, particularly those most affected by decentralisation and outsourcing, such as cooperatives, logistics, retail, tourism, catering, multi-service, and cleaning. Indeed, in such labour-intensive sectors, in which production does not require many tangible assets or a high level of competence or specific know-how to perform the contract, companies often outsource activities that are not strictly connected to their core business with the aim of reducing labour costs, with a high turnover of entrepreneurs.[47]

---

43. Andrea Lassandari, *Oltre la 'grande dicotomia'? La povertà tra subordinazione e autonomia*, Lavoro e diritto, 82-102 (2019).
44. Court of Milan, 30 June 2016, No. 1977, confirmed by the Milan Court of Appeal, 28 December 2017, n. 1885, in *DeJure*. For a similar case, *see* Court of Turin, 9 August 2019, No. 1128. *See* Giulio Centamore, *Contratti collettivi «qualificati» e trattamento economico dei soci lavoratori di cooperativa: cronaca e implicazioni di una vicenda singolare*, Labor, 237 (2017); Lucio Imberti, *Art. 36 Costituzione: in assenza di interventi legislativi chi è l'autorità salariale?*, in Lavoro diritti europa (2019).
45. Stefano Bellomo, *Determinazione giudiziale della retribuzione e individuazione del contratto collettivo-parametro tra Art. 36 Cost. e normativa speciale applicabile ai soci lavoratori di cooperative*, Rivista italiana di diritto del lavoro, II, 28-38 (2020).
46. Lucio Imberti, *Art. 36 Costituzione, supra* n. 44.
47. Roberto Riverso, *Cooperative spurie ed appalti: nell'inferno del lavoro illegale*, in Questione giustizia online (2019). The weakness of such workers is due to the instability of employment in contractor companies, which operate in a highly competitive market and whose performances are strongly influenced by the decisions of the clients. *See* David Weil, *The fissured workplace.*

[3] *Active Labour Market Policies, Training, and Unemployment Benefits*

Unemployed persons must declare their immediate availability for work in order to access job centre services. After making this declaration, they must then enter into a 'personalised service agreement' with the job centre, in which they undertake to participate in training, qualification, and professional retraining initiatives to promote their entry into the labour market. However, due to the lack of investments made and the small number of job centre operators, the agreement has thus far not lived up to its promise of personalising initiatives for the unemployed. The situation began to change in 2019, when an extraordinary plan to bolster job centres was approved. New resources have also been invested in more recent years. Following the approval of the National Recovery and Resilience Plan, a series of measures were approved to provide a more personal service to unemployed individuals seeking employment, including a programme known as the 'Workers Employability Guarantee' (GOL). For the first time, this is a reform programme having some credibility, also thanks to the significant resources made available by the EU.

When turning our attention to unemployment benefits, it should be noted that they also present critical issues.

If employees meet the statutory requirements, they are entitled to NASPI – new social insurance provision for employment (*Nuova assicurazione sociale per l'impiego*) – consisting of an amount of approximately 75% of the monthly average wage over the last 4 years. After 3 months, the benefit amount decreases by 3% per month (known as '*decalage*'). If the circumstance of unemployment occurred from 1 January 2022, the rule of *decalage* becomes more favourable: indeed, the amount of the benefit decreases by 3% per month only after 6 months, while the *decalage* commences from the eighth month for NASPI beneficiaries aged over 55.

However, this unemployment benefit is conditional: the employee must actively be seeking a job and must accept *a suitable job offer*. The notion of suitable job offer is defined by law.[48] From the economic perspective, it must pay a wage that is at least 20% higher than the unemployment benefit received; from the professional perspective, the notion of 'suitable job offer' varies, depending on whether the person has been unemployed for less than 6 months, for between 6 and 12 months, or for more than 12 months. After 12 months, the suitable job offer that must be accepted by employees may even differ greatly from their previous jobs and does not have to be linked to their skills. Finally, from the geographical perspective, in the first 12 months, unemployed persons must accept offers of jobs within 50 km from their home, while, after 12 months, offers of jobs up to 80 km from their home are considered suitable.

If a suitable job offer is rejected, the unemployment benefit is lost.

Some observations can be made on this regulation.

Why work became so bad for so many and what can be done to improve it (Harvard 2017). *See* also *Dall'impresa a rete alle reti di impresa. Scelte organizzative e diritto del lavoro* (Maria Teresa Carinci ed., Giuffrè 2015); Matteo M. Mutarelli, *Riassunzione nell'avvicendamento di appalti e jobs act*, Il diritto del mercato del lavoro, 293 (2015).

48. Art. 25, legislative decree No. 150/2015 and Ministerial Decree 10 April 2018.

First, the logic behind the *decalage* system is debatable, in cases where the unemployed person has actively been seeking a new job. This issue remains problematic even though the regulation has been made more favourable. This regulation risks excessively penalising individuals who have previously received a low wage. In order to prevent a situation where unemployed persons receive benefits that do not allow them to make ends meet, those who receive a NASPI below a certain threshold and demonstrate that they have been actively seeking work may be exempted from the *decalage*.

Second, it is problematic to determine a suitable job offer on the basis of the amount of the unemployment benefit. Given that NASPI can be much lower than the individual's most recent wage, a worker in VUP Group 1 could be 'forced' to accept a job offer with very low remuneration, even lower than the remuneration earned in their previous job. Moreover, as the notion of suitable job offer becomes broader over time, there is the risk of forcing persons into jobs that are less well-paid and at lower professional level.

An active policy measure, namely the *individual job placement allowance*, was recently reinstated. This allowance consists of a voucher – available for unemployed persons who have been in receipt of NASPI for at least four months, provided that they take part in vocational retraining courses, and beneficiaries of the 'Citizen's Income' – which can be spent on obtaining intensive job placement support, including vocational retraining courses, at public or private accredited entities. Moreover, in such cases, there are measures to encourage the development of employee skills, as well as incentives both for employees who accept a suitable job offer and for the employer hiring the employee. From 1 January 2022, this measure became part of the 'Workers Employability Guarantee'. Under this scheme, which will be implemented in the coming months – it appears that unemployed persons who have been in receipt of NASPI for at least four months and beneficiaries of the 'Citizen's Income' will be entitled to the individual job placement allowance, although this will depend on the measures adopted by the Regions.

§4.03 VUP GROUP 2: SOLO AND BOGUS SELF-EMPLOYMENT

[A] Composition and In-Work Poverty Risk

Starting with more general data, according to EU-SILC, in 2018 13.5% of employed persons were self-employed with no employees.

This employment status is not associated with more secure and well-paid jobs. Self-employed persons actually experience a higher risk of in-work poverty than employed persons (18.6% vs. 12.2% in 2018). Furthermore, while this risk has slightly reduced compared to the immediate aftermath of the economic and financial crisis (20.3% in 2013), it has not returned to pre-crisis values (16.2% in 2007).

Shifting the attention to individual variables, there is a particular risk of in-work poverty for the 18-34 and 34-49 age groups (respectively, 20.6% and 21.2% in 2018). More specifically, the likelihood of being at risk of poverty for the 18-34 age group has increased constantly over time (+7.5% since the pre-crisis level). Conversely, for the group aged over 50, the risk is lower (15.4% in 2018); this category demonstrates that it is more capable of recovering from the effects of the crisis (indeed, compared to 2013, the rate has decreased and is now much closer to pre-crisis values).

Considering the *gender variable* in this group, women are less likely than men to be at risk of in-work poverty (13.8% vs. 20.7%). This somewhat surprising fact should be viewed very carefully. Indeed, women were consistently under-represented within the group compared to men (30.8% vs. 69.2% in 2018). Therefore, the sharp difference in the risk of in-work poverty may be explained by the lower representativeness of the group.

Nationality appears to be strongly associated with a much higher possibility of being poor while in work. In 2018, 45.8% of non-Italian self-employed persons with no employees were at risk of in-work poverty (vs. 17% of Italians). Furthermore, over time, the in-work poverty risk for non-Italians has constantly increased (+16.6 pp from 2007 to 2018).

When considering *education levels*, persons who are highly qualified are not automatically protected from the risk of in-work poverty. In 2018, this risk is much higher among those with a low level of education (26.3%) compared to those with medium and higher levels (respectively, 18% and 12.1%); however, the latter two values are still rather high by comparative standards. Furthermore, while the risk decreased slightly for the low-skilled persons between 2013 and 2018, it constantly and sharply increased over time for the highly-educated. This data confirms the scarce economic returns of education in Italy.[49]

Shifting the focus to *household variables*, in 2018 the risk of in-work poverty is much higher for single-member households (21.4%) than for those with two or more members (respectively, 11.2% and 18.7%). Furthermore, for the latter category, the risk decreased between 2013 and 2018, while it increased for single-member households. Accordingly, the risk of in-work poverty appears to be much higher in single-earner families (29.9%) than in dual-earner households (9%). The risk for both types of household has remained rather constant over time. The data once again confirms that the old-fashioned male-breadwinner family model exacerbates in-work poverty risks.

Finally, the data demonstrates that the risk of in-work poverty is associated with the number of children in the household. Before the crisis, the risk was extremely high (28.7%) for households with more than one child and worsened with the crisis (36.3% in 2013). In 2018, the situation improved, and the rate decreased to 25.8%, a level even lower than the pre-crisis period. Interestingly, for those families with one child, the risks constantly increased over time, albeit slightly.

---

49. Silja Häusermann, Thomas Kurer, & Hanna Schwander, *High-skilled outsiders? Labor market vulnerability, education and welfare state preference*, Socio-Economic Review, 13:2, 235 (2015).

[B] Legal Framework

[1] Notion

The employment contracts relevant to VUP Group 2 are hetero-organised collaborations (*lavoro eterorganizzato*), semi-subordinate employment contracts (*lavoro parasubordinato*), and solo self-employment contracts.

Starting with hetero-organised collaborations, pursuant to Article 2 of Italian Legislative Decree no. 81/2015, subordinate employment protections also apply to these collaborations 'which take place mainly through personal work and continuous work, the methods of which are organised by the client'.

Their characterising features are: prevalent personality, continuity, and hetero-organisation. '*Prevalent personality*' occurs when the collaborator's personal work prevails over the work of auxiliaries and the use of tools and machinery, both quantitatively and qualitatively. This requirement is not fulfilled if the worker uses a complex organisation, particularly in the form of a company. *Continuity* occurs when the service is not occasional but lasts over time and involves a constant commitment by the worker to perform activities in favour of the client over a certain period.[50] *Hetero-organisation* is the functional integration of the worker into the client's production organisation – arranged unilaterally by the client itself – such that the work performed can be suitably and structurally linked to this organisation.[51] The collaboration is deemed to be hetero-organised if the client determines the collaborator's working methods.

For hetero-organised collaborations, Article 2, paragraph 2 establishes several exclusions from the scope of application of subordinate employment protections. The most important exclusion concerns employment relationships regulated by national collective agreements signed by the comparatively most representative trade unions at national level, which envisage a specific regulatory framework on wages and regulatory treatment in view of the specific production and organisational requirements of the sector or industry.[52]

There has been a lively debate on the issue of classifying *hetero-organised collaborations*. According to some scholars, Article 2 identifies a new sub-type of

50. These notions have already been set out by case law with respect to coordinated and continuous collaborations pursuant to Art. 409. On the concepts of main personality and continuous work, *see, for instance,* Cass. 26 July 1996, n. 6752; Cass. 9 March 2001, n. 3485.
51. Cass. n. 1663/2020, which concerns the case of Foodora riders. On work on demand via apps *see* VUP group 4.
52. This provision enables collective bargaining to select collaborations that will not be subject to subordinate employment protections. Other exceptions are the following: collaborations consisting of professional intellectual work, for which workers are required to be registered with specific professional bodies; activities carried out, in the performance of their duties, by member of corporate bodies; activities performed, for institutional purposes, in favour of amateur sports associations and clubs affiliated with national sports federations, associated sports disciplines and sports promotion bodies recognized by the C.O.N.I.; collaborations provided in the field of production of shows and performances by music sector foundations; collaborations by operators working in the field of mountain and speleological rescue.

subordinate employment, thus extending the subordination category,[53] while others consider these collaborations to be self-employment relationships, to which subordinate employment protections should be extended.[54] However, the practical effect of the reform is 'to extend the subjective scope of application of the legal protection previously intended only for subordinate work'.[55]

The notion of *semi-subordinate employment* (*lavoro parasubordinato*) is identified in the new wording of Article 409, no. 3 of the Italian Civil Procedure Code. According to this provision, this sub-type includes collaborations consisting of continuous and coordinated work (*co.co.co*), mainly personal, though not in the form of a subordinate employment relationship. The amendment made by Italian Law no. 81/2017 specified the meaning of coordination, which is the distinguishing feature of such collaborations, thus clarifying the distinction between coordination and hetero-organisation. By asserting that collaborations are coordinated when, in compliance with the coordination methods agreed by the parties, the worker autonomously organises his/her work, the legislator has identified this distinguishing element as the 'co-determination of organisational constraints'. In *co.co.co.* arrangements, the worker is obliged to carry out the activity in accordance with the methods of organisation agreed in the contract so that his/her work is integrated into the client's production organisation; however, any power of direction or interference by the client in the performance is excluded.[56]

Italian Law no. 81/2017 has also introduced some measures to protect *solo self-employment*.[57] Pursuant to Article 1, the protections identified in this law apply to non-entrepreneurial self-employed workers, namely self-employed workers as defined in Article 2222 of the Italian Civil Code, with the exclusion of entrepreneurs. A person is self-employed when he/she performs a task or work in return for payment and is not subject to any subordination towards the other party. In this case, the legislator's aim

53. Luca Nogler, *La subordinazione nel d.lgs. n. 81/2015: alla ricerca dell' 'autorità dal punto di vista giuridico'*, WP C.S.D.L.E. 'Massimo D'Antona'. IT, No. 267 (2015); Michele Tiraboschi, *Il lavoro etero-organizzato*, Diritto delle relazioni industriali, 978-987 (2015); Tiziano Treu, *In tema di Jobs Act. Il riordino dei tipi contrattuali*, Giornale di diritto del lavoro e di relazioni industriali, 155-181 (2015).
54. *See* Adalberto Perulli, *Il lavoro autonomo, le collaborazioni coordinate e le prestazioni organizzate dal committente*, WP C.S.D.L.E. 'Massimo D'Antona'. IT, No. 272 (2015); Roberto Voza, *La modifica dell'Art. 409, n. 3 c.p.c., nel disegno di legge sul lavoro autonomo*, WP C.S.D.L.E. 'Massimo D'Antona'. IT, No. 318 (2017); Mariella Magnani, *Autonomia, subordinazione, coordinazione nel d.lgs. n. 81/2015*, WP C.S.D.L.E. 'Massimo D'Antona'. IT, No. 294 (2016). On the debate on the classification of hetero-organised collaborations, *see* Riccardo Diamanti, Diamanti, *Il lavoro etero-organizzato e le collaborazioni coordinate e continuative*, Diritto delle relazioni industriali, 205 (2018).
55. Massimo Pallini, *Towards a new notion of subordination in Italian labour law?*, Italian labour law e-journal,12:1 (2019).
56. On the contrary, when such co-determination is absent and the client unilaterally imposes methods of organisation, the collaboration must be regarded as hetero-organised.
57. On this regulation, *see* Giuseppe Santoro-Passarelli, *Il lavoro autonomo non imprenditoriale, il lavoro agile e il telelavoro*, Rivista italiana di diritto del lavoro, I, 369-396 (2017); Adalberto Perulli, *Il jobs act degli autonomi: nuove (e vecchie) tutele per il lavoro autonomo non imprenditoriale*, Rivista italiana di diritto del lavoro, I, 173-201 (2017); Stefano Giubboni, *Il Jobs act del lavoro autonomo: commento al capo I della legge n. 81/2017*, Giornale di diritto del lavoro e di relazioni industriali, 471-495 (2017).

is to introduce some minimum protections for self-employed workers who are in a position of contractual weakness.[58]

[2] Labour Law and Social Security Standards

As envisaged by Article 2 of Italian Legislative Decree no. 81/2015, hetero-organised workers are entitled to the same protections as those granted to subordinate employees, including the right to fair remuneration. However, doubts have arisen with regard to the identification of the applicable provisions. Indeed, according to some scholars, only certain provisions can be extended, as these collaborations are sub-types of self-employment.[59] Conversely, according to the consolidated interpretation, also approved by Employment Ministry Circular no. 3/2016, the entire regulation of subordinate employment applies, including the social security provisions. In ruling no. 1663/2020, meanwhile, the Court of Cassation found that extending the protections applicable to subordinate employees was – on balance – reasonable in order to protect workers who are weaker due to the imbalance in their relationship with the client.

Although coordinated and continuous collaborators do not enjoy the same protections available to employees, they are covered not only by the same labour dispute regime as subordinate employees (Article 409, no. 3 of the Italian Civil Procedure Code), but also by other legal protections, namely: Article 2113 of the Italian Civil Code, on waivers and settlements by employees of the rights provided by mandatory rules of law or collective agreements, which are not valid; mandatory social security provisions (Article 2, paragraph 26 of Italian Law no. 335/1995 extended the scope of application of social security provisions to *co.co.co.*, making the latter eligible to receive the services provided by the INPS separate pension scheme); provisions on maternity and paternity protections, including the right to an allowance for maternity leave and parental leave; sickness protections; mandatory employers' insurance for workplace injuries and occupational diseases (Article 5 of Italian Legislative Decree no. 38/2000) and health and safety regulations, when the work is performed in the client's workplace (Article 3, paragraph 7 of Italian Legislative Decree no. 81/2008); unemployment benefits, namely the right to DIS-COLL (Article 15 of Italian Legislative

58. Fabrizio Ferraro, *Le misure a tutela del lavoro autonomo non imprenditoriale*, in Diritto e processo del lavoro e della previdenza sociale, 356 (Giuseppe Santoro Passarelli, Utet Giuridica 2020); Marco Peruzzi, *L'ambito di applicazione del primo capo della l. n. 81/2017: identikit del 'lavoro autonomo non imprenditoriale'?*, Variazioni su temi di diritto del lavoro, 661-684 (2018). For this reason, Art. 1, para. 2, explicitly excludes entrepreneurs from the scope of application of the protections. An entrepreneur, as defined by Article 2082 c.c, is a person who professionally performs an organized economic activity for the purpose of producing or exchanging good and services. Also, small entrepreneurs are excluded from the scope of application of law no. 81/2017. According to Article 2083 c.c., small entrepreneurs are those working as farmers, craft workers, small traders and those who perform a professional activity, mainly organised as personal work or with the help of his or her family members.
59. Arturo Maresca, *Coordinazione, organizzazione e disciplina delle collaborazioni continuative*, Massimario di giurisprudenza del lavoro, 133-141 (2020).

Decree no. 22/2015);[60] active policy provisions for enterprises experiencing times of economic crisis (Italian Law no. 296/2006).

Similarly, Italian Law no. 81/2017 introduced some protections for non-entrepreneurial self-employed persons, such as protection in commercial transactions; a provision protecting inventions of the self-employed; the right to deduct costs for training and vocational education; protections against unfair clauses, i.e., clauses that allow the client to amend the contractual terms and conditions unilaterally or, in the case of a continuous collaboration, to withdraw from the contract without adequate notice, and clauses in which the parties establish payment terms exceeding 60 days; in addition, any refusal by the client to stipulate the contract in writing can be regarded as abusive conduct. In such cases, the worker is entitled to be compensated in the form of damages. The law has also stabilised the application of DIS-COLL to workers enrolled on the INPS separate scheme. If the worker performs continuous activity for the client, then maternity, illness, and work-related injury will not give rise to termination of the employment relationship, which will be suspended for a period not exceeding 150 days in one year. It also establishes the right to maternity and parental allowances for workers enrolled on the INPS separate scheme who have paid contributions for at least 3 months in the preceding 12-month period. Furthermore, with a view to aligning supply and demand, it places an obligation on job centres and employment agencies to create a self-employment branch, with the task of reporting professional opportunities and providing information on the procedures for starting autonomous businesses and taking part in public contract procedures.

However, Italian Law no. 81/2017 does not provide any minimum wage guarantees.[61] Indeed, it is debatable whether minimum wage regulations are applicable to these workers. Although the right to fair remuneration is traditionally only guaranteed for subordinate employees, and the self-employed are not covered by minimum wages agreed in collective agreements, some scholars highlight the opportunity to extend the scope of application of Article 36 to dependent self-employment. Indeed, pursuant to Article 35 of the Constitution, 'the Republic protects work in all its forms and practices' and not only subordinate employment. Regarding dependent and solo self-employment, in particular, workers may be in a condition of economic dependence and contractual imbalance towards a single client, which would justify this protection. However, with some exceptions, no statutory provision has, to date, laid down the right to fair remuneration for these workers, and Italian case law still excludes self-employment from the scope of application of Article 36 of the Constitution.[62]

60. Law. 30 December 2021, No. 234, art. 1, co. 223 has increased the maximum duration from 6 to 12 months.
61. Marco Ferraresi, *Il lavoro autonomo dopo la l. n. 81/2017: nuovi equilibri tra fattispecie e disciplina*, Variazioni su temi di diritto del lavoro, 629 (2018).
62. *See* Cass. 30.12.2011, n. 30590; Cass. 28.06.2017, n. 16213.

[3] Unionisation and Application of Collective Agreements

The role of collective bargaining with regard to self-employment has rarely been investigated, although - particularly in recent decades - some trade unions have established special divisions to represent these workers. These include Nidil-Cgil (*Nuove identità di lavoro*), Felsa-Cisl (*Federazione lavoratori somministrati autonomi ed atipici*), and UILTemp, which represent non-standard workers, namely agency workers, semi-subordinate workers, and the self-employed. Moreover, trade-union confederations have established associations such as CISL Vivace, a freelancers' association offering individual services, i.e., business advice, legal assistance, and financial and tax support.[63]

Collective bargaining has played a crucial role in self-employment, intervening in accordance with Article 2, paragraph 2, letter a) of Italian Legislative Decree no. 81/2015 on the matter of hetero-organised collaborations. Indeed, through this provision, the legislator confers upon collective bargaining the power to regulate collaborations despite the law: Article 2, paragraph 2, letter a) excludes the applicability of subordinate employment protections to hetero-organised collaborations when national collective agreements signed by the comparatively most representative trade unions at national level provide a specific regulatory framework on wages and regulatory treatment. This provision was immediately applied, for instance, in the call centre sector, which often relies on collaborations and where the activity is usually organised by the client, and in many sectors where the activities performed could be regarded as hetero-organised work, but where applying the subordinate employment regulations - and the associated labour costs - may lead to the cessation or outsourcing of the activities. Indeed, in the 2015-2017 period alone, almost 20 collective agreements introduced a specific provision to regulate hetero-organised collaborations.[64]

§4.04 VUP GROUP 3: FIXED-TERMERS, AGENCY WORKERS, INVOLUNTARY PART-TIMERS

[A] Composition and In-Work Poverty Risk

According to EU-SILC, in 2018, 15.8% of employed persons were temporary workers or involuntary part-timers. Interestingly, there was a clear increase in this trend over time. Once again, the data are not surprising as many of the jobs created in recent decades have been atypical.

63. There are also some associations representing professionals, such as ACTA, a 'quasi-union' promoting many political actions and social initiatives. *See* Orsola Razzolini, *Collective action for self-employed workers: a necessary response to increasing income inequality*, WP CSDLE 'Massimo D'Antona'. INT, No. 155 (2021).
64. Lucio Imberti, *L'eccezione è la regola?! Gli accordi collettivi in deroga alla disciplina delle collaborazioni organizzate dal committente*, Diritto delle relazioni industriali, 393-430 (2016); Paolo Tomasetti, *Il lavoro autonomo tra legge e contrattazione collettiva*, Variazioni su temi di diritto del lavoro, 717-760 (2018).

As expected, temporary workers are much more likely to be at risk of in-work poverty than standard employees (21.5% vs. 12.2% in 2018). Furthermore, this risk constantly increased over time and did not reduce when the economy began to recover from the recession in the early 2010s. The data thus suggest that in-work poverty among the VUP3 Group is a structural problem.

Shifting the attention to individual variables, the in-work poverty risk particularly affected the 35-49 age group, while it was lower among the younger groups (respectively, 24.8% and 17.7% in 2018). However, the risk increased constantly for all age groups over time. These data can be explained when considering household characteristics. Indeed, younger workers – who usually receive meagre wages – still tend to live with their parents.[65] In other words, the family acts as a *shock absorber*, thus softening the side effects of atypical jobs.

When considering the *gender variable*, it is interesting to note that women are less likely than men to be at risk of in-work poverty (18.6% vs. 25.2%). For men, however, the risk changed only slightly over time, while it increased substantially for women. In other words, female temporary workers and involuntary part-timers were affected by the economic crisis, and they have not managed to recover (between 2007 and 2018, the in-work poverty risk increased by 7 pp, from 11.6% in 2007 to over 18.4% in 2013 and 18.6% in 2018).

Nationality appears to be strongly associated with a much higher possibility of being poor while in work. In 2018, 34.7% of non-Italian temporary workers and involuntary part-timers were at risk of in-work poverty (vs. 18.3% of Italians).

When considering *education levels*, in comparison to VUP Group 1 and VUP Group 2, education seems to have a stronger and more positive effect. In 2018, the in-work poverty risk among workers with a low education level (29.8% in 2018) was almost double that of those with a medium level (17.4% in 2018) and triple that of those with a higher level (10.2% in 2018). For lower-educated workers, the risk remained rather stable over time, while it increased sharply and constantly for the highly-educated (approximately +8 pp from 2007 onwards).

Shifting the focus to *household variables*, in 2018 the risk of in-work poverty was higher for single-member households (34.4%) than for those with two or more members (respectively, 15.5% and 20.2%). However, regardless of their size, the economic situation deteriorated for all households, with the risk of in-work poverty substantially increasing compared to the pre-crisis level.

Accordingly, the risk of in-work poverty appears to be much higher in single-earner families (38.9%) than in dual-earner households (9.2% in 2018). The risk for both types of households constantly increased in the aftermath of the economic crisis (respectively, from 33.5% and from 6.6% in 2007). The data confirms that the old-fashioned male-breadwinner family model exacerbates in-work poverty risks, particularly when considering temporary workers and involuntary part-timers, who often receive a lower and more insecure wage than standard employees.

---

65. Paolo Barbieri, Giorgio Cutuli, & Stefani Scherer, *In-work poverty in Southern Europe: The case of Italy*, in *Handbook on in-work poverty*, 312 (Henning Lohmann & Ive Marx eds., Elgar 2018).

Finally, the data demonstrates that the risk of in-work poverty is associated with the number of children in the household. Compared to pre-crisis levels, the risk of in-work poverty for those with more than one child increased by 4.6 pp, moving from 26% to 31.6%. Conversely, the risk increased only slightly among households with just one child (from 18% in 2007 to 21.6% in 2018) – although it remains at a relatively high level by comparative standards. These values suggest that family policy measures, in-kind and not in-kind, applied by Italian governments have little effect in lowering the risk of in-work poverty.

[B] Fixed-Term Employees: Legal Framework

In recent decades, the regulation of fixed-term employment relationships has been reformed on several occasions. The Jobs Act recently amended the previous regulation, repealing the provisions on compulsory identification of specific reasons to justify the use of a fixed-term contract. Under the regulation established in Italian Decree Law no. 34/2014 ('*Decreto Poletti*'), as well as in Italian Legislative Decree no. 81/2015, fixed-term contracts were no longer viewed unfavourably, largely based upon the idea that there is a link between more flexible employment relationships and a rise in employment levels. Today, the fixed-term contract is regulated by Article 19-29 of Italian Legislative Decree no. 81/2015, as amended by Italian Decree Law no. 87/2018, converted with amendments by Italian Law no. 96/2018 (so-called *Decreto Dignità*). According to the preamble of the '*Decreto Dignità*', *this reform aimed to combat growing job insecurity, increasing the restrictions and conditions on entering into fixed-term* – and agency employment – *contracts, thus favouring permanent employment contracts.*

There are many provisions aimed at preventing misuse of the fixed-term contract.

The first concerns the *maximum duration* of the employment contract which stands at 24 months, while the original formulation of Article 19 envisaged 36 months. More precisely, *for employment contracts lasting a maximum of 12 months, there is no requirement for the employer to specify the reasons to justify using a fixed-term contract.*

According to Article 19, paragraph 1, the contract can be further extended after this period – up to a maximum of 24 months – provided that the contract is being used for at least one of the following reasons: a) to meet temporary and objective needs, *unrelated to the ordinary business activity*, or the need to replace other employees;[66] b) to meet needs relating to temporary, significant and *unpredictable increases* in the ordinary business activity.

66. The first, concerning temporary and extraordinary needs, and not concerning the ordinary productive cycle of the business activity, states that fixed-term contracts can be stipulated where there is no alternative, i.e., as an *extrema ratio. See* Antonio Preteroti, *Il contratto di lavoro a tempo determinato*, in *Diritto e processo del lavoro e della sicurezza sociale* (Giuseppe Santoro Passarelli ed, Utet Giuridica 2020).

Collective agreements stipulated by the comparatively most representative trade unions' and employers' associations at national level may establish exceptions on the maximum duration of the contracts.[67]

If a contract exceeding 12 months is entered into without providing these reasons, the contract itself will be converted into a permanent contract from the date on which the limit is exceeded. The contract is also transformed into a permanent contract if the 24-month limit is exceeded.

With the exception of employment relationships lasting no more than 12 days, the fixed-term nature of the contract must be stated in a written document.

The contract may only be *renewed* if the conditions required under Article 19, paragraph 1 are met.[68] In addition, the first renewal within a 12-month period is subject to the conditions of Article 19. If the contract is renewed within 10 days of the expiry date of a previous fixed-term contract lasting up to 6 months – or within 20 days from the termination of a contract of more than 6 months – it is converted into a permanent contract.

The contract may be freely *extended* in the first 12 months but, thereafter, may only be extended if the conditions referred to in Article 19, paragraph 1 are in place. However, the duration of a fixed-term contract may be extended, with the employee's consent, only when the term of the initial contract is less than 24 months, and, in any case, up to a maximum of 4 times over a 24 month period.[69] If these provisions are breached, then the contract will be converted into a permanent contract.[70]

The fixed-term employment relationship may *continue beyond the expiry of the term*. In this case, the employer must pay the employee an allowance for each day of continuation beyond the established term equal to 20% of the wage up to the 10th subsequent day, and 40% for each additional day. However, if the employment relationship continues beyond the 30th day for contracts lasting less than 6 months, or beyond the 50th day in other cases, the contract will be converted into a permanent contract from the expiry of the aforementioned terms.[71]

In order to prevent employers from abusing the fixed-term contract, there is also a *quantitative limit*: the number of fixed-term employees may not exceed 20% of the permanent workers in the workforce.[72] Any breach of this percentage restriction will not result in the contracts concerned being transformed into permanent contracts; instead, the employer will be fined.

In order to ensure the quality of fixed-term work and equal treatment for fixed-term workers – in compliance with Council Directive 1999/70/EC – Article 25 of

---

67. *See also* Circular of the Ministry of Labour, n. 17 of 31 October 2018, which also specifies that, on the contrary, collective bargaining cannot intervene with regard to justifying reasons for fixed-term contracts.
68. The renewal implies the stipulation of a new fixed-term contract.
69. The number of lawful extensions within a 24-month period has been reduced from 5 to 4 by the so-called *Decreto Dignità*.
70. Art. 21 of legislative decree No. 81/2015.
71. Art. 22 of legislative decree No. 81/2015.
72. Art. 23. For employers with up to five employees, it is always possible to enter into fixed-term employment contracts.

Legislative Decree no. 81/2015 lays down the principle of non-discrimination: according to this principle, fixed-term employees must not be treated less favourably solely because they have a fixed-term contract, unless different treatment is justified on objective grounds. If the employer fails to comply with the non-discrimination obligations, then it will be fined.

Fixed-term employees are entitled to a right of priority. Indeed, unless otherwise specified in collective agreements, an employee who has worked for the same employer under one or more fixed-term contracts for longer than 6 months has a right of priority, for the following 12 months, in any hiring processes for permanent contracts concerning the role carried out under the fixed-term relationship(s). The right of priority must be expressly indicated in the employment contract.[73] If the right of priority is breached, consolidated case law states that the employee is not entitled to the stipulation of an employment contract, but only to receive compensation for damages.[74]

Moreover, Article 26 of Italian Legislative Decree no. 81/2015 stresses the importance of training for fixed-term employees, to enhance their skills, career advancement and to improve their occupational mobility. To this end, it states that *collective agreements may envisage methods to facilitate access for temporary workers to adequate training opportunities*. In this way, the Italian legislator has entrusted this task to collective bargaining, in order to comply with clause no. 6, paragraph 2 of Directive 1999/70/EC. However, the main collective agreements do not appear to introduce rules to encourage the effective training of fixed-term employees.[75]

Temporary employees are entitled to social security benefits, similarly to employees having permanent contracts. However, certain difficulties may arise in the event of any fragmentation of working careers. This is particularly true with regard to unemployment benefits: NASPI is granted to employees who have paid social security contributions to INPS for at least 13 weeks in the 4 years preceding the unemployment period and for at least 30 days in the previous 12 months. This means that those workers who have been employed under very short-term contracts may be excluded from the scope of application of this measure.

The current regulation of fixed-term employment represents a compromise solution: a reason must be provided to justify the use of fixed-term arrangements for contracts exceeding one year and for any renewal, but this reason does not have to be specified for the first fixed-term contract lasting under one year. In this way, *the legislator aims to discourage the frequent and continuous use of fixed-term contracts to*

73. Problems arise if the contract makes no mention of such right. *See* Cristina Alessi, *Il contratto di lavoro a tempo determinato. Commento agli artt. 19-23, d. lgs. n. 81/2015*, in *Codice Commentato del Lavoro*, 2770 (Riccardo Del Punta & Franco Scarpelli eds, Wolters Kluwer 2020). *See also* Court of Rome, 10 September 2019, No. 7311, in De Jure. According to Art. 24 of legislative decree n. 81/2015, also employees hired on a fixed-term basis for the performance of seasonal activities have right of priority.
74. Supreme Court, 26 August 2003, No. 12505, in De Jure; Court of Teramo, 24 October 2018, No. 766, in De Jure; Court of Frosinone, 10 October 2018, in Laws of Italy.
75. *See, for example,* CCNL metalworker industry, CCNL trade for employees in tertiary, distribution, and services companies of 30 July 2019 and CCNL for chemical sector of 19 July 2018.

satisfy long-term economic needs. However, as this regulation does not restrict the use of the first short fixed-term contract – the duration of which must not exceed one year – *it does not actually address the issue of precariousness. On the contrary, it risks contributing to the higher turnover of employees, thus exacerbating job insecurity.*[76]

With regard to the role of social partners, meanwhile, this has been reduced compared to the past. Today, collective bargaining can regulate many issues concerning fixed-term employment relationships, such as training, waiver of the right of priority or quantitative limits, and maximum duration.[77] *Thus, collective bargaining intervenes – and has intervened – in facilitating the use of fixed-term contracts, despite the 'new' restrictive rules laid down in Italian Legislative Decree no. 81/2015.*

[C] Temporary Agency Workers: Legal Framework

Temporary agency work is actually regulated in Italian Legislative Decree no. 81/2015 (Articles 30-40), as recently amended – with the aim of reducing flexibility and precarious employment relationships – by the *Decreto Dignità.*

Pursuant to Article 30, an agency employment contract is a permanent or fixed-term contract by which an authorised agency makes one or more workers available to a user;[78] workers assigned to a user operate under the supervision and control of the latter. It is a *triangular relationship* – between the *employment agency*, the *user*, and the *worker* – governed by *two contracts*, the *agency contract* and the *employment contract*. Both the employment contract (between the agency and the worker) and the agency contract (between the agency and the user) may be fixed-term or permanent. If the agency contract is permanent, then the employment contract must also be permanent. Therefore, permanent agency work is not synonymous with precariousness.

There are certain provisions aimed at *preventing misuse of agency work.*

There is a quantitative limit: pursuant to Article 31, the number of workers employed under a permanent agency employment contract may not exceed 20% of the number of permanent workers in the user's workforce, while the number of workers hired under fixed-term contracts or fixed-term agency employment contracts may not

76. Maria Paola Aimo, *Lavoro a tempo, on demand, 'imprevedibile': alla ricerca di una 'ragionevole flessibilità' del lavoro non standard*, Working Paper C.S.D.L.E. 'Massimo D'Antona'. IT, No. 431 (2020); Pasquale Passalacqua, *Il contratto di lavoro subordinato a tempo determinato e la somministrazione di lavoro alla prova del decreto dignità*, Working paper C.S.D.L.E. 'Massimo D'Antona'. IT, No. 380 (2018); Massimiliano Marinelli, *Contratto a termine ed attività stagionali*, Lavoro diritti europa, n. 1 (2019); Cristina Alessi, *Il contratto di lavoro a tempo determinato, supra* n. 73.
77. Circular of the Ministry of Labour n. 17 of 31 October 2018. On this issue, *see* Arturo Maresca, *Coordinazione, organizzazione, supra* n. 59; Antonio Preteroti, *Il contratto di lavoro, supra* n. 66. This is the case, for instance, with regard to collective agreements for the cinematographic industry on 31 July 2018 and for temporary agency work signed on 21 December 2018, which provided for a maximum duration of more than 24 months.
78. The agency must have specific administrative authorisation, which is only issued to those companies that comply with certain requirements concerning their reliability and economic stability.

exceed 30% of the number of permanent workers employed by the user. Collective agreements may introduce a different quantitative limit. Unlike fixed-term contracts, if the quantitative limits are exceeded, agency workers can ask to be categorised as permanent employees employed by the user.

Article 35 of the Decree establishes a principle of non-discrimination towards agency workers. Indeed, agency workers are entitled to economic and regulatory treatment no inferior to the treatment enjoyed by the user's employees in the same production unit having the same duties, as well as being entitled to the same social and welfare services. However, the *tertium comparationis*, i.e., the comparable employee, is difficult to define: indeed, if agency work is an instrument of the outsourcing process, there may be no comparable employees within the user. Furthermore, in some cases, the equal treatment principle envisaged with regard to agency employment makes it more convenient for users to rely on procurement contracts rather than on agency work. Indeed, there is no statutory provision establishing a general principle of equal treatment to protect a contractor's employees, with the exception of those concerning public procurement and transnational posting of workers.

The employment contract between the agency and the worker may be permanent or fixed-term.

If workers are hired by an agency on a permanent employment contract, the subordinate employment regulations apply. In this case, the worker is entitled to an *availability allowance* for periods during which he/she is not assigned to work at a user. The amount of this allowance is determined by way of collective agreements and may not, in any case, be lower than the rate fixed by Decree of the Minister of Employment and Social Policies. The national collective agreement signed on 21 December 2018 by the comparatively most representative trade unions in the sector establishes the amount of the availability allowance at EUR 800 per month. If the collective agreement does not apply, Italian Ministerial Decree of 10 March 2004 fixes the amount of the availability allowance at EUR 350 per month.

For fixed-term employment contracts, the provisions referred to in Articles 19-29 of Italian Legislative Decree no. 81/2015 apply. This regulation is very different from the one previously in force, where the fixed-term contract between the agency and the worker was subject to specific provisions.[79] Now, however, the provisions established for the fixed-term contract arrangement are applied generally, with the following exceptions: it is not necessary to wait for a certain period of time between one fixed-term contract and the next; there is no maximum number of fixed-term contracts; the right of priority in hiring processes is not granted to temporary agency workers. Therefore, after the first 12 months, a specific reason for using the fixed-term contract must be indicated, in reference to the user,[80] and, in any case, the contract may last for up to 24 months.

79. Pasquale Passalacqua, *Il contratto di lavoro subordinato a tempo determinato*, *supra* n. 76; Andrea Bollani, *Contratto a termine e somministrazione nelle scelte del legislatore del 2018*, Diritto e pratica del lavoro. Inserto, No. 40 (2018).

80. The more restrictive governance of the fixed-term contract arrangement with an agency seems to comply with EU law and the jurisprudence of the Court of Justice of the European Union. *See*

Article 35 establishes the *joint liability* of the user and the employment agency for wages and social security payments.

At the end of the agency arrangement, the user may hire the agency worker; any clause aimed at limiting this right for the user, even indirectly, is invalid. This restriction is legitimate only when the worker has received adequate compensation, as established by the collective agreement applicable to the user.

The legislator has introduced some guarantees concerning trade union rights for agency workers and has involved collective bargaining in regulating temporary agency employment. Pursuant to Article 36, agency workers are granted the trade union rights and collective guarantees envisaged by Italian Law no. 300/1970, as well as the right to participate in union meetings held at the user. In addition, in order to guarantee that the trade-union representatives can monitor the use of agency work, each year, the user must notify the trade-union representatives within the company or at local level of the number and duration of agency employment contracts in place, as well as the number and qualifications of the agency workers.[81]

In the context of collective agreements on agency work, the provisions on vocational education are particularly interesting. If certain agency workers are hired on a permanent contract but no job opportunities arise, the regulations governing collective dismissal do not apply. The national collective agreement for agencies of 27 February 2014, renewed on 21 December 2018, establishes a complex procedure to be applied in these circumstances. This procedure involves paying remuneration to support the worker and the participation of the latter in professional retraining initiatives. The agency may only dismiss the worker at the end of the procedure.

Article 38 deals with the consequences of any illegitimate use of agency employment. If the agency contract is not stipulated in writing, the workers must be regarded as employees of the user. If the agency arrangement is unlawful – in that it violates the limits and conditions envisaged by Articles 31, 32, and 33 – the worker may demand the establishment of an employment relationship with the user, which becomes effective from the beginning of the agency arrangement.

[D] Involuntary Part-Timers: Legal Framework

The original purpose of regulating part-time work was to facilitate a better work-life balance. This purpose has only been partly achieved as, over time, the regulation of part-time work has become more flexible in terms of adapting the work to meet the needs of the employer. The role of the collective agreement has also changed over time: although collective agreements play an important role in regulating the flexibility of

Luca Ratti, *Natura temporanea del lavoro tramite agenzia e limiti derivanti dal diritto europeo*, Rivista italiana di diritto del lavoro, II (2021).

81. A breach of such obligations is regarded as constituting anti-union conduct pursuant to Art. 28 of the Workers' Statute. *See* Alberto Lepore, *Trasferimento d'azienda, Outsourcing, somministrazione del lavoro ed appalto*, in *Diritto e processo del lavoro e della previdenza sociale*, 1806 (Giuseppe Santoro Passarelli ed., Utet Giuridica, 2020).

part-time contracts, unlike the past, the law gives greater flexibility to the employer, in the absence of collective agreements.

Part-time work is actually regulated by Articles 4-12 of Italian Legislative Decree no. 81/2015, which define the part-timer as an employee with fewer normal working hours than a comparable full-time worker, usually amounting, in accordance with Article 3 of Italian Legislative Decree no. 66/2003, to 40 hours per week.[82] Part-time work does not require a minimum number of working hours in the day, week, month, or year.[83]

The part-time contract must be stipulated in writing, in order to prove its existence, and must contain *details* of the *working hours* and *their arrangement with regard to the day, week, month, and year*. If there is no proof that a part-time employment contract has been signed and if the duration of working hours is not specified in writing in the contract, the employee may request the judicial conversion of the part-time employment contract into a full-time contract. If the omission only concerns the arrangement of working hours, the judge will determine these details, taking account of the employee's *family responsibilities*, his/her *need to supplement the income* by carrying out other working activities, and the needs of the employer.

The law introduces a sort of 'rigid flexibility', as the amount of hours and the arrangement of working hours must be established in advance in the contract. The law then allows for the regulation to be made more flexible with the possibility of introducing *extra-hours work* (*lavoro supplementare*), *overtime work* (*lavoro straordinario*), and *flexible clauses*.

With regard to the arrangement of working hours, in compliance with the provisions of collective agreements and within the limits of normal working hours, the employer may request the performance of additional work, i.e., extra-hours work. If the collective agreement regulates extra-hours work, the employee is obliged to provide this performance. In the past, if the collective agreement did not regulate extra-hours work, the employer could not demand that it be provided. On the other hand, if applicable collective agreements do not regulate this issue or if collective agreements are not applicable to the employment relationship, the employer may now require the employee to perform extra-hours work up to a maximum of 25% of the agreed hours of work per week. In this case, the employee may only refuse to provide extra-hours work on the basis of proven work, health, family, or vocational training grounds. Employees who work extra hours are entitled to an allowance equal to 15% of the hourly wage.

The employer may also request the performance of *overtime*, i.e., work exceeding normal hours. If the applicable collective agreement regulates overtime work, the

82. Collective agreements may provide for normal hours of work of less than 40 hours per week. In this case, part-time work means contracts with less hours than the normal hours provided for by the collective agreement.

83. Both employees who work 38 hours a week and those who work 2 hours per week are part-timers.

employee must perform this work within the limits and under the conditions established in the collective agreement. Otherwise, overtime work requires an agreement between the employee and the employer, and it must not exceed 250 hours per year.[84]

The employer is granted some flexibility in part-time arrangements by way of *flexibility clauses*, which allow the employer *unilaterally to amend the duration or schedule of working hours*. The primary regulatory source of these clauses is the collective agreement. If the applicable collective agreements do not regulate this issue or if collective agreements do not apply to the employment relationship, flexibility clauses can be stipulated at individual level, before a certifying commission and in written form.[85] Under penalty of invalidity, flexibility clauses must set out the terms and conditions for amending the duration and schedule of work. However, the employer may only change working hours with at least 2 working days' notice, and up to a maximum of 25% of annual part-time work. In these cases, the employee is entitled to a 15% increase in the hourly wage. If the work is performed in application of flexibility clauses without respecting the conditions and limits envisaged by law or by collective agreements, then employees are entitled to compensation for damages.

In order to ensure that employees genuinely consent to these arrangements, Article 6, paragraph 8 also states that any refusal by an employee to accept changes to working hours does not constitute justified grounds for dismissal. The issue concerns situations where an employee's consent is requested when establishing the employment relationship. Indeed, this makes it difficult to guarantee truly free and genuine consent.

The law envisages for the employee the 'right to reconsider' the flexibility clause. This right is only recognised for employees suffering from cancer or chronic-degenerative diseases or employees with disabled children aged under 13.

Despite the attempt to guarantee minimum protection to employees, the limits on the employer's power to arrange working hours as it sees fit do not seem sufficient. On the contrary, the current regulation of part-time work makes the employment relationship flexible and adaptable to the employer's needs, hindering opportunities for employees to organise their time freely – thus preventing a reasonable work-life balance – or to take on additional work to supplement their income. Indeed, this regulation may even lead to a deterioration in the living conditions of part-time workers.[86]

The equal treatment principle is provided with the aim of granting fair treatment. Pursuant to Article 7, part-time employees must not be treated less favourably than full-time employees employed in the same position and at the same level. Indeed, part-timers are entitled to the same rights as comparable full-time workers and their economic and regulatory treatment is determined based upon the *pro rata temporis* principle, i.e., the reduction of working hours.

84. *See* Art. 5, Legislative Decree No. 66/2003.
85. The employee has the right to be assisted by a representative from his or her trade-union association.
86. Massimiliano Delfino, *Il lavoro part-time nella prospettiva comunitaria. Studio sul principio volontaristico* (Jovene 2008); Vincenzo Bavaro, *Il tempo nel contratto di lavoro* (Cacucci 2008).

Part-time employees are entitled to the payment of social security contributions in proportion to the hours worked.[87]

§4.05 VUP GROUP 4: CASUAL AND PLATFORM WORKERS

[A] Casual Workers: Notion and Relevant Legal Framework

A casual worker is a worker whose work is irregular or intermittent. This category includes intermittent work (*prestazione occasionale*) and on-call work (*lavoro a chiamata*).

[1] Intermittent Work

Voucher-based work (*lavoro occasionale*) was introduced in 2003 by Italian Legislative Decree no. 276/2003 in the framework of occasional accessory work (*lavoro occasionale accessorio*). Originally, voucher-based work relationships were intended to be occasional, as they were only allowed in specific sectors and for certain activities, and only for certain categories of people at risk of social exclusion or unemployed persons. The many reforms deregulating the use of vouchers, thus expanding their scope of application, led to an extraordinary increase in the number of vouchers used every year. Therefore, the regulation of voucher-based work was strongly criticised, with vouchers often being misused.

Today, intermittent work is regulated by Article 54-bis of Italian Decree Law no. 50/2017.[88] Voucher-based work is a particular form of employment in which the employer pays workers for an occasional service with a voucher. The employer purchases a voucher to be used as payment for each hour of activity performed by the worker, covering both pay and social security contributions; the worker then presents the vouchers at the competent offices to receive cash.

There are different 'schemes' of voucher-based work: the so-called *Libretto Famiglia*, which can be used by private individuals to pay workers who provide domestic and care services,[89] and the '*occasional work contract*' for workers employed in small firms, having no more than five employees.[90] However, there are some limits on the 'purchase' of occasional work: the maximum yearly voucher-based income for each worker may not exceed EUR 5,000; each user may not use vouchers for payments exceeding EUR 5,000; for work performed by a worker for the same user, the amount may not exceed EUR 2,500 in one calendar year. In addition, the duration of the work

87. Marco Papaleoni, *Il nuovo part-time. Nel settore privato e pubblico* (Cedam 2004).
88. Francesca Marinelli, *Il lavoro occasionale in Italia. Evoluzione, disciplina e potenzialità della fattispecie lavoristica* (Giappichelli 2019).
89. This is the case, for instance, of gardening, cleaning, maintenance works, babysitting, or care services for elderly or sick people.
90. Law Decree No. 87/2018, converted with amendments by Law No. 96/2018, provided that hotel and tourism sector companies employing up to eight workers and agricultural business with up to five employees can also use such occasional work contracts.

or service may not exceed 280 hours in one calendar year. The aim of these limits is to prevent vouchers from replacing other forms of employment.

If the legal limits are breached, the employment relationship is converted into a full-time permanent subordinate employment relationship.

The hourly wage amount to be paid using vouchers is established by the legislator. For this reason, some academics regard it as a sort of statutory minimum wage. For small companies, this amounts to EUR 9, while for the *Libretto Famiglia* the payment is higher, in the net hourly amount of EUR 10.00. These payments are exempt from taxation; they do not affect unemployment status, and they can be calculated for determining the income required to obtain a residence permit.

With regard to access to social security measures, such workers have limited protections. They are entitled to INPS national insurance for invalidity, old-age, and survivors' benefits[91] and INAIL[92] insurance for workplace accidents and occupational diseases. However, they are excluded from sickness cash benefits, maternity allowance, unemployment benefits, and family allowance.

[2] On-Call Work

On-call work (*lavoro intermittente*) is regulated by Articles 13-18 of Italian Legislative Decree no. 81/2015. It takes the form of a permanent or fixed-term employment contract where the employer can 'use' a worker's activity intermittently or irregularly. This means that the employee declares his/her availability to work over a certain period of time, during which he/she may be called in to work, even for a few days, at short notice. There is no provision concerning a minimum and/or a maximum number of working hours.

There are two different types of on-call work. In the first – and most frequent – the employer can call the employee, who is not obliged to answer the call (on-call work with no obligation to answer the call). During periods when the worker is not employed, he/she is not entitled to receive a wage or other benefits. In the second type of arrangement – on-call work with obligation to answer – if the employer calls the employee, he/she is obliged to answer. In this case, he/she has the right to an availability allowance, the amount of which is established by collective agreements; however, it may not be lower than the minimum rate determined by the Ministerial Decree, adopted following consultation with the comparatively most representative trade unions.[93] For sickness or other events meaning that the worker is temporarily unable to work, he/she must inform the employer, specifying the duration of the hindrance. During this period, the worker is not entitled to any availability allowance. If the worker fails to inform the employer, he/she loses the right to the availability allowance for a period of fifteen days. Any unjustified refusal to work may constitute

91. They are enrolled in separate insurance scheme.
92. INAIL is the Italian national institute for insurance against accidents and occupational disease at work.
93. The Ministerial Decree 10 March 2004 still determines the availability allowance amount, setting it at 20% of the salary provided for by the applicable collective agreement.

grounds for dismissal and for return of the portion of availability allowance covering the period after the refusal.

On-call work arrangements may be entered into in two situations: first, in the cases identified by collective agreements or, in the absence of collective agreements, in the cases identified by Ministerial Decree.[94] Second, the contract may also be entered into with workers under 24 years old – provided that the work is performed in the 25th year – or those aged over 55.

The employment contract may not exceed 400 days of work over 3 years. If the duration of work continues for a longer period, the relationship is converted into a full-time subordinate employment relationship. The aforementioned limit does not apply, for example, to the tourism or entertainment sectors, where the law allows this type of contract to be used on an unlimited time basis.

The legislation ensures equal treatment for on-call workers compared to standard employees. In accordance with Article 17, they must not be treated less favourably than comparable permanent workers, obviously on a *pro rata temporis* basis, in light of the work actually performed.

Since on-call employment relationships are usually established for the performance of a short-term service, these workers struggle to access unemployment benefits, although the current regulation of this matter is more favourable than in the past.

[B] Platform Workers: Notion and Relevant Legal Framework

A platform worker is an individual who uses an app or a website to match him/herself with customers, in order to perform specific tasks or to provide specific services in exchange for payment. There are two different sub-types of platform workers: workers-on-demand via app (the most common type in the Italian legal system) and crowd-workers.

[1] Workers On-Demand via App

The *legal status* of platform workers has been the subject of great debate, particularly with regard to food delivery riders. Indeed, food delivery platforms generally use semi-subordinate employment contracts or occasional self-employment contracts, in view of the fact that workers are not restricted in terms of workplace and working hours. This classification leads to a lack of protection for such workers: often the platforms are used to adopt piecework based pay and, as workers are thought of as being self-employed, there is no statutory coverage for workplace accidents.[95] Despite this classification, in many cases the employment relationship of these workers is similar to subordinate employment, as they are subject to managerial power and are

---

94. Ministerial Decree 23 October 2004 that refers to a 1923 decree.
95. Feliciano Iudicone & Michele Faioli, *Country Background; Italy'*, *DON'T GIG UP! State of the Art Report* (Institut de Recherchese Economiques et Sociales 2019).

economically dependent on the employer, who 'often unilaterally determines the terms and conditions of work without any scope for negotiation'[96] and coordinates the work performance.

This debate also emerges in case law: indeed, the first ruling on this issue considered riders to be semi-subordinate workers,[97] while subsequent decisions classified them as hetero-organised workers with the consequent application of the subordinate employment regulation.[98] In another decision, the court considered platform workers to be subordinate employees.[99]

Italian Decree Law no. 101 of 3 September 2019, converted with amendments by Italian Law no. 128/2019, intervened in the regulation of riders' employment relationships. It amended Article 2 of Italian Legislative Decree no. 81/2015 and, in addition, established protections for work via digital platforms, introducing specific provisions in Chapter 5-bis of Italian Legislative Decree no. 81/2015.

According to the 'new' formulation of Article 2 of Decree no. 81/2015, the regulation and protections envisaged for subordinate employment relationships also apply to those collaborations that result in mainly personal and continuous performances, the methods of which are organised by the client, even if this takes place via digital platforms. Thus, it explicitly allows for employees working on demand via apps to be included among hetero-organised workers.

As stated in Article 47-bis, chapter V-bis of Italian Legislative Decree no. 81/2015, the legislator intended to ensure, beyond the scope of Article 2 paragraph 1, *minimum protection levels for self-employed workers engaged in delivering goods on behalf of others*, in urban areas and using bicycles or motor vehicles, via platforms, including digital ones. It means that other gig-workers are excluded from the scope of application of this regulation. The following provisions lay down regulations concerning form and information (Article 47-ter); payment (Article 47-quater); prohibition on discrimination (Article 47-quinquies); mandatory insurance against workplace accidents and occupational diseases (Article 47-septies).

Regarding payments – representing the most problematic issue – Article 47-quater states that collective agreements stipulated by the comparatively most representative trade unions' and employers' associations at national level may define criteria for determining the overall remuneration. However, piecework based remuneration is prohibited. Indeed, in the absence of a specific collective agreement, riders

96. European Commission, Study to gather evidence on the working conditions of platform workers, Final Report, 13 March 2020, 245.
97. Court of Turin, 7 May 2018, No. 778. *See* Gionata Cavallini, *Torino vs. Londra il lavoro nella gig economy tra autonomia e subordinazione*, Sintesi, 5, 7 (2018); Pietro Ichino, *Subordinazione, autonomia e protezione del lavoro nella gig-economy*, Rivista italiana di diritto del lavoro, II, 294 (2018).
98. *See* Supreme Court, 24 January 2020, No. 1663 – on this judgment, *see* Mariella Magnani, *Al di là dei ciclofattorini. Commento a Corte di Cassazione n. 1663/2020*, Lavoro Diritti Europa, 1 (2020); Giuseppe Santoro Passarelli, *Sui lavoratori che operano mediante piattaforme anche digitali, sui riders e il ragionevole equilibrio della Cassazione 1663/2020*, WP C.S.D.L.E. 'Massimo D'Antona'. IT, No. 411 (2020) – and Court of Appeal of Turin, 4 February 2019, No. 26.
99. Court of Palermo, 24 November 2020, no. 3570.

may not be paid on the basis of deliveries made; such workers must be guaranteed a minimum hourly wage based on the minimum rates determined by national collective agreements for similar or equivalent sectors signed by the comparatively most representative trade unions' and employers' associations at national level.

With the spread of platform work, many spontaneous coalitions of workers have been established[100] and many collective agreements have regulated the employment relationship of platform workers. On 18 July 2018, the trade unions Filt-CGIL, Fit-Cisl, and Uil Trasporti signed a supplementary agreement for subordinate riders, attached to the renewed National Collective Agreement for Logistics, Transport of Goods and Shipments. It includes provisions on health and social security insurance for those workers and establishes the working hours at 39 hours per week. On 2 November 2020, Filt-CGIL, Fit-Cisl, and Uil Trasporti signed another Protocol attached to the National Collective Agreement of Logistics, Transportation of Goods and Shipments, implementing the provisions of Chapter 5-bis of Italian Legislative Decree no. 81/2015. It provides for the application to self-employed riders of rights and protections applicable to their subordinate counterparts as envisaged by the annex to the 2018 National Collective Agreement for Logistics, Transport of Goods and Shipments for subordinate riders.[101]

On 15 September 2020, Assodelivery[102] and UGL signed a 'National Collective Agreement regulating the deliveries of goods on behalf of third parties by self-employed workers, known as riders'. This agreement provides a regulatory framework for self-employed riders, pursuant to Article 47-quater, paragraph 1, as well as Article 2, paragraph 2, letter a) of Italian Legislative Decree no. 81 of 2015. The latter allows the national collective agreements signed by the comparatively most representative trade union associations at national level to exclude hetero-organised collaborations from the labour law protections. The Assodelivery-UGL agreement ratifies the autonomous nature of the relationship, based on the flexibility that characterises the working activity of these workers and the possibility for riders to accept or reject deliveries throughout the entire relationship. In this way, these workers are precluded from accruing extraordinary remuneration, additional monthly payments, holidays, and severance indemnities, sickness payments, and maternity allowance. Furthermore, Articles 10 and 11 of the Collective Agreement attempt to waive the prohibition on piecework pursuant to Article 47-quater of Italian Legislative Decree no. 81/2015, stating that the rider will receive fees based on the deliveries completed, with the only

100. These include, for instance, 'Riders Union Bologna', that in 2018 signed the 'Charter of fundamental rights of digital work in the urban context.' It was signed by the mayor of Bologna, Riders Union Bologna, the three most important national trade union Confederations (CGIL, CIISL, UIL) and the managers of two local food delivery platforms (Sgam and MyMenù). The Charter laid down minimum protections applicable to workers who use a platform to perform their job, regardless of the classification of the employment relationship. Further examples of spontaneous coalitions are Deliverance Project, Deliverance Milano, and Riders Union Firenze.

101. On this and on problematic issues of such an extension, *see*, Paolo Tosi *La tutela dei riders, carenze legislative ed eccedenze interpretative*, Lavoro diritti europa, 1 (2021).

102. It is the employer's association representing some food delivery companies, such as Deliveroo, Glovo, Social Food, and Uber Eats.

corrective provision being that he/she is guaranteed, in any case, minimum remuneration for one or more deliveries – determined on the basis of the estimated time for completing that delivery – equivalent to EUR 10.00 gross per hour. This means that the minimum hourly remuneration of EUR 10.00 per hour is only guaranteed for working hours and not for the availability periods between one delivery and the next, thus derogating from the statutory provision referred to in Article 47-quater, paragraph 1, applicable in the absence of any regulation by collective agreements. Another problematic issue concerning this agreement is the comparative representativeness of Ugl Rider and Assodelivery, which is questionable.[103]

[2] Crowdworkers

Crowdwork has not received the same attention given to work on-demand via apps. Indeed, due also to the lack of attention from the media, crowdwork is excluded from the statutory protections envisaged by Italian Decree Law no. 101 of 3 September 2019, converted with amendments by Italian Law no. 128/2019.

Crowdworkers are usually programmers, freelancers, or professionals who make themselves available to perform different jobs from home or from other locations via online platforms.[104] Crowdworkers perform their work online – and therefore potentially anywhere – making it difficult to identify the particular state's law to which they are subject. Usually, 'traditional' economic entities use crowdwork as a form of outsourcing. Online outsourcing processes concern both microwork and freelancing.

Trade unions have paid less attention to these workers and no collective agreement has addressed the arrangement. Only a few union experiences have emerged, consisting of communities spontaneously arising on the web, such as 'Vivace' – a community created by CISL to give a voice to freelancers – or ACTA – the Italian freelancers' association – aimed at creating a network and fostering cooperation among freelancers, in order to represent, protect, and enhance autonomous professional activities.

---

103. For this reason, the Ministry of Labour addressed a note to Assodelivery, in which it highlighted that the unions signing the agreement seem not to satisfy this requirement. For a comment on this collective agreement, *see* Gionata Cavallini, Il *Ccnl Rider Ugl-Assodelivery. Luci e ombre di un contratto che fa discutere*, Sintesi, 5 (2020); Franco Carinci, *Il CCNL rider del 15 settembre 2020 alla luce della Nota dell'Ufficio legislativo del Ministero del lavoro spedita a Assodelivery e UGL, firmatari del contratto*, Lavoro europa diritti, 1 (2021). The Court of Bologna (30 June 2021) considered unlawful the Deliveroo's direction, imposing on its riders the acceptance of the collective agreement stipulated with UGL in September 2020, as a condition for continuing the collaboration. The court also excluded that UGL was a comparatively more representative trade union.

104. *See* Davide Dazzi, *GIG Economy in Europe*, in Italian Labour Law Journal, 12:1, 67 (2019).

§4.06 MEASURES INDIRECTLY INFLUENCING IN-WORK POVERTY

It is also important to consider the indirect measures, since the notion of in-work poverty involves the equivalent household disposable income. The following considerations emerge from an analysis of nine areas: social assistance; family benefits; means-tested monetary benefit; housing policy; childcare services; healthcare; long-term care policies; education; and life-long learning – referring to four types of households.[105]

The first aspect to emerge is that most of these measures have a potential indirect effect on all four VUPs, regardless of the household composition. Universal measures, such as healthcare and education, indeed provide social rights based on citizenship (or residency) and are therefore disconnected from employment status and the household size. At the same time, policies based on the selective universalism principle – such as the minimum income guarantee – provide means-tested benefits which do not, however, discriminate on the grounds of an individual's particular employment. At first sight, the Italian Welfare State seems to be effective in giving equal protection to a varied range of occupational groups and households. However, a more in-depth analysis paints a less optimistic picture. Some considerations can be provided in this regard.

First, the fact that no major differences emerged between household types does not necessarily mean that the system is equal. On the contrary, the diverse composition of households has an influence – negative or positive – on the likelihood of individuals experiencing in-work poverty. It is, accordingly, reasonable to consider that more at-risk households should receive higher protection. The data suggest that this is only partially the case in Italy. Single-parent households receive better treatment when looking at means-tested benefits or in the case of family allowance, but there is no *ad hoc* measure specifically applied to them.

Second, as already mentioned, in the family area – concerning both cash transfers, leave, and services – the system is far from being equal, and the impact for the various VUPs is likely to differ.

With regard to cash transfers, until 2021, *family allowance* (*Assegno al nucleo familiare*, ANF) was earnings-related, being inversely connected to the household income, increasing as the number of family members grew. It was also financed through contributions. However, there was an occupation-based eligibility criterion that excluded a broad number of workers. Only employees and semi-subordinate employees (in this case, with some significant restrictions) were entitled to this benefit. Consequently, self-employed persons (VUP2) and casual and platform workers (VUP4) were completely or partially excluded.[106] Family allowance, like all other cash transfers based on household income, had a 'familiarising effect': ANF could have an indirect negative effect for (male) single-earner households – particularly for those likely to

105. Single-earner, single-parent household with childhood, one earner couple with childhood, and household composed of two workers with childhood.

106. These groups could benefit only the *Birth Allowance* and the *non-contributory family benefit* for the third child.

receive a low wage – reinforcing a vicious cycle in which, for women, it is not convenient to work as the economic return is limited.

The *tax credit for dependent family members* (*detrazioni fiscali per familiari a carico*) represents another cash-transfer measure expected to have a different effect on the four analysed VUPs. The benefit is given to all workers, and the amount depends on the individual taxable income. The higher the income, the lower the final credit will be. However, those receiving a low income are very likely not to be able to benefit from this measure or only to do so partially (so-called *incapienti*). This may be the case for platform workers (VUP4) or some atypical workers, for example, fixed-term workers with several months of unemployment.

In March 2021, a new universal family benefit (the *Universal and Unique Family Allowance*) – which replaced family allowance, deductions for dependent children, and birth-related allowance – was approved. The measure provides the family with a monthly allowance for all children, regardless of the parents' employment status, from the seventh month of pregnancy to twenty-one years of age.[107] Starting from 1 March 2022, the allowance is paid monthly, and it is linked to the ISEE (Indicator of Equivalent Economic Conditions, which takes account of both income and wealth) and the number of children. If the ISEE is not provided or if it is higher than EUR 40,000, the household will only be entitled to the minimum amount (EUR 50 per child). The maximum amount is EUR 175 per child if the household ISEE does not exceed EUR 15,000. If the ISEE exceeds EUR 15,000, the amount gradually reduces. At least on paper, the measure represents a significant change towards an equal system, although we must await its actual implementation before assessing its effect.

In 2018 a minimum income guarantee was introduced for the very first time – the Inclusion Income (*Reddito di Inclusione* – REI) – which has, in turn, been replaced by a new measure (more generous in terms of cash benefits) known as the Citizenship Income (*Reddito di Cittadinanza* – RdC).[108] The RdC is expected to pay up to EUR 780 per month to individuals with no income, adjusted to take account of the household composition. This measure is conditional on engaging in job seeking and training initiatives, despite the fact that job seeking and training programmes are inadequate in many regions. Thanks to the RdC, the distribution capacity of the Welfare State has increased over the last three years.[109] However, the RdC is another measure that shows no favour to more disadvantaged households, as it tends to benefit families with one single person without children more so than families with two parents and one or more children.

---

107. For dependent adult children, up to the age of 21, it is required that they attend at a school or professional training course, or a degree course; or carry out an internship or work activity with an income lower than 8.000 euro per year; or are unemployed or carry out the civil service. For dependent children with disabilities, there is no age limit.
108. Vincenzo Ferrante, *Reddito di cittadinanza, retribuzione e salario minimo legale*, Rivista giuridica del lavoro e della previdenza sociale, 414-452 (2021).
109. Anna Alaimo, *Il reddito di inclusione attiva: note critiche sull'attuazione della legge n. 33/2017*, Rivista del Diritto della Sicurezza Sociale, 3, 419 (2017); Giovanni B. Sgritta, *Politiche e misure della povertà: il reddito di cittadinanza*, Politiche Sociali, 1, 39-56 (2020).

Shifting the attention to leave periods, differences between the VUPs can also be identified here. Maternity leave is guaranteed to all workers but in a very different manner. Semi-subordinate workers are entitled to maternity leave and to the respective allowance, but the right to parental leave only applies until the child is 3 years old, whereas, for employees, it applies until the child is 12. For self-employed women, the right to the allowance is subject to a previous contribution. Fixed-term employees are protected only if they have an active contract at the beginning of the leave. Those who have unstable jobs are often excluded from the benefit or receive a negligible amount if they have paid contributions in other separate pension public schemes. Furthermore, the various forms of fixed-term work, even with all legal protections, can make parental leave and maternity leave risky in terms of working continuity. In other words, it seems that only low-skilled workers in standard employment (VUP1) can fully benefit from these measures.

Finally, with regard to services, childcare for children aged 0-3 is *de jure* universal, but *de facto* – as the recent reforms have not ruled out co-payment – occupational status and household composition indirectly affect the actual entitlement to this service. In the public sector, fees are controlled, making the service affordable for low-wage workers (and thus for all four VUP categories). However, as the public provision of this service is minimal, most families are forced to rely on private sectors, where the prices are higher. Although there are several vouchers – at central and local administration level – to reduce the cost of the fees, enrolment priority – in both public and private sectors – is usually given to children with both parents working. This means that, in reality, all four categories of VUPs in single-earner households are likely to have more limited access to the service. It is not surprising that, given the design of the policy, in 0-3 childcare, the higher social classes are overrepresented.

The final consideration concerns the capacity of social policies to mitigate the effects of in-work poverty, which varies depending on the regions analysed. Indeed, as social assistance and healthcare have been devolved to regional and local governments, strong geographical differences have arisen between northern and southern regions, with the latter displaying lower levels in terms of measures/resources available and quality of services. Therefore, all four VUP categories may experience a very different 'mitigation effect': while this is higher in the northern and central regions – for example, regarding access to affordable public childcare – it is lower in the southern regions. In other words, the historical north-south divide that characterises the Italian Welfare State has led to fragmented social citizenship and thus to differences in the effectiveness of those social policies, which indirectly alleviate the everyday problems experienced by the working poor.

§4.07 CONCLUSIONS

Some concluding remarks can be made with regard to the VUP Groups.

In relation to measures that directly affect in-work poverty, low or unskilled standard employees (VUP Group 1) are the most protected workers, although, in recent years, many reforms have compounded their precariousness and their working conditions, for instance, by weakening the protection against unfair dismissal. In addition, unemployment benefit regulations often risk excessively penalising low or unskilled standard employees who have previously received a low wage, 'forcing' them to accept a job offer with very low remuneration and pushing them towards lower level professions. Another issue concerns wage-setting mechanisms, particularly pirate collective agreements, which often lead to strong reductions. This results in employee wages often being inadequate.

With regard to VUP Group 2, demands for protection of solo and bogus self-employment have gradually emerged for those economically dependent self-employed workers facing economic-social weakness. This has led to the extension of significant statutory protections, particularly for so-called hetero-organised workers. However, coordinated and continuous collaborators and solo or non-entrepreneurial self-employed persons are still excluded from many protections, such as minimum wage guarantees.

The regulations on fixed-term employment, although recently amended with a view to reducing flexibility and irregular employment relationships, do not actually address the precariousness issue and, conversely, actually risk exacerbating job insecurity. Moreover, certain difficulties may arise with regard to access to social security benefits: indeed, those workers who have been employed on very short-term contracts risk being excluded from the scope of application, for instance, of unemployment benefits, which are only granted to employees who have paid social security contributions for a minimum period of time. The regulation of part-time work also does not provide adequate protection, as the possibility for the employer to introduce extra-hours work, overtime work, and flexible clauses may hinder the employee in arranging and scheduling his/her working hours. Clearly, this has a particular impact on involuntary part-timers, who work part-time as they are unable to find full-time work, reducing their chances of performing other work and earning adequate remuneration to make ends meet. Even the principle of non-discrimination – established by the law with regard to employees of VUP Group 3 – often fails to ensure that they are not treated less favourably than comparable permanent or full-time employees or than the user's employees assigned to the same duties, as it is often problematic to identify so-called comparable employees.

Finally, the employment relationships of casual workers included in VUP Group 4 are characterised by job insecurity and precariousness. Indeed, despite the minimum protections and the limits laid down by law to prevent such job arrangements from replacing other forms of employment, it may be difficult for these workers to enjoy minimum standard protections and to access social security measures. It largely depends on the very short duration or the occasional nature of the performance of a service. Some positive measures that have improved the situation are those ensuring a form of minimum wage for voucher-based work and a minimum amount of availability allowance for on-call workers, as well as the statutory regulation of riders' employment relationships laid down in Italian Decree Law no. 101 of 3 September 2019.

The outbreak of the COVID-19 pandemic has compounded the situation. In general, VUP Group 1 employees received very strong protection during the epidemiological emergency, although the remuneration of these low-wage employees is still lower than before, as the wage guarantee fund only pays a portion of the salary. Self-employed workers, as well as casual workers, were probably most affected by the COVID-19 pandemic crisis and least protected against its socio-economic consequences, receiving only limited income-support benefits. The pandemic has definitely emphasised the need for more inclusive social shock absorbers and social security measures.

When interpreting these findings in combination with some characteristics of the production system, the resulting picture is far from optimistic. The Italian production and labour market systems have driven a race to the bottom: indeed, investments in research and development remain scarce, along with the demand for highly skilled workers, who are more likely to be paid higher wages. The bulk of new jobs are low-skilled and precarious, with atypical jobs increasing after the economic recession. The characteristics of the production system also have an impact on education: indeed, the economic returns from higher education are lower compared to other European countries.

Shifting the attention to the labour market, the deregulation implemented in recent years has not been supported by ad hoc measures for combating in-work poverty. Since 2012 no policy measures have been introduced explicitly to address in-work poverty.[110] One indirect measure that may assist in alleviating in-work poverty is the RdC, which is much more generous than the previous measure. This measure appears to be rather effective in covering the needs of the working poor, albeit it has been applied more as an unemployment benefit than as a fully-fledged minimum income scheme.[111] However, the pillar for the activation of RdC has been poorly designed. It follows that an 'active inclusion' which supports access to quality employment is still absent.

Finally, in-work poverty is more likely to affect those households with only one parent employed, that is, single-parent and breadwinner family models. This means that a move towards a dual-earner family model is a crucial aspect for preventing in-work poverty. However, such a move requires the already mentioned obstacles to female employment being removed. Thus far, access to real, universal childcare and to a leave system which promotes gender equality is, unfortunately, still limited.

In conclusion, it seems reasonable to state that the micro-drivers of in-work poverty are generated, preserved, and strengthened by distortions in the Italian system. In this context, the outbreak of the COVID-19 pandemic – and its resulting economic crisis – has only exacerbated the situation.

110. The only – and however 'partial' exception is the '*bonus 80 euro*', a supplementary income-support measure, consisting in a special deduction applicable to employees' income tax. Michele Raitano, Matteo Jessoula, Emmanuele Pavolini & Marcello Natili, *ESPN thematic report on in work poverty – Italy* (European Social Policy Network – ESPN 2019).

111. Armando Vittoria, *La scomparsa dei poveri. Una prima valutazione di policy sul Reddito di Cittadinanza*, Politiche Sociali, 3, 525 (2020).

CHAPTER 5

In-Work Poverty in Luxembourg

Antonio García-Muñoz

The chapter presents the situation of in-work poverty in Luxembourg, with a focus on specific groups of workers that are in a more vulnerable position in the labour market, the Vulnerable and Under-Represented Persons (VUP) Groups. The introduction provides the reader with an overview of the situation of in-work poverty in Luxembourg and the different elements in the labour law and social security regulation that may play a role. Subsequent sections provide a targeted analysis on each of the four selected VUP Groups. For each such groups, the relevant legal framework, composition, and impact of in-work poverty are assessed. The conclusions offer a summary of the main findings and ideas in the chapter.

§5.01 INTRODUCTION

The study of in-work poverty in Luxembourg is as fascinating as difficult. In the common imaginary, poverty is associated with weak economies, unemployment, crisis, or underdevelopment. Is not the case of Luxembourg, one of the strongest, more developed, and best performing economies of the world, almost untouched by recent crisis, with the highest GDP per capita in the European Union (EU).[1]

And yet, the researcher is confronted with one of the highest levels of in-work poverty in the EU and has difficulties to identify the reasons behind, so many determinants having an influence on it. Indeed, in-work poverty is, per se, a complex reality influenced by several and interrelated factors that demand an extra effort to those researchers looking to understand the influence of one of them in particular.

1. According to Eurostat data, the Luxembourgish GDP per capita in 2021 was 86,550 euros, already higher than pre-pandemic levels. Ireland, the second-best, had a GDP per capita of 70,920 euros, https://ec.europa.eu/eurostat/databrowser/view/sdg_08_10/default/table?lang=en.

From the design and limitations of existing indicators to the very special characteristics of the Luxembourgish economy or the lack of data regarding casual or informal workers, there are many uncertainties and open questions that call for further research.

The present chapter focuses on the role of labour law and social security regulation and, more in particular, how these regulations shape and impact the working conditions of particular groups of workers, the VUP Groups, representing individuals more vulnerable to the risk of in-work poverty. The following paragraphs of this introduction aim to present the complexities of the topic and its study in Luxembourg, providing some information to contextualize the chapter. The subsequent sections are dedicated to the four VUP Groups under study: low or unskilled standard workers in low-wage sectors (VUP Group 1), solo self-employed (VUP Group 2), atypical workers (VUP Group 3), and casual and platform workers (VUP Group 4). The last section offers some conclusions.

[A] The Many Paradoxes of In-Work Poverty in Luxembourg

The study of the role that the current legal framework may play in the existence and reproduction of in-work poverty in Luxembourg is particularly challenging.

First, as for any other country, in-work poverty is a complex reality influenced by several and interrelated factors. The focus of the present book, i.e., labour law and social security regulation, is just one part of the many factors shaping in-work poverty. It is not only that other legal realms, such as tax law, also play an important role, but also, as explained in the introductory chapter of the present volume, that regulation is only one element among many others. The socio-demographic characteristics of individual workers, the composition of the household where the worker lives, the economic structure of the country, etc., are also important drivers in the occurrence of in-work poverty.

Second, Luxembourg can be described as a paradoxical case of study, due to a series of statistical 'abnormalities' in relation to in-work poverty that defy common sense. On the one hand, despite being a successful and robust economy, the level of in-work poverty in Luxembourg is among the highest in the EU, and it has steadily increased over time in the last decades. The share of employed persons living in poor households in 2019 was 12.1%, which makes Luxembourg the third worst EU performer after Romania and Spain.[2] At the same time, however, Luxembourg performs quite well compared to other EU countries in terms of material deprivation. In fact, the share of employed people living in households experiencing severe material deprivation is very low (0.9%), while the corresponding value for social and material deprivation is 2.4%.

Third, while the level of in-work poverty has increased over time in the last years, the labour law and social security regulatory framework has remained remarkably stable, and little affected by recent crisis. Indeed, despite the abrupt fall in the GDP

2. The rate of at-risk of in-work-poverty for employed persons in Luxembourg was 9.3% in 2007 and 11.2% in 2013. The source of these data is Eurostat (ilc_iw01).

following the 2008 crisis, employment adjustment remained small. Reforms on labour law and social security regulation were also minimal. The same seems valid in relation to the recent COVID-19 crisis. The successful and extensive use of reduced working hours' schemes and considerable financial support by the State may be part of the explanation. In any case, the described increase in the levels of in-work poverty does not seem to be related to legal reforms. This is a challenging scenario for the study of the role of regulation, since one of the variables of the study varies while the other seems, at first sight, stable.

[B] A Protective Regulation ... for Indefinite Workers

When compared to other EU Member States, the labour law and social security regulation of Luxembourg can be described as protective. The indefinite contract of employment continues to be the most common form of employment in Luxembourg: in 2019, 'only' 7.4% of the employed workers in Luxembourg were on temporary contracts.[3] Likewise, working full-time is still the norm: part-time work occupied 17% of the employed resident persons in 2019, among which many are probably second-earners working part-time to strike a balance with care and housework.

Furthermore, labour law legislation provides, in comparative perspective, for a limited degree of flexibility in the use of atypical work contracts (temporary, part-time, and agency work). Casual work, platform work, and on-call work (which conforms VUP Group 4) are forms of employment that remain marginal or outside the legal framework in Luxembourg.

The legislator favours the indefinite contract, which is the 'default' form of work contract, as established in Article L.121-2 of the Labour Code.[4] The use of temporary contracts is limited by law: in principle, fixed-term contracts can be used only for the execution of a particular task of limited duration,[5] although there are some exceptions. The limitation in the use of temporary contracts is complemented by a number of legal measures to prevent abuse, such as a maximum duration of two years for the fixed-term contract (with some exceptions), a maximum number of renewals (two), and a temporal break for the use of successive fixed-term contracts.

A weakness in the system in relation to in-work poverty may come from the extension and content of Active Labour Market Policies (ALMP) strongly oriented to activation and employment creation. From the point of view of in-work poverty, the fact that ALMP allow on many occasions to deviate from the law, establishing or

3. The source of all data in this introduction is Eurostat, EU-SILC, unless otherwise indicated. The percentage of 7.4% of temporary workers includes temporary agency workers, which are a small number in Luxembourg.
4. Article L.121-2 Labour Code: 'Le contrat de travail est conclu sans détermination de durée. Toutefois, dans les cas et sous les conditions visées au chapitre 3 du présent titre, il peut comporter un terme fixé avec précision dès sa conclusion ou résultant de la réalisation de l'objet pour lequel il est conclu'.
5. Article L.122-1 Labour Code: 'Le contrat de travail à durée déterminée peut être conclu pour l'exécution d'une tâche précise et non durable; il ne peut avoir pour objet de pourvoir durablement à un emploi lié à l'activité normale et permanente de l'entreprise.'

favouring lower salaries (or allowances), the use of temporary contracts, etc., may result in the creation of employment of lower quality, increasing the risk of in-work-poverty. Further research, particularly on the capacity of ALMP to favour transitions into 'standard' employment, is needed in order to assess the concrete impact of these policies in relation to in-work poverty.

But despite the potential impact of ALMP, it can be said that labour law is relatively successful in limiting the use of temporary employment, thus favouring indefinite employment. To have an indefinite employment contract still protects against the risk of in-work poverty in most cases, although a little bit less in some particular sectors characterized by low-wage salaries (as is the case for workers in VUP Group 1).

The system is less successful, however, in protecting temporary and part-time workers. The risk of in-work poverty is, at 27.7% (2019), more than double among temporary workers than among those with an indefinite contract. Likewise, the in-work poverty levels of part-time workers are considerably high (20.1% in 2019). The combination of temporary and part-time employment results in a very low level of protection against in-work poverty, since almost one of every two of part-time workers with a temporary contract is at risk of in-work-poverty in Luxembourg. More details are provided in the analysis of VUP Group 3, in section §5.04 of this chapter.

[C] The Role of Minimum Wage

In Luxembourg, there is a statutory minimum wage that applies to all workers, irrespective of the sector or contractual situation, although there are differences in the amount of the minimum wage depending on two criteria: age and qualification.[6] This results in a floor for wages, i.e., wages cannot go below the minimum established. Moreover, in absolute terms this floor is very high, particularly when compared to the minimum salaries in other EU Member States. From October 2021, the gross monthly minimum wage is set at 2,256.95 EUR for an adult unskilled worker, or 2,708.35 EUR for an adult skilled worker. Shouldn't this be enough to prevent in-work poverty? Unfortunately, the answer to this question is negative, for several reasons.

First, as explained in the introduction to this volume, research shows that there is no strong correlation between low salaries and in-work poverty. The concept of low-wage worker in Europe is *relative* (because it depends on the distribution of wages in the population) and *individual* (the situation of the household as a whole is not considered). In addition, low pay is measured on gross hourly earnings, while poverty is based on equivalent household disposable income measured over a full year. Even if it is true that the risk of poverty is higher for a low-paid worker, there is a weak

6. According to Article L.222-5 Labour Code, the minimum wage of teenagers below 18 years old is fixed as a percentage of the standard minimum wage, namely at 75% of the minimum wage for teenagers aged 15 and 16, and 80% for teenagers aged 17. For 'qualified' adult workers, the applicable minimum wage results from a 20% increase in the standard minimum wage. Qualified employees are those who exercise a profession that entails professional qualification, usually acquired through studies or formation and accredited by an official certificate.

correlation between these two indicators.[7] Many low-paid workers are secondary earners in a household, and the first earner ensures that the household is not below the poverty line.[8] Therefore, the minimum wage can only be part of a policy mix composed of several instruments to fight in-work poverty, as it will only have incidence in one of the risk factors, and not the most decisive one: low wages.

Second, the minimum wage is not an optimum instrument to protect those at risk of in-work-poverty because of low work intensity, which is the case not only for part-time workers, but also for temporary workers experiencing periods of no-work in-between contracts and for casual workers. Since the minimum wage is paid in its integrity only to full-time workers, any situation short to full time becomes problematic.

Third, although in absolute and comparative terms the minimum wage in Luxembourg can be considered to be very high, its level (for non-skilled) workers is fixed almost at the poverty line for Luxembourgish standards. This is problematic for some groups in particular, such as in the case of single-earners households with children. The differentiation between skilled and unskilled workers may be also particularly problematic for some workers in certain economic sectors where it is difficult to comply with the legal requisites to be considered qualified. These sectors are more likely to be low-wage sectors (VUP Group 1), where the occurrence of in-work poverty is higher.

Therefore, the minimum wage, although useful and helpful to maintain a decent level of salaries and prevent low salaries to go below the poverty line (among other functions) has its limitations to fight in-work poverty. In any case, it cannot be the only weapon, as there is not a single silver bullet to put an end to such a complex problem as in-work poverty is.

§5.02 VUP GROUP 1: LOW OR UNSKILLED STANDARD EMPLOYMENT

Although workers included in VUP Group 1 are relatively better off when compared to workers in other VUP Groups, still the in-work at-risk-of-poverty level of VUP Group 1 is significantly higher (19.6%) than the general in-work at-risk-of poverty level of the entire workforce employed full-time with permanent employment contracts (9%).[9]

---

7. Bertrand Maître, Brian Nolan, & Christopher T. Whelan, *Low-pay, in-work poverty and economic vulnerability: a comparative analysis using EU-SILC*. Manchester School, 80(1), 99-116 (2012); Salverda, W., 'Low earnings and their drivers in relation to in-work poverty', in *Handbook on In-Work Poverty*, 26-49 (Henning Lohmann & Ive Marx eds., Edward Elgar Publishing 2018).
8. Marco Gießelmann & Lohmann Henning, The different roles of low-wage work in Germany: regional, demographical and temporary variances in the poverty risk of low-paid workers, in *The Working Poor in Europe*, 96-123 (Hand-Jürgen Andreß & Henning Lohmann eds., Edward Elgar Publishing, 2008).
9. Data of 2019. Source: EU-SILC, Eurostat. Workers included in VUP Group 1 for Luxembourg are workers in occupations at level 1 and 2 as defined by the ILO in the International Standard Classification of Occupation (ISCO-08) working in the following sectors: 'accommodation and food service activities'; 'administrative and support service activities'; 'wholesale and retail trade and repair of motor vehicles and motorcycles'; 'arts, entertainment and recreation'; 'other service activities'. Only workers employed in enterprises with more than 10 employees are considered.

This may seem paradoxical at first sight. First, because in Luxembourg there is a minimum wage that is applicable to all workers and is set to a (relatively) high level. This minimum wage, as discussed in the introduction, should protect particularly those working full-time, as is the case of workers in VUP Group 1. However, the fact that the minimum wage is set at a lower level for unskilled workers (being this level close to the poverty threshold), results in a disadvantage specially for the workers considered in VUP Group 1. In this sense, making the minimum wage level dependent on the level of skills does not help to protect unskilled workers, or in any case the protection afforded to them is less powerful against in-work poverty (to the extent that it may be linked to low wages). Second, because full-time standard employment, that is the preferential form of employment in the Luxembourgish legal order, is supposed to provide for a decent standard of living and high standards of protection, also in terms of access to social security benefits. Obviously, to certain extent, this is not the case, particularly for workers belonging to VUP Group 1. The question is why is this so.

The present section attempts to provide some materials to better understand this apparent paradox. It seems that the structure of the economic sector and the individual socio-demographic characteristics of the workers play an important role on the level of in-work at-risk-of-poverty for VUP Group 1.

Workers included in VUP Group 1 in Luxembourg are concentrated in a few economic sectors. If we would limit ourselves to those sectors defined in the WorkYP Project as 'poor', i.e., those sectors where more than 20% of the employees are low-wage earners, only two sectors should be included in the analysis for Luxembourg, namely 'accommodation and food service activities' and 'administrative and support service activities' '. The sector 'wholesale and retail trade; repair of motor vehicles and motorcycles', with 18.54% of low-wage earners in 2018, and employing a relevant number of workers in Luxembourg (11%) comes next.[10] Other relevant economic sectors in Luxembourg such as 'construction', 'professional, scientific and technical activities' and 'financial and insurance activities', employing each around 10% of the total of employees in the country, have a much lower share of low-wage earners. This seems to indicate that the problem with low or unskilled standard employment is very much located in some specific sectors, despite the fact that, as the next sections show, there are no particularities that deviate from the general rules in the labour law regulation of work in the sectors included in VUP Group 1.

[A] Composition of VUP Group 1

Who are the workers belonging to VUP Group 1 in Luxembourg? In 2019, roughly one of every ten workers in the country belonged to VUP Group 1.[11] The proportion of

Due to data constraints, low-skilled workers in the sectors 'real estate activities' and 'professional, scientific and technical activities' have been included in VUP Group 1.

10. These data refer to employees in enterprises with at least 10 workers. Source: Eurostat, Structure of Earnings Survey (earn_ses_pub1; earn_ses18_02).
11. Workers in VUP Group 1 represented 9.5% of the employed population.

young, non-Luxembourgish and less educated persons is higher in VUP Group 1 when compared to the employed population as a whole.

Women are overrepresented in this group. In 2019, 47.5% of workers in VUP 1 were women. This is close to the proportion of women in the whole population of employees (46.8%, *see* table 5.1), but considerably higher than the proportion of women in the population of employees in full-time and permanent jobs. This seems to indicate that in-work poverty in VUP Group 1 has a gender dimension.

In light of these data, individual factors, particularly the socio-demographic characteristics of the workers, seem to play a relevant role.

Table 5.1 Workforce Composition of VUP Group 1 in Luxembourg (2019)

	Employed Persons	*Employees Only*	*Full/time and Permanent Employees*	*FT and Permanent Employees in Low-skilled Occupation*	*VUP Group 1*
Proportion of employed population	100	95.4	70.8	28.4	9.5
Age group					
18-34	30.8	31.5	33.1	32.3	37
35-49	43	42.8	42.8	41.6	41.9
50 +	26.2	25.7	24.2	26.1	21.1
Gender					
Women	46.5	46.8	37.8	31.6	47.5
Men	53.5	53.2	62.2	68.4	52.5
Nationality					
Luxembourgish	45.4	45.2	43.8	40.7	27.8
Not Luxembourgish	54.6	54.8	56.2	59.2	72.2
Education					
Lower secondary/primary	20.6	21.2	19.1	41.5	39.8
Upper secondary or post-secondary	36.3	36.5	35.1	49	47.6
Tertiary	43.2	42.3	45.8	9.6	12.5

Source: EU-SILC, Eurostat.

[B] Relevant Legal Framework

There are no particularities in the labour law regulation affecting the labour conditions of full-time employees with permanent employment contracts in different sectors. Neither there are specificities affecting workers of VUP Group 1 when it comes to ALMP, vocational training, or unemployment benefits.

The only statutory provisions worsening working conditions that may affect some economic sectors are on the rules for the use of temporary contracts, so they do not affect VUP Group 1 workers.

The fact that the minimum wage differentiates between skilled and unskilled workers, setting a lower amount for the second group, affects negatively VUP Group 1, since the floor of salaries for this group is lower than for skilled workers.

The role of collective bargaining is more difficult to assess. Data on trade union density and collective bargaining coverage in Luxembourg are not easy to find and the variations between different datasets are important.

When it comes to trade union density, the International Labour Organization (ILO) data for year 2016 estimated that 32% of employees (including non-residents) in paid employment were union members.[12] Organisation for Economic Co-operation and Developmant (OECD) data show a trade union density of 28.2% for year 2019,[13] whereas the Institutional Characteristics of Trade Unions, Wage Setting, State Intervention and Social Pacts (ICTWSS) database estimates union density at 31.8% in 2018,[14] but only considering workers living in Luxembourg. The most recent data provided by the ILO on collective bargaining coverage for Luxembourg estimate a coverage of 55% of employees (including non-resident employees) in year 2014.[15] The OECD estimates a collective bargaining coverage of 56.9% in 2018.[16]

To get an idea of collective bargaining coverage of workers in VUP Group 1, table 5.2 shows the proportion of workers covered by collective pay agreements in Luxembourg (for companies with at least 10 employees) for the year 2018.[17] The data in table 5.2 are found in the Structure of Earnings Survey, that provides information on collective agreements by sector of activity.

12. ILO. ILOSTAT https://www.ilo.org/shinyapps/bulkexplorer4/?lang=en&segment=indicator&id=ILR_TUMT_NOC_RT_A.
13. OECD. Trade Union Dataset, https://stats.oecd.org/Index.aspx?DataSetCode=TUD.
14. Jelle Visser, ICTWSS Data base. Version 6.1. Amsterdam: Amsterdam Institute for Advanced Labour Studies AIAS. November 2019.
15. ILO. ILOSTAT, https://ilostat.ilo.org/topics/collective-bargaining/.
16. OCDE, https://stats.oecd.org/index.aspx?DataSetCode=CBC.
17. The percentages in table 5.2 refer to the proportion of employees that have the right to collective bargaining for which pay and or conditions of employment are determined by collective agreements.

Table 5.2 Proportion of Workers Covered by Collective Pay Agreements in Luxembourg (Enterprises with At Least 10 Employees), 2018

Sector	*Industry Agreement (%)*	*Company or Aingle-employer Agreement (%)*	*No Collective Agreement (%)*
Accommodation and food service activities	17.8	0.6	81.6
Administrative and support service activities	81.8	2	16.2
Wholesale and retail trade; repair of motor vehicles and motorcycles	17.3	27.2	55.5
Human health and social work activities	76.8	1.8	55.5
Real estate activities	NA	NA	NA
Transportation and storage	38.5	28.7	32.8
Manufacturing	4	62.6	33.3
Construction	64.4	9.8	25.8
Other service activities	9	10.4	80.6
Water supply; sewerage, waste management, and remediation activities	34.1	NA	26.4
Arts, entertainment, and recreation	29	12.1	58.9
Professional, scientific, and technical activities	NA	13.9	84.5
Information and communication	2.6	23.8	73.5
Financial and insurance activities	66.7	7	26.2
Education	86.7	6.8	6.5
Public administration and defence; compulsory social security	100	0	0

Source: Eurostat, Structure of Earnings Survey (earn_ses08_01).

Note: NA indicates data are not available. The activity sectors shown in the table are ordered by the proportion of low-wage earners from the highest to the lowest.

Data in table 5.2 show that it is not easy to find a clear relation between collective bargaining coverage and low-wage earnings. In the sector with the highest proportion of low-wage earners (*accommodation and food service activities*), 81.6% of the employees are not covered, but in the second sector with higher low-wage earners' proportion (*administrative and support service activities*) 83.8% of the employees are covered by collective agreements. In the other end, in two of the sectors with the lowest percentage of low-wage earners (*professional, scientific, and technical activities; information and communication*) collective bargaining coverage is also very low, whereas in financial and insurance activities more than 66% of the workers are covered by collective agreements.

The data in table 5.2 seem to indicate, therefore, that the role of collective bargaining may not be as important as other characteristics of the particular sector.

[C] Impact Analysis

Working in one of the sectors defined as poor entails a higher poverty risk for workers in Luxembourg, but this affects differently different groups of workers depending on factors such as the household composition and other socio-demographic characteristics.

In terms of age, the risk of in-work poverty is the highest for older workers: of those aged 50 and more in VUP Group 1 in year 2019, 25.1% are considered in-work at-risk-of- poverty, whereas for workers aged 35-49 this percentage is 16% and 19.7% for the younger workers (aged 18-34).[18] This differs from the general population of full-time and permanent employees, where the risk of in-work poverty is higher for workers aged 35-49 (9.6%) and the differences between the different cohorts of workers are not so stark.

The in-work poverty rate of VUP Group 1 is higher for women than for men, namely 20.9% of women in VUP Group 1 were at-risk-of-poverty in 2019, whereas the proportion reached 18.5% for men. This is an interesting difference with the general population of employees, for which there are no significant differences in the proportion of risk of in-work poverty between women and men.

Nationality and educational level are among the most relevant characteristics affecting in-work poverty levels. Regarding nationality, 12.2% of the workers in VUP Group 1 who were Luxembourgish were at-risk-of-poverty in 2019, whereas this percentage reached 22.6% among not Luxembourgish workers. When it comes to education, the highest the level of education, the lowest is the risk of in-work poverty. The proportion of workers in VUP Group 1 with lower secondary or primary education that were at-risk-of-poverty was 24.9%, whereas among those with tertiary education this proportion was 14.5%

Last but not least, the household composition matters. The size of the household, the number of children, and the number of workers in the household have an important effect on in-work poverty levels in Luxembourg. The risk of in-work poverty is much lower if there is more than one worker in the household (11.7% in 2019) than when the workers in VUP Group 1 are the only person working in the household

18. The source of all data in this section is EU-SILC, Eurostat.

(37%). When it comes to children, the risk of in-work poverty of workers in VUP Group 1 increases with the number of children: for households without children, the rate on in-work poverty is 17.5%, whereas it increases up to 24.1% in households with more than one child.

§5.03 VUP GROUP 2: SOLO AND BOGUS SELF-EMPLOYMENT

VUP Group 2 groups together solo/economically dependent and bogus self-employed. This group can be only imperfectly captured, as European Union Statistics on Income and Living Conditions (EU-SILC) statistics only distinguish between self-employed without employees and self-employed with employees. Those self-employed that are 'dependent', irrespective of them having employees or not, are therefore not visible, although we assume that most dependent self-employed are solo self-employed. As for bogus self-employment, due to its very nature, this category remains outside statistical information. Therefore, in the following analysis, VUP Group 2 is restricted to self-employed without employees.

The relevance of VUP Group 2 is limited in Luxembourg, where it represented only 2.3% of the resident workforce in 2019.[19] Although the risk of in-work poverty among the self-employed without employees (13.6%, 2019) is higher than for the general population of employees (12%), the difference is rather small. This departs from the situation of other EU countries, where VUP Group 2 suffers a particularly higher risk of in-work-poverty than the general population of employees (*see* other national chapters in this book).

The legal framework in Luxembourg is very strict in distinguishing self-employed from employees. The application of labour law and social security rules is strictly limited to employees, and there is no any intermediate category. Technically, bogus self-employment is seen as a problem of misclassification and the legal sanction is re-qualification.

[A] Composition of VUP Group 2

This section tries to understand the composition of VUP Group 2 in Luxembourg. Several socio-demographic and professional dimensions are considered. As has been said, the analysis of VUP Group 2 is restricted to self-employed without employees, that is the closest we can get, with the existing data, to the original VUP Group 2.

Solo self-employed in Luxembourg are older, on average, than employees. In 2019, 51.1% of the self-employed without employees were aged between 35 and 49 years old, while this age group represented only 43% of the employees.[20]

From a gender perspective, women are under-represented among the self-employed (with or without employees) in Luxembourg, since they represented only

19. Eurostat, EU-SILC.
20. The source of all the data in this section is Eurostat, EU-SILC. All data are referred to year 2019 unless otherwise indicated.

40.3 % of the total in comparison to 46.5 % of women in the employed population. However, if we focus only in solo self-employed, women represented 51 % of the total, having experienced a significant increase over time: women were only 35.2 % of the solo self-employed in 2007 and 47.2 % in 2013.

When it comes to nationality of the solo self-employed, most persons in this group are not Luxembourgish nationals (56.7 % of the solo self-employed in 2019 were not Luxembourgish). Furthermore, a stark decreasing trend is observed in the participation of Luxembourgish nationals in this group. In 2007, 63.4% of the solo self-employed were Luxembourgish. This is a stronger decrease than the one experienced in the general population of employees, where the proportion of Luxembourgish has shrunk from 52.1 % in 2007 to 45.2 % in 2019.

Solo self-employed have on average a higher educational level than the general population of employees. In 2019, 59.8 % of the solo self-employed had tertiary education, in comparison to 42.3 % of the employees. The self-employed are also more present in occupations that require a high level of skills compared to the employee's population (although there are no representative data on this last aspect for solo self-employed).

Last but not least, self-employed are concentrated in some particular sectors, namely real estate activities; professional, scientific, and technical activities; administrative and support service activities; human health and social work activities; and arts, entertainment, and recreation and other service activities.

[B] Legal Framework

The Luxembourgish legal framework is rather strict in its binary approach to the classification of workers: a person is either an employee or a self-employed. There are no intermediate categories. The key criterion to differentiate these two different legal categories is the existence of subordination. The definition of self-employed is a negative definition: are self-employed those workers that are not considered employees.

This division between subordinated workers (employees) and independent workers (self-employed) is central to define the scope of application of labour law. In a speech at the European Council in December 2020,[21] the Luxembourgish Minister of Labour stated that Luxembourg is contrary to introduce third categories of workers between employees and self-employed. In some cases, the legislator has intervened to clarify the status of certain groups of workers, such as professional sportsmen and trainers (that are considered self-employed) and performance workers (*intermittents du spectacle,* that are considered employees).[22]

In Luxembourg, there is no generally applicable definition of contract of employment, and the case law fills this gap by determining in each case whether there is an

21. https://www.consilium.europa.eu/en/meetings/epsco/2020/12/03/.
22. Putz, J.L. (2016), *Le travail flexible et atypique,* Larcier, 2016.

employment relationship (subordinate employment) or a service relationship (independent self-employed).[23] The courts have established in their case law a definition of labour contract where there are three elements to be considered for a contractual arrangement to be qualified as labour contract: 'provision of work', 'in exchange of a salary', and 'under the subordination of another person'.[24] The qualification as an employee will depend therefore on an analysis of the relevant elements of the material reality of every contractual arrangement. Subordination is the key element of the analysis.

The concept of subordination refers to the ability of an employer to give orders, supervise and give instructions, check the achieved results and, eventually, sanction the non-performance.[25]

In this legal framework, bogus self-employment is understood as a problem of incorrect qualification of the employment relationship: if a person is not a self-employed, then he/she is an employee. Re-qualification of the contractual arrangement into an employment relationship is the legal answer to bogus self-employment in Luxembourg.[26]

Solo self-employed are considered as any other self-employed. They do not have any special status under Luxembourgish law. Economic dependency does not have any legal consequences, although it may be an indicator of subordination.

In this legal framework, there are obvious obstacles to the application of labour law and social security standards to workers in VUP Group 2. Since labour law is only applicable to employees, no labour law rules and standards are applicable to solo self-employed.

The situation is different when it comes to social security standards. Self-employed are obliged to affiliate and contribute to the social security system for some contingencies. This results in self-employed having access to most of the standard social security benefits, including monetary benefits for parental leave or pensions. Nevertheless, the social security regime of the self-employed differs in some important aspects from that of employees, for example in the access to unemployment benefits. The self-employed can claim unemployment benefits when they have stopped their activity because of economic and financial problems, health problems, or 'force majeure'. To be eligible, they must prove at least two years of compulsory insurance (whereas for an employee the requisite established in Article L.521-6 is to have been employed a minimum of 26 weeks in the last 12 months).

23. Putz, J.L. (2017), 'The concept of "Employee": The Position in Luxembourg', in Waas, B., van Voos, G.H. (Eds), *Restatement of Labour Law in Europe. Volume 1. The Concept of Employee*, Hart, Blomsbury.
24. CJS, cassation, 2 February 1989, WENZEL c/S.A TEXACO Luxembourg, where the labour contract is defined as 'la convention par laquelle une personne s'engage à mettre son activité à la disposition d'une autre, sous la subordinationde laquelle elle se place, moyennant rémunération'.
25. Putz, J.L. (2017), 'The concept of "Employee"', *supra* n. 23.
26. Putz, J.L. (2016), *Le travail flexible, supra* n. 22.

[C] Impact Analysis

It is necessary to be cautious when studying in-work poverty in VUP Group 2, because the measurement of income from self-employed is difficult.[27] Incomes of this group are often not constant over time and intertwine with business income. The coverage rate of self-employment income in relation to the national accounts is low.[28] This could partly explain why self-employed workers have a higher risk of income poverty in general than employees but do not necessarily have a higher rate of material deprivation (or do even have lower material deprivation rates in some countries).[29]

The at-risk of in-work-poverty rate for self-employed without employees in 2019 was 13.6% compared to 12% for employees.[30] An interesting trend is that while the in-work poverty rate increased for employees in the last decade (from 10.1% in 2013 to 12%), it has strongly decreased among self-employed without employees (from 22% in 2013 to 13.6% in 2019). Material deprivation was lower among self-employed without employees (0.5% in 2019) compared to employees (2.5% in 2019).

The risk of in-work poverty is much higher for men than for women for VUP Group 2. The rate of risk of in-work poverty was 16.5% for men who are solo self-employed whereas it only affected 10.8% of the women in this group.

Nationality plays also an important role. Solo self-employed who are Luxembourgish have a much lower risk of in-work poverty (3.1% in 2019) than foreigners belonging to this group (21.7%).

A somewhat counterintuitive result is observed in relation to educational level. The risk of in-work poverty for solo self-employed increases with the level of education (whereas the opposite trend occurs for employees). In 2019, 17.3% of the solo self-employed with tertiary level of education were at risk of in-work-poverty. For solo self-employed with secondary or lower education level, the rate of risk of in-work-poverty was 8.3%.[31]

Finally, the household dimension plays an important role and, particularly, the number of children. Solo self-employed with children are at higher risk of in-work poverty (23.7 % in 2019) than those without children (5.7% in 2019).

---

27. Horemans, J., Marx, I. (2017) 'Poverty and Material Deprivation among the Self-Employed in Europe: An Exploration of a Relatively Uncharted Landscape. *IZA Discussion Paper Series, n 11007.*
28. Atkinson, A., Guio A-C., Marlier, E., (2017), 'Monitoring the evolution of income poverty and real incomes over time', in Atkinson, A., Guio A-C., Marlier, E., (Eds) *Monitoring social inclusion in Europe.* Publications Office of the European Union.
29. Horemans, J., Marx, I., (2017) 'Poverty and Material Deprivation' *supra* n. 27.
30. The source of all the data in this section is Eurostat, EU-SILC.
31. This may be related to the aforementioned reasons regarding the difficulties to measure income for the self-employed. Furthermore, the sample for self-employed without employees is small, which can favour distortions.

§5.04 VUP GROUP 3: FIXED-TERM, AGENCY WORKERS, INVOLUNTARY PART-TIMERS

VUP Group 3 includes the 'typical' forms of atypical employment: fixed-term work, temporary agency work, and part-time work.

[A] Fixed-Term Workers

[1] Legal Framework

The Luxembourgish legal order is rather restrictive with the use of fixed-term work. The reference is the open-ended contract, that in principle must be used unless there is a cause not to do so.

Fixed-term contracts can only be concluded for the accomplishment of a specific and non-permanent task of the company. The law further specifies that fixed-term contracts cannot be used to provide work related to the normal activities of the company.

The law enumerates, in a non-exhaustive list, a number of situations where the use of fixed-term contracts is possible: replacement of temporarily absent employees; seasonal employment; accomplishment of occasional tasks that do not form part of the core business of the company; execution of urgent works linked to security reasons and prevention of accidents; employment of unemployed persons registered at the public employment agency of Luxembourg (ADEM, *Agence pour le développement de l'emploi*) and taking part in insertion or reinsertion programmes; some types of professional training contracts; employment of professors and researchers at the University of Luxembourg; and employment of students with some conditions. The use of temporary contracts is also admitted for contracting in particular economic sectors where the use of temporary contracts is widespread and systematic: audio-visual sector; some tasks in the banking sector; formation; professional sports; construction and public works; expositions; forestry; modelling; spectacles, musicians.

With the aim of preventing abuse, the regulation of fixed-term contracts includes a number of further limitations in their use and functioning consisting of maximum length of the temporary contracts; maximum number of renewals and limits to the succession of contracts. All temporary contracts must specify a minimum duration. Zero-hour contracts are not possible in Luxembourg.[32]

First, temporary contracts have a maximum duration. The maximum length of a temporary contract is 24 months, including renewals and probation period (Article L.122-4 (1)). Seasonal contracts depart from this rule: they can be concluded for a maximum of 10 months within a reference period of 12 months, renewals included (Article L.122-4 (2)). An exception to this rule is employment at the University of Luxembourg and other public research institution, where temporary contracts with a maximum duration of up to 60 months are possible.

---

32. Putz, J.L. (2016), *Le travail flexible, supra* n. 22.

Second, temporary contracts can be renewed only twice within the period of maximum duration. The seasonal contracts may include a renewal clause for the following season. There are a number of exceptions in the limit to renewals for some cases when the employer is the State, the municipalities, or the University of Luxembourg.

Third, there is also a legal limitation to the succession of contracts. Once a temporary contract has ended, the general rule is that, for the same position, a new temporary contract with the same or with a different employee cannot be concluded before a lapse of time equal to 1/3 of the duration of the first contract has passed. However, a number of exceptions are contemplated in the law, the most relevant of which are seasonal contracts, contracts of replacement in case of a new absence of the replaced employee, and temporary contracts related to employment policies as defined in the law.

In those sectors where the use of temporary contracts is widespread and systematic, the limits for the use of temporary contracts do not apply, which may be problematic in terms of in-work poverty.

A general principle of equality between temporary and indefinite workers applies: all the legal and conventional provisions applicable to indefinite workers are also applicable to temporary workers. This includes all the conventional provisions in collective agreements. The law explicitly establishes that conventional provisions applicable to indefinite workers are also applicable to temporary workers unless otherwise indicated by law (Article L.122-10).

The sanction in case of violation of the rules regulating the use of temporary contracts is re-qualification of the temporary contract into an indefinite contract.

ALMP have the potential to be a Trojan horse for the idea of a limited use of temporary contracts. The rational of these policies is activation of unemployed workers, in the idea that offering them any type of job will work as a stepping stone into standard, non-subsidized, employment.[33] To this end, ALMP in Luxembourg allow from easing in the rules of the use of temporary contracts (and of pay) that may be problematic from the point of view of in-work poverty. For instance, the 'employment reintegration contract, the employment support contract, or the employment initiation contract are all temporary contracts. The key in this point is to assess whether these contracts are really easing transitions from unemployment into standard employment or failing to do so and becoming traps of precarity (and, possibly, poverty). This analysis, that possibly will demand longitudinal studies on work transitions not available yet, is beyond the scope of the present chapter and must therefore be left unanswered.

33. European Commission, https://ec.europa.eu/info/sites/default/files/european-semester_thematic-factsheet_active-labour-market-policies_en.pdf.

[2] Group Composition and Impact Analysis

Temporary employment is relatively low in Luxembourg when compared to other EU countries. In 2019, 7.4% of the employed in Luxembourg were on temporary contracts.[34]

Temporary workers are, on average, younger than the general population of employees, since 45.9% of the workers in this group were aged 18-34 years old, compared to 31.5% of employees in this same age group when the general population of employees is considered.

The gender distribution is similar for the group of all employees and for temporary workers. Temporary workers tend to be more often non-Luxembourgish, with lower educational level, and employed in low-skilled occupations than the general population of employees. The rate of foreign workers among the temporary workers was 61.2% in 2019 compared to 54.8% among the general population of employees. Up to 32.4% of the temporary workers had a low level of education (vs. 21.2% of the employees) and 65% of the temporary workers had a low-skilled job, whereas this was the case for 44.7% of the employees.

Workers with a fixed-term contract are at a much higher risk of experiencing in-work poverty than workers with indefinite contracts. Indeed, temporary employment is one of the factors that more clearly multiplies the risk of in-work poverty in Luxembourg. The at-risk of in-work-poverty rate for temporary employees in Luxembourg was as high as 27.7% in 2019. Moreover, it has grown significantly over time, at higher speed than the increase of the risk of in-work-poverty experienced by the general population of employees. In the year 2007, the risk of in-work-poverty was 14% for temporary workers, whereas it was 9% for employees. This data show that, among temporary employees, the risk of in-work-poverty has almost doubled since 2007, whereas it has increased from 9% to 12% among employees.

The effect of in-work poverty on temporary workers is also unevenly distributed between different groups when socio-demographic and household dimensions are considered. While the risk of in-work-poverty of men and women is similar when all the population of employees is considered, it is significantly higher for men than for women among the temporary workers (31.1% for men in 2019 compared to 23.9% for women).

Temporary workers are more likely to be at risk of in-work-poverty when they are not Luxembourgish (30.3%) than when they hold the Luxembourgish nationality (21.3%).

Although a higher level of education protects also temporary workers against in-work poverty, the risk of in-work poverty is higher for temporary workers when compared with the general population of employees for all educational levels. Even for those with tertiary education, the in-work at-risk-of-poverty rate is as high as 14% for temporary workers (compared to less than 7% for the general population of employees).

34. The source of all data in this section is Eurostat EU-SILC.

There are also important differences within temporary employment, since the length of the contracts and the work intensity are relevant in connection with the impact of in-work-poverty. The more the number of months in employment during a reference period, the lower is the risk of in-work-poverty among temporary workers. Similarly, working full time decreases the risk of in-work-poverty also among temporary workers: the in-work poverty rate is double for part-time workers with a temporary contract than for temporary workers working full-time. Nearly one in two temporary workers working part-time is at risk of in-work-poverty in Luxembourg.

Finally, the household dimension is also decisive. Both the number of adults at work in the household and the number of children affect the risk of in-work poverty. Having at least two workers in the household reduces the risk of in-work-poverty by more than two, from 39.9% when there is a single earner in the household to 18.9% when there is more than one. On the other hand, the more children, the higher the risk of in-work poverty. The rate or at-risk of in-work-poverty of temporary workers living in households without children is 20.5%, whereas it increases to 28.5% when there is one child in the household and up to 55.1% when there is more than one child.

[B] Temporary Agency Workers

[1] Legal Framework

The basic regulation of temporary agency work is in Article 131 of the Labour Code. Article L. 131-1 defines temporary work agency as 'any person, natural or legal, whose business activity consists of hiring and remunerating employees with a view to placing them at the temporary disposal of users for the performance of a specific and non-permanent task'.[35] The law also refers to the user firm in Article L.131-4, but does not provide any definition.

There are also two collective agreements applicable to all temporary work agencies in the country. One of these agreements, signed originally in 2014 and renovated in 2018, deals with the relations between the temporary agency workers and the agencies.[36] The other applies to the permanent personnel of the agencies and, therefore, will not be analysed in this report. Both agreements have been declared of general application.[37]

The declared aim of the agreements of 2014 and 2018 is to guarantee the coordination of working conditions and the social peace in the companies of the sector

35. Article L.131-1 Labour Code : '... est considéré comme «entrepreneur de travail intérimaire»: toute personne, physique ou morale, dont l'activité commerciale consiste à embaucher et à rémunérer des salariés en vue de les mettre à la disposition provisoire d'utilisateurs pour l'accomplissement d'une tâche précise et non durable, dénommée ci-après «mission»'.
36. *Convention collective pour les travailleurs intérimaires des enterprises de travail intérimaire.* The 2018 agreement is available (in French) at http://www.fes.lu/wp-content/uploads/2018/09/Conventions-collectives-du-9-juillet-2018-applicables-aux-travailleurs-int%C3%A9rimaires-des-entreprises-de-travail-int%C3%A9rimaire.pdf.
37. *Règlement Grand-ducal* 28 April 2014. Available online at https://legilux.public.lu/eli/etat/leg/rgd/2014/06/10/n2/jo.

while contributing to fight unfair competition and informal work. For the rest, it generally follows the same contents of the law, adding some detail to the principle of equality and its application.

Only authorized temporary work agencies can place workers at the disposal of third companies. The use of agency work is restricted to the same cases and for the same purposes that temporary contracts. Therefore, a 'mission' contract can only be concluded in the same cases and for the same purposes than those established for a standard temporary contract. The aim of the legislator is to restrict the use of temporary agency work to the temporary needs of user firms. However, the regulation of temporary agency work deviates from the regulation of 'standard' temporary contracts in one key aspect: the maximum duration of the mission contract is limited to 12 months, instead of the 24 months' maximum duration of temporary contracts. This maximum duration includes renewals. There is also a limitation in the number of renewals of the contract of mission: within the aforementioned 12 months, the contract of mission can be renewed a maximum of 2 times.

Another rule that tries to avoid abuses in the use of agency work is established in Article L.131-11, providing that at the end of a mission contract there can be no recourse to the use of yet another mission contract, with the same or another worker, for the same task or position, before a time lapse of minimum 1/3 of the duration of the first mission has passed. The same exceptions in the application of this rule than in the case of fixed-term contracts are established (seasonal contracts, contracts of replacement in case of a new absence of the replaced employee, use of agency work in one of the sectors where the use of temporary contracts is widespread and systematic or temporary contracts related to employment policies).

The temporary work agency is responsible for the payment of the salaries to the agency workers. These salaries cannot be inferior to those of a worker with the same or comparable qualifications in the user firm. If there is not a comparable worker, the salaries cannot be inferior to those established in the sectoral collective agreement applicable in the company for the position of the particular agency worker or, in any case, to the salary perceived by a worker with the same or comparable qualification in other company. Social contributions and taxes are also responsibility of the temporary work agency. On its part, the user firm is, during the execution of the mission contract, responsible for the application of all health and safety rules, as well as for the application of all other legal, conventional, and contractual rules regarding the working conditions of the agency workers.

The workers' representatives of the user firm must be consulted by the employer before using agency work. In addition, in case he/she is requested to do so, the employer must facilitate the service contracts for provision of work concluded with the agency to the workers' representatives. However, the role of these workers' representatives is only consultative, and they cannot prevent the employer to use agency workers.

There are different types of sanctions in case of violation of the rules to use agency work. The first is requalification of the mission contract into an indefinite contract between the agency worker and the temporary work agency. However, this sanction is interpreted narrowly by the courts that have been reluctant to apply the re-qualification of the mission contract into an indefinite one.[38] Re-qualification cannot be decided in relation to the user firm, as declared by the Court of Appeal in its judgment of 21 March 2013.[39] The second possible sanction may be applied when the provision of workers is considered an illegal provision of labour, which is the case when any employer different than a temporary work agency places workers at disposal of another company. In this situation, both the provider and the user of illegal labour are jointly liable for the payment of the wages and their accessories, as well as the allowances and the related security charges and taxes.[40] Finally, it is possible to apply other sanctions in several situations when there is a violation of the rules regulating the use of agency work. These sanctions may consist of fines or, in case of reiteration, even imprisonment of up to six months.

The principle of equal treatment is explicitly incorporated in the regulation of agency work in connection to salaries and equal access in the user firm, in the same conditions as indefinite workers of that company, to collective facilities, particularly restoration services and transport facilities.

The collective agreement further specifies this principle of equality, establishing, for example, that agency workers also have the right to the same work and security equipment that permanent workers have in the user firm. In connection to salaries, the collective agreement adds several interesting provisions. First, the contract of service must have an indication of the remuneration in the user firm for a permanent employee with the same or an equivalent remuneration of the agency worker.[41] Second, Article 10 specifies that the remuneration of agency workers must include all the elements of remuneration existing in the user firm, including bonuses, primes, and accessory remuneration such as meal vouchers, transport costs, etc. It also states that any upgrade of the salaries applicable to the permanent employees of the user firm must be applied as well to agency workers.[42]

However, the courts have established some limitations to the application of the principle of equality in relation to salaries. For instance, when a bonus or premium is payable in a certain moment of the year when the agency worker was still not in the user firm, then the agency worker is not entitled to it.[43] Likewise, a bonus established in the collective agreement is only payable if the agency worker is in the user firm in the moment of payment.[44]

Temporary agency workers have the right to be informed by and consult the workers' representatives of the user firm. However, they do not have the right to be represented in the user firm, since Article L.413-6 Labour Code establishes that

38. Putz, J.L. (2016), *Le travail flexible, supra* n. 22.
39. CSJ, 3e, 21 March 2013, 37491.
40. Article L.133-3 Labour Code.
41. Article 3.1 of the convention collective du 9 julliet 2018 applicable aux travailleurs intérimaires des entreprises de travail intérimaire.
42. Article 10 sections 1 and 4 of the convention collective du 9 julliet 2018 applicable aux travailleurs intérimaires des entreprises de travail intérimaire.
43. CSJ, 8e, 8 March 2012, 36504.
44. CSJ, 3e, 14 March 2013, 38706.

temporary agency workers do not have the right to vote or to be elected to the workers' representative bodies.

Despite the existence of two collective agreements applicable to temporary work agencies, there are some objective elements in the nature of temporary work that make it more difficult for trade unions to adequately represent temporary agency workers, such as the temporal element and the high rotation of these workers. In addition, in Luxembourg most temporary agency workers are 'frontaliers' which adds further difficulties.[45]

[2] Impact Analysis

The number of temporary agency workers in Luxembourg is low. According to data elaborated by the main Luxembourgish trade union (OGBL), only around 2% of the workers in Luxembourg, which is around 9,000 workers at a given moment, are temporary agency workers. Although given the high fluctuation of agency work in the first 6 months of 2018, a total of 18,000 workers were employed by temporary work agencies.[46] Therefore the relevance of these workers in VUP Group 3, and in Luxembourg in general, is limited. Moreover, during the COVID-19 pandemic, the use of agency work diminished by 2/3.[47]

Who are the temporary agency workers in Luxembourg? Data from the general inspection of the social security of 2020 show that temporary agency workers are very much concentrated in the construction and industrial sectors, and only 25% of them reside in Luxembourg.[48]

Due to the fact that, from a EU-SILC perspective temporary agency workers are included in the category of 'temporary workers' unless they are employed by the temporary work agency with an indefinite work contract, there is no information on the effect of in-work poverty for this subgroup of workers, although possibly some of the observations made for temporary workers above are valid also for agency workers.

[C] Involuntary Part-timers

[1] Legal Framework

As in many other jurisdictions, part-time work is defined in Luxembourg in a negative way: every worker who works less hours per week than a full-time worker in a particular company is considered to be a part-time worker.[49] This results in an

45. Putz, J.L. (2016), *Le travail flexible, supra* n. 22.
46. OGBL (2018), Intérim, Le travail intérimaire au Luxembourg Quels sont mes droits? http://www.ogbl.lu/syndicat-services-energie/files/2018/09/interim_brochure_fr.pdf.
47. Luxemburger Wort. 24/08/2020, available at https://www.wort.lu/fr/economie/l-interim-fait-les-frais-de-la-crise-5f4397f1da2cc1784e364463.
48. *Ibid.*
49. Article L.123-1 Labour Code : 'Est considéré comme salarié à temps partiel le salarié qui convient avec un employeur, dans le cadre d'une activité régulière, un horaire de travail dont la durée

extremely heterogeneous group that includes people working extremely low hours and some other working almost full time. Part-time workers can do so under a fixed-term or indefinite contract. The effect of in-work poverty is different for the different groups of part-time workers, as shown in the next section.

VUP Group 3 includes those part-time workers that are in working part-time against their will, i.e., involuntary part-timers. There is no legal definition of involuntary part-time. Some of the rules regulating part-time in Luxembourg aim at guaranteeing that people working part-time are doing so voluntarily. Such is for instance the spirit of the rule in Article L.123-3 Labour Code that seeks to facilitate the transition from part-time to full-time work if this is the will of the worker, or the rules limiting the possibilities to increase the duration of working time. Interestingly, the 1993 law that regulated part-time work for the first time in Luxembourg was titled law of voluntary part-time work.[50]

Eurostat defines involuntary part-timers as those persons who explain that they work part-time because they cannot find a full-time job.[51] According to Eurostat LFS data for the year 2019, 17% of employed persons aged 15 to 64 years are in part-time employment in Luxembourg, which represents a lower percentage than in neighbouring Germany, Belgium, and Netherlands and a similar percentage than in France. Among them, 12.9% affirmed that they work part-time because they cannot find a full-time job.

However, the definition of involuntary part-time job is debatable. First, it is possible that people who report working part-time in order to care for children or dependent adults are not really doing so 'voluntarily', but because of the lack of any (affordable) alternative. To define who are the involuntary part-time workers included in VUP Group 3, following the methodology used in the research project *Working, Yet Poor,* a broad definition of involuntary part-time is adopted. In the data on part-time work in EU-SILC, the following reasons for working part-time are offered as possible answers to the participants: 1) undergoing education or training, 2) personal illness or disability, 3) wants to work more hours but cannot find a job(s) or work(s) of more hours, 4) do not want to work more hours, 5) number of hours in all job(s) are considered as a full-time job 6) housework, looking after children or other persons 7) other reasons. Workers whose answers are 3, 6 or 7 are included, for the purposes of the present chapter, in VUP Group 3 as involuntary part-timers.

The regulation of part-time work in Luxembourg is rather complex. Rules on working time allow for a relatively high degree of flexibility. The law establishes that part-time workers can still work longer hours than those indicated in the contract per day or per week on the condition that they do not work on average more hours than what is stipulated in their contracts within a reference period of four months (Articles

hebdomadaire est inférieure à la durée normale de travail applicable dans l'établissement en vertu de la loi ou de la convention collective de travail sur cette même période.'

50. Loi du 26 février 1993 concernant le travail volontaire à temps partiel.
51. Eurostat (2020), EU labour force survey -methodology, Statistics explained, https://ec.europa.eu/eurostat/statistics-explained/index.php?title=EU_labour_force_survey_-_methodology#EU-LFS_concept_of_labour_force_status.

L.123-2 and L.211-6 Labour Code). Unless otherwise provided for in the contract of employment, the actual daily and weekly working time of a part-time employee resulting from the possibility to work longer hours may not exceed by more than 20% the actual daily and weekly working time of the part-time employee. In an attempt to prevent abuse, the work contract of the part-time employee has some mandatory contents that include: a mention of the agreed working-time; the distribution of the working time in the different days of the week (this can only be modified if there is agreement of both parties); the limits and modalities for supplementary working time (that only can be modified at a later stage if there is agreement of both parties); the limits and modalities for surpassing the daily and weekly working time agreed in the contract.

An important instrument affecting the execution of part-time contracts is the working time plan regulated in Article L.123-1(4) of the Luxembourgish Labour Code. This working time plan is a legal obligation for all companies in Luxembourg. This plan consists on the description, at least one month in advance in those companies where the period of reference to calculate working time limits is longer than one month, the foreseeable working time schedule for every employee, thus making it possible for the workers to know in advance when they have to work.

In order to open a part-time position, the employer must inform in advance to the worker's representatives, who have a consultative role. Another relevant provision is Article L.123-3 Labour Code, that establishes the obligation to inform in advance about all new part-time or full-time positions to be opened in the company to those workers that have communicated their desire to work part-time (when they are working full-time) or full-time (when they are working part-time), provided that the new positions correspond to their qualifications and experience. However, this obligation to inform does not entail an obligation for the employer to hire the internal employees.[52]

Luxembourgish law explicitly establishes a principle of equality between part-time and full-time workers. Article L.123-6 Labour Code states that part-time workers benefit from all the rights recognized to full-time workers in the law and applicable collective agreements, although at the same time opens the possibility that collective agreements may establish some exceptions.[53] The law also establishes a principle of equal remuneration between part-time and full-time employees, proportional to the time actually worked (Article L.123-7). For seniority rights and benefits, the law establishes a legal fiction by which part-time workers will be considered for these purposes as if they had been employed full-time. This is also the case concerning qualification for the application of minimum wages: the case law has established that the professional experience of part-time workers is calculated as if they had worked full-time.[54]

52. Putz, J.L. (2016), *Le travail flexible, supra* n. 22.
53. Article L.123-6 Labour Code: 'Les salariés occupés à temps partiel bénéficient des droits reconnus aux salariés à temps complet par la loi et les conventions collectives de travail applicables à l'établissement, sous réserve, en ce qui concerne les droits conventionnels, de modalités particulières prévues pour leur exercice par la convention collective de travail applicable.'
54. TT Luxembourg, 14 julliet 2015, n.2975.

[2] *Workforce Composition and Impact Analysis*

The category of involuntary part-timers is not perfectly captured by existing statistics. Some part-timers who have worked 30 hours or more were not therefore questioned about the reason for part-time work, but may still be involuntary part-timers (the normal working time in Luxembourg in the private sector is 40 hours per week). Other part-time workers did simply not answer the question on the reasons to work part time. There is, therefore, a risk of underestimating the total number of involuntary part-timers. With the caveats mentioned in the previous section about how we do define involuntary part-timers using EU-SILC data for this chapter, we would obtain that, being a total of 17.3% of all employed persons in Luxembourg working part-time in 2019, a total of 5% would be involuntary part-time workers, with the mentioned risk of under-estimation.[55]

Disaggregated data show that women are strongly overrepresented among part-time workers. Up to 84.9% of part-time workers in 2019 were women, which seems to indicate an important gender dimension of part-time work. This very high proportion of women working part-time indicates that, due to gender roles, gender pay gap, and other structural reasons women tend to be still more often second earners in the household, prioritizing (voluntarily or not) care work over full-time work. However, the proportion of men working part-time has increased over time (from 6.3% in 2017 to 15.1% in 2019).

Compared to the general population, part-time workers are more often Luxembourgish citizens (52% of part-time workers, versus 45.5% of Luxembourgish nationals when the general employed population is considered).

Part-time workers are also more likely to be less educated and to have a low-skilled occupation than the general employed population, although a higher proportion of involuntary part-timers have a tertiary education when compared with the total population of part-time workers.

Part-time workers are less frequently the only worker in the household when compared to the general employed population (29.9% of the part-timers are the only income earners of the household compared to 36.9% among the employed population). They are also more likely to be parents of two or more children, especially those in involuntary part-time (as defined for this chapter, i.e., including in this group those working part-time because of 'housework, looking after children or other persons'). These data seem to confirm that a high percentage of involuntary part-time workers in Luxembourg are women, and work part-time, because family responsibilities make it impossible, or very difficult, to hold a full-time job.

Table 5.3 shows the impact in percentages of in-work at-risk-of-poverty of involuntary part-timers in comparison with some other groups in Luxembourg, also taking into consideration different socio-demographic characteristics and the household dimension.

55. The source of all data in this section is Eurostat, EU-SILC.

Table 5.3 In-Work At-Risk-of-Poverty of Involuntary Part-Timers and Some Other Groups in Luxembourg (2019) in Percentage (%)

	Employed Persons	*Employees Only*	*Part-time Workers*	*Involuntary Part-timers*
All	12.1	12	20.1	21
Age group				
18-34	11.7	11.8	27.6	25.4
35-49	12.7	12.7	21.7	25.4
50 or +	11.5	10.8	14.1	10.8
Gender				
Women	12	12	19	s.s
Men	12.1	11.9	26.3	s.s
Nationality				
Luxembourgish	6.7	6.6	12	12.1
Not Luxembourgish	16.4	16.2	28.9	30.8
Education				
Lower secondary/primary	24.3	23.9	33.1	27.7
Upper secondary or post-secondary non-tertiary	10.8	10.9	16.9	18.4
Tertiary	6.9	6.4	12.9	15.8
Occupation				
High skill (ISCO-08 level 3 and 4)	5.3	4.8	7.4	12.4
Low skill (ISCO-08 level 1 and 2)	20.8	20.8	30.4	27.9
Contract				
Permanent	–	10.3	16.3	s.s
Temporary	–	27.7	48.5	s.s
Number of in-work persons in the household				
1	18.8	18.9	35.6	42.3
> 1	8.1	8	13.5	13.7
Number of children (< 18)				
0	9.1	9.1	19.7	20.1
1	14.8	14.9	22.4	15.8

	Employed Persons	*Employees Only*	*Part-time Workers*	*Involuntary Part-timers*
> 1	17.8	17.4	18.7	25.5

Source: EU-SILC, Eurostat.

Note: s.s: small sample size.

The at-risk of in-work-poverty of part-time workers is higher than that of the employed population, more than 20% in 2019. In fact, part-time workers are, together with temporary workers, the most vulnerable group regarding in-work poverty risk in Luxembourg.

From a gender perspective, part-time workers who are men face a higher risk of in-work poverty than female part-time workers, probably due to the second-earner nature of many female part-time workers.

Nationality is also relevant: part-time workers who are Luxembourgish nationals experience a lower risk of in-work poverty than foreign part-time workers.

Educational attainment is a protective factor against in-work poverty for part-time workers (voluntary and involuntary). The in-work poverty rate of low-educated part-time workers went up to 27.7% in 2019, whereas it was 15.8% for part-time workers with tertiary education. To have a high-skilled job also protects against in-work poverty, although a little bit less in the case of involuntary part-time workers. Still, the risk of in-work at-risk-of-poverty of involuntary part-time workers in high-skill occupations was 12.4% in 2019 compared to 27.9% for the same group in low skill occupations.

The type of work contract is also very relevant. Indeed, for part-time workers the risk of in-work poverty is three times higher for those working on temporary contracts than for those working on indefinite contracts. The combination of part-time and temporary employment results in the most precarious group of workers in terms of in-work poverty in Luxembourg. Almost one of every two part-time workers with a temporary contract was at-risk of in-work-poverty in the year 2019 in Luxembourg (48.5%)

Finally, as for all the other VUP groups, the household dimension is relevant. Being the only worker in the household greatly increases the risk of poverty for part-time workers (voluntary or involuntary). For involuntary part-time workers living alone, the risk of in-work poverty in 2019 was 42.3%, whereas for the same group of workers living in a household with more adults at work this risk decreased to 13.7%.

A trend that differentiates part-time workers from all the other VUP Groups is that the effect of the number of children does not necessarily contributes to the increase of the risk of in-work poverty. Indeed, the risk of in-work poverty of part-time workers with one child is lower (15.8%) than the same risk for part-time workers without children (20.1%).

§5.05 VUP GROUP 4: CASUAL AND PLATFORM WORKERS

The study of VUP Group 4 in Luxembourg is not easy. The main problem is the lack of data, which limits any attempt to assess the situation of workers in VUP Group 4. Statistics at EU, international and national level do not seem to capture a significative presence of casual and platform workers in Luxembourg. Eurofound reports on 'new forms of employment' do not consider Luxembourg in the scope of their analysis.[56] Likewise the JRC'S COLLEEM Survey does not report any data from Luxembourg.[57] Different hypothesis try to explain why platform and other 'new' forms of work remain limited in Luxembourg. As in other countries, it may be the case that part of the platform workers have informal arrangements and do not declare their activities with platforms.[58] Other authors argue that the micro nature of the tasks performed via platforms, having as a consequence a low level of remuneration, would explain the low spread of such forms of employment in Luxembourg, due to the high cost of living.[59]

The legal framework is also restrictive: no legal definition of casual and/or platform workers exist in Luxembourg. The law does not regulate these forms of work.

Despite these limitations, the following sections attempt to provide some information about VUP Group 4 workers.

[A] Composition of VUP Group 4

A specific characteristic of VUP Group 4 in Luxembourg may be the presence of foreign workers operating from neighbouring countries. The JRC'S COLLEEM Survey, provides some insights on the socio-economic profile of platform workers that can be extrapolate to Luxembourg (with all due cautions).[60] The quoted report found that platform workers are, on average, younger than employees and self-employed. Women are under-represented. The level of education seems to be higher than that of the general population.

[B] Casual Workers: Notion and Relevant Legal Framework

This category includes two distinct subcategories: intermittent work and on-call work.

56. Eurofound (2015), *New forms of employment,* Publication Office of the European Union; Eurofound (2018) *Employment and working conditions of selected types of platform work,* Publication Office of the European Union. *See also* Fabo, B., Beblavy, M., Kilhoffer, Z., Lenaerts, K. (2017), An Overview of European Platforms: Scope and Business Models. Publication Office of the European Union.
57. Pesole, A., Urzi Brancati, M.C., Fernandez Macias, E., Biagi, F., Gonzalez Vazquez, I., (2018), Platform Workers in Europe Evidence from the COLLEEM Survey, EUR 29275 EN, Publications Office of the European Union, Luxembourg.
58. CEPS, EFTHEIA, and HIVA-KU Leuven (2020), Study to gather evidence on the working conditions of platform workers. European Commission.
59. Putz, J.L., (2016), *Le travail flexible, supra* n. 22.
60. Pesole, A., Urzi Brancati, M.C., Fernandez Macias, E., Biagi, F., Gonzalez Vazquez, I., (2018), Platform Workers in Europe Evidence, *supra* n. 57.

Intermittent work has no legal basis in Luxembourg. There are no contracts of intermittent work in the Luxembourgish legal order, and the case law has systematically considered invalid attempts to establish work contracts of intermittent work.[61]

Seasonal work exists in Luxembourg, but seasonal work arrangements cannot be considered intermittent work. The seasonal contract can, however, incorporate a clause that foresees the continuation of the relation for the next season or campaign. In these cases, and when the seasonal contract is repeated for more than two seasons, the temporary contract at the origin of season work is transformed in to a contractual relation with an indefinite global duration (*relation a durée globale indéterminée*) as foreseen in Article L.122-5(2) of the Labour Code. In any case, the use of seasonal work is very limited in Luxembourg, because these contracts can only be used in some particular sectors, namely agriculture, viticulture, and tourism.[62]

The so-called intermittent contracts in the performance sectors (*intermittents du spectacle*) are not forms of intermittent work, but a succession of fixed-term contracts.[63]

There are no legal provisions on on-call work in Luxembourg. In the Luxembourgish national conference on in-work poverty organized with stakeholders in June 2021 by WYP Project, trade unions denounced that some contractual practices in some sectors, such as on-call companies, incorporate provisions of extreme flexibility in the working time that, in practice, are almost equivalent to on-call. There are provisions in Luxembourgish labour law that would allow preventing these situations, such as the '*plan de organisation du travail*', regulated in Articles L.211-7 and following of the Labour Code.

[C] Platform Workers: Notion and Relevant Legal Framework

There is no regulation on platforms or platform workers in Luxembourg. It seems that most existing platforms face difficulties in qualifying the contracts with their collaborators. The clear division between employees and self-employed, with no intermediate categories, make it hazardous to qualify these collaborators as self-employed.

Despite the absence of statistical evidence on the number of platform workers, their status and their needs, the Workers Chamber (CSL) elaborated in December 2020 a legislative proposal to regulate platform work and submitted it to the Parliament.[64] The proposal shares the idea that platforms are to be considered intermediaries in the labour market.[65] Because platform workers, despite remaining statistically invisible, may hide a situation of bogus self-employment, the CSL' proposal advocates for a

61. Eurofound (2020), Labour market change: trends and policy approaches towards flexibilization. Challenges and prospects in the EU series. Publication Office of the European Union.
62. Règlement grand-ducal du 11 juillet 1989 portant application des dispositions des articles 5, 8, 34 et 41 de la loi du 23 mai 1989 sur le contrat de travail.
63. Putz, J.L. (2016), *Le travail flexible, supra* n. 22.
64. https://www.csl.lu/wp-content/uploads/2021/02/proposition-de-loi-de-la-csl_-travail-fourni-par-lintermediaire-dune-plateforme-francais-1.pdf.
65. Ratti, L. (2020), 'Les deux faces du travail sur plateforme numériques : crowdwork et work on-demand' in *Revue Pratique de Droit Social,* 6/2020.

system of presumptions that would help to discourage the use of bogus self-employment disguised as platform work. The proposal includes rules on 'virtual' displacement that considers application of the labour law rules of the country of the person that benefits from the work of the platform worker. Therefore, Luxembourgish labour law would apply when the service or work is received in Luxembourgish territory. In any case, this is just a proposal and has not been so far approved by the Parliament, that is not obliged to take a vote on the proposal. Moreover, legislative proposals coming from social partners or professional chambers do not even need to be discussed.

Existing rights and obligations of platform workers depend finally on the legal qualification of their contractual arrangement. There are two possible scenarios: platform workers are considered either independent contractors or employees.

When platform workers are considered independent contractors, the parties are entirely free to determine their mutual obligations, following civil law rules applicable to contracts in general. The only obstacle might come from the need to check whether individuals performing micro-tasks in a professional way could be required to get an *autorisation d'établissement*, which is an administrative license to exercise professional activities in Luxembourg. Furthermore, the tax and social security regimes of independent contractors may also have an impact on the spread of platform work.

If platform workers are considered employees, then labour law and social security rules would be applicable in full.

The current scenario of platform work in Luxembourg is still of legal uncertainty. The EU proposal for a Directive on improving working conditions in platform work[66] will, in case of approval, contribute to develop a legal framework for platform workers in Luxembourg.

§5.06 CONCLUSIONS

Due to the complexity of in-work poverty, a study focusing only on the role of labour law and social security regulation, as is the case in the present chapter, is necessarily limited in the description of the problem. Aspects such as the particularities of tax law, the structure of the economic sectors in Luxembourg, the lack of affordable accommodation, the income distribution, etc., play a very important role, but are outside the scope of the study. Therefore, the picture is partial and incomplete. Still, the preceding pages provide some hints of the in-work poverty situation in Luxembourg and some clues as to where the main problems lie, at least in relation to the groups studied.

A profile of the typical working poor, deriving from individual and household circumstances and situation in the labour market, can be traced: single earners with children, non-Luxembourgish workers, low-skilled workers employed in low-wage sectors, and those working part-time and/or with a temporary contract are the most at-risk of in-work-poverty. On the contrary, persons living in households without

66. European Commission, Proposal for a Directive of the European Parliament and of the Council on improving working conditions in platform work, COM (2021) 762 final.

children and with more than one earner, Luxembourgish nationals, highly qualified workers, and people working full-time with standard employment contracts have the lowest risk of becoming working poor.

In-work-poverty is concentrated in few sectors in Luxembourg, particularly, as we have seen in the analysis of VUP Group 1, in those with higher levels of low-wage workers. Within these sectors, unskilled workers are at a higher risk of poverty, particularly older workers, women and low-educated workers who are not Luxembourgish. For workers in VUP Group 1, living in a single-earner household with children also increases the risk of experiencing in-work poor. The standard employment contract, that is, indefinite and full-time work contract, is less protective for workers in VUP Group 1 than for the average worker. Being sector-specific legislation almost inexistent and without evidence of a decisive role of collective bargaining, it seems that the role of regulation is limited in connection to the situation of VUP Group 1. However, the fact that the minimum wage for unskilled workers is set at a lower level than for skilled workers affects negatively workers in VUP Group 1, and it can be very problematic in those particular sectors where the chance to get what the legislator considers as 'qualified' professional skills are very low. The structure of the economic sectors and the individual socio-demographic and household characteristics seems to play a very important role.

Despite these sector-specific problems, the labour law regulation in Luxembourg can be described as protective in comparative terms. It can also be said that, even if it is successful in limiting the use of temporary contracts, it fails to protect atypical workers, and particularly temporary workers.

Temporary employment and low work intensity are both important risk factors in relation to in-work poverty. Workers included in VUP Group 3 (and possibly a similar situation is true of those workers in VUP Group 4) are those experiencing a higher risk of in-work poverty of all the groups studied. When part-time employment is also temporary, the risk of in-work poverty is extremely high: almost one in two of these workers is at risk of being working poor.

Some gaps in the rules limiting of the use of temporary contracts may be problematic. First, the fact that in some sectors the use of temporary contracts is considered systematic and widespread, led the legislator to accept that the limitations in the use of temporary employment do not apply in them. This may result in the precarisation of those sectors. In light of the data on in-work poverty levels among temporary employment, we can suspect that in these economic sectors the prevalence of in-work poverty is high. Second, ALMP as designed in Luxembourg allow for deviations on the rules that limit the use of temporary employment, which may be also problematic.

With all the described caveats in relation with the data on incomes of the self-employed, the situation of workers in VUP 2 seems to be relatively acceptable, with a risk of in-work-poverty only slightly above the existing risk for all the employed population. This departs from the situation in other jurisdictions, where solo self-employed tend to be in a very precarious position. Furthermore, the size of this group in Luxembourg is relatively small, so their weight in the population of working poor is accordingly limited.

Finally, regarding VUP Group 4, little can be said, as the limitations in available data are difficult to overcome. The size of this group of workers seem to be rather small in Luxembourg, but it is also possible that it hosts some of the most precarious workers, including what could be described as 'informal' workers, and therefore remain 'invisible'. To a great extent, for those workers in VUP Group 4 that are 'formal', the applicable rules would depend on their qualification as employees or self-employed, with possible important consequences on the incidence of in-work poverty in this group.

To sum up, in-work poverty does not affect evenly all workers, since the risk to suffer in-work-poverty is considerably higher for some groups, as this chapter shows. It is difficult to assess what exactly the role of labour law regulation is, but some problems have been highlighted in connection to low-wage sectors, temporary work, and part-time work.

CHAPTER 6

In-Work Poverty in the Netherlands

Mijke Houwerzijl, Nuna Zekić, Sonja Bekker & Marion Evers

This chapter presents a summary of the Dutch National Report, which analyses the regulatory structures affecting the working conditions for the vulnerable and under-represented persons (VUP) and assesses different aspects of regulations that can have a direct and indirect impact on the situation of in-work poverty for such workers. Data on poverty risks in relation to various individual and household variables of the four VUP Groups is presented and discussed, and the analysis includes the legal framework and conclusions drawn from data on the VUP Groups.

§6.01 INTRODUCTION

Setting the scene

The Dutch economy has proven to be quite resilient in the past decade, both during the financial crisis of 2009-2013, and during the economic downturn following the COVID-19 pandemic (up to the end of 2021).[1] However, a low unemployment percentage might mask the difficulties that some groups of workers have in finding a decent, well-paid, secure job. The Netherlands is known to have an 'inclusion problem': employers are less likely to hire (younger) workers with a lower educational attainment and people who are distanced from the labour market, let alone on standard contracts. According to the European Commission, the degree of flexibility and segmentation at the Dutch labour market lead to vulnerability, for instance if adverse

1. Cremers, J., Bekker, S., & Dekker, R. (2017). *The Dutch polder model – Resilience in times of crisis*. In Igor Guardiancich & Oscar Molina (Eds.), *Talking through the crisis* (pp. 189-212) (24 p.). Geneva: ILO.

economic shocks occur.[2] Also the Organisation for Economic Co-operation and Development (OECD)[3] has warned for lower job security and job quality for workers. Early 2020, a Dutch committee advising the government argued that the current 'Dutch design' of regulation (and practice) of work not only is morally wrong, but also harms economic, social, and societal development.[4] Following up on this, the Dutch Social and Economic Council (*SER*), has in June 2021 advised to limit labour market flexibility in the Netherlands.[5]

Moreover, despite wage growth in the past decade, frequent calls have been made to further increase wages in order to support household purchasing power and internal demand. In about half a million jobs (about 5.9% of all jobs), the workers have an income at or below[6] the minimum wage. However, there are also many jobs that are only slightly above minimum wage, thus still falling within the category of low-paid jobs. For instance, 1 million Dutch jobs (about 12%) fall within the scope of 110% of minimum wage or lower, and 2.2 million jobs (about 26%) fall within the range of 130% of minimum wage or lower. The poverty threshold in the Netherlands is calculated annually by Statistics Netherlands (*CBS*), and it was EUR 1,090 net per month for a single-person household in 2019.[7]

Based on Eurostat data (2019), 5.5%[8] of all in-work persons in the Netherlands were at risk of poverty and 1.1%[9] even lived in severe material deprivation. This is an indicator of structural poverty.[10] Irrespective of the employment status, the poverty risk for the whole population of the Netherlands is 13.2%, which suggests that being an active part of the workforce still decreases the risk of poverty. Furthermore, within the whole working population those with the highest education have the lowest risk of poverty and those with a low education level run the highest risk of poverty (obviously those with medium level of education are in between).[11]

Household variables show that the poverty risk for single-person households is much higher (9.9%) than for households with two (4%) or more (5%) persons. Notably, if only one person in the household works, there is a poverty risk of 12.3%,

2. EC (2020), Country report the Netherlands, SWD(2020) 518 final, Brussels, 26.2.2020.
3. Baker, M., & Gielens, L., (2018), Making employment more inclusive in the Netherlands, Econ. dept. working papers No. 1527, OECD.
4. H. Borstlap et al. (January 2020). *In wat voor land willen wij werken? Naar een nieuw ontwerp voor de regulering van werk.* Eindrapport van de Commissie Regulering van Werk, Den Haag.
5. SER (2021), Advies 2021-2025, *Zekerheid voor mensen, een wendbare economie en herstel van de samenleving.*
6. Which can be explained by a considerable amount of younger workers earning minimum youth wages.
7. CBS, 2019: https://opendata.cbs.nl/statline/#/CBS/nl/dataset/83932NED/table?%20ts=1565008102724.
8. EU average: 9.2%.
9. EU average: 3.2%.
10. Data Eurostat. Material deprivation refers to the inability of individuals or households to afford those consumer goods and activities that are normal for a society at the time (to pay bills, keep the home warm, eat meat/fish/protein equivalent every other day, have a car, a washing machine, internet access, etc.).
11. Almost half of the individuals in the Dutch working population have a high level of education (46.8%). A further 38% has an intermediate education level, and only 15.2% has a low education attainment.

while if more than one person in the household is employed, the risk drops significantly to 2.7% (year 2019). Finally, also the number of dependent children slightly affects the poverty risk. Having no dependent children is connected to a 5.4% poverty risk. One dependent child leads to, surprisingly enough, a slightly lower risk of poverty (5.2%), which might be the effect of child-related benefits. If there are two or more dependent children in the household, then the risk of poverty rises to 6%, indicating that there may be some factors related to (child-)benefits that have no positive effect (or even a negative effect) on household income.

Notably, the immediate effects of the COVID-19 crisis on the loss of jobs and income have not been translated into current statistics yet.[12] However, first explorations suggest that the most vulnerable groups on the labour market have been affected the most.

Chapter structure

Against this backdrop, the chapter presents main findings of the Dutch National Report of the WorkYP project. First, important regulatory structures affecting the working conditions for the four VUP Groups are briefly addressed, including a selection of instruments that can have a direct and indirect effect on the situation of in-work poverty for such workers (section § 6.02).[13] Second, data on poverty risks in relation to various individual and household variables of each of the four VUP Groups are presented, including relevant aspects of the legal framework and conclusions drawn from data on the VUP Groups (sections § 6.03 – 6.06). The chapter ends with a summarizing conclusion (section § 6.07).

§6.02 ROLE OF THE LEGAL FRAMEWORK

[A] The Binary Divide Between Employees and Self-Employed

It should be stressed from the onset that the legal system in the Netherlands has a binary divide: according to Dutch labour law and the general contract law, a worker is either an 'employee' or a 'self-employed person'. Whereas the worker with an employment contract has an entrance ticket to the 'solid fortress of labour law', the solo self-employed worker (VUP Group 2 workers) remains outside and generally lacks this protective shelter. The employment contract is also the entrance ticket to another fortress of specific social security schemes for employees. In contrast, the solo-self-employed worker is subject to the general rules of contract law, in which party autonomy and freedom of contract are the core principles. As an effect, the consequences of being defined as a solo self-employed worker can be quite invasive, since labour and social security law regulations do (with some exceptions) not apply.

12. Bekker, S., Buerkert, J., Quirijns, Q., & Pop, I. (2021). In-work poverty in times of COVID-19. In E. Aarts, H. Fleuren, M. Sitskoorn, & T. Wilthagen (Eds.), *The new common: How the COVID-19 pandemic is transforming society* (pp. 35-40). Springer.
13. For an elaborate overview, *see* Part I of the national report: Houwerzijl, M.S., Zekić, N., Evers, A.A. and Bekker, S. WORKING, YET POOR; NATIONAL REPORT: NETHERLANDS, Tilburg university and Utrecht University, 26-07-2021.

When all the elements of the definition in the Dutch Civil Code (Article 7:610 and 7:659 DCC) are met, there is an employment contract, regardless of whether the parties wanted to conclude an employment contract. The most important economic element of the employment contract is (periodic) payment of remuneration. 'Authority' or 'subordination' is also considered key element in determining an employment relationship.

The solo self-employed worker works on the basis of a different type of (commercial) contract. The DCC regulates several types of commercial contracts. The most important ones are the agreement to 'make a work' (*overeenkomst tot aanneming van werk*), as regulated in Article 7:750 DCC, which is traditionally mostly used in the construction sector, and the agreement for services (*overeenkomst van opdracht*), as regulated in Article 7:400 DCC. This contract was traditionally associated with 'the liberal professions', notably medical doctors, notaries, and lawyers. Nowadays, contractual arrangements of most solo self-employed workers are based on contracts for services.

The distinction between the contract of employment and the contract for services is subordination. However, determining whether there is subordination can be difficult. Another distinctive element is that the self-employed contractor does not necessarily perform his or her work personally. This is only the case when parties specifically agree to that, or when it is clear that the contract was concluded because of the specific qualities of a specific contractor (Article 7:404 DCC). In case of a dispute that is brought before the court, the assessment as to whether there is an employment contract or a contract for services, is made on the basis of an evaluation of all circumstances of the case, which in the Netherlands is called the 'holistic assessment'.[14] Until recently, 'all circumstances' was generally understood as including the intentions of the parties when they concluded the contractual relationship, as well as their societal position and the way in which parties executed the agreement in practice.[15] This led to very differing decisions by lower courts in cases with sometimes large factual similarities. In November 2020, in its Judgment 'X/Gemeente Amsterdam', the Supreme Court clarified that the intention of the parties does not play a role in the question of whether the agreement must be regarded as an employment contract.[16] According to this recent judgment, it must first be examined which rights and obligations the parties have agreed upon. Only when that has been established, the court can assess whether the agreement has the characteristics of an employment contract or not. In short: it is the actual operation of the arrangements made by the parties which will be decisive in determining the true nature of the contractual relationship.

Notably, in the Netherlands, the same standards are applied in assessing whether an employment contract exists across the three legal areas of labour law, social security law, and tax law.[17]

---

14. More elaborate *see*, Samiha Said, *Digital Platform Work in Dutch Labour Law*, working paper prepared for LLRN4, Santiago de Chile May 2019.
15. Dutch Supreme Court (*Hoge Raad*), 14 November 1997, ECLI:NL:HR:1997:ZC2495 (*Groen/Schoevers*).
16. Dutch Supreme Court (*Hoge Raad*), 6 November 2020, ECLI:NL:HR:2020:1746, para 3.2.3.
17. Dutch Supreme Court (*Hoge Raad*), 25 March 2011, ECLI:NL:HR:2011:BP3887 (*Gouden Kooi*); S. Said, 'Werknemer of zelfstandige? Drie keer raden!', *ArA* 2017/1, p. 55 e.v.

Regarding the Dutch social security system, it is important to know that it is composed of a set of compulsory universal schemes (at minimum flat rate level), covering all (economically active and non-active) persons legally residing in the Netherlands, as well as a set of compulsory schemes only available to employees. Hence, the Netherlands has a hybrid system of social security protection. So, in the social security perspective, the binary divide between employees and self-employed only concerns employee benefit schemes. As a default, solo self-employed workers are not covered by these schemes. However, there are in social security legislation some extensions to the employee-concept.[18] The reason behind this is that the legislator deemed it necessary to bring not only persons with an employment contract under the employee insurance, but also those who, from a socio-economic point of view, should be equated with employees, because they are equally economically dependent on work for one principal. The extensions to an employment relationship are laid down in the personal scope of the employee benefit schemes.[19] Under the condition that they fulfil certain requirements, e.g., home workers, musicians, artists, professional sportsmen, and 'other persons, who perform personal work for remuneration,' are covered under the employee insurance schemes; they have an employee-like status. So, from the perspective of the WorkYP project, for instance, the Dutch unemployment benefits (UB) used to be rather accessible for certain self-employed who meet the criteria for being classified as employee-likes (which boil down to employee-like economic dependency).

[B] Main Sources of Labour Law Protection and the Role of Collective Bargaining

Since 1983, the Dutch Constitution includes two provisions concerning employment protection of working people by labour law. Article 19 (1) of the Dutch Constitution[20] stipulates that it shall be the concern of the authorities to promote the provision of sufficient employment. Next to that, Article 19 (2) requires the Dutch Government to enact rules concerning the legal status and social protection of working persons and concerning co-determination. Most important from the perspective of the WorkYP project, is Article 20 of the Dutch Constitution,[21] which in its first paragraph stipulates that it shall be the concern of the authorities to secure the means of subsistence of the population and to achieve the distribution of wealth.[22] The minimum adequate living

18. There are also some exceptions to an employment relationship laid down in Articles 6 and 6a of the Sickness Benefits Act. These are not relevant for the subject of this Chapter.
19. Articles 4 and 5 of the Sickness Benefits Act (*Ziektewet*) and the Decree on Employment Relationships ('Rariteitenbesluit') based on Article 5 of the Sickness Benefits Act.
20. Extensively M. Houwerzijl & N. Zekić, Commentary on Art. 19: De grondwet | Artikel 19 – Werkgelegenheid en arbeidskeuze.
21. Extensively M. Houwerzijl & F. Vlemminx, Commentary on Article 20 (in Dutch): De grondwet | Artikel 20 – Bestaanszekerheid.
22. Notably, constitutional law has never played a dominant role in litigation since Article 120 of the Dutch Constitution prohibits the judiciary to test laws and treaties against the constitution, as this is considered a prerogative of the legislature. Moreover, there is no constitutional court in

standard that should be guaranteed refers not only to social security benefits but also, for example, to the minimum wage.

Substantive Dutch employment law is not consolidated into a single code, but it is laid down in many different legal sources.[23] Apart from protective labour law rules laid down in the Dutch Civil Code (e.g., dismissal law protection), important public labour law protection is applicable to all employees who are working (even temporarily such as posted workers) on Dutch territory.[24]

For our purposes, the Minimum Wage and Minimum Holiday Allowance Act (*WML: Wet minimumloon en minimumvakantiebijslag*) is the most important legal instrument. The WML sets a minimum wage floor in the Dutch labour market, which helps to establish a minimum subsistence level. The statutory minimum wage is automatically linked to the development of the general level of wages. Every six months Netherlands Statistics (*CBS*) calculates the average level of wage rises in the (collective labour agreements) CLAs of Dutch workers, and the minister subsequently adjusts the minimum wage with the same percentage by Royal Decree.[25] Once in a while economic scholars have pleaded to lower the statutory minimum wage, in order to stimulate employment, but this has never been embraced by the government. However, in the period 1983-1995 (when the Dutch economy suffered from a persistent level of high and long-term unemployment), the automatic linkage to the rise of average wages has been interrupted several times. The long-lasting effect of this former policy is that the current level of the minimum wage, measured in terms of purchasing power, is still reduced if compared to the minimum wage level in the 1970s (corrected for inflation).[26]

On 1 July 2021, the monthly minimum full-time gross wage was EUR 1,701 per month for an adult full-time worker (everyone who is 21 years of age and older). Employees are also entitled to a minimum of 8% holiday allowance (paid once a year).[27] Notably: the normal weekly working time may vary between 36 and 40 hours a week, depending on the sector of the economy. Therefore it is not possible to give a general applicable hourly minimum wage, but on average it is about EUR 11 an hour. The Dutch largest trade union FNV, together with some other stakeholders, taking into consideration the increasing amount of working poor in the Netherlands, have started a campaign to increase the minimum wage to a 'living wage' level of 14 euro an hour, which would be 60% of the average wage in the Netherlands, as it was originally

---

the Netherlands. This gap is filled by international (social) rights treaties, which are quite an important source of law, due to the Dutch monistic system.

23. For an elaborate overview of Dutch labour law in English, we refer to: *Labour law in the Netherlands*, by Antoine Jacobs, 2020, Wolters Kluwer. We also draw on Bouwens, Houwerzijl, Roozendaal, *Schets van het Nederlandse arbeidsrecht*, Wolters Kluwer 2021.
24. This concerns the Minimum Wage and Minimum Holiday Allowance Act; the Working Hours Act; the Health & Safety (Working Conditions) Act; the Placement of Personnel by Intermediaries Act; and the Equal Treatment Act.
25. As observed by Jacobs, *Labour law in the Netherlands* 2020, p. 138: The procedure for adopting the minimum wage is very simple and depoliticized, it never stirs political debate.
26. Jacobs, *Labour law in the Netherlands,* 2020, pp. 257-259, 141.
27. https://www.rijksoverheid.nl/onderwerpen/minimumloon/bedragen-minimumloon/bedragen-minimumloon-2021.

intended.[28] In 2018, the scope of the Minimum Wage Act was extended to solo self-employed workers, unless they provide their services in the pursuit of a business or in the independent pursuit of a profession (Article 2 (2) (b) WML). The idea is to cover bogus self-employed workers but not genuinely self-employed persons.

From 1 January 2017 onwards, it is, in principle, prohibited for employers to deduct any other costs from the minimum wage than employees' wages statutory wage tax, national insurance, and employee insurance contributions, along with – if applicable – contributions to occupational pension schemes or similar secondary employment conditions).[29] Generally, this means that it is no longer permitted to withhold expenses relating to real costs (e.g., housing, work clothes, and travel expenses) from the minimum wage (Article 13 *WML*). The measure was introduced to prevent (sometimes very serious) underpayment and other abuses, occurring mainly with regard to posted workers and migrant workers in low-wage sectors. The aim is to guarantee that the employee is always entitled to at least the statutory minimum wage. It is also laid down in law that only a limited amount of income can be garnished to pay debts or other duties. The seizure-free amount used to be 90% of the statutory minimum wage level in order to allow for an adequate minimum decent standard of living.[30]

Besides private and public labour law, there are Acts on more collective aspects of labour law (on the right to collective bargaining, the extension of a collective labour agreement (CLA), collective dismissals and co-determination rights of employees in undertakings). Trade unions, employers' organizations (social partners), as well as individual employers may conclude CLAs, principally or exclusively setting out the terms of employment. Social partners also have an important role in the Dutch consultation model (*Poldermodel*) within the industrial relations system. Apart from their consultation, lobbying and advising roles at national level and their collective bargaining activities at sectoral and company level, social partners play an important role in fostering compliance and enforcement of rules. For instance, if provisions from (often) universally binding CLAs are not observed, then employees and/or social partners may institute an action against the non-compliant employer.

As trade union density is only 19%,[31] many sectoral CLAs cannot reach a 'sufficient' level of coverage through membership alone.[32] Therefore, the majority of employers use clauses in the individual employment contract to bind the employees to sectoral collective agreements (i.e., *incorporatiebeding*). Because of the wide use of

28. https://www.voor14.nl/voor_14_is_mogelijk.
29. Under strict conditions (and in line with Art. 7:631 & 632 DCC) deductions for housing & utility or service costs are allowed up to 25% of the Minimum Wage level after written authorization by the employer and employee. *See* Art. 2a(1)(a) *Besluit Minimumloon en Vakantietoeslag* (Decree Minimum Wages & Holiday Allowance).
30. As of 1 January 2021, an Act on the simplification of the seizure-free threshold (*Wet vereenvoudiging beslagvrije voet*) has entered into force.
31. https://www.cbs.nl/nl-nl/nieuws/2018/25/bijna-een-op-de-vijf-werknemers-lid-van-een-vakbond. *See also* Keune (2021) Inequality between capital and labour and among wage-earners: the role of collective bargaining and trade unions. *Transfer, 27*(1), 29-46.
32. W. Gielen en J. Floris, 'Wie is er nog lid van een vakbond? Inzicht in lidmaatschap, belang en tevredenheid', *CBS Statistische Trends* 2018.

such clauses and because most sector-level collective agreements are made generally binding by a government decree, more than 80% of the Dutch employees is covered by a CLA. Hence, the rather low unionization in the Netherlands does not stand in the way of a high collective agreement coverage. Notably, many statutory provisions are three-quarter mandatory, meaning that only CLA parties can deviate from these statutory standards, also to the detriment to the workers. Most CLAs therefore contain, besides better conditions than the statutory minimum standards, also some less favourable working conditions. The number of successive fixed-term contracts (important for VUP Group 3 workers) can, for example, be extended by a CLA.

All CLAs have wage scales for different job titles. The wage scales are usually designed in such a way that the employee receives a wage increase after every year in employment (annually). This means that the longer the employee has been working somewhere, the higher the wage. So, wages increase with job tenure. In these job ladders, there is usually a maximum to how high a salary can go for a certain job title. However, most often, the character of CLAs is that they provide the minimum standard. So, at company level (for all employees) and/or even in individual negotiations between employer and employee, deviation in favour of the employee is possible.[33] Other important pay-related conditions established in most CLAs are occupational pension schemes (allowing workers to build up occupational pensions on top of the basic state pension[34]), surcharges for overtime, end-of-year bonuses, et cetera.[35] In sum, CLAs use a much broader definition of pay than is applied in the *WML* with regard to the statutory minimum wage.

[C] Main Sources of Social Security, Providing Direct Income Support

Social security law provides an important source of direct income support (if need be), consisting not only of an employee benefit system and a residence-based benefit system, but of a right to means-tested social assistance (administered by the municipalities) as well, meant as a last safety net.

Since 1983, the Dutch Constitution includes a provision concerning the right to a minimum level of subsistence and social security. Most important from the perspective of the WorkYP project, is Article 20(1) of the Dutch Constitution[36] which, as already mentioned, stipulates that it shall be the concern of the authorities to secure the means of subsistence of the population and to achieve the distribution of wealth. Moreover, Article 20(2) requires the Dutch Government to lay down rules concerning entitlements

33. Also, many sector-level CLAs allow for decentralized collective bargaining arrangements 'à la carte' at company level.
34. Together, the state pension and the supplementary company pension may amount to approximately 70% of the median wage during an employees' career (this will change from 2026 onwards). Solo self-employed are sometimes allowed to opt-in, but this is rather expensive and therefore not frequently used.
35. Art. 2a Wet AVV states which components should also be guaranteed to posted workers (and which not).
36. Extensively: M. Houwerzijl & F. Vlemminx, Commentary on Article 20 (in Dutch): De grondwet | Artikel 20 – Bestaanszekerheid.

to social security by Acts of Parliament. In Article 20(3), it is stipulated that every Dutch national resident in the Netherlands who is unable to provide a living for themselves, shall have a right to social assistance from the authorities, which should be regulated by Act of Parliament. Clearly, the assumption that poverty among working people is undesirable from a policy point of view, is underpinned by this Article 20 of the Dutch Constitution. Interestingly, commitment to this fundamental right was (implicitly) addressed in both the current and the previous Dutch government's Coalition Agreement to 'fight poverty and indebtedness' and to 'make work pay'.[37]

The universal benefit schemes encompass survivorship benefits, basic state pension, child benefits, and long-term care. Everyone have access to these residence-based schemes. This is also true for the Dutch general healthcare system, which is based on private health insurance, mandatory for all residents (*Zorgverzekeringswet, Zvw*). Since the system is residence-based, it does not differentiate between different types of workers such as salaried, self-employed, or non-standard employed workers. Employers thus have no obligation to offer health insurance.[38] For residents with lower incomes, the government provides an income-dependent health insurance allowance (*zorgtoeslag*).

Employee benefit schemes cover the social risks of unemployment, sickness, and disability. All employees working in the Netherlands are compulsory insured for the employee benefit schemes. In case of job loss, such as in economic crisis situations, they are entitled to unemployment benefits (UB), provided they meet the eligibility requirements.[39] The level of these benefits amounts, as a rule, to 70%-75% of the last earned daily wage,[40] with a maximum.[41] The maximum daily wage in the Netherlands as of 1 July 2021, is EUR 225,57 per day (which amounts to EUR 4906,15 per month).[42] Until 1 January 2016, the maximum duration of UB was 38 months. The maximum duration was gradually reduced to 24 months from 1 July 2019 onwards. This reform mainly affected older unemployed persons with a longer employment history, since their maximum UB duration was considerably reduced. Unemployed persons, who do

37. Coalition agreement 10 October 2017 (*Regeerakkoord*): p. 22, 27; Coalition agreement 15 December 2021 (*Regeerakkoord*): pp. 23-25.
38. Until 2006, the *Ziekenfondswet* was in force, an employees' insurance scheme that protected employees and self-employed persons with low incomes only.
39. Apart from rights to an UB, all Dutch employees are entitled under labour law to a so-called transition allowance (*transitievergoeding*) when their employment contract ends on the initiative of the employer. The amount of the transition allowance is equal to one-third of the monthly wage for each calendar year that the contract of employment has lasted.
40. An automatic indexation mechanism for all social benefits, including UB and social assistance, does exist *(Wet Koppeling met afwijkingsmogelijkheid* (WKA) 1992). Biannually, the level of all benefits is increased by the average percentage increase in contractual wages. Although the Act on the indexation of social benefit provides for the option to freeze benefit levels in the case of a strong relative increase in the number of beneficiaries, the government did not use this option in recent economic crises.
41. On top of the compulsory employee-related benefit schemes provided for by law (illness, incapacity for work, unemployment), many sectors have concluded specific sectoral CLAs regarding supplementary benefits. For example, paying compensation in case of illness from the first sick day or topping up the statutory benefit level to 80, 90, or even 100 % of the last wage.
42. These are gross amounts. https://www.uwv.nl/werkgevers/bedragen-en-premies/detail/maximumdagloon.

not meet the requirements for UB at all, can rely on the general social assistance scheme, which is means-tested.

The most important social assistance scheme is laid down in the so-called Participation Act (*Participatiewet or PW*). The PW provides the ultimate social safety net, granting a minimum income to anyone legally residing in the Netherlands who has insufficient means to support oneself, meaning little or no other income (including other benefits) and/or a partner and few personal assets (if any). The amount of social assistance benefits is linked to the statutory minimum wage. Actually, the statutory minimum wage level is very much functioning as a 'red line' for all low incomes in the Netherlands because all minimum amounts of employee-related benefits and the social assistance level are linked to the statutory minimum wage. In principle, every two-adults household is entitled to minimum benefits at the level of one net minimum wage (in that respect the minimum wage supposedly is still based on the single breadwinner household, where it originally was based on as well). From a legal and systemic perspective, the established social minimum is 50% (married people) or 70% (single people) of the net minimum wage. This also means that nobody is obliged, in order to receive such payments, to accept or perform work below the level of the statutory minimum wage.

[D] Social-Fiscal Allowances, Indirectly Influencing In-Work Poverty

There is a range of instruments to support households with children: (income-dependent) combination tax credits, child care allowance, parental leave options, and (income-dependent) child benefits, for example. Next to the allowances to reduce the financial burden of having children, the Dutch government supports low- and middle-income households and individuals with other basic needs such as rent/housing allowance and healthcare insurance allowance. This system of so-called social-fiscal income-related allowances helps covering living costs by providing an allowance that eases the financial burden.[43] Said social-fiscal allowances do not make a principled difference between working and non-working people. In line with the 2006 new policy insight that finding a job does not always mean an escape from poverty, working and non-working groups are treated equally according to the household's ability to pay for certain services. The annual expenditure for the system of social-fiscal allowances amounts to EUR 13 billion, and the system fulfils a number of crucial functions.

However, the so-called *kindertoeslagenaffaire* now threatens to discredit the whole system of social-fiscal allowances. This political affair concerns the technicalities of the allowances system: It is based on a rather generous and easy advance-payment design combined with a strict, harsh, and disproportional recovery and anti-fraud policy. In practice, this has led to accumulated repayments occurring most frequently among poorer households and households with people in flexible employment. These households most often have differentiating income levels and also people

43. Which is no luxury in light of – in some regions – soaring high rents and high prices of child day care.

tend to report income changes less frequently and less timely than was expected. Thus, the system of advance payments and settlements showed to have unpleasant consequences for poor (working) families who were supposed to benefit the most from it, as it leads to increased income insecurity and contributes to debt problems. The recovery practice of child care allowances eventually led to huge political turmoil and as a consequence, on 15 January 2021, the cabinet decided to collectively offer its resignation, two months before the Lower House elections, in response to a report of the Parliamentary Interrogation Committee on Childcare Benefits.

Despite the critique, it must be acknowledged that the social-fiscal allowances help narrowing the gap between low-income and better-off households. The allowances also lead to a considerable increase in the social minimum for people living on welfare or minimum wage level.[44] Furthermore they facilitate demand management in the market-based systems of healthcare, housing, and childcare. It will therefore be difficult to find a suitable alternative.[45]

§6.03 VUP GROUP 1: LOW OR UNSKILLED STANDARD EMPLOYMENT

[A] Composition of VUP Group 1

As discussed in the introductory chapter of this book, VUP Group 1 consists of workers in low or unskilled jobs who have a full-time and open-ended employment contract. In 2019, 14.4% of the Dutch in-work population belongs to VUP Group 1. There are significantly more men than women in VUP Group 1: 83.3% versus 16.7%. Some 39.5% of the low-wage workers is 50 years of age or older. In addition, 33.1% is aged between 35 and 49, and 27.4% is aged between 18 and 34.[46]

Of the low-wage workers, 29.6% works in *agriculture, industry, or construction*. These are not considered to be poor sectors by Eurostat,[47] however Dutch employees working in these sectors have the highest risk of poverty: 5.9%, which is just above the Dutch average of 5.5%. A further 38.9% works in *trade, transport, accommodation, and food services or info-com*, of which trade (wholesale and retail) and accommodation and food services are considered to be poor sectors. Of the employees belonging to VUP 1 in these sectors, only 3% is at risk of poverty. The other 31.5% of VUP 1 works in 'other services', being *financial and insurance activities, real estate activities, administrative and support service activities, education, human health and social work activities, arts, entertainment and recreation, and other service activities*. Of these sectors, the ones considered poor sectors are administrative and support service, arts, entertainment and recreation, and other service activities. Workers from VUP 1

44. The lowest income earners, depending on their household situation, receive 13% to 20% of their disposable income through these social-fiscal allowances. See, Rijksoverheid (2019). *Rapport deelonderzoek 1 IBO Toeslagen*.
45. *See* Vonk et al., 'Een verkenning van alternatieve inrichtingsvormen voor het huidige stelsel van inkomensafhankelijke toeslagen', *Weekblad Fiscaal Recht* 2021/98.
46. *See* table 6.1 below in §6.03[C].
47. The Netherlands is not quite familiar with the term 'poor sector'. Moreover, not for all economic sectors sufficient data is available.

working in these sectors have a poverty risk of 4.6%. In §6.03[C] below, the composition of VUP Group 1 is linked to more detailed data on in-work poverty.

VUP Group 1 workers may have started working early, because they have low-skilled jobs for which a diploma is attained at an earlier age[48] than other educational levels.[49] In that regard it should be noted that the Netherlands has a system of youth minimum wage for workers younger than the age of 21 with significantly lower wages than the normal minimum wage. This brings us to the relevant legal framework.

[B] Relevant Legal Framework

[1] Collective Agreements Coverage

Many CLAs fall within the scope of the sectors mentioned above. In these sectors, sector-level CLAs tend to prevail. Many VUP Group 1 workers are therefore covered by sector-level CLA's, such as for the 'industry', e.g., CLA for large metal processing (*Metalelektro*), CLA for general packaging industry (*Algemene verpakkingsindustrie*), CLA for wood processing industry (*Houtverwerkende industrie*). However, there are enterprise-level CLA's as well, especially for big enterprises, such as Philips and Tata Steel. The same applies for other (groups of) low-wage sectors. There is a branch of CLA for the construction industry (*Bouw & Infra*), a CLA for the brick industry (*Baksteenindustrie*), and a CLA for carpenter industry (*Timmerindustrie*). There are relatively fewer CLAs in the arts, entertainment, and recreation branches. There is, however, a CLA for recreation (*Recreatie*), applying to tourism companies such as vacation parks, but not including hotels and restaurants, since these have a different sector-level agreement. There is also a sector-level CLA for sports for non-profit organizations that facilitate sports in the broadest sense. Moreover, there is a sector-level CLA for theatre and dance (*Toneel en Dans*), a CLA for movie theatres (*Bioscoopbedrijf*), a CLA for museums (*Museum*), and a CLA for orchestras (*Orkesten*). Finally, there are several CLA's for large media-companies and a sector-level CLA for broadcasting companies (*Omroeppersoneel*). Hence, also in this group of low-wage sectors there are many CLA's.

[2] Recent or Pending Labour and Social Security Law Reforms

Labour law reforms may affect the VUP Group 1 employees' working conditions, improving or worsening their precariousness and/or their working conditions. In the

48. Until the age of 16, all persons have to follow compulsory education (secondary school). In principle, if a person aged 16 does not have a diploma from a secondary level vocational education, then education is compulsory until 18 years old.
49. Although workers in 'low- or unskilled standard employment' might also be overqualified. Actually, only 25.1% of VUP group 1 workers have a low education and 15.9% have a high education. The largest part of the low-wage workers (59%) has an intermediate level of education.

last decade, this concerns the reforms that occurred in the aftermath of the financial crisis and of the COVID-19 pandemic.

In 2015, the Act on Work and Security (*Wet Werk en Zekerheid*) changed Dutch labour law, aiming to make flexible or temporary contracts less flexible and the open-ended contracts less permanent. However, the dominant perception is that where dismissals may have become less costly, since severance payment has been lowered, the dismissal procedure has remained rather rigid with increased (litigation) risks for employers.[50] In 2018, new changes were introduced with the Act on Labour Market in Balance (*Wet Arbeidsmarkt in Balans*). For VUP Group 1 workers, the main feature is the introduction of a so-called cumulating ground for dismissal in order to make it (a bit) easier to dismiss employees. All in all, the new legislation seems to have worsened the position of the VUP Group 1 workers only slightly. Having an open-ended full-time contract in the Netherlands still provides solid labour law protection.

An issue that is still pending is the issue of the monthly statutory minimum wage. Since the same monthly statutory minimum wage applies in all sectors, even though the full-time working hours can differ per sector and even per employer, having no hourly minimum wage means that workers with a 40 hours working week have to work more hours for the same amount of money than workers with, for example, a 36 hours working week. It has been calculated that an employee working in a sector where the normal working time is 40 hours earns 11% less per hour than an employee working in a sector where the normal working time is 36 hours. There are, therefore, pay differences at the minimum wage level that are only caused by the difference in normal working hours per sector and the absence of a minimum hourly wage. There is a bill pending in the Parliament to introduce an hourly minimum wage.

[C] Descriptive Data and Impact Analysis

[1] Workforce Composition Related to In-Work Poverty

In order to assess to which extent VUP Group 1 workers are exposed to poverty, table 6.1 provides an overview of the Eurostat data in the most recent year (2019). The number in brackets reflects the share (%) of a variable in this group. For example, 27.4% of low-wage workers with a standard employment contract is 18 to 34 years old. The number on its left is the percentage of people in this category that are at risk of poverty. For example, 2%* of the low-wage workers aged 18 to 34 lives below the poverty threshold.

50. *See also* Nuna Zekić, 'Reforming labour laws in the Netherlands: An assessment of the redistributive effects', in V. Pulignano, & F. Hendrickx (Eds.), *Employment relations in the 21st century: Challenges for theory and research in a changing world of work* (Bulletin of Comparative Labour Relations; No. 107), Kluwer Law International 2019, pp. 77-89.

Table 6.1 VUP 1: Low-wage Workers (Low or Unskilled in Standard Employment), NL, 2019 (%)

% of in-work population	(14.4)		
In-work at risk of poverty	4.4		
Individual variables		**Household variables**	
Age group		**Household size**	
18-34	2* (27.4)	1	< 1(18.4)
35-49	8.5 (33.1)	2	0.7 (29.4)
≥50	2.6 (39.5)	> 2	8 (52.2)
Gender		**No. of in-work persons in the household**	
Women	0.2* (16.7)	1	6.2 (33.7)
Men	5.2 (83.3)	> 1	3.4 (66.3)
Education		**No. of children (< 18)**	
Low	4.8 (25.1)	0	0.3 (65.5)
Medium	4.6 (59.0)	1	6.7* (14.5)
High	2.2* (15.9)	> 1	15.9* (20)

Source: Eurostat data.

Note 1: extremely low poverty percentages that are derived from small sample sizes are reported as < 1.

Note 2: *nationality* and *number of months work* cannot be reported on due to extremely small sample size (< 50).

Note 3: based on the definition of this group, the variables 'full-time/part-time', 'permanent/temporary contract' and 'occupational skill level' are not reported in the table; 100% of them is employed full-time, in low-skilled occupation, and on a fixed-term contract.

* Careful interpretation, low sample size (N = 100–200).

As mentioned earlier, 14.4% of the Dutch in-work population in 2019 was employed in a low-skilled profession, on the basis of standard employment (VUP Group 1), with 4.4% of them being at risk of poverty. This percentage is below the national average of 5.5%. Some aspects stand out from the data on these low-wage workers. First of all, there is a striking difference in at-risk-of-poverty percentage between the age groups. The middle age group of 35 to 49 years has by far the highest risk of poverty, with a percentage of 8.5%, compared to 2% of the younger group and 2.6% of the older group. This higher risk of poverty cannot be explained from the data itself, but might be explained by the simple reasoning that people in this age category (35-49 years) are more likely to have dependent children living with them, and thus having more mouths to feed with the same income, than individuals from the other age categories.

Next to that, from the significantly more men than women in VUP Group 1 (83.3% versus 16.7%), the men have a much higher at-risk-of-poverty percentage of 5.2% against 0.2% of the women. An explanation of this large difference is that Dutch women most often work part-time. If women have a full-time and permanent job at a lower-skill level, they are hardly ever experiencing poverty. This might be due to their household composition.

That household size seems to play a prominent role can also be seen in the figures of the entire working population (employees and self-employed) of the Netherlands (Table 6.2). Among the Dutch working population, single-person households have a greater risk of poverty than people in a two- or multi-person households (see table), as discussed in § 6.01.

Table 6.2 At Risk of Poverty, All Employed Persons, Including Employees and Self-Employed, NL 2019 (%)

Household Size	*% of Population*	*At Risk of Poverty*
1	16.6	9.9
2	30.4	4
> 2	53	5
No. of in-work persons in household		
1	29.4	12.3
> 1	70.6	2.7
No. of children (< 18)		
0	60.2	5.4
1	15.3	5.2
> 1	23.5	6

Source: Eurostat data.

The data of VUP Group 1, however, does not correspond with this. According to this data, single persons with a low-wage job would have close to 0% chance of being below the poverty line (*See* table 6.1). The question is why, because the overall tendency in the Netherlands is that persons in a single household run the highest risk of poverty. In addition, the poverty rate of just 0.7% for two-person households in the VUP Group 1 does not correspond with the overall poverty rate of two-person household in the Netherlands (4%). Finally, the risk of poverty for a household of more than two persons in VUP Group 1 is 8%. This is a relatively high percentage compared to the other two household compositions. The data gives no explanations, but it could be the taxation systems for low-income groups that explain the findings. Next to household size, also the number of in-work people in the household of a low-wage worker influences the risk of poverty. If there is one employed person in the household the poverty risk is 6.2%, but if more than one person is employed, this chance is reduced to 3.4%. Finally, the number of dependent children living at home also affects the poverty risk. The majority of low-wage workers (65.5%) has no dependent children living at home. Of them, only 0.3% has a risk of poverty. Of the workers with one dependent child, this chance is 6.7%. Most striking is the risk of poverty of the low-wage workers with more than one dependent child living at home: 15.9%. This indicates that low-wage workers with (especially multiple) children have a high chance of poverty. This is a striking deviation from the average national statistics: for the three categories, they show poverty risks of 5.4%, 5.2%, and 6%. This might indicate that children-related costs are not covered well enough by the available benefits for workers with a low wage, despite having a full-time job and a (most likely) stable income.

In short, according to these data, low-wage workers belonging to the VUP Group 1 overall have a lower than average risk of poverty. For VUP Group 1 workers who live in a household with more than two persons, or who have two or more dependent children, face the highest risk of poverty. It is striking, however, that low-wage workers in a single-person household virtually have no risk of poverty, contrary to the national trend. The main take away thus seems to be that broadly speaking, having a 'normal' open-ended and full-time contract helps against the effects of having a very low income. This conclusion, however, loses its validity as soon as the household size increases, and there are children living at home. This might be due to, e.g., failing child-related policies for low-income groups and merits further research.

[2] Impact of the Financial and Corona Crisis

The Eurostat data shows that the overall poverty risk of persons in VUP Group 1 was lower before the financial crisis (3.5%) than it was after the financial crisis (5.3%). For all employed persons in the Netherlands, this risk was slightly lower after the crisis (from 4.6% to 4.5%). What is most striking is that the poverty risk of single-persons households of VUP Group 1 however significantly dropped, from 3.1% to less than 1%. Furthermore, the persons belonging to VUP Group 1 living in a more-than-two-person household went from a 4.5% poverty risk to an 8.5% poverty risk. This means that after the crisis, the larger households had a higher risk of falling below the poverty line. Furthermore, households with one in-work person also experienced an increase in risk of poverty, more than households with more than one in-work person. This signals that the financial crisis had a larger effect on the single-earner households. Finally, the risk of poverty rose in a similar amount for households with and without dependent children; however for households with more than one dependent child, it rose slightly more. This indicates that income for households with more than one dependent child decreased and/or expenses rose more than for households with no or just one dependent child.

To mitigate the socio-economic impact of COVID-19, several schemes have been introduced. The Emergency Bridging Measure for Sustained Employment (*Noodmaatregel Overbrugging Werkgelegenheid: NOW* 1) was the first and most important one (also from a budgetary perspective). Under this scheme, which ran from March until June 2020, employers that received government subsidies were enabled to continue to pay the wages and were not allowed to dismiss workers for financial reasons. *NOW* 2, 3, and 4 were introduced as an extension on *NOW* 1.[51] Employers could apply for compensation of wages for employees with permanent or fixed-term contracts as well as for employees with other flexible contracts. Hence the workers in VUP Group 1 and 3 generally were protected via their employer by the *NOW* schemes.

§6.04 VUP GROUP 2: SOLO AND BOGUS SELF-EMPLOYMENT

[A] Composition of VUP Group 2

In 2019, 9% of the Dutch in-work population was solo self-employed. Almost half of the solo self-employed (47.3%) were 50 years or older, whereas the 35 to 49-year-olds made up 37.2% of the solo self-employed. The smallest part (only 15.5%) of the solo self-employed is aged between 18 and 34.[52] A possible explanation for the large proportion of older (especially 50 +) solo self-employed is that due to their age, they often have a much smaller chance of finding employment, thus being forced into self-employment. Moreover, at a later age the wish to become an entrepreneur might be stronger, while experience and the financial position of the household (e.g., having a second earner in the family, and no longer having care and financial responsibilities for dependent children) might allow for starting up a business. In §6.04[C], the composition of VUP Group 2 is linked to data on in-work poverty, but first we turn to the relevant legal rules.

[B] Relevant Legal Framework

[1] Fiscal Support for (Solo) Self-Employed

Several fiscal policy instruments lower the threshold to start a company and stimulate in particular solo-entrepreneurship in the Netherlands. The following three instruments are most often used in practice: the self-employed tax deduction, the starter's deduction, and the small and medium-sized enterprise (SME) profit exemption. All these tax deductions reduce taxable income without the need for expenses incurred in generating that income, which is quite unique in comparison to other countries.[53]

The self-employed tax deduction (*ZA: zelfstandigenaftrek*) is meant to reduce the taxable income of self-employed. When working for their company for at least 1,225 hours a year (about 25 hours per week), one could (in 2021) deduct EUR 6,670 from their profits when filing their tax returns. This deduction will be gradually reduced until in 2036, it will be set at EUR 3,240, with the aim to harmonize tax conditions for

51. The NOW-scheme did run until Autumn 2021. *See*, https://www.uwv.nl/werkgevers/overige-onderwerpen/now/index.aspx.
52. *See* table 6.3 in §6.03[C] below.
53. OESO (2015). 'Taxation of SMEs in OECD and G20 countries', OECD Tax Policy Studies 23, Paris: OECD; Other countries generally have less generic entrepreneurial tax schemes.

entrepreneurs and employees.[54] Furthermore, the tax relief for new companies (*startersaftrek*) is an increase of the *ZA* deduction especially intended for new businesses. By temporarily sharing the entrepreneurial risk between government and companies, it is more interesting for employees or unemployed to switch to entrepreneurship. In 2019, 2020, and 2021, the starter's deduction was EUR 2,123. Finally, the SME profit exemption is a reduction of the tax rate of a given percentage that applies to every *IB* (income tax) entrepreneur regardless of the number of hours worked (since 2010) and regardless of whether a profit or loss is made.[55] It allows the entrepreneur to deduct a given percentage of his or her profits made after deduction of other fiscal support measures. From 2020 onwards, the deduction of the SME profit exemption will be gradually diminished.

An evaluative study commissioned by the Ministry of Economic Affairs in 2017 showed that the fiscal policy instruments seem to add little to the general welfare of the Netherlands.[56] Based on the CBS microdata for the period 2007-2014, the analysis showed that there is limited growth among the companies, and profits are low.[57] It seems therefore relatively easy to become an entrepreneur, and that many people do so as a solo self-employed, but that growth less often occurs.

[2] Applicability of the General Contract Law Framework

As mentioned §6.02[A], the DCC regulates several types of commercial contracts. The majority of solo-self-employed persons works on the basis of an agreement to 'make a work' (*overeenkomst tot aanneming van werk*), as regulated in Article 7:750 DCC, which is traditionally mostly used in the construction sector, or an agreement for services (*overeenkomst van opdracht*), as regulated in Article 7:400 DCC. There is not much difference between these two types of contracts for determining the legal protection of the self-employed. As a default, labour law neither applies to their contracts, nor to employee benefit insurance schemes. However, there are some exceptions.

[3] Applicability of Labour Law and Social Security Standards

Since 1 January 2018, self-employed persons are entitled to statutory minimum wage and minimum holiday allowance (*Wet minimumloon en minimumvakantiebijslag*), unless they fiscally qualify as an undertaking (an entrepreneur). The legislator's aim was to give protection to precarious self-employed workers and to prevent downward

54. 2021 Tax Plan: post-crisis tax system will be better, fairer and more sustainable | News item | Government.nl.
55. Currently 14% in the specific Box 2.1 of the Dutch tax system.
56. Ter Weel, B., Smits, T., Witteman, J., Vriend, S., & Rosenboom, N., *Evaluatie fiscale ondernemersregelingen*, SEO report for Ministry of Economic Affairs, January 2017: Evaluation fiscal entrepreneurship – SEO Economisch Onderzoek.
57. The analysis showed that every year 2% to 3% of the self-employed grow into a company with employees and that 0.7% of the sole proprietors annually grow into a company with employees and that 0.7% of the self-employed grow into a company with its own legal personality.

wage competition with employees (social dumping), to ensure every worker at the Dutch labour market an income above the poverty line.[58] However, as most self-employed persons in the Netherlands do want to qualify as an undertaking, because this has fiscal benefits, it is still not clear how effective the extended scope of the statutory minimum wage has been so far. There are also other employment items, for which the application of labour law had already been extended to self-employed persons. For example, some provisions of the Law on health and safety (*Arbeidsomstandighedenwet*) apply to self-employed persons as well. The Supreme Court has ruled that under certain circumstances employer's liability under Article 7: 658 (4) DCC also exists for principals towards self-employed persons.[59] Furthermore, female entrepreneurs have a right to a form of maternity leave (Article 3:18 and 3:20 *WAZO*).

Regarding social security, as explained in § 6.02[A], some solo self-employed have an employee-like status, because, from a socio-economic point of view, they are equally economically dependent on work for one principal. Under the condition that they fulfil certain requirements, e.g., home workers, musicians, artists, professional sportsmen, and 'other persons, who perform personal work for remuneration,' are covered under the employee insurance schemes. However, accessibility has worsened with the entering into force of the Assessment of Employment Relationships (Deregulation) Act (AERD Act: *Wet deregulering beoordeling arbeidsrelaties*) in 2016. This Act was an attempt to mitigate the negative aspects of increasing solo self-employment, such as bogus self-employment, by abolishing the legal certainty for self-employed persons regarding exemption from employee insurance. At the same time, the AERD Act created a de facto opt-out for employee-benefits insurance by those with an employee-like status, which sits uneasily with the ratio for extensions to the employee-concept.[60]

A specific social assistance scheme for self-employed is administered as of 1985 that allows for a loan for working capital and/or temporary income support, initially up to 18 months. The scheme has been modified several times and can be invoked by both starting and established self-employed (under certain conditions).[61] In 1998, the following elements were added: a trial period for unemployed starters to examine their potential markets and develop a business plan; an allowance for guidance and advice; an increase in the amount of credit; an extension of the period to award supplementary income support (until 36 months); the possibility of taking account of income from other sources (another job, partner's income) when deciding on the viability of a plan; and special provisions for persons who are handicapped or with care obligations.[62]

58. *Kamerstukken II* 2012/13, 33623, nr. 3.
59. HR 23 March 2012, LJN: BV 0616.
60. In the coalition agreement of the former but then new Government of 2017, it was agreed to replace this contested Act. However, the government has not succeeded in finding a good alternative that would reconcile (better than the Deregulation Act) the interests of solo self-employed with good tariffs and those with precarious conditions.
61. Currently applicable: *Besluit bijstandverlening zelfstandigen 2004*, Decree of 14 October 2003, Government Gazette (*Stb.*) 2003, 390, most recently adapted version published in *Stcrt.* 2020, 66672.
62. Currently the following groups of freelancers/self-employed persons are eligible to *Bbz*, to be decided upon by the municipality's social services: those starting a company, who receive

During the COVID 19-pandemic, a special temporary social assistance scheme for self-employed was introduced, called *TOZO*.[63] The scheme allowed for income support and/or a loan for working capital. The *TOZO* has been extended several times. With the first *TOZO*-scheme, no partner income test applied, however this has been changed when the *TOZO* was prolonged; if the income of the self-employed and/or of his or her partner in the months for which the claim was made is higher than the social minimum,[64] a *TOZO* benefit was no longer assigned.

[4] Application of Collective Agreements

To curb the problems with vulnerable (false) self-employed, the FNV, the largest Dutch trade union, took the initiative to advocate the conclusion of CLAs with minimum rates for solo self-employed, in order to offer them a minimum level of protection, but also to protect employees from downward pressure on wages and working conditions. When a few CLAs indeed entitled self-employed persons to invoke the tariffs or other labour conditions set out in the CLA against their clients, this led to the well-known judgment of the CJEU in 2014 in the FNV-Kiem case,[65] and in 2019 and 2020 to policy changes by the Netherlands Competition Authority (in Dutch abbreviated to *ACM*), which create more room (albeit in a cautious manner) for including (false) self-employed in the scope of collective bargaining. According the *ACM* guidelines, in principle, self-employed persons are not covered by CLAs, because they are considered undertakings. This is why competition law applies to the self-employed. However, there are situations where the competition rules do not apply or where *ACM* will not impose any fines. There are four situations in which self-employed workers are allowed to make arrangements with each other about rates and other conditions. They are allowed to do so, if:

(1) the self-employed workers work side-by-side with employees; or
(2) their turnovers and market shares are small; or
(3) the benefits outweigh the drawbacks; or
(4) the arrangements concern a rate that is not higher than necessary for safeguarding the subsistence level.[66] ACM will not impose fines on arrangements between and with self-employed workers that aim to guarantee a

welfare, UB, or incapacity benefit; established entrepreneurs who are experiencing temporary financial problems; entrepreneurs born before 1960 with a non-viable company (in Dutch); entrepreneurs who wish to end their company.

63. Decree of 17 April 2020 containing temporary rules with respect to social assistance for self-employed that are financially harmed by the consequences of the crisis; Temporary benefits for self-employed professionals (*Tijdelijke overbruggingsregeling zelfstandig ondernemers*), Government Gazette (*Stb.*) 2020, 118.
64. For a household couple, this is 100% of the minimum wage level; for a single person this is approximately 75% of the minimum wage.
65. CJEU 4 December 2014, C-413/13 (*FNV KIEM*), ECLI:EU:C:2014:241.
66. Which is approximately at the level of the statutory minimum wage. *See*, The Netherlands Authority for Consumers and Markets, 'Guidelines: Price arrangements between self- employed workers', 2019.

subsistence level for said self-employed workers. The agreed upon minimum rates may not be higher, and their scope may not be larger than necessary for being able to support oneself.

Since these guidelines were introduced, CLAs occasionally contain (newly negotiated) provisions on self-employed persons. An example of a CLA with provisions on the fees for the self-employed is the collective agreement for the Architects. According to this CLA, self-employed architects must earn at least 150% of the wage that an employee receives for the same work. The same is agreed in the CLA for Public Broadcasting. The CLA for Theatre and Dance contains a provision with 140%.

[C] Descriptive Data and Impact Analysis

[1] Workforce Composition Related to In-Work Poverty

In order to assess to which extent VUP Group 2 workers are exposed to poverty, the table 6.3 provides an overview of the Eurostat data in 2019.

Table 6.3 VUP 2: Solo Self-Employed (SSE), NL, 2019 (in %)

% of in-work population	(9)		
In-work at risk of poverty	14,3		
Individual variables		Household variables	
Age group		**Household size**	
18-34	8,3* (15,5)	1	27,2* (18,3)
35-49	9,6 (37,2)	2	12,3 (32,5)
≥50	20,1 (47,3)	> 2	10,9 (49,2)
Gender		Number of in-work persons in the household	
Women	12,1 (44,4)	1	26,9 (31,5)
Men	16,1 (55,6)	> 1	8,6 (68,5)
Education	Number of children (< 18)		
Low	8,3* (15,7)	0	15,4 (61,7)
Medium	14 (37,4)	1	10,7* (13,7)
High	15 (43,4)	> 1	13,8 (24,7)
Working time			
Full-time	3 (49,3)		
Part-time	25,1 (50,7)		
Occupation (skill level)			
High	13,3 (56,7)		

% of in-work population	(9)	
In-work at risk of poverty	14,3	
Individual variables		Household variables
Low	13,3 (43,3)	

Source: Eurostat data.

Note: *nationality* and *number of months of work* cannot be reported on due to extremely small sample size (< 50).

*Careful interpretation, low sample size (N = 100-200)

As mentioned, in 2019, 9% of the Dutch in-work population belonged to VUP Group 2. A rather large amount of them, namely 14.9% of the solo self-employed was at risk of poverty. This percentage is well above the national average of 5.5%. What stands out from the data in table 3 is that 8.3% of the youngest group (only 15.5% of solo self-employed) and 9.6% of the middle group (who make up 37.2% of the solo self-employed) have an income below the poverty line. This is much higher than the national average. However, the 50 + age group (47.3% of the solo self-employed), has an extremely high risk of poverty: 20.1% (which is 1 in 5). This might point at a (too strong) push towards self-employment rather than a free choice to become an entrepreneur. In light of the extreme risk of in-work poverty, such motivation might not always be considered the best predictor of setting up a successful business.

Furthermore, interesting results also appear when education is related to poverty. Overall, the risk of poverty is lower when the level of education is higher, as shown by the data on all employed persons in the Netherlands. For solo self-employed however, the data shows the opposite: a higher education is linked to a higher risk of poverty. Perhaps the explanation for this lies in the fact that low-skilled self-employed often have jobs in construction or agriculture,[67] where work is more constantly available and in higher volume than in the (creative cultural) services sectors.[68] Therefore, they might be more ascertained of having (full-time) work, and thus an adequate income, on a continuous base.

Another huge difference is visible between the poverty risks of part-time and full-time solo self-employed. The number of part-timers (50.7%) and full-timers (49.3%) among the self-employed is almost equally distributed, but for full-timers the risk of poverty is only 3% while it is 25.1% for the part-timers. This is quite logical: working less than full-time could lead to insufficient income no matter the profession and/or contract type. But another question is why half of the solo self-employed work part-time, while a quarter of them is at risk of poverty.

Next, the household variables show interesting data. To start with, half of the solo self-employed (49.2%) live in a household of more than two people. Interesting to

67. https://opendata.cbs.nl/statline/#/CBS/nl/dataset/82808NED/table?dl=4160.
68. Been & Keune, 2020: That is just part of being able to do my cool job: Understanding low earnings but high job satisfaction in the creative industries in the Netherlands.

see is that 'only' 10.9% has a risk of poverty, while solo self-employed in a smaller household (two persons) have a higher poverty risk of 12.3%. The greatest poverty risk is however found for the single-person households: 27.2%. Also, solo self-employed persons living in more-persons household with one in-work individual have a very high risk of poverty with 26.9% (about 1 in 4). Self-employed persons in a household with two (or more) in-work individuals have a substantially lower risk of poverty: 8.6%, which is about 1 in 12. This means that as a solo self-employed person one should be in a household with a double (or at least 1.5) income to be able to make ends meet. Being a self-employed single person or single-earner household, one has a significant chance of falling below the poverty line. Finally, the majority of the self-employed (61.7%) have no dependent children, however they run a higher risk of poverty (15.4%) than the self-employed with children living at home (10.7% and 13.8%,[69] which is still too high). This does seem counter-intuitive because one might expect that having children means having more mouths to feed and thus having a higher likelihood of being poor, but this can also be explained by the fact that the group without children at home are probably foremost the older self-employed, who are more likely to (work part-time and) be poor. In addition, the single-person households, who also have a high poverty risk, also automatically fall within the category of 'no kids at home'. These factors (age and single-person household) thus may explain the high risk of poverty among solo self-employed who have no children at home.

Altogether, according to these data, the solo self-employed with the highest risk of falling below the poverty line, are those who live in a single-person household or who are the only in-work person in the household, the self-employed who are 50 years and older, and self-employed who are working part-time.

Heterogeneous composition of VUP Group 2 complicates finding causes of poverty.

It is important to note that the solo self-employed are a very heterogeneous group, including both successful entrepreneurs and (bogus) self-employed with little other options. Participants to a national WYP workshop suggested therefore to examine more closely the motives to start up a business (genuine versus forced entrepreneurship). Likewise, reasons for a very low income among SSE could range from having few assignments or being in a race-to-the-bottom on tariffs, versus choosing a sabbatical year with little assignments. Also, the start-up years of a business could coincide with lower revenues. Therefore, long-term low income might be a helpful indicator. According to Statistics Netherlands (*CBS*) 'long-term low income' (more than four consecutive years) only applies to 2.1% of self-employed.[70]

Moreover, although no specific data can be found on poverty of 'forced solo self-employed' versus 'solo self-employed by choice', it is plausible indeed that poverty among the forced solo self-employed is higher than among the solo self-employed who have made a conscious decision to become an entrepreneur. The *Zelfstandigen Enquête*

---

69. Solo self-employed who have one child living at home have a poverty risk of 10.7%, and solo self-employed that live in a household with two or more children have a poverty risk of 13.8%.
70. https://www.cbs.nl/nl-nl/nieuws/2018/03/bijna-1-op-de-10-zzp-ers-loopt-risico-op-armoede.

Arbeid[71] (Dutch Self-employed Labour Survey) of 2019 shows that 20% of solo self-employed answered that they are not self-employed by choice. They were unable to find a suitable job as an employee, have been fired or their previous contract has not been renewed, or their employer wanted them to start working as a self-employed.

In June 2021, regarding the vulnerable position of many solo self-employed, the *SER* advised, e.g., to introduce a rebuttable presumption of an employment relationship for those whose rates are below the maximum daily wage (approximately EUR 30-EUR 35 per hour).[72] In these situations, it should be the client who must prove that there is no employment relationship. Above that rate, the reverse should apply.[73] Stakeholders disagree on whether such a measure would solve the problem of a low income. Several factors play a role explaining low incomes of SSEs, including not having enough assignments (meaning that if the tariff is high, but assignments are few, the overall income is still low), and the low barriers to become SSE in the Netherlands, which could act as a driver of in-work poverty (e.g., in order to avoid unemployment and reliance on benefits, one could become SSE without assignments).[74] Thus, the hourly income is not necessarily always the cause of poverty among solo self-employed; rather, not being able to work enough hours may lead to poverty.[75] This is also what Statistics Netherlands indicates: the fewer hours a self-employed person works, the greater the risk of poverty,[76] which is in line with table 6.3 above, showing a large at-risk poverty difference between full-time and part-time solo self-employed.

[2] Impact of the Financial and Corona Crisis

Generally, the poverty risk of VUP Group 2 workers was higher before the financial crisis (16%) than it was after the crisis (12.2%). This decrease is in line with the trend for all employed persons in the Netherlands. The explanation for the higher than average decrease for solo self-employed compared to all employed persons cannot be derived from data; however, a possible factor might be that solo self-employed with very low earnings gave up their enterprise and applied for benefits or accepted a job at an employer during the crisis. Furthermore, it is striking that the poverty risk of persons living in a household of more than two persons had a decrease in poverty risk from 18.1% to 10.4% after the financial crisis, while for the other household sizes the poverty risk hardly changed. This drop could either indicate that after the financial crisis, solo self-employed with larger households could make ends meet more easily than before the crisis, or it could point at a selection effect of the lowest earning solo

71. CBS, 2019: https://www.cbs.nl/-/media/_pdf/2019/27/zea-2019-rapport.pdf.
72. Applied as a maximum limit to the insured wage in the employee benefit schemes.
73. *See* SER, *Sociaal-economisch beleid 2021-2025, Zekerheid voor mensen, een wendbare economie en herstel van de samenleving*, Advies 21/08, The Hague June 2021, Appendix, pp. 11-12.
74. ZiPconomy, 2018: https://www.zipconomy.nl/2018/01/zzp-en-armoede-oorzaak-of-gevolg/.
75. Platform ZZP dienstverleners: https://i-zo.nl/wp-content/uploads/2018/12/document-wat-weten-we-van-de-ZZP-er.pdf.
76. CBS: https://www.cbs.nl/nl-nl/nieuws/2018/03/bijna-1-op-de-10-zzp-ers-loopt-risico-op-armoede.

self-employed withdrawing from entrepreneurship and finding other sources of income. It is likely that the crisis shook out many of the not successful solo self-employed, as a result of which their more successful colleagues (with a smaller risk of poverty) remained. Finally, somehow households of VUP Group 2 workers with dependent children had more income or less expenditure than households without dependent children, or they for other reasons had a smaller risk of falling below the poverty line. This could also be explained by the mentioned 'shake-out' effect of the crisis: Solo self-employed who are responsible not only for themselves but also for children cannot afford taking as much financial risk as solo self-employed who have no others depending on their income. So, solo self-employed with children may leave entrepreneurship sooner and look for a job with more income security.

The coronavirus impact on solo self-employed may be evidenced by the use of *TOZO*: By April 30 2020, about 343,000 applications were submitted,[77] demonstrating the huge need for income support. Solo self-employed also reported that they received fewer assignments.[78] Consistent with this finding, similar groups reported a strong decrease of their income: 69% of the low-income self-employed workers, and 49% of the high-income self-employed workers.[79] Interestingly, the *TOZO* seems to make a chance to become a structural arrangement. In light of the large vulnerability of many solo self-employed, as was highlighted by the corona crisis, the *SER* advised in June 2021 to make it a permanent arrangement for self-employed. According to the *SER*, the scheme should be transformed from social assistance into a contributory scheme. Self-employed should pay contributions to this scheme themselves.

§6.05 VUP GROUP 3: FIXED-TERM, TEMPORARY AGENCY, INVOLUNTARY PART-TIME WORK

[A] Composition of VUP Group 3

VUP Group 3 concerns flexible workers, consisting of fixed-term workers, agency workers, and involuntary part-timers. Taken together, in 2019, 22.5% of the working population worked as a flex worker. Flex work thus is very common in the Netherlands. In 2019, 8.8% of flex workers worked less than 12 months of the year. This group most likely consists of agency- and seasonal workers. Most of the flex workers are young (35.4%) or middle-aged (38.7%), just over a quarter (25.9%) is 50 years or older. Furthermore, women form a large majority within the group of flex workers with 77.2%, men are a minority at 22.8%.[80]

77. FNV, 2020: https://fnvzzp.nl/nieuws/2020/04/beroep-op-tijdelijke-overbruggingsregeling-zelfstandig-ondernemers-tozo-groeit.
78. Bekker, S., Buerkert, J., Quirijns, Q., & Pop, I. (2021). In-work poverty in times of COVID-19. In E. Aarts, H. Fleuren, M. Sitskoorn, & T. Wilthagen (Eds.), *The new common: How the COVID-19 pandemic is transforming society* (pp. 35-40). Springer. https://doi.org/10.1007%2F978-3-030-65355-2_5.
79. *Ibid.*
80. *See* table 6.4 in section §6.05[E] below.

In §6.05[B], [C], and [D], the relevant legal frameworks for these three subgroups are described separately, as they work under partially different labour and social security conditions. Finally, in §6.05[E], a general impact analysis based on data for the whole group of flex workers is provided.

[B] Fixed-term Employees

[1] Relevant Legal Framework

The Dutch Civil Code (Article 7:667 DCC) stipulates that fixed-term employment contracts end by operation of law (*ipso jure*). Fixed-term contracts can be renewed only three times in a row; the fourth fixed-term contract is converted in to an open-ended contract by law (Article 7:668a DCC). The same occurs when successive fixed-term contracts exceed the period of three years. Employment contracts are considered successive when the intervals between the contracts do not last longer than six months. The maximum overall duration for successive fixed-term contracts is thus three years, intervals up to six months included.[81] There is no objective reason required for concluding or renewing fixed-term contracts. They are also used for structural demand of work.

Contrary to employees with an open-ended contract, fixed-term workers used to lack any rights to a compensation in terms of severance payment when their employment comes to an end. This changed in 2015, when a new law (*Wet werk en zekerheid*) introduced a right to a severance payment – called: transition allowance – for all employment contracts that end 'at the initiative of the employer'. From 2020 onwards, severance payment is due also in case the employer does not continue a (series of) fixed-term contract(s) irrespective of the duration of the contract. The employment history does matter for the amount of this transition allowance, which is calculated as one-third of the monthly wage for every working year.

Fixed-term employees are in principle entitled to the same employee insurance benefits as standard employees. Fixed-term employees with short contracts might be at a disadvantage regarding UB since everybody needs to satisfy the so-called weeks of employment requirement: one has to have worked at least 26 of the last 36 weeks prior to unemployment.[82] The worker is then entitled to three months of UB. After that there is the 'years of employment requirement': To meet this requirement, the employee should prove that in the five years immediately prior to the year in which the unemployment started, he or she has performed paid work during at least four years of at least 208 hours in each of those years.[83] This criterion is relatively easy to meet.[84] If the employee meets the employment history requirement, then the minimum payment duration of three months is extended by one month. Together, basic entitlement and

81. It is possible to conclude a one-off fixed-term contract of more than three years.
82. For some workers there are exceptions, such as artists or musicians or employees who are not in regular employment.
83. The year in which unemployment occurs is not counted, since this is (partially) part of the eligibility criterion.

the extension lead to a duration of the UB in months similar to the employment history in years. So, a person who has worked for eight years is entitled to a benefit for eight months.

[2] Data and Impact Analysis

During the first emergency-scheme after the outbreak of COVID-19 pandemic, the NOW 1, that ran from March until June 2020, organizations could claim financial support for both employees with permanent contracts and also employees for whom the employer was not obliged to continue paying wages. In this way, employees with flexible employment contracts were protected against immediate loss of income. Nevertheless, there are indications that despite the financial support by the Dutch government, still many fixed-term contracts were not renewed.

In 2020, 18.1% of all employees were temporary workers. This includes fixed-term employees and temporary agency workers (the latter only being 16.3% of temporary workers). Interestingly, for 28.8% of fixed term workers the main reason for having a fixed term contract is 'probation', indicating that temporary employment contracts are used as a sort of prolonged probation period. Another 25.3% indicates that they have a fixed-term contract because they cannot find a permanent job yet, 14.5% indicates that they do not want to have a permanent job, and a small minority of 3.4% indicates that they had a fixed-term job because they are mainly involved in education or training.

The evaluation of the Law on Work and Security (*Wet werk en zekerheid*) showed that the length of stay of employees in the so-called flexible shell had increased on average since its introduction in 2015.[85] Especially the low-educated employees were found in 2020 to be working longer in flexible jobs, while the period in flexible jobs of the higher-educated workers had not changed.

[C] Temporary Agency Workers

[1] Relevant Legal Framework

The definition of the Dutch agency work employment contract is stipulated in Article 7:690 DCC. The law provides for many exceptions regarding agency workers.[86] For example, Article 7:649 DCC where discrimination on the basis of the temporary nature of the employment contract is prohibited, does not apply to temporary agency workers.

84. The paid work of 208 hours a year can be met by weekly working 5 hours or with a full-time (40 hours a week) job for 6 weeks and everything in between. Students with side jobs will often acquire employment history already during their studies.
85. A. Heyma et al., 'Evaluatie Wet werk en zekerheid (Wwz)', June 2020, p. 5.
86. The applicable law with its many exceptions for the temporary agency workers, is also referred to as a 'lightened' or 'relieved' employment law regime in the doctrine, meaning to indicate that the legal regime contains a lighter 'burden' on employers in this sector than usual. *See*, e.g., J.P.H. Zwemmer, *Pluraliteit van werkgeverschap* (Plurality of employership), Deventer: Kluwer 2012.

The main feature that distinguishes a temporary agency contract from other contracts is the possibility to include a so-called agency clause in the contract in the first 26 working weeks (prolonged by the collective agreement to 78 working weeks). This means that the employment contract ends automatically when the user company declares that they do not need the worker any longer, or when, for example, the agency worker becomes ill.[87] Depending on the employment history, the agency worker is entitled to sickness benefits via the *UWV* (Employee Insurance Agency) from the third day of illness. Temporary agency workers with short contracts might be at a (slight) disadvantage regarding UB since everybody needs to satisfy the 'week employment and year employment requirements' (*see* §6.05[B][1] for an explanation). In this case, the duration of the benefit depends on the unemployment history. The benefit will be payable for as many months as the number of years the person was employed with a maximum of 24 months.

Collective agreements for temporary agency workers are very important for the legal position of these workers, because in the absence of a CLA, the stricter statutory regime would apply. For example, according to the CLA for temporary agency worker, a temporary worker can be employed on the basis of fixed-term contract for the duration of five and a half years before an open-ended contract must be concluded. In practice, most agency workers are covered by a CLA, because the ABU-CLA (ABU is the biggest TWA employer association) is made generally binding.[88] Based on the CLAs, the temporary agency sector has its own occupational pension fund in which workers start to build up (supplementary) pension once they have worked through a temporary employment agency for 26 weeks, provided they are 21 years or older. Such a waiting period for pensions does not exist for most other employees in the Netherlands.

There are no limits on how much or how long a user undertaking can make use of temporary agency work. Initially, temporary agency work was supposed to be used for replacement of sick workers and in times of peak demand. Over the years, however, temporary agency work has become to be used for structural demand of work as well. In addition, different types of agency work have emerged over the years. Besides 'traditional' agency work, there is now also 'payrolling' and 'contracting'. These are all triangular employment relationships where the worker is seconded to user companies. As of 2020 new provisions specifically for payrolling were added to the DCC in order to improve the working position of payroll-workers. Whether the new rules (introduced

---

87. This is stipulated in the collective agreement for agency workers. It is debatable whether such provision is legal. Relatively recently, the Hague appeal court declared that such a practice is banned by the prohibition to terminate an employment contract due to illness, Appeal Court The Hague 17 March 2020, ECLI:NL:GHDHA:2020:460.
88. It should be noted that (part of) the TWA-sector is notorious for abuses and non-compliance, in particular regarding labour migrants. *See*, e.g., most recently two advisory reports that have been endorsed by the government from the 'Booster Team Protection Labour Migrants' on the working and housing conditions of labour migrants during COVID-19 in The Netherlands. *See*, Aanjaagteam Bescherming arbeidsmigranten, *Geen tweederangsburgers. Aanbevelingen om misstanden bij arbeidsmigranten in Nederland tegen te gaan*, The Hague, 30 October 2020. *See also*, Inspectorate SZW, 'State of Decent Work 2019', Ministry of Social Affairs and Employment 2019.

by the Act on Labour Market in Balance) are effective in protecting the workers remains to be seen in the years to come.

[2] Data and Impact Analysis

In the data of Statistics Netherlands (*CBS*), data on agency workers is incorporated with fixed-term employees in data on 'temporary employment'. However, individuals with a fixed-term contract make up the majority of temporary employees. Agency workers are just 16.3 % of temporary employees. Nevertheless, the annual number of temporary agency workers in the Netherlands has grown between 2006 and 2018 from 800 thousand to almost 1.2 million (including payrolling and migrant temporary agency workers).[89] Also, the amount of work the agency workers perform has increased considerably from 200 thousand to 400 thousand full-time working years.

Immediately after the financial crisis in 2008-2009, the volume of agency work first decreased. This also happened after the second economic dip in 2012-2013. Thereafter, however, the growth resumed again, and it has offset the decline in the crisis. In 2018, the number of agency workers was 18 % higher than in 2008. When we look at the number of working hours in agency work, the increase is even 50 %. Research shows clearly that during economic upturn, agency work increases, while during recession, it stays the same or it decreases slightly.[90] Since 2006, the length of stay of temporary agency workers in temporary agency work has continuously increased. In 2014, 21 % of all agency workers was working in temporary agency work longer than 3 years.[91] Compared to other temporary workers, such as fixed-term workers and on-call workers, temporary agency workers have the least stable careers, with many job changes as well as periods without work.[92]

To mitigate the socio-economic impact of COVID-19, under the Emergency Bridging Measure for Sustained Employment (*Noodmaatregel Overbrugging Werkgelegenheid: NOW* 1), which ran from March until June 2020, employers that received government subsidies were enabled to continue to pay the wages and were not allowed to dismiss workers for financial reasons. *NOW* 2, 3, and 4 were introduced as an extension on *NOW* 1. Temporary agency firms could apply for compensation of wages for temporary agency workers as well, however the scheme was more complicated to apply since it also depended on whether the user company still wanted to make use of the assigned temporary agency workers.

89. A. Heyma a.o., *De positie van uitzendwerknemers. Ontwikkelingen 1998-2019* (The position of agency workers. Developments 1998-2019), SEO Economisch Onderzoek, Amsterdam February 2020, p. 29.
90. *Idem.*, p. 30.
91. *Idem.*, p. 49.
92. W. Smits & J. de Vries, 'Employability van flexibele en vaste werknemers in Nederland', *Tijdschrift voor Arbeidsvraagstukken*, 2019 (35) 2, pp. 159-175.

[D] Involuntary Part-Timers

[1] The Notion and Measurement of Involuntary Part-Time Work

There is no definition of a part-time employment contract in Dutch law. Normally, part-time work is understood to mean work performed on the basis of an employment contract during a working time that is shorter than usual within the employer's company.[93] The Law on flexible work (*Wet flexibel werken 2016*) gives workers a right to submit a request for a reduction or an increase of the working time.

It is not easy to determine how many of part-time jobs in the Netherlands are of involuntary nature. Part-time employment is very common in the Netherlands. It is culturally accepted to work part-time; on some occasions, it could even be described as the norm.[94] It is mostly women who work part-time, but part-time work is increasing among men as well. Part-time work might be considered involuntary when an employee has made a request for increasing the working hours, and this request has been rejected. However, such data is not available.

Eurostat gives an overview of the main reason for Dutch individuals to be part-time employed.[95] It appears that 'care of children or adults with disabilities' and 'education and training' are the most common reasons for part-time employment, together with 'other reasons', which is not further defined by Eurostat. It might include people wanting to work part-time because of another job or volunteer work on the side, or because they want some time for themselves, for example, to do sports, to travel, to meet up with friends, et cetera. However, it could also be people who work irregular hours and who cannot increase their number of working hours due to the irregularity of their week schedule. Moreover, questions related to the wish to work more hours (e.g., moving from a small to a large part-time job) may be answered differently than questions on wanting to have a full-time job.[96] An interesting difference between men and women is that the care of adults with disabilities or children is the main reason for one-third of the woman working part-time, whereas for men this is only 10%. On the contrary, education or training is the main reason to work part-time for more than one-third (37.5%) of men, and for only 17% of women.

'Other family or personal reasons' (3.2%), 'own illness or disability' (4%), and 'no full-time job found' (6%) are less often the main reason for having part-time employment. The last two reasons might also be an indicator of which part of part-time employment may be considered involuntary. *CBS* also gives an indication of the

93. N. Gundt, 'Deeltijd-arbeidsovereenkomst', in J.P. Kroon & P. de Casparis (eds.), *Flexibele arbeidsrelaties*, Deventer: Wolters Kluwer.
94. Bekker, S. and Leschke, J. (2021), Fragmented labour markets in affluent societies: examples from Germany and the Netherlands, OSE Paper Series, Research Paper No.48, Brussels: European Social Observatory.
95. Eurostat, 2020: https://ec.europa.eu/eurostat/databrowser/view/lfsa_epgar/default/table?lang=en.
96. Portegijs, W. et al. (2018), *Emancipatiemonitor 2018*, Sociaal en Cultureel Planbureau, https://digital.scp.nl/emancipatiemonitor2018/wie-zorgt-er-voor-de-kinderen/.

number of involuntary part-timers in data describing the untapped labour potential.[97] They indicate that in 2020, almost 372,000 persons were 'underutilized part-time workers', being people who work part-time and who want to work more and are available for this at short notice. If certain conditions are met, nearly 8 out of 10 Dutch women with a part-time job would want to start working more hours per week. For one-third insufficient household income would be a reason to work more hours.

[2] Relevant Legal Framework

Part-time work is very common in the Netherlands, and it is almost fully integrated in employment law in the sense that part-timers as a default receive the same conditions and benefits as full-time workers, but on a pro rata temporis basis. Hence, there are very few legal norms that specifically address part-time work. The Dutch law forbids discrimination between part-time and full-time workers (Art. 7:648 DCC), however, unequal treatment can sometimes be objectively justified.

As explained earlier, the Dutch law does not provide for a minimum wage per hour, but only provides for a minimum wage per month. This can be disadvantageous for part-time workers who work on a minimum wage level, and especially those who work irregularly. Part-time workers need to calculate the minimum wage per hour. Hourly minimum wage is dependent on 'normal full-time working hours' (*normale arbeidsduur*), which ranges from 40 hours per week to 36 hours per week. So, the minimum wage per hour can vary from sector to sector, and even from company to company. Because of this, it is not always easy for people to find out what their rights are. It also makes enforcement of minimum wage law complicated. There is a bill pending in the Parliament to introduce an hourly minimum wage.

[3] Part-Time Work and Multi-jobbing

Individuals who work fewer hours in their primary job than they would like, are more likely to have a second (or even a third) job.[98] This is also referred to as multiple jobholding. In the Netherlands, a relatively high percentage of multiple jobholders still has multiple jobs one year later (> 60%). Particularly in the period 2010-2017, there is also a relatively high outflow into unemployment or inactivity.[99] Multiple jobholders in the Netherlands have lower hourly earnings compared to single jobholders.[100] Findings seem to indicate a downward wage mobility particularly related to workers with medium educational attainment levels. In 2018, 7.4% of all employees had more

97. CBS, 2020: https://www.cbs.nl/-/media/_excel/2021/21/onbenut-arbeidspotentieel-naar-regio-2020.xlsx.
98. W. Conen, 'Multiple jobholding in Europe. Structure and dynamics', AIAS-HSI Working Paper Series, WP 10, April 2020, p. 33.
99. *Ibid.*
100. *Ibid.*, p. 34.

than one paid job.[101] Two-thirds of them have a second job as an employee, one-third has a second job as self-employed.

Combining multiple jobs can have different reasons. First, workers can have multiple jobs because they cannot work more hours in their first job. Approximately 21% of the multi-jobbers has multiple jobs to get by financially, while 29% has multiple jobs for earning something extra. A second reason for multi-jobbing is that the variety in tasks and social contacts increases job satisfaction (25%) or contributes to the acquisition of different types of knowledge and skills (16%). Third, some multi-jobbers have multiple jobs because it protects them from unemployment (*hedging*). This is the reason for 10% of them.

Research shows that multi-jobbing has a positive effect on labour participation. Compared to single-jobbers, multi-jobbers actually had more months of paid work during a follow up period of five years. However, they appeared to be less economically independent than people with only one employment relationship. Multi-jobbing can thus be a good strategy for staying connected to the labour market (job security), but not for income security.

On the other hand, the Dutch UB are relatively adapted to modern employment relationships, such as for employees with a non-standard contract, including those with marginal part-time jobs or on-call work (VUP Groups 3 and 4) and multiple jobholders. For instance, if an employee has not lost all employment, the number of working hours that the employee still has in a given calendar week is compared with his or her average number of working hours in the last 26 calendar weeks (Article 16(2) WW). That this average is used as a basis for calculation is particularly important in the case of employment contracts that fluctuate in terms of hours (e.g., on call jobs). As mentioned, in principle, the loss of working hours must amount to at least five hours. However, to give UB entitlements also to part-time workers with an average of less than ten working hours per calendar week, unemployment also arises when a person has lost less than five working hours, but at least half of his or her average working hours per calendar week. When assessing whether there is a relevant loss of paid working hours in such situations, the non-insured work performed by the employee in the last 26 calendar weeks must also be included in the assessment.[102]

[4] Impact of the Corona Crisis

To mitigate the socio-economic impact of COVID-19, under the *NOW*, employers that received government subsidies were enabled to continue to pay the wages and were

101. CBS (Stef Bouwhuis, Goedele Geuskens): https://longreads.cbs.nl/dynamiek-op-de-nederlandse-arbeidsmarkt-2019/combineren-van-banen/.

102. This can be illustrated as follows: if the person concerned only had a 4-hour job as an employee and lost it, the rule applies that he has lost more than half of his working hours, and he is therefore unemployed. However, if someone is an independent accountant for 36 hours per week and in addition works for 4 hours in a side job as an employee, and he loses this side job, he has no entitlement to *WW*. Although an employee loses more than half of his working hours, it is taken into account that he still works 36 hours as an accountant, so in fact he is in the same position as an employee who loses 4 hours.

not allowed to dismiss workers for financial reasons. Employers could apply for compensation of wages for employees with permanent or fixed-term contracts, so both part-time workers with an open-ended contract and those with a fixed-term contract should have been protected against income loss and unemployment if their employer applied for *NOW*. Notwithstanding, statistics Netherlands (CBS) shows that the COVID-19 crisis sparked the wish of workers with a small part-time job to work more hours per week (it increased by 71 thousand, 50 thousand of whom currently have a job of less than 12 working hours per week).[103]

[E] Descriptive Data and Impact Analysis

[1] Workforce Composition Related to In-Work Poverty

In order to assess to which extent VUP Group 3 workers (all together) are exposed to poverty, the table 6.4 provides an overview of the Eurostat data in the most recent year (2019).

Table 6.4 VUP 3: Flex Workers (Fixed-Term, Agency Workers and Involuntary Part-Timers), NL, 2019 (in %)

% of in-work population	(22,5)		
In-work at risk of poverty	6,9		
Individual variables		**Household variables**	
Age group		**Household size**	
18-34	8,8 (35,4)	1	17 (13,1)
35-49	6,1 (38,7)	2	6,8 (23,5)
≥50	5,4 (25,9)	> 2	4,8 (63,4)
Gender		**No. of in-work persons in the household**	
Women	5,3 (77,2)	1	18 (26,3)
Men	12,3 (22,8)	> 1	2,9 (73,7)
Education		**No. of children (< 18)**	
Low	11,1* (11,8)	0	8,3 (48,6)
Medium	6,5 (43,8)	1	5,6 (19,6)
High	4,9 (44,4)	> 1	5,5 (31,8)
Working time			
Full-time	5,7 (22,7)		
Part-time	7,2 (77,3)		

103. CBS (2021), Meer werkenden met kleine deeltijdbaan, Press release, 17-6-2021.

% of in-work population	(22,5)
In-work at risk of poverty	6,9
Occupation (skill level)	
High	3,2 (49,0)
Low	9,7 (51,0)
Contract	
Permanent	4,1 (53,6)
Temporary	9,8 (46,4)
No. of months work (during reference period)	
12	6,2 (91,2)
Less than 12	13,3* (8,8)

Source: Eurostat data.

* Careful interpretation, low sample size (N = 100-200

Of the Dutch flex workers (fixed-term workers, agency workers, and involuntary part-timers together), 6.9% is at risk of poverty, which is above the national average of 5.5%. The data shows that the risk of poverty is higher for younger than for older flex workers. Furthermore, women form a large majority within the group of flex workers with 77.2%, men are a minority at 22.8%. The difference in poverty risk is striking: for the women in VUP Group 3, this is 5.3%, which is actually below the national average of all in-work persons (5.5%), while for the men this is as much as 12.3%. What also stands out is that the low-educated individuals in VUP Group 3 have quite a high risk of poverty compared to the average- and high educated individuals: 11.1% compared to 6.5% and 4.9%. This aligns with the national trend.

Flex workers that work full-time have a much higher risk of poverty than Dutch full-timers in general: of all in-work individuals in the Netherlands, full-timers have a 2.9% risk of poverty, while this is 5.7% for full-time flex workers. This is a striking difference. It shows that as a flex worker, full-time employment gives considerably fewer financial resources than working full-time on a permanent employment contract. The part-timers of VUP Group 3 on the other hand have a poverty risk that is almost equal to that of all in-work individuals who work part-time (even slightly less): 7.2% compared to 8.7%.

The poverty risk of the group that works all 12 months is with 6.2% slightly higher than the national average of 5.5%; the poverty risk of the flex workers who work less than 12 months however is 13.3%.[104] This latter group in 2019 amounted to 8.8% of flex workers. It can logically be expected that this much higher risk of poverty can

104. This difference is not far off from the national data on all in-work persons (5.1% for individuals that worked 12 months, 12.1% for individuals that worked less than 12 months).

be explained by a lower total income, given that they work less during the year. This too supports the idea that working too few hours is more likely to influence the existence of a low income, than the hourly earnings. It is important to note that many of the flex workers working less than 12 months most likely consist of agency- and/or seasonal workers. The group of seasonal workers often remains hidden in Dutch data (e.g., because they are counted as part of the group of temporary agency workers and/or hired in other ways). There is virtually no data on the number of seasonal (migrant) workers as a separate labour market group. The reason for this is that migrant seasonal workers who work a maximum of four out of six months in the Netherlands are not obliged to register in the *BRP* (*Basisregistratie Personen*; Civil Registry Database), and those who stay longer often do not (know they should) register.[105] Statistics Netherlands (CBS) bases their statistics on immigrants only on those who are registered, so a considerable amount of seasonal workers are not visible in data. The only indication of the amount of seasonal workers by Statistics Netherlands can be derived from one of their articles stating that in 2019 the agricultural sector accounted for 29,800 full-time jobs for people who are not regularly employed.[106] However, it is not clear whether these are Dutch seasonal workers, foreign workers, or both. Regarding poverty, table 6.4 shows however that not being employed for 12 consecutive month means a higher at-risk of poverty rate, which could hint at the financial position of seasonal workers as well.

The household variables show some interesting data as well. Flex workers living in a single-person household have a poverty risk of no less than 17%. This indicates that VUP Group 3 workers on their own often do not earn enough to make ends meet. Flex workers in a household of two persons have a much lower poverty risk of 6.8%. An additional income and being able to share certain costs thus lowers the risk of being poor. The majority (63.4%) of flex workers lives in a household of more than two persons, with a 4.8% poverty risk. That so many flex workers live in a bigger household can be explained by the fact that many are living-at-home students or pupils, who work via a (student) employment agency or have a temporary/part-time contract at a shop or supermarket. They most of the time fall within the 'more-than-two-persons' households, and because of their parents' income as supplementing income they do not fall below the poverty line (and even score better than the 5.3% national average for more-than-two-persons-households). Furthermore, when the flex worker is the only breadwinner in the household (for example, he or she is single or has a non-working partner and/or child), the risk of poverty is as much as 18%. This is much higher than the poverty risk of all the in-work individuals in the Netherlands who are the only in-work person in the household (8.9%). However, as soon as there is a compensating second (or more) income, this risk is tremendously lower at 2.9% (and close to the national average for all persons with the same household situation which is 2.7%). Lastly, it is striking that the trend for VUP Group 3 in 2019 seems to be that the risk of poverty is decreasing when the number of dependent children is increasing.

105. Rijksoverheid,2021: https://www.rijksoverheid.nl/binaries/rijksoverheid/documenten/rapp mfa.pl-arbeidsmigranten.pdf.
106. CBS, 2020: https://www.cbs.nl/nl-nl/nieuws/2020/15/bijna-30-duizend-contractbanen-in-de -landbouw.

This does not match the national trend among all in-work individuals (no dependent children: 5.4% poverty risk, 5.2% for one child, and 6% for more two or more children). Also, the VUP Group 3 trend of 2019 is not in line with the trends in 2013 and 2007. There is no clear explanation for these divergences based on this data.

Altogether, the flex workers with the highest risk of poverty, according to these data, are the flex workers who are male, who work less than 12 months a year, who live in a single-person household, and/or who are the only working person in the household.

[2] Impact of the Financial and Corona Crisis

The Netherlands has a high degree of flexibility on its labour market. Especially the flexible workers belonging to VUP Group 3 run a higher risk at becoming unemployed or inactive than standard workers. During both the financial crisis and the corona crisis, people in the most insecure jobs more often lost their jobs, and they had insufficient protection from the employee-benefits scheme.[107]

Regarding the financial crisis, what we can see in the data is that generally, the poverty risk of flex workers belonging to VUP Group 3 was lower before (4.7%) than after the financial crisis (6%). This increase contrasts with the trend for all employed persons in the Netherlands, where the poverty risk dropped with 0.1 percent point, thus remaining relatively stable. Interestingly, the poverty risk of persons living in a two-person household increased with 1.8 percent point after the financial crisis, and that of individuals in a household of three or more persons, on the contrary, decreased with 0.2 percent point. This might indicate that after the financial crisis, flex workers living in larger households could make ends meet more easily than before the crisis. Moreover, for flex workers living in a household with only one in-work person, the poverty risk increased with 4.2 percent point, from 14.6% before to 18.8% after the financial crisis, while the poverty rate of households with more than one income only just increased with 0.1 percent point. This indicates that the crisis seems to have worsened the financial position of flex workers in single-earner households. Finally, it stands out that only for the households without dependent children the risk of poverty significantly rose (3.5 percent point); for the households with dependent children (one or more) however, the poverty risk decreased, with 0.6 percent point. This suggests that after the crisis, somehow flex workers without dependent children in the household had much more trouble making ends meet, and that flex workers with children had a better financial position than before.

During the first emergency-scheme after the outbreak of COVID-19 pandemic, the *NOW* 1, that ran from March until June 2020, organizations could claim financial support for both employees with permanent contracts and also employees for whom the employer was not obliged to continue paying wages. In this way, employees with

107. Beek, van der, J.W.M., and Zwemmer, J.P.H., 'NOW: Flexwerknemers (en flexwerkgevers) tussen wal enschip en de TOFA-regeling', *Tijdschrift voor Arbeidsrecht in Context*, November 2020, nr. 3, 1-5. Also S. Bekker and J. Leschke, 'Social security innovation for inclusive worker support during the corona crisis?' Blog post *Journal European Social Policy*, 29-07, 2020.

flexible employment contracts could be protected against immediate loss of income as well. *NOW* 2, 3, and 4 were introduced as an extension on *NOW* 1. Employers could therefore apply under the *NOW* schemes for compensation of wages of all VUP Group 3 workers until Autumn 2021. There are indications that despite the financial support by the Dutch government, still many fixed-term contracts were not renewed and for temporary agency workers, applying the scheme was more complicated as the employing temporary agency was also dependent on the willingness of the user company to keep making use of the assigned agency workers.

§6.06 VUP GROUP 4: CASUAL AND PLATFORM WORKERS

[A] Composition of VUP Group 4

As described in the introductory chapter of this Book, VUP Group 4 covers casual work and new forms of (casual) employment: intermittent work, on-call work, and platform work. Not all the types of casual work are in a contractually recognizable way present on the Dutch labour market and/or known under a specific name in practice. Whereas on-call work is regulated already for a long time in the Dutch Civil Code, intermittent work is not regulated in a specific contractual form in the Netherlands. Eurofound describes intermittent work as a form of employment often related to an individual project, specific task, or seasonally occurring job.[108] Based on this notion, there seems to be overlap both with on-call work and with what is referred to as 'contracting' in the Netherland, implying a triangular relationship, such as with temporary agency work.

[B] Relevant Legal Framework

[1] On-Call Work

An employee has an on-call employment contract when the contract does not contain a fixed number of working hours either (a) per time unit of up to a month, or (b) per time unit of up to a year, and the wage is not spread evenly over that time unit (Article 7:628a lid 9 DCC). This means that the employee has an on-call employment contract when his or her contract does not stipulate a fixed number of working hours and his or her wage can vary every month. An employee also has an on-call employment contract when he or she does not have a right to a wage per time unit (e.g., per month) when he or she has not performed labour, hence, when the right to wages has been excluded. Additional rules may be issued by Royal Decree (Article 7:628a sub 9 DCC). An on-call employment contract can be either a fixed-term or an open-ended contract. In practice, there exist different on-call contracts. The zero-hour contracts and the so-called min-max contracts are the most common. The latter stipulate both a minimum and a

108. It is defined in Eurofound's 2015 research, New Forms of Employment, as being characterized by a fixed-term period, which either involves fulfilling a task or completing a specific number of days' work.

maximum number of hours a week that the worker is prepared to/may be requested to work.

As of 1 January 2020, whenever the on-call contract has lasted 12 months, the employer is obliged to offer the employee an employment agreement with fixed hours at least equal to the average amount of working hours in the preceding 12-month period (Article 7:628a sub 5 DCC). Already since 1999, on-call workers can invoke a *legal presumption* of the number of working hours (Article 7: 610b DCC). If an employment contract has lasted at least three months, the agreed working hours in any month are presumed to have a scope equal to the average number of working hours per month in the three preceding months. The on-call employee also has a right to wages of three hours per call, even if the employee worked less than three hours (Article 7:628a lid 1 BW).

While on-call workers do not have different eligibility conditions for UB compared to other employees, they do face higher obstacles in fulfilling them.[109] The eligibility conditions for UB are (i) a loss of a relevant number of paid working hours (at average, 5 hours) and (ii) a week requirement (having worked in 26-out-of 36 weeks before the first day of unemployment (Articles 16 and 17 *Werkloosheidswet* (Unemployment benefit act)). The week requirement is particularly hard to meet for employees working irregularly and with weeks without calls, even though there are specific rules to adjust the calculation for employment contracts that fluctuate in hours (*see* §6.05[D][3].[110]

[2] Intermittent Work

As described earlier, intermittent work is not regulated as a specific contractual form of work in the Netherlands. 'Intermittent work' may be agreed upon in employment contracts with flexible hours that fall outside the scope of on-call work as defined in the DCC. This means that the rules regarding on-call work do not apply. Such contracts contain a fixed minimum number of working hours on an annual basis and evenly spread wages, but the working hours are flexible, so the employee has great uncertainty throughout the year about the times to be worked. However, because there is income security, the legislator decided to exclude such contracts from the scope of legal protection of on-call work. Occasionally, a certain group of workers is excluded in a collective agreement from certain employee benefits, for example, 'vacation workers' (*vakantiekrachten*) or 'helpers' (*hulpkrachten*) who work during the weekend.

[3] Workers On-Demand via App

Many of the people doing offline work on-demand via app have the (tax) status of being solo self-employed. There are many solo self-employed in the Netherlands (*see* §6.04

109. *See also,* S. Burri, S. Heeger-Hertter and S. Rossetti, *On-call work in the Netherlands: trends, impact, and policy solutions*, ILO Conditions of Work and Employment Series No. 103, p. 28.
110. *Idem.*, p. 31.

on VUP Group 2 workers), and it has been suggested that the most recent rise in the number of solo self-employed can be partially explained by the rise of platform work.[111]

Courts in the Netherlands have already ruled on several occasions about the legal qualification of workers on-demand via app. Case law on platform work is still very much in flux. Until now, most important verdicts seem to be the rulings on Deliveroo-riders. The Amsterdam Court of Appeal ruled in the beginning of 2021 that Deliveroo's meal delivery riders and drivers work on the basis of an employment contract, rather than being self-employed.[112] The Court of Appeal paid attention to inter alia the fact that the wages were set unilaterally by Deliveroo, which is an indication of an employment contract. Furthermore, the Court found that Deliveroo has far-reaching monitoring possibilities, mainly through continuously tracking the driver's GPS location, which the Court considers to be a form of authority. The payment model established unilaterally by Deliveroo also points to Deliveroo's interference in the delivery process and therefore to a relationship of authority. Deliveroo has also announced that it will appeal to the Court of Cassation against the ruling.

Furthermore, in September 2021, the Amsterdam Court of Appeal ruled on the employment status of Helpling workers.[113] It found that Helpling workers are in fact temporary agency workers. In first instance, the lower Court had ruled that circumstances point to a contractual (employment) relationship between the worker and the household; however, the Appeals Court found more and heavier circumstances pointing to a contract between Helpling and the worker. Because the worker is structurally deployed at the households and Helpling has no control over the work to be performed, but leaves that to the households, the Appeals Court found that the contract does not qualify as a 'normal' employment contract, but instead as a temporary agency contract.

[4] Crowdworkers

Compared to platform work performed on location (work on-demand via app), very little is known about crowdworkers (so, digitally performed platform work) in the Netherlands. Crowdwork is usually divided into two types of work: (i) micro-tasks, such as completing surveys, participating in experiments, or rating online content, and (ii) larger and more substantive tasks where the worker usually needs some kind of qualification, such as translation work or programming for IT companies. The payment for the micro-tasks is generally especially low. Just like with work on-demand via app, the legal qualification needs to be determined per case. There is no Dutch case law yet on crowdwork, which is not surprising given the unfamiliarity and invisibility of this kind of work. Dutch trade unions have focused so far on platform workers (on-demand via app) performing offline work only.

111. W. Pieterson, 'Peer Country Comments Paper - The Netherlands', Directorate-General for Employment, Social Affairs and Inclusion Peer Review on 'Platform Work', EC September 2020.
112. Amsterdam Court of Appeal 16 February 2021, ECLI:NL:GHAMS:2021:392.
113. Amsterdam Court of Appeal 21 September 2021, ECLI:NL:GHAMS:2021:2741.

[C] Descriptive Data and Impact Analysis

[1] Data from National Sources

Because Eurostat does not contain data on VUP Group 4 workers (casual workers and platform workers), the data were collected using national sources. Table 6.5 below provides an overview of the data on VUP Group 4 from the most recent years, and thus most representative: 2019 for casual workers and 2020 for platform workers. The data has been collected from different sources; a dataset on VUP Group 4 in its entirety was not found unfortunately. The SEO (2020) stated in a study specifically focused on the gig economy (*klusseneconomie*) that 80,577 persons are working as platform worker in the Netherlands. The data on on-call and zero-hour workers was derived from a dataset on the Dutch labour force from Statline (CBS). Combining the information on both groups, it turns out that VUP Group 4 makes up about 7% of the Dutch working population and thus concerns a relatively small group. This is even more true because there might be an overlap with the other VUP Groups, as the platform workers for instance fall within the category of solo self-employed (since they are put to work most often as solo self-employed up to now) or combine different types of employment relationships (*see* the explanation of the multiple job holder phenomenon in §6.05 [D][3]). This applies especially to platform workers: 66% of them indicates that platform work is not their main activity (SEO, 2020). The majority of VUP Group 4 will often not depend on the earnings via the platform or the on-call contract but may use this to cover the gaps in household budget.

Table 6.5 shows the data on VUP Group 4 as set out above. Based on the national data collected, it appears that on-call and zero-hour workers make up 6.1% of the working population. Of them, 10.2% is at risk of in-work poverty. The platform workers appear to be a very small group: less than 1% of the working population is a platform worker. They have a poverty risk of an estimated 5.25%, which is similar to the 5.5% average of the whole working population. Unfortunately, there is no national data on poverty relating to household composition for VUP Group 4.

Table 6.5 VUP Group 4: On-Call, Zero-Hours and Platform Workers, NL, Estimates

	No. of Persons	*% In-work Poor Individuals*	*Percentage of Working Population*
Total working population	*8,953,000*	*5.5%*	*100%*
On-call / zero-hours workers	545,000	55.590 (10.2%)	6.1%
Platform workers	80,577	5.25%	0.9%
Total (estimate)	**625,557**	**15.45%**	**7%**

Sources: SEO 2020; CBS 2019.

[D] Poverty Among VUP Group 4 Workers[114]

[1] Platform Workers

SEO (2020)[115] divides platform work into two groups: those providing physical (offline) services (workers on-demand via app) and those providing online tasks (crowdworkers). The report includes figures about the average gross income per month for different types of platform work. This shows that the group of crowdworkers that performs 'other online tasks' has the highest earnings. Their average salary is EUR 1000 per month. The group of crowdworkers with the lowest earnings are those who collect, verify, or transcribe data. They earn an average of EUR 417 per month. Regarding workers on-demand via app, the average reported gross monthly income was EUR 651.[116]

The total average gross monthly income of all platform workers is about EUR 677. The monthly income from platform work thus is below the poverty line of EUR 1,090 net per month (Dutch definition of poverty threshold in 2019). In practice, as mentioned before, platform work is almost never the only source of income (*SEO*, 2020). A percentage of 66% of the platform workers is estimated to combine platform work with other paid work, and this 66% collects only a small part (< 25%) of the income from paid work through platforms. It therefore is likely that the platform work is used to supplement the main income from other jobs. However, there are also four 'types' of platform workers who have no other income (from work or social security benefits). These are the housewives/housemen (1.5%), volunteers (1.5%), informal carers (0.75%) *(mantelzorgers)*, and 'others' (1.5%). If they are a single-person household and would have no additional second income, then they could be the ones representing the platform workers living below the poverty line.

[2] On-Call/Zero-Hours Workers

For on-call and zero-hour workers, data on income was also hard to find. However, data from Statistics Netherlands (*CBS*) shows that the average gross income of an on-call/zero-hours worker is EUR 11,100 on an annual basis, which is a monthly income of EUR 925.[117] If this were their only source of income, it would mean that many on-call/zero-hours workers fall below the poverty line of EUR 1,090 net per month (Dutch definition of poverty threshold for a single person). The average standardized monthly income of on-call/zero-hours workers however is no less than EUR 2,717. This means that the group on-call/zero-hours workers, corrected for

114. Because there are no known percentages of poverty of either platform workers or on-call and zero-hour workers, this had to be derived from other sources and/or calculated on the basis of collected data.
115. SEO, 2020: https://25cjk227xfsu3mkyfg1m9xb7-wpengine.netdna-ssl.com/wp-content/uploads/2020/10/2020-04-Meting-kluseconomie.pdf.
116. Based on delivery services, household services, passenger transport, professional services, and other physical services.
117. CBS, 2019: https://opendata.cbs.nl/#/CBS/nl/dataset/83686NED/table?dl=4CA62.

differences in household size and composition, has an income of well above the poverty line. Many of them will thus have an additional income from their household, and another explanation might be the share of scholars and students with on-call/zero-hours contracts: they often still live at home, which means that they fall under the household of their parents, and/or they receive a study loan or grant as well, and therefore do not belong to the group of people at-risk of in-work-poverty. According to the report by *CBS* (2019), less than 20% of the on-call and zero-hours workers can support themselves financially, but this often concerns young people with a job next to their studies/education. The *SCP* reported in 2018 that most working poor work either as self-employed, part-time worker, or as on-call worker (so a mixture of VUP Group 2, 3, and 4 workers).[118] According to this report, 10.2% of on-call workers are below the poverty line.[119]

§6.07 CONCLUSIONS

Based on the foregoing analysis, general conclusions on in-work poverty are drawn regarding the Dutch labour market (§6.07[A]) and the Dutch legal framework (§6.07[B]), next to more specific conclusions concerning the four VUP Groups (§6.07[C]). The chapter ends on a positive note with a brief outlook on some promising recent developments (§6.07[D]).

[A] General Conclusions on the Dutch Labour Market

As stated in the introductory section to this Chapter, the Netherlands has quite a strong and resilient economy and labour market. Compared to other EU countries, unemployment rates did not increase dramatically during both the financial- and the COVID-19 crisis. Moreover, in-work-poverty rates for workers are much lower than for the entire Dutch population, meaning that having a job is still an important factor to move out of poverty. Eurostat data shows that there is a rather low level of severe material deprivation in the Netherlands (1.3% in 2013, 1.1% in 2019, and even 0.9% in 2020). This means that despite the fact that 5.5% of the working population faces some degree of poverty, only around 1% of the working population lives in such severe poverty that they cannot afford the very basic needs. The European average severe material deprivation rate is 3.2% (EU28, 2019, estimate), indicating that employees in the Netherlands have a relatively good financial position.

At the same time, some groups of workers at the Dutch labour market deserve attention as are more likely to experience in-work-poverty than others, particularly those with flexible jobs. They are also more vulnerable for economic setbacks. A related problem is that consecutive generations that are flowing from school to work have been increasingly confronted with temporary jobs as a first employment relationship. Moreover, they stayed in this position for longer. As a result, the financial

118. SCP, *Als werk weinig opbrengt*, 2018, p. 26.
119. Based on research data of 2014.

situation of the younger generations may be less favourable and less stable, leaving them more exposed to the risk of in-work poverty. Also for workers with a distance to the labour market, the flexibilization of the labour market affects the sustainability of created jobs, particularly in jobs which require a low skill level. Compared to 2003, the amount of low-skilled workers with a flexible contact or in self-employment was twice as high in 2019. It contributes to the existence of groups of workers who get caught in a constant cycle of being in-work and out-of-work.

[B] Role of the Dutch Legal Framework in Relation to Workers' Risk of Poverty

The Dutch monthly statutory minimum wage serves as social minimum because all minimum amounts of employee-related benefits and the social assistance level are linked to the statutory minimum wage. This also means that nobody is obliged, in order to receive such payments, to accept or perform work below the level of the statutory minimum wage.

Social partners and collective bargaining are highly relevant in setting wages and thus have quite an impact on workers' standard of living. The Netherlands has multi-employer bargaining with high coverage: despite relatively low union density (which currently is around 19%), collective bargaining coverage is stable at around 80% of workers, largely through sectoral agreements and mechanisms to extend these. This high coverage assures that the vast majority of workers has a decent protection in terms of both decent wages and (supplementary) protection in case of unemployment, sickness, and other situations of suspension of work. High collective bargaining coverage might thus be a factor in explaining the relatively low overall Dutch at-risk-of-poverty and severe material deprivation rates.

However, even if hourly wages are reasonably adequate when having a full-time job, the high incidence of part-time work in the Netherlands begs the question whether monthly incomes are sufficient, and whether people have enough opportunities to access jobs with enough working hours per week. Think of workers with irregular working hours per week due to zero-hour or on-call contracts, who thus have an irregular income.

Another group of workers who are more likely to experience in-work poverty are the solo self-employed. The Dutch system of tax credits creates (too) strong incentives to become self-employed, so the number of solo self-employed has been growing strongly in the past decades. Even though there are many genuine entrepreneurs who successfully operate within their market, others struggle to make ends meet, particularly if they are reliant on one client or operate in markets with fierce competition on price. Action is required to protect these vulnerable groups of workers, for example, as advised by the *SER* in June 2021, by reducing the tax incentives for solo self-employed and introducing a rebuttable presumption of an employment relationship for those whose rates are below a certain level. In these situations, it should be the client who must prove that there is no employment relationship.

Looking at social security, this does not always fits the needs of workers, particularly those who have low wages and/or irregular income. For instance, the UB scheme is not accessible for self-employed, while their access to social assistance (welfare) might be constrained because this is means-tested. UB does provide a relatively easy access for employees with the most common types of non-standard contracts; however, since the height of UB is proportional to the number of hours of previous employment, it does not always provide substantial income security for them. In addition, the duration of UB was strongly reduced in recent years, which, together with some other changes to the legal framework, might worsen the income security, particularly of older workers.

A strong feature of the social security system is that the universal schemes provide all residents with e.g., healthcare insurance, and a pension at social minimum level. Also, a system of social-fiscal allowances exists in the Netherlands, which makes no distinction between working and non-working people either and which is based on broad income limits, resulting in about 7.5 million allowances being given to more than 5 million households (almost 60% of Dutch households). This system of additional income support on top of the social minimum, actually contributes to a more balanced income distribution, ensuring that the gap between poorer and richer households does not widen further. Paradoxically, at the same time, the design of payments in advance and related retrievals, increases income insecurity and debt problems in particular for people who are most in need of said allowances. The system of social-fiscal allowances is now broadly discredited because of its disproportionate application. Noteworthy, an expert meeting with people experiencing in-work poverty in the Netherlands demonstrated that processes of accessing and getting social security does not match well with volatile incomes from flexible jobs, creating difficult periods of getting not enough or getting too much income support, the latter resulting in needing to pay back part of income support.[120]

[C] Conclusions on In-Work Poverty among the Selected Groups of Workers

Based on data from Eurostat, it can be concluded that across the whole working population, as well across the selected VUP Groups, in-work poverty is especially an issue for persons in a single-person household or a household with only one in-work person, in particular when there are dependent children in the household. Looking specifically at the VUP groups, it can be concluded that the solo self-employed and flex workers (so the VUP Groups 2 & 3) are most often at risk of in-work poverty, partly due to them not being able to work for sufficient hours. The table 6.6 gives a summarizing overview of the poverty risks for the Dutch working population as a whole, as well as for the separate VUP Groups.

120. Stakeholder meeting observations, organized for WorkYP, Netherlands, April 2021.

Table 6.6 In-Work at Risk of Poverty, All Employed Persons (Including Employees and Self-Employed) and Separate VUP Groups, NL, 2019

	% of In-work Population	*In-work at Risk of Poverty*
In-work population	100%	5.5%
VUP 1	14.4%	4.4%
VUP 2	9%	14.3%
VUP 3	22.5%	6.9%
VUP 4	7%*	Unknown

Source: Eurostat data, SEO, 2020; CBS, 2019.

* Estimates, compiled from sources SEO, 2020; CBS, 2019.

Regarding standard workers in low-wage and low-skilled occupations (VUP Group 1), it was observed that the Dutch design of calculating with monthly statutory minimum wages and not with an hourly minimum wage creates inequality in (minimum) wages that are not explainable. Moreover, individuals at risk of in-work poverty within VUP Group 1 are identified as being a) persons who live in a household of more than two persons, and b) persons who have more than one dependent child at home. An important take away from the data on VUP Group 1 is that, broadly speaking, having a 'normal' permanent and full-time contract helps against the negative financial effects of having a very low income. However, this finding is not fully valid for households with more than one dependent child living at home.

The analysis of the solo/bogus self-employed (VUP Group 2) shows that these workers face certain challenges and risks at in-work-poverty, partly due to the number of hours they can work. Moreover, solo self-employed are as a default not covered by labour law and collective agreements and, as a consequence, have less access to protection in terms of wage regulation, social security insurances, and pension schemes (although they are insured for health care and for a basic pension at social minimum level). The group of solo self-employed is, however, heterogeneous, so individual circumstances can differ widely. Moreover, whereas solo self-employed have high poverty risks, these workers have a quite low severe material deprivation rate. This indicates that for this group of workers, the in-work poverty measurement might not always be suitable for assessing their actual standard of living. This is supported by national data showing that despite the 14.3% poverty rate, only 2.1% of self-employed face long-term poverty. To conclude with, self-employed in a single-person household have a significantly high risk of in-work poverty, and also the older (50+) self-employed and those who are working part-time are significantly more at risk of poverty.

VUP Group 3 comprises the flex workers, including fixed-term, temporary agency, and involuntary part-time workers. Remarkably, the data show that male flex workers have a much higher risk of poverty (12.3%, versus 5.3% for women). Also flex workers working less than 12 months a year have a high risk of poverty (13.3%). Specific categories of households that are at risk of in-work poverty within VUP Group 3 are flex workers who are in a single-person household and flex workers who are the only working individuals in the household. This indicates, similar to the self-employed, that a flex worker without a compensating second income of a partner can often not make ends meet properly.

Finally, VUP Group 4 consists of various casual workers, including platform workers. For this group, it is difficult to assess the extent of the problem of in-work poverty since no information on these workers is available in Eurostat. We used national data sources to gain insight into the number of on-call and platform workers in the Netherlands and their financial situation. What can be concluded is that VUP Group 4 concerns a relatively small group (about 7% of the in-work population). There is also a considerable overlap with other VUP Groups, for instance, because people combine different employment statuses, or because platform workers are most often labelled as solo self-employed. Workers of VUP Group 4 face a very low monthly income (below the poverty threshold), but for both the on-call workers and the platform workers it is highly likely that they have these jobs to supplement their main income. Even though the number of persons that are fully dependent on platform work for their living is likely to be small, those who would be dependent on this form of work are quite vulnerable due to their unclear legal status in relation to labour law protection and social security schemes.

[D] Outlook

To end on a positive note, after we finished our National Report in July 2021, the attention for the issue of in-work poverty in the Netherlands has further increased. For instance, in October 2021, the largest Dutch trade union FNV launched an action plan against poverty at the local level, in light of the fact that more than a million people in the Netherlands live in poverty, including 300,000 children. FNV calls on municipalities to include the points in its Action Plan in a municipal agreement.[121] Among other things, the FNV proposes that people living on less than 150% of the Social Minimum should be exempted from paying municipal taxes. This should not only apply to benefit recipients but also include the working poor. They should also be able to make use of municipal facilities such as special assistance for unforeseen, necessary medical expenses. In many municipalities, the threshold now stands at 110% to 130% of the Social Minimum Entitlement.

Furthermore, on 10 January 2022 a new government has taken office, which endorses the Advice of June 2021 from the *SER*, referred to at several places in this chapter. In this advice, the main stakeholders of the Dutch 'polder model' provided building blocks for solving the issue of a too-flexible labour market and the lack of social protection for vulnerable (bogus) solo self-employed workers. Moreover, in

---

121. https://www.fnv.nl/nieuwsbericht/sectornieuws/uitkeringsgerechtigden/2021/10/fnv-presenteert-plan-voor-lokale-armoedebestrijding.

September 2021, the *SER* published an explorative report on how to create work without poverty.[122] This study focuses on ensuring that people can generate sufficient income from their jobs, have enough working hours, and have a stable income. Concretely, it advices to increase the minimum wage (and compensate employers for higher expenditure on wages in order to prevent the loss of jobs). Moreover, the advice is to improve governmental services to workers and benefit recipients, combining digital services with reliable and personal support, and reducing the complexity of rules. The national government, municipalities, employers, and trade unions should jointly work towards an improved system. These recommendations are already put high on the Agenda of the Minister of Social Affairs and a new dedicated Minister for Poverty Reduction Policies.

122. SER, 2021, *Werken zonder armoede, The Hague: SER.*

CHAPTER 7

In-Work Poverty in Poland

Monika Tomaszewska & Aleksandra Peplińska

The phenomenon of in-work poverty in Poland has been relatively recently subject to theoretical and empirical research in the area of the labour market and employment policy. This chapter is one of the few that present the analysis of the scale and causes of in-work poverty in Poland. It seems that the main reason lies in a rather limited scope of operation of labour law. Covering the work performed with effective protection depends on obtaining the status of an employee, which is interpreted restrictively. Contrary to individual labour law, the range of protection in collective labour law has been extended, thanks to international law influence, to cover all dependent workers, including those providing services in the form of self-employment. This disparate standard of protection in one branch of law leads to difficulties in seeking protection that labour law provisions ensure.

Further differences are noticeable between the employment status in labour law and the insurance status in Poland, which makes the phenomenon of in-work poverty encompass many spheres of law and policy at the same time. In assessing the causes of in-work poverty, one cannot overlook the access to social benefits which protect against the occurrence of an incapacity for work determined by various personal risks.

This chapter also comments on deficiencies in the legal regulations which contribute to increasing inequalities between the employed. The explanation of the in-work poverty phenomenon in Poland cannot solely rely on legal analyses. The objectives of the employment policy, limiting the scale of unemployed people, and finally, social policy focusing on helping households, are of equal importance here.

In the process of stabilising labour market in Poland, the right to a fair wage and guarantees the rate of minimum wage for non-employees plays a crucial role. Spreading Polish experiences regarding remuneration and the mechanisms that influence its determination has been a part of the mainstream discussion undertaken at the transnational level on adequate minimum wages in the European Union (EU).

§7.01 INTRODUCTION: OVERVIEW OF INFLUENTIAL FACTORS IMPACTING IN-WORK POVERTY IN POLAND

This introduction presents the essential elements of the Polish regulatory context, directly or indirectly impacting in-work poverty. It is estimated that in 2019 the number of people at risk of poverty or social exclusion (AROPE rate) was 6.691 million, which accounted for 18.2% of the entire population in Poland. Against this background, the in-work poverty (AROP rate) slightly decreased currently to 9.9% of the total number of workers.

The legal, economic, and social analyses indicate several factors that fundamentally determine the condition and scope of in-work poverty in Poland. The risk factor that mainly threatens working people and affects their well-being lies in various types of atypical and unsustainable forms of employment. Commonly accepted in the doctrine of labour law and statistical information is the interpretation of an atypical employment as deviate from the standard employment model. This targeted model of employment is a full-time contract for an indefinite period. Therefore, the atypical concept embraces all forms of a flexible employment contract, such as part-time employment, a contract for the duration of a specific job or a fixed-term contract. However, the atypical grounds for employment are primarily related to the exclusion from or limitation of the scope of protection provided by the labour law in connection with the absence of an employee status.

The legal status of an employee and conditions for its acquisition are determined by the provisions of the Labour Code (Article 2 and Article 22). Such employee status entails the broadest and most effective protection of both the basis of employment and the conditions under which the work is provided. Yet, obtaining the status of an employee requires meeting a number of conditions and is generally interpreted restrictively. What is symptomatic of the Polish system is an apparent dissonance between individual labour law and collective labour law. The legislator extended the protection of collective interests to non-employees, i.e., persons providing dependent work and the self-employed. Despite fundamental changes to the collective representation of the interests of employed persons, the above changes did neither improve unionisation (i.e., the membership of trade unions) nor the number of trade unions established by persons without the status of employees.

The distinguishing feature of the Polish labour market is a large percentage of people employed outside the protection of the labour law system (approx. 18%-20%). Various types of civil law contracts and self-employment regulated by branches other than labour law are applied for this purpose. A selection of legal grounds for performing work depends on many factors. The continuous increase in civil law contracts and self-employment proves that, apart from bogus self-employment, there are other essential considerations informing the choice of such basis. It seems that a significant choice of an atypical employment tends to result from calculating labour costs related to public and legal burdens, flexibility and scheduling the working time independently. In the case of the Polish legal system, non-employee forms of employment offer more favourable payroll taxes and determination of social security contributions than employment contracts. Consequently, a flexible form of employment is seen as more attractive for both parties: the employer incurs fewer costs, and the employee receives a salary higher than the one under an employment contract. Interestingly, a constant increase in the statutory minimum wage for employees did not reduce the number of contractor's workers and did not significantly tip the scale of poverty among employed persons. This evidences the fact that there is a weak correlation between increasing salaries and reducing in-work poverty.[1]

The parameter that accompanies the risk of poverty is low or even negligible work intensity, which results from a significant flexibility of employment conditions under previously mentioned part-time contract, fixed-term contract, work by a temporary employment agency, or employment under civil contract where the hours of work are not defined. It is shown by the highest risk-of-poverty rate noted by households with the lowest intensity of work. However, over the years from 2017 to 2019, the rate dropped in Poland by 7.1% (in 2019).

Compared with other countries, Poland shows a significant correlation between the percentage of in-work poverty and the level (low) of education,[2] which is closely related to performing work in sectors that do not require special qualifications (the so-called poor sectors). A similar relationship/dependence can be observed regarding the place of residence. Due to the unbalanced level of development of specific regions in Poland, the number and availability of jobs significantly affect the legal ground, quality, and conditions of employment.

The household composition related to the number of its members and structure thereof (the fact of having children, the number of children, and the number of working adults in each household) is among the factors that can markedly contribute to the occurrence of in-work poverty among economically active people in Poland. Undoubtedly, the highest, despite social benefits, in-work poverty rate (within the framework of all analysed years, i.e., 2014-2019) was presented by single parents with dependent children (in 2019, it reached 16.2%). Similar situation results from the lack of income of the other parent, which has a significant bearing on the observed income risk rate in comparison with other households. Furthermore, socio-economic analyses conducted in recent years indicate a slightly increased risk of poverty among single-person households. The above phenomenon may be related to the lack of access to social support programs, which are generally addressed to families with dependent children.

1. Wiemer Salverda, Low earnings and their drivers in relation to in-work poverty, in Handbook on In-Work Poverty 26-49 (Henning Lohmann & Ive Marx eds., Edward Elgar Publishing 2018).
2. While in general the highest at-risk-of-poverty rate over all of the analysed years was obtained by workers with the lowest level of education, the at-risk-of-poverty rate for workers with the lowest qualifications in Poland indicates downward trends (from 28.7% in 2011 to 20.4% in 2019).

Provided that in-work poverty is a complex and multidimensional phenomenon, the present chapter advances the characteristics of an employment relationship and features that distinguish it from a civil law relationship (§7.01[A]). The latest amendments to the Act on Trade Unions evidently extending the scope of protection of collective interests to the self-employed are analysed in §7.01[B]. A critical element of this protection is the negotiation capacity of the content of autonomous sources of labour law. Trade unions play an essential role in determining the working conditions, especially the amount of remuneration on the national level in terms of the minimum wage and at the company level (§7.01[C]). The chapter points to the basics of determining the charge of social security contributions which show apparent differences in the burden of said contributions between employee and non-employee forms of employment (§7.01[D]).

Section 7.02 offers a legal and sociological analysis linking to some particular groups of workers, referred to as 'vulnerable and under-represented persons' (from VUP1 to VUP4 groups). It is articulated in an overview of the national legal framework in connection to in-work poverty, including statutory minimum wages, collective bargaining (coverage, role in wage-setting, etc.), and most relevant social security benefits. Subsequently, this part includes a study of the regulation affecting each of the four VUP groups. This part shows the composition of each single VUP group, explaining the applicable legal basis for the assigned group and assessing the impact of regulation on the incidence of in-work poverty therefor.

[A] The Scope of Protection by Polish Labour Law: Characteristics of the Employment Relationship

Labour law in Poland belongs to the branch of law codified into the framework act of the Labour Code adopted in 1974.[3] The Labour Code governs the scope of the labour law regulations and the most important legal institutions such as sources of labour law, employment relationship,[4] status of an employee and an employer; stipulates their rights and obligations and form of their collective representation. Labour law is not the only field of law that sets forth work performance in the Polish legal system. The engagement under civil law agreements, which is the most competitive to the engagement under employment agreements, concerns performance of work based on civil law agreements regulated by the Civil Code[5] (such as e.g., a mandate contract or a contract for a specific task) and as self-employed.

The factor that decides on the coverage with labour law protection relates to the acquisition of an employee status on the grounds of entering into the employment

3. Act of 26 June 1974 Labour Code (Consolidated text of the Journal of Laws of 2020, item 1320 z as amended)
4. Monika Tomaszewska, Ewolucja instytucji umowy o pracę [Evolution of the institution of the employment contract] [in:] System prawa pracy [The Labour Law System], ed. K.W. Baran, 224-270, (Woltes Kluwer Poland Warszawa 2021)
5. Act of 23 April 1964 Civil Code, Consolidated text of the Journal of Laws of 2020, item 1740 as amended (here the Civil Code).

relationship.[6] A set of work qualities determines the legal qualification of a performed work as an employment relationship i.e., (a) voluntary, (b) subordinate, (c) paid, (d) provided in person, (e) cooperated (team), (f) obligating the employee to provide work, and (g) without the risk for performance of the obligation.[7] In compliance with Article 22 § 1^1 and 1^2 of the Labour Code, employment under conditions corresponding to said qualities is of an employee character irrespective of the name of the agreement concluded by the parties. It is also inadmissible to replace employment agreements with agreements of other character with unchanged terms and conditions of providing work. The wording of this provision is an illustration of several important assumptions in labour law:

- the legislator's strive for elimination of the improper practice of forcing employed persons to agree to the resignation from an employee status,
- counteracting apparent contracts,
- recognition of employment with employee subordination qualities as employment relationship irrespective of the name of the agreement concluded by the parties.[8]

The provisions of Article 22 of the Labour Code do not eliminate admissibility of providing work under civil law agreements (specifically under the mandate contract), if it is compliant with the will of the parties who conclude such agreements. Provisions of the Polish law have not introduced in the legal system the presumption of concluding the employment relationship.[9] Since no employment relationship is presumed, a specific basis for employment depends, in fact, on the parties' free will. Consequently, the form of employment relies not so much on the character of the work performed as it is stimulated by other factors such as the economic benefits achieved due to the lower public-law burden when choosing non-employee grounds.

What transpires from Polish regulations is that subordination is a feature that allows differentiating the employment relationship from other non-employment forms of activity (civil engagement and self-employment). Elements that prove the dependency of the person performing work as an employee are, for example:[10] definite period of time of providing work and place of the performance of activities; signing time sheets;[11] subordination to the rules and regulations of work and orders given by the management regarding the time, place, and manner of performing work and the

6. In compliance with the Labour Code, the employment relationship can be entered into on the grounds of an employment agreement (Article 25 of the Labour Code), appointment (Article 68 of the Labour Code), nomination (Article 76 of the Labour Code), election (Article 73 of the Labour Code), and agreement for cooperative employment (Article 77 of the Labour Code).
7. Jakub Stelina, Monika Tomaszewska, Marta Zbucka-Gargas, Introduction to Polish Labour Law with Cross-Border Aspect, 6-7 (C.H. Beck Warszawa 2021).
8. Judgement of the Supreme Court of 07.04.1999, I PKN 642/98.
9. Judgement of the Supreme Court of 28.01.1998, II UKN 479/97.
10. *See* judgement of the Supreme Court of 11.01.2008, I PK 182/07.
11. Judgement of the Labour and Social Security Court in Lodz of 25.11.1975, I P 848/75, Sł. Prac. 1976/4, p. 38.

obligation to comply with the work standards;[12] the obligation to execute orders given by superiors;[13] performance of shift work and permanent availability;[14] exact specification of the time and place of performance of the entrusted task and performance thereof under manager's supervision.[15]

In practice, the above elements of subordination more rarely happen simultaneously. There is also a tendency to define the work performed through achieved results and effects, with no indication of the time for an employee to be at the employer's disposal, which is very symptomatic of a remote working. The complex nature of social and economic relations and work organisation modifications (e.g., remote work) only increase doubts about the unequivocal legal qualification of a given type of employment.

In case of a dispute over the legal nature of employment, only a court can determine the existence or non-existence of a legal relationship or the right (Article 189 of the Code of Civil Procedure).[16] However, the judicial path is long-lasting. On average, the trial concerning an employment relationship takes approximately three years. Trials for determination of the legal nature of employment, while it is pending, are rare as the employees fear the consequences. Employees usually make their claims only after termination of their employment.

[B] Scope of Protection by Collective Labour Law: The Concept of an Employed Person and Autonomous Sources of Law

What is symptomatic of the Polish system is an apparent dissonance between individual labour law and collective labour law. There, crucial breakthrough in the sphere of collective rights was due to the extension of the personal scope of such rights. A significant legal change is related to the judgement of the Constitutional Tribunal of 02.06.2015, K 1/13,[17] which defined the constitutional 'freedom of association' in light of Convention ILO no. 89 extending collective rights beyond the rights belonging only to employees. As a result, the judgement issued by the Constitutional Tribunal, K 1/13 amended the Act of 23 May 1991 on trade unions.[18] Article 1^1 of the Act on trade unions (hereinafter: the Act on trade unions) introduces the concept of a person performing gainful work, which means that an employee and also a person provide work for remuneration on other grounds than the employment relationship, if they do not employ other persons for this type of work, irrespective of the employment basis, and enjoy the same rights and interests related to the performance of work, which translates to them being represented and defended by a trade union (Article 1^1 of the Act on trade unions). Consequently, the legal situation of the self-employed and those

12. Judgement of the Supreme Court of 27.02.1979, II URN 19/79, NP 1981/6, p. 82.
13. Judgement of the Supreme Court of 11.04.1997, I PKN 89/97, OSNAPiUS 1998/2, item 35.
14. Judgement of the Supreme Court of 11.09.1997, II UKN 232/97, OSNAPiUS 1998/13, item 407.
15. Judgement of the Supreme Court of 22.12.1998, I PKN 517/98, OSNAPiUS 2000/4, item 138.
16. Act of 17 November 1964 Code of Civil Procedure Consolidated text of the Journal of Laws of 2021, item 1805 as amended.
17. OTK-A 2015/6, item 80.
18. Act of 23 May 1991 on Trade Unions, Journal of Laws of 2018, item 1608.

working under civil contracts changed in both establishing and joining trade unions and the right to negotiate collective agreements.

In practice, the amendment to the Act on trade unions was followed neither by an increase in the number of the employed joining the existing trade unions, nor by encouraging this group to establish independent and autonomous trade unions. It results from the lack of protection of contractors because legal provisions do not provide for a legal protection comparable to that of the employment relationship. There are also severe doubts about the legal nature of agreements concluded by the self-employed with the unions and about the subject of such agreements. Consequently, the amendment to the Act on trade unions did not improve the working conditions of this group of employed persons.

The essence of trade unions' activity lies in the capacity to be a party to collective labour agreements or to hold the right to negotiate the content of the so-called specific sources of labour law. Various types of so-called specific sources of labour law evidence the autonomy of labour law, which guarantees the influence on the determination of working conditions by the stakeholders, i.e., by employers and employees represented by their representatives. The majority of specific sources of labour law have an intercompany character. Supra-company collective labour agreements and certain collective agreements are an exception to the above rule.

Specific sources of labour law, in particular collective labour agreements and rules and regulations of remuneration serve to determine the rules (methods) of remunerating employees at the company level, whereas acceptable deviations from the universally binding provisions can only occur to the benefit of an employee. It means that regulations of specific sources of labour law improve both the terms and conditions of work and the amount of remuneration with regard to the universally binding provisions. Therefore, their role is to raise the standard of protection. Recognising under Article 9 of the Labour Code specific acts as sources of the labour law means that they simultaneously become the substance of the employment relationship.

Article 9 of the Labour Code, in which the principle of favour is included, defines relations between specific sources and universal sources of labour law. The principle of a privilege of an employee defines the relation between collective agreements (and other legal activities shaping the employment relationship) and labour law provisions.[19]

In 2016, 79 company collective agreements and 896 additional protocols were registered, which in turn are used to amend already registered collective agreements.[20] It is worth juxtaposing certain values such as the number of employees covered by company collective agreements at just over 38,000 employees with the population working in the national economy in 2016 at 15.7 million people.[21] It leads to the conclusion that collective agreements do not constitute a primary mechanism for

19. Jakub Stelina, Monika Tomaszewska, Marta Zbucka-Gargas, Introduction to Polish Labour Law with Cross-Border Aspect, 35-26 (C.H. Beck Warszawa 2021).
20. The data presented are taken from the National Labour Inspectorate activity report for 2016.
21. CSO Report Employees and wages in the national economy in 2016 – preliminary data.

regulating work and pay conditions, even though in the hierarchy of sources of law, they are on top and are applied before all specific sources of labour law.

Some parts of specific labour law provide for the employer's right to amend the terms and conditions of work and pay leading to the reduction of the benefits to which the employee is entitled, including the amount of remuneration. The Labour Code stipulates three types of suspensive agreements which include derogation clauses. Common features of said three types of agreement concluded between the employer and trade unions are temporary duration and collective character. If there are no unions, the employees are represented by a representative selected in accordance with the procedure adopted by the employer – ad hoc (Article 9^1 of the Labour Code and Article 23^{1a} of the Labour Code).

- Article 9^1 of the Labour Code – agreements to suspend the application of company regulations and statutes.
- Article 23^{1a} of the Labour Code – an agreement to suspend the application of less favourable conditions of employees' employment than those arising from employment contracts.
- Article 241^{27} § 1 of the Labour Code – an agreement to suspend the provisions of a collective agreement, which can only be concluded by the parties to the collective agreement.

The change of employment conditions to the detriment of employees may concern contractual provisions and provisions included in specific sources of labour law, which means that suspensive agreements could not diminish the level of protection provided by generally applicable labour law.

Mechanisms that render working conditions set forth in the Labour Code more flexible were applied in the Act of 02.03.2020 on specific solutions related to preventing, counteracting, and combating COVID-19, other infectious diseases and resulting crisis situations.[22] Agreements on using less favourable employment conditions refer their effect to both, persons with an employee status and a status of persons employed under civil law agreements. A premise for conclusion of an agreement is a decrease in business turnover as a result of COVID-19 outbreak, as well as the absence of public-law arrears.

[C] Concept of a Fair Remuneration: a Guarantee of a Minimum Wage in the Polish Legal System

The right to a fair remuneration derives from two provisions of the Constitution of the Republic of Poland[23] – Article 33 stipulating the right of men and women to the same remuneration for work of the same value and Article 65 par. 4 introducing the

22. Consolidated text of the Journal of Laws 2021, item 1842, as amended – hereinafter referred to as the Act on COVID-19.
23. Constitution of the Republic of Poland of 2 April 1997, Journal of Laws 1997, item 483 as amended.

obligation of a statutory specification of a minimal amount of remuneration. Normative grounds for the right to fair remuneration are set forth in Article 13 of the Labour Code. Due to its programmatic character, Article 13 does not create legal ground for individual claims. In judicial decisions, it was expressly indicated that the right to fair remuneration under Article 13 of the Labour Code is only an interpretative guideline and thus, does not constitute the basis for employees' claims for increasing remuneration over the level of a minimum wage.[24] Therefore, it is only that part of remuneration which is defined by separate regulations as minimum that is of a claim and warranty nature.

In the Polish legal system, the amount and the manner of calculating minimum wage are provided for in the Act of 10.10.2002 on minimum wage[25] (the Act on minimum wage). In light of this act, a universal and uniform manner of determining components of the minimum wage is binding in Poland and one minimum wage rate is set for all employees (irrespective of the sector). The aim of the act is to ensure a specific amount of remuneration which refers to the costs of maintenance rather than to the type or quality of the work performed. Therefore, the amount of the minimum wage and the hourly rate are vested due to the employment not only on the grounds of an employment relationship, but also under civil law agreements such as a mandate contract or an agreement for providing services.

The minimum wage rate has been the subject of annual negotiations within the Council of Social Dialogue in compliance with the procedure stipulated in the Act on minimum wage (Article 2 par. 1 of the Act on minimum wage). If social partners do not reach an agreement on the amount thereof, then the right to specify it is vested in the Council of Ministers. The amount of the minimum wage is subject to publication in the Official Gazette of the Republic of Poland 'Monitor Polski', by the announcement of the Prime Minister until 15 September each year (Article 2 par. 4 of the Act on minimum wage). The amount of the remuneration of an employee employed for a full-month of work cannot be lower than the amount of the minimum wage. In order to calculate the amount of the employee's remuneration, the remuneration components and other benefits resulting from the employment relationship are vested in an employee (on employment basis) with the exception of:

- anniversary award;
- severance pay for the employee with regard to retirement or social security pension due to the incapacity for work;
- remuneration for overtime;
- night work allowance;
- seniority premium (from 01.01.2020) vested due to the long-time service.

The aforementioned five components of the remuneration are not included in the basis for calculating the amount of the minimum remuneration.

24. *See* Judgement of the Supreme Court of 29.05.2006 I PK 230/05, OSN 2007 nos. 11-12, p. 155.
25. Consolidated text of the Journal of Laws of 2018, item 2177.

The scope of the Act of the minimum wage was extended to persons with a non-employee status by the Act of 22 July 2016.[26] Consequently, since 2016, the forms of calculating minimum remuneration have applied to work performed on contracts of mandate (Article 734 of the Civil Code) and for the provision of services to which the provisions on mandate apply (Article 750 of the Civil Code). The contractors were guaranteed, among other things, at least a minimum rate per hour of service provision (in 2021 - PLN 18.30). In this way, the position of the self-employed was partially equalised with employees. However, this Act limits its scope of application only to specific nominate civil law contracts.

In the system of Polish labour law, the standard of the minimum wage is increased by specific autonomous sources of labour law. However, due to a negligible degree of unionisation and a very complicated and lengthy conclusion procedure, the collective agreements do not constitute a formal method of increasing remuneration. In practice, employer's remuneration regulations are more commonly used at the company level which content are also consulted with the unions. In the absence of trade unions, the regulations are consulted with an ad hoc employee representative. A weak side to the remuneration regulations is their limited scope of regulation covering only a single employer. Therefore, they cannot constitute a mechanism of regulating the remuneration that pertains to a specific industry or region for the employees.

There are no legal obstacles extended in respect of the working conditions provided for in specific sources of labour law (such as collective agreements or work and remuneration regulations) to persons who do not hold the status of employees. However, there are several limitations to this solution. First, such regulations cannot be issued exclusively for non-employees because they lose their character as a source of labour law. Second, it is possible to extend the subjective scope of the only existing labour regulation, i.e., one adopted for employees. In practice, it is sporadic that the specific sources of labour law are extended to include non-employees.

[D] The Social Security System as a Mitigation of Poverty and Social Risk

The social security system in Poland has not been codified yet; however, it achieved a significant level of coherence and pivots on four relevant legal acts:

- Act of 12.10.1998 on social security system.[27]
- Act of 17.12.1998 on retirement and social security pensions from the Social Insurance Fund.[28]
- Act of 25.06.1999 on cash social security benefits in respect of sickness and maternity.[29]

26. Journal of Laws of 2016, item 1265.
27. Journal of Laws of 2020, item 266.
28. Journal of Laws of 2020, item 53.
29. Journal of Laws of 2020, item 870.

- Act of 30.10.2002 on social security against accidents at work and occupational diseases.[30]

A fundamental importance should be attributed to the Act of 13 October 1998 on social security system, which hinges on two principle characteristics of this system i.e., the principle of commonness of social security and the principle of equality. These are the main features of social insurance. The first one is related to the intention of covering all persons performing gainful work with social insurance, who due to the existence of the same or similar fortuitous events are subject to the protection provided for by social security. Whereas, the principle of equality stipulates the requirement of equal treatment of entities in similar situations and, simultaneously, eliminates from the system the unjustified differentiation due to personal characteristics of a human being such as: sex, race, ethnicity, nationality, marital status, and family status.

In reliance upon the principle of the commonness of social security system, statutory provisions seek to cover with obligatory insurance persons performing almost every type of gainful work. Therefore, the legislator prefers to use the concept of an insured person which covers with its scope all types of the work performed. What is important, the legislator shapes for the purposes of social security a separate, with regard to the provisions of the Labour Code, definition of an employee (Article 8 par. 2a of the Act on social security). The extension of the scope of subjects considered on the grounds of the Act on social security as employees attaches to two situations. The first one comprises providing work on the grounds of one of the enumerated civil law agreements by the mandatary to the benefit of his or her employer. The second one consists in providing work under one of such agreements by a person, who concluded the enumerated agreement with a third party, performing under such an agreement work to the benefit of the employer with whom he or she is in the employment relationship. The premise deciding on considering such a person to be an employee pursuant to the security act consists in the fact that, while being an employee linked to a given employer on the grounds of an employment relationship, he or she simultaneously provides work to his or her benefit under a civil law contract directly or through the agency of a third party.

An independent title to cover persons with the social security obligation is performing work under an agency agreement (Article 758 par. 1 of the Civil Code), a mandate contract (Article 734 par. 1 of the Civil Code), or other agreement on providing services (Article 750 of the Civil Code). This applies to cases when a mandate contract or other civil law agreements are an exclusive basis for providing work. Social security law provisions collectively define such group as contractors (mandataries). Mandataries are a specific category of the insured situated in factual and legal terms between employees and the self-employed. Therefore, a mandatary is subject to a retirement pension and social security pension obligatory contribution. Whereas contribution on accident insurance depends on where the work is performed, sickness insurance being entirely voluntary for said persons. The above differentiation of both the basis and the amount of social security contributions for contractors is explained in

30. Journal of Laws of 2019, item 1205.

reliance upon the type of such contracts and the circumstances of concluding them. Due to the voluntary character of the sickness insurance contribution and, for the most part, of the accident insurance, some persons employed under civil law agreements decide to not pay the contribution and thus keep a part of their remuneration.

Non-payment of the sickness insurance contribution carries far-reaching consequences primarily in the event of the incapacity for work and a loss of the sources of income. The most frequent cases of incapacity for work are occasioned by illness, care for family members (children), or motherhood. Enumerated categories of insurance risks constitute grounds for payment of sickness benefit or care allowance on the condition of previous payment of sickness insurance contributions. In further perspective, the presented division of insurance obligations can disadvantage persons who do not pay all insurance contributions. The willingness to increase the amount of income by the part of unpaid public levies is attractive primarily to mandataries and service providers who receive very low remuneration or to relatively young people not yet burdened with family obligations.

Unfortunately, it is not the final list of exemptions from paying social security contributions. The provisions introduce an important exception to persons employed under a mandate contract until becoming 26 years old since these persons are not subject to social insurance (Article 6 par. 4 of the Act on social security system). This provision is intended to have a beneficial impact on employers by encouraging them to employ young people without relevant professional experience. The consequence of the above solution is predominantly the employment of young people under a mandate contract, as service under an employment contract gives rise to a comprehensive obligation to pay contributions to the full extent.

In the Polish legal system, collective labour agreements cannot be seen as the source of increasing social insurance protection, even though they constitute the most crucial source of labour law. It results from the character of social security law as absolutely binding administrative provisions. An essential feature of social insurance is the acquisition of rights according to the pre-defined premises, in compliance with the principle of formal equality of subjects.[31] A weakness to this solution lies in the absence of the possibility to adjust provisions in specific, isolated cases which have not been covered with the scope of the regulations. The retirement-social security pension authority does not exercise, therefore, the freedom to assess granting or not granting a specific benefit.

Nonetheless, the foregoing solution shows its negative consequences as well, for example in the form of increasing the number of persons employed under unstable forms of employment. In turn, instability of work does not favour stabilisation of life and financial situation. It also exerts an impact on postponing the decision on starting a family, hinders purchase of an apartment due to the relatively low capacity of repaying a large loan.

---

31. Inetta Jędrasik-Jankowska, Pojęcia i konstrukcje prawne ubezpieczenia społecznego [Legal Concepts and Structures of Social Insurance], 43-45, (Wolters Kluwer Warszawa 2020).

§7.02 REASONS AND EFFECTS OF IN-WORK POVERTY WITH REGARD TO DIFFERENT VUP GROUPS: A STATISTICAL AND ANALYTICAL STUDY

[A] VUP Group 1: Low- or Unskilled Standard Employment

[1] Composition of VUP Group 1

VUP Group 1 is focused on low- or unskilled employees with standard employment contracts employed in poor sectors. The characteristics of this group may therefore include people with a low level of education, low level of qualifications, and employment in poor sectors on full-time contracts. According to Eurostat data,[32] in 2019, workers employed in low-skilled occupations and at the same time in poor sectors accounted for 8.3% of all workforce (persons aged more than 18 years, employed on a permanent, full-time basis and having been employed for more than 6 months in the year preceding the survey). This result remained higher by about 2 percentage points when compared to previous years, i.e., 2007 - 7.0% and 2013 - 6.5%. At the same time, 5.4% of this group of employees were directly at risk of poverty in 2019, and 2.0% were experiencing material deterioration. While the percentage of people employed in low-skilled occupations and poor sectors rose in 2019, the poverty and deprivation rates mentioned above have declined markedly since 2007.

Table 7.1 In-Work Poverty and Deprivation among VUP Group 1 in Poland, in 2019

	All Employed	*Employees Only*	*VUP 1: Employees in Low-Skilled Occupation and in Poor Sectors*
% of the employed (in-work) population	100	79.6	8.3
In-work poverty	9.7	5.3	5.4
Severe material deprivation	1.8	2.0	2.0

Source: EU-SILC/Eurostat.

Reading guide: Among the employed, in Poland, in 2019, 9.7% are at-risk-of- poverty.

In 2019, the largest group of employees in low-skilled occupations and poor sectors were those in the 35-49 age range (42.9%) and, importantly, this indicator increased compared to previous years (2007 - 36.7%; 2013 - 39.2%). The data also

32. EU-SILC, 2007, 2013, and 2019.

show that the share of the youngest workers employed in low-skilled occupations and in poor sectors has been gradually decreasing over the years (2019 – 32.7%; 2013 – 38.7%; 2007 – 48.5%). In 2019, however, poverty risk rates for different age categories were similar, ranging from 5.6% (for the 18-34 and 35-49 age groups) to 4.8% (for the oldest age category of employees more than 50 years of age).

Table 7.2 Composition of VUP Group 1 in Poland, in 2019[33]

	All Employed	*Employees Only*	*VUP 1: Employees in Low-Skilled Occupation and in Poor Sectors*
Age group (%)			
18-34	7.7 (29.0)	5.4 (31.1)	5.6 (32.7)
35-49	10.1 (42.8)	5.1 (42.3)	5.6 (42.9)
> =50	11.2 (28.2)	5.4 (26.6)	4.8 (24.4)
Gender (%)			
Women	8.7 (48.0)	4.5 (49.5)	5.4 (61.1)
Men	10.7 (52.0)	6.0 (50.5)	5.4 (38.9)
Nationality (%)			
Country of residence	9.7 (99.3)	5.3 (99.3)	s.s.[34]
Other	12.7 (0.7)	5.8 (0.7)	s.s.
Education (%)			
Lower secondary/Primary of less	20.4 (5.1)	13.3 (4.6)	6.9 (5.0)
Upper secondary or post-secondary non-tertiary	12.0 (59.9)	6.6 (58.5)	5.5 (79.3)
Tertiary	4.3 (35.0)	2.2 (36.8)	4.8 (15.7)

Source: EU-SILC/Eurostat.

Reading guide: In 2019, in Poland, 61.1% of low-skilled employees (permanent and full-time contract) in poor sectors are women. Among these women 5.4% are at risk of in-work poverty.

The analysis by gender shows that women dominated among workers in low- or unskilled employees, with standard employment contracts, employed in poor sectors

33. Data in brackets – % of total employees in a given category.
34. The decomposition by nationality – too small sample to construct statistics – EU-SILC, 2007, 2013, and 2019.

(2019 – 61.1% of the total; 2013 – 54.8%, 2007 – 52.3%). However, the risk-of-poverty rate for both genders was identical and amounted to 5.4%.

In 2019, 79.3% of the employed in low-skilled occupations and at the same time poor sectors were people with secondary and basic vocational education (level 3-4 according to the Organisation for Economic Co-operation and Development (OECD)-11 classification) with 5.5% of workers at risk of poverty.[35] Moreover, 15.7% of those employed in low-skilled professions and poor sectors said they had a university degree (of which 4.8% were at risk of poverty).

According to the European Union Statistics on Income and Living Conditions (EU-SILC) report, in 2019, 71.9% of workers in low-skilled and poor occupations were employed in sectors related to wholesale and retail trade; repair of motor vehicles and motorcycles; transport and storage; accommodation and food services activities; information and communication (Trade/Transport/Accommodation and food services/info-com). Approximately 6.5% of those employed in this economic sector category were at risk of poverty. The remainder of workers from this domain (28.1%, with 2.5% at risk of poverty) were employed in other service categories. Furthermore, these results remain at similar levels over the subsequent years analysed (i.e., 2007, 2013, 2019). Due to the small sample size, it is not possible to analyse this category of employed workers by nationality or number of months of work in the year preceding the survey.

The household characteristics of workers in VUP group 1 allow to complete the characteristics of this group of workforce. In 2019, 72.5% of them were members of households comprising more than two persons (of which 4.9% were at risk of poverty).[36] Approximately 21.2% were workers from households with exactly two occupants (poverty risk ratio 6.4%), while 6.3% were single-person households. The highest risk-of-poverty rate (8.7%) was observed in the case of the last group. Moreover, 67.2% of workers in VUP Group 1 lived in a household with another worker, and the risk-of-poverty rate for this category was 2.4%. The remaining part (32.8%) covered those being the only employed person in the household, and the risk-of poverty rate for this category amounted to 11.5%.

Among the employed in VUP Group 1, 57% were those not providing for any children under the age of 18 and the risk-of-poverty rate for this category of workers was 4.3%. Almost 18.1% of the total of this category of workers were those with more than 1 child under the age of 18, of which 4.9% were at risk of poverty.

[2] Relevant Legal Framework

Poland's statutory regulations do not define low- or unskilled employees. However, this concept is used for various statistical studies. In line with the International Standard Classification of Education (ISCED), a low-skilled worker is one who is characterised by an incomplete primary or primary (level 1) or lower secondary (1st

35. EU-SILC, 2007, 2013, and 2019.
36. *Ibid.*

degree secondary – level 2) education. This indicator should be adjusted to Polish conditions and the reform of the education system in 2015. Lower secondary schools were successively phased out, and the low qualification level (1 and 2) included an incomplete primary education covering eight classes.

Low qualifications may also be indicated by an occupation, or more precisely, by the lack of occupation, described in compliance with the valid Classification of Occupations and Specialities and standards of ISCO-88 (International Standard Classification of Occupation). Accordingly, low-skilled workers are those who perform low-complexity jobs.

Another attempt to define the scope of low- or unskilled employees, with standard employment contracts, employed in poor sectors is reliance upon statistical data denoting remuneration where more than 20% of the employed earn below the median two-third earnings. Polish statistical data show that the average monthly gross salary in enterprises with more than nine employees in 2019 was PLN 4,920.09. For example, salaries in the *Accommodation and Catering section* ranged from PLN 3,231.40 as opposed to the ones in the *Information and Communications section*, where average remuneration started from PLN 8,441.14. It was respectively 34.3% less and 71.6% more than the average gross monthly salary. In Poland, the sectors considered as traditionally poor do not differ from those indicated in the Eurostat statistics. These include in particular: accommodation and catering, other service activities, administration and support activities, construction, transport and warehouse management, and activities related to entertainment and recreation.

Unfortunately, specific sources of labour law are rarely used to enhance working conditions or remuneration in this particular group. This is mainly because collective agreements do not generally constitute a primary mechanism to regulate the conditions of work and pay, even though in the hierarchy of sources of law, they applied before all specific sources of labour law. As indicated by the statistical data contained in the Report of the National Labour Inspectorate from 2016, a negligible number of company collective agreements also occur in poor sectors: accommodation and catering – 0, other service activities – 1, administration and support activities – 1, construction – 2, transport and warehouse management – 8, activities related to entertainment and recreation – 1.

[3] Impact Analysis

Compared to other countries, in Poland, there is a significant correlation between the percentage of in-work poverty and the level (low) of education, which is closely related to performing work in sectors that do not require special qualifications (the so-called poor sectors). The data available from the *Central Statistical Office* (CSO) report 'Structure of wages by occupation' of 2019,[37] which are essential in this respect, do not reflect the accurate scale of the in-work-poverty in poor sectors, which transpires from

37. https://stat.gov.pl/en/topics/labour-market/yearbook-of-labour/methodological-report-statistics-on-labour-market-wages-and-salaries,5,1.html.

the adopted data collection methodology which covers only employers with more than nine employees if their employment basis is an employment contract. Whereas civil law contracts or self-employment dominate as the basis for work in most poor sectors such as accommodation, catering, entertainment, and recreation. The minimum remuneration rate is binding upon the parties to the contract if it is an employment contract. Whereas, in the case of civil law contracts, it is imperative only for selected types of contracts, such as commission or provision of services. In view of the fact that some part of the employed in the poor sectors perform their work as non-employees, the scale of poverty may be underestimated.

[B] VUP Group 2: Solo and Bogus Self-Employment

[1] Composition of VUP Group 2

For many years, Poland has been in the forefront of the EU countries in respect of the number of the self-employed. For several years now, Poland has invariably occupied the third place among the Member States, after Greece and Italy. Eurostat data show that the number of the self-employed not employing others amounted to 2.4 million people, which constituted 14.3% of all the employed.[38] Moreover, 28.9% of the self-employed were at risk of poverty, and 1.8% were experiencing material deprivation. It is worth noting, however, that while the at-risk-of-poverty rate unfortunately did not improve significantly from 2007 till 2019, the material deprivation rate has clearly declined (2007 – 15.9%; 2013 – 7.5%; 2019 – 1.8%).

Table 7.3 In-Work Poverty and Deprivation among VUP Group 2 in Poland, in 2019

	All Employed	*All Self-Employed (Including Family Workers)*	*VUP 2: Self-Employed Without Employee*
% of the employed (in-work) population	100	20.2	14.3
In-work poverty	9.7	27.3	28.9
Severe material deprivation	1.8	1.3	1.8

Source: EU-SILC/Eurostat.

Reading guide: Among the employed, in Poland, in 2019, 9.7% are at risk of poverty.

38. EU-SILC, 2007, 2013, and 2019.

In 2019, the group of the self-employed (not employing workers) were mostly men (58.9%), of whom up to 29.7% were at risk of poverty. For women (41.1% of all self-employed without employees), the risk of poverty in 2019 was 27.8%. The largest group both in 2019 and previous years i.e., 2007, 2013 were people in the age category of 35-49 years. Unfortunately, at the same time, as many as 29.3% of this group were at risk of poverty in 2019. High rates of the self-employed suffering from poverty were also seen in other age categories. In terms of educational achievement, the largest group in 2019 were people with upper secondary education, basic vocational and post-secondary non-tertiary education. The smallest group of the self-employed are those with the lowest educational achievement. In 2019, 66.3% of the self-employed in VUP Group 2 were people with a medium level of education (upper secondary, basic vocational and post-secondary non-tertiary according to ISCED-11 level 3-4 classification). Among the group with the medium level of education, as many as 33.4% of the self-employed in VUP Group 2 were at risk of poverty. Based on the Table 7.3, we can see that the higher the level of education, the lower the risk-of-poverty rate. Among the group with the lowest level of education, as many as 42.9% of the self-employed in VUP Group 2 were at risk of poverty in 2019. Regarding working hours for the self-employed in VUP Group 2 in 2019, 89.6% of them worked full time, of which 29.3% were at risk of poverty. Almost 76.9% of the self-employed in 2019 had a high level of qualifications, of which 34.3% were at risk of poverty.

Table 7.4 Composition of VUP Group 2 in Poland, in 2019[39]

	All Employed	*All the Self-Employed (Including Family Workers)*	*VUP 2: the Self-Employed Without an Employee*
Age group (%)			
18-34	7.7 (29.0)	21.7 (20.2)	23.0 (19.0)
35-49	10.1 (42.8)	28.8 (45.1)	29.3 (45.1)
> =50	11.2 (28.2)	28.7 (34.7)	31.6 (35.9)
Gender (%)			
Women	8.7 (48.0)	27.8 (42.4)	27.8 (41.1)
Men	10.7 (52.0)	26.9 (57.6)	29.7 (58.9)
Nationality (%)			
Country of residence	9.7 (99.3)	s.s.[40]	s.s.
Other	12.7 (0.7)	s.s.	s.s.

39. Data in brackets – % of total employees in a given category.
40. The decomposition by nationality – too small a sample to construct statistics; EU-SILC, 2007, 2013, and 2019.

	All Employed	*All the Self-Employed (Including Family Workers)*	*VUP 2: the Self-Employed Without an Employee*
Education (%)			
Lower secondary/Primary or less	20.4 (5.1)	40.0 (6.7)	42.9 (7.2)
Upper secondary or post-secondary non-tertiary	12.0 (59.9)	31.2 (65.3)	33.4 (66.3)
Tertiary	4.3 (35.0)	15.0 (28.0)	13.5 (26.5)
Occupation			
High skill (ISCO-08 level 3 and 4)	3.5 (37.1)	12.6 (27.4)	10.9 (23.1)
Low skill (ISCO-08 level 1 and 2)	13.4 (62.9)	32.9 (72.6)	34.3 (76.9)

Source: EU-SILC/Eurostat

Reading guide: In 2019, in Poland, 41.1% of the self-employed without an employee are women. Among these women, 27.8% are at risk of in-work poverty

The economic sector analysis allows the conclusion that the largest group of the self-employed in 2019 were those working in the sectors of mining and quarrying, manufacturing, electricity, gas, steam and air conditioning supply, water supply; sewage, waste management and remediation activities, construction (64.5%), of whom 31.1% were at risk of poverty. It is worth noting, however, that this kind of data fall into single economic sector industries with a high level of internal differentiation (e.g., mining with construction) which, in general, means that they strongly differ in their motivation for undertaking potential self-employment. In the mining industry, for example, becoming self-employed would entail the loss of many cash allowances.

According to Eurostat,[41] in 2019, among the self-employed (not employing workers), 76% were people from households with more than 2 persons, 29.7% of whom were the groups at risk of poverty. Single-person households in the self-employed group accounted for only 7%, of which as many as 30.8% were at risk of poverty. The result regarding households with more than two members is also alarming - since 2007, a slight increase in the risk of poverty in this group has been observed and still practically every third household of a self-employed person is at risk of poverty. Including data on having children under the age of 18, the dominant group of self-employed in VUP Group 2 in 2019 were childless households (52.4%), of which 29.4% were at risk of poverty. In the other distinguished groups (i.e., those with 1 child

41. EU-SILC, 2007, 2013, and 2019.

and those with more than 1 child), the poverty risk rate remained at a similar level (29.5% and 27.2% respectively).

[2] Legal Framework: Notion; Obstacles to the Application of Labour Law and Social Security Standards; Unionisation and Application of Collective Agreements

There is no legal definition of self-employment in the Polish legal system. For commentaries and statistical purposes, there have been two takes on the term of self-employment. In a narrower but more prevalent sense, self-employment is construed as one-person activity as it indirectly transpires from the legal context of Article 304 of the Labour Code. As such, self-employment is subject to the Act of 6.03.2018 – Business Activity Law.[42] Business activity in self-employment can be undertaken after applying to the Central Registration and Information on Business (Article 17 of the Business Activity Law). An entry in the register has far-reaching legal consequences, e.g., it enjoys a presumption of the accuracy of the data entered, which is particularly important for the protection of third parties, e.g., consumers using the services of the entrepreneur. In addition, the self-employed acts as a professional in business transactions. Similarly, for its research and reports on the state or health of employment, the CSO assumes that self-employment means people who are running a business on their own.

In a broader sense, self-employment serves to analyse all atypical forms of employment as being competitive to the employment contract. For example, the *Labour Force Survey (basic survey)* and *Workforce in atypical forms of employment* conducted by the CSO[43] of 2016 define self-employment as non-typical forms of employment. In both documents, the non-typical work is viewed as all forms of employment other than the employment contract. As a result, the study embraced all types of civil law contracts governed by the Civil Code (i.e., mandate contracts, contracts for specific work, managerial agreements, and other civil law contracts, so-called innominate contracts), and self-employment means a person running their own business. The analysis of the structure of people working in atypical forms of employment (in their primary place of work) has shown that the most popular form was mandate contract – 65.7% of the total atypical employment and 2.9% of the total number of employed. The second group in terms of percentage participation were the self-employed – 16.1% and 0.7% of the entire workforce. For 92.5% of those declaring their main job under civil law contracts, this was the only work they performed at that time.[44]

The foregoing data should be compared with the information received from the social insurance institution which differentiates between contributions paid by the solo

42. Journal of Laws of 2021, item 162.
43. https://stat.gov.pl/obszary-tematyczne/rynek-pracy/pracujacy-bezrobotni-bierni-zawodowo-wg-bael/pracujacy-w-nietypowych-formach-zatrudnienia,21,1.html
44. *Ibid.*

self-employed and contributions paid for employed subcontractors. Data on contributors obtained from the Social Insurance Institution show that already at the beginning of 2012, the percentage paying social insurance contributions only for themselves was 67.78%; however, by mid-2020, the rate was already 71.08%. In the analysed period, the group of self-employed increased by 362,789 people. These figures confirm that almost 2 million employees pay social security contributions as solo self-employed. Such a large scale of the self-employed is influenced by the favourable rules for determining the base for the calculation of contributions contingent on the insured's declaration, which in fact comes down to the minimum wage basis and not the actual income. Moreover, the regulations limit compulsory contributions to social pension and retirement insurance.

In view of the growing scale of persons engaged under civil law agreements, specifically mandate contracts (Article 735 of the Civil Code) or contracts for the performance of services (Article 750 of the Civil Code), the legislator stipulated for said contracts a guarantee of the right to remuneration, amending to this end the act on minimum wage.[45] In compliance with Article 8a par. 4 of the Act on minimum wage 'The mandatary or the service provider cannot waive the right to remuneration in the amount resulting from the amount of the minimum hourly rate or transfer the right to this remuneration to another person.'

[3] Impact Analysis

Vast majority of the self-employed (80.2%) worked in this form not by choice. Regarding 51.3% of people in this group, the employer declared that the assignment of work was conditional on their establishing a business. The remaining 48.7% of people decided to take up this form of employment on their own (the employer did not require them to set up a business or this form of employment was more beneficial than other forms).

The displayed figures confirm that almost 2 million employees pay social security contributions as the solo self-employed. The same tendency emerges from European statistics. VUP Group 2 includes solo and bogus self-employed persons. In EU-SILC, the only distinction available is between the self-employed with employees and those without employees. A particular part of solo self-employed is bogus self-employed, but there is no guidance that could help determine how large this percentage is.

Such a large percentage of the self-employed (paying social insurance contributions only for themselves) is not reflected in the National Labour Inspectorate audits that question the legality of the legal basis for providing work. Pursuant to the provisions of the Labour Code, the replacement of an employment contract with non-employment forms, mainly civil law contracts, amounts to an offence against the employee's rights. The above offence, under Article 281^1 of the Labour Code, is punishable by a fine from PLN 10,000 to PLN 30,000. Figures displaying labour law

45. The Act of 22 July 2016 amending the Act on the minimum wage for work and certain other acts (Journal of Laws, item 1265, as amended).

violations have not shown a large scale of the self-employed. The National Labour Inspectorate report for 2019[1] shows that offences related to a bogus self-employment account for only 1.6% of the total violations against employee rights.

This low rate may indicate an ambiguous determination of the nature of a given employment and the ineffectiveness of the methods of self-employment control applied so far. In addition, numerous incentives for the self-employed established in both the social insurance system and the tax system mean that both parties to the contract do not show any interest in properly determining the nature of their relationship.

[C] VUP Group 3: Fixed-Term, Agency Workers, Involuntary Part-Timers

[1] Composition of VUP Group 3

VUP Group 3 includes fixed-term workers, agency workers, and involuntary part-timers. For statistical analysis, this group is represented in total (VUP 3) and divided into two groups – temporary workers (composed of fixed-term and temporary agency workers) and involuntary part-timers. Surveying the data, we have to remember that some individuals are both involuntary part-timers and temporary workers.

In 2019, VUP Group 3 represents in total 16.6% of workers in Poland.[46] According to Eurostat data, people in temporary employment accounted for 16% of the total workforce, 9% of whom were at risk of poverty. Involuntary part-timers accounted for only 1.2% of the total workforce, but 18.7% of them were at risk of poverty. Analysing the data for 2007 and 2013, we can notice a gentle decrease in both employment in this form (2007 – 20.2%; 2013 – 22.7% of total employment) and the risk-of-poverty rate (2007 – 12.3%; 2013 – 12.0%).

Table 7.5 In-Work Poverty and Deprivation among VUP Group 3 in Poland, in 2019

	All Employed	*Temporary Workers*	*Involuntary Part-Timers*	*VUP 3*
% of the employed (in-work) population	100	16.0	1.2	16.6
In-work poverty	9.7	9.0	18.7	9.1
Severe material deprivation	1.8	4.8	9.4	4.8

Source: EU-SILC/Eurostat.

Reading guide: Among the employed, in Poland, in 2019, 9.7% are at risk of poverty.

46. EU-SILC, 2007, 2013, and 2019.

Eurostat data exhibit that the group most often employed in flexible forms of work (temporary or part-time employment) were the youngest workers, i.e., up to 34 years old (in 2019, they represented 46.1% of the total employed in this category, of whom 7.7% were at risk of poverty). People aged 50 and above are the least likely to be employed in this category, accounting for 20.3% of all jobs in 2019. However, unfortunately, it was this group that manifested the highest poverty risk rates (11.2%). In 2019, 52.3% of all those employed in VUP Group 3 were women, 8.5% of whom were at risk of poverty. Data presented in Table 7.6 show also a predominance of people with secondary education (2019 – 64.5% of whom 9.4% were at risk of poverty), followed by higher education (26.9% of whom 5.2% were at risk of poverty). This form of employment thus hardly concerns people with the lowest level of education. Yet, it is worth noting that on the basis of the figures presented here – it is in this category, i.e., people with the lowest level of education, that the highest risk-of-poverty rate was recorded (18.7%). Such data may indicate that practically every fifth person employed in this form – who has the lowest level of education – is at risk of poverty. However, a high level of education does not necessarily imply high skills. Indeed, as the cited Eurostat data show, 75.3% of all temporary workers or part-timers in 2019 were low-skilled, 11% of whom were at risk of poverty. In 2019, 12.6% of this category of workers (i.e., temporary workers or part-timers) worked less than 12 months a year, 15.6% of whom were at risk of poverty. The vast majority of people in this employment category worked for the entire calendar year preceding the survey.

Table 7.6 Composition of VUP Group 3 in Poland, in 2019[47]

	All Employed	*Temporary Workers*	*Involuntary Part-Timers*	*VUP 3*
Age group				
18-34	7.7 (29.0)	7.7 (47.2)	12.7 (27.8)	7.7 (46.1)
35-49	10.1 (42.8)	9.9 (32.8)	13.5 (41.9)	9.7 (33.6)
> = 50	11.2 (28.2)	10.5 (20.0)	31.5 (30.3)	11.2 (20.3)
Gender				
Women	8.7 (48.0)	8.5 (51.0)	s.s	8.5 (52.3)
Men	10.7 (52.0)	9.5 (49.0)	s.s	9.7 (47.7)
Nationality				
Country of residence	9.7 (99.3)	s.s.	s.s	s.s.[48]
Other	12.7 (0.7)	s.s.	s.s.	s.s.

47. Data in brackets – % of total employees in a given category.
48. The decomposition by nationality – too small sample to construct statistics, EU-SILC, 2007, 2013, and 2019.

	All Employed	*Temporary Workers*	*Involuntary Part-Timers*	*VUP 3*
Education				
Lower secondary/Primary of less	20.4 (5.1)	18.6 (8.8)	–	18.7 (8.6)
Upper secondary or post-secondary non-tertiary	12.0 (59.9)	9.3 (64.4)	23.7 (72.6)	9.4 (64.5)
Tertiary	4.3 (35.0)	5.0 (26.8)	5.6 (27.4)	5.2 (26.9)
Occupation				
High skill (ISCO-08 level 3 and 4)	3.5 (37.1)	3.3 (24.4)	5.1 (28.7)	3.4 (24.7)
Low skill (ISCO-08 level 1 and 2)	13.4 (62.9)	10.8 (75.6)	24.2 (71.3)	11.0 (75.3)

Source: EU-SILC/Eurostat.

Reading guide: In 2019, in Poland, 52.3% of workers of VUP Group 3 are women. Among these women 8.5% are at risk of in-work poverty.

In 2019, almost 69.7% of the workers in VUP Group 3 were members of households comprising more than 2 persons (of whom 8.1% were at risk of poverty).[49] Moreover 20.8% were workers from households with exactly 2 occupants (poverty risk ratio 8.9%), while 9.5% were single-person households. In the case of the last group, however, as in previous groups, the highest risk-of-poverty rate (16.9%) was observed. In 2019, 65.7% of workers in the forms of work under analysis lived in a household with another worker, and the risk-of-poverty rate for this category was 5.2%. The remaining part (34.3%) covered those being the only employed person in the household, and the risk-of poverty rate for this category amounted to 16.5%. Thus, as the data demonstrate, the absence of an additional source of income from employment in the household increases the risk of poverty. These figures look relatively similar in previous years as well.

Among persons employed in flexible work arrangements in 2019,[50] 56.9% were those not providing for any children under the age of 18, and the risk-of-poverty rate for this category of workers was 8.5%. Moreover 18.5% of the total of this category of workers were those with more than 1 child under the age of 18, of whom 8.7% were at risk of poverty. The difference between groups in terms of risk of poverty can be noticed in those with 1 dependant under 18 years of age, for whom the mentioned rate was 10.8% in 2019. Social benefits for each additional child in the family may be a factor that reduces the potential risk of household poverty. In addition, it should be

49. EU-SILC, 2007, 2013, and 2019.
50. *Ibid.*

noted that the 2019 data include actual data for 2018. The social benefit Family 500+ was extended only to every child in the family in 2019 – before this year, children without siblings (the only children) did not receive such financial support.

[2] Fixed-Term Employees

[a] Legal Framework: Notion; Equal Treatment; Working Conditions and Social Security Benefits; Unionisation and Collective Agreement Application

The Labour Code contains a closed catalogue of employment contracts, which differentiates between contracts for an indefinite period and fixed-term contracts (Article 25§1 of the Labour Code). The Articles 11^3 and 18^{3a} of the Labour Code introduce an express prohibition **of** discriminating against employees based on the duration of the contract as well as on the part-time employment. Violation of the principle of non-discrimination is treated as an employment law tort. Therefore, the principle of non-discrimination is binding not only on the legislator introducing the labour law regulations, but also on the social partners in defining the content of specific sources of labour law that include collective labour agreements, work regulations, and remuneration regulations. Employees under fixed-term contracts enjoy the same protection under collective labour law as employees on indefinite-term contracts.

There are two types of fixed-term employment contracts in Polish labour law – ordinary and special. The provision of Article 25^1 of the Labour Code limits the duration of fixed-term contracts to 33 months (2 years and 9 months), and this limitation applies to joint employment, i.e., both under one and several fixed-term contracts (ordinary fixed-term employment contract). The above mechanism was supplemented by a limit of three such contracts, with a mechanism provided for ineffectiveness of the so-called annexation of agreements to prevent circumvention of the statutory limit on the number of permissible agreements. What is worth mentioning at this point, mechanisms that limit the number and duration of fixed-term contracts have been introduced as a result of the European Court of Justice (ECJ) ruling in an answer to a preliminary question related to different periods of termination of a fixed- and indefinite-term contracts – Case C-38/13 Nierodzik.[51]

A significant protection of the effectiveness of the discussed limitations is the sanction for their violation provided for under Article 25^1 § 3 of the Labour Code. It is the transformation, by operation of law, of a fixed-term employment contract into an employment contract for an indefinite term in the event of exceeding the 33-month limit for the duration of fixed-term contracts, as well as in the case of concluding the fourth such contract within that period.

51. Judgement of the Court (Eighth Chamber), 13 March 2014 C-38/13 Małgorzata Nierodzik v Samodzielny Publiczny Psychiatryczny Zakład Opieki Zdrowotnej im. dr Stanisława Deresza w Choroszczy, ECLI:EU:C:2014:152.

The above limitations as to the number (up to 3 contracts) and time (up to 33 months) do not apply to the so-called special fixed-term contracts. These contracts concern specific grounds listed in Article 25^1 § 4 of the Labour Code (clearly articulated in the text of the contract) for which the fixed-term contract is concluded. This provision lists the following reasons for special fixed-term employment contracts:

(1) Replacement of an employee during their excused absence from work.
(2) Performance of work of a casual or seasonal nature.
(3) Performance of work for the duration of the term of office.
(4) When the employer indicates objective grounds on its side.

In all such cases, the conclusion of a fixed-term contract must serve satisfaction of a genuine periodic need and is necessary to that end in light of all the circumstances of the case. When concluding a contract for the purpose referred to in Article 25^1 § 4, the employer is obliged to notify the competent District Labour Inspector within five working days. Out of the four prerequisites enumerated above, the first three are verifiable and are subject to control by both the National Labour Inspectorate and labour courts. Failure to notify is deemed an offense against the employee's rights, punishable by a fine of PLN 1,000-30,000.

In the practice of business trading, the most common grounds used to extend the term of fixed-term contracts are so-called objective grounds on the part of the employer, who invokes permissible exceptions to the limitations on the use of fixed-term contracts (Article 25^1 § 4.4 of the Labour Code).

[b] Impact Analysis

The National Labour Inspectorate reports (for 2015 and 2016) indicate the incompatibility of such formulated derogations in Article 25^1 § 4.4 of the Labour Code with the judgement of the ECJ in case C-16/15.[52] It emerges from the above judgement that the use of an *'objective ground' as justification for temporary employment must be limited under national law to the precise circumstances characterising the activity in question and cannot be left to the discretion of the employer*. The general character of the clause in Article 25^1 § 4.4 of the Labour Code may be regarded as insufficient for Poland to realise the objectives of Directive 99/70/EC. The ECJ in the same year took the view that: '(...) *As regards the existence of an 'objective ground', it follows from the case-law that this concept must be understood as referring to precise and concrete circumstances characterising a given activity, which are therefore capable, in that particular context, of justifying the use of successive fixed-term employment contracts. Those circumstances may result, in particular, from the specific nature of the tasks for the performance of which such contracts have been concluded and from the inherent characteristics of those*

52. Judgement of the Court (Tenth Chamber) of 14 September 2016 Case C-16/15 María Elena Pérez López v Servicio Madrileño de Salud (Comunidad de Madrid), ECLI:EU:C:2016:679.

tasks or, as the case may be, from pursuit of a legitimate social policy objective of a Member State (...).

The reports conclude that the provision of Article 25[1] § 4.4 of the Labour Code allowing for exceptions is of a general nature. The substance of this provision does not allow determination of objective and transparent criteria to verify whether the re-conclusion of fixed-term contracts serves to meet the actual demand, whether it leads to the achievement of the objective pursued and whether it is necessary in this regard.[53] Thus, there is a potential risk of concluding contracts for a specified period of time above the limits set forth in the labour law and with negligible possibilities of their control by the National Labour Inspectorate.

[3] Temporary Agency Workers

[a] Legal Framework: Notion; Equal Treatment; Working Conditions and Social Security Benefits; Unionisation and Collective Agreement Application

Temporary employment agencies are a part of vital labour market institutions in Poland under the Act of 20 April 2004 on employment promotion and labour market institutions.[54] Legal foundations for the operation of temporary employment agencies were laid down by the Act of 9 July 2003 on the employment of temporary agency workers.[55] This activity is subject to the Marshall's of the Voivodeship decision and requires an entry in the register that is in the Marshall's custody of temporary employment agents. Moreover, the obligation to submit annual reports to the Marshall is a measure that enables controlling the activity of temporary employment agencies. However, such control focuses on the formal and financial aspects of running a business, as the working conditions of employees are subject to the State Labour Inspectorate.

The Act on the employment of temporary agency workers regulates the tripartite relationship between three temporary employment entities:

- temporary employment agency – employer - client;
- temporary employment agency – temporary agency worker;
- employer – client – temporary agency worker.

As the law stands at present, temporary work agencies may employ under an employment contract or a civil law contract. Further, there are no criteria according to which the agencies choose the grounds of employment to apply (Article 7 par. 2 of the employment of temporary agency workers). As a result, most temporary agency workers are employed under civil law contracts. The choice of the grounds of employment has far-reaching legal consequences because the scope of rights and

53. State Labour Inspectorate activities report for 2016, p. 71.
54. Journal of Laws of 2018, item 1265.
55. Consolidated text of the Journal of Laws of 2019, item 156 as amended.

obligations of an employee employed under a civil law contract is distributed differently. For example, Article 13 of the Act on the employment of temporary agency workers stipulated only the elements of the content of the employment contract concluded between a temporary agency employee and an agency. This provision, however, omits the elements of civil law contracts. Due to the admissibility of employment on grounds other than employment contract, there arises some doubt as to the proper application of the foregoing Article also to civil law contracts. This distinction carries important implications for the legal position of temporary agency workers and the comparability of their employment conditions.

The catalogue of differences and ambiguities between employees and contractors does not end there. For instance, the scope of information about working conditions provided to contractors is also not fully established. However, the case law is slowly paving the way for the range of information given about the conditions to contractors to be the same as those given to employees. There is no doubt whatsoever that the scope of personal liability and financial accountability of contractors is different when compared to such of the employees.

One should also notice and appreciate positive changes in the provisions of Polish law aimed at eliminating the phenomenon of so-called the chain of temporary employment agencies. This mechanism does effectively counteract the extension of a temporary work and can be seen as an instrument to correct the ever-widening poverty range among people working temporarily. It was the Act of 7 April, 2017 amending the Act on the employment of temporary agency workers and certain other acts[56] that introduced limitations to temporary work consisting in the performance of a temporary work for one employer-client for a total of 18 months within a period of 36 consecutive months. If a temporary agency worker performs work for the benefit of one employer-client on a continuous basis, which includes tasks whose performance is the responsibility of an absent employee employed by this employer-client, in such case, performing temporary work cannot exceed 36 months. Upon the expiry of this period, a temporary agency worker may complete work for the same employer-client not earlier than after 36 months.

[b] Impact Analysis

The consequences of the foregoing differences between employees and contractors employed by temporary work agencies are very well reflected by statistics. In 2018, contractors under civil law contracts (105,920) accounted for 56% of the total number of people employed through employment agencies in the national territory. The number of such people exceeded the number of people employed under a contract of employment by 22,989 (82,931). The term ‘ temporary employee’ in the Polish legal system does not always mean a person employed in reliance upon an employment relationship, and an employment under civil law contracts is not illegal.

56. Journal of Laws of 2017, item 962.

The collected data confirm that most people found employment in the following four groups of occupations, i.e., as simple industrial workers (19,532), manual packers (12,630), simple labourers (10,739), and warehousemen (10,609). In 2017, the most sizeable occupational group was that of simple labourers (30,545). The presented data suggest that most temporary agency workers are qualified according to the criteria set out in the report on VUP 1.

The consequence of employing temporary agency workers in sectors classified as so-called poor sectors is a proportionally higher incidence of violations of labour rights. The violations are related to the problem of legality of employment. Every fourth case of illegal employment or other illegal gainful activity was revealed by the National Labour Inspectorate inspectors in the trade and repair sector (23% of detected cases), followed by industrial processing (15%), construction (14%), and accommodation and food services (12%).[57]

On the other hand, there were also positive developments in law such as the above-mentioned eliminating of the phenomenon of so-called the chain of temporary employment agencies. This mechanism effectively counteracts the extension of temporary work and can be considered an instrument to correct the widening poverty scale among people working temporarily.

[4] Involuntary Part-Timers

[a] Legal Framework: Notion; Equal Treatment; Working Conditions and Social Security Benefits; Unionisation and Collective Agreement Application

There is no definition of an involuntary part-timer in the Polish Labour Code. The Labour Code regulations provide for the terms 'part-time work' and 'part-time employee'. The status of such a person is usually defined through comparisons to a full-time employee. In defining the term 'part-time', the concept of full-time is crucial. Full-time work is to be construed as a daily and average weekly standard established for a specific category of employees in the provisions of the labour code or other provisions of the labour law, including the provisions of a collective agreement, work regulations, or statutes. As a rule, full-time working hours are equal to the statutory working time standards. As pointed above, the Articles 11^{3} and 18^{3a} of the Labour Code introduce a clear prohibition of discriminating against employees based on the duration of the contract as well as on part-time employment. Violation of the principle of non-discrimination is treated as an employment law tort in Polish legal system. Therefore, it binds both the legislator and the social partners in determining the substance of the working conditions.

Determination of part-time work has an individualised character with reference to a specific employer and the conditions for a working time indicated by the labour law

57. The above data are taken from the National Labour Inspectorate Activity Report for 2019 (https://www.pip.gov.pl/pl/f/v/229168/Sprawozdanie%202019.pdf#page=121).

as full time. The extent of the reduction of working time is irrelevant, which means that there is no lower limit for determining part-time status. It can be, for example, only one hour a day. Consequently, there is no clear line between casual, occasional, and part-time work in Polish legal system.

In Polish legal system, there is a clearly expressed principle of proportionality (pro rata temporis principle) enshrined in Article 29^2 § 1 of the Labour Code. This provision stipulates that the *conclusion of a contract of employment for part-time work must not result in conditions of work and pay being established which are less favourable for the employee compared with other employees who perform the same or similar work based on full-time employment, subject to the provision that remuneration and other work-related benefits must be in proportion to the employee's working time.*

The employment dimension, as well as the amount of working time, is an essential element of any employment contract which is subject to arrangement between the parties. Pursuant to the judgement of the Supreme Court of 2 June 1995, I PR 1/95,[58] the employer is obliged to employ an employee not only in accordance with the agreed type of work and in the appropriate place, but also in the appropriate dimension and schedule of work time. In line with the labour law, it is relatively an easy transformation of a contract from a full-time to a part-time contract at the employee's initiative. The motives for which the employee submits such a request are not subject to evaluation and verification. Article 29^2 § 2 of the Labour Code contains a directional norm providing that *as far as possible, an employer should consider requests by employees to change the length of their working time defined in their respective contracts of employment.*

There are also other implications of this provision because it grants the entirety of discretion to employers to assess the feasibility of employing full-time staff. Such approaches were confirmed by the judgement of the Supreme Court of 17 February 2000, I PKN 542/99,[59] in which the Supreme Court took the position that *an employer cannot be required to continue to employ an employee on a full-time basis if this is not justified by the scope of their duties, and the employer is not in a position to assign additional work corresponding to his/her professional preparation.* The ruling stipulates that employers may not be compelled to employ a person for a full-time job, even if the employee's skills and qualifications suffice and serve the job's purpose. At the same time, neither the provisions nor the jurisprudence indicate how to assess the impossibility of employing the employees on a full-time basis. This approach to the employment dimension can become a source of unwanted part-time employment. Yet, there are no precise statistics in this regard.

Due to the fact that the employment dimension is an important element of the employment contract, a conversion of working hours from full-time to part-time requires an amending notice or an amending agreement reached between parties.

58. Judgement of the Supreme Court of 2 June 1995, I PR 1/95, OSNP 1996, no 3, item 48. http://www.sn.pl/sites/orzecznictwo/orzeczenia1/i%20pr%201-95.pdf.
59. Judgement of the Supreme Court of 17 February 2000, I PKN 542/99, http://www.sn.pl/sites/orzecznictwo/orzeczenia1/i%20pkn%20542-99.pdf.

[b] *Impact analysis*

A quite flexible transition from a full-time contract to a part-time contract at the request of an employee creates a potential risk of abuse of this possibility, primarily because the reasons for such an application are not assessed in any way. In addition, the jurisprudence, guided by the employer's entire economic and personal risk, gives him autonomy in determining the tasks that determine the size of employment. Unfortunately, there are clear statistics that would indicate that this provision was abused in a way that would force an employee to work part time.

An open exception to the principle of proportionality provisions provided in respect of part-time workers is the right to acquire overtime allowance. Following the judgement of 9 August 1985, I PRN 643/85,[60] a part-time employee is entitled to a normal remuneration for work more than the standard specified in the employment contract without any overtime allowances. Overtime allowances are payable only if the daily or weekly working time limits provided for in the applicable regulations have been exceeded. Pursuant to Article 151 § 5 of the Labour Code, *the parties shall agree on a maximum permitted number of working hours in excess of the working time defined in the contract of employment of an employee who is employed on a part-time basis; if that number of hours is exceeded, the employee shall be entitled to the overtime pay.*

Regarding involuntary part-timers, the problem lies with the overtime allowance and determining how overtime should be calculated. The ambiguity of the regulations raises further questions, e.g., whether the hours worked in excess of a part-time employee's hours, but no more than a full-time employee's hours, should be included in the annual limit of 150 hours of excess hours.

[D] VUP Group 4: Casual and Platform Workers

[1] *Composition of VUP Group 4*

Both the European and national labour market monitoring databases lack unambiguous data referring to the above group of workers/employed. Often on-call seasonal workers statistically count as temporary workers, casual workers. However, in the case of employees of online platforms, mobile applications – there is no clear data due to a great diversity of this form of work, i.e., different types of work ('departments' of the platform economy), different labour markets, different level of participation of platform employees, or different level of dependence of an employee/participant on the platform itself. However, taking account of all available, though highly scattered data, it can be concluded that the group of these workers comprises largely young people, i.e., under 35 years of age, both women and men. Assessment of the risk of poverty is difficult in this respect, inter alia, due to the fact that for part of the employed it is the only form of earning, but for a considerable part it is an additional form of earning, i.e.,

60. OSNCP 1986, z. 5, item 79.

constituting an additional supplement to income that comes from other employment or social or family benefits. Unfortunately, there is no data which would clearly indicate the percentage of people employed under this form of contract and at risk of poverty.

With regard to the education attainment and qualifications, two dominant categories of workers can be identified – those with the lowest education attainment, those performing work with the lowest level of required qualifications – i.e., simple work, manual workers, unskilled workers. This category of workers can be found primarily in agriculture, horticulture, construction, or some services – such as cleaning. It can be suspected that it is for this category of workers that this form of work will constitute their primary source of livelihood, apart from social benefits. The second category of workers are people with secondary or even higher education who perform work with relatively low qualifications and view the work as an additional or temporary earning source – in the course of education, as a break to find another, stable employment. This category of workers is very often encountered, among others, in transport services, shipping, courier services, catering industry, and tourism.

To a large extent, the category of workers analysed in this section are immigrants. According to a PARP report commissioned by the Ministry of Labour, Family and Social Policy in 2018,[61] Poland, for the third year in a row, was among the top OECD countries in terms of the number of temporary labour migrants (1.1 million permits issued to seasonal or temporary workers from outside the EU, and 27 thousand workers posted to Poland from the EU). Seasonal workers visiting Poland come mainly from third countries (Ukraine, Belarus, Moldova, Nepal, India).

[2] Casual Workers: Notion and Relevant Legal Framework

Both the legislator and the doctrine face difficulties in defining such terms as seasonal worker or casual worker. Polish law applies the notion of a casual worker in the context of a seasonal or casual work without its explanation. The term of casual work is directly used by the legislator in the provisions on the protection of health and safety of employees at work, primarily in the Regulation of the Council of Ministers of April 3, 2017 on the list of burdensome, dangerous, or harmful work for pregnant women and women breastfeeding a child.[62] In this context, casual work is understood as *manual handling of objects, loads or materials no more than 4 times per hour if the total time of performing these works does not exceed 4 hours a day* (§. 2 p. 2 Regulation). However, the proposed definition serves other purpose than identifying the instability of employment conditions.

Therefore, definition of this concept refers to the common understanding of the term 'seasonality' or 'occasionality'.[63] Seasonal work is an intermittent work that may be performed only periodically, for a specific part of the annual calendar cycle, in

61. The phenomenon of temporary work. Thematic report. PARP, 2020 https://www.parp.gov.pl/component/publications/publication/zjawisko-pracy-sezonowej (accessed 07 Feb. 2022).
62. Journal of Laws of 2017, item 796.
63. Monika Tomaszewska (in) Kodeks pracy. Komentarz [Labour Code. Commentary] Vol. 1, Art. 1-113, rev. V, ed. Krzysztof W. Baran, (Wolters Kluwer Poland, Warszawa 2020) Article 25^{1}.

connection with the characteristics of the seasons, especially weather conditions. In effect, this type of atypical form of employment is most often used in trade, industry, hotel services, and tourism.

Seasonal work, its occasional and periodic nature, determines choosing only a fixed-term contract set forth in Article 25^1 § 4.4 of the Labour Code.[64] Despite the thoroughgoing amendment to this article in 2017, this provision causes numerous interpretative problems for both employers and labour inspectors who control the performance of a casual and seasonal work.[65] This is due to the inclusion of a seasonal work in the catalogue of exceptions to the restriction on the conclusion of multiple fixed-term contracts (*see* Article 25^1 § 4.4 of the Labour Code).

Another type of temporary employment is on-call work, which occurs both in legal and economic circulation. On-call work is legally permissible, although there is no separate legal basis in Polish law. Literature defines the work on call, otherwise known as the work on demand, as not a continuous or systematic provision of work, but a work only 'on demand' and only 'on call' of an employer. With regard to the variability of work organisation consisting of intensive work and standby phases, the appropriate legal basis for its performance is a part-time contract. However, even the labour law provisions do not guarantee the minimum number of working hours per week or month for the part-timers. The regulations only require that the employee be given seven days' notice of the current working schedule, which is not equivalent to ensuring a specific work intensity.

It should be emphasised here that there are severe doubts about the qualifications of an on-call work in respect of the employment relationship. In this regard, the judgement of the Supreme Court on March 19, 2013, I PK 223/12[66] proved indeed a landmark ruling. In accordance with this ruling, '*on-call work, even with fully paid waiting time for work, does not constitute the construction of an employee employment within the meaning of Art. 22 § 1 of the Labour Code*'.

[3] Platform Workers: Notion and Relevant Legal Framework

Paid forms of work provision in the form of crowd work and work on demand via applications are the subject of few publications in the Polish doctrine. Web applications' paid provision of on-demand work is a crowdwork form of organisational work. Freelancers involved in this work process can use their expertise or specific skills (such as language skills) to work on online platforms. What differs between the two forms of working by the platform is the type of work performed, which in web applications' paid work requires more unique knowledge and qualifications.

The relationship between platform workers and principals is characterised by the absence of direct links between the parties. The contractor may not even be known to the principal. This work organisation and performance form is not qualified under the

64. *Ibid.*
65. National Labour Inspectorate Report 2018, p. 290. https://www.pip.gov.pl/pl/f/v/211637/Sprawozdanie%202018%20r.#page=286.
66. OSNP 2014, No. 1, item 4.

labour law as an employment relationship. Such approach justifies the absence of such necessary elements of any employment relationship as the direct provision of work and a personal subordination to the employer. Moreover, most of said people are genuinely autonomous at their work and can use platform work as a way to develop their entrepreneurial activities.

Since this relationship does not qualify as an employment relationship, these contractors (platform workers) are not covered by labour law protection. Therefore, the conditions pertinent to, for example, working time, rest time, principles of health and life protection, paid annual leave, and other leaves related to parenthood do not apply to platform workers.

[4] Impact Analysis

The vast majority of the employed from VUP Group 4 which covers various categories of temporary work, ranging from seasonal and occasional work to non-uniform forms of work on the e-platform, are classified under VUP Group 2. Most of such people are genuinely autonomous at their work and can use platform work as a way to develop their entrepreneurial activities. This type of provision of work is symptomatic of platform group workers therefore, their legal status should be specified as genuine self-employment predominantly in the form of one-person business activity. As such, self-employment is subject to the Act of 6.03.2018. – Business Activity Law[67] according to Polish law. Business activity even in solo self-employment can be undertaken upon applying to the Central Registration and Information on Business (Article 17 of the Business Activity Law).

§7.03 CONCLUSIONS

The presented analysis shows a relatively limited scope of the Polish labour law, which excludes a large group of employed people from its protective mechanisms. A fundamental legal act for labour law, the Labour Code, was adopted in 1974 and is based on a traditional model of the employment relationship and the rights and obligations between its parties. The work performed is ensured adequate protection conditional upon obtaining the status of an employee, which, in turn, is interpreted quite restrictively in Polish law. This is visible in the interpretation of the concept of subordination which is key to distinguishing an employment relationship from self-employment.

With the political and economic changes that took place in Poland in the early 1990s, the model of the employment relationship provided for in the labour code underwent only minor modifications. Therefore, adaptation to the principles of a free market economy was effected through a broad consent of the legislator to atypical forms of employment. As a result, there has been a significant increase in atypical forms of employment in Poland, specifically fixed-term employment contracts and

67. Journal of Law of 2021, item 162.

self-employment. The range of atypical forms of employment has even grown to uncontrollable sizes (up to 2.5 million employees). This state of affairs was influenced by numerous privileges for the self-employed in the form of low social security contributions and exemptions, or preferential taxation rules, which only strengthened the 'attractiveness' of non-employee employment relationships.

It was only at the beginning of 2016 that the legislator decided to extend some protective mechanisms to people who do not have the status of employees. This concerned, for example, the minimum wage rate that the self-employed are entitled to or the right to collective protection of their interests. However, the protection instruments are selective and inconsistent. As a consequence, they did not in any way mitigate the effects of atypical forms of work in the form of instability or ensuring the intensity and regularity of work that guarantees an adequate standard of living, and typically shield against in-work poverty.

CHAPTER 8

In-Work Poverty in Sweden

Ann-Christine Hartzén

The present chapter presents the problem of in-work poverty in Sweden, the main drivers, and the specific situation of the four different Vulnerable and Under-Represented Persons (VUP) groups. The introduction explains why wage levels in Sweden are not an issue of concern in relation to in-work poverty, but instead, various forms of non-standard employments that generate lower numbers of working hours in combination with gaps in social security schemes need attention. The situation for the four different VUP groups is thereafter accounted for, highlighting specific issues and problems that face the VUP groups where in-work poverty risks are more pertinent. The conclusions highlight the main findings and further stress the most problematic issues in relation to some recent and future potential legislative changes that could have an impact on the situation concerning in-work poverty in Sweden.

§8.01 INTRODUCTION

To understand the issue of in-work poverty in Sweden, a brief introduction to the Swedish model of labour market regulation is needed. The Swedish model originates from a system where employment conditions and relations were, and to a high degree still are, regulated through collective bargaining and collective agreements. Traditionally the legislator has only intervened when the social partners have been unable to agree on regulations or when the situation on the labour market and in society has been turbulent or in crisis in a manner that has necessitated legislative intervention in order to avoid increasing problems. Such interventions have generally been framed in a manner so as to grant the social partners a retained scope of action for regulation through collective agreements. This has been achieved by making the adopted legislation semi-discretionary, which means that the social partners are free to derogate from the legislation in collective agreements. Such semi-discretionary rules are for example found in relation to working-time regulations, temporary employment contracts, negotiations with trade unions, and other forms of regulations governing certain aspects of working conditions. However, issues concerning just cause for dismissal, prohibitions of discrimination, and protective mechanisms with minimum requirements cannot be undercut through collective agreements. It is generally required that the collective agreement is concluded at industry level, but if the industry level agreement allows for further adaptations through workplace collective agreements, this is also legally acceptable.[1]

The result is a system with strong social partners granting a collective agreement coverage rate of about 90%, leaving only 10% of Swedish employees without the protection offered by a collective agreement despite the unionisation rate amounting to roughly 70%. Since the public sector is fully covered by collective agreements, the workplaces lacking collective agreements are to be found within the private sector for which the collective agreement coverage rate is 83%.[2]

The Swedish model has also generated a system without legislation on minimum wages; instead wages are set through negotiations between the social partners and regulated in collective agreements. If there is no applicable collective agreement at the workplace, then there will be no minimum wage level, and the wage will instead be set in agreement between the employer and the worker.[3] In these situations, case law has defined that the wage shall be reasonable, but this definition would allow some deviation from the wage levels defined in the relevant collective agreement for the sector concerned. If there is a considerable difference between the wage level in the relevant sectoral collective agreement and the wage paid to the worker, then the court would consider the wage unreasonable and the worker would be entitled to have the wage adjusted and to be compensated for his/her loss. Such court cases are rare and the actual existence of unreasonable wages at workplaces not covered by collective agreements is difficult to estimate, especially since the interpretation of 'considerable difference' is not entirely clear.[4] In other words, lacking a collective agreement applicable and therefore a minimum wage, the wages set in collective agreements for the specific sector in question will be used as a benchmark in case of dispute.[5] Wages

1. Mats Glavå and Mikael Hansson, Arbetsrätt, pp. 69-71 (Studentlitteratur, 2016) and for an explanation of the historical background establishing the Swedish model *see* Axel Adlercreutz and Birgitta Nyström, Labour Law in Sweden, pp. 50-51 (Wolters Kluwer, 2015).
2. Swedish National Mediation Office, Avtalsrörelsen och lönebildningen 2018, Medlingsinstitutets årsrapport, pp. 166-168 (Swedish National Mediation Office, 2019).
3. Petter Hällberg and Christian Kjällström, Collective agreements and minimum wages, pp. 1-2 (Swedish National Mediation Office, 2020).
4. The most recent is probably the case from 2007 concerning two foreign workers who were temporarily employed for berry picking by an employer who did not have a collective agreement, where the Swedish Labour Court concluded that the individual employment contracts should be interpreted to include wages in accordance with the collective agreement most suitable for the work conducted, *see* AD 2007:1. Previous cases include AD1991:26 and AD 1983:130.
5. *See, for example,* the AD 1982:142 where the Labour Court concluded that the calculation of an adequate wage level shall be based on the collective agreement for the specific sector concerned

are thus generally set at sectoral level, but company level collective agreements may contain additional clauses. It is not possible though to locally negotiate lower wages than those set in the sectoral agreements.[6] The wages set in the sectoral agreements can therefore be considered as minimum wages. Wages are revised regularly and the practice on the Swedish labour market is that the levels of wage increase, as defined in the sectoral agreement for the manufacturing industry, are used as benchmark for all other sectors.[7]

From an international perspective, the minimum wages set in collective agreements are high, with minimum wages in general above 60% of the median income.[8] It is thus worth stressing that the wage setting model in Sweden should not be conceived as a risk in relation to in-work poverty. Indeed, studies have shown that it is not low-minimum wages that cause in-work poverty in Sweden. Instead, the main reasons seem to be connected to low-work intensity, intermittent employment contracts, or specific lower wages for young and inexperienced workers.[9] There might also be problems relating to the rather few workplaces that are not covered by collective agreements, but the extent of this is very difficult to assess due to lack of reliable statistics.[10] An additional remark is that the Swedish labour and social security legislation is more or less in flux at the time being. Various changes intended to better adapt the legislation to the increasing need of flexibility on the labour market are under discussion, recently introduced or soon to be introduced. Providing an account of all changes under discussion is not possible here, but those relevant to the discussion in this chapter will be referred to.

[A] Atypical Employment Contracts

The connection between in-work poverty and work intensity in Sweden calls for a brief account of the legislation governing fixed-term and part-time employments since both forms of employment affect the number of hours worked. Even though the main rule is that an employment shall be for an indefinite duration according to Article 4 Employment Protection Act (EPA), the legislation governing fixed-term employment forms is fairly flexible. There are two issues that specifically contribute to this flexibility. First, Article 5 EPA regulating fixed-term employment forms, such as substitute employments and seasonal employments, also stipulates a specific form of

---

or AD 1986:78 where the Labour Court provided similar reasoning when deciding that compensation for inadequate wages can be granted for up to two years back in time.

6. Adlercreutz and Nyström, *supra* n. 1 at 190-192.
7. Swedish National Mediation Office, *supra* n. 2 at 191.
8. Hällberg and Kjellström, *supra* n. 3 at 3-4.
9. *See*, for example, Kenneth Nelson and Johan Fritzell, ESPN Thematic Report on In-work poverty Sweden (European Commission, Directorate-General for Employment, Social Affairs and Inclusion, 2019).
10. This problem is also highlighted in Swedish National Audit Office, Statens insatser mot exploatering av arbetskraft – regelverk, kontroller samt information och stöd till de drabbade RIR 2020:27, pp. 28-31 (Swedish National Audit Office, 2020).

temporary employment called general temporary employment. This form of employment does not require any specific reason for its temporary duration;[11] instead, the employer is free to make use of it when s/he sees a need for a temporary position. Second, the measures for preventing abuse as stipulated in Article 5 a EPA consist of a complex set of requirements that will generate a transformation of the temporary employment into a permanent employment. In short, a fixed-term employee who, during a period of five years, reaches a total period of employment of two years or more with the same employer, shall have his/her contract of employment automatically transformed into a permanent employment contract. The transformation rules apply to employees reaching the two-year period on either substitute contracts or contracts for general temporary employments, with the two forms of employments counted separately, i.e., one year as substitute and one year as general temporary employee will not count as two years in this respect. Neither numerical limits for temporary contracts, nor limitations for a minimum duration of a temporary contract exist in legislation. These flexible rules on fixed-term contracts have generated a situation where more precarious forms of temporary employments, such as intermittent employments, have become more common. As such, the character of temporary contracts has become increasingly precarious with shorter and less-stable fixed-term contracts making up an increasing part of temporary employments.[12]

Relating to part-time work, there is no legislation limiting the use of part-time work, nor any legislation stipulating full-time work as a main rule. What does exist are regulations governing rights for workers to work part-time when having small children.[13] There is also an obligation for employers to consider whether it is possible to increase working hours of part-time employees before recruiting new personnel. It is for the employer to decide whether such a solution is possible, and it also requires that the part-time employee has notified the employer of his/her wish to increase working hours.[14] There is in other words no established right to full-time work, and the combination with flexible rules on fixed-term work can be considered a clear risk in relation to in-work poverty since it does allow for the use of employment contracts that are not generating stable and secure incomes.[15]

---

11. Adlercreutz, and Nyström, *supra* n. 1 at 80.
12. For discussion *see*, for example, Government White Paper 2019:5, Tid för trygghet – Slutbetänkande av utredningen för ett hållbart arbetsliv över tid, pp. 261-265 and Tomas Berglund, Kristina Håkansson, Tommy Isidorsson and Johan Alfonsson, *Tidsbegränsat anställdas framtida arbetsmarknadssituation*, 2(23) Arbetsmarknad & Arbetsliv 47-66 (2017).
13. Articles 6 and 7 Parental Leave Act.
14. Article 25 a Employment Protection Act.
15. Current legislative debate might generate changes in this regard. Even though there is no Government Bill presented as of yet, there is a strong wish from the private sector social partners in Sweden as well as politicians to introduce changes to the EPA. In relation to fixed-term and part-time work, the changes could imply improvements from the perspective of in-work poverty. For fixed-term work, the transformation rules would be sharpened and framed in a manner that would make it easier for intermittent employees to reach the qualification period for permanent employment. In relation to part-time work, there is a suggestion of a general presumption of full-time work unless the party claiming otherwise can provide proof of a part-time contract. This suggestion also includes a requirement for the employer to provide the reasons for part-time work when requested by the employee. These and the other suggested changes to the EPA are

[B] Challenges Arising from the Construction of Unemployment Benefits

Apart from flexible forms of employment, another issue of concern in relation to in-work poverty is the construction of certain social security schemes. To start with the unemployment benefit system, it needs to be pointed out that the historically strong protection offered through structures based on the Gent system, underwent rather drastic changes in the aftermath of the 1990s crisis, making it more difficult for persons to qualify for unemployment benefits.[16] However, additional changes took place during the 2000s when eligibility criteria for the unemployment benefit were made stricter and membership fees were increased in order to strengthen incentives for unemployed to find work.[17] These changes resulted in a huge drop of membership in the unemployment benefit funds, from previous levels of around 90% to levels around 70%.[18] Even though subsequent adjustments concerning the membership fees for unemployment funds have been made, membership rates have not fully recovered. The changes also caused a decline in the share of unemployed that access unemployment benefits from 80% of the unemployed in 2006 to 40% in 2013.[19] Since then, membership has increased in terms of numbers of members, but such an increase corresponds mainly to an increase of persons active on the labour market, meaning that the membership rate as such has not recovered. In December 2019, the membership rates for the age group 16 to 64 years old were 73% for women and 69% for men.[20] There have been some temporary changes in response to the COVID-19 pandemic, and some of those changes are under discussion of becoming permanent. These changes relate to qualification requirements and the caps for the benefit. Worth noting is that the changes have generated a higher increase of members during 2020, with a bit over 260,000 persons being members of an unemployment benefit fund in September 2020 compared to September 2019.[21] The increase of members do not necessarily mean a similar increase of persons covered by the scheme, because the eligibility criteria for unemployment benefits involve requirements based on certain amounts of previous work and the person being available for work on the labour market.[22] For those not

presented and discussed in Ministry Publications Series 2021:17 En reformerad arbetsrätt – för flexibilitet, omställningsförmåga och trygghet på arbetsmarknaden. The draft bill was handed over to the Council on Legislation on 27 January 2022, see Government draft bill, Lagrådsremiss: En reformerad arbetsrätt – för flexibilitet, omställningsförmåga och trygghet på arbetsmarknaden of 27 January 2022.

16. Caroline Johansson, *Occupational Pensions and Unemployment Benefits in Sweden*, 3(36) International Journal of Comparative Labour Law and Industrial Relations, 339-360 (2020).
17. Government Bill 2006/07:15 En arbetslöshetsförsäkring för arbete.
18. Anders Kjellberg, Den svenska modellen i en oviss tid: Fack, arbetsgivare och kollektivavtal på en föränderlig arbetsmarknad, pp. 12-15 (Arena Idé, 2020).
19. Ursula Berge, Året då A-kassan blev lägre än försörjningsstöd – Om hur trygghetssystem har kollapsat och försörjningsstödet tar smällen (Akademikerförbundet SSR, 2014).
20. IAF (The Swedish Inspection for Unemployment Benefits) statistics, taken from https://www.iaf.se/statistikdatabasen/arsstatistik/3-653-948-personer-ar-medlem-i-en-arbetsloshetskassa/ last accessed 04/11/2020.
21. IAF statistics, taken from https://www.iaf.se/statistikdatabasen/Arbetsloshetsforsakringen-i-siffror/ last visited 04/11/2020.
22. As regulated in Article 9, 44 and 44 a of the Unemployment Benefit Act with certain aspects further defined in the Swedish Inspection Authority for Unemployment Benefits Regulation

qualifying for the income-related unemployment benefit system, there is the possibility of receiving a basic unemployment benefit on the condition that the person fulfils the general requirements of being an active jobseeker and the requirement of previous work.[23] This benefit is subject to significantly lower caps of the daily amount though, normally set at 365 SEK per day, but temporarily during the pandemic increased to 510 SEK per day.[24]

In addition to the decreasing number of persons covered by the income-related unemployment benefits system, the construction of this system with fixed caps for the daily amounts provide challenges for standard employees becoming unemployed. In practice, very few actually do receive benefits corresponding to 80% of their previous salary and the actual benefit paid will be close to the poverty threshold, unless the person is also covered by benefits provided through transition agreements or is a member of and holds an income insurance with a trade union.[25] However, fixed-term, part-time, and especially casual workers face specific challenges both in relation to fulfilling qualification requirements and in relation to rules governing how to calculate the benefit to be paid. For casual workers, there are challenges in relation to the qualification requirement of previous work, since this requirement involves a minimum number of weekly working hours during a certain period of time. In addition, even though in some circumstances the unemployed are allowed to take up a temporary employment and afterwards go back to unemployment benefits, the assessment of the person's availability for work might be negatively affected. The reason is that in order to receive unemployment benefits a jobseeker also needs to fulfil a requirement of being available for work on the labour market. The assessment of that availability requires a certain extent of free hours for taking up work every week. If casual work would cause the jobseeker to have too few hours of availability for work, then the casual employment would be considered as an obstacle for the person's availability on the labour market.[26]

For part-time workers the cap for the basic benefit will be set in proportion to the person's previous working hours, i.e., for someone who has worked 75% of full time the basic benefit will be cut down to 75% of the maximum amount for this benefit.[27]

No. 2015:3. In relation to the requirement of the jobseeker having to be available for work on the labour market and as such being subject to an obligation of applying for suitable jobs, the Swedish Inspection authority for Unemployment Benefits (IAF) has criticised the Public Employment Services for not assuring that the assessments of a suitable job are well-founded enough, *see* Swedish Inspection for Unemployment Benefits, Report 2017:16 Tillämpningen av regelverket för lämpligt arbete.

23. The construction of the unemployment benefit system as consisting of a basic or minimum level and an income-related part is discussed in, for example, Government White Paper 2020:37, Ett nytt regelverk för arbetslöshetsförsäkringen, p 110. For a discussion in English *see* Johansson, *supra* n. 16.
24. As stipulated in Article 3 of the Regulation concerning Unemployment Benefit (RUB), with the temporary changes during the pandemic stipulated through Regulation 2020:220.
25. TCO, Svensk a-kassa allt sämre: En rapport om utvecklingen inom EU och Norden de senaste 20 åren (TCO, 2021).
26. As discussed in Government White Paper 2019:5 *supra* n. 12 at 203-206. *See also* Government White Paper 2020:37 *supra* n. 23.
27. Article 3 of the Regulation concerning Unemployment Benefit (RUB).

Since the income-related benefit is calculated as a daily benefit on the basis of previous income and previous normal working hours, the income-related benefit will also be affected by the lesser number of working hours for part-time workers becoming unemployed.[28] For someone being part-time unemployed, there is also a limit of 60 weeks during which it is possible to combine part-time employment and part-time unemployment benefits.[29] In addition to the issues that fixed-term and part-time workers face in terms of unemployment benefits, another problematic case concerns self-employed, since they need to show that their business is inactive in order to qualify as unemployed. If a self-employed would take up unemployment benefits and afterwards go back to running the business, then there will be a period of five years during which s/he would have to liquidate the business completely in order to be able to take up unemployment benefits again.[30] The caps in the unemployment benefit system as well as its gaps in terms of coverage and adaptability for non-standard workers are very likely to increase the risk of in-work poverty for workers with less-stable employments and who face periods of unemployment in between periods of work. In addition, self-employed have limited possibilities to be covered in case of temporary difficulties or down periods in the business through unemployment benefits. The temporary measures to support self-employed, introduced during the COVID-19 pandemic, have not led to persistent changes in this regard.

[C] Challenges Arising from the Construction of Sickness Benefits

The second part of the social security structures of particular relevance in relation to in-work poverty in Sweden concerns sickness benefits, where the most important aspects relate to eligibility requirements involving also an assessment of a person's decreased working capacity due to illness. For standard employees, the first two weeks of illness are in general fairly uncomplicated since the first 14 calendar days are covered by sick pay that the employer pays in accordance with the Sick Pay Act. Self-employed are as such excluded from the right to sick pay, and the eligibility rules applicable for employees with short-term contracts of less than a month exclude these workers from the right to sick pay during the first 14 days of employment.[31] For such workers, the protection granted through the regulations governing sickness allowance are therefore of high importance. The regulations on sickness allowance are provided by the Social Security Code, and currently there are on-going legislative discussions of changes in relation to these issues. The reason for the legislative debate is that the system with sickness allowance to a great extent has been developed relating to standard full-time employments, and with increasing variations of employment forms on the labour

28. The calculation, as taking into account both the previous income and the previous normal working hours, is regulated in Article 25 UBA.
29. Article 7 RUB.
30. As regulated in Article 34, 35, and 35 a UBA.
31. Articles 1 and 3 Sick Pay Act. *See* Lotti Ryberg-Welander, Socialförsäkringsrätt: Om ersättning vid sjukdom pp. 101-102 (Norstedts Juridik, 2018) for a brief discussion.

market, there have also been increasing problems with persons falling outside the scope of the social security system.[32]

Self-employed face specific challenges in relation to sickness allowances due to a somewhat complicated income assessment in establishing the income base for calculation of the benefit.[33] In addition, they may be subject to a higher number of qualifying days, during which no allowances will be paid, compared to employees, depending on what level of social security contributions the self-employed has registered for. There are indications, however, that the self-employed registering for longer qualification periods, and thus lower social security contributions, are less likely to be dependent on their business as the main source of income.[34] Nevertheless, the difficulties in foreseeing the actual amount paid as sickness allowance due to the complexity of income assessment may result in specific challenges for self-employed and potential increased risk of in-work poverty in case of illness.

Similar and perhaps even worse challenges relating to foreseeability concerning the amount paid as sickness allowance exist for casual workers. These workers face difficulties due to their less stable income and irregular working patterns. In addition, they have until recently been subject to uncertainties as to how their eligibility for sickness allowance shall be assessed with rules applying for unemployed persons falling sick have applied depending on the circumstances of the case.[35] In some situations, the casual worker has been considered as ill during employment and received sickness allowance in relation to how many hours of work were lost during the period of illness.[36] In other situations, the casual worker has been considered as sick during unemployment and subject to calculations of the sickness allowance based on what the person would have received as unemployment benefit with a much lower cap than is the case for sickness allowance relating to income from employment.[37] With the on-going legislative debate, some steps have recently been taken in order to seek to improve the situation for intermittent workers, by assuring that these workers are entitled to sickness allowance on the basis of income from work during the first 90 days of illness. The requirement is that it shall be reasonable to assume that the worker would have performed work unless the person was ill.[38]

---

32. *See* Government White Paper 2019:5 *supra* n. 12 at 86 and Government White Paper 2020:26 En sjukförsäkring anpassad efter individen, pp. 61-63.
33. Ryberg-Welander, *supra* n. 31 at 82-83 (Norstedts Juridik, 2018).
34. Government White Paper 2019:41 Företagare i de sociala trygghetssystemen, pp. 83 and 85-88.
35. The rules for calculation of sickness allowance are found in Sections 27 and 28 Social Security Code, but explaining them in detail would require a lot more space than is deemed suitable for the purposes of this text. The concrete challenges and risks for casual workers are discussed in Government White Paper 2020:26 *supra* n. 32 at 38-40, 43 and 61-65.
36. Section 27 Articles 10-11 Social Security Code.
37. Section 28 Article 11 Social security Code and for discussion *see* Ryberg-Welander, *supra* n. 31 at 156.
38. The new rules were introduced on 1 February 2022 through the insertion of new articles in the Social Security Code, for this specific issue *see* Section 27 Article 16 a, Social Security Code. The reasons for the changes were framed in line with the previous discussions on the uncertain situation for workers with a form of employment that is becoming more and more common on the labour market. *See* Government Bill 2021/22:1 Budgetpropositionen för 2020, Utgiftsområde 10 – Ekonomisk trygghet vid sjukdom och funktionsnedsättning, especially pp. 57-66.

The final, and possibly, most important issue of concern in relation to sickness benefits and in-work poverty would rather relate to the eligibility requirements involving an assessment of decreased working capacity due to the illness. This assessment may be related to the person's actual work, other work for the employer with whom the person holds an employment, or any work normally available on the labour market, depending on the person's employment status and/or for how long the person has been ill. For workers with a stable employment, there is a time line establishing that the decreased working capacity shall be assessed in relation to the work the person normally conducts during the first 90 days of illness, in relation to other work that the person could do for the employer during the period of day 91-180 of illness and from day 181 in relation to work that normally exists on the labour market.[39] Even though the regulations do not specifically address self-employed, it is expressed in preparatory works that the assessment of decreased working capacity for self-employed shall be conducted in relation to their regular work during the first 180 days of illness and after that in relation to work that normally exists on the labour market.[40]

Even though recent changes have been introduced, it is worth pointing out that casual workers have faced difficulties in terms of the assessment of decreased work capacity and in relation to what work such an assessment shall be conducted. For these workers, the assessment has depended on the circumstances in each specific case since a casual worker falling ill while having work scheduled may have had his/her decreased working capacity assessed in relation to that scheduled work. If no work was scheduled, then the result may instead have been that the person had the decreased working capacity assessed according to the rules applicable for unemployed that is in relation to any work that normally exists on the labour market. The assessment in relation to any work that normally exists on the labour market is generally stricter than an assessment in relation to specific work, due to the much broader range of work tasks, making it less likely that a person will be considered as having decreased working capacity in relation to the labour market as a whole.[41] For a person working with elderly care, where the tasks may involve physically demanding lifts, a strained ankle or injured shoulder would likely be considered to decrease the working capacity in relation to the work, but in relation to any work normally available on the labour market the assessment could result in the opposite. Also in this respect, recently introduced changes are likely to improve the situation for intermittent workers since these are now to have their working capacity assessed in relation to the intermittent

39. This is often referred to as the rehabilitation chain and is regulated in Section 27 Articles 46-49 Social Security Code. For explanation and discussion, *see* Government White Paper 2020:26 *supra* n. 32 at 32-35 and Ryberg-Welander, *supra* n. 31 at 143-145.
40. Government White Paper 2020:26 *supra* n. 32 at 37.
41. *Ibid.*, at 62-65. Worth noting is that from 1 September 2022, the notion of 'work that normally exist on the labour market' will be changed to 'work within a specified occupational group that contains work that normally exist on the labour market' in order to assure that the National Social Security Agency will have to specify what form of occupation is used as the basis for the assessment and as such increase transparency and foreseeability for the assessment. *See* Government Bill 2020/21:171 Angiven yrkesgrupp – åtgärder för en begriplig sjukfärsäkring.

work during the first 90 days of illness.[42] It is, however, difficult to fully assess the outcome of these changes before case law has developed.

The share of applications for sickness allowance that have been rejected is also significantly higher for the group of unemployed and others where the assessment of the decreased working capacity is conducted in relation to work that normally exists on the labour market. This issue clearly indicates the problems that on-call workers have faced in relation to the issue of sickness and social security benefits.[43] There has also been a significant increase in the share of rejected applications from 2015 when the Swedish National Social Security Agency implemented objectives for decreasing the number of sick days.[44] The issue has become more and more debated, not least since persons suffering from illness and being unable to work are nevertheless being denied sickness allowance and as such at high risk of ending up in poverty.[45] In this debate, the issue of persons suffering from illness that result in a partial decreased working capacity and thus in need of part-time sickness allowance has also been highlighted. The discussion has highlighted that the application of rules governing partial sickness allowance has rendered difficulties with rigidity concerning the distribution of partial sick leave. The lack of flexibility for partial sick leave has been considered to have resulted in a high degree of rejected applications for part-time sickness allowance. It is not unlikely that there is an increasing share of involuntary part-time workers for whom sickness is the reason for part-time work, but for whom sickness allowance will not cover the loss of income due to illness.[46] Legislative inquiries and initiatives for changes have been launched, but what the results will be remain to be seen. In the following sections, the situation concerning the four different VUP Groups are further discussed, highlighting some of the main risk factors for the groups.

§8.02 VUP GROUP 1: LOW- OR UNSKILLED STANDARD EMPLOYMENT

Due to the fairly high wage levels in Sweden, there are less issues concerning in-work poverty for this group of workers than would be the case from a European perspective. There are in fact no sectors in Sweden falling under the European Union definition of a poor sector.[47] In relation to this, it is worth highlighting the fact that wages below

42. The new rules were introduced on 1 February 2022 through the insertion of new articles in the Social Security Code, for this specific issue *see* Section 27 Articles 49 b and 49 c, Social Security Code. The reasons for the changes were framed in line with the previous discussions on the uncertain situation for workers with a form of employment that is becoming more and more common on the labour market. *See* Government Bill 2021/22:1 Budgetpropositionen för 2020, Utgiftsområde 10 – Ekonomisk trygghet vid sjukdom och funktionsnedsättning, especially pp. 57-66.
43. Government White Paper 2020:26 *supra* n. 32 at 62-65.
44. *Ibid.*, at 93-96.
45. For further discussion on the consequences and experiences of individuals in relation to this *see* Niklas Altermark, Avslagsmaskinen: Byråkrati och avhumanisering i svensk sjukförsäkring pp. 107-112 (Verbal, 2020).
46. Government White Paper 2020:26 *supra* n. 32 at 110-111.
47. This is based on Eurostat: earn_ses_pub1n, extraction 18.01.2021 with definitions of sectors in accordance with NACE rev. 2 classification. See EUROSTAT, *Statistical classification of economic*

60 % of the median wage are rare. A report from the Swedish National Mediation Office concerning minimum wages showed that the total proportion of employees earning a wage below 60 % of the median wage was a mere 0.9 %. Nevertheless, lower wages were more common for workers in three occupations: restaurant personnel (7.9 %); customer services personnel etc. (3.6 %); and private sector cleaners (1.6 %). However, the majority of those workers were either younger than 20 years, worked less than 40 % of full-time, or had variable supplements to their salary that raised their pay above 60 % of the median wage. When employees of young age, having a low-work intensity or being subject to variable supplements were excluded, the proportion of employees earning less than 60 % of the median wage dropped significantly and for the whole labour market it was as low as 0.3 %.[48] The strong link between the number of working hours and in-work poverty in Sweden is thus of importance to bear in mind when discussing this group of workers, who as per definition work full-time.

[A] Composition of VUP Group 1

Workers in low-wage and low-skilled occupations employed full-time on a permanent employment contract make up a fairly small proportion (7.5 %) of the entire in-work population in Sweden.[49] The majority of these workers are male (62 % in 2019), but in comparison to workers in standard employment in all low-skilled occupations, there is a higher share of female workers in poor sectors (38 % compared to 33 % in all low-skilled occupations). In general, younger workers are also over-represented in this group, with higher shares of workers aged 18-34 (but also higher share of workers aged 35-49) than the workforce as a whole. A vast majority (64.7 %) of the workers in this VUP Group 1 have a medium-level education. Due to the small sample size, it is not possible to deduce what share of these workers have a low or high level of education, However, it is reasonable to assume that the level of education is lower for this group of workers than for the overall in-work population since low-skilled sectors in general show a very low share of higher educated workers in comparison to the labour market as a whole. In terms of nationality of standard employed persons in low-skilled and low-wage sectors, it is difficult to make any assessments because the sample size is too small. For low-skilled sectors in general, the share of standard employed persons with non-Swedish citizenship is only slightly higher than the share of in-work persons with non-Swedish citizenship overall (7.9 % compared to 7.7 %). However, the share is higher than the share of non-Swedish citizens among permanently, full-time employed persons in all sectors (5.9 %).[50]

---

activities in the European Community, part. IV, *Structure and Explanatory Notes*, in *https://ec.europa.eu/eurostat/documents/3859598/5902521/KS-RA-07-015-EN.PDF.*

48. Hällberg and Kjellström, *supra* n. 3 at 4.
49. *See* Table 8.1 below. The information in this section is based on data from Eurostat, EU-SILC, 2019. The responsibility for all conclusions drawn from the data lies entirely with the author. The exploitation of the EU-SILC data has been done by the Luxemburgish partner of the 'Working, Yet Poor' project. If not specifically mentioned as relating to another year, the data presented in the text refer to the year 2019.

Table 8.1 In-Work Poverty Rates for VUP Group 1 in Comparison to All in Employment

Sweden		
	Employed Persons 2019	*VUP1 2019*
% of the employed (in-work) population	*(100)*	*(7.5)*
In-work at risk of poverty	(7.8)	(8.0)
Severe material deprivation rate	(0.7)	(1.0)
Individual variables:		
Age group		
18-34	10.8 (29.1)	10.5 (33)
35-49	7.8 (35.5)	6 (41.7)
> =50	5.3 (35.4)	8.1 (25.3)
Gender		
Women	6.7 (46.5)	6.7 (38)
Men	8.6 (53.5)	8.8 (62)
Education		
Medium	5.9 (50.9)	5.2 (64.7)
Economic sector		
Trade/Transport/Accommodation and food services/info-com	7.2 (22.9)	8.3 (61)
Others services	7.5 (51.1)	7.6 (39)
Household variables:		
Number of in-work persons in the household:		
1	13.5 (39.7)	12.9 (45.1)
> 1	4 (60.3)	4 (54.9)
Number of children (< 18):		
0	7.2 (60.3)	6.3 (59.4)
1	8.4 (16.8)	10.5 (40.6)
> 1	8.6 (22.9)	

Source: Eurostat, EU-SILC, 2019. Where there are two different numbers indicated, the numbers in parenthesis show the percentage share of the selected population and the other number show the in-work poverty rate. The responsibility for all conclusions drawn from the data lies entirely with the

50. Eurostat, EU-SILC, 2019. The responsibility for all conclusions drawn from the data lies entirely with the author. The exploitation of the EU-SILC data has been done by the Luxemburgish partner of the 'Working, Yet Poor' project. If not specifically mentioned as relating to another year, the data presented in the text refer to the year 2019.

author. The exploitation of the EU-SILC data has been done by the Luxemburgish partner of the 'Working, Yet Poor' project.

From the statistics in Table 8.1, it seems fairly clear that this group of workers do face certain risk of in-work poverty, albeit in-work poverty rates do not differ significantly from those of the overall employed population.

[B] Relevant Legal Framework

With the Swedish labour and social law system being structured on the premise of standard employment, these workers are the VUP Group that are exposed to the fewest risks of in-work poverty, at least in terms of legal uncertainties or gaps. Some issues, nevertheless, generate risks for these workers due to their lower wages, and those issues are connected to the decrease of income during periods of illness or unemployment due to the frequently applied rule of social insurance schemes covering 80% of the income loss.[51] There are thus risks that these workers may fall below the poverty threshold during periods where the worker temporarily takes up social security benefits. In relation to unemployment benefits, it is especially noteworthy that the requirement of accepting a suitable job, involves a threshold of a wage as low as 90% of the unemployment benefit paid as a minimum for deeming the income from the job suitable.[52] This means that these workers, who will be subject to fairly low unemployment benefits, face risks of having to accept job offers with a wage at such a low level as to increase their risk of in-work poverty even further. Even though it is doubtful that a job involving a wage that is significantly lower than wage levels applied in collective agreements would be considered suitable and minimum wage levels in general tend to be set above the poverty threshold,[53] the lack of case law as to what is a suitable job in relation to the wage offered for that job causes a specific risk for these workers.

Since collective agreement coverage is generally high, at 100% in the public sector and around 83% in the private sector,[54] these workers are also to a fairly high

51. The principle of covering loss of income in case of illness, parental leave, and so on is in general applied with a formula of calculation generating social security benefits at approximately 80% of the worker's income, with certain caps. The calculation of benefits is regulated in the Social Security Code and the various sections covering different social security benefits, except for unemployment benefits which are subject to separate regulations in UBA, RUB, and adjacent legislation.
52. As regulated in Swedish Inspection Authority for Unemployment Benefits Regulation No. 2015:3 (IAFFS 2015:3).
53. On minimum wage levels in collective agreements in relation to poverty thresholds *see* Hällberg and Kjellström, *supra* n. 3. The application of the criteria for assessing the suitability of a job offer has been investigated and discussed in Inspection for Unemployment Benefits (IAF), Report 2017:16 Tillämpningen av regelverket för lämpligt arbete. However, the issue of what is a suitable wage level was not explored in detail, and there is a lack of case law offering clear conclusions in relation to this issue.
54. Swedish National Mediation Office, *supra* n. 2 at 166-168.

extent covered by supplementary protection mechanisms from collective agreements, involving among other things potential support for training and transition on the labour market in case of redundancies.[55] There are risks, however, that some workers within this group may fall outside the scope of the protective structures that the Swedish model offers since the collective agreement coverage rate is significantly lower within smaller companies, especially in private sectors where wages are lower and also trade union membership is lower. For example, within other services in the private sector, there has been a decline of trade union membership from 71% in 2006 to 50% in 2019,[56] and collective agreement coverage for smaller companies with less than 50 employees in this sector was as low as 22% in 2015.[57] Unfortunately, current available statistics do not provide information detailed enough to do more than to point at potential risks.

[C] Impact Analysis

Trying to assess the situation for these workers on the basis of relevant legal framework and the available statistics on in-work poverty found in Table 8.1, some remarks can be made. Among these workers, it is slightly more common to live alone or to live in a household with only one person in work than it is for the whole in-work population.[58] Even though the overall in-work poverty rate for this group of workers is comparable to the whole group of employed persons in Sweden, it is possible to see specific categories within this VUP group that face higher risks of in-work poverty. In particular, in-work poverty rates higher than the overall figure for this group are found among: young workers aged 18-34; single person households; workers living in a household with only one in-work person; and households with children. Younger persons are more likely to be single, live alone, and potentially also more likely to earn a wage close to the minimum level set in the collective agreement, or even subject to a specific lower-wage level for young workers. Single person households could thus be more likely to be subject to issues in relation to periods of sickness or unemployment where the benefits paid fall below the poverty threshold, which could be an explanation of the higher in-work poverty rates for young and single persons in this VUP group.

For a worker in this VUP group, living either as a single parent or in a household where only one parent is working, the situation seems fairly similar. It is possible to see

55. For an account and discussion of such collectively agreed benefits, *see* Johansson, *supra* n. 16.
56. Kjellberg, *supra* n. 18 at 134.
57. *Ibid.*, at 175.
58. The following assessments relating to common traits for workers in this group and in-work poverty rates are based on data from Eurostat, EU-SILC, 2019, as presented in Table 8.1. The responsibility for all conclusions drawn from the data lies entirely with the author. The exploitation of the EU-SILC data has been done by the Luxemburgish partner of the 'Working, Yet Poor' project.

that households with only one person in-work have significantly higher rates of in-work poverty (12.9%) than households with two working persons (4%). We also see that having children in the household increases the in-work poverty rate with a little more than four percentage points.[59] It seems as if the relatively lower wage levels for the workers in this VUP group are not always sufficient for assuring a living standard above the poverty threshold if the wage is to support a family. These difficulties are likely to be increased if the working person in the household faces a period of sickness or unemployment.

§8.03 VUP GROUP 2: SOLO AND BOGUS SELF-EMPLOYMENT

The case of VUP Group 2 is a problematic case to study. First, there are difficulties in retrieving reliable statistics, since available statistics cover the broader group of self-employed without employees. To what extent the self-employed without employees are dependent or bogus self-employed, however, is highly difficult to assess. Second, the actual declared income for self-employed seems not to be indicative of their socio-economic situation in terms of material standard. Despite these workers being subject to very high in-work poverty rates of well above 20%, they are not affected by severe material deprivation at all.[60] As such it is possible to point at some risks that have been identified, but conclusions as concerns the extent and impact of in-work poverty for this VUP Group can at best be considered indicative.

[A] Composition of VUP Group 2

As already mentioned, it has not been possible to find statistics that specifically cover this VUP Group, albeit some figures concerning self-employed without employees exist. Self-employed without employees make up a small share of about 6% of the in-work population in Sweden, which means that VUP2 reasonably will be smaller than that.

59. *See* Table 8.1.
60. In 2019, self-employed without employees were subject to an in-work poverty risk of 24.3%, whereas the severe material deprivation rate was zero. Data from Eurostat, EU-SILC, 2019, as presented in Table 8.2. The responsibility for all conclusions drawn from the data lies entirely with the author. The exploitation of the EU-SILC data has been done by the Luxemburgish partner of the 'Working, Yet Poor' project.

Table 8.2 In-Work Poverty Rates for Self-Employed Without Employees in Comparison to All in Employment

Sweden		
	Employed Persons 2019	*VUP2 Broadly 2019*
% of the employed (in-work) population	*(100)*	*(6.1)*
In-work at risk of poverty	(7.8)	(24.3)
Severe material deprivation rate	(0.7)	(0)
Individual variables:		
Age group		
18-34	10.8 (29.1)	25 (51)
35-49	7.8 (35.5)	
> = 50	5.3 (35.4)	23.6 (49)
Gender		
Women	6.7 (46.5)	22.5 (32.1)
Men	8.6 (53.5)	20.3 (67.9)
Education		
Low	17.3 (12.1)	25.0 (70.6)
Medium	5.9 (50.9)	
High	5.5 (36.9)	21.3 (29.4)
Working time		
Full time	6.4 (81.5)	24.1 (79.4)
Part time	13.4 (18.5)	22.5 (20.6)
Economic sector		
Agriculture/Industry/Construction	6.3 (19.9)	23.1 (51.4)
Trade/Transport/Accommodation and food services/info-com	7.2 (22.9)	
Others services	7.5 (51.1)	23.8 (48.6)
Not defined	13.8 (6.1)	
Household variables:		
Household size		
1	11.3 (24.6)	29 (63.9)
2	5.9 (31.2)	
> 2	7.1 (44.2)	16 (36.1)
Number of in-work persons in the household:		
1	13.5 (39.7)	43.8 (40.6)

Sweden		
	Employed Persons 2019	*VUP2 Broadly 2019*
% of the employed (in-work) population	*(100)*	*(6.1)*
In-work at risk of poverty	(7.8)	(24.3)
> 1	4 (60.3)	11 (59.4)
Number of children (< 18):		
0	7.2 (60.3)	25.9 (66.4)
1	8.4 (16.8)	26.6 (13.2)
> 1	8.6 (22.9)	17.8 (20.5)

Source: Eurostat, EU-SILC, 2019. Where there are two different numbers indicated, the numbers in parenthesis show the percentage share of the selected population and the other number show the in-work poverty rate. The responsibility for all conclusions drawn from the data lies entirely with the author. The exploitation of the EU-SILC data has been done by the Luxemburgish partner of the 'Working, Yet Poor' project.

As can be seen in Table 8.2, self-employed without employees are in comparison with the whole in-work population, more likely to be male, 50 years or older and living in a household of one or two persons without children below the age of 18. Another characteristic that differs slightly for this group is that they are somewhat less likely to have a higher-level education. They are also more likely to work in the broad spectrum of agriculture, industry, construction or trade, transport, accommodation and food service, and information and communication sectors, where more than 50% of self-employed without employees are occupied.

[B] Legal Framework: Notion; Obstacles to the Application of Labour Law and Social Security Standards; Unionisation and Application of Collective Agreements

Swedish labour law is a binary system where a person performing work for another party is either considered an employee and thus protected under labour law or considered an assignment worker who is not protected. The term self-employed is on the other hand not specifically defined in the law; instead, the presumption would be that a self-employed person is a person who performs work under conditions that would classify that person as an assignment worker according to labour law.[61] Such an assessment could also be the case for a solo self-employed person even though increasing dependence and subordination towards one main client could also lead to

61. For further discussion, *see* Annamaria Westregård, Digital collaborative platforms: A challenge for the social partners in the Nordic model, NJCL 1(2018), 89-112 (2018).

increasing reasons for classifying the person performing work as an employee.[62] As for bogus self-employed, the presumption is that the self-employment is used as a façade in order to circumvent labour law legislation, and in a situation where the work relationship would be examined in court under labour law, the work performing party would be classified as an employee.[63] However, such an assessment would only happen in case there would be a dispute in court and in practice a self-employed and his/her client would most likely structure their relations on the basis that employment law does not apply for the work performing party.

Since the Swedish Co-Determination Act includes dependent contractors within its scope, it could from a labour law perspective be possible to include dependent self-employed in the scope of application for collective agreements. If so, the self-employed would also be covered by the protection that collective agreements provide concerning working conditions. However, since such an inclusion is generally perceived as in breach of competition law this has not been a strategy adopted by Swedish trade unions.[64] Nevertheless, some trade unions do also hold self-employed as members. The trade unions that allow self-employed to be members of the organisation are, in general, either trade unions directed at occupations where self-employment is more common or trade unions organising white-collar workers or professionally trained academics where the professional identity is an important focus for the organisation.[65] The largest white-collar workers' union, Unionen, has reported to have approximately 10,000 self-employed among their members, but the main interests of these members are not to achieve collective agreement coverage. Instead, the self-employed that are members of Unionen tend to be members in order to access certain forms of insurances and advice services granted to members of the trade union.[66] Trade union membership for self-employed in Sweden can thus be seen rather as a form of additional security for the individual member than as a way to organise workers.

---

62. The criteria and the overall assessment are discussed in detail in, for example, Glavå and Hansson, *supra* n. 1 at 93-95.
63. An example of such an assessment is found in the case AD 2013:92 where a transportation company was found not to be able to circumvent the employers' responsibilities for a lorry driver by means of using an intermediate service providing company (with similar ownership as the main transportation company) to sign agreements on provisions of services with the individual lorry driver. The circumstances in the case instead showed that the work conducted was performed under conditions of an employment relationship, and the lorry driver was considered to be an employee of the transportation company.
64. For a discussion on these legal issues *see* Annamaria Westregård, *Protection of platform workers in Sweden. Part 2 Country report*, Nordic future of work project 2017-2020: Working paper 12. Pillar VI, pp. 14-17 (Fafo, 2020). The opinion that competition law prevents the inclusion of self-employed within the scope of collective agreements was expressed by several trade union representatives during the work with Swedish national workshops within the 'Working, Yet Poor' project.
65. This issue was to some extent discussed with trade union representatives during the Swedish national workshops for 'Working, Yet Poor'. Occupational identity and self-employment being more frequent within a specific occupation were identified as main contributing factors for trade unions to decide to open up membership also for self-employed.
66. This issue was taken up during the Swedish national workshops for 'Working, Yet Poor' where representatives of different trade unions that also allow self-employed as members were present and expressed the intentions of opening up for membership for self-employed.

As has been indicated earlier, there are specific challenges and insecurities for self-employed in relation to social security schemes, especially as concerns the more complex rules and administration for calculation of income base and the amount to be paid. In addition, the practical problems that these workers face in terms of being absent from work and adjacent risks of losing the client might also decrease these workers' willingness to take leave in case of, for example, sickness or becoming a parent. The restrictions placed on business activities in relation to unemployment benefits, as mentioned earlier, will make it difficult for these workers to assure themselves possibilities for getting back in employment by means of their own business if they take up unemployment benefits.

[C] Impact Analysis

The situation for solo and bogus self-employed persons in relation to in-work poverty is very difficult to assess both due to the lack of reliable statistics for this specific group and because of the contradiction between high in-work poverty rates and zero percent severe material deprivation.[67] Studies concerning self-employed in Sweden also indicate that this group of workers tends to work more and earn less than employees in the same occupation,[68] but whether this also implies that they are in a more socio-economically vulnerable position is very difficult to assess. At the same time, even though these workers may not be subject to issues of severe material deprivation, the challenges they face in relation to practical difficulties and uncertainties in relation to social security benefits may cause vulnerabilities that increase longer-term poverty risks for this group.

§8.04 VUP GROUP 3: FIXED-TERM, AGENCY WORKERS, INVOLUNTARY PART-TIMERS

Due to the strong connection between the number of worked hours and in-work poverty in Sweden, atypical employments where workers may end up not reaching sufficient number of working hours also show increasing risk of in-work poverty. However, the situation differs to some extent between the three subgroups of atypical forms of employment, which specificities are discussed separately. Statistics covering fixed-term workers and involuntary part-time workers grouped together show the precarious situation these workers potentially face in terms of in-work poverty risks.

67. See Table 8.2.
68. This has been a significant trend among freelancers in various occupations and for a study on how freelance journalists' strategies for coping with the situation *see* Maria Norbäck, and Alexander Styhre, *Making it work in free agent work: The coping practices of Swedish freelance journalists*, Scandinavian Journal of Management, 4(35), Article 101076 (2019).

Table 8.3 In-Work Poverty Rates for Fixed-Term and Involuntary Part-Tie Workers in Comparison to All in Employment

Sweden		
	Employed Persons 2019	*VUP 3 Narrowly 2019*
% of the employed (in-work) population	*(100)*	*(12.2)*
In-work at risk of poverty	(7.8)	(19.5)
Severe material deprivation rate	(0.7)	(3.5)
Individual variables:		
Age group		
18-34	10.8 (29.1)	23.8 (51.5)
35-49	7.8 (35.5)	22.2 (25.4)
> =50	5.3 (35.4)	7.2 (23)
Gender		
Women	6.7 (46.5)	19.5 (58.5)
Men	8.6 (53.5)	19.5 (41.5)
Nationality		
Local	6 (92.3)	12.9 (78.1)
Other	26.6 (7.7)	43.3 (21.9)
Education		
Low	17.3 (12.1)	32.2 (20.2)
Medium	5.9 (50.9)	13.8 (48.9)
High	5.5 (36.9)	14.1 (30.9)
Occupation (skill level)		
High	5 (51.1)	16.5 (36.2)
Low	10.7 (48.9)	21.5 (63.8)
Economic sector		
Trade/Transport/Accommodation and food services/info-com	7.2 (22.9)	20.4 (19)
Others services	7.5 (51.1)	20.9 (59.3)
Number of months work (during the reference period):		
less than 12	17.8 (6)	18.3 (18.9)
12	7.1 (94)	19.8 (81.1)

Sweden		
	Employed Persons 2019	*VUP 3 Narrowly 2019*
% of the employed (in-work) population	*(100)*	*(12.2)*
In-work at risk of poverty	(7.8)	(19.5)
Household variables:		
Household size		
1	11.3 (24.6)	29 (29)
2	5.9 (31.2)	16.9 (26.6)
> 2	7.1 (44.2)	14.9 (44.4)
Number of in-work persons in the household:		
1	13.5 (39.7)	30.2 (48.6)
> 1	4 (60.3)	9.4 (51.4)
Number of children (< 18):		
0	7.2 (60.3)	19.2 (61.5)
1	8.4 (16.8)	16.3 (22.5)
> 1	8.6 (22.9)	25.2 (16)

Source: Eurostat, EU-SILC, 2019. Where there are two different numbers indicated, the numbers in parenthesis show the percentage share of the selected population and the other number show the in-work poverty rate. When s.s. is indicated instead of a number, the sample size has been too small for generating reliable data. The responsibility for all conclusions drawn from the data lies entirely with the author. The exploitation of the EU-SILC data has been done by the Luxemburgish partner of the 'Working, Yet Poor' project.

From Table 8.3, we can see that fixed-term and involuntary part-time workers are subject to significantly higher rates of in-work poverty than the whole population of employed persons, regardless of which category we look at. In addition, they are also subject to a higher rate of severe material deprivation, indicating that for these workers there are more challenges in making ends meet than working persons in general would face in Sweden. Young workers, women, and foreign-born workers are over-represented among fixed-term workers and involuntary part-time workers. Low-skilled occupations are more common for these workers as is a low level of education. In addition, they are more likely to live alone and as such also more likely to be the only working person in the household.

[A] Fixed-Term Employees

As was discussed in the introduction, the legislation on fixed-term employment in Sweden is very flexible, and the issue is continuously debated. The total share of fixed-term employees has remained fairly stable throughout the years,[69] thus indicating that the flexible rules are not necessarily eroding the idea of a permanent employment as the main form of employment. However, it seems that the character of fixed-term contracts used on the labour market has gone from stable forms such as longer substitute contracts towards less secure and short-term intermittent forms of fixed-term contracts, especially within blue-collar occupations.[70] In addition, the total share of fixed-term employments is also on the increase for blue-collar occupations, in comparison with white-collar occupations where there has been a tendency of a slight decreasing share of fixed-term contracts instead.[71] With less probability for transitioning from a fixed-term contract to a permanent employment for workers employed with precarious forms of fixed-term contracts,[72] the risk of getting stuck in a situation of various forms of fixed-term employments in combination with periods of unemployment have increased. In relation to this and in the light of the COVID-19 pandemic, the elderly care services sector has been granted specific attention in the Swedish debate, and working conditions within this sector have been highlighted as problematic.[73] This is a sector where the share of fixed-term employments is significantly higher than for the labour market in general. Worth noting is that there are differences depending on whether the employer running the elderly care services organisation is public or private, where the share of fixed-term employments was 27% and 37% respectively in 2017, compared to 16% for the whole labour market.[74] Even though the higher share of fixed-term employments in this sector to some extent can be explained by difficulties for employers to find personnel with the required qualifications for permanent employment,[75] it is unlikely that the full share of fixed-term employments can be explained by shortage of staff.

[1] Legal Framework: Notion; Equal Treatment; Working Conditions and Social Security Benefits; Unionisation and Collective Agreement's Application

With the flexible rules on fixed-term employments that exist in Sweden, it is also worth highlighting that the protection offered to these workers through the prohibition of direct and indirect discrimination relates specifically to pay and working conditions[76]

69. Kjellberg, *supra* n. 18 at 164.
70. Johan Alfonsson, Alienation och arbete: Unga behovsanställdas villkor i den flexibla kapitalismen, pp. 157-162 (Arkiv, 2020).
71. Kjellberg, *supra* n. 18 at 164.
72. Berglund et al., *supra* n. 12.
73. The issue of employment conditions within the elderly care sector was specifically addressed in Government White Paper 2020:80 Äldreomsorgen under pandemin.
74. Hampus Andersson, Så mycket bättre? 2018 – En jämförelse av anställningsvillkor och löner i privat och kommunalt driven äldreomsorg, pp. 14-15 (Kommunal, 2018).
75. The problem of finding relevantly trained and educated staff for certain occupations as an important explanation for high shares of fixed-term employments has been highlighted by employers' representatives during 'Working, Yet Poor' project workshops with stakeholders in Sweden.
76. Articles 3 and 4 Act on prohibition of discrimination of part-time and fixed-term employees.

but not to other areas such as social security or unemployment benefits. Improving the situation for fixed-term workers in relation to social security and unemployment benefits therefore requires the sort of legislative changes that currently are under discussion and as mentioned earlier, to some extent recently introduced. With coming legal changes through which the qualification time for having a fixed-term employment transformed into a permanent employment will be shortened from two years to twelve months, there could be a potential change.[77]

The proposed changes to the EPA will be framed in the form of semi-discretionary law that is common in Sweden, enabling the social partners to deviate, also in pejus, from the law through collective agreements. In relation to this it is worth highlighting an issue concerning mainly blue-collar workers in private sector education, health and care services, for which collective agreements often include a peculiar form of deviation. The deviation consists of a clause allowing fixed-term employees to renounce the right to become permanently employed by signing an individual contract with the employer on renouncing that right for six months. The requirement is that the initiative for such an agreement shall be taken by the employee. In most such cases, the collective agreement also allows for several such individual contracts to be agreed upon.[78] The reasons for implementing such clauses are questionable since an employee is always free to resign from a position as long as the period of notice is respected. Therefore, the only party in the employment relationship that could gain from these clauses is the employer and, therefore, there is a risk that the employer will exert pressure on fixed-term employees to initiate the signing of an individual agreement to renounce the right to have the employment transformed into a permanent employment. Such a risk is particularly prominent when there are insufficient mechanisms for control of these individual agreements by the trade union. The above-mentioned higher share of fixed-term employees found in private sector elderly care services, compared to public sector elderly care services, could possibly indicate that these forms of individual agreements on renouncing the right to transformation into permanent employment are also used. There is thus a need for social partners to address this issue and take responsibility for assuring that clauses in collective agreements do not open for practices that worsen conditions for fixed-term employees.

The role of the social partners, therefore, serves some additional attention, especially due to various forms of supplementary social security benefits regulated and granted through collective agreements. Such additional benefits exist for example in connection to parental leave benefits or in relation to transition and unemployment support in case of redundancies, but they are generally conditioned on a certain length

77. These changes are at the time being in the process of being reviewed by the Council of Legislation, *see* Government draft bill, *supra* n. 15.

78. *See*, for example, Article 3 para. 2 in Almega Vårdföretagarna and Kommunal, Kollektivavtal, allmänna villkor och löner – Bransch Äldreomsorg (Collective agreement covering blue-collar workers in private sector elderly care services) or Article 3 paragraph 5 in Almega Tjänsteföretagen and Kommunal, Kollektivavtal – Friskolor (Collective agreement covering blue-collar workers in private sector education).

of the employment, which fixed-term employees are less likely to fulfil.[79] Therefore such additional benefits do not really serve to highlight the value of collective agreements for fixed-term workers. This is not an issue to be ignored because there are increasing problems concerning trade union representation of fixed-term workers in Sweden.

These problems are mainly related to the lower level of unionisation among fixed-term workers than among permanent employees. Differences in unionisation between fixed-term and permanent employees have existed for a long time in Sweden. This difference has also increased along with the overall trend of decreasing trade union membership. This is specifically noteworthy in relation to fixed-term, blue-collar workers for which trade union membership rates have dropped from 63% in 2005 to 37% in 2018. This can be compared to permanently employed, blue-collar workers for which the membership rates have dropped from 83% in 2005 to 67% in 2018. Similar developments can be seen for white-collar workers with a stronger decrease of trade union membership rates for fixed-term employees, which have dropped from 68% in 2005 to 53% in 2018 in comparison to white-collar permanent employees where the rates have dropped from 80% in 2005 to 75% in 2018.[80] At the same time the share of temporary employed has increased among blue-collar workers from 20.6% in 2005 to 23.4% in 2019. If full-time students are excluded from the statistics, then the increasing share of temporary employees among blue-collar workers is less, from 18.2% in 2005 to 19.9% in 2019. For white-collar workers, the share of fixed-term employees has instead dropped, especially when excluding full-time students from the statistics, 9.9% in 2005 whereas in 2019 the share of fixed-term employed white-collar workers was 8.2%.[81] The combination of decreasing trade union membership among fixed-term employees and the increasing share of temporary contracts among blue-collar workers call for concern. Both trade unions and employers need to take action in order to assure that collective agreements offer better protection and the relevance of trade union membership become more apparent for fixed-term workers.

[2] Impact Analysis

Trying to assess the situation of in-work poverty for fixed-term workers is subject to some uncertainties since statistics do not distinguish fixed-term workers with more stable and long-term contracts from fixed-term workers on short-term contracts. In addition, the available statistics, group fixed-term workers and involuntary part-time workers together. Some risk factors may be identified from Table 8.3, such as young age, having a low level of education, being foreign-born, working in an occupation with a low skill level, living as a single person, or being the only working person in the

79. For a discussion concerning pension and transition benefits, *see* Johansson, *supra* n. 16. For a discussion concerning parental leave benefits, *see* Jenny Julén Votinius, *Collective Bargaining for Working Parents in Sweden and its Interaction with the Statutory Benefit System*, International Journal of Comparative Labour Law and Industrial Relations, 3(36), 367-386 (2020).
80. Kjellberg, *supra* n. 18 at 164.
81. Ibid.

household.[82] The relatively young age of the workers in this group in combination with the fact that it is slightly more common for these workers to live alone, could indicate that single person households in this group more often consist of a young person. The higher rates of in-work poverty for both these categories also indicate that single person households to a higher extent combine fixed-term work with periods of unemployment, which, as mentioned above, is very likely to increase poverty risks. Even though it is plausible that a fair share of young fixed-term workers are in the process of establishing themselves on the labour market, the segmented labour market in Sweden, with higher thresholds for gaining a stable position especially for foreign-born workers,[83] generates risks for these groups. It seems as if young and foreign-born workers risk becoming trapped in a situation of in-work poverty for longer periods, and the difficulties they face in accessing sufficient support through social security structures therefore need attention. These problems become even more pressing when considering the class structures of the segmented labour market in terms of disadvantages for those with low level of education and those working in occupations with low skill level. For a fixed-term worker living as a single parent with one or more children or being in a household of two parents with children as the only working parent, the same risks in relation to fulfilling criteria of length of employment in order to access various benefits exist. In addition, having one wage for making a living causes additional risks, which is visible in the difference of more than 20 percentage points in in-work poverty rates between households with one and households with more than one person working.[84]

[B] Temporary Agency Workers

Temporary agency workers are not singled out in statistics, thus relevant in-work poverty rates are as such not available, nor are there reliable data available concerning the work-force composition of temporary agency workers. What can be said is that temporary agency workers tend to be younger and also more often foreign-born than what is the case for the labour market in large. In 2019, 40% of temporary agency workers were under the age of 29, and 27% were foreign born.[85] Despite these groups generally showing higher risks of in-work poverty, there are certain specificities concerning the situation for these workers on the labour market in Sweden that may give rise to somewhat less concern in relation to in-work poverty.

82. The following discussion is based on the statistics available in Table 8.3.
83. For further discussion *see*, for example, Arbetsmarknadsekonomiska Rådet, Arbetsmarknadsekonomisk rapport – Tudelningarna på arbetsmarknaden (AER, 2017); Kåre Vernby, and Rafaela Dancygier, Employer discrimination and the immutability of ethnic hierarchies: A Field Experiment. Working Paper 2018:17 (IFAU Institutet för arbetsmarknads- och utbildningspolitisk utvärdering, 2018); or Lina Aldén, and Mats Hammarstedt. Integration of immigrants on the Swedish labour market – recent trends and explanations. Report 2014:9 (Linnaeus University Centre, Labour Market and Discrimination Studies, 2014).
84. *See* Table 8.3.
85. Kompetensföretagen, Därför behövs kompetensföretag (Kompetensföretagen, 2020).

[1] *Legal Framework: Notion; Equal Treatment; Working Conditions and Social Security Benefits; Unionisation and Collective Agreement's Application*

Temporary agency work is regulated in the Act on temporary agency work, which entered into force in 2013. The relevant terms are defined in Article 5 and the principle of equal treatment is set out in Article 6. Temporary agency work is not specified in relation to social security or unemployment benefits, where potential problems are rather related to the form of employment as such and not whether the employer is a temporary work agency. In the Swedish context, it is worth noting that working conditions for temporary agency workers have been regulated in collective agreements well before the implementation of the Temporary Agency Work Directive.[86] The employers' organisation representing temporary work agencies has been very active in seeking to improve the reputation and legitimacy of temporary work agencies on the Swedish labour market. This strategy has focused also on assuring a high degree of collective agreement coverage for temporary work agencies, and in 2017 approximately 97% of the workers employed by temporary work agencies were covered by collective agreements.[87] There is thus a very high collective agreement coverage rate despite younger and foreign-born workers being over-represented and the unionisation rates thus likely lower among these workers.[88] In addition to the high coverage of collective agreements, the contents of these agreements also tend to offer protection which can be considered as decreasing risks of in-work poverty for temporary agency workers. Clauses on wages for blue-collar temporary agency workers are based on the average hourly wage for comparable workers at the user undertaking, which tends to generate a higher wage for the often younger and less-experienced temporary agency worker than the wage they would have received as employed directly by the user undertaking.[89] Clauses limiting the use of casual employment contracts are also frequent as well as obligations on employers to inform trade unions about the use of temporary contracts.[90]

[2] *Impact Analysis*

Lack of statistics make impact assessments very difficult, but it is worth pointing out that temporary agency work holds a fairly small part of the Swedish labour market. In

86. Annika Berg, Bemanningsarbete, flexibilitet och likabehandling: En studie av svensk rätt och kollektivavtalsreglering med komparativa inslag, pp. 254-256 (Juristförlaget i Lund, 2008).
87. Arbetsmarknadsekonomiska Rådet, Arbetsmarknadsekonomisk rapport – Olika vägar till jobb, p 67 AER,2018).
88. For the higher share of young and foreign-born workers, *see* Kompetensföretagen, *supra* n. 85. Concerning trade unionisation rates, *see* Kjellberg, *supra* n. 18 at 46-48.
89. This is the case in the main collective agreement for blue-collar temporary agency workers Bemanningsavtalet between Almega Bemanningsföretagen and LO-förbunden. For discussion on these wage clauses *see* Berg, *supra* n. 86 at 254-258.
90. *See*, for example, Clause 3 Section 1 Bemanningsavtalet between Almega Bemanningsföretagen and LO-förbunden or Clause 2.2.2 Allmänna anställningsvillkor, Avtal för tjänstemän, between Almega Bemanningsföretagen, Unionen and Akademikerförbunden.

2018, the temporary work agencies affiliated to the employers' organisation Kompetensföretagen employed about 93,000 full-year equivalent workers[91] or roughly 2% of the labour market force. In addition, the potentially higher risk normally affecting blue-collar workers due to lower-wage levels are lessened due to the tendency of a positive wage gap, whereby these workers tend to earn a higher income than comparable blue-collar workers in a more standard form of employment.[92] The in-work poverty risks for these workers in Sweden therefore seem less pertinent than for other groups of atypical workers.

[C] Involuntary Part-timers

Due to the strong connection between the number of hours worked and in-work poverty, the situation for part-time workers is of more importance to highlight in the discussion. The figures presented in Table 8.3 above indicate that foreign-born, female and/or young workers could be over-represented among involuntary part-time workers. The majority (59.3%) of these workers are also found in the category of other services, where health and care services and social activities services are found, which are female-dominated sectors. Based on more detailed information on which specific sectors that hold the highest shares of part-time employees, it is possible to see that within certain sectors (health and care services, food and accommodation services, trade including retail, but also accommodation) at least 25% of the employees are part-time workers.[93] The fact that part-time work is more common among women than men is visible in statistics from SCB (Statistics Sweden), where figures from 2019 show that 26.6% of women and 10.8% of men work part-time. In actual numbers, part-time working women are more than twice as many as part-time working men.[94] Understanding how many of these are to be considered involuntary part-time workers requires taking into account how many of them would prefer working more hours than they actually do. SCB provides some statistics in relation to so-called underemployed part-time workers showing that around 100,900 women and around 62,400 men that work part-time would like to work for more hours.[95] This means that 17.3% of the women and 22.5% of the men that work part-time could be considered as involuntary part-time workers. The main reason for part-time work is that it has not been possible to find full-time work, but high physical or psychological demands of the job or

91. Kompetensföretagen, Årsrapport 2018 (Infront Data, 2019).
92. Joakim Hveem, Are temporary work agencies stepping stones into regular employment? IZA Journal of Migration, 2(21), pp. 1-27 (2013).
93. Svenskt Näringsliv, Allt fler jobbar heltid – Förekomst och utveckling av heltid och deltid på arbetsmarknaden, p 9 (Svenskt Näringsliv, 2017) and Joa Bergold, Ulrika Vedin, and Ulrika Lorentzi, Sveriges jämställdhetsbarometer 2020: Tid, makt och pengar – jämställda och jämlika möjligheter att försörja sig livet ut, pp. 13-14 (LO, 2020).
94. Source: SCB. Based on tables as presented on https://www.scb.se/hitta-statistik/temaomraden/jamstalldhet/ekonomisk-jamstalldhet/arbetskraftsdeltagande-och-sysselsattning/?showAllContentLinks=True#130363 (last accessed 22.04.2021).
95. Source: SCB. Based on tables as presented on https://www.scb.se/hitta-statistik/temaomraden/jamstalldhet/ekonomisk-jamstalldhet/arbetskraftsdeltagande-och-sysselsattning/?showAllContentLinks=True#130368 (last accessed 22.04.2021).

personal health issues are also frequent reasons. For blue-collar female workers, which is the group with the highest share of part-time workers, three out of ten have reported not being able to find full-time work, and two out of ten have stated the demands of the job or their own health as the reason for not working full-time.[96]

[1] *Legal Framework: Notion; Equal Treatment; Working Conditions and Social Security Benefits; Unionisation and Collective Agreement's Application*

Swedish legislation holds a definition of the concept of a part-time worker in Article 2. Act on prohibition of part-time and fixed-term employees and part-time workers are also subject to the prohibition of direct and indirect discrimination in Articles 3 and 4 of the same act. In addition, there are different forms of protective rules governing for example, the number of extra hours an employer is allowed to request from part-time workers,[97] and employer obligations to investigate the possibility for increasing working hours of part-time workers before recruiting new staff if part-time workers have registered interest in increasing working hours.[98] There is no limitation for the minimum hours of part-time work though, even though collective agreements may contain clauses whereby employers are encouraged to assure that part-time contracts amount to at least 50% of full-time work.[99] The coming probable changes of the EPA will also introduce additional legislation of relevance for part-time workers. First, the reform will define full-time work as the main form of employment with adjacent requirements on employers to provide a written statement of the reasons for part-time work on the request of the worker. The intention is to make full-time work the norm on the labour market and call for more thorough reflection before decisions on using part-time contracts.[100] Second, protective measures will be adopted in order to assure that in situations where the employer reorganises work by reducing the working hours of the employees, the employer needs to offer the new positions with lower working hours in order of seniority of employment, and there will also be a requirement for the employer to respect a period of notice before the application of the lower number of working hours in the contracts.[101] It remains to be seen what the effect of this for part-time work in Sweden will be though.

In relation to social security benefits, part-time workers face certain difficulties, mainly due to their lower income. Since the income base for social security benefits

96. Bergold etal., *supra* n. 93 at 13-14.
97. Articles 10 and 10 a Working Time Act limits the number of general extra hours to 200 per year and additional extra hours to 150 per year respectively.
98. Article 25 a Employment Protection Act.
99. For example, Clause 3 section 5 Kollektivavtal, allmänna villkor och löner – Bransch Äldreomsorg between Almega Vårdföretagarna and Kommunal and Clause 3.3 Butiksavtalet between Livsmedelsföretagen and Handels.
100. To be implemented in a new Article 4 a EPA, *see* Government draft bill, *supra* n. 15.
101. In accordance with the proposed new Article 7 a EPA, *see* Government draft bill, *supra* n. 15.

depend on the income that the worker has,[102] that income base will naturally become lower for part-time workers, meaning that the allowances paid will be lower. It is also worth noting that the regulations allowing for taking up partial parental allowance are also part of the reasons for part-time work. Part-time work is in general much more common among women than men, and it is also more common for women to take part-time parental allowance.[103] Even though involuntary part-time work is an issue for both men and women, the dominance of women within the group of part-time workers highlights this issue as a question of importance for equality.

In terms of collective agreements, part-time workers are covered in the same manner as full-time workers and in general qualification rules for additional benefits relate to employment time[104] and do as such not exclude part-time workers even though such benefits would also be lower for part-time workers due to their lower income. Whether or not part-time workers are unionised to the same extent as full-time workers is more difficult to say though since specific statistics for part-time workers have not been found. If part-time workers follow the same pattern that other groups with a less stable position on the labour market do, then they are likely to be subject to lower unionisation rates than full-time workers. Part-time work is more common in female-dominated sectors such as retail and health care services. However, whereas retail is a sector where unionisation rates are relatively low, health care services tend to hold higher unionisation rates.[105]

[2] Impact Analysis

The challenges for involuntary part-time workers in relation to in-work poverty are strongly linked to the number of hours they work, regardless of the household they live in. To some extent an involuntary part-time worker living in a working couple household with children and where the other working person has a full-time employment, will face less risks since such a couple is more likely to reach a disposable income above the poverty threshold.[106] However, considering that part-time work to such a high degree is an issue for women, there are other forms of social risks involved for

102. The regulations on calculation of income base for social security allowances are generally connected to the present working income based on the workers current employment and the income generated from that employment will thus be used for calculation of the benefits. The basic premises for how the income base for social security benefits is to be decided are found in Section 25 Social Security Code and additional specific rules for the various forms of social benefits are found in the sections governing each respective benefit.
103. Even though the increased number of days that are reserved for each parent have cause fathers to take out more days of parental leave, there is still a significant difference in how parental leave is divided between men and women. For further discussion. *see* Swedish National Social Security Agency, Socialförsäkringsrapport 2019:2 Jämställd föräldraförsäkring: Utvärdering av de reserverade månaderna i föräldraförsäkringen (Försäkringskassanm 2019).
104. As mentioned in relation to fixed-term workers earlier.
105. Kjellberg, *supra* n. 18 at 31-33.
106. Approximately 76% of full-time employment has been stated to generate an income above the threshold for in-work poverty, *see* Axel Cronert, and Joakim Palme, *Approaches to Social Investment and Their Implications for Poverty in Sweden and the European Union*, Global Challenges Working Paper Series, No. 4, pp. 9-10 (CROP, 2017).

part-time working women that would face a situation of poverty without the full-time working partner. Household types subject to the highest risks of in-work poverty as such, would most likely be single-parent households (i.e., one working person with children) and couple households with children where the involuntary part-time worker is the only person in work.[107]

The different forms of social security benefits, will also be set at lower levels for these workers due to their lower income, thus increasing the challenges for this group in case of, for example, sickness or unemployment. In addition, not having found a full-time job is also the main reason for working part-time, thus indicating that this group might be partially unemployed. However, partial unemployment benefits are subject to a stricter time frame than full-time unemployment benefits,[108] which could affect the situation of these workers in a negative sense from the perspective of in-work poverty. Not being able to cope with high demands in the job and/or personal health issues are also prominent as reasons for part-time work. In this regard it is worth highlighting the debate concerning the assessment of decreased working capacity as part of eligibility for sickness allowance and that the share of applications subject to rejections have increased, possibly generating a situation where there are persons feeling too sick to work full-time, but at the same time not being considered eligible for part-time sickness allowance.[109] It remains to be seen to what extent suggested legislative changes will result in a decrease of part-time work, because such a decrease could also quite likely contribute to a decrease of in-work poverty due to the strong link between working hours and in-work poverty. Trying to tackle the issue through other forms of changes in labour or social security law would possibly require changes to underlying principles, for example, the loss of income for which social security benefits are intended to cover.

§8.05 VUP GROUP 4: CASUAL AND PLATFORM WORKERS

The last VUP group is most likely also the group facing the highest vulnerability in relation to in-work poverty. However, also here some difficulties exist as concerns lack of reliable statistics. It is not unlikely that some of the workers included in the statistics on fixed-term and involuntary part-time workers in Table 8.3, could be casual or platform workers, but it is not possible to say how many are employed on shorter and/or intermittent temporary contracts, nor whether they are performing platform work. What is clear though, is that these workers do face specific challenges and risks for in-work poverty partly due to the form of employment as such and also due to legal uncertainties and potential misclassifications of their legal status.

107. Based on the figures found in Table 8.3.
108. The limit for part-time unemployment benefits is set at 60 weeks, compared to 90 weeks for full-time unemployment benefits in accordance with Article 7 Regulation on Unemployment Benefits.
109. A detailed picture of the problems for persons feeling too sick to work, but at the same time not being considered to have a decreased capacity for work and as such be denied sickness allowance, is provided in Altermark, *supra* n. 45.

[A] Composition of VUP Group 4

A clear idea of the composition of this VUP group is impossible to provide due to the difficulties with statistics. What could possibly be stated is that platform work seems to be more common among men than women, and a majority of those active in platform work are young.[110] Platform work is still a marginal part of the labour market in Sweden, and very few of those taking up platform work do so with the intention of having platform work as the main income.[111] However, there seems to be an increasing positive interest among jobseekers, and it is likely that it will become more common in the future.[112]

In relation to casual workers SCB do report statistics relating to intermittent and on-call workers aged 15-74 years, by including these workers in the category of hourly and on-call work.[113] However, those statistics include persons employed on general temporary employment, which can also be a long-term temporary contract for full-time work, as well as school holiday employments. What can be said based on those statistics is that: hourly and on-call employments are the most common forms of temporary employments in Sweden; more women than men are employed on these forms of contracts; in sectors dominated by women, foreign-born and young workers, such as health and care services and food and accommodation services, these forms of employments are much more common.[114] Even though hourly and on-call contracts are more common for workers below 25 or above 65 years old, it is an employment form that affects workers of all ages.[115]

Casual workers are also less likely to be members of a trade union. In 2017, 28% of the temporary employed without agreement on weekly working hours were members of a trade union, compared to 39% in 2006. For female, casual workers the most common sectors of activity are: health and care services; retail; hotel and restaurants; and education. For men, the most common industry sectors are: financial and business services; health and care services; transport; and retail.[116] With the exception of health and care services, where collective agreement coverage is high, the other sectors of activity are likely to be subject to lower rates of collective agreement coverage.[117] It is therefore not unlikely that these workers are subject to risks associated with not being covered by a collective agreement.

---

110. *See* Jenny Wahlbäck, Delningsekonomin och digitala plattformar – begrepp, omfattning och arbetsrättsliga regler, pp. 21-22 (SACO, 2018) and Linda Weidenstedt, Andrea Geissinger, and Monia Lougui, Varför gigga som matkurir? – Förutsättningar och förväntningar bakom okvalificerat gig-arbete, pp. 21-23 (Ratio, 2020).
111. Weidenstedt, et al., *supra* n. 110 at 21-23; Jon Erik Dølvik, and Kristin Jesnes, Nordic labour markets and the sharing economy – Report from a pilot project, TemaNord 2018:516, pp. 46-49 (Nordic Council of Ministers, 2018).
112. *See* Wahlbäck, *supra* n. 110 at 21-22, and Weidenstedt, et al., *supra* n. 110 at 21-23.
113. SCB, Utvecklingen för tidsbegränsat anställda 2005-2019, Sveriges officiella statistik, Statistiska meddelanden, p 8 (SCB, 2020).
114. *Ibid.*, at 2, 9-11 and 24.
115. Government White Paper 2019:5 *supra* n. 12 at 235-238 and SCB, *supra* n. 113 at p 1.
116. Government White Paper 2019:5 *supra* n. 12 at 240-245.
117. Exact figures for collective agreement coverage rates for different sectors of activity has not been found, but some indications could possibly be found based on figures for smaller

[B] Casual Workers: Notion and Relevant Legal Framework

The very flexible rules on temporary contracts in Sweden allow for intermittent forms of employment on the basis of both the general temporary employment and substitute employment, since neither of these employment forms holds requirements of the length of the contract, nor on minimum working hours. Current legal restrictions are therefore limited to the transformation rules for substitute and general temporary employment, whereby twelve months of temporary employment give priority for further reemployment with the employer, and more than two years of employment within a period of five years for the same employer will generate a transformation to a permanent employment.[118] However, since it is only time in employment that counts for the transformation, on-call or intermittent workers, who are only considered as employed when they are conducting work, will face longer periods before they reach this limit.[119] In this respect the proposed changes to the EPA, most likely to be implemented before the end of 2022, will provide important improvements for these workers. First, time in between employments will be counted as time in employment if the worker has had three or more separate temporary employments within one calendar month for the same employer.[120] The time in employment for transformation to a permanent contract will also be shortened to 12 months.[121] It is not unlikely that these changes will improve possibilities for intermittent workers to gain access to more stable employments. In addition, the new rules directed at intermittent employees concerning sickness allowance, as discussed earlier, will also serve to improve the loss of income protection for these workers in case of illness. However, one issue still remains to be solved and that is the unclarity concerning the number of weekly working hours an intermittent employee becoming permanently employed should be entitled to. This issue is as of yet not regulated and case law does not provide clear guidance.[122]

[C] Platform Workers: Notion and Relevant Legal Framework

In relation to platform work, the flexible Swedish legislation on temporary employment do give ample room for platform companies to make use of intermittent employment contracts, but it is not clear to what extent platforms engage persons as employees or

---

companies, with caution given to the fact that the share of smaller companies vary between sectors. For statistics, *see* Kjellberg, *supra* n. 18 at 134 and 175.

118. Articles 25 and 25 a EPA.
119. Government White Paper 2019:5 *supra* n. 12 at 234-238.
120. Article 3 paragraph 2 in the new EPA. The form of temporary employment referred to is the new specific temporary employment intended to replace the general temporary employment (Article 5 point 1 in the new EPA). To prevent abuse it will also be forbidden to employ on substitute contracts in order to evade this rule on calculation of employment time, Article 5 paragraph 2 in the new EPA. *See* Government draft bill, *supra* n. 15.
121. The shortened period of twelve months will apply for specific temporary employments, but for substitute employment the limit of two years will remain. Article 5 in the new EPA. *See* Government draft bill, *supra* n. 15.
122. Government White Paper 2019:5 *supra* n. 12 at 348-350 and 366-369.

as assignment workers (who could be conducting the work as self-employed). Media coverage concerning platform work has indicated that some companies take advantage of the very flexible regulations on temporary employments, hiring platform workers on short-term temporary contracts.[123] Practices are likely to vary between platforms and the legal classification of workers in accordance with the Swedish binary system could result in different outcomes depending on the business model of the platform.[124] A growing form of platform companies in Sweden is so-called umbrella companies, initially targeting persons wishing to take on assignments as self-employed, without having to set up their own business. In such cases, the worker and the client will agree on the work to be conducted and the remuneration for this work, assuring that the client signs a contract with the umbrella company. The umbrella company will take on the role as an employer for the duration of the agreed work and will sort out the invoicing of the client and pay salary to the worker after having deducted taxes, social security contributions, and a commission for its services from the payment of the client.[125]

There have been discussions as to whether umbrella companies should be considered to fall under the definition of a temporary work agency in the Temporary Agency Work Act,[126] but no cases have so far clarified this. Current developments seem to involve umbrella companies as an intermediate administrative employer on a more regular basis as a way for other platform companies to evade employer responsibilities. At the time being there is an interesting case pending concerning this construction, where a Foodora delivery rider was first employed by Foodora. However, when changing from bike to moped, the rider instead received a contract from the umbrella company Pay Salary in spite of the performance of work being continuously directed and supervised by the same managers at Foodora. The law suit against Foodora has been filed by the trade union Transport seeking to establish that the delivery rider shall be considered to have been employed by Foodora all the time.[127] In addition to being a highly interesting case for the further developments of platform work in Sweden, it is worth noting that the parties involved are also parties to a landmark collective agreement for the platform economy in Sweden.[128] The increasing attention and action

123. Examples of media coverage are the article series on gig-work in Sydsvenskan initiated with the article based on a journalist's own experiences as a bicycle delivery rider. *See* Dan Ivarsson, *Så pressar Foodora sina cykelbud att trampa fortare*, Newspaper article in Sydsvenskan, published 18.10.2020, available at https://www.sydsvenskan.se/2020-10-18/sa-pressar-foodora-sina-cykelbud-att-trampa-fortare (last accessed 03.06.2021).
124. Westregård, *supra* n. 61.
125. Government White Paper 2017:24, Ett arbetsliv i Förändring – hur påverkas ansvaret för arbetsmiljön?, pp. 161-165.
126. Westregård, *supra* n. 61.
127. The case is number A 154/21 in the Swedish Labour Court and the preparatory hearing is scheduled for late March 2022.
128. The first collective agreement specifically adapted to digital platforms was concluded between Transport and Foodora on 25 February 2021. The agreement consists of the blue-collar transport sector national agreement with a supplement adapted specifically for bicycle and moped delivery riders. This supplement is in other words a company specific collective agreement. Transportarbetareförbundet (2021) Budavtalet – Cykel och mopedbud.

taken by trade unions[129] is accompanied with rising interest among platform companies to improve credibility and legitimacy, which is a development that shows commonalities with the historical developments concerning temporary work agencies.[130] This could indicate that regulation of platform work in Sweden may very well be solved between the social partners, within the Swedish model, in a not too far future.

[D] Impact Analysis

The absence of reliable statistics makes it very difficult to draw any conclusions concerning in-work poverty for casual and platform workers in various households. What can be said is that the vulnerabilities and risks, found for fixed-term workers and part-time workers in relation to in-work poverty, are most likely exacerbated for casual workers due to the unpredictable working hours and income. For platform workers, this may be even worse since they may also be affected by a misclassification as self-employed. Even though there might be groups among these workers who are not having work as their main income, but rather as a complement for other forms of occupations such as studying, those that are depending on their income from work for their living are indeed in a precarious situation. Quite likely, it is among these groups of workers that we find some of those facing the worst problems of in-work poverty. The recently introduced changes in relation to on-call workers and sickness allowance[131] will provide better foreseeability for casual workers falling ill and could as such be considered an improvement. In addition, the coming changes to the EPA, shortening the time frame for when a temporary employment shall be transformed to a permanent employment and also increasing the possibility for intermittent workers to reach the time in employment required for transformation,[132] could further improve the situation.

§8.06 CONCLUSIONS

What can be concluded concerning in-work poverty in Sweden is that the problem is not related to the wage level as such. There may be some workers that fall outside the protective mechanisms of the Swedish model, and there are good reasons for the

129. For example, the white-collar workers union Unionen has directed attention towards these categories of workers, and the blue-collar workers union in the transport sector, Transport, has had specific campaigns directed at platform delivery riders. Information from trade union representatives during the Swedish national workshops for 'Working, Yet Poor'.
130. Carl Fredrik Söderqvist, and Victor Bernhardtz, Labor Platforms with Unions: Discussing the Law and Economics of a Swedish collective bargaining framework used to regulate gig work, Working paper 2019:57 (Swedish Entrepreneurship Forum, 2019).
131. As regulated in Section 27, Articles 16 a, 49 b and 49 c, Social Security Code. Briefly explained in the introduction earlier.
132. Notably a shorter time frame for the transformation from temporary to permanent employment, possibility for intermittent employees to have time in between employments counted for the transformation rules, and full-time work expressly being the main rule. *See* Government draft bill, *supra* n. 15.

Swedish social partners to intensify their strive to assure higher unionisation and collective agreement coverage rates. However, the problem of in-work poverty seems more strongly connected to the number of hours worked than to workplaces with very low wages. The regulatory structure that provides ample room for very flexible forms of employment in combination with social security structures designed on the basis of standard employment have generated a situation where workers with fixed-term and/or part-time employment face specific challenges. With less predictable working patterns and less stability in the employment, the worker will face higher risks of in-work poverty. Even though a large group of the workers facing the highest risks in these regards are likely to be younger workers in the process of establishing themselves on the labour market, those are not the only ones affected. Instead, workers with children, especially single parents or workers being the only in-work person in households with children are also affected by increased risks of in-work poverty.

Furthermore, women and foreign-born workers, who are over-represented among workers with unstable forms of employment and/or part-time work are facing specific vulnerabilities in relation to in-work poverty risks. The reason is that these workers are also to some extent more likely to be employed in sectors where collective agreement coverage is lower, and they also have a lower probability of trade union membership. In that sense, these workers will be less likely to be covered by the protection that the Swedish model is generally providing through collective agreements and strong social partners and instead left with the protection offered through legislation. In such a situation, it becomes of even higher importance to assure that legislation offers a strong protection.

The recently implemented changes in relation to sickness benefits for intermittent workers and the coming changes concerning transformation of fixed-term contracts and full-time employment as the main rule could thus generate changes that will also affect in-work poverty rates in Sweden. However, it remains to be seen what the consequences of the coming changes will be, not least since the semi-discretionary character of Swedish legislation allows the social partners an ample room for manoeuvre via collective agreements. It is thus also of importance that the social partners in Sweden start to address the issue of in-work poverty, with its causes and its consequences, in collective bargaining in the future. The current situation, where protection and benefits are less accessible for casual and or atypical workers, is a result of both legislation and collective agreement clauses being poorly adapted to the increased use of flexible forms of employment on the labour market. In relation to this both trade unions and employers' organisations need to take responsibility for finding solutions. It is for the social partners to assure that workers subject to flexible forms of employment are also able to gain from benefits regulated in collective agreements. Without such incentives for joining trade unions, atypical workers will remain unlikely members, and difficulties for turning decreasing membership trends will persist and continue to challenge the strength of the Swedish model. Unless the social partners manage to take responsibility and deal with some of the problems caused by the current blank spot of the Swedish model, the risk is that they actually undermine their own legitimacy for being the main regulators of the Swedish labour market.

CHAPTER 9
Working, Yet Poor: A Comparative Appraisal

Christina Hiessl

The present final chapter describes, compares, and analyses the situation of Vulnerable and Under-represented Persons (VUPs) in relation to in-work poverty in the seven countries studied in the 'Working, Yet Poor' project (Belgium, Germany, Italy, Luxembourg, the Netherlands, Poland, and Sweden). It connects the findings of the preceding chapters to empirical insights and broader considerations of the factors influencing poverty for each of the four focus groups. Based on these findings, it examines the potential of measures to tackle in-work poverty as part of an overall policy approach to combatting poverty.

§9.01 INTRODUCTION

As has been expressed throughout the chapters of the present book, paid labour stands out across countries as the overriding major pathway to avoiding poverty. In-work poverty rates of around 9% across the European Union (EU) as described in the introductory chapter compared to poverty rates close to 50% for the unemployed and almost 30% for the inactive.[1] As long as such a clear relationship between work and poverty reduction can be assumed to hold true in general, the pivotal element in any strategy to alleviate poverty may reasonably be to boost labour market participation. Yet, the emergence and persistence of vulnerable groups who are likely to fail to escape poverty through work puts such approaches into perspective – particularly where they

1. *See* Eurostat data at https://ec.europa.eu/eurostat/databrowser/view/ILC_LI04__custom_2223204/default/table?lang=en.

aim to make job creation simpler or more attractive by removing certain forms of protection for the worker.

In fact, since 2013, there has been a continuous increase in employment rates and fall in unemployment (including long-term unemployment) rates across the EU, and these developments continued even through 2020 in respect of employment and long-term unemployment.[2] These trends hold true for all of the countries studied in this book, although some countries display slightly later peaks (in 2014/15) for (long-term) unemployment. The share of people living in households with very low-work intensity[3] – as one component of the EU's AROP (at risk of poverty or social exclusion) indicator – has been on the decline since 2014. Such declining tendency can also be observed at least as from 2016 in all countries studied except Luxembourg and Sweden (which had under-average values to begin with).[4] During the same period, AROP rates for the general population have remained largely unchanged, even increasing slightly according to provisional data for the latest years.[5]

In other words, moving more people into employment has not resulted in a reduction of poverty rates – indicating that, for many, out-of-work poverty has been replaced by in-work poverty. The fact that this was accompanied by a decrease in severe material deprivation (SMD) levels indicates that this development has contributed to alleviating the worst forms of poverty, but not allowed more households to reach an income level which does not compromise their full participation in society. It thus appears all the more important to focus on the situation of VUPs, and to discuss how policy choices affect the reasons for their high risk to be working, yet poor.

In what follows, this chapter examines the situation of workers in the four VUP Groups as described in the introductory chapter, as it presents itself in the Belgian, Dutch, German, Italian, Luxembourgish, Polish, and Swedish context. For each of the VUP Groups, this examination is built around questions relating, *i.a.*, to the role played by the characteristics that make those groups vulnerable (a low skills level, the legal qualification as self-employed, or the low-hour or non-continuous nature of their work), but also to the reasons for workers to be part of those groups in the first place. Section 9.06 offers some tentative conclusions about the potential for policy approaches to avoid that, in an increasingly inclusive labour market, out-of-work poverty is merely replaced by in-work poverty for those excluded from various protective mechanisms.

---

2. *See* Eurostat data at https://ec.europa.eu/eurostat/databrowser/view/tesem010/default/table?lang=en; https://ec.europa.eu/eurostat/databrowser/view/tesem120/default/table?lang=en; and https://ec.europa.eu/eurostat/databrowser/view/tesem130/default/table?lang=en.
3. I.e., where working-age household members' combined working time is equal or less than 20% of their total work-time potential: *see* Eurostat definition at https://ec.europa.eu/eurostat/statistics-explained/index.php?title=Glossary:Persons_living_in_households_with_low_work_intensity.
4. *See* Eurostat data at https://ec.europa.eu/eurostat/databrowser/view/tipslc40/default/table?lang=en.
5. *See* Eurostat data at https://ec.europa.eu/eurostat/databrowser/view/tespm010/default/table?lang=en.

§9.02 VUP GROUP 1: LOW- OR UNSKILLED STANDARD EMPLOYMENT

[A] What Role Do Skills Play for Labour Market Perspectives?

The Italian contribution is the most instructive in terms of pointing out the inherent connection between the development of economic activity in different sectors, the consequent creation of a demand for skilled work, and the resulting return on educational investment. Arguably, in countries where a thriving business environment creates a high demand for skilled work, skill upgrades constitute a promising pathway to better paid employment, and those left to perform lower- or unskilled work will generally possess greater bargaining power relating to their wages. Conversely, inappropriate labour market opportunities for employment in higher-skilled occupations are likely to increase competition for low-skilled jobs and weaken such bargaining power to the point where workers will regularly be forced to accept poor wage levels to escape unemployment. While there are self-evidently numerous factors influencing the demand for skilled work, a discussion of which would go beyond the analysis conducted in the framework of the WorkYP project, several points are worth mentioning in this respect.

First, issues of skills mismatches and overqualification are commonplace in all countries studied. As analysed in a recent Eurofound study,[6] labour shortages are on the rise across the EU, fuelled, *i.a.*, by demographic change. Between 2013 and 2019, the EU-wide job vacancy rate doubled to 2.3%, and stood at a level over 3% in six countries including Belgium, Germany, and the Netherlands. As pointed out most illustratively in the German contribution, such skill shortages are often most salient in areas that do not necessarily require tertiary education, but are critically dependent on vocational training with a strong practical component (notably work-based learning leading to formally recognised qualifications). Belgium, where individuals with completed tertiary education make up almost half of the workforce, has the second highest job vacancy rate in the EU,[7] and more than 40% of jobseekers are long-term unemployed (the fourth highest value EU-wide).[8] This is the likely reason for the fact that European Union Statistics on Income and Living conditions (EU-SILC) data do not indicate a particularly significant correlation between poverty and 'low-skilled work' under the broad definition described in the introductory chapter. By contrast, in all countries, workers whose educational attainment does not surpass the lower secondary level are the most susceptible to poverty both in and out of work. In Belgium, Germany, and Poland, a low level of education emerges as the single most important factor increasing the risk of in-work poverty in the EU-SILC extracts – both for all employed persons and for the subset of low-skilled employees, and notably also for

6. *See* Eurofound, Tackling Labour Shortages in EU Member States (2021), https://www.eurofound.europa.eu/publications/report/2021/tackling-labour-shortages-in-eu-member-states.
7. *See* Eurostat data at https://ec.europa.eu/eurostat/statistics-explained/index.php?title=Job_vacancy_statistics.
8. *See* Eurostat data at https://ec.europa.eu/eurostat/statistics-explained/index.php?title=Unemployment_statistics_and_beyond.

non-standard forms of employment. Finally, it is apparent from several country chapters that the connection between demand and supply is not unidirectional. In other words, countries with vocational training systems that 'produce' a workforce with readily usable skills in sectors with a significant growth potential are also more likely to stimulate the development of business activity in need of those skills.

All in all, a focus on skills development appears to have a considerable potential for reducing in-work poverty in a long-term, sustainable manner, apart from other beneficial effects, e.g., in terms of job quality and economic development. This raises the question whether VET (vocational education and training) systems in their current form succeed at encouraging and empowering those able and willing to upgrade their skills – focusing both on those in and out of employment.

[B] Are Workers Enabled and Encouraged to Acquire Relevant Skills and Develop Them Further Throughout Their Lives?

All country chapters point to the uneven offer of VET and life-long learning, which tends to exacerbate differences. Across countries, low-skilled workers are the least likely to be offered further training, despite the fact that they would stand to benefit most from skills upgrades. Across the EU, less than a quarter of adults (aged 25-64) whose education level is lower secondary or below are participating in VET. Persons with an upper secondary degree are almost twice, tertiary degree holders almost thrice as likely to be involved in such training.[9] There are, however, sizeable differences among countries.

Poland is a particularly noteworthy example of a country with a high educational attainment among its population,[10] which may however be insufficiently nourished by skills development throughout working life. In 2016, the level of participation in adult training was overall just more than half of the EU average, and particularly low for those with a lower education level (5.4%, i.e., less than a quarter of the EU average). This indicates a high risk of workers with a high potential being trapped in low-skilled jobs because their skills are not adapted to the demands of the labour market. The contribution notes that employees have no right to training or its financing vis-à-vis the employer, so that companies may in practice continue to focus their training investment on higher-skilled workers. At the other end of the scale, Sweden stands out as the EU country with the highest overall level of participation in adult training, and most notably the participation of the group with the lowest education level (over 45%) is twice as high as the EU average. This may be instrumental in avoiding long-term unemployment (where the Swedish share among the unemployed is the lowest in the

9. *See* Eurostat data at https://circabc.europa.eu/ui/group/d14c857a-601d-438a-b878-4b4cebd0e10f/library/ac6f3889-ab25-4f75-9c7a-de997f65e2db?p = 1&n = 10&sort = modified_DESC. Note that the most recent available Eurostat data stem from 2016 and are to be updated in 2022.
10. *See* Eurostat data at https://ec.europa.eu/eurostat/databrowser/view/EDAT_LFSE_03__custom_1739499/default/table?lang = en.

EU[11]) as a major source of poverty, which risks causing downward wage pressures and consequentially in-work poverty risks. Germany and the Netherlands in turn stand out as the only two EU countries where more than half of all companies employ IVT (initial vocational training) participants (notably apprentices).[12] This focus on training provided by companies certainly plays a key role in assuring the relevance of skills and keeping unemployment at a very low level[13] despite high labour costs.

A common feature of vocational training systems in the three countries just highlighted is a high degree of ownership by the social partners. This seems highly relevant for ensuring that VET is both geared towards including the skillsets desired by employers and focused on not leaving vulnerable groups such as VUP 1 workers behind. Germany, the Netherlands, and Sweden are also among the frequently quoted best practice examples of mechanisms for collective bargaining-based anticipatory re-skilling in the context of collective redundancies,[14] such as the transition agreements mentioned in the Swedish contribution.

A Belgian initiative obliging employers with ten or more employees to provide training during at least two days per year has not yet been subject to a thorough evaluation of effectiveness. A mechanism even more difficult to evaluate are general legislative or case law-based duties for employers to offer training that prevents a worker's redundancy. The fact that the Netherlands and Sweden, where this is an express statutory duty, excel compared to other EU countries with a view to low-skilled workers' participation in training may indicate that this constitutes an important stimulus for employers to proactively train their workforce before skills become obsolete.

Another measure evaluated as effective in several country chapters is the provision of targeted financial support for employees undergoing training while remaining in employment, through cost compensation and/or wage subsidies. The Italian contribution describes the introduction and evolution of a right to an individual job placement allowance, conditional upon participation in vocational retraining. As the system in its current form has become applicable only as from 2021, an evaluation may be premature. By contrast, first encouraging evaluations indicate the effectiveness of reforms in 2018/19 in Germany, which expanded instruments of public cost compensation and wage subsidies for in-work training participation for low-skilled workers. A complex set of criteria is to ensure channelling most support towards small and medium-sized enterprises (SMEs) (which are otherwise most reluctant to provide

11. *See* Eurostat data at https://ec.europa.eu/eurostat/databrowser/view/une_ltu_a/default/table?lang=en.
12. *See* Eurostat data at https://ec.europa.eu/eurostat/databrowser/view/trng_cvt_34s/default/table?lang=en.
13. *See* Eurostat data at https://ec.europa.eu/eurostat/databrowser/view/UNE_RT_A_H__custom_1183575/bookmark/table?lang=en&bookmarkId=ae3e21b6-7566-4f19-a7ea-31c0031ab579.
14. *See*, e.g., EESC, Social dialogue as an important pillar of economic sustainability and the resilience of economies taking into account the influence of lively public debate in the Member States. Exploratory opinion, 2021/C 10/03 (2021), https://eur-lex.europa.eu/legal-content/EN/TXT/?uri=uriserv%3AOJ.C_.2021.010.01.0014.01.ENG&toc=OJ%3AC%3A2021%3A010%3ATOC.

training), those workers most in need of training, and training programmes most likely to enhance employability.

Several country chapters refer to efforts to stimulate training participation during furlough or short-time work in the COVID-19 crisis. A German evaluation raised concerns about employers' pronounced reluctance to provide training in light of economic uncertainties, triggering a reform to enhance incentives for companies. A Dutch initiative obliged employers to enable training activities among workers for whom wage subsidies were received, subject to oversight by the works councils. Demand for government-funded advice and training schemes for this purpose was high.

[C] Are Workers Enabled and Encouraged to Find Employment That Matches Their Skills?

Measures to enable jobseekers to find suitable employment range from placement services and training measures to subsidies encouraging the hiring of jobseekers facing difficulties due to their skills level and/or the duration of unemployment. Substantial differences in the level of ambition of active labour market policies (ALMPs) are indicated by comparative statistics on ALMP spending (ranging, among the countries studied, from 0.42% of GDP in Poland to 1.25% in Sweden).[15] At the same time, all of the countries studied combine such mechanisms of support with those which gradually increase the pressure to end a situation of unemployment. Such pressures are generally based on the threat of facing poverty in unemployment – through benefit sanctions for failure to comply with job search criteria, and through depreciation in the benefit level over time. The countries studied differ widely both regarding the concept of *suitable work*, which the beneficiary must actively search and accept, and, perhaps even more crucially, regarding the speed and extent to which an unemployed person's income decreases in typical cases.

At one end of the scale, Belgium, which generally excels in terms of low in-work poverty rates across the board, only obliges beneficiaries to accept work corresponding to their usual occupation or to a related profession. Beneficiaries' skills and training remain relevant throughout the period of receiving unemployment insurance benefits. While the amount of the benefit and its relation to past wages decrease over the period of receipt, there is a non-means-tested minimum for which there is no temporary limit.

By contrast, in Germany, Poland, and Sweden, the majority of the unemployed today is not even receiving any insurance-based benefits.[16] In Germany, the discussion about a system under which more than two-thirds of the unemployed depend on a fully means-tested assistance benefit (because they do not fulfil the conditions for insurance benefits in the first place, have exhausted their period of entitlement, or would remain below the existence minimum with the benefit amount) is particularly vocal and fuels current reform debates. As is common for means-tested assistance benefits in all

15. *See* OECD data at https://www.oecd.org/employment/activation.htm.
16. *See* OECD data at https://www.oecd.org/els/soc/SOCR_UBPseudoCoverageRates.xlsx.

countries, they are set far below the relative poverty line, and benefit sanctions might make the amount undercut the SMD level. The Swedish contribution describes a concerning trend of declining membership in the (voluntary) unemployment funds, with low-wage workers most likely to drop out of coverage. This adds to general risks of jobseekers being driven into low-skilled, low-paid work, as constituted also by benefit conditionality mandating the take-up of work providing wages as low as 90% of the unemployment benefit. Such concerns are even more preeminent for the situation in Poland, where just more than 15% of the unemployed are entitled to insurance-based benefits.[17]

All in all, driving overqualified jobseekers into low-skilled, underpaid jobs appears a questionable approach to problems of misalignment of a worker's skills with labour market needs. Arguably, such policies threaten to result not only in in-work poverty for those concerned, but also to even more severe poverty among the low-educated, who are 'crowded out' of low-skilled jobs and end up in long-term unemployment.

[D] What Are the Main Instruments to Prevent Poverty for VUP 1 Workers?

[1] Instruments Concerning the Wage Level

Minimum wage systems fulfil the crucial function of creating a wage floor for those whose individual bargaining power is limited, *i.a.*, due to the skills level of the occupation. The German chapter points to the (unsurprising) outcome that 'poor sectors' with a high share of low-skilled work were most affected by the introduction of a statutory minimum wage in 2015.

Considering that, at present, none of the countries studied meets the first 'Kaitz' criterion (minimum wage of 60% of the median wage), earning a minimum wage will not necessarily protect against falling below the relative poverty line set at 60% of the medium household income. Sweden – a country where minimum wages are set exclusively via collective bargaining – is one of only two countries in the EU meeting the second 'Kaitz' criterion (50% of the average wage).[18] This already points to the core importance of coverage by collective agreements for VUP 1 workers' risk of being affected by poverty. In all of the countries studied except Poland, collective agreements have a major role to play in determining working conditions and notably wage levels. While union membership has dwindled to levels around or beneath 20% in three of the seven countries and now includes more than half of the workforce only in Belgium and

17. Ibid.
18. *See* European Commission (2020), Impact assessment accompanying the Proposal for a Directive of the European Parliament and of the Council on adequate minimum wages in the European Union, Commission Staff Working Document, SWD/2020/245 final. Available at https://eur-lex.europa.eu/legal-content/EN/TXT/?uri=CELEX%3A52020SC0245, pp. 4 et seqq.

Sweden (and about a third of it in Italy and Luxembourg),[19] the importance of collective agreements reaches far beyond this. Due to mechanisms such as sector-wide extension of agreements and erga omnes application by covered employers, collective agreement coverage rates are put at around or more than half of the workforce in all studied countries except Poland (reaching levels around 90% in Belgium and Sweden). Moreover, these coverage rates frequently underestimate the wider impact of collectively agreed standards through mechanisms such as employer's voluntary adoption, references in individual labour contracts, conditionality in public procurement, or judicial interpretation.

While statistics on the specific unionisation and/or collective bargaining coverage rates of VUP 1 workers are missing, the Swedish contribution refers to differences between white-and blue-colour workers as a particularly relevant proxy for skills levels. In this regard, the general decline in unionisation levels in the Swedish private sector over the past 15 years was substantially more pronounced for blue-collar workers. This is relevant for collective bargaining coverage, as in Sweden there are no sector-wide extensions of collective agreements. Poor sectors in turn are linked to below-average or even negligible collective bargaining coverage in most countries. In Poland, where collective bargaining generally happens on the company level and is largely restricted to large companies and the public sector, coverage is virtually absent in poor sectors. By contrast, the systematic sector-wide extension of collective agreements in Belgium and the Netherlands even in sectors with very low union affiliation ensures extensive coverage also in most poor sectors.

The significance of collective bargaining coverage for low-skilled workers is emphasised notably in the German chapter: while the above-mentioned (*see* last subsection) reform of German unemployment benefits, which exacerbated pressures to accept every job offer, is found to have been instrumental in maintaining a very large low-wage sector[20] at times of strong economic growth, its original expansion happened much earlier and coincided with the beginning of strong decline in collective bargaining coverage rates.

It needs to be stressed that, despite the overall link between collective bargaining coverage and wage adequacy, not all collective agreements provide protection against low wages, particularly for low-skilled workers. The Italian contribution highlights the emergence of 'pirate' collective agreements (i.e., those signed by non-representative unions) and their inadequate wage scales. Also, derogations *in peius* are a common feature of collective agreements in several countries, and sometimes affect wage levels – e.g., by means of derogations from sector-level agreements by collective bargaining at company level. Poland stands out by enabling even the suspension of provisions in individual employment contracts by 'suspensive agreements' between the employer and a trade union or ad hoc representatives, which are widely used in practice.

Particular attention is warranted for employees not covered by any form of minimum wage standard. In light of the universal applicability of statutory minimum

19. Ibid, pp. 6 et seqq.
20. *See* Eurostat data at https://ec.europa.eu/eurostat/databrowser/view/earn_ses_pub1s/default/table?lang=en and https://ec.europa.eu/eurostat/web/labour-market/earnings/database.

wages (with few exceptions) in five out of the seven countries studied, this is primarily an issue concerning Italy and Sweden. In Italy, well-established case law deduces fair wage standards from pertinent collective agreements signed by the most representative social partner organisations, even if the employment relationship at issue is not covered by any particular agreement. By contrast, in the Swedish system with its strong union movement and employers' widespread membership in employers' associations, cases in which employers are neither bound by a collective agreement nor adjusting their wage policy to the rates in relevant collective agreements, have apparently been rare so far. Yet, scattered court decisions evidence that the sectoral collective agreement is used as a benchmark for determining wage entitlements in case of a 'considerable difference' between the contractual stipulations and the minimum envisaged for the sector.

[2] Instruments Concerning Wage-Replacing Benefits

As standard employees, VUP 1 workers are basically covered by all benefit entitlements under labour law and social security. Belgium is the last country to gradually abolish differences between white- and blue-collar employees under statutory law. Such differences continue to be relevant for entitlements based on collective agreements in several countries, though. Moreover, domestic workers as a particularly vulnerable subgroup of VUP Group 1 are likely to be excluded from the scope of some legislative protections, as pointed out by the Belgian contribution in relation to sick pay and suspension due to economic causes.

As emphasised by the Swedish contribution, even if VUP 1 workers have the same entitlements as other workers, more frequent and longer spells of sickness or unemployment put them more at risk of exhausting maximum durations, and lower wage levels mean that any less-than-100% replacement rate may push them close to or below the income poverty level. Although some countries' benefit systems are coined to take low wages and the family constellation into account so as to avoid poverty, none of them excludes entirely that the reduction of income in these situations causes the household's income to fall below the threshold of (relative) income poverty. This holds true even for Belgium, where the benefit system is characterised by a high degree of awareness of poverty risks in this respect.

Most recently, crisis-related measures such as short-time work have self-evidently had consequences in terms of reduced income for the employees affected, though to different degrees in the countries studied. Those were designed with specific attention for low-wage workers risking to fall below the poverty line in some but not all countries. The German chapter specifically refers to criticism directed at a short-term work system with flat-rate benefits and no minimum allowance for those at risk of poverty.

[E] Conclusions

As highlighted in the Italian contribution, among the four focus groups, VUP Group 1 appears as the one comparatively best protected against risks of in-work poverty. Focusing on this group underscores, first, the key relevance of policies countering declining trends in collective bargaining, especially tendencies for the most vulnerable, most 'replaceable' categories of workers to be excluded. At the same time, it evidences the potentially crucial role of skills policies and ALMPs – so as to provide opportunities for higher-skilled work for those able and willing to do it, and avoid that an 'inflation of qualifications' among applicants for low-skilled jobs make those with an actually low level of education even more vulnerable to exploitation. In this context, policy approaches exerting excessive pressure on the unemployed to accept the 'first best job' are of particular concern.

The findings discussed in this section also illustrate the importance of studying different VUP groups together. Notably, the extent to which performing low-skilled work in poor sectors increases the risk of poverty is particularly pronounced in Luxembourg, i.e., the one country where standard employment still covers more than 70% of the workforce. It is much less evident in the Netherlands, where the share of VUP 1 workers among the workforce is 2-3 times lower than in Luxembourg. This indicates that, in a country with strong protections for standard employment and few barriers to self-employed and atypical work, the most precarious forms of low-skilled work may have been largely moved outside the scope of VUP Group 1.

§9.03 VUP GROUP 2: SOLO AND BOGUS SELF-EMPLOYMENT

[A] Why do Workers Choose to Work as Self-Employed?

Across the EU, one in seven employed persons is self-employed. The share of self-employed workers among the EU's workforce has been gradually declining in recent decades, by about 1.5 percentage points since the early 2000s.[21] With the sole exception of Belgium, the countries studied in the WorkYP project are characterised by either very high or very low shares of the self-employed among their workforce: Italy, the Netherlands, and Poland are among the top four countries (with shares of 18%-21%), whereas Germany, Luxembourg, and Sweden are three out of just four EU countries with a share below 10%. The overall decreasing trend holds true for all these countries with the notable exception of the Netherlands, where the share of self-employed workers has increased by more than 4 percentage points in the last 15 years.

Much caution is called for when basing conclusions about the effects of regulation on such trends in overall numbers. As has been stressed elsewhere,[22] those are

21. *See* Eurostat data at https://ec.europa.eu/eurostat/databrowser/view/LFST_HHSETY__custom_1957254/default/bar?lang=en.
22. *See* Christina Hiessl, National Approaches to Collective Bargaining for the Self-Employed, in Collective Bargaining for Self-Employed Workers in Europe (Bernd Waas & Christina Hiessl ed. 2021) 266.

likely to obscure important developments – e.g., where the decline of 'traditional' forms of self-employed activity (e.g., agricultural) counterbalances a surge in 'new forms' of self-employment in the service sector. To obtain a better understanding of the impact of regulation as described further in this section, it is thus useful to additionally pay attention to the question of voluntariness of self-employed work performance.

First, the numbers themselves evidence that self-employment tends to decrease at times of favourable labour market developments, which create opportunities for being hired as an employee. This already indicates that, when given the choice, the majority of workers will shy away from self-employment. Results from the EU's 2017 Labour Force Survey (LFS)[23] imply that one in six self-employed persons would prefer to work as an employee, whereas the opposite is true for just one in eleven employees. For economically dependent solo self-employed workers as defined by that LFS,[24] the share of such involuntary self-employment is almost one-third. The LFS does not provide reliable country-specific data for most of the countries studied. While the Dutch involuntariness rate appears slightly below average in the survey, national data of 2019 as referred to in the country chapter evidences that 20% are not solo self-employed by choice. More than a quarter of the Belgian, and more than 40% of the Italian solo self-employed surveyed in the LFS indicated wishing to work as employees.[25] The Polish survey cited in the country chapter even indicates that the vast majority of self-employed workers would prefer hired labour; one in two has become self-employed at the request of the principal.

Regulation in turn influences the choice between employed and self-employed work in a twofold way: first by impacting the parties' motives to prefer one type of contract over the other, and second by limiting the choice of contract in light of the factual situation.

[1] Motives to Prefer Self-Employment over Employment – For Workers and Principals

The conclusion of an employment contract entails a variety of obligations for the employer, most notably under tax, social security, and labour law. In all European jurisdictions, these obligations can be (partly) limited or avoided by a principal working with independent contractors instead. However, national systems diverge widely as to how much more favourable this option turns out for the principal compared to hiring employees, and as to whether it also entails (perceived or actual) benefits for the worker.

A prime example of a country where the 'cost advantage' of self-employment is significant is the Netherlands. Under Dutch law, self-employed activity is connected

23. *See* Eurostat data at https://ec.europa.eu/eurostat/statistics-explained/index.php?title=Self-employment_statistics#in_2_self-employed_persons_highly_satisfied_with_their_current_job.
24. I.e., solo self-employed workers who have worked during the last 12 months for only one or for a dominant client, with the latter determining even their working hours.
25. *See* Eurostat data at https://ec.europa.eu/eurostat/databrowser/view/LFSO_17PSCB__custom_1791320/default/table?lang=en.

not only to lower social security contributions, but also to a significantly lower tax burden. The fact that lower taxes make the self-employed option appear very attractive not only for principals but also for workers is seen as a key reason for the rapid growth of the share of the self-employed in the Netherlands. As indicated in the last subsection, the share of involuntary self-employment is much lower than in the other countries where the self-employed make up an unusually large share of the workforce.

A sizable (short-term) cost advantage exists also in Germany, where the exclusion of the self-employed from social insurance is most comprehensive, so that the self-employed are by default not even required to pay contributions for pension insurance. However, other than in the Netherlands, this advantage appears much more as a strict quid pro quo in return for social protection being reduced to a minimum (fully means-tested social assistance benefits far below the relative poverty line in case of insufficient reserves for sickness, unemployment, old age, or economic crisis). Therefore, the debate in Germany focuses less on problems of privileges which would make self-employment unjustifiably attractive, and more on the very high poverty risks of those who fail to sufficiently invest in alternatives to state social security.

[2] Legal Limits to Choosing the Form of Contract

Self-employment is essentially a residual category, which may be performed under different forms of civil law contracts not regarded as an employment contract. All European jurisdictions stipulate the principle of primacy of facts in some form: the legal consequences of an employment relationship can never be avoided simply by a contractual designation. There are significant differences between countries, though.

First, there are nuances as to whether the will of the parties has any influence on the legal characterisation of a contract in case of doubt. Approaches in the countries studied range from including the will of the parties as a formal statutory criterion (as in Belgium) to an express rejection of attributing any importance to it (as in the Netherlands after a recent judicial turnaround). Second, self-evidently, legal definitions of the employment contract are not uniform across countries. While an in-depth comparison of individual definitions applied in the countries studied would be beyond the scope of this report, it is evident from comparative research on their interpretation in case law[26] that notably the following examples of 'strategies' for avoiding a classification as an employment contract will likely have different chances of succeeding in different jurisdictions: payment per completed assignment instead of hourly remuneration; free determination of working hours and methods by the worker; use of own materials and equipment; permission to use substitutes or assistants to perform the work; work under framework contracts with no formal obligation to complete individual assignments; lack of concrete instructions and control mechanisms for the employer. Third, in all countries except Belgium and Luxembourg, certain distinctions

26. *See* Christina Hiessl, Case Law on the Classification of Platform Workers: Cross-European Comparative Analysis and Tentative Conclusions, in Comparative Labour Law & Policy Journal 42.2 (2021).

exist also within the group of self-employed workers. Therefore, misclassifications – with significant consequences for the contract's 'costliness' for the principal on the one hand and the worker's protection (*i.a.*, against poverty) on the other – are an issue even if the contractual relationship does genuinely not imply the existence of an employment contract. Such a 'layered' approach is particularly pronounced in Germany and Italy, where the law defines a number of subcategories to which various stipulations of social security and/or labour law are made applicable in a piecemeal fashion. However, as of today, certain deviations exist also in jurisdictions with a basically binary approach to the employment/self-employment dichotomy, such as the Netherlands and Sweden. In this context, the will of the parties is irrelevant in all countries.

The criteria of relevance for self-employed persons to fall under a legally defined category entitled to certain protections are essentially the following:

- (mainly) personal work performance: employee-like persons in Germany; non-entrepreneurial self-employment, 'co.co.co' and 'hetero-organised' work in Italy; 'persons performing gainful employment' in Poland; dependent contractors in Sweden;
- duration/continuity of the contractual relationship: co.co.co and hetero-organised work in Italy;
- organisation of work methods by the principal: hetero-organised work in Italy;
- prior agreement on work methods with the principal: co.co.co in Italy;
- dependence on one dominant client: employee-like persons in Germany; dependent contractors in Sweden;
- absence of an own business structure of a certain complexity and/or working in a way similar to employees: contractors falling under the Dutch Minimum Wage Law; hetero-organised work in Italy; persons performing gainful employment in Poland; dependent contractors in Sweden;
- absence of a registered business: civil contracts in Poland (including those falling under the Minimum Wage Act);
- work under specific types of contract (mandate or comparable): workers falling under the Minimum Wage Act in Poland;
- work in specific sectors or occupations. This can be either a positive criterion for inclusion in protective standards (e.g., pension insurance in Germany) or a basis for exemption (e.g., from the concept of hetero-organised work in Italy).

The Italian example is perhaps most noteworthy in terms of targeted policy emerging in reaction to the 'popularity' of hiring independent contractors. A number of relatively recent developments in legislation and case law, which introduced new mandatory dividing lines within the group of self-employed workers, have extended the definition of existing groups, and strengthened their rights vis-à-vis the principal and under social security. Similar forms of targeted measures have more recently been enacted in the other two countries whose share of self-employment among the workforce is particularly high in European comparison: the Netherlands and Poland. In fact, as discussed *infra* at §9.03[B][1], Italy, the Netherlands, and Poland are the only ones among the example countries which (after relatively recent reforms) have some form of minimum wage standard in place for self-employed workers. By contrast, the numerous distinctions among the self-employed under German law are less recent and mainly serve to delimitate access to aspects of social security rights, which in other countries would often be guaranteed to all entrepreneurs. Similarly, the Swedish concept of dependent contractor has been in existence for a long time. While both countries have granted collective bargaining rights to a subcategory of the self-employed for decades, the practical importance of collective wage-setting for the self-employed has never extended to the vast majority of sectors and occupations (*see infra* at §9.03[B][1]).

Another aspect which cannot be exhaustively discussed within the ramifications of this chapter is the existence of effective remedies against bogus self-employment. One major challenge in this respect is the complexity of the notion of employee in all countries. In this respect, also administrative procedures for obtaining certainty about the classification of a contractual relationship in advance may play a non-negligible role. In most countries, such procedures only exclude a retroactive reclassification of the purportedly self-employed worker as an employee by the social security institutions (not the courts), and only in case of truthful and complete reporting of all aspects and later changes of the contractual relationship. By contrast, the Dutch system, which is very widely used in practice and originally granted full protection against later reclassification, is considered to have contributed to the rise in solo-self-employment in the recent past (contrary to international trends). A related aspect is invoked in the Polish contribution, which refers to the scarcity of fines for inaccurate classification.

A more drastic measure to curb bogus self-employment in a particularly sensitive sector was taken in Germany. In the wake of sizeable outbreaks of COVID-19 infections in slaughterhouses, companies of 50 or more workers have been prohibited as of 2021 from engaging self-employed contractors in the core business of the meat industry. Similarly, Luxembourg law defines the status for certain occupations by default – to the effect that professional sportsmen and coaches are considered self-employed, while artistic performers have the status of employees.

[B] What Are the Main Instruments to Prevent Poverty for VUP 2 Workers?

[1] Instruments Concerning the Wage Level

Statutory minimum wage regulation applies to the self-employed only in exceptional cases. This includes the probably ‘most protected’ of all subgroups of self-employed in the countries studied – hetero-organised workers in Italy. Their rights are – according to the prevailing interpretation – almost indistinguishable from those of employees, and accordingly include fair wage standards. Other groups of self-employed do not have access to the right to a fair wage – which in Italy serves as a vehicle for minimum wage protection via judicial interpretation. In 2016, i.e., one year after the introduction of pertinent regulation in Italy, Poland included self-employed persons working under a mandate or similar contract in the scope of its Minimum Wage Act. In 2018, the Netherlands followed suit, including non-entrepreneurial self-employed persons in the scope of the Minimum Wage law. In all three countries, these reforms ensure the applicability of the same wage level as for employees to a subgroup of the self-employed. Since, in a country like the Netherlands, gross wages for the self-employed would actually need to be higher than for employees to make up for lacking social insurance coverage (*see infra* next subsection), a recent social partner proposal suggests the introduction of a presumption of employee status in case of an hourly rate beneath EUR 30-35. Such regulation would be unique among the countries studied and arguably constitute a functional equivalent to a minimum wage where the principal seeks to avoid the applicability of the legal presumption.

Minimum wage protection via collective agreements is somewhat more important for the self-employed than statutory wages. Yet, although trade union representation of the self-employed is an emerging phenomenon in all of the countries studied except Luxembourg, its meaningfulness in terms of establishing protective standards based on collective agreements remains very limited and typically concentrated in certain sectors. With statistics on unionisation rates among the self-employed usually not available, these can only be estimated based on membership information provided by individual trade unions. Even for Sweden, which was the first country to introduce bargaining rights for the self-employed, the white-collar union's self-employed membership of 10,000 would amount to less than 2.5% of all self-employed in the country.

Concerns about violations of competition law constitute a barrier to collective bargaining activities for the self-employed in most of the countries studied.[27] Only in the Netherlands competition authorities have strived to provide clarity about the criteria for the legality of agreements. Apart from such concerns, national law in most of the countries studied allows for collective bargaining activities for the self-employed either comprehensively (Italy, the Netherlands) or for specific subgroups of the self-employed: employee-like persons and home workers in Germany, persons performing gainful employment in Poland, and dependent contractors in Sweden – i.e., effectively groups working without (significant) help from auxiliaries, in a way comparable to employees. The Belgian contribution emphasises the lack of a legal basis regulating the effect of the agreements that are concluded for the self-employed in practice.

At present, major collective agreements for the self-employed in individual sectors or occupations exist in Germany, Italy, the Netherlands, and Sweden, but there are no signs of a larger-scale spill-over to other sectors. By exception, a vitalisation of collective bargaining activities seems to have been achieved by an Italian measure which included hetero-organised contractors into all protections available for subordinate employees, but at the same time allowed the social partners to flexibly and comprehensively deviate from this rule. This regulation, introduced in 2015, led to the conclusion of almost twenty collective agreements for this category of contractors in

27. *See* Hiessl, *supra* n. 22 at 266 et seqq.

the two years that followed. In the Netherlands, a small number of collective agreements contain minimum remuneration rates both for employees and for self-employed persons – currently for the areas of architecture, public broadcasting, and theatre and dance.

[2] Instruments Concerning Wage-Replacing Benefits

As of today, all countries studied provide for mandatory social insurance at least for certain groups of self-employed workers in certain branches of insurance. Apart from that, the self-employed are usually entitled to tax-financed social benefits in the same fashion as employees. Mandatory wage-replacing benefits paid by the employer extend to self-employed workers only in exceptional cases – as in that of hetero-organised work in Italy. German home workers and employee-like persons are entitled to annual and care leave on the same basis as employees. The general lack of coverage by employer-sponsored benefits affects sick pay entitlements in all countries, but may have further consequences particularly in countries where top-up benefits to social security entitlements are regularly granted through collective agreements (as in Sweden).

In line with Directive 2010/41/EU, all countries envisage some form of maternity benefit also for the self-employed, possibly with an alternative right to a qualified replacement. Family benefits are typically universal or means-tested, and thus granted irrespective of employed or self-employed status. Apart from this, a main dividing line can be drawn between countries which generally cover the self-employed either under the same schemes as employees (or analogous schemes) for all main branches of social insurance, and those which, as a rule, exclude them from the wage-replacing benefit schemes in case of sickness, invalidity, unemployment, old age, and death.

The latter is most notably the case for Germany, where the self-employed are only obliged to obtain healthcare insurance (from a private provider with risk-dependent premiums) and must otherwise fall back on social assistance if their income sinks below the existence minimum (which essentially corresponds to severe material deprivation). The only category included in the scheme applicable to employees (including contribution payment by the principal) is the small group of home workers. For some other categories defined by their occupation or a very pronounced form of dependence on a single client, inclusion in pension systems and/or accident insurance is provided. For other categories, even access to voluntary coverage under the state social security system is limited. At present, among the self-employed in Germany, insurance coverage for sickness and unemployment is unusual, and old-age provision has been found insufficient in three out of four cases. Dutch law provides only for mandatory inclusion in the (flat-rate benefit) pension system on the same basis as employees. In Poland, civil law contractors are included in the pension and industrial injury system, but contribute based on the minimum wage or a declared amount.

In the other countries studied, all branches of social security extend to all self-employed persons (with the exception of insurance against industrial accidents and occupational disease, which is reserved to employees in Belgium). Yet, also in these countries, some more or less significant differences exist in the individual branches. Generally, sickness, disability, industrial accident, and parental leave allowances tend to follow similar rules regarding their full or modified extension to self-employed workers, with the aforementioned exceptions. The Belgian contribution points to differences in benefit amount compared to employees' entitlements, as maternity, paternity, and long-term incapacity benefits are granted as flat-rate rather than income-dependent benefits. In Sweden, the self-employed are entitled to benefits only after a waiting period.

Unemployment benefits are the one benefit type for which certain differences between employees and self-employed exist in all countries. The Luxembourgish contribution refers to minor aspects in this respect; the Swedish chapter to the impossibility to combine partial unemployment benefits with part-time self-employed work, whereas a comparable combination is possible for employees. In Italy, co.co.co and non-entrepreneurial self-employed are entitled to benefits calculated just as for employees, but with a shorter maximum duration. The same is true for Belgium, where the right to unemployment benefits for employees is basically unlimited. As emphasised by the Dutch chapter, wage standards for the self-employed do not alleviate poverty risks related to periods without assignments. Such periods, according to Eurostat, are reported by 12.3% of self-employed as main difficulty faced in their professional activity (the second most frequently cited difficulty after administrative burdens).[28] Effectively, self-employed going through a difficult patch may be deterred from applying for unemployment benefits if this requires them to fully give up on their business activity – as would generally be the case in the countries studied. The one notable exception is Belgium, where a 'bridging right' for self-employed persons facing economic difficulties due to certain events existed already before the onset of the COVID-19 crisis. The lack of comparable provisions in other countries may be a core reason for self-employed persons to forgo entitlements when their income falls below the poverty line.

In Germany, where the vast majority of self-employed persons is not covered by unemployment insurance, even application for social assistance may be particularly challenging for them. Notably if they have built up old-age savings instead of participating in pension insurance, then applications for social assistance risk being rejected for failure to use up existing assets first. The Swedish contribution stresses that existing mechanisms of the social security system are generally less well suited to address the situation of the self-employed, e.g., with regard to the more complex administration and income assessment, the consequences of being absent from work, or processes of rehabilitation from health-related incapacity without support from an employer.

To address the consequences of the COVID-19 crisis, all countries studied eventually introduced specific benefit schemes to address income shortfalls of self-employed persons, even if those were basically not covered by a short-time work

28. *See* Eurostat data at https://ec.europa.eu/eurostat/statistics-explained/index.php?title=Self-employment_statistics.

system or equivalent. The Belgian system stands out for providing income-dependent benefits, which additionally take the family situation into account, based on a pre-existing system. Other countries generally used flat-rate benefits and/or compensation for fixed operating expenses or lost revenue. Most of these benefits were enacted in March 2020 or soon after, although pay-out procedures could be lengthy. By contrast, the self-employed in Germany could exclusively apply for compensation of business-related fixed expenditure for almost one year. A systematic compensation for income losses became available only in February 2021 – leaving those self-employed who are essentially 'selling their labour' without any benefit for almost a year.

[3] Consequences of the Non-Applicability of Protective Mechanisms

Empirical insights on poverty rates can be seen as a pronounced indication of the relevance of different protective mechanisms under labour law and social security.

Most notably, this applies to the seemingly contradictory finding that exceptionally high AROP levels compare to inconspicuous or even relatively low SMD levels (*see infra* at §9.03[C]). This likely relates to the fact that all countries operate social assistance schemes to alleviate material deprivation, and problems of non-take-up and loopholes in coverage (e.g., for migrants) concern employed and self-employed workers alike. By contrast, as described *supra* at §9.03[B][1], mechanisms such as minimum wages and collective bargaining are regularly inapplicable to the self-employed. The sizable differences in AROP rates in all countries could be seen as a confirmation of the key role that those mechanisms play in reducing those rates for employees. Another striking commonality between all countries is the much weaker effect of a high level of education, performance of a high-skilled occupation, and full-time working hours on poverty levels of the self-employed. This points to a decisive influence of regulation which, for employees, ensures that every hour worked is remunerated at least at the minimum wage level, and collective agreements' wage scales that reward higher education and high-skilled work.

An evaluation of countries' different strategies to address the COVID-19 crisis' impact on self-employed workers would be premature. Survey data is available for Germany, as a particularly noteworthy example of a country where the self-employed were excluded from all social insurance-based protections and long not granted alternative benefits to address income losses as such. These show that 15% of employees, but almost 60% of self-employed persons experienced a decline in earnings during the crisis, with self-employed women most affected.

Finally, it seems crucial to stress that the loopholes in coverage by wage-replacing benefits do not necessarily result in higher in-work poverty rates. After all, once a former self-employed worker is out of work due to unemployment, durable health impairment or old age, they are by definition not in-work poor. In this regard, the German contribution refers to 'hidden' in-work poverty in the numerous cases where a self-employed person's net income lies above the poverty line, but effectively remains below it if the amount necessary to avoid poverty over the life cycle is set aside. Arguably, this applies not only to pension insurance (for which the lack of any coverage for a large share of the self-employed in Germany is exceptional among the countries studied), but also to lacking or insufficient provision for risks of unemployment and disability.

[C] Conclusions

The countries studied illustrate the variety of policy approaches to the risks connected to self-employed activity, which result in in-work poverty rates almost (for all self-employed) or more than (for the solo self-employed) three times higher than for all employed persons. Those approaches range from deterring the use of self-employed contractors and partly even prohibiting it to the successive expansion of protective mechanisms to various subgroups of the self-employed. While the second approach may risk making bogus self-employment even harder to combat in an increasingly complex system, the former may put the 'genuine' self-employed at even higher risk of poverty.

Section 9.03[B] has evidenced the challenges faced by all countries when it comes to the transposition of instruments that effectively alleviate poverty risks for employees to cases of (genuine) self-employment. The fact that these issues are currently on the policy agenda of various governments may be illustrated by a number of recently implemented reforms or reform discussions as described in this section. At least in relation to the development of collective bargaining-based protection, which is currently connected to substantial difficulties and uncertainties in all countries, the European Commission's recent Guidelines regarding the application of competition law[29] may prove a significant stimulus for further development in the national context.

§9.04 VUP GROUP 3: FIXED-TERM, AGENCY WORKERS, INVOLUNTARY PART-TIMERS

[A] Why Do Workers Choose to Work in Atypical Jobs?

[1] Fixed-Term Employment

Across the EU-27, the share of temporary (i.e., fixed-term) work has stably amounted to around 15%-16% of all employees over the last two decades, with a slight decrease in the context of the COVID-19 crisis.[30] Among the countries studied, this share varies from very low values in Luxembourg (generally below 10%, though with an increasing tendency in the long term) and the Netherlands, where it has surpassed 20% in several years (and, after a decreasing trend since 2017 and through 2020, has spiked to an all-time high of more than 27% in 2021).

---

29. *See* draft guidelines at https://ec.europa.eu/commission/presscorner/detail/en/ip_21_6620.
30. Down to 13% in the second quarter of 2020, but increasing since: *see* Eurostat data at https://ec.europa.eu/eurostat/databrowser/view/LFSQ_ETPGA__custom_1818481/default/table?lang=en.

As national law rarely stipulates very significant barriers for an employee to resign from an open-ended employment relationship (apart from possible consequences in terms of severance pay and/or unemployment benefits), the party interested in concluding an employment contract for a fixed term is regularly the employer.

An in-depth description of regulation on dismissal protection, which an employer can avoid by resorting to fixed-term contracts, would be beyond the scope of the present chapter. Suffice to say that dismissal regularly requires justification, notice well in advance, information and consultation, in the Netherlands even the permission of an authority or judge. For groups such as parents, sick, and disabled employees, workers' representatives etc., additional barriers for dismissal apply. Another aspect concerns severance pay, which national law or collective agreements frequently stipulate for regular employees. In this respect, a 2015 reform in the Netherlands included fixed-term workers in the scope of severance pay regulation, first after two years of employment. Since 2020, all employees have been entitled to the payment of one-third of their monthly wage per year of employment. An evaluation cited in the chapter does not find the original reform effective in bringing down the number of those staying in the 'temporary shell' for prolonged periods. A major factor for the attractiveness of fixed-term contracts also concerns the ease with which such contracts can be entered into and upheld for longer times without risking sanctions, as discussed *infra* at §9.04[C][1].

For the employee, fixed-term work is regularly involuntary. The share of temporary workers consciously choosing for fixed-term employment ranged from 1.4% in Italy to 31.4% in Sweden in 2020.[31] With the exception of Germany and the Netherlands, where the country samples are dominated by apprentices and probation workers, respectively, the majority of respondents in all countries studied (as well as in the EU as a whole) indicated that they had not found a permanent job. In Italy, that share was close to 80%, evidencing that more than 12% of all employees were involuntary fixed-term workers.

Apart from these general motivations, fixed-term employment is particularly sensitive to the economic circle. Notably in situations of crisis, fixed-term contracts will be left to expire, whereas job offers in a subsequent period of uncertainty are especially likely to be only temporary. LFS data show that the share of fixed-term work in the EU fell by two percentage points within just over a year during the global financial crisis and even more rapidly during the COVID-19 crisis (down to an all-time low of 13% in the second quarter of 2020).[32] Nowhere was this fluctuation as pronounced as in the Netherlands.

31. *See* Eurostat data at https://ec.europa.eu/eurostat/databrowser/view/lfsa_etgar/default/table?lang=en.
32. *See* Eurostat data at https://ec.europa.eu/eurostat/databrowser/view/LFSQ_ETPGA__custom_1818481/default/table?lang=en.

[2] Temporary Agency Work

Largely similar considerations apply to temporary agency workers, who have consistently constituted about 2% of the EU's workforce since measurements began in 2008, with a slight slump during the global financial crisis. Among the countries studied, the rate ranged between 0.5% in Poland and 3% in the Netherlands in 2020.[33]

Again, a company relying on temporary agency work rather than standard employment benefits from the non-applicability of core stipulations of dismissal law. Moreover, a cost advantage may stem from deviations from the equal treatment principle as allowed by Article 5 of the TAWD,[34] which in several countries are regularly envisaged by collective agreements with near-universal coverage (*see infra* at §9.04[C][2]). For workers, temporary agency work may fulfil a role as a stepping stone into the labour market (notably for foreigners and young workers, as noted in the Swedish contribution). At the same time, its performance over a long time is rarely motivated by anything but the lack of other options. Termination by the user regularly implies either falling back to low remuneration levels in the agency pending placement or, even more frequently, the termination of fixed-term employment with the agency (*see infra* at §9.04[C][2]).

[3] Involuntary Part-Time Employment

Involuntary part-time work is by definition not wanted by the employee. The share of part-time employees overall has constantly been slightly (Italy, Luxembourg) or rather significantly above the EU average of 17%-18% in all countries studied except Poland – with the Netherlands, Germany, and Belgium constituting three out of the top four countries in the EU.[35] For the employer, unlike with temporary work arrangements, part-time work is usually not per se more or less advantageous than full-time work. Several country chapters note that part-time employees are in practice particularly vulnerable to underpayment– especially due to higher actual than contractually stipulated working time and unpaid overtime. In Germany, regular unpaid overtime is by far the most frequent form of non-compliance with the statutory minimum wage, and concerns 'only' 10% of full-time, but 38.5% of part-time employees, and even more than 50% of mini-jobbers (*see infra* at §9.04[C][3]).

When asked to state a reason for working less than 30 hours per week, only a minority of workers indicate not wanting to work more. This option has been selected by only 10%-20% of EU-SILC respondents across the EU since 2006, when the question

33. An unlikely spike to 5.4% in Germany in 2020 as indicated in the data at the time of writing (which would lift the EU average to an unprecedented 2.6%) contradicts national statistics as mentioned in the contribution. *See* Eurostat data at https://ec.europa.eu/eurostat/databrowser/view/LFSA_QOE_4A6R2__custom_1828104/default/table?lang=en.
34. Directive 2008/104/EC of the European Parliament and of the Council of 19 November 2008 on temporary agency work, *OJ L 327, 5.12.2008, p. 9–14.*
35. *See* Eurostat data at https://ec.europa.eu/eurostat/databrowser/view/LFSQ_EPPGA__custom_1819754/default/table?lang=en.

was first included in this form.[36] The most frequently indicated reason has in all years been that of having failed to find longer-hours work – more than 30% of respondents in some years, but down to an all-time low slightly below 25% in 2020. Two more reasons indicating potential involuntariness – house- or care work and 'other reasons' – have each consistently been selected by around 20% or more of respondents. Among the countries studied, the importance of the individual reasons varies widely. Luxembourg has always stood out for a very high share of genuinely voluntary part-time workers (not wanting to work more), Sweden for a high share of health-related part-time work, the Netherlands for the importance of education and training as a reason for part-time work. By contrast, Italy has always been among the countries most concerned by involuntary part-time employment in the narrow sense, with the share of those having failed to find full-time employment increasing almost constantly to now almost two-thirds of all part-time workers. Germany and the Netherlands are both among the top three EU countries in relation to family care-related part-time, and Poland (with its extremely low share of part-timers) is the only EU country where more than half of respondents referred to 'other reasons' for working less than thirty hours per week.

The Dutch and Swedish chapters emphasise the gender differences. Involuntary part-time work in the narrow sense is more relevant for men – having concerned more than 40% of the EU's male part-time workers in some years, now at a historic low of 31.5% in 2020 (but almost 80% in Italy). Conversely, care-related part-time work plays only a minor, albeit slowly increasing role for men – reaching its historic peak of 5.5% in 2020. The 12% rate in Luxembourg is on top of the EU ranking, followed by the Netherlands. By contrast, family care is the reason indicated by more than a quarter of female part-timers, and it has become the most important reason after 2016 due to the continuous decline in involuntary part-time work in the narrower sense. Several chapters give more insights into how these motivations are influenced by the regulatory environment. A Dutch survey asking part-timers if they would work more hours provided that certain conditions are met finds this to be the case for nearly eight out of ten female part-timers. These conditions include working hours that are better aligned with private responsibilities or options to work from home, availability of high quality and affordable childcare, a concrete request to work more by the employer, and finding a job offering the desired number of working hours. Survey data from Germany allowing the female respondents to select more than one motive underlines the dominance of family care obligations (86% for children, 10% for other family members), 'joint consideration with my spouse' (60% – *see infra* for the tax law particularities playing a role here), and simply accepting working hours as suggested by the employer (35%). A Swedish survey confirms the particular relevance of health-related part-time.

An exhaustive discussion of the policy instruments playing a role for these motives would be beyond the scope of the present chapter. This notably applies to

36. *See* Eurostat data at https://ec.europa.eu/eurostat/databrowser/view/LFSA_EPGAR__custom_1829275/default/table?lang=en.

measures to improve the employment opportunities of the disabled, or investment to boost the provision of affordable child and/or elderly care. For measures to enable and encourage involuntary part-timers in the narrower sense to obtain skills that are more in demand and may qualify them for full-time work opportunities *see supra* at §9.02[B]. Another borderline case of voluntariness relates to financial disincentive to increasing working hours, notably due to the withdrawal of means-tested benefits or a favourable tax treatment in case of income gains. These might be most crucial when compared to the costs incurred, e.g., due to increased reliance on paid services to provide care for children or other care-dependent household members, as emphasised for Germany.

Apart from social benefits, the German contribution points to the role of the tax system, and especially the joint tax assessment of spouses – under which a higher income of the part-time working spouse frequently increases the tax rate applied to the main earner. Moreover, Germany presents an example of conscious regulatory intervention to increase the attractiveness of jobs with very low working hours, by exempting earnings of up to EUR 450 per month ('mini jobs') from taxes and social security affiliation. This system has come under fire in the light of data strongly indicating that financial advantages regularly accrue for the employer much rather than for the workers, *i.a.*, as a result of hourly remuneration below the low-wage threshold and unpaid overtime. In surveys, a third of mini-jobbers have expressed a wish to find a job subject to social security contributions, and a significant share indicated their employer's opposition as the main barrier to increasing working hours.

[B] How Much of Their Wage-Earning Potential do VUP 3 Workers Lose due to Involuntary Low-Hours or Non-Continuous Work?

The degree to which atypical work increases poverty risks crucially depends on whether it prevents employees from working to the degree necessary to obtain an adequate income – either by continuous but too low working hours, or by (repeated) interruptions of employment or placement for work. As for the latter, both the duration of temporary employment or placement and the likelihood of a swift transfer to new (especially permanent) work are decisive. For temporary agency workers, an additional factor consists in the permanency of their employment contract with the agency and their entitlement to wages in periods when they are not assigned to a user. Across the EU, about one-third of fixed-term contracts last for less than six months, another third for 6-12 months, and less than 10% beyond three years.[37] While workers employed for 'long-term fixed terms' enjoy more stability momentarily, they also continue to face the disadvantages of an uncertain employment situation for a protracted period of time. Those disadvantages include, beyond the aforementioned differences in dismissal protection, e.g., difficulties in obtaining loans or rental contracts, insecurities when starting a family, a lower probability to benefit from

37. *See* Eurostat data at https://ec.europa.eu/eurostat/databrowser/view/LFSA_ETGADC__custom_1860913/default/table?lang=en.

training opportunities, or a high likelihood to exploitation, as described in the German contribution.

The Dutch contribution cites data on the likelihood of workers in different forms of employment to become unemployed or inactive. While temporary workers with an outlook at an open-ended contract even have a slightly lower likelihood than employed persons overall to be out of work one year later, all other categories of fixed-term and temporary agency workers were about twice as likely to be unemployed or inactive at that point. This indicates the heterogeneity of a group which ranges from workers on a fixed-term probation track for potentially well-paying, stable jobs to those who find themselves trapped in insecure employment arrangements over a prolonged period of time. *See also infra* at §9.05[B] regarding the situation of intermittent employment.

Eurostat data on the probability of transitions from fixed-term to permanent employment[38] are incomplete in respect of several countries, preventing the determination of a European average value in this respect. Among the other WorkYP countries, the Netherlands and Sweden shows rather high transition rates about or above 15% of fixed-term workers securing a permanent position each quarter. Italy and Poland display rather low values, generally below 10% – indicating a significant risk of being trapped in temporary work precisely in countries with rather high shares of fixed-term contracts. The Swedish contribution remarks that such risks seem to concern primarily young and foreign-born workers with difficulties of establishing themselves on the labour market, while the Dutch contribution highlights the situation of temporary agency workers as those with the least stable careers in the country. Regarding part-time work, LFS data[39] display particularly high shares of workers in very low-hour employment contracts for the Netherlands and Germany, whereas part-time work is frequent but usually involves more than 30 weekly working hours in Belgium and Sweden.

Similar to concerns about 'hidden in-work poverty' among VUP 2 workers due to insufficient social insurance or savings for times of need, data for VUP 3 workers do not depict the long-term consequences which involuntary low-hour or non-continuous work over a prolonged period may have for the workers' careers (scarring effect). Several chapters also note that VUP 3 workers were significantly more likely to lose their jobs during the COVID-19 crisis – notably due to the easy termination of fixed-term and temporary agency work contracts, and of the non-applicability of short-time work schemes, e.g., to German mini-jobbers (half of whom lost their jobs in 2020).

---

38. *See* Eurostat data at https://ec.europa.eu/eurostat/databrowser/view/LFSI_LONG_E09__custom_1834564/default/table?lang=en.
39. *See* Eurostat data at https://ec.europa.eu/eurostat/databrowser/view/LFSA_QOE_3A4__custom_1834775/default/table?lang=en.

[C] What are the Main Instruments to Restrict Involuntary Part-Time and Temporary Work Performance?

[1] Fixed-Term Employment

EU Member States' obligation to take measures to prevent the abuse of fixed-term work under the Fixed-Term Work Directive (FTWD)[40] has been addressed in different ways and frequently been subject to reform in the countries studied. These measures typically involve a combination of the instruments envisaged by Clause 4 of the Framework Agreement.

Fixed-term contracts without a justifying reason can be concluded in all countries but Luxembourg. In this case, there is frequently a maximum overall duration of two years, but only one year in Italy. By contrast, fixed terms can last up to 33 months in Poland and even 3 years in the Netherlands. Pending reform bills aim to reduce the maximum to 12 months in Sweden and 18 months in Germany. Within these periods, Swedish law currently allows for an unrestricted number of repeated contracts, whereas the number of renewals is limited to a total of three (Germany, the Netherlands, Poland) or four (Belgium, Italy) in the other countries. Only Belgium prescribes a minimum duration (of three months) of each contract within this framework. As for the justification of fixed terms by an objective reason, Court of Justice of the European Union (CJEU) case law (e.g., Case C-177/14 – *Regojo Dans;* C-331/17 – *Sciotto*) has held that these may notably relate to the nature of the task or social policy objectives. In Belgium, Germany, and Poland, no temporary threshold applies to contracts justified by certain objective reasons; in Italy, the existence of such reason only extends the maximum duration to two years. A German reform bill foresees the introduction of an absolute threshold of five years also for fixed-term contracts based on an objective reason. Luxembourg stands out as the only country regularly requiring both a justifying reason and adherence to the maximum (two-year) threshold, in addition to having the lowest cap on the number of renewals.

In all jurisdictions, lists of justifying reasons include reasons related to the nature of the activity, such as seasonal work, extraordinary temporary needs, or the replacement of other employees, partly with further specifications and/or exceptions. The stipulation of probationary periods with particularly flexible termination is allowed for up to two, three, or six months. Regarding aims of a social policy nature, some countries have more liberal rules for employers hiring employees facing particular difficulties, such as registered jobseekers in insertion or reinsertion programmes in Luxembourg, or former apprentices, long-term unemployed and jobseekers above age 52 (after four months of unemployment) in Germany. Another justification not related to the nature of the work are the exceptions granted for start-up companies, e.g., in Germany and Italy. Justifying reasons subjects to criticism (and frequently doubts as to their compatibility with the FTWD include jobs in economic sectors where temporary

40. Council Directive 1999/70/EC of 28 June 1999 concerning the framework agreement on fixed-term work concluded by ETUC, UNICE, and CEEP, *OJ L 175, 10.7.1999, p. 43–48.*

contracts are 'widespread and systematic' (Luxembourg), limited budgets in the public sector (Germany), and objective reasons 'as indicated by the employer in the contract' in Poland.

An upper threshold for the share of fixed-term employees in the workforce of a company exist only in Italy at present (20%, with exceptions). In Germany, a stricter threshold of 2.5% in companies with a staff of more than 75 is envisaged by the aforementioned pending reform bill. Some countries do not consider follow-up contracts to constitute a successive fixed-term contract if certain minimum periods have passed. These may be of a fixed duration (e.g., six months in the Netherlands), or a share of the contract duration (one-third in Luxembourg – with exceptions). Swedish law uses a reference period of five years, within which fixed-term contracts between the parties cannot exceed the aforementioned limit of two years. A reform proposal likely to be implemented before the end of 2022 aims to ensure for the time between three or more separate temporary contracts to be counted as continued employment towards the new maximum of twelve months.

Collective agreements can and frequently do deviate from the statutory framework in Germany, Italy, the Netherlands, and Sweden. Such deviations may notably concern the maximum duration and/or number of possible renewals. Swedish social partners are granted the most far-going autonomy to flexibly set up alternative forms of fixed-term contracts with different requirements. The contribution voices concerns over a provision allowing blue-collar employees in education and healthcare to waive their right to permanent employment. As opposed to this, the social partners' leeway has been limited by a Dutch reform in 2015, *i.a.*, by the introduction of a justification requirement. In Belgium, an extension to three years is possible with the permission of the competent authority; in Germany, no additional restrictions apply for fixed terms determined by court settlements. In some countries, exceptional extensions of fixed-term contracts were permitted temporarily in the context of the COVID-19 crisis.

[2] Temporary Agency Work

Temporary agency work tends to be subjected to even more complex regulation to balance aims of boosting employment opportunities with abuse prevention. In most countries, workers can only be hired out by registered or authorised agencies (with the notable exception of the Netherlands), and frequently there are formal requirements such as written contracts with further specified contents.

Italy and Luxembourg essentially extend the measures to prevent the abuse of fixed-term contracts to temporary agency work, so that hiring in employees via an agency is subject to the same maximum periods and requirements for justification. In Belgium, the system for temporary agency work is even more restrictive than that for fixed-term work, in that every assignment requires a justifying reason – although there is an additional option to justify the arrangement by the intent of filling a vacancy permanently. Other countries apply specific regimes with maximum thresholds and/or justifying reasons required. In Germany, the Netherlands, and Sweden, these are heavily determined by collective agreements covering almost the entire sector and supplementing or deviating from the statutory framework.

In the Netherlands, this regime allows for even longer periods of temporary hiring than via fixed-term contracts, with even more flexibility for the duration of individual assignments. The pertinent collective agreement allows for the stipulation of the automatic termination of employment at the end of a particular assignment, including in case of premature termination by the user without any justifying reason, throughout the first 76 weeks of employment with the agency. A right to an open-ended contract exists only after five and a half years. Both in Germany and Poland, the maximum duration of a temporary agency worker's assignment to a specific user is generally set at 18 months and thus shorter than for fixed-term work not justified by a specific reason. However, German law allows for further placement with the same user after an interruption of only three months, as well as an extension of the maximum period by collective agreement. By contrast, the Polish 18-month limit applies within a 36-month reference period (whereby both the limit and reference period are doubled in case of replacement of an absent employee of the user). Sweden does not stipulate any specific thresholds for assignments, although the rules regarding fixed-term contracts remain applicable to the employment contract with the agency. In addition, the collective agreements covering 97% of temporary agency workers contain specific provisions against casual or intermittent work – so that temporary agency workers are effectively more likely to have a permanent or long-term temporary contract than those employed directly by the user, and receive a guaranteed wage between assignments. Apart from this, notably the main collective agreement for blue-collar workers entitles agency workers to wages equivalent to those of employees with average seniority in the user undertaking – and thus frequently higher payment than a newly-hired direct employee would receive.

Both Belgium and Germany allow temporary agency work in the construction sector only to a very limited degree. A prohibition to use temporary agency work in German companies with a staff of 50 or more for the core business of the meat industry was added very recently after major outbreaks of COVID-19 cast a spotlight on working conditions in that sector. Again, Italy stipulates a maximum threshold for the share of temporary workers per undertaking – 20% for temporary agency work alone, and 30% when taken together with fixed-term employment. A similar rule exists in Belgium. In Sweden, the collective agreements applicable to potential user companies frequently contain clauses requiring negotiation with the local union before making use of temporary agency work. In most other countries studied, employee representatives at user undertakings have a right to information and consultation about various aspects of the use of temporary agency workers, as mentioned e.g., in the Italian contribution.

[3] Involuntary Part-Time Employment

Concrete legal barriers to the conclusion of part-time contracts as such are rare, but some country chapters cite measures aimed at curbing particularly precarious or abuse-prone forms of part-time work. Belgium is the only country to outlaw very low-scale part-time work, as contracts are basically (with various exceptions) prohibited from stipulating weekly working hours below a third of a full-time job. In Sweden, various collective agreements require employers to avoid part-time employment for less than half of the full-time level. Italy stands out by strict requirements for stipulating part-time working hours in writing, failure of which entitles the employee to demand recognition as a full-time employee or the determination of working hours in line with the employee's needs (financial as well as family-related). Similarly, the Swedish legislator plans to introduce a duty for employers to stipulate the reasons for part-time work in writing and observe a notice period, if working hours are to be reduced.

Regarding involuntary part-time work, most countries have transposed Clauses 5 (2) and (3)a of the Framework Agreement annexed to the Part-Time Work Directive (PTWD)[41] expressly in their domestic law, thus requiring employers to accommodate wishes to transfer between full-time and part-time work 'as far as possible', and stipulating that an employee's refusal to change their working hours to full-or part-time should not 'in itself' constitute a valid reason for dismissal. A concretisation of these rights and duties is provided notably by Dutch and German national law. A Dutch provision introduced in 2016 gives employees with a seniority of 26 weeks the right to request an increase or decrease in their working hours, which need not be motivated. The employer in turn must motivate a rejection by compelling interests, lack of which entitles the employee to consider the request approved after a month. The law lists examples of compelling reasons, just as the corresponding German provision, which prescribes also procedures and timeframes for re-application. More specific rights to change from full-time to part-time exist for parents and carers. In these cases, Article 9 of the Work-Life Balance (WLB) Directive 2019/1158 (which is due for transposition by 2 August 2022) specifies that the employer must enable return to full-time work as agreed, and must 'consider' a justified request for early return. Italian law stipulates a priority rule which employers are bound by when filling full-time positions in the area of work of employees wishing to return from a childcare-related part-time arrangement. A right to a reduction of working hours may also arise in the context of the employer's obligation to provide reasonable accommodation for disabled employees under Article 5 of Directive 2000/78/EC, and national law may extend this to employees with health issues more generally or in specific cases. In such cases, a concrete right to return to full-time when the employee's health condition improves is usually not expressly provided for.

The obvious difficulties faced by employees wishing to enforce the described rights on an individual basis indicate the importance of employer's duties not only to inform employees about concrete available work opportunities, but also to inform and consult workers' representatives regarding plans for filling vacancies. Whereas clear obligations to this end may be difficult to deduce from the formulation of Clauses 5 (3)a of the Framework Agreement, national law tends to be more specific notably regarding information and consultation duties.

41. Council Directive 97/81/EC of 15 Dec. 1997 concerning the Framework Agreement on part-time work concluded by UNICE, CEEP, and the ETUC – Annex: Framework agreement on part-time work, *OJ L 14, 20.1.1998, p. 9–14.*

[4] Effectiveness of Measures

Developments in the share of fixed-term workers among the workforce display a remarkable degree of correlation with the legal limitations as described. As mentioned *supra* at §9.04[A][1], among the countries studied, the share of fixed-term workers is lowest in Luxembourg (the only country which stipulates both a justification requirement and a two-year limit for every fixed-term contract) and highest in the Netherlands and Poland, which allow fixed terms without a justifying reason for the longest duration. As several chapters indicate that some but not all previous reforms have influenced the number of fixed-term contracts concluded, the recent and planned reforms as described for several countries will warrant close evaluation.

As for temporary agency work, the highest shares among the WorkYP countries have regularly been found in the Netherlands, followed by Germany. In both countries, the law allows for its use without specific justification, and for workers to be employed under fixed-term contracts that are synchronised with the duration of placement with a specific user, which has become almost ubiquitous practice. On top of this the Dutch system stands out by the unusually long maximum duration of 5.5 years combined with fully flexible termination over the first 78 weeks, while the German system is characterised by large-scale derogations from the equal pay principle, for a duration which exceeds the period of most assignments. It seems important to note in this context that an important risk for circumvention of the regulation of temporary agency work consists in the difficult distinction between agency work and subcontracting, to which such regulation is not applicable. In the Netherlands, the conclusion of 'payrolling' agreements used to be a particularly popular strategy to avoid the application of these rules, until a recent reform subjected such agreements to the same rules as agency work as from 2020.

Regarding involuntary part-time workers, a comparative discussion based on empirical insights is difficult due to the heterogeneity of the group, the different importance of different dimensions of involuntariness in the countries studied and the multitude of influencing factors (*see supra* at §9.04[A][3]). At any rate, the aforementioned measures taken in Belgium and Sweden to avoid very low-hours part-time employment are reflected in data showing the scarcity of such employment in these countries despite overall high shares of part-timers – as opposed to the very high prevalence of low-hour work in Germany and the Netherlands. As for the described instruments entitling employees to request an increase of working hours with their employer, case law both at EU level (cf. Case C-221/13 – *Mascellani*) and in the countries studied is scarce and provides little concrete guidance, and empirical information about the frequency of requests to increase working hours seems to be missing. Doubts about the effectiveness of the system in enabling workers to assert their interests regarding working hours are voiced, e.g., in Italy.

[D] What Are the Main Instruments to Prevent Poverty for VUP 3 Workers?

[1] Instruments Concerning the Wage Level

As workers hired under an employment contract, VUP 3 workers are regularly covered by statutory minimum wages and collective agreements, in addition to the specific equal treatment provision as envisaged by EU law. They are also included in the scope of company-level representation by works councils – although an adequate representation of temporary agency workers' interests is complicated by the triangular nature of their employment relationship, and national law may restrict workplace-level representation to either the agency or the user undertaking. In practice, collective agreements cover an important share of VUP 3 workers; temporary agency workers even stand out by a particularly comprehensive coverage by collective agreements in most of the countries studied. However, the consequences of coverage by collective agreements may be very different for VUP 3 workers compared to the workforce overall, which puts its general role as a key instrument to ensure adequate wage levels into perspective.

As described, such agreements frequently contain deviations from legal protections which may increase poverty risks – such as the derogations from the equal pay principle in Germany and Sweden, or the permission of successive assignments subject to termination at will by the user in the Netherlands (*see supra* at §9.04[C][4]). Both for Germany and the Netherlands, the conclusion of collective agreements with trade unions of questionable representativeness has become an issue – since such agreements are nonetheless broadly applicable in the sector, via ministerial extension (the Netherlands) or widespread reference in individual employment contracts (Germany). These questions of representativeness seem all the more pertinent when considering that – particularly in those countries where the social partners are regularly and significantly deviating from statutory standards for fixed-term and temporary agency workers (Germany, the Netherlands, Sweden) – these categories of workers are particularly unlikely to be union members.

All in all, on the one hand the trade union movement in several countries has in the recent past become more active in seeking to represent the workers concerned by atypical employment rather than exclusively aiming to curb its use. The fact that the social partners have been given a broad leeway for tailor-made solutions may also have worked as an important stimulus for initiating collective bargaining activities for poorly unionised groups of workers. At the same time, the above indicates that certain non-derogable standards may be essential to avoid that these workers' interests are traded off against better rights for the 'core workforce'. In Germany, the low-wage sector includes 21% of all employees, but 33% of fixed-term workers, 39% of temporary agency workers, and even 47% of part-timers with working time below 20 hours per week. This has made atypical workers (notably temporary agency workers and mini-jobbers) the greatest beneficiaries of the introduction of a statutory minimum hourly wage in 2015.

Apart from express derogations from equal pay standards, a number of difficulties in their application may result in VUP 3 workers facing overall lower wage levels, which add to the poverty risks linked to low-hour or non-continuous employment. One of those difficulties concerns seniority-based remuneration, which is regularly an issue for those working fixed-term periods for different employers (this is precisely the aspect in which the Swedish standard for blue-collar agency workers differs from other systems). Regarding part-time workers, a slower progression on the wage scale is not necessarily prohibited by European law (cf. CJEU case law, e.g., in cases Case C-109/88 – *Danfoss*, C-17/05 – *Cadman*), but may be excluded by national law (e.g., in Luxembourg). A group covered neither by statistics on temporary work nor by specific principles of equal treatment are temporary agency workers with a permanent contract in stand-by periods pending placement to a user undertaking. Again, the quasi-universal Swedish collective agreements ensure a non-negligible level of hourly wages to be provided to workers during such periods As opposed to this, Italian temporary agency workers are only entitled to an availability allowance of EUR 800 or even just 350 per month, indicating a high risk of poverty in case of a longer time-lapse between placements. A phenomenon particularly difficult to capture by statistics or regulation is the aforementioned (*see supra* at §9.04[C][4]) practice of outsourcing of tasks to subcontractors, which may evade not only the application of sector- or company-size-specific regulation, but notably the application of collective agreements with their important role for wages.

Finally, the Polish contribution stresses that every fourth case of illegal employment, which is naturally prone to underpayment, involved illegal temporary agency work.

[2] Instruments Concerning Wage-Replacing Benefits

Also with regard to social security benefits, VUP 3 workers do not face a situation akin to VUP 2 workers' far-going exclusion from protective mechanisms. The only group facing comprehensive exclusion from insurance-based social security systems are mini-jobbers in Germany, who are by default covered only by pension insurance, but with an opt-out possibility used in more than 80% of cases.

But also VUP 3 workers benefitting from full social security coverage may encounter difficulties in claiming benefits. To begin with, all countries' unemployment insurance systems make the right to benefits conditional upon prior periods of work within specific framework periods. Failure to meet minimum requirements typically implies having to fall back on social assistance or low flat-rate benefits; short insurance periods regularly result in a short duration of benefit entitlement. Accordingly, a situation of unemployment is very likely to cause the household income to drop below the poverty line either immediately or after a short time. The duration of employment also regularly plays a role for the right to (and possibly the duration of) sick and/or parental leave; in Germany also for the voluntary continued affiliation with social insurance schemes that are mandatory for employees. Paid annual leave will regularly be replaced by an allowance in lieu in case of short fixed-term contracts.

Differences appear even more pronounced with a view to entitlements beyond the statutory minimum level. Both the Swedish and the German chapters note that collective agreements frequently stipulate entitlements regarding leave rights and dismissal compensation based on a duration-of-work criterion, and the same is true for entitlements provided for in transition agreements or social plans in case of collective redundancy. In the same vein, the Dutch contribution refers to occupational pensions, which provide an important addition to the country's flat-rate public pension scheme. The Swedish contribution notes difficulties in establishing based on available data what share of temporary workers would be excluded from benefits based on a length-of-employment criterion, and estimates are further complicated by the applicability of different collective agreements with individual preconditions for supplementary benefits. Even where temporary workers fulfil the requirements for benefits paid by the employer, they may face termination of employment in situations where other employees would be protected from it (illness, parenthood, etc.). In the Netherlands, this does not only concern cases of regular expiry of a fixed term, but even premature termination of a contract for temporary agency work by the user.

As for measures to address these difficulties, Belgium stands out by giving specific consideration to the situation of temporary workers with interrupted periods of work or irregular working hours in its social security system. For them, alternative calculation methods exist for incapacity and maternity benefits, to allow for building up entitlements over a longer period and/or based on the number of hours rather than days of work in the past year. As for benefits provided by employers, the Dutch temporary agency work sector has established an own occupational pension fund. For some sectors or categories of workers, centralised funds are established by collective agreements or even the law (e.g., Belgium) to grant paid leave and/or severance pay under a system that benefits employees with frequently changing employers.

Depending on the reasons for their low working hours (*see supra* at §9.04[A][3]), part-timers may be eligible for benefits for partial incapacity, part-time parental leave, or partial unemployment. Particularly with regard to the latter, the countries studied display substantial differences as to its existence and generosity. The Swedish chapter stresses that partial benefits are subject to a stricter time frame of 60 weeks, implying a risk of exhaustion over prolonged periods of involuntary part-time. As for access to sickness or invalidity benefits, the Swedish contribution invokes concerns over the criteria used in work capacity assessments, which often leave workers feeling unable to work full-time without partial wage-replacing benefits to top up their incomes.

In the context of the COVID-19 crisis, some of the mentioned issues have been temporarily alleviated by measures which waive or reduce requirements for social security benefits. In Poland, the main instruments to protect jobs in the pandemic did not support temporary agency workers. In relation to a German reform that included temporary agency workers in short-time work schemes for the first time, the still significant reduction of their share indicates that the measure may have alleviated but not eliminated their substantially higher risk of becoming unemployed. Mini-jobbers in turn continued to be excluded both from unemployment insurance benefits and from short-term allowance schemes. As a result, mini jobs accounted for an absolute majority of all jobs lost between early 2020 and early 2021, despite constituting only one-fifth of all employment contracts.

[E] Conclusions

Similar to VUP Group 2, VUP Group 3 is a highly heterogeneous category. As pointed out in several country chapters, it includes a significant number of workers for whom a low or unstable labour market income is not liable to lead to poverty risks in the household context, as in the case of fixed-term working students living with their parents (cf. the large share of young workers) or part-timers with a full-time working partner assuming family care obligations (cf. the high share of women as mentioned *supra* at §9.04[A][3]). However, the extraordinarily high SMD rates for this group evidence that, among those who are concerned by poverty in their respective household context, a particularly high share are so far below the poverty line that not even the most necessary expenses of daily living are secured.

Another commonality with VUP Group 2 is that VUP 3 workers' vulnerability to poverty goes beyond what can be captured by measurements that are strongly conditional on the momentary employment and family situation, as all forms of atypical employment described in this section are particularly likely to have consequences for a worker's future career and social security entitlements. Experience in the WorkYP countries indicates the effectiveness of regulatory restrictions to curb the incidence and duration of fixed-term and temporary agency contracts, whereas approaches to avoiding involuntary part-time work will differ widely across countries depending on the prevailing reasons for its existence.

The principle of equal treatment acts as the key instrument to alleviate poverty risks which go beyond the inherent consequences which non-continuous and/or low-hour work has on the workers' income situation and are more related to their weak bargaining power. Weak bargaining power and representation also make the role of collective bargaining less straightforward for VUP 3 workers, as national law tends to use far-going derogation options as a stimulus for the social partners to conclude agreements for these groups. In the case of temporary agency workers – whose situation tends to be most decisively determined by the applicable collective agreement – the Swedish union movement seems exceptional in terms of successfully assuring protective standards for atypical workers, which also prevent the latter from constituting a cheap alternative to workers that form these unions' key constituents.

§9.05 VUP GROUP 4: CASUAL AND PLATFORM WORKERS

[A] Why Do Workers Choose to Work as Casual or Platform Workers?

[1] Intermittent Work

Intermittent work effectively amounts to a particularly short form of a fixed-term work relationship. For employers, it obviously indicates an even higher degree of flexibility than more extensive periods of fixed-term work, and it may be attractive not only for extraordinary tasks but also for regularly occurring needs that are difficult to predict. Thereby, recruitment costs can be minimised if some form of framework arrangement exists with (a number of) workers who can be contacted at short notice if such need arises. The delimitation with on-call employment (based on one continuous contract rather than a series of fixed-term contracts) may therefore be blurred.

Apart from the obvious role played by the legal limits described *infra* at §9.05[C][1] for the attractiveness of using the legally possible forms of intermittent work, the German and Italian chapters refer to dedicated schemes which make its use particularly advantageous for employers. In Germany, a variant of the aforementioned mini job scheme consists in limiting work to 70 days per calendar year. This results in the same non-applicability of income tax and social security coverage. In Italy, private households and micro-enterprises with up to five employees can rely on voucher-based work, which is exempted from income tax and parts of social insurance, and subject to a low uniform minimum wage rate of EUR 9 or 10. The principal also benefits from significant administrative simplification regarding the payment of social security contributions (as the employer pays the gross wage in vouchers, which the employee can cash in for their net wage with the competent authority). Both countries' schemes reduce costs and increase legal certainty about the permissibility of repeated short-term contracts for the parties involved (cf. the risks of retroactive insurance contributions imposed in cases of bogus self-employed work performance).

These dedicated schemes may also make those types of work appear particularly attractive for workers, notably due to the described exemption from tax and social security contributions. German and Italian jobseekers can also engage in work within the limits of the described schemes without losing their right to unemployment insurance benefits. Apart from such particular advantages, the performance of intermittent work more generally may be voluntary and even desirable for workers, notably if they are able to use it as a top-up income-earning opportunity, which they can align with their individual schedule. The lack of reliable comparative data makes it difficult to assess the share of intermittent workers who are actually free to accept or refuse intermittent offers of work assignments, and what share are forced to take up such forms of work for lack of other options.

[2] On-Call Work

Essentially the same considerations as for intermittent work may hold true for on-call work arrangements. As described at §9.05[C][2], all countries studied impose various legal limits to the use of on-call arrangements, which will be key in determining its attractiveness for employers. In Belgium, the use of flexi-jobs (*see infra*) gives employers the additional advantage of a lower minimum wage standard of just over EUR 10 per hour and a special social security contribution of 25%.

In the 2004 LFS, almost two-thirds of employees working exclusively on call in the EU (less than 1.8% of all employees, but with data lacking for half of the member states) indicated that this type of work was convenient for their personal work situation.[42] That share was even more than 90% in Sweden, but just more than 50% in Poland, and as low as 14% in Italy. Self-evidently, any concrete conclusions based on information on a single year predating significant economic and regulatory developments in all countries seem dubious. At any rate, these data indicate the relevance of the country context for whether on-call work constitutes an opportunity for better work-life balance or rather a risk of involuntary, precarious work performance for those without options for more stable employment.

[3] Platform Work

As platform work is regularly based on intermittent work performance, reference can essentially be made to all considerations presented *supra* at §9.05[C][1]. Measures of national law which consciously increase the attractiveness of platform work for either party are rare. Such an effect can, however, be assumed for a Belgian law passed in 2016, which expressly excludes platform work performed as a side job for up to EUR 6,390 per year from social security coverage. Just as the above-described German and Italian schemes for small-scale intermittent work, this may reduce both costs and risks in case of misclassification (*see infra* at §9.05[C][3] on the emergence of litigation over bogus self-employment among platform workers). Attempts at further deregulation have been invalidated by a judgment of the Constitutional Court.

[B] How Much of Their Wage-Earning Potential do VUP 3 Workers Lose due to Involuntary Low-Hours or Non-Continuous Work?

Despite the virtual absence of empirical data, it may be safe to assume that incomes from intermittent, on-call and platform work are regularly insufficient in themselves to sustain a living above the poverty line. Whereas this may be in accordance with the worker's needs and capacities and not necessarily lead to poverty risks for the household, the income from such work will usually be a part of the household income at high risk of being lost or dropping to a very low level. Considering that employers and principals are typically using casual work for fluctuating needs, the jobs of VUP 4 workers are even more dependent on the economic cycle – notably at times of crisis. The COVID-19 pandemic has been another example of this.

Both the Swedish and the Dutch contributions refer to findings indicating that VUP 4 workers face high risks of being trapped in intermittent or on-call employment, or to become unemployed. Dutch data for 2018 show that 15% of on-call workers were unemployed or inactive a year later – the highest share among all observed groups.

42. *See* Eurostat data at https://ec.europa.eu/eurostat/databrowser/view/LFSO_04ONCWISNA__custom_1869962/default/table?lang=en and https://ec.europa.eu/eurostat/databrowser/view/LFSO_04WK1PNA11__custom_1870054/default/table?lang=en.

[C] What Are the Main Instruments to Restrict Casual and Platform Work?

[1] Intermittent Work

Most countries' laws basically allow for the conclusion of very short fixed-term contracts – although Belgian and Luxembourgish law require a justifying reason in all cases, Luxembourgish regulation also the stipulation of a minimum period. However, as indicated *supra* at §9.04[C][1], the possibility of repeated fixed-term contracts between the same parties is limited in most countries. By exception, Sweden generally allows an unlimited number of renewals if the upper threshold of two years of fixed-term work within five years is respected.

Among the other countries, Belgium, Germany, and Poland allow an unlimited number of fixed-term contracts between the same parties in case of the existence of a justifying reason for each successive agreement (*see supra* at §9.04[C][1]). In these countries, just as in Sweden, a potential reclassification of repeated short-term contracts as a continuous contract must be decided on a case-by-case basis. In Poland, an exception from the general regime for fixed-term employment applies in case of seasonal work, which the labour inspectorate has found prone to abuse due to the broad and ill-defined notion of seasonal work. In Italy with its basically rather strict approach to repeated fixed-term contracts, there is an exception for the aforementioned system of voucher-based employment. If the conditions (*see supra* at §9.05[A][1]) are fulfilled, the contract is reclassified as a full-time continuous relationship only when surpassing the threshold of 280 hours per year. Other violations of the limits described *supra* may lead to the non-applicability of the advantages of the voucher-based system, and failure to timely notify the competent authorities of working hours is sanctioned by monetary fines.

Only the Dutch and Luxembourgish rules do not provide for exceptions to the rule that fixed-term contracts may not be renewed more than twice or thrice, respectively. Arguably, the required interruption of one-third of contract duration before concluding a new (series of) contract(s) in Luxembourg may be easy to achieve in case of intermittent short-term contracts; yet, a justifying reason is always required. Luxembourgish case law is strict in this regard, and even seasonal work may be reclassified as employment with an 'indefinite global duration' if clauses about a renewal for the next season are stipulated more than twice between the same parties. Exceptions exist only for special contracts in the framework of public social programmes.

[2] On-Call Work

Regarding on-call arrangements, one key distinction concerns the question whether employees are obliged to be available for work on call, or rather free to accept or refuse a call to work. In the latter case, most countries do not impose particular limits on voluntary overtime (within the boundaries of working time regulation) or shift changes as agreed ad hoc between the parties of an employment contract. If this leads to a certain regular pattern of work performance, courts may find the contract to have been amended by tacit agreement, entitling the employee to continued employment with working hours amounting to past practice (yet the Swedish contribution also stresses that case law on this point is very scarce). Where there is no obligation on either of the parties of a contract to offer or accept any minimum number of work assignments or hours, the contract will often be classified as a mere framework agreement for individual fixed-term contracts or self-employed work performance. In this respect, there may be significant legal uncertainty as to the conditions under which courts may reclassify such arrangements as uninterrupted employment contracts - as evidenced by the difficulties in classifying platform work (*see infra* next subsection). By exception, Italy stipulates a concrete limit of 400 days of work within 3 years, which leads to a reclassification as full-time employment contract even where the employee has never been obliged to accept a call to work.

With the exception of Luxembourg, all countries studied conditionally permit on-call work in the narrower sense, i.e., contracts under which no regular contractual work pattern is identified in advance, the employer is entitled to determine working hours ad hoc or at short notice, and the employee is obliged to follow a call to work.

Both Belgian and Italian law envisage contract types which can essentially amount to zero-hours contracts without an obligation to notify working hours in advance, albeit only in specific circumstances. In Belgium, 'flexi-jobs' can be used only for employees in hospitality, catering, retail, beauty care or bakery, who have worked at least four-fifth of normal hours for a different employer in the third quarter preceding the agreement. It is thus effectively only possible either as a small-scale side job or for a limited number of months after a job change of a former full-time employee. In Italy, on-call work is possible in specific cases identified by collective agreement or ministerial decree, or with workers aged either below 25 or above 55. The main limitations are a maximum threshold of 400 days of work within three years, the employer's obligation to pay an availability allowance during the stand-by period, and the prohibition of its use six months after collective redundancies or the use of short-time work.

In the Netherlands, the conclusion of zero-hours contracts is not limited to certain categories of workers, but basically requires notification about working hours at least four days in advance. The employee is entitled to wages based on the notification (even if the employer eventually fails to call the employee), and for at least three hours per call. After one year, the employee has a right to an employment contract with fixed working hours in accordance with past practice. Collective agreements can shorten the notification period down to 24 hours and exclude seasonal work - whereby the practical importance of these options is not yet clear due to the recent introduction of the legal framework in 2020. A basically very similar scheme - including the four-day notification period and three-hour shift duration - has existed in Germany for a longer time already, but it does not allow for zero-hour-type flexibility regarding the number of working hours. The law basically only permits fluctuations up to 25% above a stipulated minimum, or alternatively up to 20% below a stipulated maximum duration of weekly working hours. However, the social partners can and frequently do derogate both from these limits to fluctuation and from the employee's right to be informed four days in advance. Times during which an employee is required to remain available on call are not remunerated in either country.

Virtually no statutory restrictions for the use of on-call (including zero-hours) contracts exist in Poland and Sweden (where collective agreements frequently include conditions for the use of on-call work, though).

Whereas on-call agreements in the narrower sense are thus subject to certain concrete ramifications in all countries except Poland, a similar degree of flexibilisation can often be obtained by the combination of very low-hour part-time contracts with regular overtime determined by the employer. Some countries' laws consider the employer by default entitled to order a certain number of overtime hours also for part-time workers – up to 25% of part-time hours in Italy (subject to a 15% wage supplement), 200 hours (increased by a further 150 hours in case of unpredictable circumstances) per year in Sweden, and a not clearly specified number of hours according to Dutch case law. As opposed to this, Luxembourgish part-timers can be asked to work overtime hours only in exceptionally justified cases, and never beyond the normal working time of a comparable full-time employee.

Even where no such automatic right to impose overtime is envisaged, the (collective or) individual agreement may stipulate obligations to perform overtime in all countries. Most have no concrete limit as to the number or share of overtime hours that would be considered abusive if agreed this way, or which would entitle the employee to a requalification of the contract into a full-time contract. By exception, Italian law stipulates a restriction of up to 250 hours of extraordinary overtime work per year. The excessive use of such overtime may be disincentivised to some degree by wage supplements for overtime, but such are not envisaged, e.g., in Poland. Overtime hours can usually be communicated at relatively short notice (e.g., two days in Italy and three days in Luxembourg, with concrete timeframes missing in most countries).

Apart from (or in addition to) the reliance on overtime, a considerable degree of flexibility can also be achieved in all countries via the stipulation of reference periods over which working hours need to correspond to the regular weekly number only on average, often via tools such as 'working time accounts'. Under Luxembourgish law, specific stipulations to this end in the employment contract are not needed as long as working hours do not exceed 120% of the contractually stipulated hours in each week. The Dutch contribution confirms that such reference periods can amount to up to a full year, during which the employer may be free to distribute the agreed aggregate annual working hours over the individual weeks or months. If a stable income is paid to the employee throughout this period, the aforementioned rules on on-call work do not apply. This effectively holds true for all countries, although shorter maxima (e.g., four months in Belgium and Luxembourg) tend to apply for reference periods. In most countries, the limits (if any) to the fluctuation of working hours in this context are highly sector-specific, due to the key role of collective bargaining in determining the framework for working time flexibilisation.

[3] Platform Work

All of the regulation described in two previous subsections may in principle be relevant for platform workers if those are classified as employees. Since, however, a majority of platform workers at present are solo or bogus self-employed, reference may be made to measures described *supra* at §9.03[A][2] for VUP Group 2. This concerns notably the existence of effective mechanisms to rectify bogus self-employment.

The question whether and when arrangements which platforms present as self-employed work should be reclassified as employment contracts has been assessed by courts, labour inspectorates, and/or social security bodies in all countries studied but Poland, at least in relation to certain types of platforms. With the exception of Germany, these cases have concerned exclusively on-demand work via apps. Notably food delivery riders have been categorised as employees by a second-instance judgment in the Netherlands, one first-instance ruling in Italy, and a Belgian social security body. A number of Italian courts including the Court of Cassation have opted for a classification of riders as 'hetero-organised' workers (with rights similar to employees), whereas self-employed status has been confirmed by a Belgian court and the Luxembourgish labour inspectorate. Cleaners have been qualified as temporary agency workers by a Dutch second-instance decision, whereas a Swedish administrative court overruled the reclassification of providers of private household-related tasks as employees by the labour inspectorate. Uber has been found to be the employer of its drivers by a Dutch court and a Belgian social security body, and a platform hiring out 'freelancers' to businesses, *i.a.*, in the care and hospitality sector has been considered a temporary work agency by the Dutch labour inspectorate. As for crowdwork, a single case of on-location microtask performance has been found to constitute an employment contract by the German Supreme Court.[43]

The uncertainty emerging from such scarce and partly contradictory case law is increased by the fact that almost all non-final cases of reclassification are still subject to appeal. The Italian example shows that even where a series of court decisions agree on the classification of platform workers (as hetero-organised workers), they may not necessarily agree on the consequences in terms of their rights.

Yet, the emerging litigation targeting platform companies, which is particularly likely to move through to higher-instance courts due to its pertinence for large numbers of workers, may be of crucial relevance also for other forms of intermittent and on-call work. Notably the case law issued in higher-level courts in Germany, Italy, and the Netherlands as mentioned in the preceding paragraphs evidences a tendency of reconsidering the importance traditionally given to certain criteria, such as the lack of a contractual obligation to accept an offer to work or the use of own material, as opposed to other indicators of subordination and dependence. These considerations could arguably challenge the current classification of various forms of non-platform-based work as self-employed activity based on the voluntariness of accepting work assignments on an intermittent or on-call basis.

---

43. *See also* Hiessl, *supra* n. 26.

The only platform type where (some) major providers in several countries are reported to 'voluntarily' hire their workforce under open-ended employment contracts are food delivery businesses. Even in these cases, platforms may be reluctant to perform employer functions, as evidenced by German and Italian court decisions forcing platforms to provide equipment or enable the establishment of a works council or board-level participation. Italy is the only country where the legislator has repeatedly aimed to clarify the status and rights of one category of platform workers – by an express reference to delivery riders in the legal definition of hetero-organised work as well as the introduction of specific rights irrespective of their classification. These rights concern notably coverage by collective bargaining, information rights, the prohibition of piece-based remuneration, entitlements to accident insurance, and wage supplements for work on weekends and in adverse weather conditions

Pending the progress of the European Commission's legislative initiative to prescribe a presumption of employee status at EU level,[44] Luxembourg is currently the only country where the introduction of such a presumption is being discussed based on a proposal of the Workers' Chamber. In Germany, the labour ministry has announced the enactment of specific protections for platform workers, including platforms' responsibility for their workers, improved social protection, transparency, control, and effective implementation. Several more concrete and previously rejected moves by the parliamentary opposition may become relevant again after the recent change of government. The introduction of special protective measures for platform workers is also planned by the Belgian government.

[4] Effectiveness of Measures

As evident from the above description, most countries' legal framework imposes certain limits to the most precarious forms of on-call work, which require employees to be available for assignments (without a right to decline) over long periods without being guaranteed a certain number of hours or amount of income. Those consist either in the non-permissibility of zero-hours-type complete unpredictability of working hours, or, where this is allowed, in its effective limitations to (specific circumstances and) a maximum duration). An issue of concern apparent in the above-described schemes, which cannot be exhaustively discussed in this context, is the lack of an effective right to disconnect in most countries' on-call regulation. Concerns over work-life balance therefore exist even where poverty risks are reduced by regulation that avoids a drop in income in periods of low-work intensity (by limits to the fluctuation of weekly working hours or a guarantee of a stable income irrespective of working hours over one year). None of the countries stipulates a concrete limit to the period during which on-call hours or mandatory overtime work can be scheduled, and only Italy provides an incentive for such limits by requiring the employer to pay an availability allowance.

44. *See* full text of the proposal at https://ec.europa.eu/social/BlobServlet?docId=24992&langId=en.

As mentioned in the last paragraph of subsection §9.05[C][2], the restrictions established for on-call work in the strict sense may be of limited effectiveness if employers can achieve a similar or larger degree of flexibility via alternative means. The brief overview of regulation relating to combinations of part-time with overtime work evidences that such alternatives exist virtually in all countries studied. In this respect, the German contribution notes that limits to the fluctuation of working hours in case of on-call employment have been introduced by a 2019 reform in reaction to abusive practices. However, the majority of agreements in practice are based on the combination of low-hour part-time, working time accounts, and overtime.

Apart from such concerns, most restrictions to on-call work apply only where employees are required to be available for assignments as ordered by the employer. By contrast, arrangements under which the employee is free to accept or reject an offer of work performance basically appear to entail no problems of work-life balance. To the contrary, they may entail significant benefits for workers who, for whatever reason (work-, family-, health-related etc.) need or appreciate an ad hoc decision about each deployment. The aim of providing opportunities for the labour market participation of individuals whose personal situation does not allow for more regular forms of employment is also key in all the described (*see supra* at §9.05[A][1] and §9.05[A][3]) dedicated schemes which make small-scale intermittent or platform work particularly attractive. Depending on the legal context in each country, such arrangements may be generously allowed either as repeated intermittent fixed-term contracts, specific on-call contracts or part-time work with voluntary overtime. In this respect, Italy stands out as the country where all these types are subject to concrete limits to the possible degree of flexibilisation. Still, the contribution notes serious doubts about the system's capability to prevent exploitative flexibilisation practices.

One dilemma faced by the legislator in this context is certainly that restrictions for flexible employment contracts may result in an extra stimulus to make use of contracts for (formally) self-employed work performance. Reference could for instance be made to schemes such as voucher-based employment in Italy, which targets private households and micro-enterprises with intermittent work needs. Arguably, in the absence of such a scheme, these employers may be particularly likely to resort to bogus self-employment or even informal employment, which – other than the high-profile cases about bogus self-employment in the platform economy – may be very unlikely to ever be rectified. Similar concerns apply to certain sectors which are particularly vulnerable to undeclared work such as hospitality and retail, which are targeted by the Belgian flexi-job regime. Balancing such considerations with risks of abuse is self-evidently difficult.

Another key difficulty lies in the very concept of relying on voluntariness in relation to a segment of the workforce which – despite the scarcity of data – can safely be assumed to be disproportionally affected by in-work poverty. Platform work is arguably a type of work organisation 'perfecting' the model of offering intermittent work opportunities to a pool of workers who can be contacted at short notice, without any necessity to legally oblige a particular worker to assume a particular assignment. From the perspective of the worker, the voluntariness of accepting the assignment is obviously put into perspective when the opportunities are limited and their income depends on it. In this respect, the prominence of platform work can be argued to have shone a light on practices of intermittent and on-call work which have long existed in the offline world, and the questionability of allowing agreements to be classified as self-employed work mainly due to the lack of an obligation to work. The emergent case law which re-evaluates the notion of employee in light of work realities in the platform economy may thus serve to alleviate the legal uncertainties which may be assumed to prevent many bogus self-employed intermittent workers from claiming their rights.

[D] What Are the Main Instruments to Prevent Poverty for VUP 4 Workers?

[1] Instruments Concerning the Wage Level

The above-described difficulties that VUP Group 4 may pose in terms of the workers' legal classification as employees, self-employed, or a tertium genus are of key relevance for the applicability of statutory and collectively agreed wage standards. Apart from the basic wage, this may also concern cost compensation for (or provision of) the equipment necessary for work performance or health and safety protection (including additional precautions due to the pandemic). The importance of such components can be underlined by reference to court decisions in Germany and Italy ensuring their enforcement for employed platform riders. As emphasised *supra* at §9.05[C][4], the emerging litigation targeting platform companies may be of central relevance also for clarifying the classification and rights of other intermittent and on-call workers.

Italy stands out by its degree of regulatory intervention to bring one vulnerable group of platform workers (delivery riders) under the scope of wage standards set by collective bargaining). This is supported by regulation to avoid underpayment of these workers, relating, e.g., to information rights, the prohibition of piece-based remuneration, entitlements to accident insurance, and wage supplements for work on weekends and in adverse weather conditions. As opposed to this, the regulation pertaining to Italian voucher-based work and Belgian flexi-jobs expressly allows for undercutting otherwise applicable minimum wage standards (*see supra* at §9.05[A]).

Concrete data about unionisation rates are generally non-existent for VUP 4 workers, but there is a common understanding that these are likely even lower than for VUP Group 3. Only Swedish data calculate separate unionisation rates for temporary workers without working hours stipulated in advance, evidencing levels far below those of the general workforce, and decreasing more rapidly. Nonetheless, a nascent unionisation of at least certain parts of the on-demand workforce is reported for all countries but Luxembourg and Poland. Some chapters provide examples of trade union initiatives to mobilise specifically platform workers.

No country chapter offers concrete data or estimates regarding the coverage of VUP 4 workers by collective agreements. At present, collective agreements with a specific focus on platform workers are applicable to delivery riders in Italy and Sweden, while negotiations to that end have been discontinued in Belgium. These collective agreements regulate aspects such as wages and supplements, collective insurances, and the provision of equipment. Notably the Swedish contribution sees a great potential for collective bargaining to take charge of the regulation of platform work in line with national traditions. In Italy, existing agreements expressly cover self-employed platform workers. In both countries, some platform workers are covered by general sectoral collective agreements. Works council agreements have been concluded by platforms recognising their employer status in Germany. In Belgium and the Netherlands, where collective agreements are typically universally applicable for a sector, coverage is implied by decisions qualifying platform workers as employees. Unions are usually also a key driving force (apart from labour inspectorates and social security bodies) behind a push for rectifying bogus self-employment for entire categories of workers, via strategic litigation in exemplary cases. Notably in Italy and the Netherlands, cases for the reclassification of platform workers have been brought specifically with a view to ensure the applicability of collective agreements

The concerns about the role of collective agreements invoked above for VUP Group 3 apply also, and perhaps even more, to VUP Group 4. While workers' representatives, including works councils and unions playing a central role in determining working time arrangements at company level, may contribute significantly to the avoidance of abuse of casual work, they may also be reluctant to prioritise the rights of a group with low levels of unionisation.

Such reluctance may, first of all, result in unions agreeing to exceptions from protective standards for VUP 4 workers. The Dutch contribution notes that some collective agreements exclude certain categories of intermittent workers from their scope or that of specific benefits stipulated therein. Perhaps even more importantly, concerns are raised with a view to the social partners' use of derogation possibilities to create very flexible on-call regimes. In Italy, a court decision has confirmed the insufficient representativeness of a trade union which signed a widely applicable collective agreement making use of a particularly far-going derogation options for delivery riders. Just like for VUP 3 workers such as temporary agency employees, these issues may be the flipside to the successful stimulation of collective bargaining activities for groups at the margins of the labour force. While these examples evidence the key importance of representativeness requirements in collective bargaining, the Belgian contribution also notes that such requirements may dilute the voice of unions specialising in representing the interests of VUP 4 workers in collective bargaining.

An emerging phenomenon are intermediaries offering to assume the role of employer when freelancers work (intermittently) with self-chosen customers. This applies to the Belgian SMart cooperative, which simultaneously acted as a trade union for its workers in relation to the delivery platform that hired them, and notably to umbrella companies, which have become increasingly relevant in the Swedish labour market.

Finally, the vulnerability of intermittent and notably platform work, which typically attracts a workforce mainly consisting of 'labour market outsiders' and especially those with a migration background, to illegal practices is noted in several country chapters. This underlines the importance of effective enforcement mechanisms in protecting the wage levels of VUP 4 workers.

[2] Instruments Concerning Wage-Replacing Benefits

Considering that the great majority of VUP 4 workers will be either solo or bogus self-employed or employed under a fixed-term and/or part-time contract, reference can largely be made to the considerations mentioned for VUP Groups 2 and 3.

Several country chapters note that accessing social security benefits can be exceedingly difficult for VUP Group 4. This is most obvious in relation to the groups expressly excluded from coverage by insurance-based social security schemes as mentioned *supra* at §9.05[A] – intermittent mini-jobbers in Germany, small-scale platform workers in Belgium, and partly voucher-based workers in Italy. The latter are included in industrial accident and pension insurance, but not entitled to sickness, maternity, or unemployment insurance benefits. As opposed to this, the Belgian flexi-job scheme – which is based on a similar logic of offering a lower tax burden and administrative simplification – does not compromise the employee's social security rights.

Beyond such specific exclusions, qualification periods (for sickness, invalidity, unemployment benefits etc.) will be particularly challenging in case of intermittent work with highly irregular working hours and potential interruptions over longer periods. Even the determination of a situation of unemployment can be challenging if zero-hour workers or on-call workers with highly variable weekly working hours are not called to work by the employer for some time, or the number of deployments drops to a negligible level. In relation to sickness and invalidity, the Swedish contribution points specifically to work capacity assessments, which may be unfavourable for VUP 4 workers who are denied an assessment in relation to their past professional activity. Reference is made to an ongoing reform process, which has recently given casual workers a right to sickness allowance on the basis of income from work during the first 90 days of illness. During sickness and on public holidays, on-call employees are especially likely to forego payment if it is not clear that they would otherwise have been called to work on that day.

All in all, VUP 4 workers may be particularly likely to need to fall back on income- or means-tested subsidiary benefits. Some country chapters therefore point to general concerns over the effectiveness of these benefits in alleviating poverty. In this respect, the Swedish contribution highlights the particular difficulties faced by VUP 4 workers unable to predict their irregular incomes when applying for income-tested benefits.

These general difficulties have in many cases been exacerbated by the COVID-19 crisis, during which VUP 4 workers have been especially prone to losing their jobs. For instance, the Luxembourgish contribution notes that platform workers may have benefitted from measures neither targeting subordinate workers nor those in place for the self-employed. In this regard, the crisis measures in Italy stand out by entitling voucher-based workers and on-call employees to a repeatedly extended flat-rate monthly allowance of first EUR 600, then EUR 1,000, under rather generous minimum requirements (30 days of on-call employment within a year).

[E] Conclusions

VUP Group 4 could be seen as a category which assembles the most vulnerable subgroups of all other VUP Groups – with the majority being either dependent (and potentially bogus) self-employed or fixed-term and/or part-time employees, and the few standard employees (working on call or via platforms) very likely to be low-skilled. The virtually complete absence of data regarding AROP or SMD levels for this group allows only for speculation about the poverty risks faced by those whose main labour market income stems from casual or platform work.

The various schemes enabling 'simplified' smaller-scale employment or contracts with flexible working hours illustrate a general dilemma of policies aiming to alleviate poverty. Such schemes are usually meant to create attractive alternatives to forms of work that are particularly susceptible to poverty, such as bogus self-employment and informal employment, or practices of unpaid overtime. If, however, the use of these schemes threatens to substitute regular employment, the overall impact on poverty risks may turn out negative. The same can once again be said about collective bargaining, which – just as for VUP Group 3 – is challenging in respect of a very weakly unionised group of workers, for which the legislator allows partly very far-going deviations in peius.

As shown by the comparative overview, in most countries there is no coherent approach to casual work, and strict limitations of certain forms of contract can regularly be circumvented by relying on other instruments which provide a similar degree of flexibility for employers. Perhaps even more than for VUP Group 3, questions of voluntariness appear to be key – as the greatest degree of flexibility can be achieved when principals rely on a pool of workers who are formally free whether and when to work, but may in fact be forced to accept every available offer. At least in respect of platform work, which is regularly based on this concept, the European Commission's Proposal for a directive on working conditions in platform work[45] may prove a key instrument in avoiding that this reliance on voluntariness leads to an exclusion from the benefits of an employment contract – and the associated safeguards against poverty risk.

§9.06 GENERAL CONCLUSIONS

A global look at EU-SILC data available for VUP Groups 1-3 evidences a remarkably uniform 'distribution' of poverty risks in the seven countries studied in this book. Notably, VUP 2 workers consistently show the highest AROP rates, whereas VUP 3 workers are significantly more affected by high SMD levels. These findings apply consistently across countries despite the otherwise sizeable differences in terms of

45. Full text available at https://ec.europa.eu/social/BlobServlet?docId=24992&langId=en.

poverty rates and their development over time. The sole exception is Luxembourg, which – for country-specific reasons as discussed in the chapter – is generally characterised by unusually high AROP rates for employees, which turn out slightly higher for VUP Group 3 than for VUP Group 2. If data were available for VUP Group 4, they might reasonably be assumed to produce the even higher rates of in-work risk of poverty and severe material deprivation than for the other groups.

The comparative overview provided in this chapter has sought to sketch out the complex challenges which legislators face in terms of ensuring protections for different groups of vulnerable and under-represented workers – while avoiding that costly or complex regulation triggers the recourse to forms of work that are even more precarious, or result in more unemployment or inactivity as the status which imply the severest poverty risks.

As highlighted throughout this chapter, there are numerous ways in which the legal framework influences the likelihood of workers belonging to one of the VUP Groups to receive adequate wages and wage-replacing benefits. For all workers, this includes most notably the degree to which social security and collective bargaining systems are actively designed to take account of the situation of VUP workers, or to the contrary exacerbate the insider-outsider divide. The latter is true for instance if the social partners consciously deviate from legally envisaged protections for them in return for advantages for better represented workers, or if access to social security is denied, perhaps despite prior contribution payment (e.g., because VUP 3 or 4 workers fail to meet certain thresholds, or VUP 2 or 4 workers lose accrued entitlements the moment they become self-employed). As described, the countries studied diverge widely in this respect.

Sizeable differences have also been evidenced in respect of the degree to which the legal framework enables VUP workers to move into a more secure status. This includes, *i.a.* (for VUP Group 1) skills development policies and measures influencing pressures on jobseekers to accept the 'first best' job, (for VUP Group 2) the adaption of the notion of employee to capture situations of vulnerability as well as measures for countering bogus self-employment, (for VUP Group 3) measures to prevent the abuse of temporary work and to address the various (family-/labour market-/health-related) reasons for working part-time, and (for VUP Group 4) a coherent approach to limiting the permissibility of on-call work with mandatory availability and avoiding the exclusion of work based on voluntary availability from the benefits of a continuous employment relationship.

As apparent from the country chapters on which the analysis presented in this chapter is based, not all of these aspects currently receive particular attention in national-level policy debates. Yet, as described, a number of recent changes, pending reforms, and developments in collective agreements and case law indicate that awareness of their importance is increasing at least in some countries in regard of each of the mentioned areas of regulation. In Germany and the Netherlands, recently elected governments have made aims of combatting poverty and exploitation in the labour market a core commitment for the upcoming legislative period. The measures envisaged in that context are partly aimed at addressing country-specific particularities (such as the excessively strict means-tested benefit system for jobseekers and the comprehensive exclusion of the self-employed from social insurance in Germany, or the excessive incentivisation of the use of self-employed and atypical work in the Netherlands); others are setting innovative new standards (such as the planned one-off increase of the German minimum wage to a level above 60% of the median, or the potential introduction of a presumption of employee status in case of low remuneration in the Netherlands). The Swedish contribution notes more generally that 'labour and social security legislation is more or less in flux at the time being'. Certain forms of work are subject to reform proposals for enhanced protection in more than one country - such as fixed-term employment (in Germany and Sweden) or platform work (in Belgium and Germany).

All in all, it is apparent from the analysis throughout the chapters of the present book that a phenomenon as complex as in-work poverty is influenced by a multitude of factors, part of which are barely amenable to legal regulation. Among the various aspects in which the regulatory environment (including *i.a.*, economic, tax, infrastructural, and family policies) determines poverty risks, this book has sought to highlight the most immediately relevant rules of labour law, labour market policies, and social security. More than anything, the analysis focusing on vulnerable and under-represented groups may have served to illustrate that policy approaches to combat poverty are by no means determined exclusively by the 'generosity' of certain protective measures. Instead, many of the most immediate challenges for a policy mix to comprehensively address poverty risks might be to ensure that protective measures are actually applicable to and accessible for those who would be most in need of them.

BCLR - BULLETIN OF COMPARATIVE LABOUR RELATIONS

Vol. Author/Title/Year/ISBN

1. Roger Blanpain, *Individual Employment Contracts: Collective Agreements*, 1970.
2. Roger Blanpain, *Social Planning*, 1971 (ISBN 90-312-0018-2).
3. Roger Blanpain, *Guaranteed Income Funds*, 1972 (ISBN 90-312-0019-0).
4. Roger Blanpain, *Employee Participation at the Level of the Enterprise*, 1973 (ISBN 90-312-0020-4).
5. Roger Blanpain, *Vastheid van Betrekking: Staking en Bezetting*, 1974.
6. Roger Blanpain, *Labour Law and Industrial Relations (International Bibliography)*, 1975 (ISBN 90-312-0023-9).
7. Roger Blanpain, *Multinational Enterprises*, 1976 (ISBN 90-312-0024-7).
8. Roger Blanpain, *Worker's Participation in the European Company*, 1977 (ISBN 90-312-0044-1).
9. Roger Blanpain, *Women and Labour*, 1978 (ISBN 90-312-0077-8).
10. Roger Blanpain, *European Conference on Labour Law and Industrial Relations: Multinational Enterprises*, 1979 (ISBN 90-312-0091-3).
11. Roger Blanpain, *Job Security and Industrial Relations*, 1980 (ISBN 90-312-0147-2).
12. Roger Blanpain, Greg Bamber & Russell Lansbury, *Technological Change and Industrial Relations: An International Symposium*, 1983 (ISBN 90-312-0205-3).
13. Roger Blanpain, James Janssen van Raay & A. Moulty, *Worker's Participation in the European Community: The Fifth Directive*, 1984 (ISBN 90-654-4187-5).
14. Roger Blanpain, *Equality and Prohibition of Discrimination in Employment*, 1985 (ISBN 90-654-4215-4).
15. Roger Blanpain, *Restructuring Labour in the Enterprise: Law and Practice in France, F.R. of Germany, Italy, Sweden and the United Kingdom*, 1986 (ISBN 90-654-4283-9).
16. Roger Blanpain & E. Kassalow, *Unions and Industrial Relations: Recent Trends and Prospect: A Comparative Treatment*, 1987 (ISBN 90-654-4294-4).
17. Roger Blanpain & Marco Biagi, *Trade Union Democracy and Industrial Relations*, 1988 (ISBN 90-654-4394-0).
18. Roger Blanpain & Jelle Visser, *In Search of Inclusive Unionism*, 1990 (ISBN 90-654-4439-4).
19. Roger Blanpain, *Flexibility and Wages: A Comparative Treatment*, 1990 (ISBN 90-654-4461-0).

20. Roger Blanpain, Stephen Frenkel & Oliver Clarke, *Economic Restructuring and Industrial Relations in Industrialised Countries,* 1990 (ISBN 90-654-4488-2).
21. Roger Blanpain & Friedrich Fürstenberg, *Structure and Strategy in Industrial Relations,* 1991 (ISBN 90-654-4559-5).
22. Roger Blanpain, Amira Galin & Ozer Carmi, *Flexible Work Patterns and Their Impact on Industrial Relations,* 1991 (ISBN 90-654-4572-2).
23. Roger Blanpain, *Workers' Participation: Influence on Management Decision-Making by Labour in the Private Sector,* 1992 (ISBN 90-654-4600-1).
24. Roger Blanpain, Brian Brooks & Chris Engels, *Employed or Self-Employed,* 1992 (ISBN 90-654-4613-3).
25. Roger Blanpain & Tiziano Treu, *Industrial Relations Developments in the Telecommunications Industry,* 1993 (ISBN 90-654-4642-7).
26. Roger Blanpain & Marco Biagi, *Industrial Relations in Small and Medium Sized Enterprises,* 1993 (ISBN 90-654-4696-6).
27. Roger Blanpain & Marco Biagi, *Participative Management and Industrial Relations in a Worldwide Perspective,* 1993 (ISBN 90-654-4769-5).
28. Roger Blanpain, Jacques Rojot & Hoyt N. Wheeler, *Employee Rights and Industrial Justice,* 1994 (ISBN 90-654-4804-7).
29. Roger Blanpain & Ruth Ben-Israel, *Strikes and Lock-Outs in Industrialized Market Economies,* 1994 (ISBN 90-654-4841-1).
30. Roger Blanpain, Kazuo Sugeno & Yasuo Suwa, *The Harmonization of Working Life and Family Life,* 1995 (ISBN 90-411-0064-4).
31. Roger Blanpain & Laszio Nagy, *Labour Law and Industrial Relations in Central and Eastern Europe,* 1996 (ISBN 90-411-0298-1).
32. Roger Blanpain, *Labour Law and Industrial Relations in the European Union,* 1997 (ISBN 90-411-0527-1).
33. Taco Van Peijpe, *Employment Protection under Strain,* 1998 (ISBN 90-411-0528-8).
34. Roger Blanpain, Takashi Araki & Ryuichi Yamakawa, *The Process of Industrialization and the Role of Labour Law in Asia,* 1999 (ISBN 9-041-1104-7-X).
35. Roger Blanpain & Marco Biagi, *Non-standard Work and Industrial Relations,* 1999 (ISBN 90-411-1117-4).
36. Roger Blanpain, *Private Employment Agencies: The Impact of ILO Convention 181 (1997) and the Judgment of the European Court of Justice of 11 December 1997,* 1999 (ISBN 90-411-1118-2).
37. Roger Blanpain, *Multinational Enterprises and the Social Challenges of the XXIst Century: The ILO Declaration on Fundamental* Principles *at Work, Public and Private Corporate Codes of Conduct,* 2000 (ISBN 90-411-1280-4).
38. Roger Blanpain, Ryuichi Yamakawa & Takashi Araki, *Deregulation and Labour Law: In Search of a Labour Concept for the 21st Century,* 2000 (ISBN 90-411-1370-3).
39. Roger Blanpain, *The Council of Europe and the Social Challenges of the XXIst Century,* 2001 (ISBN 90-411-1543-9).

40. Roger Blanpain, *On-Line Rights for Employees in the Information Society, Use & Monitoring of E-Mail & Internet at Work*, 2002 (ISBN 90-411-1626-5).
41. Roger Blanpain, *The Evolving Employment Relationship and the New Economy: The Role of Labour Law & Industrial Relations*, 2001 (ISBN 90-411-1691-5).
42. Roger Blanpain, *Involvement of Employees in the European Union, Works Councils, Company Statute, Information and Consultation Rights*, 2002 (ISBN 90-411-1760-1).
43. Michele Colucci, *The Impact of the Internet and New Technologies on the Workplace: A Legal Analysis from a Comparative Point of View*, 2002 (ISBN 90-411-1824-1).
44. Roger Blanpain, *White Paper on the Labour Market in Italy: The Quality of European Industrial Relations and Changing Industrial Relations*, 2002 (ISBN 90-411-1841-1).
45. Roger Blanpain, Russell D. Lansbury & Young-Bum Park, *Impact of Globalisation on Employment Relations: A Comparison of the Automobile and Banking Industries in Australia and Korea*, 2002 (ISBN 90-411-1850-0).
46. Roger Blanpain & Antoine Jacobs, *Employee Rights in Bankruptcy: A Comparative-Law Assessment*, 2002 (ISBN 90-411-1942-6).
47. Roger Blanpain, Takashi Araki & Shinya Ouchi, *Corporate Restructuring and the Role of Labour Law*, 2003 (ISBN 90-411-1949-3).
48. Roger Blanpain, *Collective Bargaining, Discrimination, Social Security and European Integration*, 2003 (ISBN 90-411-2010-6).
49. Roger Blanpain & Luis Aparicio-Valdez, *Labour Relations in the Asia- Pacific Countries*, 2004 (ISBN 90-411-2239-7).
50. Roger Blanpain & Ronnie Graham, *Temporary Agency Work and the Information Society*, 2004 (ISBN 90-411-2252-4).
51. Roger Blanpain, *The Actors of Collective Bargaining: A World Report*, 2004 (ISBN 90-411-2253-2).
52. Roger Blanpain & Michele Colucci, *The Globalisation of Labour Standards: The Soft Law Track*, 2004 (ISBN 90-411-2303-2).
53. Roger Blanpain, Takashi Araki & Shinya Ouchi, *Labour Law in Motion: Diversification of the Labour Force & Terms and Conditions of Employment*, 2005 (ISBN 90-411-2315-6).
54. Roger Blanpain, *Smoking and the Workplace*, 2005 (ISBN 90-411-2325-3).
55. Roger Blanpain, *Confronting Globalization: The Quest for a Social Agenda*, 2005 (ISBN 90-411-2381-4).
56. Roger Blanpain, Thomas Blanke & Edgar Rose, *Collective Bargaining Wages in Comparative Perspective: Germany, France, the Netherlands, Sweden and the United Kingdom*, 2005 (ISBN 90-411-2388-1).
57. Roger Blanpain & Anne Numhauser-Henning, *Women in Academia & Equality Law: Aiming High - Falling Short?*, 2006 (ISBN 978-90-411-2427-6).
58. Roger Blanpain, *Freedom of Services in the European Union: Labour and Social Security Law: The Bolkestein Initiative*, 2006 (ISBN 978-90-411-2453-5).
59. Roger Blanpain, Frans Pennings & Nurhan Sural, *Flexibilisation and Modernisation of the Turkish Labour Market*, 2006 (ISBN 978-90-411-2490-X).

60. Roger Blanpain & Boel Flodgren, *Corporate and Employment Perspectives in a Global Business Environment*, 2006 (ISBN 978-90-411-2537-X).
61. Roger Blanpain, Shinya Ouchi & Takashi Araki, *Decentralizing Industrial Relations and The Role of Labor Unions and Employee Representatives*, 2007 (ISBN 978-90-411-2583-3).
62. Roger Blanpain, *European Framework Agreements and Telework: Law and Practice: A European and Comparative Study*, 2007 (ISBN 978-90-411-2560-4).
63. Roger Blanpain, Jim Kitay, Leanne Cutcher & Nick Wailes, *Globalization and Employment Relations in Retail Banking*, 2007 (ISBN 978-90-411-2620-1).
64. Roger Blanpain, Russell Lansbury, Jim Kitay, Nick Wailes & Anja Kirsch, *Globalization and Employment Relations in the Auto Assembly Industry: A Study of Seven Countries*, 2008 (ISBN 978-90-411-2698-6).
65. Roger Blanpain & Michele Tiraboschi, *The Global Labour Market: From Globalization to Flexicurity*, 2008 (ISBN 978-90-411-2722-8).
66. Roger Blanpain, Michele Colucci & Frank Hendrickx, *The Future of Sport in the European Union: Beyond the EU Reform Treaty and the White Paper*, 2008 (ISBN 978-90-411-2761-7).
67. Roger Blanpain, Linda Dickens, *Challenges in European Employment Relations: Employment Regulation, Trade Union Organization, Equality, Flexicurity, Training and New Approaches to Pay*, 2008 (ISBN 978-90-411-2771-6).
68. Roger Blanpain, Hiroya Nakakubo & Takashi Araki, *New Developments in Employment Discrimination Law, 2008* (ISBN 978-90-411-2782-2).
69. Roger Blanpain, Andrzej Marian wiątkowski, *The Laval and Viking Cases: Freedom of Services and Establishment v. Industrial Conflict in the European Economic Area and Russia*, 2009 (ISBN 978-90-411-2850-8).
70. Roger Blanpain, William Bromwich, Olga Rymkevich, Silvia Spattini, *The Modernization of Labour Law and Industrial Relations in a Comparative Perspective*, 2009 (ISBN 978-90-411-2865-2).
71. Roger Blanpain, Juan Pablo Landa & Brian Langille, *Employment Policies and Multilevel Governance*, 2009 (ISBN 978-90-411-2866-9).
72. Roger Blanpain, European Works Councils; *The European Directive 2009/ 38/EC of 6 May 2009, 2009* (ISBN 978-90-411-3208-6).
73. Roger Blanpain, William Bromwich, Olga Rymkevich & Silvia Spattini, *Labour Productivity, Investment in Human Capital and Youth Employment: Comparative Developments and Global Responses*, 2010 (ISBN 978-90-411-3249-9).
74. Greg J. Bamber & Philippe Pochet, *Regulating Employment Relations, Work and Labour Laws: International Comparisons between Key Countries*, 2010 (ISBN 978-90-411-3199-7). General Editor: Roger Blanpain.
75. Roger Blanpain, Desislava Nikolaeva Dimitrova, *Seafarers' Rights in the Globalized Maritime Industry*, 2010 (ISBN 978-90-411-3349-6).
76. Roger Blanpain, Hiroya Nakakubo & Takashi Araki, *Regulation of Fixed- Term Employment Contracts*, 2010 (ISBN 978-90-411-3356-4).

77. Roger Blanpain, William Bromwich, Olga Rymkevich & Iacopo Senatori, *Rethinking Corporate Governance*, 2011 (ISBN 978-90-411-3450-9).
78. Roger Blanpain & Frank Hendrickx, *Labour Law between Change and Tradition: Liber Amicorum Antoine Jacobs*, 2011 (ISBN 978-90-411-3424-0).
79. Roger Blanpain, Thomas Klebe, Marlene Schmidt & Bernd Waas, *Trade Union Rights at the Workplace*, 2012 (ISBN 978-90-411-3460-8).
80. Roger Blanpain, William Bromwich, Olga Rymkevich & Iacopo Senatori, *Labour Markets, Industrial Relations and Human Resources Management: From Recession to Recovery*, 2012 (ISBN 978-90-411-4004-3).
81. Roger Blanpain, Hiroya Nakakubo & Takashi Araki, *Systems of Employee Representation at the Enterprise: A Comparative Study*, 2012 (ISBN 978-90-411-4080-7).
82. Roger Blanpain & Frank Hendrickx, *Temporary Agency Work in the European Union and the United States*, 2013 (ISBN 978-90-411-4769-1).
83. Roger Blanpain, Toker Dereli, Y. Pınar Soykut-Sarıca & Aslı en-Tabaı, *Emerging Patterns of Work and Turkish Labour Market Challenges under Globalization: Readings on Labour and Employment Relations*, 2014 (ISBN 978-90-411-4983-1).
84. Roger Blanpain, Pablo Arellano Ortiz, Marius Olivier & Gijsbert Vonk, *Social Security and Migrant Workers: Selected Studies of Cross-border Social Security Mechanisms*, 2014 (ISBN 978-90-411-4770-7).
85. Roger Blanpain & Nikita Lyutov, *Workers' Representation in Central and Eastern Europe: Challenges and Opportunities for the Works Councils' System*, 2014 (ISBN 978-90-411-4746-2).
86. Roger Blanpain, Ulla Liukkunen & Chen Yifeng, *China and ILO Fundamental Principles and Rights at Works*, 2014 (ISBN 978-90-411-4984-8).
87. Roger Blanpain, *The Use of Languages and Employment Relations*, 2014 (ISBN 978-90-411-5606-8).
88. Roger Blanpain, Hiroya Nakakubo & Takashi Araki, *Protection of Employees' Personal Information and Privacy*, 2014 (ISBN 978-90-411-5608-2).
89. Roger Blanpain, Jan Wouters, Glenn Rayp, Laura Beke & Axel Marx, *Protecting Labour Rights in a Multi-polar Supply Chain and Mobile Global Economy*, 2015 (ISBN 978-90-411-5662-4).
90. Roger Blanpain & Stefania Marassi, *Globalization and Transnational Collective Labour Relations: International and European Framework Agreements at Company Level*, 2015 (ISBN 978-90-411-4748-6).
91. Roger Blanpain, Frank Hendrickx & Petra Herzfeld Olsson, *National Effects of the Implementation of EU Directives on Labour Migration from Third Countries*, 2016 (ISBN 978-90-411-6257-1).
92. Roger Blanpain, Frank Hendrickx & D'Arcy du Toit, *Labour Law and Social Progress: Holding the Line or Shifting the Boundaries?* 2016 (ISBN 978-90-411-6747-7).

93. Roger Blanpain & Frank Hendrickx, *Reasonable Accommodation in the Modern Workplace: Potential and Limits of the Integrative Logics of Labour Law*, 2016 (ISBN 978-90-411-6258-8).
94. Roger Blanpain, Frank Hendrickx & Bernd Waas, *New Forms of Employment in Europe*, 2016 (ISBN 978-90-411-6239-7).
95. Roger Blanpain, Frank Hendrickx, Hiroya Nakakubo & Takashi Araki, *The Notion of Employer in the Era of the Fissured Workplace: Should Labour Law Responsibilities Exceed the Boundary of the Legal Entity?*, 2017 (ISBN 978-90-411-8470-2).
96. Elena Sychenko, *Individual Labour Rights as Human Rights: The Contributions of the European Court of Human Rights to Worker's Rights Protection*, 2017 (ISBN 978-90-411-8629-4).
97. William Bromwich & Olga Rymkevich, *Improving Workplace Quality: New Perspectives and Challenges for Worker Well-Being*, 2017 (ISBN 978-90-411-8628-7).
98. Sarah De Groof, *Work-Life Balance in the Modern Workplace: Interdisciplinary Perspectives from Work-Family Research, Law and Policy*, 2017 (ISBN 978-90-411-8630-0).
99. Sylvaine Laulom, *Collective Bargaining Developments in Times of Crisis*, 2018 (ISBN 978-90-411-8999-8).
100. Frank Hendrickx & Valerio De Stefano, *Game Changers in Labour Law: Shaping the Future of Work*, 2018 (ISBN 978-90-411-9953-9).
101. Ivana Palinkaš, *The Legal and Institutional Framing of Collective Bargaining in CEE Countries: Between Europeanisation and Decentralisation*, 2018 (ISBN 978-90-411-9199-1).
102. Jeremy Waddington, *European Board-Level Employee Representation: National Variations in Influence and Power*, 2018 (ISBN 978-90-411-9202-8).
103. Jan Pichrt & Kristina Koldinská, *Labour Law and Social Protection in a Globalized World: Changing Realities in Selected Areas of Law and Policy*, 2018 (ISBN 978-94-035-0093-5).
104. Matthew W. Finkin, *American Labor and the Law: Dormant, Resurgent, and Emergent Problems*, 2019 (ISBN 978-94-035-0654-8).
105. Giuseppe Casale & Tiziano Treu, *Transformations of Work: Challenges for the Institutions and Social Actors*, 2019 (ISBN 978-94-035-0891-7).
106. Miguel De la Corte-Rodríguez, *EU Law on Maternity and Other Child-Related Leaves: Impact on Gender Equality*, 2019 (ISBN 978-94-035-1452-9).
107. Valeria Pulignano & Frank Hendrickx, *Employment Relations in the 21st Century: Challenges for Theory and Research in a Changing World of Work*, 2020 (ISBN 978-94-035-1764-3).
108. Matteo Bottero, *Posting of Workers in EU Law: Challenges of Equality, Solidarity and Fair Competition*, 2021 (ISBN 978-94-035-2860-1).
109. Bernd Waas & Christina Hießl, *Collective Bargaining for Self-Employed Workers in Europe: Approaches to Reconcile Competition Law and Labour Rights*, 2021 (ISBN 978-94-035-2373-6).

110. Mathias Wouters, *International Labour Standards and Platform Work: An Analysis of Digital Labour Platforms Based on the Instruments on Private Employment Agencies, Home Work and Domestic Work*, 2022 (ISBN 978-94-035-4024-5).
111. Luca Ratti, *In-Work Poverty in Europe: Vulnerable and Under-Represented Persons in a Comparative Perspective*, 2022 (ISBN 978-94-035-4996-5).